THEY MARCHED

DAVID MARANISS

SIMON & SCHUSTER

INTO SUNLIGHT

WAR AND PEACE
VIETNAM AND AMERICA
OCTOBER 1967

New York   London   Toronto   Sydney   Singapore

SIMON & SCHUSTER
Rockefeller Center
1230 Avenue of the Americas
New York, NY 10020

The author and publisher gratefully acknowledge permission
to reprint "Elegy" from *Archeology of the Circle,* by Bruce Weigl.
Copyright © 1999 by Bruce Weigl. Used by permission of
Grove/Atlantic, Inc.

SIMON & SCHUSTER and colophon are registered trademarks
of Simon & Schuster, Inc.

For information regarding special discounts for bulk purchases,
please contact Simon & Schuster Special Sales
at 1-800-456-6798 or business@simonandschuster.com

Book design by Ellen R. Sasahara
Maps designed by Gene Thorp

Picture Section Credits
Tom Grady photos: 1, 11, 19, 24. *The Daily Cardinal:* 2, 30, 32, 35, 42. Allen Family photo album:
3, 5. First Infantry: 4, 6. 28th Regiment photo: 7, 8, 9, 10, 16. Army Signal Corps photo: 12. Sikor-
ski family photo album: 13, 14. Tom Hinger photo album: 15. Clark Welch collection: 17, 18.
Verland Gilbertson: 20. Richard Calef: 21, 22. Ed Amorosi collection: 23. Fagan Publishing Co.
postcard: 25. Jane Brotman photo album: 26. Betty Menacher photo album: 27. *The Capital
Times:* 28, 29, 31, 33, 43, 44. *Wisconsin State Journal:* 34, 36, 37, 38, 39, 40. *Connections:* 41. David
Maraniss: 45. Consuelo Allen: 46. Linda Maraniss: 47.

Manufactured in the United States of America

10   9   8   7   6   5   4   3   2   1

Library of Congress Cataloging-in-Publication Data

Maraniss, David.
   They marched into sunlight : war and peace, Vietnam and America,
October 1967 / David Maraniss.
       p.   cm.
     1. Vietnamese Conflict, 1961–1975—United States. 2. Vietnamese Conflict, 1961–1975—
Protest movements—United States. 3. United States—Politics and government—1963–1969.
I. Title.
DS558.M35 2003
959.704'31—dc21   2003052885

ISBN 0-7432-1780-2

To Elliott and Mary Maraniss, my parents

Contents

Cast of Characters

VIETNAM STORY

Albin, Ray: Delta weapons platoon mortars plotter

Allen, Consuelo: Oldest daughter of Terry Allen Jr.

Allen, Jean Ponder: Wife of Terry Allen Jr.

Allen, Terry, Jr.: 2/28 Black Lions battalion commander

Allen, Terry, Sr.: World War II First Infantry Division commander

Arias, Michael: Alpha radiotelephone operator

Barrow, Clarence: Delta first sergeant

Blackwell, James: Black Lions intelligence officer

Bolen, Jackie: Delta squad leader

Breeden, Clifford: Alpha rifleman, first man killed in October 17 battle

Buentiempo, Ernest: Alpha radiotelephone operator

Bunker, Ellsworth: U.S. ambassador to South Vietnam

Burrows, George: Reconnaissance platoon rifleman

Byrd, Dwayne: Delta acting platoon leader

Cash, John A.: Military historian of October 17 battle

Colburn, Tom: Delta rifleman from C Packet

Coleman, William: First Infantry assistant division commander

Coonly, Bill and Bebe: El Paso friends of Terry Allen Jr.

Costello, Joe: Alpha grenadier

Cron, Doug: Delta rifleman from C Packet

DePuy, William: Hay's predecessor as First Infantry Division commander

Dowling, Francis: Black Lions sergeant major

Durham, Harold (Pinky): Delta artillery forward observer

Eastman, Phil: Doctor at Ninety-third Evacuation Hospital

Edwards, Peter: Alpha platoon leader

Erwin, Bill: Reconnaissance platoon leader

Farrell, Michael: Alpha radiotelephone operator from C Packet

Gallagher, Michael: Alpha rifleman

Garcia, Melesso: Delta rifleman from C Packet

Gavin, James G.: Retired general and war critic

George, Jim: Alpha Company commander from C Packet

Giannico, Paul: Delta rifleman from C Packet

Giap, Vo Nguyen: Commander in chief of the North Vietnamese Army

Gilliam, Jim: Delta radiotelephone operator

Grady, Tom: Alpha executive officer from C Packet

Grider, Edward: Alpha rifleman

Griego, Santiago: Delta rifleman from C Packet

Grosso, Gerard: Black Lions air operations officer

Hay, John H.: First Infantry Division commander

Hinger, Tom: Alpha medic

Ho Chi Minh: Leader of North Vietnam

Holleder, Don: First Brigade operations officer, former Army football star

Johnson, Willie C.: Alpha platoon leader

Jones, Bernard Francis: Special Forces captain

Jones, James: Alpha forward observer aide

Kasik, Jim: Bravo Company commander

Kirkpatrick, Fred: Delta point man

Lam, Nguyen Van: Commander of C-1 Company, Eighty-third Rear Service Group

Landon, Gregory: Delta radiotelephone operator from C Packet

Laub, David: Delta radiotelephone operator

Locke, Eugene M.: Deputy ambassador to South Vietnam

Lovato, Joe, Jr.: Delta Company medic

Luberda, Andrew: Delta platoon leader

McGath, Bill: Delta rifleman from C Packet

McMeel, Frank: Delta rifleman from C Packet

Miller, Peter: Delta rifleman from C Packet

Mullen, Thomas V.: Alpha platoon leader

Newman, George: First Brigade commander

Phillips, Raymond: Delta radiotelephone operator

Reece, Ronnie: Delta rifleman from C Packet

Reese, Thomas: Charlie Company commander

Schroder, Jack: Delta rifleman from C Packet

Scott, Jimmy: Delta radiotelephone operator

Scott, Paul D.: Delta radiotelephone operator

Sena, Faustin: Delta rifleman from C Packet

Shelton, Jim: Black Lions operations officer

Sikorski, Daniel: Delta machine gunner and squad leader

Sikorski, Diane: Danny's little sister in Milwaukee

Sloan, John: Black Lions operations officer

Smith, Mark: Reconnaissance platoon sergeant

Stroup, David: Delta platoon leader

Tallent, Doug: Delta weapons platoon from C Packet

Taylor, Mike: Delta rifleman from C Packet

Thompson, Gerald: Delta squad leader

Tizzio, Pasquale: Black Lions radiotelephone operator

Triet, Vo Minh: VC First Regiment deputy commander

Troyer, Mike: Delta rifleman from C Packet

Valdez, José: Alpha first sergeant

Warner, Terry: Delta weapons sergeant from C Packet

Welch, A. Clark: Delta Company commander

Westmoreland, William C.: Military Assistance Command, Vietnam, commander

Weyand, Frederick C.: III Corps commander

Woodard, Carl: Alpha squad leader

WISCONSIN STORY

Archer, Sandra: San Francisco Mime Troupe actor

Bablitch, William: UW law student and demonstration observer

Beutel, A. P. (Dutch): Washington lobbyist for Dow Chemical Company

Boll, James: Dane County district attorney

Brandes, Stuart: History doctoral student and observer

Brandt, E. N.: Dow Chemical Company director of public relations

Brotman, Jane: UW freshman from New Jersey

Bunn, Peter: UW assistant dean of students

Center, Charles: UW business school professor

Cheney, Lynne: UW doctoral student in English literature

Cheney, Richard B.: UW graduate student in political science and future vice president

Cipperly, Jack: UW assistant dean of students

Cohen, Robert: UW graduate student and leftist orator

Coyote, Peter: San Francisco Mime Troupe actor

Davis, Ronald G.: San Francisco Mime Troupe director

Dietrich, Cathy: UW student politician and Soglin girlfriend

Doan, Herbert Dow: Dow Chemical Company president and grandson of founder

Dow, H. H.: Dow Chemical Company founder

Edelson, Morris: UW English graduate student and *Quixote* editor

Emery, William: Madison chief of police

Fleming, Robben: UW chancellor before Sewell

Gabriner, Bob: UW history graduate student and *Connections* editor

Gabriner, Vicki: UW graduate student and mime artist

Genack, Judy: UW senior and March on the Pentagon participant

Gerstacker, Carl: Dow Chemical Company chairman

Goldberg, Harvey: UW professor of European history

Goodman, Jerilyn: UW freshman and observer

Goodwin, Everett: UW music school student at Dow demonstration

Hanson, Ralph: UW chief of protection and security

Harrington, Fred Harvey: UW president

Harrington, Jack: Police inspector

Haslach, Henry: UW Students for a Democratic Society leader

Hendershot, William (Curly): Dow Chemical Company college recruiter

Julian, Percy: Madison lawyer representing student activists

Kaplan, William: UW junior and antiwar activist at Dow demonstration

Kauffman, Joseph: UW dean of student affairs

Keene, David A.: UW graduate student and Young Americans for Freedom chairman

Krasny, Michael: UW English teaching assistant and Dow demonstration observer

Steiner, Alison: High school senior and March on the Pentagon participant

Stielstra, Jonathan: UW junior who cut American flag cable atop Bascom Hall

Wagner, Dave: UW student and *Connections* writer

Wheadon, Dave: Worker at Oscar Mayer and March on the Pentagon participant

Williams, William Appleman: UW history professor and theorist on American imperialism

Zeitlin, Maurice: UW sociology professor and antiwar activist

WASHINGTON STORY

Califano, Joseph: White House assistant to the president

Cater, Douglass: White House assistant to the president

Christian, George: White House press secretary

Christopher, Warren: Assistant attorney general

Clark, Ramsey: Attorney general

Fortas, Abe: Supreme Court justice and LBJ confidant

Helms, Richard: Director of the Central Intelligence Agency

Johnson, Lady Bird: First lady of the United States

Johnson, Lynda Bird: Daughter of the president

Johnson, Lyndon Baines: President of the United States

Johnson, Tom: Assistant press secretary, note taker

Katzenbach, Nicholas: Deputy secretary of state

Kissinger, Henry: Harvard professor and Johnson administration consultant

Leonhart, William: Assistant to the president

McNamara, Robert S.: Secretary of defense

Robb, Charles S.: Marine Corps major, Wisconsin graduate, future LBJ son-in-law

Rostow, Walt V.: National security adviser

Rusk, Dean: Secretary of state

Wheeler, Earle G.: Joint Chiefs of Staff chairman

A BRIEF PREFACE

THIS BOOK is shaped around two events that occurred contemporaneously during two days in the sixties—October 17 and 18, 1967. The first was an ambush in Vietnam that occurred when the Black Lions, a renowned battalion of the First Infantry Division, marched into the jungle on a search-and-destroy mission forty-four miles northwest of Saigon. The second was a demonstration at the University of Wisconsin where antiwar protestors staged a sit-in aimed at preventing the Dow Chemical Company, manufacturers of napalm, from recruiting on the Madison campus. The title is taken from the first line of "Elegy" by Bruce Weigl, a poem about U.S. infantrymen in Vietnam marching into sunlight on their way to a deadly ambush. But the image applies to all the people of this book who were caught up in the battles of war and peace during that turbulent era. Soldiers in Southeast Asia, student protesters in the United States, President Johnson and his advisers at the White House—they lived in markedly different worlds that were nonetheless dominated by the same overriding issue, and they all, in their own ways, seemed to be marching toward ambushes in those bright autumn days of 1967.

BOOK ONE

Some say that we shall never know and that to the Gods we are like flies that the boys kill on a summer day, and some say, on the contrary, that the very sparrows do not lose a feather that has not been brushed away by the finger of God.

—Thornton Wilder, *The Bridge of San Luis Rey*

CHAPTER I

SAILING TO VUNG TAU

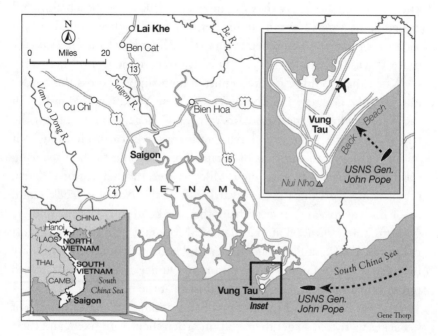

Gene Thorp

THE SOLDIERS REPORTED one by one and in loose bunches, straggling into Fort Lewis from late April to the end of May 1967, all carrying orders to join a unit called C Packet. Not brigade, battalion, or company, but packet. No one at the military base in Washington State had heard of C Packet until then. It was a phantom designation conceived by military planners to meet the anxious demands of war.

The early arrivals were billeted on the far northern rim of the army base in a rotting wooden barracks with flimsy walls known derisively as "the pit." Many of them checked in at night after long flights and bus rides from forts in Louisiana and Texas or home leaves in the Midwest, and for them morning sunlight revealed an ethereal vision. Out the window, in the distance, rose majestic Mount Rainier. But after gaping at the snowcapped peak, they had little to do. Some were attached temporarily to an engineering battalion, the 339th, but they had no duties. A captain named Jim George, trim and handsome, a marathon runner fresh from the Eighth Infantry Division in Germany, led them through morning calisthenics and long-distance running, which was a drag except for the sight of flaccid lieutenants wheezing and dropping to one knee. One lazy Saturday they organized a picnic at the beach club and grilled hamburgers but ran out of beer, so a young officer rounded up a squad of privates and marched them to the PX and back on a mission for more. It was perhaps the best executed training maneuver of their stay.

When they could, the bored enlisted men slipped across the border into Canada. Gregory Landon of Vestal, New York, who wound up in the infantry after dropping out of Amherst College, rented a car for the trip and paid cash, not even having to use a credit card. He thought it odd to be provided a means of escape from Tacoma to the sheltering north but returned as scheduled. Mike Troyer, drafted out of Urbana, Ohio, while working the graveyard shift at the Navistar truck plant, made his way to Vancouver with another weekend squad. Some soldiers got drunk and climbed atop a memorial fountain before being run off politely by the Canadian police. Peter Miller, drafted out of the assembly line of a Procter & Gamble soap factory in Quincy, Massachusetts, found himself in jail in Seattle following a dustup at the bus station.

After a few weeks of this military being and nothingness, the men of C Packet were told to get their wills in order, their teeth fixed, and their dog tags ready because they were being shipped to Vietnam as permanent overseas replacements in the First Infantry Division. Most of them knew what was coming, but some were taken by surprise, and the news provoked a round of concerned calls to the base from relatives, congressmen, and clergy.

"Morale of the men is fairly good considering the situation we're in, but there is an underlying gloom," Greg Landon wrote home to his parents. There had been no attempt by the military to explain the war, he reported, and he felt "relatively ignorant" about jungle warfare even though there had been a Vietnam focus to his advanced infantry training at the notorious Tigerland compound at Fort Polk, Louisiana. What he thought he knew was discouraging. "Vietnam seems to be a real hellhole," he lamented, reciting a litany of horrors: Viet Cong (from *Viet*

Nam Cong San, meaning Communist Vietnamese), poisonous snakes and plants, mysterious diseases, leeches, chiggers, ticks, tigers, contaminated water. With all that, he was shipping off to a war that from his "lowly Pfc's viewpoint" could not be won short of a miracle because the Viet Cong could "easily blend into the populace while the large American" could not.

The one certainty Landon confronted was morbid. "Sad to think that a certain percentage of people here are sure to die in Vietnam," he wrote. In a P.S. he confided that he could sense even then who would die and who would survive and that he had to "extricate" himself from the doomed so that he would not die with them. Mike Troyer had similar thoughts. The favorite epigram of a gruff Tigerland drill sergeant stuck in his mind: It's not your duty to die for your country. It's your duty to make an enemy soldier die for his.

Most of the enlisted men in C Packet entered the military as draftees or volunteers for the draft. Few had attended college. Even fewer were from professional, comfortably middle-class homes like Landon, whose father, an Amherst graduate, was a lawyer for IBM, or Troyer, who had studied psychology at Urbana College and whose dad was a labor leader at the truck plant. They were working-class kids drawn from a handful of states scattered around the country: Landon, Peter Miller, David Halliday, and Frank McMeel among a group from New York and Massachusetts; Faustin Sena and Santiago Griego part of a cluster from New Mexico; Troyer, Bill McGath, Doug Cron, Terry Warner, and Tom Colburn, five of the large contingent from Ohio and Michigan; Michael Taylor from Alaska; Doug Tallent from North Carolina; and Jack Schroder in a group from Nebraska and Wisconsin.

Schroder was a quiet young man with reddish blond hair who had entered the army at nineteen after studying to be a dental technician at the Career Academy in Milwaukee. His aim was to own a lab and make false teeth. He had volunteered for the draft mostly out of a sense of duty and family tradition, partly from frustration. His girlfriend, Eleanor Heil, a nursing student, had become pregnant but at first did not feel ready for marriage. She feared that her father in the small northern Wisconsin town of Edgar would disown her if she tried to come home, so she chose to keep the pregnancy a secret until she could put the baby up for adoption. In early March, when her boy was born, Heil realized that she could not give him away. She felt instantly grown up and ready to marry Jack, who had gone off to the army a few months earlier and was finishing infantry training at Fort Bliss, Texas. Jack was elated by her change of heart. They got married on his first furlough and spent a few days together as a family before he reported to C Packet. When Eleanor learned that the packet was being shipped to Vietnam, she traveled to Fort Lewis to be with her new husband for his last few weeks stateside. They shared a mobile home in a trailer park near the fort with two other married couples. On her final day there, as she was saying good-bye, Jack blurted out that he would not come home a cripple.

Four days later, on the day after the Fourth of July, Private Schroder started keeping a daily journal. "Was woke up this morning at 0515, had Reveille at 0600 and chow following," the first entry began. "Had formation at 0800, the captain telling us that we had approximately 24 more hours till we leave Fort Lewis, Washington. He said to plan on leaving base at 0300 in the morning. There is a lot to do and a short time to do it in."

Schroder returned to his bunk and packed his large green duffel bag—four issues of khaki uniforms, still the stateside version, with heavier cotton than jungle fatigues, plus two pairs of boots, socks, and underwear. Then he walked to the post exchange with a pal to "get some personal items" he might need in Vietnam. After standing around while his buddy "called his 3 girl friends and took plenty of time to tell them good-bye," Jack phoned his parents. No one was home. He tried Eleanor. "But it seemed she wasn't home either, anyway no one answered, she and my son Lawrence Wayne probably went shopping in town." Mail call brought a letter from his mother urging him to be careful and have a "fast trip back to the States" at the end of twelve months.

That evening a posse of privates sat for haircuts, an outing described by Michael Taylor in a letter to his parents in Cordova, Alaska. "Everybody went haircut crazy. . . . Some guys got mohawks, some had rings going around their heads, others got polka dots. One guy had his look like wings. . . . Of course, we all have to have another haircut because the Old Man won't go for it." It was, if nothing else, another way for the young soldiers to express their conflicted feelings about the military before they departed for the unknown.

"Men are anxious to leave now," Schroder signed off his diary that night. "I don't blame them much." Officers included: at their own private going-away party, sixteen war-bound lieutenants emptied four cases of champagne.

The soldiers were mustered at one the next morning and ordered to turn in their bedding and clean the barracks before being divided into three groups for the bus ride to the air field. "It was a very cloudy rainy & dreary day plus cold," Schroder wrote. He talked to two stewardesses on the commercial flight to San Diego, but still it was "not a good trip," lasting "4 hours and some odd minutes." A charter bus brought them to the navy pier, where other replacement packets, some army aviators, and a vast contingent of marines waited to board the ship that would sail them all to Vietnam. It was the USNS *General John Pope,* an old bucket named for the Civil War general who was relieved of command by Lincoln after the second Battle of Bull Run.

The USNS *Pope* had made its first Pacific run in December 1943 carrying troops from San Francisco to New Caledonia and was pulled out of mothballs by the Military Sealift Command for Vietnam service. It was a General Class transport ship: 623 feet long, with a maximum speed of twenty-one knots and room for 5,289 men. When sunlight hit at certain angles, massive dents became visible in the hull. "Is this what the *Reluctant* looked like?" asked C Packet lieutenant Tom Grady, a graduate of Lasalle University in Philadelphia, when he caught sight of the creaky vessel. Grady was reminded of the hapless supply ship that Henry Fonda and Jack Lemmon were stuck on in the dark World War II comedy *Mister Roberts.*

The C Packet troops waited three hours before they were allowed aboard. They marched up the plank to the huzzahs of a brass band, but once they reached deck, there was another delay before chow, because twenty-seven hundred marines ate first. The next morning Schroder hustled to the breakfast line before the mob of marines. The ship was scheduled to leave port at one that afternoon, but the loading took several hours more, which seemed providential to the men. "All day there were young women & girls here at the dock trying to get the GIs to whistle and talk to them and they did," Schroder noted. "Some even missed chow because of the girls. I don't know what they are going to do when they get a leave in December for R.R. (Rest & Recuperation)."

Not long after they shoved off, there was an abandon-ship drill and another meal. The food was not bad, Schroder wrote touchingly, as if he had been living in domestic bliss for years, but "not anywhere near the cooking at home I get from my wife Eleanor." For Michael Taylor and Bill McGath, two C packet troops assigned KP duty, the comparison to home cooking was beyond imagining. One of their jobs was to help navy chefs prepare scrambled eggs for breakfast, which involved climbing up a metal ladder to crack 122 dozen eggs into a massive kettle. They staged contests to see who could crack the most eggs at once, with shell shards flying unappetizingly into the mix. McGath noticed from the crates that the eggs were not fresh but had been in cold storage for fourteen months. What struck Mike Troyer most about breakfast service was that meals awaited them on prestacked trays: eggs that were stuck to the bottom of one metal tray would be scraped onto the plate below.

The enlisted men were also stacked, floor to ceiling, row after row, seven berths high. The first few nights at sea were all rocking and rolling. Troyer's bunk felt like a stomach-turning amusement park ride. His feet would rise above his head, then his head would rise above his feet, up and down, all night long. "A lot of the men was sick during the night. The sea got plenty rough last night and has been almost all day," Schroder's July 8 entry began. "After chow almost everyone has been hanging over the sides vomiting." Doug Cron, from an Ohio dairy farm, had never been on a boat before. He felt queasy as soon as the ship left port and stayed sick most of the way, spending more time on deck than in the mess hall. Santiago Griego discovered danger at the rail. His first time there he looked up barely in time to duck vomit streaming down at him from a deck above.

Seasickness was what passed for excitement. The daily routine grew so tedious so quickly that Fort Lewis seemed hectic in retrospect. The soldiers went to movies, read paperbacks, prepared quarters for inspection, sunbathed when the weather turned hot, peeled their skin, began taking malaria pills, did more calisthenics, attended Vietnamese language classes, or skipped them, went to Bingo Night on Tuesday and Thursday, and jostled with the scruffy, tattooed marines. "Everywhere you go there are Marines, most of them are good men but there are a few that could stand to be thrown overboard," wrote Mike Troyer. They also played poker in the latrines, organized boxing matches, wrote letters and notes in journals, talked endlessly about what they would do on R&R or when they got back home, and slept. Lieutenant Grady, who under normal circumstances prided himself on the ways he could avoid physical exertion (he was one of the winded officers during the long-distance runs at Fort Lewis), became so bored that he started looking forward to physical training twice a day.

The only good part of the voyage, Grady told the troops, was that time aboard ship was subtracted from the one-year Vietnam tour. "Hey, look, it's not that bad," he often said, trying to raise spirits. "That's three weeks you don't have to spend *there*." With his gregarious nature, and without rigid regard for rank, Grady, who volunteered for the draft and was commissioned at officer candidate school, often talked freely to the kids in the packet and made friends among them. He grew especially fond of Michael Farrell, a nineteen-year-old draftee from New Orleans, who had a "bubbly and optimistic nature." Farrell was the sort of young buck who thought he was invincible. He confided to Grady that he wanted to be a machine gunner in Vietnam. "Why in God's name would you want to do that?" the lieutenant asked.

On the twelfth Jack Schroder wrote in his diary: "Well, today is my birthday, and what a place to be spending it out on a ship in the middle of the Pacific Ocean miles from nowhere." Private Landon, who also kept a diary of the voyage, described the atmosphere that day as "battle ship gray all the way." He had been pulling guard duty on deck since they left port five days earlier and had "yet to see another ship." On the thirteenth, as they crossed the International Date Line, he spotted a small whale three hundred yards away. What he saw most often were sweaty, bored men in T-shirts and caps, overheated privates looking for places to catch a breeze but lounging in all the wrong places. "Constantly shooing troops off equipment etc. Tedious job," Landon wrote. "Other guards let the rule go to seed, making the job that much tougher. Hate having to be the son-of-a-bitch, but these privates stick together like glue."

Tom Colburn, another C Packet man with guard duty, was more lenient, allowing soldiers to sprawl on deck for five minutes or so before asking them to leave. Colburn, whose pals took to calling him Baby-san, was the youngest of the bunch, a high school dropout from Pontiac who had just turned eighteen and barely carried a hundred pounds on his five-nine frame. Faustin Sena, who guarded a freezer, was more substantial but also easygoing. He loved nothing more than to sit above the hatch chugging on liberated cans of Hershey's chocolate milk.

News from the outside world arrived in a shipboard newspaper known as the *Pope Pourri,* which had a twelve-man staff of editors, reporters, and illustrators and included wire reports from the Armed Forces Press Service and United Press International. It was a straightforward sheet, with little attempt to propagandize. Day after day came reports of deadly race riots in Newark, the arrest of segregationist terrorists in North Carolina, the difficult aftermath of the Six-Day War in the Middle East, fighting in the Congo, the debate over a national tax increase, and of course the news about Vietnam. On the Saturday morning of July 15, the men of C Packet read the latest unsettling figures: 282 Americans had been killed in battle during the previous week, the third-highest weekly total since the war began. The trend seemed to be more of the same. "More Troops to Vietnam—LBJ," read the banner headline that day over a story noting that President Johnson, after two days of meetings with his generals at the White House, had decided to send more battalions into the war.

Considering where the soldiers were coming from, and where they were going, it was inevitable that tensions would play out aboard ship. There were fights every day, mostly minor scrapes. But on the nineteenth Landon reported "a small riot on the deck, drawn along racial lines." Not surprising, he thought, since fires of black rage were burning in so many inner cities that summer. "This tied in with the concurrent unrest in Newark, N.J. The problem grows with the length of the trip and as the climate grows hotter and thicker. Thank God for the air conditioning in the compartments."

That last sigh of relief was something that Captain Jim George could not utter. He was stuck in a small cabin with three other captains, a room without air conditioning that soared above one hundred degrees and was unbearably sticky even on windy days. George was fastidious about washing his underwear but was warned by the ship captain that they were using too much water and might have to start rationing. Some officers played poker at night, but George did not know how. He consistently lost at bingo, but at least won at Monopoly once. For George, who prepared for an officer's career at Wofford College in his home-town of Spartanburg, South Carolina, the long trip was another re-minder of the occasional frustrations of the military bureaucracy.

First the army cut short his command of a tank company in Germany to rush him to Vietnam, then they made him wait and do nothing at Fort Lewis for two months, and then they put him on this slow voyage across the Pacific. "I just feel as though I've wasted so much valuable time and also the taxpayers' money just sitting around," the earnest officer wrote home to his wife, Jackie. "I'm not doing much and ready to get on with the task at hand." He was a bright officer, only twenty-five, with two young sons, John and Jay, and a wife whom he dearly missed. In one letter home to Jackie at 155A Pine Grove Manor in Spartanburg, his mind drifted back to their first apartment and how they "worked to-gether to prepare it for a happy marriage"; and to the day he rode a mo-torcycle up on the porch of their little house on Vernon Street and how

Jackie "raised H——L" with him for buying it; and to the first night in their apartment in Germany and little John's afternoon naps; and to all the good times they'd had in five married years "even though outside factors such as college, money, parents and the Army" had put some pressure on them "from time to time."

These wistful daydream remembrances were welcome interruptions to the sounds of war rumbling in his brain. In spare hours he read books about combat, first *The Last Battle,* a narrative describing the final Allied push toward Berlin in World War II, then *Dateline: Vietnam,* an account by Scripps-Howard war correspondent Jim G. Lucas of the fighting zone to which George was headed. During nightly bull sessions in the airless cabin, the captains talked about what to expect in Vietnam and how they would fare in battle. George wanted to command his own infantry company in Vietnam and was surprised to learn that some officers had no desire to lead troops into combat.

The brutal reality of man killing man, he confided in a letter to Jackie, now dominated his conscious and subconscious thoughts. "I've had a lot of time to engage in deep thinking and it's really sickening how the world is so full of conflict and what's more how we're so much a part of it. At times I feel so guilty and know I could do more to make it a better place. I'll do what I can, and pray that God will lead me. I've already started to dream of killing and am already tired of the smell of death. Life is so short at times but too long at others. We're all a 'bunch of nuts' I guess. I'm just out on a limb by myself today and have no one to talk to who has the patience to understand me or will let me try to understand them. I'll endure what I must and remember that I must be a good 1) soldier, 2) gentleman, 3) lover and 4) Christian. The most important, of course, is #4 and the others as apropos."

Thoughts of killing also raced through the mind of Private Troyer. He wondered if he could take a human life. Peter Miller had the same question. Like the others, he had grown up playing army and watching John Wayne movies. Was that version different from the real thing? Bill McGath wondered too but felt a moral obligation. In his eleventh-grade speech class at Mifflin High in suburban Columbus, he had chosen the pro side in a war debate, and he believed still what he had said then— that the United States had to "protect its allies, fight communism, and let free policy reign." Terry Warner, off a livestock farm in western Ohio, had "no feelings about the war one way or the other" but knew enough to be scared. Alaskan Mike Taylor was already sick of the military. "This

Army is something else," he had written home to his parents after his records had been mixed up with two other Michael Taylors. "They are always screwing up something."

Whether it was mass dyslexia, hope for some spiritual blessing for the year ahead, or most likely just soldierly sarcasm, some troops aboard soon reversed the name of their ship and started calling it not the *John Pope* but the *Pope John.* Not that they treated the vessel with more reverence after that. Somewhere along the Tropic of Cancer in the vast Pacific stretch past Midway Islands, one soldier felt so trapped that he jumped overboard, a suicidal escape attempt that was thwarted when the ship turned around and picked him up. He was the second would-be escapee from the USNS *Pope* that year. During the January voyage a soldier in the Ninth Infantry Division had gone overboard to his apparent death.

They reached Okinawa at nine on the Saturday morning of July 22, the first land in two weeks. The troops were allowed off ship but ordered to return by 1800 hours. Mike Troyer and his pals marched up the hill to the enlisted men's club, where they drank scotch for twenty-five cents a glass and played slot machines. Landon was forced to stay on board because an officer decided his hair was too long. In his diary he recorded the harbor scene: no gunboats; two cargo ships, one coming, one going ("war keeps them pretty busy"); bright white sand; turquoise water spotted with jellyfish; the wreckage of a four-motor airplane from World War II hulking on the beach; a storm approaching from the south.

Vietnam was a few days distant and closing fast in Landon's mind. "The daily reports of action in the war seem so common now," he wrote on his lonely watch, reciting news from the *Pope Pourri,* "200 enemy dead in a sweep . . . 15 American dead and 50 casualties etc. etc. It is as if we will never see the end. If N Viet Nam is bluffing, it backs up its bluff. Politics in S Viet Nam hardly help. Until there can be 2 sides to this war, and not 50,000 shades of commitment, this war cannot and will not be won. The populace is obviously confused and divided. These people must decide and decide soon or the U.S. will tire to the point of despair in tiptoeing through the morass of politics while ducking improvised weapons of Viet Cong and barrages of Russian-made artillery fire. Maybe."

The troops who scrambled off that morning stumbled back up the gangplank on their afternoon return. Lieutenant Grady said he never saw so many drunk kids in his life, almost every single one dead drunk. One smacked an officer and ended up in the brig. Another sauntered aboard toting a cheap guitar case, which when searched contained not an instrument but a fifth of whisky. A third pulled up in a taxi and stumbled out naked, claiming he had gone swimming and someone had stolen his clothes. Another wobbled halfway up the plank and keeled overboard. *How's the water?* some buddies yelled down. *Just fine,* he answered, squirting an arch of spray from his mouth, and with that a few jumped overboard to join him. The officers were for the most part sympathetic: *Just get these kids back in,* Grady said. *They know where they're going. Let's not make this any tougher than it is.*

Captain George had spent six hours in port. He wrote to Jackie that it was dirty and smelled "worse than Germany." Even though he was impressed by the low prices of clothing in the PX, he passed them up, but he could not resist buying a Japanese steel string guitar for only ten fifty, which he would strum until his fingers went raw. He also went to a geisha house with the other captains and got a bath and a massage for a buck eighty, an enjoyment he described to his wife without hesitation: "It was real unusual. The woman started by walking up and down our backs."

Schroder wrote in his diary that he stayed away from the bars, choosing instead to go swimming. He got cut by coral, managed to avoid the jellyfish, but could not avoid his sloshed compatriots at the end of the day. "There were a lot of fellas they were so drunk they had to be carried back. 90% of them. There were several fights. A fight here in the compartment, two men on one. They beat him up while he was asleep in bed, he got messed up pretty bad he got kicked in the face. Nobody would break it up, so I broke it up, don't like the odds 2 against one."

As the ship steamed down into the South China Sea, the weather turned from torrid to unbearable. One hundred degrees during the day and one hundred at night. The air conditioning system broke, which was when many soldiers first realized that the ship *had* air conditioning. Although sleeping on deck was prohibited, the rule was obliterated by necessity, and for a few nights a thousand or more men slept in the open air. "As many as could fit went up there," Landon noted. "It looked like we were boat people."

The morning sunrise was soothing, the water a shade of dark blue the soldiers had never imagined and perfectly smooth. "I've never seen Indian Lake as calm as what this water is," Mike Troyer reported to his parents, referring to a small Ohio lake of his boyhood. Flying fish were everywhere, and occasional whales. Four days past Okinawa, the ship reached Da Nang, Vietnam, where the rest of the marines off-loaded, leaving the mess hall at last to Schroder and the GIs. Jim George heard "artillery or mortar fire" when they pulled into Da Nang, but "it was about 10 or 15 miles away and I think it was ours." Peter Miller stood at the rail and watched the marines march away, and surveyed the harbor with its exhilarating bustle of ships and boats, a riot of smells and colors, and here came barefooted Vietnamese men unloading cargo. It all seemed exotic to him, nothing like the soap line at the factory in Quincy. "Hoo boy," he said, taking it in. "This is a different world."

Two days later, after a final leg south at the end of the six-thousand-mile voyage, the ship came to a stop a few hundred yards from the beach at Vung Tau, an old resort town known during colonial days as Cap St. Jacques, about sixty miles southeast of Saigon. Late that night Faustin Sena saw bright lights in the distance and remarked that it must be a big city out there. The lights were not from a city, he was told. Those were the lights of war—bombs and tracers. A chill went up his back. "Oh, mama," he whispered.

The next morning, in the bright dawn of July 29, this latest batch of American infantrymen clambered down Jacob's ladders into old World War II–style landing boats and came ashore.

THE WATER WAS SMOOTH and easy, barely disturbed by the crafts plying back and forth from the big ship. The sand of Back Beach, white and clean, invited these young Americans in, with the verdant rise of Nui Nho, the little mountain, framing the vista at the southern end of the peninsula, its three rusted, thirty-three-ton French naval guns offering only an intimation from on high of the war-torn history of this slender land.

For most U.S. enlisted men in Vietnam, history tended to begin anew the day they stepped foot "in country" and to end the day they left. Evocative war stories were passed down from one group to the next, but few historical facts. Back Beach might have meant nothing to the men of C Packet, just an insignificant point of entry, a brief stop on the way to somewhere else. But in the legend of the First Infantry Division's service in Vietnam, the white sands of Vung Tau represented the first station of the cross. It was here, less than two years earlier, during the early days of

October 1965, that the main force of the First Division reached Vietnamese soil—9,600 troops and their equipment brought over on twenty ships as part of Operation Big Red. Army cameramen were at the beach October 7 and recorded that day's arrival on 35-millimeter film. Their grainy footage of the seminal scene, as viewed later, flickered eerily between color and black-and-white, as though caught forever between present and past.

Soldiers line the deck of the U.S.S. *General Daniel I. Sultan,* green duffel bags slung over their shoulders, waiting their turn to board landing craft, many of their faces pubescent, unmarked. On their shoulder sleeves, the proud Big Red One insignia, an olive drab shield two and a half inches wide, three and three-quarters inches high, with a red Arabic numeral one in the middle. Placid waters, blinding sand, a welcoming party of big brass on the beach, including the architect of the American buildup, General William C. Westmoreland, commander of the Military Assistance Command, Vietnam, neatly attired in starched fatigues with a MACV patch on his left sleeve, his blue-gray eyes gleaming under a baseball cap. Behind him, an ethereal array of Vietnamese girls holding lotus flowers, each dressed in an *ao dai* of pure white. White, black, Latino—the soldiers disembark and march up the beach, their figures dissolving into brightness.

The four-star general and the *ao dai* wisps were nowhere to be seen as the replacement troops from the USNS *Pope* came ashore twenty-two months later. A Vietnamese teenager chased after Doug Tallent as he reached the beach and tried to take his watch. Another group of local boys stood nearby yelling, "Fuck you, GI!"

Greg Landon, with his deadpan sarcasm, said all he needed was a corncob pipe to feel like General MacArthur staging his dramatic return to the Philippines. The beach swarmed with six hundred men, some in formation, others roaming the sand, uncertain where they should go. There were now nearly a half million American forces in Vietnam and more arriving daily by air and sea. Battalions were growing from three rifle companies to four, which was what the packets were all about—a means of quickly providing fresh troops for the additional companies. C Packet was being divided into two units that would be assigned to different battalions within the Big Red One.

First Lieutenant Clark Welch and First Sergeant Bud Barrow came upon this hectic shoreline scene looking like a modern-day Don Quixote and Sancho Panza, the officer stooping slightly next to his shorter sidekick, who carried a makeshift flag that they had fashioned the day be-fore—blue cloth attached to a bamboo pole with crossed rifles braced by the words D Company above and the numbers 2/28 below.

"Where's Delta Company? Are you Delta Company?" Welch asked the first beachmaster he encountered carrying a clipboard. These were not companies, they were packets, he was told. A navy officer finally pointed him toward a unit of men standing at attention in fatigues, "a beautiful formation, with this beautiful captain"—officers in front, ser-geants in back, duffel bags at their sides, the ship behind them in the glimmering sea. It was the unit led by Captain George.

"There's only one commander here, and it ain't you," Welch told George in his invariably direct manner after they were introduced. C Packet existed no more. These men were now part of Delta Company, the fourth and final company of a battalion that made up half a regiment known as the Black Lions. What a storied history these Black Lions had: formed in 1901, the first American unit committed to combat in World War I, twice awarded the croix de guerre with palm, France's highest military honor, named in the aftermath of their most famous battle there, when they became known as the Black Lions of Cantigny. Welch addressed the newest members of that proud lineage. He gave little thought to the fact that George was the superior officer, captain to lieu-tenant. He never was much on rank; he rarely even wore his rank on his battle uniform.

Welcome to Vietnam. He was Lieutenant Welch, commander of Delta Company. They were now Delta Company, Second Battalion, Twenty-eighth Infantry Regiment, First Infantry Division. They would move from Vung Tau to the Big Red One base at Lai Khe by C-130 air-plane. No time to waste. But first Welch needed a guidon bearer, some-one to carry the blue Delta banner. No one stepped forward. "Okay, goddamit, you!" the lieutenant bellowed, pointing to the tallest soldier in the rear. "Wherever I go, you go. Hold that banner high!" And with that he marched ninety-three of his new men, plus several dozen others who were as yet unassigned, off the sand, into the sunlight, toward the airfield and the transport planes that carried them to their strange new home.

It was raining when they arrived at Lai Khe, but the division band was at the airstrip to greet them. Drum rolls and trumpets for the arriv-ing heroes. *Wow, this is special,* Greg Landon thought. Then abruptly he found himself loaded into the back of an old deuce-and-a-half, a heavy supply truck, where he and the other Delta recruits slipped around on a truck bed as muddy as the hoof-slopped earth beneath a feeding trough for dairy cows in the aftermath of a midsummer thundershower. So much for feeling special. Captain George and the other new officers were taken another direction, to headquarters of the Big Red One's Third Brigade. A colonel was waiting for them. He seemed eager to give them an unsentimental lecture on the facts of life in the war zone. Enlisted men could not be trusted, he said. Enlisted men were nothing but sons of bitches.

Sons of bitches. Jim George was stunned. His "blood boiled" as he thought to himself, "Aren't those the guys pulling the triggers and doing the fighting and dying?"

CHAPTER 2

TRIET'S MARCH SOUTH

Vo Minh Triet had been fighting in the war fields between Saigon and the Cambodian border for more than six years by the summer of 1967. To the American soldiers at Lai Khe, he was the enemy, out there somewhere beyond the concertina wire, and all they had to do was go out and find him.

Each of us has our own situation, Triet once explained, and his went like this: He was a southerner, the sixth child born into a farm family in the district of Ba Tri near the mouth of one of the Nine Dragons, or branches, of the Mekong River. Near the end of the summer of 1945, when he was fifteen, his life was reshaped by circumstances beyond his adolescent horizon. The wartime Japanese occupiers had left, a declaration of independence had been issued in Hanoi, and the long struggle to rid Vietnam of the French colonialists had begun anew. Ba Tri was a stronghold of the liberation movement. Less than a mile from Triet's rural home stood the revered tomb of Nguyen Dinh Chieu, the great blind poet of the South whose patriotic verse a century earlier had inspired his countrymen as they took up arms against foreign occupation. "Better to die fighting the enemy and to return to our ancestors in glory / Than to survive in submission to the Western strangers."

Triet quit school and joined the resistance against the French, just as his father had done. First he was in a youth brigade, later in the army of the Viet Nam Doc Lap Dong Minh Hoi, the Allied Vietnamese Independence League known as the Viet Minh. He was wounded in the right shin in 1952 during a battle in Kien Giang Province, but kept fighting until the French were defeated in 1954. At that point much of Vietnam was controlled by the Viet Minh, but its fate was determined by outsiders. The larger Communist powers, led by the Soviet Union and China, pushed the Viet Minh to accept the Geneva accords dividing Vietnam in two. It was to be a temporary separation until elections could be held to reunify the nation in the summer of 1956. Triet and his unit marched north to await the national elections, which never happened. The government in the South, with the Eisenhower administration its primary benefactor, declared that the North's aggression in the aftermath of Geneva negated the agreement.

In the first days of 1961 Triet took the first steps toward the final battlefield of our story, walking back toward his native South with one of the first units of North Vietnamese forces to take up the fight against the U.S.-supported Saigon regime. He was thirty by then, an old warrior by military standards but one of the younger men of a squad whose average age was thirty-five. His comrades, like him, were transplanted southerners who had fought the French. For twenty nights before leaving, they had trained for the winding journey down Vietnam's treacherous spine by walking three hours through the countryside beyond the Xuan Mai barracks south of Hanoi. Triet, weighing 121 pounds, trained by hauling a pack loaded at nearly half his weight. It was drudgery, he thought, but there was gratification at the end of each outing when they returned to camp and were given limeade and porridge and maybe some beer or *quoc lui,* rice whisky that to them tasted finer than Russian vodka.

In the official military history of Triet's regiment, published decades later, there is mention of a final meeting in Hanoi with the two leading figures of the Vietnamese revolution, Communist Party chairman Ho Chi Minh, referred to affectionately as Uncle Ho, and Senior General Vo Nguyen Giap, hero of the defeat of the French at Dien Bien Phu. It was reported that Giap, after briefing these southbound troops on their duties, "chatted with them cordially and open-heartedly" and asked, "Comrades, once in the South, where will you find guns to fight the enemy?" To which came the reply, "General, we will carry guns from the North to kill the enemy and take their weapons." Later that evening Uncle Ho gave the soldiers four pieces of advice. First, maintain unity. Second, preserve secrecy. Third, act in coordination with new comrades. And fourth, be prepared "to go anywhere and do any work assigned by

the party . . . and refrain from making demands." The troops were said
to be "extremely moved" by Ho's "sagacious instructions" and promised
to heed his teachings. So went the myth.

The poetic and the harsh converge in Vietnam. From that glorified
rendition of a noble sending-forth followed two months and twenty-
seven brutal days. Triet and his comrades were transported by truck
down Route 1 to Ha Tinh, then west toward the mountains near the
border with Laos, and from there they walked more than six hundred
miles south through the wilderness along the Truong Son range. They
carried French-made MAS (modern army supply) rifles, a few Thompson submachine guns, radio equipment, and medical supplies. There
was no road, only the most primitive semblance of what Americans later
would call the Ho Chi Minh Trail. The route over and around densely
forested mountains was marked by broken twigs left by advance scouts.
Three weeks of training gave Triet little warning of how exhausted he
would feel after only the first day. His boots made his feet swell, so he
took them off and tied them around his shoulders, then threw them
away altogether and replaced them with rubber-tire sandals.

The sandals were less slippery on mountain slopes and also more effective when it came to tree leeches. If a soldier wore boots, the tree
leeches could dig in, but with sandals at least they could be spotted immediately. The sight and sound of tree leeches haunted every man who
marched down the Truong Son trail. Triet saw no tigers along the way,
nor did he encounter enemies from the Saigon Special Forces, but he
would never forget the tree leeches. They lived under leaves that fell
from the trees, and when troops came by, the creatures smelled a human
feast approaching. Triet and his comrades would hear a cranky *yrrow,*
yrrow sound and see the trail move and the leaves rustle, and they knew
that beneath the leaves tens of thousands of leeches were heading toward
them en masse. The audacious bloodsuckers were about the size of pen
tips before they gorged. They attached themselves in spherical hordes.

Salt was among the most precious rations Triet carried. It was meant
for cooking, but he used it for another purpose. At the end of the day he
wrapped a piece of cloth around the tip of a stick and soaked it in salted
water. This became his leech-removing prod for the next morning; the
salt would make leeches jump from his feet. Instead of salt for flavoring,
Triet and his squad often used the ash from charcoal to flavor their
meals, which usually consisted of pressed rice along with greens they
had picked along the way. Every hour they took a ten-minute break to

gather food for dinner, collecting what they could find at the side of the trail: mostly bamboo sprouts and greens known as machete heads and airplane heads. When they reached camp for the night, they gathered and washed the greens, boiled them, spread them out on two nylon ponchos, and took out their chopsticks for a communal dinner.

Lunch was a small portion of pressed rice, if available, and for energy in the early afternoon Triet reached into his pocket and pulled out a tiny piece of the hundred grams of ginseng that he had bought in a traditional medicine shop in Hanoi. At an aid station in the Central Highlands, where there was no rice, his squad was provided a can of corn. It was divided evenly among the men, twenty kernels per soldier a day. During one stretch near the end of the march, they went seven days without rice. The storage bins at an aid station were empty, and the commander decided that if they waited around for rice, they might all get sick and die and have no one to bury them, so they kept moving. For morning sustenance they relied on what they jokingly called *ca-phe doc,* which means "hill coffee"—not the sort one would buy at the market. Every night, if possible, Triet and his squad camped next to a stream, which meant they were in a low-lying drainage area and the walk the next morning would be on a steep incline up the next mountain. They usually walked uphill from dawn until ten or eleven before reaching a crest, and this difficult ascent was their hill coffee because it unfailingly woke them up.

The first southbound troops reached their destination on March 27. Triet's squad arrived weeks later. Their new headquarters were at two base camps, one hidden deep in the jungle of War Zone C near the Cambodian border above Tay Ninh, about sixty miles to the northwest of Saigon, and another across the Saigon and Song Be rivers to the northeast in War Zone D. The camps were on the rim of a larger region of Vietnam called Eastern Nam Bo, where many native southerners had fought the French in the early 1950s. Abandoned tunnels and trenches from that earlier struggle were still evident. "Eastern Nam Bo is full of hardships but exudes gallantry," troops had sung as they left the region to relocate in the North in 1954. Now they were back in this familiar landscape where they would fight and die for another fourteen years.

Once in the South, the soldiers were reorganized into fighting units, part of the People's Army of Vietnam (PAVN). Vo Minh Triet, whose war name was Bay Triet, became part of a regiment with the code name Q761, a designation taken from its official founding in July 1961. A few months later, on the second of September, the national day in the North, Triet and his comrades were officially designated the First Regiment at a ceremony in the shadows of Nui Ba Den, the Black Virgin Mountain, where they recited ten solemn oaths of faithfulness and solidarity and promised to fight to the end for the liberation of South Vietnam and national reunification. Over the next few years Triet's regiment would take on other aliases, most notably the Binh Gia Regiment, an honorific bestowed upon it after a decisive battle in late 1964 against the South's ARVN (Army of the Republic of Vietnam) units near Saigon. American intelligence reports later identified it consistently as the 271st Regiment, though this was a name the unit itself never used. Q761, yes; First Regiment, yes; Binh Gia, yes; 271st, no. There never *was* a 271st, Triet later insisted.

After the victory at Binh Gia, nearly four years into the fight against what they called the puppet troops of Saigon, Triet and his comrades believed their opponents were near defeat. It was an assessment shared by the Johnson administration in Washington, and soon thereafter, starting with the landing of elements of the U.S. Ninth Marine Expeditionary Force at Da Nang in early March 1965, the forces of the communist-led People's Army of Vietnam found themselves in a new sort of strategic war, dealing with ever-increasing numbers of American infantrymen on the ground and B-52s overhead.

The first full division of soldiers from the U.S. Army sent into Eastern Nam Bo in the summer and fall of 1965 belonged to the First Infantry, the old and proud Big Red One. By September 2, when Triet's First Regiment was incorporated into the newly founded Ninth VC Division, his commanders knew much about these arriving Americans: the order of battle, the names and histories of generals and colonels, all the way down to the height and weight of the average soldier (1.8 meters and eighty kilos, compared to 1.6 meters and fifty kilos on their side). *The Big Red One* was translated into Vietnamese as "Big Red Brothers." It was described in PAVN documents as an awesome force that had "a long history of warfare and had performed in an outstanding manner . . . in our military terminology, a unit that won a hundred battles in a hundred fights." An exaggeration, perhaps, but close enough for propaganda.

There was concern that the Americans, with their vast supply of armored vehicles, helicopters, big guns, and bombs, were invincible. One VC Ninth Division colonel even claimed that with inferior firepower and equipment, he gave his men the option of not fighting the Americans if they felt overwhelmed. (He reported later that fifteen of two hundred soldiers took this offer.) "Would the division be able to handle the Americans? How should it fight to beat them? These were extremely pressing questions," Ninth Division historians reported later. When Triet heard that the Americans were coming, his first thought was that the war would be "terrible and fierce." As to whether it would be a long war or a short war, he was less certain. From Hanoi radio he had heard reports of the incipient antiwar movement in the United States and pronouncements from Uncle Ho that the disquiet within America might be as important as armed conflict in Vietnam. Shaping public opinion was a strategic aspect of the political struggle, which was always waged in concert with the war itself.

As for the Big Red Brothers, Triet thought they were strong in firepower but also had potential weaknesses. What did they know about the people they were fighting and the land on which they fought?

CHAPTER 3

LAI KHE, SOUTH VIETNAM

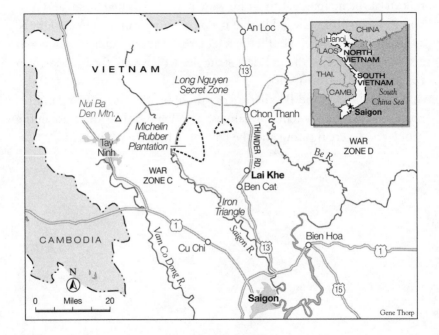

Gene Thorp

L AI KHE, pronounced *lie kay*. It was at once a small Vietnamese
village, a French rubber plantation, and an American military
base camp, three cultures interwoven by history and circumstance if not trust. Fences encircled the local village, which was swallowed whole by the larger oval of the military base. Who the fences were
supposed to protect, or keep in or out, was never obvious. Villagers
worked for the Big Red Brothers, washing laundry, cleaning rooms,
burning shit, cutting hair, serving drinks, providing sex, but many were
quietly supporting the other side, the Viet Cong. The French managers
of the Michelin plantation rarely showed up, though they seemed to
have scouts who knew everything; if rubber trees were cut down to give

24

mortars a cleaner arc into the nearby jungle, an invoice was sure to arrive soon thereafter billing the First Division a few hundred dollars per felled tree. While damning the French, the Americans took full advantage of the splendid remains of the colonial plantation; the officer corps occupied a resortlike villa of white stucco and red tile houses complete with recreation center and swimming pool. That some of the larger buildings came with oversized basins once used for rubber experiments was but a minor inconvenience.

Slicing vertically up the center of Lai Khe was Route 13, an unpaved highway made of rocky red laterite soil that ran from the outskirts of Saigon, some thirty-two miles to the south, to the Cambodian border, another forty miles north. Thunder Road, as the Americans called the highway, was a critical supply line that the First Division spent considerable firepower trying to control, with limited success. Like much of that section of Vietnam, it tended to belong to the South during the day and the Viet Cong at night. Big Red One engineers, protected by rifle companies, worked on the road relentlessly, clearing it of mines and using wooden planks to make passable stretches that had been ravaged by monsoon-season craters. Before a massive repair job in 1966, an engineering report said that it "looked as if the whole road would shortly sink into the swamp."

Within the uneven perimeter of Lai Khe, a loop approximately three miles long and a mile wide, division, brigade, and battalion headquarters were situated to the west side of Route 13, or to the left of the road driving north, as were the village, the helicopter pads, the aviation units, known as the Robin Hoods of Sherwood Forest, and several rifle companies, including Alpha Company of the Black Lions. A perforated steel airstrip ran south-north on a parallel line less than a hundred yards to the east of the highway. It was also on that side, up on the far northeastern section of the perimeter, that Clark Welch set up base camp for his new Delta Company, a good two-mile hike from division headquarters and the village. Though it was not entirely within his power to decide where to locate his men, it certainly was appropriate for Welch to be apart from the crowd.

There was no one comparable in the Black Lions regiment, few in the entire First Division. Long and sinewy at six foot two and 160 pounds, his frame always tilting forward slightly, ready to move, with his rough-hewn face topped by crew-cut black hair, his deep authoritative voice and fierce blue-eyed gaze softened by a sheepish smile, Welch was a soldier's soldier in the most elemental sense. He was an innate leader who earned his own rifle company by sheer ability in the field. It was not out of West Point that he became a lieutenant, nor officer training school. His only academic degree then was from Oyster River High in Durham, New Hampshire, in 1957. After excelling as a Green Beret sergeant, he was commissioned as an OBV2 lieutenant on December 15, 1965, with his father, a retired Corps of Engineers colonel, administering the oath. The acronym meant that he was an obligated volunteer who could serve as an officer for two years but was not guaranteed anything more. "In other words, 'Don't plan on keeping it,'" is how Welch half jokingly defined his lieutenancy.

The last thing Welch expected was to become a line commander in an infantry division. He had worn the green beret since it was authorized by President Kennedy in 1961, taking part in Special Forces operations in Lebanon, Laos, Venezuela, and Central America, and anticipated more of the same in Vietnam. He had studied Vietnamese at language school in Monterey, California, and had taken psychological operations training, all in preparation for what was known as Project Gamma, an ill-conceived project that envisioned small Special Forces teams consisting of two Americans and four Vietnamese living in villages near the demilitarized zone and collecting information on the enemy. By the time Welch arrived in the last days of April 1967, a few Gamma teams had been wiped out by the Viet Cong and the operation was scrapped. At the same time, the First Infantry Division desperately needed officers and was drawing them from anywhere possible. The realities of Vietnam and the demands of war changed Welch's assignment. He was going to the 2/28 Black Lions in Lai Khe.

The change surprised and upset him. At the First Division's rear headquarters in Di An, where he stopped on his way to Lai Khe, he pounded on an officer's desk and argued that this had to be a mistake. He was special. He had been trained for special things. He was still wearing his Green Beret uniform. From behind, an authoritative voice declared, "Lieutenant, I'm sure you'll be happy in my old division." Welch turned around to see the tough little former commander of the Big Red One, Major General William E. DePuy.

"Oh, yes, sir. I'm sure I'll be happy," Welch answered.

"Get rid of that silly hat," DePuy said, and that was the end of that.

From the moment he arrived at Lai Khe, Albert Clark Welch began making a special name for himself, even without his green beret. On his second day in camp, he was sent to an area several miles to the southwest where the Viet Cong functioned in an elaborate network of under-ground tunnels. A Black Lions unit had killed three enemy soldiers and three more were trapped in a tunnel, but the battalion interpreter had left earlier that week and Welch was the only American on the scene who knew some Vietnamese. "I talked 3 VC into surrendering," he reported in a letter to his wife, Lacy Welch, a nurse then living in Fort My-ers, Florida. (He wrote to her virtually every day—long, evocative accounts in the legible print lettering of an engineer.) "I told them they were surrounded and we had a flamethrower and they scrambled right out. They came out with their weapons and said all the others had es-caped. We blew up the tunnel and the 3 VC were flown back to Brigade." Welch was a modest man, there was a bit of the Jimmy Stewart aw-shucks quality to him as he detailed his accomplishments, but he was also a proud soldier who wanted to share his feelings with his wife. He thought he had made "quite a first impression" with his new battalion.

Two days later the Viet Cong launched a mortar attack on Lai Khe, and Welch's instinctive reaction further enhanced his reputation. After all the training he had done, it was almost as if he had been through it before, he told Lacy. He was in the mess hall drinking coffee when the rockets hit outside, blowing open the doors to the building. It was the first enemy attack at Lai Khe in weeks. Instinctively realizing that it was incoming mortar fire, Welch jumped up and yelled, "Get in the bunker!" He pushed his fellow soldiers out toward the bunker, then ran to the command bunker and asked where the mortar alarm was. No one had pushed it yet. "I was leaning on the siren when the XO (executive officer) ran in," Welch wrote to Lacy. "He said that was the first time he'd been beaten to his own bunker—and to be beaten by a 'newly-arrived lieutenant' who not only beat him but was there sounding the alarm—was not what he expected. I think I can do well here, Lacy."

That assessment was shared by his superior officers. At a ceremony at the end of Welch's first week, a brigade lieutenant colonel told the new troops that some "might be in combat before the sun set today and oth-ers would never see a shot fired during 12 months"—then cited the ex-ample of a new lieutenant who had already qualified for a Combat Infantry Badge. Welch was "looking around, like everyone else" to see who that might be, when the officer added, "I mean that lieutenant who got 3 VC to give themselves up earlier this week."

Welch was made the leader of the Black Lions' recon (reconnaissance) platoon, an elite unit that before he took over had served primarily as a protective guard for the battalion. He swiftly transformed it into a hot unit ready for action and led his men into their first firefight on May 16. A few hours after the battle, he struggled to describe what it felt like. "This morning I actually led my men in combat," he wrote to Lacy. "I guess it should be one of the greatest things I've ever done—I've worked towards it for so long. I just can't say what it's like. This war is really affecting the whole world, but it's only being fought right here along a very thin line separating combat soldiers from the Viet Cong. Much of this business is just plain awful—the people getting hurt and crying and even dying; but I saw men at their finest this morning. The infantry in close combat is just something else. . . . Although I've been sure that I could perform when I had to, now I know that I can lead, even under fire."

After another firefight a few weeks later, Welch again tried to relate to Lacy what it was like. Again he feared that he would not find the words. "We just gathered and shot at anything that moved because we knew we were the only good guys around. . . . For a few minutes it was like the whole world was right there with us, all my life, everything I've ever done or thought about was right there. After it was over and we dared to talk or look around, we just couldn't comprehend that we were all alive and that the VC had really been that close. They were close, Lacy, and there was a hell of a lot of them."

During his first month in Lai Khe, Welch led his platoon on twelve missions and made contact with the Viet Cong eleven times. His unit of sixteen soldiers had killed "between 10 and 20 VC" without losing a man and had captured a pile of weapons, ten tons of reinforcing rods that the enemy used to make claymore mines, twenty tons of rice, salt, and oil, a stash of clothes, and a file cabinet of VC tax rolls and payroll vouchers, with the last entry May 1967. His men by then had a nickname for him—Big Rock. He was the talk of the camp, always in the middle of things. "That's one old son of a bitch that's got his shit together," he overheard a soldier say of him one night, and he considered it the ultimate compliment.

"I keep thinking of what the news reporter wrote about me many years ago, when my trombone got bent and I couldn't play my solo," he reminisced in a letter to Lacy about his New Hampshire school days. "Something about, 'Young Welch seems to be able to get in trouble very easily, but always gets out again just as easily.'" Soldiers from other companies now wanted to get into his platoon, believing that with him they would be safe yet never bored, an uncommon set of circumstances.

When Welch was out in the field, he had the habit of never being too far from his point squad. If there was action, he wanted to see it and be part of it. Men who walked with him considered him hyperalert, sensitive to any unexpected noise, yet an important part of his leadership style was to present himself as a cool operator. As he moved through camp, Big Rock carried in a holster under his shoulder a battle-scarred pistol with a bullet mark on the left side, and on a sleeve across his chest he sheathed a K-Bar fighting knife. For a rifle he seldom used the new M-16, preferring a Car-15 commando automatic, which was slightly shorter and easier to carry. But another of his weapons truly defined him—an old Thompson submachine gun that came his way with its own tale of America and Vietnam. One day when he was leading the recon platoon in an area southwest of Lai Khe near the Thi Tinh River, a sergeant emerged from the tree line and got shot in the shoulder. Welch ran to help and was cradling the sergeant in his arms when a Viet Cong soldier dressed in black shorts with no shirt came "running out of the woods screaming, just screaming," and firing a Thompson submachine gun. The bullets sprayed wildly around Welch, who calmly picked up his gun, fired one shot, and "put a tiny little hole" in his attacker that "killed him real good." A few days later his men presented him with a plaque that read:

SHOOTOUT AT THI TINH
LT. WELCH 1 VC 0.

They also gave him the Thompson, which they had retrieved. The name Dodd was carved on the side, clearly not a Vietnamese name. Welch heard that it had been brought over by American OSS agents in 1945 and given to Ho Chi Minh's men to fight the Japanese. He often took the Thompson with him into the field after that; his sergeants said they could tell where he was by the distinctive *brrrrrn* contrasted with the M-16's much faster *zzzzzt*. There was also a special rack for the submachine gun on his jeep as he and his bodyguard rambled around Lai Khe.

Welch carried a small radio on which he picked up the *BBC News* when he could, and he preferred the folk music of the Kingston Trio, Joan Baez, and Peter, Paul, and Mary to rock or country. One cool commander, yet Clark Welch should not even have been in the army. He was a chronic asthmatic who had hidden the condition from doctors at his induction physical ten years earlier to prevent being classified 4-F. His parents, preferring that he go to college, thought asthma would surely keep him out of the service and were surprised when he passed. Later, when he went overseas, Lacy routinely sent him small glass inhalers in protective green plastic, which he carried in his pocket and occasionally used after ducking behind a tree to avoid being seen. The dust and vegetation of Vietnam made him wheeze but never disabled him.

During his command of the recon platoon, Welch found himself in situations where his rough comprehension of Vietnamese proved useful. His squad was occasionally assigned to patrol a section of Route 13 between Lai Khe and Ben Cat, ten miles to the south, where they encountered local men on bicycles or motorbikes who aroused suspicion. As he reported in his deadpan style to Lacy, the phrase he often used on such occasions was "Gentlemen, you must go quickly now or all us gentlemen will have to tie you up and put you in jail, please." One day on road patrol he asked an old man in Vietnamese why he had stopped at the side of the highway closest to the brigade headquarters. The "papa-san" responded that his motorbike was broken. When Welch stepped on the pedal, the motor started right up. A search of the man's belongings turned up "drawing instruments in a little silk bag in the bottom of his lunch pail." They arrested him and discovered during questioning that he had been taking "angle measurements, distances etc." around brigade headquarters—details the Viet Cong used for their mortar attacks.

More often Welch found himself swarmed by Vietnamese children, who were fascinated by everything about him, his crew cut, the hair on his arms, his height, his clothes, his language skills, and what seemed like a big heart inside this big American. One day he visited a Catholic school in Ben Cat with the battalion chaplain and said, after peering in a classroom, "All of the children look very smart. What are they studying?" At least that is what he meant to say, he explained in a letter to Lacy. "The class just broke up with everybody giggling and pointing. [The teacher] said very good and showed me a simple book that a little girl was writing in. I read a little bit out of it and everybody giggled again and the little girl grabbed my arm and wouldn't let go while I walked around and looked at what the rest of the class was doing. A group of boys were reading out of what looked just like a *Tarzan* comic book. I picked it up and read and then turned the page and sure enough—*Tar-san cac con truong,* Tarzan, leader of all the animals . . ."

Welch was soon surrounded by hundreds of children. He had heard a story once that if there were a number of little children around, you were safe, the VC wouldn't try to shoot near you. "Well," he wrote home, "I was the safest I've ever been in my life, because we were waist-deep in kids, we left the courtyard trailing a wake of yelling, waving little kids."

TWO MONTHS INTO HIS TOUR at Lai Khe, Welch was called to division headquarters. They were increasing the number of rifle companies from three to four, Welch was told. They wanted all the company commanders to be captains, but they had been watching Welch carefully and decided to make an exception. They wanted him to form and lead the new Delta Company of the 2/28 Black Lions. The day he was given the assignment, July 6, was the very day the USNS *Pope* departed San Diego, carrying many of the men who later would join his company. He couldn't seem to stay anywhere for long, Welch wrote Lacy, "but this is almost an unbelievable thing. I'll be able to choose a cadre of NCOs from units already here and then we'll move into the woods, set up our tents, start building a place to live, eat, and work, and after a sixty-day training program I'll have another infantry rifle company trained and ready to go."

For a soldier in Welch's position to win a commission in the field was uncommon enough; for him to command a rifle company was extraordinary. He would be the only lieutenant with his own company in the entire First Division, one of only a handful in all of Vietnam. He considered it an honor and a challenge. When he began putting the company together, it amounted to nothing more than "one infantry Lt. (AC Welch) and a large section of rubber plantation," as he described it to Lacy. Within a week he had a first sergeant, two tents, and a latrine, and soon he had a mess hall, an orderly room, and his first batch of soldiers—twenty veteran infantrymen from other companies handpicked with two thoughts in mind. First, Welch wanted men with combat experience who could steady the nerves of the FNGs, the fucking new guys, as new arrivals were called. And second, he was looking for soldiers with mechanical or electronic skills who could help him construct the Delta camp. There was no shortage of prospects. As word spread around Lai Khe that Big Rock was getting a company, men started volunteering. One night five jeeps pulled up to the orderly room and a band of men jumped out. They were looking for the new Delta commander. "I came out to see what the commotion was about," Welch reported in a letter home. "It was Recon—all those little bastards—wanting to come with me to the new company. That really got to me." Afraid to show emotion, Welch barked at a sergeant to take his men home "before the VC find out that Black Lions Recon are all in one bunch and send in a suicide squad to get us all."

His rise from the noncommissioned ranks left Welch with a deep appreciation of sergeants, whom he considered the forged steel of the army. He would go nowhere without the new first sergeant of Delta Company, Clarence (Bud) Barrow. Square of face, with a burr haircut and southern Indiana twang, Barrow was an army lifer. Back in 1948, before some of his buck privates were born, he had escaped from Bloomington and a difficult stepmother by quitting school at age sixteen and enlisting after forging his date of birth on the birth certificate. By the summer of 1967, when he received orders for Southeast Asia, he had served nineteen years in the army, including nine with the Big Red One in Germany, without facing combat. He was one year from retirement but not ready to fade away. His military career would never seem complete, he believed, unless he did a Vietnam tour. When he at last reached the war zone in Lai Khe, he lost himself a bit, not unlike the C Packet boys on shore leave in Okinawa. "We've got First Sergeant Barrow," Welch was told over the phone one night. He was expecting the new man to report, so he said, "Good, bring him up." "You don't understand," came the response. Barrow was locked up. The sergeant had had too much to drink. The two men first caught sight of each other between the bars of the military jail.

From the moment Welch arranged his release, Sergeant Barrow became his unfailingly loyal and effective top aide. As the company would fill out, Delta's young platoon lieutenants all would outrank Barrow, but Welch left no doubt that his first sergeant was to take over if he became a casualty. Barrow would also serve as the company's daily organizer (taking the morning report, assigning the day's details), its best provisioner (he had a way of making sure there were morning pastries no matter where they were in the field), and father figure. During his days as a drill sergeant at Fort Jackson, South Carolina, he had kept a sign on his desk about tact: an ability to tell a person to go to hell and make him glad to be on the way. The men might not like to hear Barrow's bark, but better his than the commander's, and they would more often turn to him when they received troubling news from home or felt uneasy. He took pride in being pivotal to the operation, but it was also a heavy burden. And he had his own concerns about the alien world he was now in. On his first patrol in country, he fell asleep on an ammo box and awoke with a start when he felt something hairy running over his arm. Was it a monkey or a rat? He never saw it, but for that second he was "scared half to death."

Not much else scared Bud Barrow after that. He became the only person in Delta not intimidated by Welch, and thus the only one with the courage to rouse the commander in the morning. After starting the coffee and finding pastries, Barrow would approach Big Rock with a swagger stick and touch him very lightly two or three times while saying softly, "Lieutenant Welch, time to get up." Then he would gingerly step to the side as Welch bolted upright and grabbed his gun, ready to shoot.

The base camp that Welch and Barrow established for Delta Company was about the size of five football fields. It was situated entirely within a grove of mature rubber trees planted in perfect rows running east-west, with spaces of eight yards between rows. Welch planned to house his men in fortified tents jumbled unevenly among the rubber trees. He insisted that they not be set up in neat rows along the lanes because that would make them easier targets. The treetops formed only a light canopy overhead, allowing a cool breeze to blow through and sunlight to dapple the ground. When there was sunlight, that is: the camp was built during the rainy season. "There's water everywhere (much more even than in Florida) and that means mud, mud, mud," Welch noted in mid July. In a largely futile effort to keep their boots dry, they put down sidewalk planks made from baseboards and wooden ammo boxes. A concertina wire fence ran around the perimeter, and there were open areas for the sight line of mortars and M-60 machine guns.

Division engineers paved a company street and put up three permanent structures—the mess hall, orderly room, and a little headquarters building, twenty feet wide and fifty feet long. Welch designed it himself. When you walked in the front door, the company clerk's desk was to the left, First Sergeant Barrow's desk to the right, and a hallway down the middle led to the commander's office, which had a map table, desk, bookshelf, and what looked like a clothes closet but actually was a private entrance to Welch's hideaway sleeping area. There were phones next to the desk and bed "so I can always be on top of things no matter where I am." Further down the hall were the operations room and library, and it was only a few steps out the back door to an underground TOC (tactical operations center) and command tent.

By July 26 Welch and his skeleton crew had consumed their first full day of meals in the mess hall. "BREAKFAST: bacon, eggs, french toast, pancakes, toast, french pastry breakfast rolls, butter, honey, jams, jelly, coffee, orange juice, milk (awful). LUNCH: fried ham, potato, rice, beans, corn, bread, hot rolls, salad, butter, jams and jelly, peaches with whipped cream, coffee, iced tea, milk (awful), Kool-Aid. DINNER: hamburger, cheeseburger, french fries, lima beans, rice, hot toasted buns, bread, ketchup, mustard, mayonnaise, ice cream! Cake! Coffee, iced tea, Kool-Aid." The next day a truckload of weapons arrived. "We've got quite an arsenal here," he reported to Lacy. "A rifle company is really a powerful force! I'm really looking forward to getting these people and the equipment together and ready so we can get out and help fight the war."

Big Rock had lost twenty-five pounds since he arrived in Vietnam and had gone through one bout of pneumonia, but now he felt well fed and healthy and raring to go. Two days later he and Bud Barrow hopped on a C-130 and flew down to Vung Tau to meet the soldiers of C Packet.

"WE ARE CALLED the Black Lions," Jack Schroder wrote home to Eleanor in one of his first letters from the Delta Company base camp amid the rubber trees. "We have a 500 piaster bounty on our heads for any member of the Black Lions. Charlie loves to cut your ears off and your Black Lions patch. We found a medic that had been completely skinned alive and hanged by his heels and had the patch cut off and [stuffed] in his mouth—not a pretty sight."

Not an entirely factual one, either. It took only a few days of hanging around the war-hardened soldiers of Lai Khe, drinking with them and listening to their stories, for the quiet dental technician to take on the bravado of his environment and send it along to his unsuspecting young wife back in the States. Everything Schroder reported in that gruesome account had some truth to it—the bounty, the cut ears and patches happened at some point somewhere—but not during his first week there. It was part of the lore of Lai Khe, spread night after night, month by month, in the bars and hooches, an expression of that part of human nature that adjusts to a frightening situation by mixing mythology and re-

ality. Mike Troyer wrote home to his parents in Ohio with another version of the same legendary story. "The unit I am in is called the Black Lions. I'll send you one of the patches that we wear on our left fatigue shirt
pocket. The V.C. are so scared of us that they have a bounty on us of
some 30 piasters . . . to collect it they have to take the Black Lion patch
and a left ear as proof that they have killed a famed Black Lion. No big
thing because Charlie is so scared to mess with us, whenever we are out
on patrol he would just as soon leave us alone."

Things were rough enough and would get worse than the new soldiers could imagine, yet still there was an odd sense of comfort in em-
bellishment. In Jack Schroder's new world, as he transformed it in his
letters, the rain fell nonstop for six months during the monsoon season,
in the dry season the temperatures ranged from 120 to 140 degrees, and
every night they were taking mortar hits from the Viet Cong that were
killing five or ten or fifteen of his buddies—all stretches of fact that reflected his absorption of a fundamental truth, one that he related in his
first letter home. "They aren't playing games over here," he wrote. The
most threatening of the events Schroder wrote about, the mortar attacks,
truly happened, beginning on the first night he stayed in Lieutenant
Welch's new camp, though the casualties were fewer than he reported.

A more subdued account came from Greg Landon, the Amherst
dropout. "Mud is everywhere and so are the V.C., I am told," he wrote
after a few days in Lai Khe. "We have mortars every night and sometimes a few injuries. . . . We have a covered trench next to the tent which
we jump into when attacked by the mortars." A week later Landon was
reeling from the hyperbolic stories coming at him. "I really don't know
what to believe over here. People just in from the field say that the 1st
battalion 16th infantry just had 100% casualties. Must have meant a
company (rather than a larger battalion) and 200 men in a company
killed or injured is fantastic in itself."

Sometimes the truth stretching was so over the top that word got
back to the commander. "One had written his mother that he'd been a
point man on 50 patrols and been wounded 4 times and was now in the
hospital—he said that his C.O. had visited him in the hospital and said
to recover quickly because they needed him back as a point man," Welch
recounted in a letter to Lacy. "He told his mother he was ready to give
his life for his country but he was getting a little tired of always being a
hero. This kid has been an assistant cook (handles gravy + salad + cold
drinks) since he got here, has never left the perimeter, and the only time

he's been near the hospital is when he goes on sick call (about twice a week)!! His mother wrote to me to ask if he hadn't done his share and couldn't he please come home instead of going back to war. I wrote a letter to her today, saying that her boy had done 'a good job in his specialized area and was quite an asset to our company. We need him right in the job he's in now and couldn't let him come home early because the company couldn't train a replacement that quickly.' I wrote some more like that and showed the letter to the boy. He's writing a letter tonight to tell his mother something a little closer to the truth so she won't worry so much. After he shows me the letter tomorrow—we'll mail both of them."

Since he only picked up 93 men at Vung Tau instead of the 140 he had been expecting, Welch was allowed to pluck some more experienced troops from other units in the division to reach his full complement of soldiers. For his four platoon leaders—three rifle platoons and the weapons (mortar) platoon—he had two battlewise officers and two untested young lieutenants. He tried to keep that same half-and-half ratio down through his squad leaders, but troop demands in Vietnam were so strong that summer, and the supply of experienced infantrymen so depleted, that he ended up short nine sergeants. *Who wants to be a sergeant?* he had asked at the end of the first day in camp. It would not be an official promotion, he could not pay them any extra, but at least they would get to eat in the sergeant's mess tent. A few of his pseudosergeants were too young to vote.

Working from a division handbook, Welch and his cadre of seasoned men trained the newcomers in jungle warfare: how to board helicopters, how to respond to enemy fire from the left or right, how to set an ambush, how to recognize booby traps and pungi sticks, and how to dig the famed DePuy bunker, named for the former division commander, which featured a berm in front and rifle holes angling left and right so that enemy attackers faced interlocking fire. Welch was a stickler about where to locate the bunkers at NDPs (night defensive positions), often moving them two or three times before the arrangement felt exactly right. His men eventually learned to mark temporary locations with their rifles and sandbags and not dig in too deeply until their finicky commander had walked the perimeter several times and given his final approval.

Greg Landon, with his Amherst background, uncommon for an enlisted man in the infantry, was called Professor by his bunkmates. He was assigned to carry the radio as an RTO (radio telephone operator), a job about which he had mixed feelings. "The job is rather risky in a fight since the radio is the first or second target, the other being the squad leader," he wrote. On the other hand he would get to know what was going on, which he considered "imperative," and "get familiar with tactics that may become useful in later parts of the war." It also might help him avoid other annoying assignments like listening post, for which a few men sat outside the perimeter all night listening for enemy approaches. "The radio is rather heavy with its extra battery, being over 30 pounds, but I'll bear it somehow," Landon reported. "Just so long as we stay out of ambushes as much as possible I'll be fairly safe. But that damned 10' aerial is a dead giveaway."

Jack Schroder trained on the M-60 machine gun. His squadmates started calling him Machine Gun Red. In his letters home he alternated between trying to reassure Eleanor, by telling her that the training would keep him out of harm's way for several weeks (and that after that he would try to get assigned to Lai Khe's dental lab), and alarming her with increasingly hard-edged stories. One night, he said, VC mortars came in near the airstrip as he was making the long walk to Delta from the village. "I ran all the way back to base camp. I never knew I could run as fast as I did. Over here speed counts." Another day he described walking through a rice paddy and finding himself "up to my ass in human waste," which he said was used as fertilizer.

The central themes of his letters became revenge, comradeship, and drinking, and the three seemed inextricably linked. He was undergoing the transformation of a soldier facing battle, his world shrinking from his country down to his division, then battalion, then company, then platoon, then squad, and finally the men he knew and lived with every day, the guys to the left and right of him. They were what he would fight for.

In his first letter the enemy was the aggressor to be feared; now Schroder was the predator. "We had a beer party last night. I got drunk and they said I went hunting Charlie with the M-60," he wrote. "I'm glad they found me. I am going to get Charlie one way or the other for he killed 7 of my buddies." In another letter he said he was eager to go on patrol at the perimeter that night. "I am going to try to find me a Viet Cong," he boasted, adding that the last VC they captured was skinned alive and had his throat slit. This was followed by an account of how a friend was killed by a mine and how they scooped up his remains and placed them in a bag.

Sprinkled amid the bloody tales were comments about the delicious fudge that Sarge got from home, dreamy thoughts of meeting for an R and R in Hawaii, and requests for rolls of 126 color film and Kool-Aid, and then sign-offs about how much rougher it was than he had expected and how much he loved his wife and baby son and wanted to come home.

Mere days in country and already many new Delta Company soldiers felt alienated from the world around them. "Nothing but bars and whores," Mike Taylor told his parents after making his first visit to Lai Khe village. "Got a haircut and massage. They slapped the ——— out of my ass. That's the last of those."

From the distance of his fourteen-man tent under the rubber trees, Greg Landon wrote to his brother, America seemed "very far away." So far away that he wished he were "in Peoria, Illinois, right now." But they were stuck in Lai Khe and the surrounding jungles. "What bothers me is that we will not be able to get to Saigon, ever. It's off limits to the 1st Division now." As for the fighting, Landon wrote, the Viet Cong had "the upper hand in this goddamned war," and it seemed that "by one means or another" every peasant had been contacted and "asked to perform duties for the V.C. against us." His sardonic streak was growing darker. Vietnam, he mused, "would be an OK country except for the Vietnamese. Since they pledge no allegiance to the govt., they pick the winner, the V.C. by default, and give us a tough time. We had three women spies in here yesterday pacing off distances and spotting troop areas on the pretense they were looking for a job. It's impossible to tell who is and is not a V.C. sympathizer. Right now we're in the process of killing everyone one way or another. So that the insects can have the place to themselves."

Here was a common theme among the enlisted men, the notion that they were being used by both the Vietnamese and their own government. "I've seen what it's like over here," Mike Troyer told his family on a three-inch reel-to-reel recording that he sent home at the beginning of his tour. "Not that I feel like marchin' in any protest march against Vietnam, but this war is worthless. These people over here are playin' both ends against the middle. They got it made, man. If Charlie won't give it to 'em, the Americans will. If the Americans won't give it to 'em, Charlie will. The comparison is like a divorce. They both want custody of one child. One parent gives it to 'em if the other won't. So they think, why the hell should I go with you? . . . I'll tell the president himself, this damn war, it just ain't worth it."

Natural beauty all around, yet the most descriptive word was *shit*. "Here it's used for everything," Lieutenant Welch explained in a letter home. "They call a Chinook helicopter a shit-hook. When the firefights first begin is when the shit starts and when things are really going hot and heavy, you're in the shit. The code name for our officer that's the preventive medicine officer (checks for flies, correct latrine maintenance, clean garbage etc.) is Shithouse 6. And if a guy gets drunk he is shitfaced."

Some things were shittier. The men heard stories about soldiers stepping on pungi sticks laced with human feces, and about puddle jumper bugs that bit out chunks of human flesh, and about the three-step viper, a snake that bites you and three steps later you're dead. They had daily encounters with the water buffalo, an animal that snorted at the sight of Americans and seemed incontrovertibly on the side of the VC. There were mosquitoes everywhere, voracious red ants, yellow spiders as large as your fist, dogs and monkeys with rabies, and during the long summer nights, through twelve hours of heartless darkness, the soldiers could hear little lizards, in voices soft and clear and matter-of-fact, calling out to them over and over again, with a refrain that sounded like *fuck you, fuck you, fuck you.*

THERE WERE ALWAYS fucking new guys to hear the lizards call out their names at Lai Khe. New soldiers arrived every day, and old soldiers left every day, their identities in large measure determined by their DEROS, which was both a noun and a verb: *D*ate *E*ligible for *R*eturn from *O*ver *S*eas. Every soldier knew his DEROS, and when he left he was *derossed*. The simultaneous arrival of so many 2/28 Black Lions from the troop ship that summer was unusual. By 1967 most soldiers were flown to Vietnam. They traveled together on chartered commercial jets with meal service and movies and stewardesses, diversions that could be pleasing but also discordant with what awaited them on the ground. The three weeks at sea might have seemed like an endless purgatory, but for those who arrived by plane, the transition from one world to another was swift and unsettling.

Tom Hinger, a Black Lions medic from Latrobe, Pennsylvania, the son of a steelworker, flew to Vietnam that July with two vastly contrasting images in his mind. The last thing he had seen on television while waiting to board a chartered 707 at Fort Ord, California, was the major league all-star game, a memorable contest won by the National League on Tony Perez's home run in the top of the fifteenth inning. That was something to talk about. But the last thing he had read at the airport before saying good-bye to his parents was a front-page account that by eerie coincidence focused on the medics of the 2/28 Battalion of the First Infantry Division and how dangerous their jobs were. That was nothing to talk about at all, and in fact enough to make Hinger fib to his parents, telling them not to worry about him because he would be safe in Vietnam, working at a hospital. On the way over, the plane stopped in Hawaii and Okinawa, and Hinger noticed that on each leg of the trip the meals got sparer and the stewardesses older.

Joe Costello, an eighteen-year-old Alpha Company grenadier from Long Island, the son of a Manhattan insurance executive, arrived at Bien Hoa Air Base by civilian jet late on a summer's night. As flight attendants instructed him to lock his tray table and put his seat back in the upright position, he could see flashes of gunfire in the darkness and explosions in the distance. Before he enlisted, Costello had never traveled farther from home than Pennsylvania. Now this: first rocket fire, then overpowering smells, a jangling bus ride, straw hats, pajamas, bare feet, women carrying wares on perfectly balanced poles, the company out on maneuvers at Lai Khe, someone taking him to the enlisted men's club, where soldiers tell grisly war stories about something called Operation Billings. *Wow, is it going to be like that?* Then another soldier escorting him to the plantation and demonstrating how they harvest rubber, cutting a diagonal slice through the bark and watching the fluid run down the slit like white sap or milkweed, or some sort of purified blood.

Michael Arias, a Mexican-American from Douglas, Arizona, was delivering laundry detergent and mouthwash door to door in Phoenix when he got drafted. He flew from Phoenix to Oakland to Anchorage with a final stop in Japan on his way to Bien Hoa that March, then was sent up to Lai Khe to join Alpha Company, which was out on Operation Junction City in War Zone C when he arrived. They tried to keep him occupied at jungle training school, which was thought to be a last, safe transitional interlude before going out in the field, but he and Jesús Razo and Ralph Carrasco quickly found themselves in a tense standoff with some other Black Lions when they tried to take a few beers that were stashed in a Coke machine. M-16s were locked and loaded, bayonets at the ready, until cooler heads prevailed.

Steve Goodman, a Black Lions mechanic from Brooklyn, the son of a Jewish milkman and the grandson of a pasta salesman, flew TWA to Vietnam on a bouncy, seemingly endless trip from New York with stops in California, the Philippines, Guam, Wake Island, and Long Binh. The entire journey "scared the shit" out of him, but that was nothing compared to his first encounter at Lai Khe. He reached Headquarters Company just as they were "hoisting down an American GI's body" from the watchtower. When the lifeless soldier neared the ground, "his insides came out and were all over the ladder and everything else and just slopping down on the ground—red, purple, black." He had been killed by the unfriendly friendly fire of a Big Red One comrade, plugged with twenty rounds as he was jokingly screaming, "I'm Ho Chi Minh! I'm Ho Chi Minh!"

Three hundred sixty-four days to DEROS.

Whatever bonds the soldiers made with comrades on the way over were usually broken as soon as they reached the replacement center at Bien Hoa and were assigned to different divisions, brigades, battalions, companies. Doc Hinger had been seated next to Jerry Saporito and shared stories with him for seventeen hours, then saw him again only once more in his life. Here was a paradox of army life. So much effort was put into stripping men of their individualism to make them effective parts of the killing machine, so much emphasis was placed on the fraternity of the squad and platoon, so much faith and trust was invested in the relationships of buddies on the fighting line, all of this was indisputably essential and true, yet each man also moved through Vietnam in his own distinct world, hundreds of thousands of individual overlapping years, each with its own beginning and unique end, a serial number and a date eligible for return.

Last name: Sikorski
First name: Daniel
Home of record: Milwaukee
State: WI
Sex: Male
Race: Caucasian
Marital status: Single

Branch: Army
Rank: SP4
Serial number: RA16889558
DEROS: March 8, 1968

Danny Sikorski was another gunner in Delta Company, an experienced hand who helped teach Jack Schroder how it was done. Machine Gun Red and Ski, as his army buddies called Sikorski, were the same age, twenty, with connections to Milwaukee and a tendency to drink to ease their boredom or anxiety. Sikorski, in country since March, was one of fifteen Black Lions transferred from Alpha to Delta to help train the new guys from the ship. "The only good thing about it is we stay out of the field for 15 days training this new company," he reported in a letter to his sister Diane. Otherwise it was an uneventful assignment. "Well, there isn't too much to talk about because we aren't doing anything except training these new fellows. I sure am drinking a lot of beer lately. Our club opens at noon and closes at 10 that's where I spend half of my day. P.S. Please send the Booze."

Diane Sikorski, two years younger than her brother, cringed when she read the P.S. In every letter home since Danny had arrived in Vietnam, he had begged or demanded that she send him a bottle of rum. Diane loved her brother deeply. When he wrote in one letter that she should call WOKY "and ask them to play a request for a boy in V.N., I want them to play Mercy Mercy, I really like that song," she was happy to oblige, but sending him rum was a different matter. Back during his last year at home on Eighth Street on the south side of Milwaukee, after their mom had died and she became the "homemaker," her tasks included cleaning his upstairs bedroom each week. On the floor behind his bed she had come across stale vomit of rum and coke that made her gag and she had screamed at him that she never wanted to see or hear the word *rum* again.

Each soldier with his own story, yet if there was a prototype of the young men from Wisconsin who fought in Vietnam, it might be Daniel Patrick Sikorski. He was a third-generation Polish immigrant, the son of Edmund Sikorski, himself one of twelve children born to Joseph and Stella Sikorski, who came to Milwaukee from Krakow. Edmund Sikorski quit school after sixth grade and went to work, spending most of his career as a filler on the assembly line at Miller Brewing Company. He married Stella Kubiak, another southsider, and together they raised

Danny and Diane in the familiar patterns of the Polish working class. They had a dog named Penny, vegetables in the backyard, a color portrait of Jesus in the living room, and latch hooks on the side door. There was a little cottage on Lake Lucerne up in Crandon where they enjoyed a two-week vacation every July and where Danny and Diane swam and fished, climbed the watchtower, and fed the deer. At Christmas they hung stockings on the fake fireplace, attended midnight mass and shared the *oplatek,* the blessed Polish wafers. Danny and Diane broke bread and exchanged good wishes and held their breath as they kissed cheeks and toasted with Mogen David wine. They went to church at Saint John Kanty and attended parish school in the early years. No one called him Ski on the south side. There would be no way to tell him apart from anyone else. His classmates in eighth grade were Tarczewski, Kucharski, Mikolajewski, Arciszewski, Mrochinski, Badzinski, Odachowski, Banaszynski, Kumelski, Benowski, Kitowski, Witowski, Szapowski, Kawczynski, Szutowski, Jaskolski, Moczynscki, Zlotkowski, Czerwinski, Kulwicki, and Danielewski.

In preparation for life as a tradesman, Danny attended Milwaukee Boys Tech, where he played football and took an apprenticeship at Harnischfeger, a tool manufacturing plant. He was extremely close to his mother, a light-hearted talker like him. They shared a love for professional wrestling, and when matches came to the Milwaukee Arena, where he worked part-time as an usher, he made sure that she got tickets. He fell into a depression when his mother died suddenly at age forty-three, before he had finished high school. Neither he nor Diane knew anyone in their neighborhood who had gone to college. When he got his draft notice, Danny and a buddy enlisted in the army. His last trip home before heading for Vietnam was a furlough in late February. By then his father had remarried and moved to the north side and there was no bedroom for him, so he slept in the cold basement. He rode the city bus back to his old neighborhood and visited the Saint John Kanty priest, Father Czaja, and confessed that he thought he was going to die.

That weekend he surprised Diane by popping in at her favorite hangout, Wyler's teen bar. He sat at another table and watched her talk with friends until the end of the night, when he approached her table and asked her to dance. A slow song. "Are you sure you want to dance with me?" she asked. "Well, you're my little sister, aren't you?" It was their first dance together. Diane felt awkward at first, but Danny reassured her. He gave her advice about how to deal with boyfriends and what to do about their father and their new stepmother, and together they remembered the smell of their mom's homemade soups. Back when Danny was born, his father had planted a pine tree by the side of the house on Eighth Street. Now, when the young soldier took a trip back to the old neighborhood, he noticed that the new owner had cut the pine tree down.

Diane started getting migraine headaches after Danny left, and she worried about their father, who would sit in his chair for hours and stare into space. She prized the letters her brother sent home, but no matter how cute he got about it (one letter ended with "G-O-T-S-A-S-T-B; Get on the stick and send the booze") that was one thing she would not do.

WHEN CLARK WELCH took command of Delta Company on the beach at Vung Tau, it meant that officers who came over on the ship would find different assignments at Lai Khe. To Lieutenant Grady it seemed at first almost like Fort Lewis all over again, with no one knowing quite what to do with him except show him a bed. He stood around the Black Lions headquarters until nightfall, and then it washed over him how different this was from any place he had been. Staring into the darkness, knowing nothing about what was out there, he grew anxious and wondered to himself, *Where are the bad guys?* Nearby, under mosquito netting, Captain George sat on his bunk and wrote home that he had found a weapon and "the nearest bunker to get in" if they got hit. The next morning at five Grady and George were awakened by the sound of artillery. *What's going on?* Grady asked. *Wakeup rounds,* he was told. H and I firings—harassing and interdiction—which involved having the big guns fire into the countryside at predetermined spots without knowing whether enemy or water buffalo were roaming around out there. H and I's were popular at Lai Khe and other American base camps, so much so that they would soon become an issue with the generals in Saigon, who were catching flak from the Pentagon for spending too much money on ammunition.

On the second day in camp Grady was getting ready to attend combat indoctrination school, and looking forward to a gradual transition to his new workplace, when he and George were told to hop on a supply helicopter and join the battalion command and two companies out in the field near Phu Loi. Grady had his new assignment, S-2 for the battalion, which meant chief intelligence officer. Looking back on that posting with his self-deprecating humor, he would call himself "the worst intelligence officer in the history of the U.S. Army," which he certainly was not, but he was on the mark when he called himself "green as grass" and "an intelligence officer who didn't know a thing." That was part of the reality of the United States Army in Vietnam in the summer of 1967, when men were pouring in faster than seasoned officers could be found to lead them, a situation greatly exacerbated by the Pentagon policy of rotating not only enlisted men but officers out of Vietnam after twelve months. Grady was fortunate that as soon as he reached the field that day, he ran into Big Jim Shelton, the battalion's S-3, or operations officer, a former football lineman at the University of Delaware who had been in Vietnam only a few weeks himself but radiated confidence and could outtalk anyone in the division. "Look, you work for me, and this is what you do," Shelton began, and Grady was more than glad to listen.

While Grady stayed back at the night defensive position (NDP) that afternoon, George went with the two companies and command unit on a search-and-destroy mission, which proved uneventful, though the day did not. When they returned from the march, the battalion commander directed George to go tell the Alpha Company commander to pack his gear and report back to headquarters, he was being fired and replaced by George. "The commander I'm replacing has only had the company for four weeks and is being relieved, so I really hope I can cut it and put the co. squared away," George wrote home to his wife. Serving as a battalion or company commander in the Big Red One during the Vietnam years was a hardship unto itself, the more dangerous equivalent of trying to manage the New York Yankees under George Steinbrenner during the early years of his ownership. Officers were constantly being moved and fired. In eight months, since the beginning of 1967, the Black Lions had already been through three battalion commanders, three Headquarters Company commanders, three Alpha commanders, three Bravo commanders, and two Charlie Company commanders. It was, said Jim Shelton, "the ass-chewingest place you've ever seen." In any case, George thought the Alpha commander hardly seemed surprised, as though "he knew that the axe was coming."

The surprise came a few hours later, when a squad of Viet Cong guerrillas slipped past the listening post and the ambush squad and launched a surprise attack on the NDP with machine gun fire and claymore mines, killing one soldier, who had been sitting atop his bunker rather than inside it, and wounding eight others. It was George's first test. "Well, I earned my CIB (combat infantry badge)," he wrote afterward. "I assumed command of the company at 1900 and at 2200 had an attack. . . . It was really something. I coulda reached out and touched the live tracer rounds. Thank God I didn't freeze and was able to make the right decisions. We had a dust off (med evac) which was hairy. I conducted it and had to help the wounded to the copter. The company did OK. The battalion CO was there but didn't do much."

The next morning the field operation was moved to a new location north of old Dog Leg Village. It was a dispiriting day, with soldiers exhausted, stung and angered by the surprise attack, the ground a mess of mud, a monsoon rain drenching them, and in the midst of this scene here came Major General John Hancock Hay Jr., the division boss, who swiftly fired the battalion commander. Two officers canned in two days. The resupply helicopter that night brought in the next leader of the Black Lions. He was a thirty-seven-year-old West Point graduate named Terry Allen Jr., who had served briefly as the battalion's operations officer earlier in his tour. "He should be real good," Clark Welch wrote to Lacy. Allen was steady and appeared seasoned. He had been in Vietnam five months by then, minus an emergency leave in June when he had returned to his native El Paso to heal an unexpected wound.

Chapter 4

El Paso, Texas

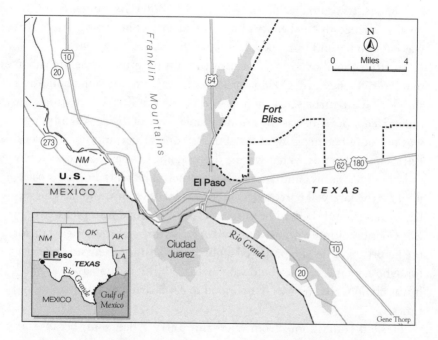

Gene Thorp

L Paso, on the verge of a boom, had a population of three hundred thousand in 1967, about a third of its census count at the end of the century, but it remained a small town in the more traditional sense, a place where the surnames were familiar, where families were defined by their histories, and where everyone in the same social set, especially the established Anglos who ran the banks, businesses, and government, seemed to know or want to know everything about everyone else. There were secrets, undoubtedly—small towns incubate secrets—but the secrets were not always as private as their originators assumed; often they were known but unspoken as part of the cultural code. El Paso took its name as the place where the Rocky Mountains parted, offering an easy valley pass from east to west. The culture of the town was a curious mix of order and disorder, shaped as it was by the Rio Grande, which ran along its southern border, separating it from Ciudad Juarez, its exotic big-sister city in Mexico, and by Fort Bliss, the U.S. Army base that sprawled across a million acres of barren beige landscape to the northeast. Sitting in the basin of the Chihuahuan desert, El Paso thought of itself as the city of the sun. It boasted of more than three hundred days of sunshine a year. Its baseball team then was the Sun Kings. Its football stadium was the Sun Bowl. Its annual Sun Carnival was ruled by the beauty of a Sun Queen and her court. All of this was enough to send some people looking for places in the dark.

In from the above-ninety heat of the sun on a mid-June afternoon that year, Genevieve Coonly picked up her ringing telephone and shrieked with surprise as soon as she heard the first words from the caller. *Hello, Bebe.* It was the unmistakable voice of Terry Allen Jr., who was not only her nephew-in-law but also one of her and her husband, Bill's, closest friends. What was he doing home? It had been only a few months since family and friends had gathered in Hart Ponder's backyard for the farewell party when Terry left for Vietnam, and now he was back even though he had been scheduled to be gone for at least a year. Bill Coonly jokingly accused his wife of "getting out the fatted calf for the favorite son" as she prepared a luncheon feast for their surprise visitor, who had asked if he could stop by to talk. But as soon as he arrived, it was obvious that he was in no mood to eat heartily or laugh about old times.

He had come home from Vietnam, Terry Allen said, because his wife, Jean Ponder Allen, the daughter of Bebe's sister, had written him a letter announcing that she was disillusioned with him and the military and the war and had left him for another man. This other man, literally a clown—Terry had heard that he was a rodeo clown who had appeared on the local television station where Jean worked—had moved into the Allen house and was living there on Timberwolf Drive with Jean and his three little girls while he was fighting for his country on the other side of the world. Terry hoped to save the marriage, but was unsure about the prospects. He thought that his mother and father, who lived in El Paso, were unaware of the scandal, so he did not want to stay with them. The Coonlys invited him to sleep in a guest bedroom at their double-winged ranch house in the upper valley while he tried to work things out with Jean, and they lent him one of their old cars for the week, a pink Cadillac.

The sudden way his life had veered off track left Allen disoriented. Not so long ago it had seemed that things were perfect, he said. His mother's family, the Robinsons, and Jean's family, the Ponders, had known one another for decades, two branches of the El Paso establishment with former mayors on both sides. The fact that Jean was thirteen years younger than he was had never given him reason for concern. How could it, when there was a twenty-year gap in the ages of his own parents, the retired general and Mary Frances, who had precisely the sort of marriage he sought to emulate? His life had followed a straight and clear path from childhood, but now here he was, out of place in his hometown, confused and lost. The first time he got behind the wheel of the pink Caddy, he drove through the streets until he ran out of gas.

TERRY DE LA MESA ALLEN JR. certainly had some choice in the life he would live, but the moments of doubt were rare. Imagine being a boy of thirteen in El Paso, and it is just before Christmas 1942, the war is on, and day after day you and your friends read and hear about the heroic deeds of American GIs fighting in North Africa against the Vichy French and the Nazis and in the Pacific against the Japanese, and you run around the neighborhood near Fort Bliss pretending to be soldiers. And then a letter arrives like the one that came from Major General Terry de la Mesa Allen Sr. postmarked 8 December.

"My dear Sonny," the old man began, using the loving nickname he called his namesake and only child, whose picture he carried with him in a leather pocket case. He was enclosing a twenty-dollar money order for a Christmas present, which he would have preferred to pick out himself but found impossible to do, given where he was and what he was doing, which was in North Africa commanding the First Infantry Division. But he had another present for his son that would be delivered especially by a staff officer heading back to the States on emergency leave. It was a flag of the Big Red One carried by his assault units when they landed in Algeria, perhaps "the first American flag to be landed on the shores." Later that same flag was "carried on a Tommy gun" by a soldier in General Allen's jeep until it was retired from service and "marked and embroidered by some of the French nuns in a nearby convent."

After urging Sonny to pay attention to his studies so that he could enroll at the New Mexico Military Institute the following year, General Allen closed his letter home with a copy of the verses of a new First Division song. "I don't know exactly what the tune is," he confessed, "but the soldiers seem to sing it to any tune that comes along."

> No mission is too difficult, no sacrifice too great
> Our duty to the nation is first we're here to state
> We're a helluva gang to tangle with
> Just follow us and see
> The Fightin' First will lead the way from hell to victory.

A battle flag and a battle song—these were not toys or imaginings but the real thing. Terry Allen the younger grew up in a veritable museum honoring the grit and glory of the United States Army. A few months before the battle flag arrived, his father had sent home a pair of special-issue rubber-soled basketball shoes that he and his soldiers had used to exercise on the deck of the transport ship that carried them from England to North Africa. The war relics were expressions of a father's love but also served as reminders of his expectations, and it was that combination that defined the bond between the two Terry Allens from the time of the son's birth on April 13, 1929. It was not intimidation and fear of disappointment, but deep affection and constant tutelage that funneled the son down the narrow chute of his family's military tradition.

The soldier's life went back another generation to Samuel E. Allen, a West Point graduate who served forty-two years as an artillery officer in the regular army, and who was married to Conchita Álvarez de la Mesa of Brooklyn, the daughter of a Spanish colonel who fought for the Union during the Civil War. Samuel Allen was said to be unassuming and conventional, traits that never came to mind at the mention of Terry Allen Sr., who began his career as a hell-raiser at West Point, where he earned his first wild nickname, Tear-around-the-Mess-Hall Allen. He hated math, found schoolwork tedious, stuttered in the classroom, and flunked out of the academy. His determination to become an army officer pushed him back to school at Catholic University in Washington, where he earned a degree and was commissioned as a second lieutenant. Over the next three decades he rose up the army ranks with a reputation as an uncommonly beloved leader who was disdainful of any rule or bureaucratic regulation that he thought inhibited the fighting spirit of his men.

During World War II, when he was commanding the Big Red One in North Africa, his freewheeling style made him a favorite of the American press. *Time* put him on its cover with a tribute to the infantry. A. J. Liebling profiled him in *The New Yorker.* Ernie Pyle occasionally slept in his tent (bedrolls on the ground, no cots for this general) and called him Terry and pronounced him "one of my favorite people"— high praise from the war correspondent who made his reputation writing about anonymous GIs rather than their famous leaders. An old jaw wound made Allen hiss through his teeth when he was riled up, emitting a sound "like a leak in a tire," as Pyle described it, and the language that came whistling out was often "so wonderfully profane it couldn't be put down in black and white" in any case. "This was no intellectual war with him," Pyle wrote. "He hated Germans and Italians like vermin, and his pattern for victory was simple: just wade in and murder the hell out of the low-down, good-for-nothing so-and-so's." Hence the nickname Terrible Terry Allen.

How his soldiers wore their uniforms, shaved their faces, and behaved in town while on furlough was less important to him than their devotion to the division and the ferocity with which they fought. While this attitude won him the unswerving loyalty of his troops, his superiors came to believe that his division was too much a separate force, individualistic and undisciplined, operating by its own rules. General Omar Bradley yanked Allen from command near the end of the Sicilian campaign, laying on him the unusual flaw of "loving the division too much." Allen was nevertheless too valuable to leave on the sidelines for the rest of the war. He returned to the States with orders to form a new division, the 104th, which was trained in time to march through France and Germany with a typical Terrible Terry battle cry leading it on, "Nothing in hell can stop the Timberwolves!"

The general's devotion to his soldiers, and their loyalty in return, was repeated tenfold in the relationship between father and son. Terry Allen Sr. was a skilled polo player whose horsemanship was legendary, going back to 1922 when as a cavalryman riding a big black army horse named Coronado he defeated the Texas cowboy Key Dunne in a long-distance horse race between Dallas and San Antonio. It was a five-day marathon that took him from the Adolphus Hotel to the Alamo and drew thousands of spectators along the rain-soaked route, inspiring press coverage matched by few sporting events in the Lone Star State outside football. Whatever he loved, he wanted his son to love as well. Sonny was only two when he was placed on his first saddle at Fort Oglethorpe in Georgia, and six when he took riding lessons while his father was stationed with the Seventh Cavalry at Fort Riley, Kansas. A love of polo was also passed along. Terry Jr. learned the game before he was ten and later became team captain and one of the best players at the New Mexico Military Institute (NMMI), his career fostered by Terry Sr. from afar. From the war zone in Europe in 1945, the general wrote a letter to Charles Meurisse and Company in Chicago placing a special order of polo sticks for Cadet Terry Allen. "I want four sticks 51" long and three sticks 52" long. . . . I want cigar-shaped maple heads of about medium weight and I particularly want these sticks to be well balanced and of the best possible grade."

Nothing but the best for Sonny.

General Allen's passionate interest in his son's polo development was surpassed only by the zeal with which he pushed for Terry Jr.'s appointment to West Point. "I have avoided seeking political influence for myself, but I feel that it is quite proper for me to do so for the sake of Terry Jr.," he acknowledged in a letter to Captain Reese Cleveland of Midland. And lobby he did, virtually nonstop starting in August 1944, when his son was only fifteen and he was back at Colorado Springs organizing the Timberwolves. He took time out then to meet with Senator Tom Connally of Texas to press for the appointment, though it was still several years off, and followed that with a letter extolling Terry Jr.'s qualifications. As the Timberwolves trudged their way through Europe, his lobbying only intensified. Letters went out regularly to influential friends and politicians in Austin, San Antonio, Houston, and Washington, all the way up to Vice President Truman. He recruited members of his staff to pull strings as well. First Lieutenant Alfred W. Wechsler of Connecticut, a loyal Timberwolf, wrote letters to several Democratic politicians in his home state, including one to State Senator Matthew Daley that pleaded the case in blunt terms. "The General has only one boy who is fifteen years of age and he is the apple of the old man's eye," Wechsler wrote. "The General's paramount wish is to have his son follow the family tradition of professional soldiering. It is also the boy's wish. . . . I would like for you to contact your friends in Washington and have them do their all in laying the foundation for the direct principal appointment . . . for this young man."

Part of the old man's motivation surely was to have his son succeed where he had failed and enjoy the long-range benefits of West Point connections that he had missed. But if Terry Jr. was more handsome and exhibited some social skills that Terry Sr. lacked, they shared an unease with math and a boredom with schoolwork. The general was at once understanding of his son's academic disposition and relentless in his gentle prodding that he strive for higher marks. In a February 1945 letter wishing Sonny luck in his high school midterms, Terry Sr. offered heartfelt advice about tests: "Above all—do not let them worry you, as you are capable of doing well if you do not get nervous about them. I just wanted to let you know that I am very happy over your progress and the fact that you are trying hard is satisfactory, insofar as I am concerned." Two months later he wrote a letter to the headmaster at NMMI expressing concern that Terry had been "dropped" from plane geometry—a course that he needed in preparation for the math heavy curriculum at West Point. When Terry Jr. sent him a strong report card at the end of that semester, the father gushed praise and noted sympathetically that studying was "a terrible bore, but is very necessary if you want not to have too hard a time when you go to West Point."

It took all of that lobbying and cajoling plus a year of remedial tutoring at another military prep school, but Terry Jr. finally made it to West Point on a senatorial appointment in 1948. As a cadet in Company H-1, he became known for "his good nature" and "burrhead haircut." He was in the Spanish club, played polo, and boxed. At Christmastime 1949, when his mother Mary Fran came to visit, she stopped by the gymnasium and distracted him just enough for his sparring partner to break his nose, an accident that later prompted a letter of reassurance to Mrs. Allen from Colonel Earl W. (Red) Blaik, the West Point football coach and athletic director. "Like boots and spurs to a cavalryman, a broken nose is a mark of manly distinction to a youngster, and in cases where they have been properly set there is no reason to worry about whether such a break will affect either the good looks or the health of the individual," Blaik wrote. Cadet Allen was regarded as "a good listener," though in a classic understatement, the *Howitzer* yearbook confided that he was "never an academic standout." In fact he finished second to the bottom of the class of 1952, one man away from being the goat of his class. It mattered not at all; he had survived West Point where his father had not, and though his personality was different from the famous general's, his classmates noticed in him many of the same leadership skills that would prove more important in his chosen career than an aptitude in mathematics. "On occasion," a classmate later wrote, "he would use a heartfelt yell and a slap on the back as a means to influence those around him."

Lieutenant Allen reached Korea with the Fifth Infantry Regiment at the end of the conflict there in 1953 and then returned home to Fort Lewis and began an ascent that paralleled his father's four decades earlier. Terry Sr. was watching his son's progress with more than casual interest, as attested to by a letter he received on December 20, 1955, from John C. Schuller, a life insurance agent in El Paso who had inside sources at the Pentagon and was able to obtain Terry Jr.'s personnel records. "Terry has an OEI (Officer Efficiency Index) of 132 as of now. This is a numerical evaluation now being given officers based on their efficiency reports. 150 is the max. 132 places him well up in the upper ONE-SIXTH of all first LTs in the army. In other words, he is highly outstanding among officers in his grade. It is relatively rare for a LT to get as high as 132." Schuller went on to assess Terry Jr.'s prospects for getting into advanced officer training courses and promotion to captain. ("Here again no worry because he has such a fine record.") All of which surely pleased the old man, who was by then retired and living in El Paso. The family ambition, shared as well by Mary Fran, was for Terry Jr. to exceed his father and someday wear the three stars of a lieutenant general or four stars of a full general.

After reaching captain, he served as a staff officer for the Continental Army Command at Fort Monroe, Virginia, and then was sent west to Colorado Springs as a junior aide to General Charles Hart at the U.S. Army Air Defense. That is where he met Bebe Coonly and her husband, Bill, who was Hart's senior aide. General Allen had stayed in Colorado Springs in 1944 while establishing the Timberwolves and was put up at the Broadmoor Hotel, where he became friends with the managers of the resort, the Tutt family. The Tutts were now quick to find Terry Jr. an apartment near the ice arena. The dashing young bachelor captain drove around town in a 1957 Thunderbird convertible with his polo boots and mallets in the back seat. He stopped over at the Coonlys' almost every day, or night, sometimes as late as two or three in the morning, knowing that he could bang on the door at any hour and feel welcome. On his way home from a party, he might "come in smiling expansively" and pronounce to the groggy Coonlys that his father had always told him never to drink alone. The life that his father had helped shape for him looked fine indeed in those final days of the fifties, and on the first of April 1959, Terry Sr.'s birthday, the loving disciple sent home a telegram that read, "My best wishes from the luckiest son in the world—Sonny."

There was one unsettling episode during his stint in Colorado Springs. Terry Jr. had fallen in love with the attractive young widow of a fallen Air Force pilot and was eager to show her off to his parents, but when the time came it proved disastrous. *Pleased ta meecha,* the woman said when she was introduced to Mary Fran, and the dignified El Paso matron, a woman who never left her house without hat and gloves, was so distraught over the coarseness of her son's lady friend that she announced that she had a terrible headache and retreated to her room. Terry Jr. was even less likely to disappoint his mother than his father, and the romance with the widow soon faded.

GENERAL ALLEN AND MARY FRAN lived in a comfortable but unpretentious house of limestone and wood at 21 Cumberland Circle within a mile's jog of the Fort Bliss front gate. On the living room wall, above a long row of polo trophies and wartime photographs, were the battle flags of the Big Red One and the Timberwolves, along with the original painting of Terrible Terry that *Time* had used for its cover. The rest of the house, with the exception of the retired general's den and Terry Jr.'s old bedroom, was painted in Mary Fran's favorite shade of art deco pink. Terry Sr. sold insurance in his retirement, though he never made much money at it, and he spent much of his time corresponding with old soldiers, coaching the polo team at Fort Bliss, and trying to keep in shape. Long before running became a fitness craze, he could be seen jogging through the residential streets in a loop that took him to the military base and then around toward the fashionable stucco homes on Pennsylvania Circle where El Paso's social elite lived. He was an unforgettable sight, decked out in army sweats with a wool wrap around his neck, carrying a medicine ball that kept his wrists supple for polo. When Jean Ponder, looking out from the backyard of her home at 230 Pennsylvania Circle, first saw this old man running down the nearby alley in the noonday heat, she went inside and asked her mother who it could be, and was told that it was General Allen.

There are conflicting accounts of when she first met the general's son. As her aunt Bebe Coonly remembered it, she and Bill threw a party for Terry when he came home from Command and General Staff College at Fort Leavenworth, a training ground for future colonels and generals

that the near-goat of West Point had become the first member of his
class to attend. Bebe's sister Alice called and asked her to invite her
daughter Jean, a gorgeous coed who had been moping around the house,
depressed about being dumped by the young man who had been her escort the previous year when she was named the lady-in-waiting at the
Sun Carnival. "And Jean walked in and looked like a million dollars,
and Terry had been laughing, drinking, and talking and then just froze
at the sight of her and that was it," Bebe Coonly recalled. Jean remembered it differently. She was home after her freshman year at the San
Diego College for Women, and her mother came up to her room and
said that Terry Allen Jr. was downstairs, would she like to meet him?
Jean said no, her mother insisted, and Jean relented, but said that she
would not change out of her Bermuda shorts. So she went downstairs
and the introductions were made, and from there "a whirlwind romance" began. They were both on the rebound, both Catholics. His
family was revered in El Paso, and she felt safe around him. To him Jean
represented the second coming of his mother, a young debutante so-
cialite who was beautiful and much younger than he was. He was 32, she
was 18. It was as though they had no choice but to accept the social
scripts that were handed to them. He proposed in July 1960 and they
were married in October.

Always on the lookout to help his son, Terry Sr. intervened in a minor fashion to ease the way for the wedding. Terry Jr. had been shipped
to Germany as an operations officer with the Eighth Infantry Division
by then and needed permission to return for the wedding, which was to
be held at St. Patrick's Cathedral in New York, with a breakfast reception at the Waldorf-Astoria. The old man wrote a memorandum to Major General Robert W. Porter, deputy chief of staff for personnel at the
Pentagon (and, not coincidentally, his old G-2 intelligence officer in the
Big Red One during the North Africa campaign), explaining that Terry
Jr. had to get married before October 5 for his bride to qualify for official dependent travel accommodations when they left for Europe. The
proper arrangements were made, and the wedding was held on October 2.
Jean wore a gown of candlelight peau de soie and lace, with a scoop
neckline and a Victorian-style skirt with a chapel train. Her face was
covered by a butterfly veil of illusion held by a small crown of orange
blossoms. As her father, James Hart Ponder, escorted her down the aisle,
he whispered, "If you don't want to do this, it's not a problem." She kept

walking toward Captain Terry de la Mesa Allen Jr., who awaited her in his dress blues. At his side stood the best man—his father.

After a honeymoon on the Riviera, Jean Ponder Allen found herself in a quaint place called Bad Kreuznach in an alien country where she knew no one and barely knew her own husband, who worked long hours in any case and usually took the car. She was utterly ill prepared for the life she faced, a beauty queen from upper-class El Paso accustomed to nothing beyond the privileged society of her youth. Her landlady, Frau Schmidt, whose husband had fought for the Nazis, took pity on her and taught her some German. She made daily strolls around the village. And in less than a year she had a baby daughter. Terry wanted to name her in honor of his Spanish grandmother, but he somehow confused the name, so it came out Consuelo instead of Conchita. In a letter to her mother-in-law in September 1962, Jean seemed to be adjusting as well as could be expected. "Terry is in the field again—for 10 days," she wrote. "Everyone is a little nervous around here, as in four days five Eighth Division people were killed. Two in an auto accident, one jumping, and a sergeant shot a captain and then killed himself! All of this took place in Mannheim—is B.K. next? Last night I played Bingo—and won ten dollars. I thought of you all night—playing with six cards! Colonel and Mrs. Peevely Rury are here and know you quite well. She says you gave a party for them when they left Fort Bliss. . . . Oh, Mary Fran, if only you could see your granddaughter now. She is cute enough to eat. She has discovered her hands now, and spends hours looking at them. This house has been blessed with a wonderful maid. I'm so delighted."

Another daughter, Bebe, named for Jean's aunt, arrived fourteen months later, and within a year of that came Mary Frances, named for Terry's mother. Jean was barely twenty-two, the mother of three little girls, overwhelmed and overtaken by postpartum depression. She was also now without the help of Frau Schmidt, the family having moved to Stuttgart and then Augsburg following Terry's assignments. His mind was very much on making it to the top. Without saying it aloud, he and Jean worked on the common assumption that someday he would be a general. His father, of the same mind, was always willing to offer advice on how to get there.

"Your considered counsel has always been a great deal of help to me," Terry Jr. acknowledged in a letter to his father in September 1963 from

Seventh Army headquarters. "I agree with your present evaluation of the situation in Vietnam as being more politically oriented. It seems to be coming even more so. My choice selection now would be to try to receive an assignment as an infantry battalion executive officer although not necessarily limited to Germany."

The old man, delighted to get that letter, fired off a reply. He recommended that his son make the move from a staff position to command duty because "extensive practical experience in troop leading is an essential basic need for any combat officer." And he concluded with a few bits of advice on the characteristics of good commanders. They "must be able to call the signals with clarity and foresight. And they must be able to imbue in their soldiers the will to fight, and the will to get the job done come hell or high water." The dutiful son moved up to become executive officer for a tank battalion of the Seventieth Armor, where he seemed to meet his father's standards of leadership. He was known as "a regular guy" who, without shouting or forcing himself upon the troops, could get men to do what he wanted out of a natural desire to please him, according to Ed O'Brien, an officer who served under him during that period.

After two years with the tank battalion, Allen was transferred to the States for a post with the U.S. Strike Command at MacDill Air Force Base in Tampa. Jean was depressed and emotionally drained by the time they got back from Europe. She was drinking to medicate herself in the evening, though that fact was hardly noticeable in a family of habitual drinkers. Terry Jr., like his father, rarely let the cocktail hour go by without two scotch and waters, which he sipped while puffing on an aromatic cigar. He was a lively storyteller and had a natural brightness to him, some called it a twinkle, that perhaps made it harder for him to see Jean's inner despair. In tandem with her drinking, she was taking amphetamines, one tablet of speed a day to help her lose weight. She was also distraught over the condition of her mother, who was in the final stages of inoperable cancer. Her mother was her emotional mainstay, but now Jean felt unable to express her distress. Jean's father had issued a family order that no one was to talk about the fatal nature of the disease, especially not in front of the mother. Alice Hicks Ponder died while Jean was in Tampa, and her father quickly remarried, making the young military wife feel even more alone.

Out of whimsy and desperation, Jean visited a fortune-teller, who put a hand on her and gave her a personal reading. Her life, she was told, was like a piece of cloth that was going to be ripped in two. Her husband might die. *Ridiculous,* Jean said to herself. *That's what I get for going to a stupid fortune-teller.* The orders came for Terry Allen Jr. to report to Vietnam on February 25. He had often told Jean that "the only way a soldier proves himself is on the battlefield." Here was his chance. Jean, in retrospect, thought she should have asked him to hold off going until she was in a better mental state, but at the time she and her husband were still operating under a different philosophy: in the military, you do what you are told to do. She still wanted to be a general's wife.

THE OLD MAN had fallen into a middle stage of dementia by then, a condition that first became noticeable during a trip to the battlefields of Holland with his old Timberwolves in 1965, when he kept wondering where he was and asking in befuddlement for Mary Fran, who had not made the trip with him. For Terry Jr., who adored his father, watching him deteriorate was like "watching the sun fall from the sky." By early 1967, when his son flew off to lead soldiers in Vietnam, the retired general was virtually unable to navigate outside his home and would lapse into periods of confusion. Holding on dearly to reminders of his glorious past, he became obsessed with the little red instructional booklets he had published during and after World War II. He carried them in his back pocket wherever he went and would hand them out to strangers and children, including little Consuelo. Among the personal items Terry Jr. took with him to Vietnam was a small brown manila clasp envelope that had "For Terry Allen jr. (All you need to fight a War)" written on the side in a palsied scrawl. Inside were three of the booklets: *Directive for Offensive Combat, Night Attacks,* and *Combat Leadership,* the final words of which were, "The battle is the payoff." In a birthday card to his father written from the Big Red One base camp in Lai Khe in late March, Terry Jr. reported that he had given copies of the booklets to the division operations officer, the brigade commander, and General Hay.

That same week, during a rare lull in his job as operations officer for the Black Lions battalion, the position he held during his first two months in Vietnam, he wrote a long letter to his young wife. "Dearest Jean," it began. "I was thrilled to receive three letters from you while on this last operation. The first letter arrived on the 19th and it was postmarked from El Paso on the 14th. This was the first letter I had received—if you had written before and included any information requiring an answer etc. please let me know. I read the letter so many times the handwriting would rightfully have come off the paper. Any break I had I would pull them out and reread them—I do miss you terribly." Jean in fact had written him almost daily in the first few weeks after his departure, loving letters in which she talked about how fortunate they were "to have such a strong bond." She was beside herself to hear that he had not received them.

The next paragraph of her husband's letter was equally warm, and it seemed apparent that he was thinking of Jean as his soulmate as he described life at the base camp. "It's good to be back to our base camp to clean up and sleep in a bed. This is the fourth night we've been able to spend here since my arrival in the battalion. It's a little relaxing and the one place I can use a fan (which I intend to buy shortly). We will be here six days before leaving on another operation. Tomorrow is Easter so I will be able to go to Mass. Our battalion chaplain is a Catholic—a Jesuit and a very fine soldier priest. We had some interesting discussions over a drink after our Junction City Operation. We both agree on so many points—wish you had been there to join us."

The remainder of the letter was all military, nothing personal, describing in great detail the last operation thirty-five miles north of Saigon as though he were filing an after action report to headquarters. If its intended purpose was to familiarize Jean with his environment, it did the opposite, only making him seem a million miles away, in a world she could not even imagine. She read his account of Operation Yorktown with increasing bewilderment and concern. "This particular area is known in the Division under the code name LAM SON (unclassified) which I've been told is the name of a 13th century Vietnamese hero. It is also the Division's contribution to the Pacification Program which is coordinated by the Division G-5 and known as the Revolutionary Development Program which sounds like a communist front organization," he wrote. "The battalion's first mission was to 'seal' a village in conjunction with a battalion from the South Vietnamese Army. The idea being to allow G5 personnel and Vietnamese National Police the chance to then screen all village males and pick up VC suspects."

Using a tactic that would have made General Allen proud, the battalion encircled the village in a night move. "One rifle company was leading followed by the command group composed of the battalion commander, myself and our radio operators, we in turn followed by the other two rifle companies. After half of the encirclement was completed we received three rifle shots from the village. Everyone hit the ground thinking we would receive further fire. Nothing happened so the move was continued. Just before the leading rifle company completed the encirclement they bumped into 15 VC running out of the village and a running battle ensued. Although some of the VC were killed we recovered only one body. Reconstruction of events the next day proved that the VC village chief, who was also the #2 communist political boss in the district, was giving a communist political class to the villagers. The three shots we heard were warning of our presence and the group of VC running out of the village were the chief and his body guard which he normally carries when traveling from village to village. The most fortunate thing was that the body we recovered was the VC chief himself."

Allen entered the village at daylight to observe the screening procedures, he told his wife. "Here the Division G5 and the South Vietnamese National Police and Army had lined up the male population over age 16. A Chieu Hoi (pronounced Chew Hoy) that is a former VC who now gives his loyalty to the government was identifying those he knew as VC. Three or four VC were rounded up this way. An additional 15 to 20 draft dodgers were also collected. While the screening took place the village males were fed GI fish and rice. Later in the day a small traveling carnival was brought in to entertain the village. The battalion remained deployed around the village while the house by house search continued. We found one VC and some weapons in a tunnel at the edge of town. I learned this village was considered about 40% VC or VC supporters. Ironically a village 10 miles away had very few VC due principally, I'm told, to the large number of Catholics."

At the end of that village roundup, the battalion moved on to a three-day search-and-destroy mission in a jungle area to the south, closer to Saigon. "It was a dirty business. We received sporadic sniper fire, made occasional contact with small groups of local VC and found a number of mines and booby traps. All told we had eleven wounded. Sniper fire did come within 3 or 4 yards of me—he was a poor shot obviously. While moving single file down a jungle trail on the second day, the Sgt. Major who was just ahead of me discovered a trip wire across the trail. The wire was rigged at either end to two 60 mm mortar rounds. An entire company had passed over the wire but fortunately it was placed too far into the ground for anyone to trip it. Although we took casualties from the booby traps many were discovered and destroyed."

The letter to his wife was so long in the writing that he continued it on Easter Sunday, before finally closing so that he could "drop this in the mail on the way to mass."

How different that world of the Black Lions seemed from what Jean was experiencing in El Paso. Terry Allen Jr. might still be playing by the script, but hers was not unfolding the way she had expected. Her mother had died. Her father had remarried within six months. Her husband was in Vietnam, encircling villages. She had three small girls to look after and no one in El Paso to whom she felt close, her childhood friends married or gone. In that difficult and isolated condition, she felt the first undirected stirrings of something else, a need to break away and reinvent herself. In a visit to the new television station in town, ABC's Channel 13, she proposed that they let her run her own weekly public affairs show. She was a striking figure in her short skirts, with long legs and flowing light-brown locks. She was also articulate and her family was well known, and such a show would cost little while satisfying the regulatory requirements of public interest broadcasting. *The Jean Allen Show* was born. It ran Sunday afternoons at two.

It was the typical local patchwork of the serious and the inane. Jean interviewed artists and authors and let local theaters perform snippets from their shows, but there was also the time a local dairy manager bragged about his best-producing cow and pulled out a picture of the cow and in a deadpan voice discussed the number of gallons she could let loose in a day. The show brought Jean into contact for the first time with people who were critical of the war in Vietnam, and day by day their thoughts altered her perspective. She noticed that people, even antiwar activists, seemed impressed that she was the wife of an army officer, but she was becoming less so. For the first time she began "to see the other side of the story in Vietnam," and she embraced it, she would say later, as naïvely as she had previously "embraced not questioning politics." She did not move to the other side gradually but suddenly, and it was more out of emotion than careful study. She was seeing life in a way she had never seen it before. Until then she had carried "abstract feelings with echoes of World War II in the background," but now, suddenly, she was "watching television and seeing body bags brought out and scenes of villages where civilians had been bombed."

This was all very different for her, and she was having a visceral reaction. As the weeks went by, in April and May, she could no longer make a distinction between her husband as a soldier and the military as a whole. If it was wrong, so was he. She began seeing the world as us versus them, and Terry Allen Jr. was one of them.

"THIS IS FOR all the women who waited for their husbands," Mary Fran Allen used to say as she started a story about what it was like to be home in El Paso while her husband was fighting in North Africa and Europe. The general's wife could be an imperious figure around Fort Bliss, expecting clerks at the PX to drop what they were doing when she entered the store and lifeguards at the base pool to take extra care in watching out for her little granddaughters, but there was an authenticity to her sense of self as the soldier's wife. One day she was swimming at the Officers' Club pool with her granddaughter Consuelo when a bugle calling "Retreat" sounded over the loudspeakers along with the end-of-the-day blast of the howitzer. She reflexively started climbing up the pool ladder so that she could stand at attention on deck, as she always did. Consuelo didn't understand and pulled at her to come back and play, accidentally scraping her grandmother's leg against the sharp edge of the ladder. Mary Fran reached down, grabbed her granddaughter, and set her down at her side, and Consuelo gaped in amazement at an early childhood vision that she would never forget—the quintessential military wife standing at attention with blood dripping down her leg.

"A very special place must be reserved in Heaven for Army wives as reward for the years of separation they have endured because of military requirements. . . . There can be no greater admiration than that of the husband to return and find, as he has hoped, that his own wife has met the test of keeping up her end of things." So began a section on how to be a proper army wife in *The Officer's Guide,* the standard bible of the soldier's profession.

Jean Ponder Allen was no longer interested in following that path to heaven. She struck up a relationship with the TV clown, started sleeping with him, and soon invited him to stay at her place, a house on a street called—of all things—Timberwolf, named after the famed division that Terry Allen Sr. led through Europe and that nothing in hell could stop. She was in a state of mind in which she felt no embarrassment and did not try to hide her relationship. Her daughters wondered who this strange man was in their house, who seemed to drink too much and who broke Bebe's tricycle, but Jean was not thinking of her children as anything more than an extension of herself. She wrote Terry Jr. a letter telling him what she was doing and how she felt. Terry called from Vietnam, but the connection was bad, figuratively and literally; it sounded as though he were on a radiophone out in the field. Soon he was getting emergency leave, flying back to El Paso, calling Bebe Coonly and making her shriek with surprise.

HE DROVE OVER TO 5014 Timberwolf in the pink Cadillac and tried to win back his wife. Feeling a need to defend her position, she overstated it, calling him a baby killer. She remembered his saying that he had grown to understand a lot of things that he hadn't understood when he first got to Vietnam and that he was taking notes and would write a book about it when he got back. He was abandoning the lifelong dream of becoming a general, he told her. He didn't know what he would do, maybe teach. The boy who considered scholarship tedious had evolved into a man who loved to read and was a voracious student of history. As Jean would remember it later, this was "in some ways maybe the most honest conversation we'd ever had between us." They sat in the bedroom, man and wife, estranged and struggling. He said that he wanted to make love to her. She wanted to but would not let him. He kept talking about the war, offering nuanced explanations of what the American military was doing and failing to do. She was not interested in complexity, only in what she had seen and heard about civilians getting killed. "It doesn't matter what you say," she told him. "It's finished." She explained to him, for the first time, how upsetting it had been for her to have three little children and make so many moves, and he said he never should have let it happen. He asked her to see a psychiatrist, and she agreed, and when the first one failed to connect with her, she went to another, one of Terry's best friends, Dr. Frank (Kiko) Schuster, who had an extraordinary ability to make anyone feel safe. She felt understood, for the first time, with him.

At night over at the Coonlys the conversations were also, inevitably, about Vietnam. "You wouldn't believe how things are going over there," Terry told Bill. It was a whole new ballgame, nothing like what they taught at command and general staff college. Senior commanders didn't seem to comprehend the reality of what was happening on the ground, in the jungles.

Bebe, a professional artist, told Terry that she had been working on a large painting out in the casita behind the house, and she wanted him to see it. The painting was her effort to show how this was a political war. The background on the canvas was an American flag, with the map of Vietnam and a hammer and sickle in the middle; superimposed on the stars in the blue-and-white upper-left corner were representations of President Johnson and the U.S. Capitol and a donkey and an elephant. Below that a helicopter was dropping napalm, and a soldier was throwing a grenade, and a medic was looking down on a dead infantryman. On the right side of the flag, amid the red and white stripes, there was a Buddhist monk praying in an orange robe, and a Vietnamese mother crying as she held a naked baby, and an American jet spraying a field with defoliant, and in the upper-right corner a rendition of a photograph Bebe had seen in *Life,* of a group of exhausted GIs. Bebe had sent the picture to an El Paso museum, which was soliciting works from local artists, but they had called her and asked her to remove it, so now it was back in the casita, hidden away among her traditional western art.

Allen studied the painting and turned away without saying a word.

He drove across town to Timberwolf again the next night, when Jean's sister Susie was babysitting the girls, and said that he just needed a minute. Susie was under instructions not to let him in, but she did. He stood in the doorway outside the bedroom and stared at his daughters as they slept, then he left. The next day he drove downtown to the end of Texas Street, where it meets Oregon, and stepped inside the First National Bank Building. He rode the elevator up to fifteen, the top floor, and found his way to Kemp Smith White Duncan and Hammond, and from there to Tad Smith's office in the northwest corner, where the picture windows lured the eye up Texas Street and on to the Franklin Mountains in the distance. Tad Smith was not a divorce lawyer, but he made exceptions for people he knew, and everyone in town knew General Allen. He encountered now the general's son, who was "pissed off." Terry said that he had staked out his wife's house and seen the car of this bozo the clown there and that he wanted a divorce and also custody of the children. Smith said that would require the development of more information about Jean's behavior, and Terry said there was a next-door neighbor who knew some things. That neighbor was a retired army officer who had told Mary Fran about the affair. It was no secret.

And the maids were talking. In El Paso, most Anglo families in the middle and upper classes had maids, and the maids knew each other. Jean's maid was talking to friends.

After Terry left his office, Smith began drafting the divorce papers and developing what he could. One of the stories the maids told him was of seeing Hart Ponder burst into tears as he tried to persuade his daughter not to do what she was doing.

Near the end of his leave Terry spent an afternoon with his girls. He was wearing a Hawaiian shirt when he picked them up in the pink Cadillac, and they went to the Campus Queen for burgers and then to the swimming pool at the Coronado Country Club. When he dropped them off and started to say good-bye, about to return to Vietnam, where he would soon become battalion commander of the 2/28 Black Lions, little Consuelo hid under a three-legged stool and started crying.

"You can't leave!" she sobbed. "You're going to die!" Terry Allen pulled his daughter up from her hideaway and held her in his arms. "Be brave," he said, "and take care of your little sisters."

BOOK TWO

Whatever may be the limitations which trammel inquiry elsewhere, we believe that the great state University of Wisconsin should ever encourage that continual and fearless sifting and winnowing by which alone the truth can be found.

—Wisconsin Board of Regents, 1894

CHAPTER 5

SONG OF NAPALM

O N THE SUNDAY MORNING of March 12, 1967, E. N. Brandt, director of public relations for the Dow Chemical Company, left his office in Midland, Michigan, the small town where the homegrown corporation was based, and caught a United Airlines flight that would carry him east for a meeting the next morning with officials at the defense department. This was Brandt's first trip to Washington and not one that he had expected to make. When he first suggested that the company meet with the military brass to present a list of concerns, he thought the mission would be appropriate for his boss, president Herbert Dow Doan, grandson of the company's founder. Doan instead simply told Brandt in his characteristically informal fashion that it sounded good, go ahead and do it.

Dow Chemical was not one of the big boys of the military-industrial complex—it ranked seventy-fifth that year in the dollar volume of its defense contracts—and its top executives in Midland were conservative Republicans, but the company nonetheless was on especially friendly terms with the Johnson administration. Directing its Washington office was A. P. (Dutch) Beutel, a legendary character known as the founding father of the Texas chemical industry. Beutel walked with a slight limp and his wrinkled, wind-burned face looked like a Lone Star topographic map delineating every river from the Red to the Rio Grande. He was a man who seemed to have the true measure of Texas, and something more: he was an old crony of LBJ's going back to 1950, when he was setting up Dow's Gulf Coast operation in Freeport. The easy relationship between Dow and the White House was now reflected in things as large as engineering contracts with the new space center in Houston and as small as the Styrofoam coffee cup holders bearing the presidential seal that Jimmy Phillips of the Freeport plant would send up as gifts to President Johnson and longtime aides Jack Valenti and Walter Jenkins. Johnson's Hill Country ranch along the Pedernales had even experimented with a defoliant Dow developed for use in Vietnam. The Texas connection served Dow well, and when word came from Michigan that the company wanted a Pentagon audience, Dutch Beutel had no trouble making the arrangements.

The public relations agenda that Ned Brandt took to Washington was at once understandable and implausible. Dow believed that the military should absolve it of responsibility for something it produced, or at least deflect the increasingly harsh criticism coming the company's way. Along with its industrial and consumer products, most notably Saran Wrap, Dow also manufactured napalm, which when packaged into a bomb became a fearsome weapon of jellied fire that sucked the oxygen out of the air and clung unmercifully to human flesh as it burned at two thousand degrees Fahrenheit.

Napalm was cheap and easy to make. The latest variation of the hellish concoction, known as napalm B, was 25 percent gasoline, 25 percent benzene, and 50 percent polystyrene mixed together in what the industry dismissively called "bathtub chemistry." Dow had begun producing napalm B at a plant in Torrance, California, in the summer of 1965 (three years after the U.S. Air Force, in its "advisory" role, began dropping napalm bombs in Vietnam), and within a year of getting the contract, it stood alone as the military's sole supplier. The weapon and the chemical company thus became inextricably linked in the public mind just as napalm was emerging as the most provocative symbol of modern warfare, with press reports and photographs chronicling its horrible effects on civilians in Vietnam and the nightly news regularly jolting viewers as violent splashes of napalm exploded in the jungles on the small screen.

Dow in turn became the most visible target of American antiwar protests, especially at colleges and universities where its corporate recruiters conducted placement interviews with seniors. The student demonstrations against Dow began in October 1966 at Wayne State University in Detroit and the University of California in Berkeley, and in the five months from then until the day Brandt left for Washington, there were forty-three anti-Dow protests staged around the country, from San José State to Wisconsin to Brooklyn College. The chant "Down with Dow!" and picketing placard "Dow Shalt Not Kill" were entering the protest lexicon alongside the napalm-inspired "Hey, Hey, LBJ, how many kids did you kill today?"

In the middle of that stretch Brandt and his associates realized the severity of their public relations dilemma. "I would hate for Dow to come out of Viet Nam with the 'Merchants of Death' label that was pinned on du Pont after the first World War; and yet, unless we come to grips with this problem, it is likely to happen," warned one Dow official in a red-flag memorandum that circulated in the company's executive offices in December 1966. The danger, according to the memo, was that Dow was being used as "a pawn in the propaganda battle of those who are for and against the war. We are being kicked around, and we are not being portrayed with sympathy in the press. Enduring this sort of treatment with silence will not cause our enemies to forget about us; it will instead encourage them to whack us some more."

Before then, as Brandt once explained, Dow's response to the protests had been to "as tactfully as possible . . . try to minimize its connection with napalm." When queried by the press or public, company officials were instructed to read a simple statement:

> The Dow Chemical Company endorses the right of any American to protest legally and peacefully an action with which he does not agree.
>
> Our position on the manufacture of napalm is that we are a supplier of goods to the Defense Department and not a policy maker. We do not and should not try to decide military strategy or policy.
>
> Simple good citizenship requires that we supply our government and our military with those goods which they feel they need whenever we have the technology and capability and have been chosen by the government as a supplier.
>
> We will do our best, as we always have, to try to produce what our Defense Department and our soldiers need in any war situation. Purely aside from our duty to do this, we will feel deeply gratified if what we are able to provide helps to protect our fighting men or to speed the day when fighting will end.

The more Dow emerged as the corporate symbol of the war, the less adequate that response alone seemed, with its subdued and somewhat evasive tone. Brandt's office quietly began developing a large-scale pub-lic relations strategy, preparing to make the case publicly concerning both napalm's use in Vietnam and Dow's corporate philosophy. At the same time it hoped to shift the heat whenever possible to the Pentagon, and that is the part of the mission that sent Brandt to Washington. The word around Midland headquarters was that the military was getting away with something; *they* were the ones using the napalm; why weren't protesters picketing *them*? What Dow executives found most exasper-ating was that the Pentagon seemed to like it that way, even if it was unfair.

The very morning that Brandt traveled to Washington, an article ap-peared in the *New York Times* that could not have pleased him more had he written it himself. The author was Dr. Howard A. Rusk, a world-renowned medical rehabilitation expert who also served as a part-time columnist for the newspaper. Under a Saigon dateline, Rusk reported that he had spent the previous week on what he called "an intensive tour" of twenty civilian hospitals in South Vietnam and had seen "not a single case of burns due to napalm." In addition, of the scores of doctors he interviewed during his trip, "many had not seen a single case of burns due to napalm and others had seen but a single case." Far more preva-lent, these doctors told Rusk, were burns from the use of kerosene in stoves and accidents involving land mines placed by the Viet Cong. His reporting led Rusk to the conclusion that "the picture that has been painted by some in the United States of large numbers of children burned by napalm in Vietnam is grossly exaggerated."

Rusk's dispatch came as a direct challenge to a report that had ap-peared in *Ramparts* magazine a few months earlier asserting that at least a million Vietnamese children had become casualties of the war, many of them victims of American napalm. The *Ramparts* piece, accompanied by harrowing color photographs of disfigured young napalm victims, served as a powerful rallying tool for campus protests against Dow. (And in fact, according to David J. Garrow's book on Martin Luther King Jr., *Bearing the Cross,* the photographs so upset the civil rights leader that they helped push Vietnam to the forefront of his moral agenda. On January 14, 1967, King was at a restaurant in the Miami air-port on his way to Jamaica when he leafed through the magazine and caught sight of the pictures, which left him nauseated and energized. As Garrow told the story, when an associate asked King why he was not eating, he replied that "nothing will ever taste good to me until I do everything I can to end the war.") The author of the *Ramparts* text was William F. Pepper, a political scientist and human rights activist who had spent six weeks in Vietnam as a freelance journalist visiting orphanages and interviewing government health officials. His report was passionate. "For countless thousands of children in Vietnam, breathing is quickened by terror and pain, and tiny bodies learn more about death every day," it began. The statistics he used were extrapolations. He said that his conclusion of a million child casualties was reached by starting with a base estimate that 415,000 civilians already had been killed in the war. Since slightly less than half of all Vietnamese were children, he figured that the number of children killed would be more than a quarter million. He then multiplied that figure by three since military statistics generally figure three times as many wounded as killed.

There were methodological flaws in both Pepper's point and Rusk's counterpoint. Pepper's base number of 415,000 civilian deaths by the end of 1966 was a guess, not a fact. The number of civilian deaths during the entire war, which lasted another six years, has never been resolved. Most estimates placed the number between 300,000 and a half million. Vietnam war expert A. J. Langguth, writing of the situation at the time of the Paris Peace Talks in 1973, six years after Pepper's article, said that the total number of civilians killed or wounded during the entire war to that point, North and South, men, women, and children, "may have run to a million." One analysis of civilian casualties—conducted by American doctors opposed to the war—later found 800 "in all the hospital beds in Vietnam" during a survey period in 1967. Pepper's assumption that slightly less than half the casualties would be children, based on their percentage of the population, was also problematic. According to statistics kept by hospitals in the Mekong Delta, where the fighting was heavy, there were 284 children among 1,141 civilian casualties admitted in January 1967, or about one-fourth of the total.

Rusk, for his part, had close connections to the military and was not an impartial observer. He based his conclusions solely on brief observations and interviews at hospitals, which could not present the full picture in a war-torn country where many civilian casualties never went to hospitals. One British physician who had been dealing with the civilian casualty issue for three years by 1967 estimated in a discussion with Jonathan Schell of *The New Yorker* that only two of ten casualties were being taken to hospitals. According to this account, there was an average of thirty war casualties a day, and ten percent of them, or three a day,

came from burns. Also Rusk offered no data to support the final assertion of his article, true or not, that American-caused civilian casualties
were "unpreventable in this type of conflict and . . . not nearly so great as
the killing and wounding of civilians by the Vietcong."

Somewhere between the two conflicting reports rested the reality of
what napalm was doing in Vietnam. Long before Pepper and Rusk visited and long after they left, respected American journalists based in
Saigon filed scores of reports on what they saw and heard in the field,
which tended to fall between Rusk and Pepper statistically but closer to
Pepper anecdotally. For those opposed to the war, one account of the
horrors of napalm could be enough.

Why would they target Dow Chemical? The answer might be found
in reports like one filed by *New York Times* correspondent Charles Mohr
describing a peasant woman he encountered in a Mekong village who
"had both arms burned off by napalm and her eyelids burned so badly
that she cannot close them." Or an article in the January 1967 *Ladies'
Home Journal* by veteran war correspondent Martha Gellhorn, who visited the provincial hospital at Qui Nhon and "saw for the first time what
napalm does."

At a cot by the door Gellhorn encountered a four-year-old boy. "Napalm had burned his face and back and one hand. The burned skin
looked like swollen, raw meat; the fingers of his hand were stretched
out, burned rigid. A scrap of cheesecloth covered him, for weight is in-
tolerable, but so is air." Gellhorn also encountered a woman from New
Jersey who had adopted three Vietnamese children. "Before I went to
Saigon, I had heard and read that napalm melts the flesh, and I thought
that's nonsense, because I can put a roast in the oven and the fat will melt
but the meat stays there," the woman said. "Well, I went and saw these
children burned by napalm, and it is absolutely true. The chemical reaction of this napalm does melt the flesh, and the flesh runs right down
their faces onto their chests and it sits there and it grows there. . . . These
children can't turn their head, they were so thick with flesh."

To the soldiers in Vietnam, there was no such thing as a benign way
to kill, or to die, or to be wounded, yet napalm still evoked a special
realm of dread. Only nine days before Brandt made his pilgrimage to
Washington, an army historian interviewed Lieutenant Colonel Alvin
R. Hylton, the chemical officer for the First Infantry Division. Hylton
talked extensively about the use of CS gas, a tear gas, in Vietnam and

said he thought his unit should be allowed to use other forms of gases as well. "There are all sorts of gases you could use here which would be more humane, for example, than burning a man up with a flame thrower that throws napalm on him."

WHEN NED BRANDT and two associates arrived at the Pentagon at ten on Monday morning, March 13, they were armed with a memo listing five actions the Department of Defense could take to help Dow. First, they wanted a statement from Defense explaining "the necessity for napalm, policies governing its use and its effect in terms of war effort." Second, they would request a letter from Secretary of Defense Robert S. McNamara, on his stationery, "stressing the need for napalm to protect American soldiers" and praising Dow's contribution in that regard. Next, they sought another letter from General Westmoreland "emphasizing the lives of American soldiers which have been saved because of napalm." Fourth, they would ask for a "visit by medal of honor winner or other battle-scarred veteran to Midland, Freeport, Torrance for personal appearances in plants. He can give first-hand reports of napalm's tactical benefits." And finally, they would ask whether they could "hire a free lance writer in Viet Nam to write battle stories where napalm played a key role in saving our boys on the front line."

Brandt assumed that his delegation might get no further than the press office or be shuffled from one low-ranking paper pusher to another. Instead they were ushered into a large meeting room where they found themselves being faced down by a panel of six colonels arrayed on the other side of a long table. The visitors were directed to sit submissively in front of the table. It was "kind of like a court martial setup," Brandt thought, and his guys were in the chairs "that normally would have been for the accused." If it was not a court martial, neither was it a freewheeling give-and-take about the relationship between the corporation and the military. For three quarters of an hour the colonels fired questions at the public relations men while revealing nothing about themselves. Brandt went into the meeting never having heard the Pentagon's position on the anti-Dow protests and went out no further informed.

As he was leaving, Brandt brought out a copy of a letter he had drafted and handed it to a Pentagon official. It was a suggested version of the letter Secretary McNamara could send to Herbert Dow Doan. (In a late revision he had even included a mention of Dr. Rusk's napalm report from Saigon.)

"Dear Mr. Doan," the draft began, "We have followed with considerable interest and concern the newspaper accounts of the demonstrations and protests that have for some time been directed against your company as a major supplier of napalm for the armed forces. It is, as you know, highly unusual for such protests to be directed against the manufacturer, rather than the military user, of a weapon, even one as emotion-laden as napalm B. In what must surely be rather trying circumstances, the conduct of your company has been exemplary . . ."

CHAPTER 6

MADISON, WISCONSIN

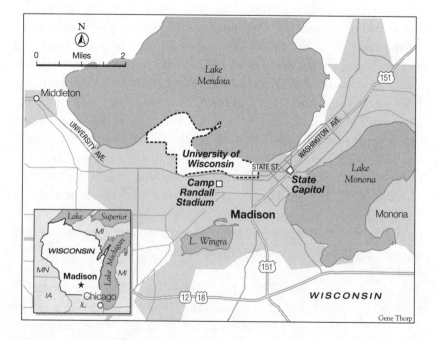

N

0 Miles 2

Middleton

Lake
Mendota

151

UNIVERSITY AVE.

WASHINGTON AVE.

**University of
Wisconsin** STATE ST.

Camp□
Randall
Stadium

**State
Capitol**

Lake
Monona

Monona

Madison

L. Wingra

151

Lake   Superior
MI
WISCONSIN

Lake Michigan

MN   MI
Madison
★
IA   Chicago
IL

12 18

WISCONSIN

Gene Thorp

T
HE 1967 FALL TERM was not yet a month old when a crowd of
rambunctious students at the University of Wisconsin spilled
from the southeast dorms of Ogg and Sellery looking for action.
It was midweek, a Wednesday, ten P.M., and the air was rapturously
warm and alluring, a welcome break from the dispiriting blanket of
gray that had settled over Madison so prematurely that year, wiping out
the last month of summer and bringing intimations of the long frozen
winter to come. Feeling free and easy in the balmy night, the young men
marched north toward Lake Mendota, skirting the Library Mall and the
Old Red Gym, then turned right and headed up the curve of Langdon
Street, picking up more recruits from fraternity houses there until they

were nearly a thousand strong. The first stop was Langdon Hall, at the time still known as a "girls" dormitory. "We want silk! We want pants! We want sex!" came shouts from the street, and out flew some panties but more rolls of toilet paper.

The crowd undulated up and down Langdon and then oozed across to State Street, passing more targets along the way. A small squad of Madison cops, some in uniform, others in plainclothes, monitored the students until they reached the sidewalk on the far side of Park Street at the bottom of State. That marked the official boundary of the university, and according to Inspector Herman Thomas, city officers would not enter the campus proper unless UW administrators formally requested their presence. Up the long rise of Bascom Hill went the student battalion, past the statue of seated Abe Lincoln and around the side of Bascom Hall onto Observatory Drive, dipping down the back slope past the Commerce and Social Science buildings, and then up again and along the ridge toward Elizabeth Waters, another dormitory for women. A score of young men were seen entering the dorm uninvited, but they scattered when spotted by a housemother, and from there the crowd dissolved in the darkness. There was minor retaliation the next night. A few hundred freshman women, mostly from Chadbourne Hall, rallied on the steps of the Memorial Union, then marched to Ogg, where they were greeted by the swoosh and splash of shaving cream and water balloons.

The culture was changing in 1967, certainly, and Madison was said to be in the vanguard, but the counterculture stereotypes later imposed on the university, as on the entire decade, fail to capture the more variegated reality of that time and place. A nocturnal panty raid was still part of the campus scene. There was not yet a glimmer of the notion that young men and women would be allowed to live in the same dormitory tower, let alone on the same floor. Visitation hours for men in the women's dorms were limited to 2:00 to 9:30 P.M. on Sundays. Three freshmen had been disciplined already that fall for breaking the women's curfew on a Saturday night. They had gone to Milwaukee to participate in a civil rights march, after which one straggled back to her dorm a shade past 1:30 Sunday morning and the others were even later. As punishment they faced a week to three weeks of restricted hours. Along Langdon Street the Greek subculture had not yet slipped into disfavor. The talk that fall was of a meningitis scare that began with a "kissing party" involving fraternities and sororities. When one young smoocher ended up at University Hospital with a mild case of the disease, panic spread and five hundred students who might have had contact with him reported to the health clinic for preventive sulfa pills.

Five years removed from past Rose Bowl glory, the Badger football team was dreadful, on its way to a winless season that inspired one loud and repetitive refrain from the student sections—"ooooohhhhhh shit!" But on the sidelines that fall, making their inaugural appearance, were sixteen pompom girls dancing in red and white miniskirts. A hundred coeds had tried out.

The crosscurrents of the times were readily evident. On the first day of fall classes, a mime troupe affiliated with *Connections,* a radical alternative newspaper, put on an early version of performance art, or guerrilla theater. Posturing as rightwing storm troopers, they barged into lecture halls, hauled out student activist compatriots, and dragged them to mock executions at the top of Bascom Hill. Two nights before the puerile panty raid, Allard Lowenstein, director of the national "Dump Johnson" movement, appeared on campus and told a gathering of students that they could be the key to his entire scenario. If they produced a strong vote against the president in the 1968 Wisconsin primary, he predicted, "there would be many political implications." *McCall's* magazine had labeled Wisconsin the number two drinking school in the nation, but that was stale news to the student newspaper, the *Daily Cardinal,* which was running a series on the mind-bending effects of LSD and other hallucinogens. The albums of the Jefferson Airplane, Buffalo Springfield, and Big Brother and the Holding Company were being sold at Discount Records and Victor Music on State Street, and the Beatles had made their cultural turn that summer with the release of *Sgt. Pepper's Lonely Hearts Club Band*—"She's leaving home, bye, bye"—but WISM in Madison and WLS in Chicago were still playing a Top 40 list that included Tommy James and the Shondells, Bobby Vinton, Bobbie Gentry, Herb Alpert, and Nancy Sinatra.

Meetings of the student senate were sparsely attended at the same time that a faculty committee earnestly considered the issue of "student power," something that student testifiers knew they lacked but could not necessarily define. The Anti-Military Ball, a counterculture tradition at Wisconsin, was held on the eve of the ROTC party and drew more students. They danced under the slogan "Anti-militarists have balls." The Madison chapter of Students for a Democratic Society usually drew more people than the student senate and had its own newsletter, but the largest campus rally earlier that year was one in which moderate students gathered under the banner "We Want No Berkeley Here"—and the largest club on campus was not SDS or Young Democrats, but Young Republicans.

Then there was the visage of Robert Cohen, a teaching assistant in philosophy who prided himself on looking like a beatnik. While Cohen was serving time behind bars at the Dane County jail on a disorderly conduct conviction stemming from an earlier protest, his scraggly black hair and beard had been buzz cut into oblivion by local barber Sam Fidele, who had volunteered his services for the occasion. Cohen complained that the sheriff had "this sexual thing" about beards and that his jailers failed "to comprehend the historical alternatives to their present non-qualitative existence." The haircut, he said, stripped him of his "philosopher's image." The sheriff said it was for "health reasons."

All part of the atmosphere of Madison, Wisconsin, 142 miles northwest of Chicago, 77 miles west of Milwaukee, surrounded by the dairy farms of Dane County on some of the richest black soil in America, connected to the world and yet a place apart. Madison, nourished by four elements: the politics of its state capitol, the intellect of its university, the calm beauty of its lakes, and the grace of its American elm trees. All seemed permanent and immutable, but they were not, not even the trees, sixty thousand elms that formed exultant archways of green over the old city streets. It turned out that they were diseased and dying, more year by year, 937 that year, up from 763 the year before, on toward an awful slaughter that would wickedly mimic the worst devastation of north country timber barons by cutting hideous bare swaths through neighborhoods that once ached with leaves. The old elms were being killed by a fungus that clogged their circulatory systems, cutting off water and sugar. It was called Dutch elm disease, and arborists said it spread from the east.

There were 5,385 freshmen at Wisconsin that fall out of a total enrollment of 33,000, and they represented—geographically, though not racially—by far the most diverse population of any public school in the Big Ten. More than 28 percent were from out of state, including 283 first-year students from New York alone. The Wisconsin Idea, conceived by leaders of the Progressive movement early in the twentieth century, was to use the UW as a "laboratory for democracy," a resource of science, agriculture, social policy, and creativity available to the government as well as to every citizen in the state. The philosophy of the

Wisconsin Idea was to reach out, rather than withdraw inward, and an unspoken but respected aspect of that was to reach beyond the state's borders to reinvigorate the social and intellectual environment, a process that had been encouraged since Charles R. Van Hise (felicitously, a rock scientist from Rock County) presided over the campus from 1903 to 1918.

A long-standing practice within that tradition was for Wisconsin to accept significant numbers of Jewish students, mostly from Chicago, Saint Louis, and the East Coast states of New York and New Jersey. For decades the student body was more diverse than the faculty, which had few Jewish professors until the early 1960s, by which time there were third-generation Jewish students following the same path their parents and grandparents had taken to the school in Madison that had welcomed them when much of the Ivy League had not. Michael Oberdorfer of Bethesda, Maryland, a graduate student in zoology and photo editor at the underground paper *Connections,* was part of that lineage. Oberdorfer's father, mother, and stepfather had all gone to Wisconsin in the late thirties. Among the family keepsakes was a letter the father had written as a young man explaining that he was heading west to Wisconsin because he had been made to feel unwelcome at Harvard.

But here was another crosscurrent: the steady infusion of students from other places, combined with the politics of the moment, had provoked a provincial response. In the aftermath of a series of antiwar demonstrations on campus, including a long but peaceful sit-in at the administration building in the spring of 1966 and a briefer occupation of the chancellor's office the following spring—both led for the most part by out-of-state students—angry alumni and state legislators pushed for a tightening of nonresident admissions. The university responded with a plan to reduce the out-of-state maximum to one-quarter of the undergraduate enrollment within three years. The 1967 freshman class marked the beginning of that process; only a year earlier, a record 38.6 percent of the new students had come from outside Wisconsin.

It was not a financial question. Any argument that Wisconsin taxpayers were subsidizing the outsiders collapsed under the weight of facts. The nonresident tuition of $1,101 per year, which might sound like a pittance to the ears of tuition-paying parents of later decades, was nonetheless $72.19 above the instructional cost per student, according to a report prepared for the board of regents. If there was a subsidy, it was going to students within state, who were charged only $350 a year to attend a first-class university. But for old schoolers like Arlie Mucks, the longtime director of the Wisconsin Alumni Association, a man who bled Badger red, there was grave concern that long-haired "outside agitators" were sullying the image of his beloved alma mater. When he expressed that fear to UW president Fred Harvey Harrington earlier in 1967, the historian turned administrator offered this reply: "Our image, Arlie, is that we are one of the great universities, high in quality, strong (very strong) in freedom of expression, a university at which we crush neither students nor faculty; a university that has had many out-of-state students since Van Hise's day; a university that has always considered itself strong enough to tolerate some dissenters and non-conformists. This 'image' is a reflection of fact and tradition that long predates me. It is a tradition of which we are all very proud. We could hardly change the 'image' without changing the institution, could we?"

The subtext of the debate, something that went unsaid in both Mucks's complaint and Harrington's response, was that a preponderance of radicals on campus seemed to be Jewish kids from the East. This was nothing new, no more so than the tension it occasionally engendered. Otto Festge, Madison's liberal mayor in 1967, had an interesting perspective on that phenomenon. He had entered the university from a farm in rural Cross Plains during another political era, the late 1930s, and remembered a common sentiment then that "if the outsiders didn't come here and stir things up, we wouldn't have these problems; the good kids of Wisconsin wouldn't do these things." Among instate undergraduates in Festge's day, many of German and Norwegian heritage, East Coast students were called "New York Indians" and the Memorial Union was known as the "Jewish emporium" because "that's where they hung out."

The hostility toward student radicals, Jewish or not, had surfaced at Wisconsin a few years before Festge arrived. On the night of May 15, 1935, a pack of two hundred students, many of them athletes, decided to disrupt a meeting of a socialist club known as the Student League for Industrial Democracy. The twenty or so people at the gathering, as well as their guest speaker, a man named Monroe Sweetland, were swallowed up by the angry crowd and carried down to Lake Mendota. Three of the young socialists were thrown in the water before the mob action was stopped by a law professor. By then more than a thousand students had gathered at the scene. Many cheered as one of the leaders of the "W" Club posse declared: "Any meeting of radicals on the university campus in the future will be stopped. We won't tolerate any reds in the university and we'll break up every gathering."

What did the University of Wisconsin represent? Jane Brotman, after graduating from Columbia High in Maplewood, New Jersey, leaned toward enrolling at the University of Maryland or Boston University but was told by her biology teacher and a patient of her father, a dentist, that she would be crazy to go anywhere but Wisconsin, which had also accepted her, and which they said was a wonderful place and a welcoming university. From another perspective, when Betty Menacher of Green Bay West announced that she wanted to go to school in Madison, her father, a lumber salesman, reacted with alarm, muttering that the campus in the state capital was little more than "a cesspool of queers."

ELIZABETH JOSEPHINE MENACHER had visited Madison twice before her college days, when the Green Bay West Wildcats made it to the state basketball tournament in the spring of her junior and senior years. The first time, she and six friends jammed into a Holiday Inn room on the northeast side of town and drove down to the university each day for the tournament at the ancient Field House next to Camp Randall Stadium. After the games they walked around the campus, and one sight from those meanderings remained etched in the young visitor's mind. She saw "a female student with long curly hair wearing a colorful poncho, probably Mexican or Guatemalan, and with sandals that laced up to her knees." The woman "looked totally cool and exotic," and Menacher knew from that moment that she "wanted to go to school where people looked like that." Wisconsin was the only school she applied to, despite her father's vituperations.

At the start of the summer between high school graduation and college, she traveled outside Wisconsin for the first time in her life, visiting relatives in Westwood, New Jersey. Several days a week she and a cousin ventured into New York City. They went to a concert in Central Park and then down to lower Manhattan, where Betty walked wide-eyed along the alien streets. "We ended up lost in Chinatown—in the rough part of it and we were also in part of Little Italy," she wrote to her friend Mary Mahaney back in Green Bay. "All these tough looking gangs of boys were gathered around every street corner. There were empty liquor bottles and beer cans all over the streets. There were all these bums sleeping right on the sidewalk (we had to step over a couple). We even went by a house where whores were outside soliciting customers. It was stinky, but I thought it was cool!" Even more exotic were the bustling sidewalks of Greenwich Village. Betty was fascinated by "the hippie scene—the people, the clothes, the ear ring shops, the music played on the streets." She had grown up in a place where everything seemed the same, every neat ranch house in her neighborhood, every attached garage and dinette, every outfit the girls wore to school, the short plaid skirts and matching tights and sweaters, *Seventeen* magazines, all the teenagers with their fake IDs going out to drink beer at the Prom Ballroom in DePere, every mother at home, no divorces, the unending if unspoken pressure to conform. There was something about Greenwich Village, like the poncho and high-laced sandals in Madison, that stirred her in a way she could not yet articulate.

No sooner had she returned to Green Bay than her father announced that he had arranged a summer job for her as a waitress at the Alpine Resort in Egg Harbor, sixty miles to the north of Green Bay in Door County. She had hoped to spend that summer with friends partying at the Prom and felt that she would be missing out on the fun, but she dutifully obeyed her father. At the Alpine she roomed in a crowded cottage with twenty other young women. They waited tables at breakfast, lunch, and dinner, then often hitchhiked five miles to the Parkway Bar and danced to Wilson Pickett songs. There was no privacy and the pay was meager. Betty netted thirty-three dollars for fifty-seven and a half hours in her first paycheck and averaged less than ten dollars a week in tips. The hard work for little reward was but one of many things she complained about in letters home to her mother—letters that were also read by her strict father, who reacted angrily. "As far as I'm concerned, you are unwelcome in this house and you don't have to write back because I don't want to hear from you," he wrote to her in mid-August.

She eventually adjusted to the resort scene by participating in minor acts of rebellion. Any waitress caught eating restaurant food was fined a dollar, a rule that became a challenge to be surmounted. "Lately everyone has been stealing food—like pies etc.," she wrote to a friend. "Then we take them (this is during the meal) to the way back part of the annex in the dining room and hide them under chairs and as soon as the people leave we eat them. Today there were 14 of the 20 waitresses eating pie back there and the owner walked by. It was really funny because everyone jumped up and started cleaning, or setting up or swatting flies, etc. He didn't know what was coming off, but he sure gave us a queer look."

After reading a story in *Seventeen* titled "Goodbye, Sweet Summer, Goodbye," she told Mary Mahaney that the headline captured exactly how she felt during those waning August days in Door County as she lived out her last summer before college. The first brush of cool air in the northern pines brought an overwhelming sensation of things coming to an end. Two or three kids left the resort every day. "Another dishwasher quit. It was the one from Manitowoc who's our age. He just left a note in the kitchen and left," Betty reported on August 19. "Then yesterday our cutest bellhop was fired. The night before he was caught (at 3 A.M.) with Candi (waitress) in his room. She had nothing on, etc. He's fired and she's on strict probation. Scandal reigns at Alpine." On August 29, the cottage's lounge was "just packed with people" there to watch the final episode of David Janssen in *The Fugitive*. Six days later it was over at last, and she went home. Her father let her back in the house, and three days later it was off to Madison.

Her parents drove her south and west down routes 45 and 151, her possessions packed in three pieces of blue Samsonite luggage that she had received as graduation presents, plus a new hatbox hair dryer and a manual typewriter. The clothes she took were mostly coordinated outfits (Villager and Lady Bug) with matching shoes. Moving day was nothing but a headache for Joseph Menacher, who was not particularly pleased to have his daughter in Madison in the first place and became even more annoyed sitting in the long line of cars waiting for a position at the loading dock of Sellery Hall. They finally unloaded, followed up with a mother-daughter shopping excursion, and then Betty, anxious to begin, nudged her parents out the door.

Her roommate in room 273 Sellery was Barb Hoffman from Nicolet High in suburban Milwaukee, a school that sent so many students to Madison every year that they had a hard time avoiding each other. Across the hall were Gail Katz and Halle Goodrich from Cleveland, and down the floor lived flocks of freshmen from New York and New Jersey. Betty might have felt intimidated by the easterners had it not been for her summer trip to New York, but of course there still were stereotypes to overcome. One New Yorker asked her if she lived on a farm. No, she said, Green Bay was a city. To Betty's shock, this person had never heard of Green Bay, home of the championship Packers. Even if she was not homesick, Betty could feel lonely, especially at mealtime; she usually tagged along with the Nicolet group until she had made friends of her own. At night the floormates smoked cigarettes, drank Tab, and had long discussions, at first about their families and high school boyfriends, but soon enough about sex and religion. Betty was Catholic but had stopped attending church and confession. She had birth control pills and a fake ID and no desire to feel guilty about her youthful adventures. As a beer drinker, if little else, she felt more experienced than the easterners, who came from states where the drinking age was twenty-one rather than Wisconsin's more lenient eighteen. There was "a lot of throwing up" in the dorm's common bathrooms in the hour after closing time. They usually went to the bars on State Street, especially the KK (Kollege Klub), but tried to avoid the Pub, with its long picture windows and all those frat boys sitting there on stools with their smug faces and beer stench and false machismo, ogling the girls passing by outside. Like many women, Betty began walking on the other side of the street just to avoid the Pub boys.

The changing culture seeped into her life almost imperceptibly. She was still the naïve freshman, not the exotic woman in poncho and sandals. She was among the freshmen women at Sellery who rushed to the window that autumn night when the boys congregated below clamoring for panties, and though she did not feel she had enough spares to throw any down, the evening was memorable enough for her to write about it in a letter to Mary Mahaney, who had enrolled at UW-Oshkosh. "Do you ever have panty raids? We had one Wed. and last night. They're cool. About 500 guys all at once begin a stampede to Sellery. They stand RIGHT outside our window (we've got a terrific view and we're only on 2nd floor) for about 2 hours—and chant and yell . . ." Her window faced Ogg Hall, she reported in another letter. "It's really cool. There are a bunch of guys who put amps up to the windows and really blast out the music—at 3 a.m. Besides ordinary music, someone recorded jungle music and sounds (roars etc.) and—get this—they have a recording of someone heaving. It's nauseating (but kind of funny if you're not feeling sick or anything!)"

Marijuana had not wafted up to her floor of Sellery yet, though Betty dated a boy who said he had experimented with dope three times. In the privacy of her dorm room she finished her paperback copy of *Valley of the Dolls,* reading it in three days, but she started to feel a pull toward the atmosphere of the Memorial Union's Rathskeller, a dark cave of shadows and whispers, with its crowd of regulars slouching behind heavy wooden tables, playing bridge, Sheepshead, and chess and talking about the Red Sox, drugs, Che Guevara, and Marcuse. After a few weeks she bought her first pair of navy-and-gray striped bellbottom blue jeans and a peasant blouse, but still wore coordinated outfits to class. She worried about whether she was "college material." She studied even on Friday nights and never skipped class in a schedule that included sociology (of the Islamic world), archaeology, French, physical education, and her 1:20 freshman composition class that met in a small room on the first floor of the Commerce Building.

During her first month on campus she had little interest in Vietnam and knew almost nothing about the war, beyond the body counts mounting on the nightly news. It had never been a topic of discussion at home. The boys in her crowd from Green Bay West went on to college, and though she had a cousin in the National Guard, he had only joined as a means of avoiding the war. The only mention of Vietnam in her letters to friends was a single sentence noting that there were more antiwar demonstrations at Madison than drunken panty raids. As she walked around the Madison campus, she saw posters about demonstrations, Dow Chemical Company, napalm. What was napalm? Betty Menacher had no idea, but she thought that anyone cool had to know, so she was afraid to ask.

JANE BETH BROTMAN followed a well-worn path to Madison. She was one of 124 New Jersey residents and among seven students from her high school who came out to Wisconsin that fall. It was a great relief to her to escape what she called the "phony, very materialistic values" of South Orange. The consumer culture of her upper-middle-class youth had left her feeling alienated, bored, depressed. Everybody in her suburb, she thought, "even though they could be very wise, very sophisticated, they all seemed to be into that whole thing of status, the fancy house, the car—it seemed to be the high school stuff." She disliked the vapidness of a social life that revolved around Crestmont Country Club, a stifling place that served as the model for much of Philip Roth's writing about the New Jersey country club set. She longed for a sense of community that she had felt only once in her life, during the summer of 1965 when she was studying Spanish and living with a family in Cuernavaca, Mexico. The "unbelievably natural sense of community there,

the organic connections between people" came as an "emotional shock."
Her response was more intuitive than intellectual, and she was not sure
what to make of it beyond a realization that life could in fact be different. It had not occurred to her until then that "one could arrange society
in a different way and, if one had different values, different social
arrangements were possible." She yearned somehow to replicate that
sense of community.

On the way to Madison, shortly after her plane lifted from the run-
way in Newark, Brotman was overtaken by anxiety. The expectations of
the society in which she was reared were that she would find a husband
in college but not necessarily her own autonomy. She knew what she
was leaving, and was glad to be leaving it, but had no idea where she was
headed. "I remember being on the plane and all of a sudden feeling the
reality of what was happening," she said later. "The denial completely
melted away and the reality set in of actually leaving home and going off
on my own to this place I had no connection with—and I was really
scared, really scared. I wanted to get off the plane." Her first environment in Madison, for better or worse, was in one sense not all that different from what she had left behind. She lived in the Towers, a plush
high-rise at the corner of State and Frances whose dining room served
prime rib sliced to your chosen thickness. Each of the University of Wisconsin's private dormitories had its own traditions and subculture. Allen
Hall attracted kids from Chicago and Michigan. Chadbourne Hall had
the most Wisconsin women. The Towers was predominantly Jewish,
East Coast, upper middle class. One of Jane's suitemates was also from
her high school. Another, from nearby West Orange, was the step-
daughter of a man who played golf with Dr. Allen Brotman, Jane's father, at Crestmont. Two more Columbia High graduates lived on the
same floor.

These reminders of her past troubled Brotman at first ("I thought, 'I
can't believe this—I come all the way out here and I can't get away!'"),
but she soon discovered that the Wisconsin campus was so big that she
would never feel trapped with the New Jersey crowd. She was on her
own most of the day, then made a point of returning to suite 405A
around nine most nights, when she and many of the other first-year
women would sit around on their beds and talk. She found her own
comforting hideaways, a study room at the Memorial Library, a table
near the back windows of the Memorial Union's Rathskeller looking out

at the terrace and Lake Mendota. And she found it surprisingly easy to ditch the last remnants of the consumer culture of South Orange. She had arrived in Madison with a trunkful of sweater and skirt outfits that she and her mother had bought late in the summer at Bloomingdale's and Lord & Taylor. "So I came out here and the first thing I saw was nobody wore these clothes. Everybody wore jeans," she recalled. "And it was like a wonderful relief. And I never wore those clothes. Never, never wore them. And it was such a wonderful feeling, a feeling of freedom, of letting that stuff go."

The beer culture of Madison puzzled her. Wisconsin was consistently ranked as the top beer-drinking school in the Big Ten, yet Brotman never had a glass of beer there and did not know anyone who drank heavily. Beer seemed more for in-state kids, the fraternity and sorority types, and students on the lower end of the academic scale, she thought. She had smoked dope once in high school, while visiting a cousin in Cambridge, Massachusetts, and felt no qualms about trying it in Madison, first at parties, then later in the year with some floormates at the Towers. They would open the windows, burn incense, and put a towel under the door to keep the telltale sweet odor from giving them away. Grass had unpredictable effects on her, sometimes easing her mind, other times inducing anxiety attacks, so she did not smoke it regularly. Nor did she consider herself part of any larger movement. She was not a counterculture hippie or a radical, and in fact found that the people who seemed most alienated from the materialistic culture were the ones who frightened her the most, especially political activists who criticized the American government. She believed that the United States was "a wonderful country that always was in the right when it did things around the world."

When she encountered people on campus "who looked and acted the part of antiwar demonstrators," they turned her off. She could not open herself emotionally to listen to anything they had to say. She classified them as "weird, strange, different, bad." Just the sight of them had a visceral negative effect on her. When she made her way through the Union on the way to the back table in the "Rat," she walked swiftly, eyes straight ahead, past the rows of political tables in the front hallway. Leaflets on the military draft, broadsheets on the Young Socialists, literature on the economic imperatives of American foreign policy—Jane Brotman "looked askance" at all of it. "If you looked at a table like that, it felt subversive," she said later, describing her state of mind in the fall of 1967. "Dangerous things could happen to you. You don't go near those people."

The sorority scene upset her even more. Caught between two distasteful worlds, she responded by pouring all of her attention into her schoolwork. She was taking French 221 and Spanish 221, two advanced classes that focused on literature, as well as gym, English, and sociology. In the first month she never missed a class and found her way to every review session, retracing the same daily path between the Towers, the library, up Bascom Hill to Van Hise for her language classes, then back down to the Rathskeller and the library and home. As much as she studied, the thought of taking her first set of six-weeks exams filled her with anxiety.

The tests were in the third week of October.

CHAPTER 7

SOGLIN'S THRILL

THE LEAD EDITORIAL in the *Daily Cardinal* of September 28 discussed the meaning of student power, which the newspaper said should involve more than "the relatively insignificant question of when to come home at night." Across from that on the opinion page was a poem portraying the University of Wisconsin as the college of big shoulders, an attempt at satire for which no apology to Carl Sandburg could have been sufficient. And down in the lower right-hand corner was the latest "Thursday's Line" column by a graduate student in history named Paul Soglin. It ran under the headline "Hi there, Badger!" and here is how it began:

> We'd like to welcome back all the students who managed to show up for the 1967–68 academic year. Through the co-operation of university officials, the city of Madison and those pursuing a suicidal course in Southeast Asia, we have scheduled another smashing calendar of events for this year. The 1967–68 year by all indications promises to be the most fun-filled, action-packed school year since university President Twombly suggested that coeds be admitted. (That was the year of the locust.) There will be more demonstrations, more cops (and bigger, though not necessarily better), higher prices, colder weather, and more bullshit from both ends of State Street.

Paul Soglin, at age twenty-two, was not yet a recognized figure on campus and went completely unnoticed in Madison at large, but he seemed determined to make a political name for himself. With his curl of unkempt black hair, mesmerizing nasal voice, and a boyish face that made him look more like a disheveled high school prankster than a bohemian grad student, he gamboled around campus in blue jeans and a sheepskin coat, pulsating with energy and self-assurance, looking for action. He had been in town five years, arriving as a freshman in 1962, and as his activism increased year by year, he watched contemporaries on the left turn away from traditional paths to power. Many of them had rejected electoral politics, preferring to organize, protest, experiment, and, in the vernacular of the era, "build a movement." Their latest intellectual forum was *Connections,* a twelve-page alternative newspaper overflowing with avant-garde poetry, radical politics, provocative illustrations, and dense, difficult prose. Soglin instead wrote for the *Cardinal,* which was more attuned to the average student, essentially mainstream and liberal, with a milder form of youthful rebellion, and his rhetoric was more easily understood as well. It is safe to say that such phrases as "action-packed" and "fun-filled," even when offered in satire, were not part of the patois of the Marcusian philosophers and movement activists at *Connections.*

While Soglin also believed in organizing, protesting, and experimenting, he was a pragmatist who could not reject entirely the established political system, for it was within that system that he envisioned his own rise. He had been elected to the student senate on the antiwar University Community Action party ticket from District VI, an off-campus district where few others, especially graduate students, seemed interested in such insular campus affairs. Also the only one of six UCA candidates elected as a delegate to the National Student Association, he attended many of its national congresses, returning each time enthralled by the political intrigue. And now, quietly, he had begun plotting a bold electoral move that might take him beyond the university environment. After analyzing voting patterns block by block in a downtown ward where many students lived but tended not to vote, he thought he saw a means of winning a seat on the Madison city council. That election was a year away. Until then there was work to be done on campus, although, as he wrote in his column, it was not typical schoolwork.

> It will be difficult for the student to attend all of this year's functions and still keep up with his classwork. The question he is going to have to ask himself is whether or not he wants a University

of Wisconsin education or a real education. For those dedicated to
the pursuit of trivia, dedicated to being spoon-fed, and not interested in an education that is relevant to what's happening, they
will find happiness and bliss in the classroom. For those of us who
are here to learn we will be out talking about the war, the shortage
of adequate housing, secret research on campus, and the meaning
of an education.

When a history professor talks about the effects of chemical
and biological warfare on the nation developing the weapons,
when a chemistry instructor discusses the moral responsibilities of
the profession, and when a university administration will explain
the limits of education in an institution that is dependent on the
federal government and large corporations for financial support,
then we can return to the classroom and learn.

Soglin and many of his contemporaries felt something in the air that
fall, their lives, politics, and culture racing toward a place unsettled. The
anticipation of this new world had intensified the previous spring, when
vociferous protests against the war in Vietnam merged with a celebra-
tory be-in at Picnic Point (Allen Ginsberg and the Fugs were there) and
a mass demonstration against a wrong-way city bus lane on University
Avenue. The civil rights movement had exploded in another direction,
toward black power and riots in the urban streets, pushing away young
white activists who had devoted years to that cause. Boston, Tampa,
Buffalo, Cincinnati, Newark, Plainfield, Detroit, Toledo, Grand Rapids,
Milwaukee, Providence, Wichita—all exploded with racial upheaval
during the summer of 1967. Many students who had headed south to organize voter registration drives at the end of school years earlier in the
decade stayed north to canvass suburban neighborhoods in an antiwar
effort called Vietnam Summer. Others piled into their cars and drove
cross country to San Francisco to partake in the hippie subculture's
Summer of Love, diametrically different choices that nonetheless
seemed part of the same sensibility that old ways had been rejected and
something new had to be tried.

There was a sense that nothing seemed impossible, good or bad. The
cultural revolution was starting to prevail—wear what you want to
wear and say what you want to say—and the political scene was taking
on an exhilarating if dangerous electrical charge. All summer long a rumor had spread through the left in Madison that the government was se-

cretly planning to round up antiwar radicals and pen them in army camps. Some thought that this meant the old order was losing its grip. Soglin and his allies in the University Community Action party, including his cochair, Bob Swacker, believed, as Swacker put it, that "the establishment had its tail between its legs and was running in every direction."

At summer's end, just before most fall terms started on American campuses, hundreds of diverse progressive and radical organizations, including the Madison chapter of the Committee to End the War in Vietnam, had assembled at the Palmer House in Chicago for the first National Conference for a New Politics. Peace movement historian Charles DeBenedetti later called it "the largest gathering of the American Left since the 1948 Progressive party convention." It turned out to be a raucous, contentious, exhausting convention, rife with walkouts, power plays, and endless posturing to see who among the three thousand delegates could look toughest. Splits became evident then that would grow into chasms in later years and decades. The issue of Vietnam was almost lost amid resolutions condemning Zionism and disparaging the Israeli victory in the Six-Day War, actions that prompted some left-leaning Jewish intellectuals to begin the turn toward neoliberalism or neoconservatism. There was also a demand by black delegates that they get as many votes and positions of power as the vastly larger number of whites. When it came to Vietnam, the mood at the convention and among leftist antiwar activists across the country was angrier and more pessimistic; there was an emerging awareness that everything that had been tried to stop the war to that point had failed. Students in this faction, as author Thomas Powers wrote in *The War at Home,* were seeking to "harden themselves for an escalating struggle." In Madison this attitude was particularly strong. As a newspaper article described some local antiwar leaders, "They have been through the acceptable protest routine (canvassing, teach-ins, incessant discussion) and emerged with their passivity gone."

JUST AS ARMY COMMANDER Terry de la Mesa Allen Jr. was shaped by the traditions of his father and grandfather before him, so too was antiwar activist Paul Richard Soglin. The military was not an institution to which members of his family felt special allegiance. Aaron Soglin, a grandfather, had grown up in Nosovich, a village in Russia, and sailed to

America in November 1912 aboard the SS *Patricia,* a ship that plied the
Atlantic in the early years of the twentieth century carrying thousands of
Eastern European immigrants to the United States from the port of
Hamburg, Germany. In immigration papers he signed after landing in
New York, Aaron Soglin listed his occupation as tailor and his age as
twenty-six. He also recorded that until then he had lived under the alias
Yankel Katzoff. As his grandson Paul later reconstructed the story, the
alias was taken so that Aaron Soglin could avoid serving in the Russian
army. The czarist army did not draft only sons, so when Aaron was born
as a second son, his parents registered his birth under the name of a
nearby married couple, the Katzoffs, who were too old to have children.
On the other side of the family, the maternal grandfather, Chaim Centora, had fled Russian-controlled Poland and sailed to America on the
same *Patricia* seven years earlier, and had also ended up in Chicago, only
to discover that his blind father, a rabbinical scholar, had been jailed in
Poland on charges that he had helped his son avoid military service.
Centora, whose name was Americanized to Hyman Century, was in
London on his way back to Poland when he learned that his father had
bribed authorities and been released.

Paul's father, Albert Soglin, grew up in the Jewish settlement around
Marshall High on Chicago's West Side. He was drafted into the army
out of college and served in the Signal Corps during World War II but
was not sent overseas. (Paul, his oldest son, was born on April 22, 1945,
which the family also remembered as the day the Russians entered
Berlin.) After the war Albert earned a master's degree in mathematics at
the Illinois Institute of Technology and was hired to teach in the
Chicago public school system. When the Illinois legislature passed the
Broyles Act, requiring a loyalty pledge from government employees,
teachers who refused to sign could continue working but would not be
paid unless they took the oath. Albert Soglin refused to sign. His wife,
Rose, taught correspondence courses for two years to earn money for the
family while he taught without pay; he relented when the state supreme
court upheld the law's constitutionality. To question the American government was the norm in the Soglin family. When Paul was four, his
mother took him along as she marched in nuclear disarmament demonstrations, protests that marked the birth of a peace movement that
would grow and transform over a generation into the movement against
the war in Vietnam. Rose Soglin named her son Paul R. in honor of Paul
Robeson, the majestic black singer, actor, and civil rights activist who

was a hero of the American left. Paul rarely saw his mother more dismayed than she was on the day that he came home from the Hyde Park school with an American Legion medal he had won for a seventh-grade essay extolling the symbolic glory of the American flag.

A few years later, when he was only fourteen, he sent away for transcripts of the House Un-American Activities Committee hearings. He read them as part civics lesson, part tragedy, and part melodrama revealing "who's squealing on whom."

By Paul's junior year in high school in 1960, his family had moved up to Highland Park in the north suburbs, among the more progressive communities outside Chicago, a town that did not have restrictive covenants against blacks and was fairly evenly divided among Catholics, Protestant, and Jews. He had some cachet among his suburban peers because he knew the hip sections down in the city near the University of Chicago. In the classroom he had a reputation as a mild rabble-rouser. His English teacher gave him an A for an entertaining speech he delivered on mathematical oddities, including how presidential candidates with double letters in their surnames historically had prevailed (Jefferson, Hoover, Coolidge, the Harrisons, the Roosevelts, Kennedy), but then dropped him a grade point when he followed that with a stirring oration in praise of Fidel Castro and the Cuban revolution. *Paul, that was a very good speech. Do you really believe what you said?* the teacher asked. *I wouldn't have said it if I didn't believe it,* he answered. He was also known for asking his teachers pointed questions about the air raid drills: *Why are we doing this?*

When it came time to choose a college, the military was a factor, in a sense. It was "a given" that Soglin did not intend to go into the service. One attraction of the University of Wisconsin, along with its academic reputation, was that it had reduced the ROTC requirement to a handful of hours while most midwestern land grant colleges still had at least a year of mandatory ROTC. Soglin arrived in Madison at age seventeen, a baby-faced kid too young to drink beer even by Wisconsin's relaxed standards. After a few months living in Kronsage Hall across from a few Wisconsin boys who trapped chipmunks along the lakeshore path and kept them in a cage, he escaped to a rooming house on North Henry Street, which offered a decidedly more bohemian atmosphere.

By his second semester Soglin was secretary of the local branch of SNCC, the Student Nonviolent Coordinating Committee, which at Wisconsin then was mostly white. On the first day of school in his sophomore year in 1963, he participated in a moment of silence on Bascom Hill in memory of four black children killed in the racially motivated September 15 bombing of the Sixteenth Street Baptist Church in Birmingham, Alabama. The next month, on the afternoon of October 18, he attended the first major protest at UW against the incipient war in Vietnam. The demonstration drew 350 people to the front of the Union, where speakers denounced U.S. government support of South Vietnamese President Ngo Dinh Diem and accused Diem of running a tyrannical regime that committed atrocities against dissident students and Buddhist monks. Placards at the rally urged "U.S. Out, U.N. In" and "Diem Out, People In."

An editorial in the *Cardinal,* whose editor-in-chief was future political journalist Jeff Greenfield, noted that while the protest's sponsors—ranging from the Young Democrats to the Young Socialist Alliance—had differing viewpoints and no solutions, they showed that they could "put aside differences of opinion to make a stand on achieving common goals." (Greenfield also wrote an accompanying column that said FBI director J. Edgar Hoover was wasting his time worrying about whether student radicals were communists. "This is, of course, absolute nonsense," he wrote. "They don't stand a chance of winning over college students. The reason for this failure is obvious—they dress badly." According to Greenfield's analysis, "the college audience demands not only a better world, but a cooler world.") In a front-page photograph of the demonstration, Soglin could be seen standing in the middle of the crowd, trying to look cool, smoking a cigarette.

TWO WEEKS LATER Diem was assassinated in a military coup orchestrated by the CIA and backed by the Kennedy administration. His death marked not an end but another bloody beginning in America's entanglement in Vietnam.

One noontime later that November, Soglin emerged from an eleven o'clock calculus class and had reached Bascom Hill when he noticed that the campus walkways were desolate at what normally was the busiest time of day. *Where is everybody?* he asked someone standing outside South Hall. *Didn't you hear?* came the reply. *Kennedy's been shot.* Soglin raced down the hill and across Park Street into the side door of the Union until he reached the entrance to the Rathskeller, where in the dimness he found a group of students at two tables near the archway, huddling around Harvey Goldberg, a young history professor who had started teaching in Madison only that fall but was on his way to becoming the guru of the student left. Soglin later described the scene: "By this time it is known that Kennedy's dead, and everyone was around Goldberg and he was talking quietly, very quietly, you could barely hear him, and he was genuinely mortified by what had happened, maybe not with Kennedy personally, but with the implications of a rightwing coup, and was it the end of democracy, and where does this fit with revolutions of Europe and the revolution of 1848 and the assassination of the archduke and the flow of history and meantime people are running up and down to the second floor where the television sets are—and then just everybody disappeared."

Thanksgiving was coming, and no one could study, so they went home. That was always part of the reality, or unreality, of student life. One could simply leave.

Soglin began college with a premed curriculum, heavy in the sciences, but he was slowed by mononucleosis in his sophomore year, failed calculus, and nearly flunked out altogether. He gradually switched his concentration to history, which was closer to his political interests and at Wisconsin meant that he could choose from an illustrious cast of professors, from William Appleman Williams and William Taylor on American foreign policy to the charismatic Goldberg on French social history to Merle Curti on American intellectual history to John R. W. Smail on Southeast Asian studies to George Mosse on European history and the lessons of nationalism. What mattered most to Soglin and his activist classmates was what they called relevance. They looked for analogies between the abolitionists of the nineteenth century and antiwar activists of the sixties. They studied abolitionist William Lloyd Garrison's argument that in fighting for a moral cause, one must be an irritant, shake up the social order, and call for immediate change rather than gradualism. They analyzed Thoreau's philosophy of civil disobedience, holding that there was a higher law than the law of the land—the law of conscience—and that when the two laws were in conflict, one must choose the law of conscience and accept the consequences. They became interested in educational policy and the question of whether a university could ever be neutral. They hungered for connections between imperialism and modern American foreign policy.

The history department at Wisconsin was renowned for a distinctive school of thought deeply rooted in midwestern values: progressive, democratic, scornful of the eastern establishment, and somewhat isolationist. As one colleague described it only half jokingly, it was "history from the viewpoint of South Dakota," which happened to be the home state of one of its practitioners, American colonial historian Merrill Jensen. The modern department was built by Fred Harvey Harrington. Before his rise to the presidency of the university, Harrington's field had been U.S. foreign policy, and his central theme was that economic imperialism served as the engine that drove the United States into the world, especially into Asia. He and his disciples, including William Appleman Williams, who was much sharper in his critique of American foreign policy, in a sense constructed their work on the foundation laid by Frederick Jackson Turner, whose portrait greeted visitors to the history department offices. Turner's thesis at Wisconsin became the seminal document on how westward movement into the always shifting frontier shaped the American democratic character. Once that expansionism moved beyond the nation's borders, the Wisconsin historians argued, it lost its larger purpose and became a manifestation of corporate greed.

Williams, a Naval Academy graduate and World War II officer who grew up on a dirt farm in Iowa, was especially strong in making the historical connections between traditional western liberalism, trade, and U.S. policy in Vietnam, what he called "the tragic ambitions of Empire." "No one can be certain, but it is highly probable that the first Americans to reach what we now call Vietnam were various masters and sailors who, seduced by the lure of wealth and adventure, became international pirates during King William's War (1689–97)," Williams once wrote. "They returned with gold and silver and other exotic wealth to flaunt their success in the streets of Boston and other ports south to Charleston. They indulged themselves in colorful and garish costumes, and made bold advances to women of all classes." That, said Williams, presaged centuries of imperial expansion during which "American leaders were chasing the nightmare of a global Pax Americana. It was a mindless hunger that led . . . finally to intervention in Vietnam."

Goldberg and Mosse drew the largest crowds, their lecture halls buzzing with hundreds of students filling the aisles and leaning over the balconies. Radical students formed a cult around Goldberg and sat spellbound as he delivered lectures laced with revolutionary allusions, cultural anecdotes, literary references, reflections on the day's *New York Times,* and arcane sociological data from French archives. Described by Madison writers Dave Wagner and Ron McCrea as "small, scrawny to the point of being cadaverous . . . all animation, elfish, with a droll smile and a pair of eyebrows that sent out a semaphore of confidential signals when he was amused or appalled," Goldberg was pure performance, yet his scholarship, and the sort he encouraged in his graduate school disciples, was based on the assiduous accumulation of fact. Soglin preferred Mosse.

With his heavy German accent and appearance of quizzical bemusement, Mosse, a wealthy Jewish refugee who had spent much of his career studying the dangerous rise of nationalism, fascism, and Nazism, was far less ostentatiously leftist than Goldberg, and less taken by the idea of empire than Williams. In his memoir written decades later, Mosse said that he and Williams "spent many a night debating whether terms like mercantilism could simply be transferred from 17th century Europe to 19th century America." Williams thrived on those connections, but Mosse thought "concepts could not be applied to different centuries and continents." He was also often curmudgeonly in his disapproval of student behavior. While receptive to what he saw as the new left's search for "a third way between Marxist materialism on the one hand and capitalism on the other," he never shied away from criticizing radical students when he saw them falling into fascistic tendencies, suppressing the speech and dismissing the thoughts of others. It was Mosse's dream to make "the power of reason" the centerpiece of liberal and leftist thought and to "put the autonomy of man into the center of socialism—man was the *end* and must never become a *means.*"

Few students who took his courses could forget Mosse's lectures. He had the ability of all spellbinding teachers to make subtle connections and allusions and bring intellectual coherence to the physical chaos of the world. His underlying themes were the uses and meaning of violence in the modern world, attacks on liberalism from left and right, the question of how good men could survive amid evil, and the many seductions of nationalism. One of his lectures was on mass casualties and the "domestication of war" in the twentieth century. He used the image of military cemeteries between the two world wars to make his points:

What then were the ways in which the tragic reality of war was made manageable, acceptable?

Central to the confrontation with mass death was the cult of the fallen soldier, and like all the sacred in our civilization it was not something new or invented for the purpose, but based upon ancient religious feeling; the adaptation of Christian piety to the war experience. The death of the fallen, their sacrifice for the nation, was often linked to the passion and resurrection of Christ. This was symbolized for example by the design of English war cemeteries, all of which contain the Cross of Sacrifice: a cross upon which a sword was superimposed. Sometimes such a cross faced a chapel of resurrection. Such linking of national sacrifice and Christian sacrifice no doubt made it easier to come to terms with the tragedies of war.

Military cemeteries symbolized this confrontation with mass death. As places of national and Christian worship they made it easier to accept death by transcending it. The distinction between soldiers' cemeteries and bourgeois cemeteries, made in Germany as early as 1915, is important here: bourgeois cemeteries were said to be materialistic in the exaggerated boastfulness of their monuments, but in soldiers' cemeteries simplicity symbolized wartime camaraderie and, so we are told, led into a serious and reverential mood. . . .

Always such cemeteries must symbolize the eternal, sacred nature of the nation and its heroes. Built into this masking of death was a longing for rest, a preindustrial nostalgia which eventually would benefit the European right. . . . The victorious nations could be quietest in their cult. In Germany and Italy the radical right took up this heritage. I can illustrate this no better than by the chorus of the Hitler Youth on Memorial Day: "The best of our people did not die that the living might die, but that the dead might come alive." The cult of the fallen became not only a masking of death, of transcending the horror of war, but a call to domination and revenge. The cult as the worship of the nation was in the forefront here, rather than, as in the victorious nations, the cult as helping to assimilate the staggering human cost of war. . . .

Even while continuing to honor the memory of the fallen, we must never lose our horror, never try to integrate war and its consequences into our longing for the sacred. . . . If we confront mass death naked, stripped of all myth, we may have slightly more chance to avoid making the devil's pact with that aggressive nationalism whose blood trail has marked our century.

Soglin was by nature more politician than ideologue, with that peculiar politico's mix of self-centeredness and worldly curiosity. He was fascinated by what moved crowds and what defined a leader, and he wanted to know what the other person, the other side, was thinking, if not feeling. That is precisely what Mosse encouraged in historians. "One cannot understand one's own history or the history of one's ethnicity without trying to understand the motivations of others, whether they are friendly or hostile," Mosse once wrote. "A historian, if he is to get history right, cannot be bigoted or narrow-minded. Empathy is for me still at the core of the historical enterprise, but understanding does not mean withholding judgment." Soglin was not an intellectual and was never part of the coterie of brilliant young doctoral students whom Mosse nurtured during that era, but he was nonetheless a devoted admirer. He was so enthralled by Mosse that he often sat in the back of the hall and stared directly at the professor over the lowered heads of hundreds of classmates furiously scribbling notes. He would just listen, without taking notes, a true believer in what Mosse called his faith. "What man is," Mosse would say, "only history tells."

As much as Soglin and his friends dismissed the fraternity crowd, they had their own predictable patterns that differed mostly in style. After classes each day, Paul would go down to the Union to "see what was happening," and then as soon as the cafeteria opened at four forty-five he ate dinner, and by five fifteen he was at the library studying, then off to a political meeting and home by ten or eleven, where he and his roommates would sit around and talk and drink or smoke dope and try to put the moves on girls, and then repeat the process the next day. A second pattern would begin at noon Friday, when Soglin started looking for a game of bridge in the Rathskeller, where he would play until eight or nine that night, then walk upstairs to listen to music in the Great Hall or go down the street to Lorenzo's or the 602 Club or the Uptown Café, where jazz flowed until two or three in the morning. The "one rule," Soglin recalled, "was that nothing interfered from roughly noon on Friday until you studied on Sunday night. We often used to say that when the revolution came, it wasn't going to start until after noon, because everybody was sleeping, and it certainly wouldn't take place on a weekend. Which may have sounded like we were being selfish, but in a way it was really important that we set aside Friday night through Sunday morning just to socialize or whatever." In spring and fall there was a regular softball doubleheader on Sunday mornings at a playing field at the corner of Dayton and Frances, the drug freaks against the politicos.

Some fragments of the American dream still held; young men who harbored revolutionary fantasies traded those in for a few hours of being Yaz or Lou Brock.

LIKE 2.4 MILLION OTHER college students, Soglin was protected from military service with a student deferment during his undergraduate years, but the draft was an unavoidable part of the Vietnam discussion. He had decided that if the Lake County, Illinois, draft board ever tried to call him up, he would refuse to serve on grounds that he opposed the war. He did not consider himself a conscientious objector, nor did he want to go to Canada. His choice, he told friends, was jail, though it was a rhetorical option that he never had to take. When fifty students at Wisconsin signed a full-page advertisement in the *Cardinal* declaring that they would refuse to be drafted, Soglin was not among them. He was still in the second or third tier of student activists, not a major player in the movement, though he wanted to be. He was "crushed, just crushed," that he had missed out, and later reflected, "How could they have been circulating it and I missed it? Was I stoned for two days?"

The antiwar movement's position on the draft was a jumble of contradictions. Young men who did not want to serve and did not want the university to cooperate with the Selective Service in any way nonetheless criticized the system for its inequities and the protection it provided them in contrast to minorities and working-class whites who did not attend college. For all the talk of revolution on campus, the proletariat was fighting another war, in Vietnam. In the spring of 1966 Congressman Alvin O'Konski conducted a survey of one hundred military inductees from his northern Wisconsin district and determined that not one of them came from a family with an average income over five thousand dollars.

It was the draft that provoked the largest demonstration on campus during Soglin's undergraduate career, coming only a few weeks before his graduation in May 1966. The issue was whether UW officials should provide grades and class rankings to the Selective Service, which had announced that deferments from the draft would be based on academic performance and that men in the lower half of their class would have to score well on a new test to avoid being drafted. Members of SDS and the Ad Hoc Committee on the University and the Draft presented demands to President Harrington and Robben W. Fleming, the chancellor, that the school stop cooperating with draft boards and that they call an emergency meeting of the faculty to revise the university's policy. There was intense debate over how to proceed with the protest after the demands were presented, and though a majority of those attending an SDS meeting, including Soglin, voted against holding a sit-in, a smaller faction decided to go ahead with one anyway. The sit-in, which began on May 16 at the new Peterson administration building on Murray Street, soon took on a life of its own. "Everyone, regardless of their initial position," joined in, Soglin recalled, and "within the night and the next day the place was packed." Along with similar sit-ins that month at the University of Chicago and City College of New York, the takeover of the administration building in Madison marked another turning point in the antiwar movement: students were now occupying campus buildings as a means of protest.

The demonstration ebbed and flowed for several days and nights. It was peaceful and at times jovial. Professor Williams stopped by one night to talk to the protesters, who found him supportive in theory but not in practice and in any case uncharacteristically incoherent. Students traded jokes with campus police and tried not to interfere with the personnel who worked there. Jim Rowen, a junior from suburban Washington, D.C., who stayed the whole time, was struck by the way friendly workers would bring food for students during the protest marathon; someone gave him a carton of milk—"very Wisconsin." There were long discussions about the draft. Often there would be two or three self-appointed student leaders holding forth at the same time in different parts of the room, though the rhetoric was usually dominated by Bob Cohen, who made the most dramatic speeches. When things dragged, delegations were sent up the hill to confer with the administration. The city police force was kept away, as were antidemonstrators.

For William Kaplan, a freshman from Wilmette, this was his first major demonstration, and he found it "pretty euphoric." He "met a lot of people, had fun," and felt part of an "instant peer group"—something he had never experienced at New Trier, his suburban Chicago high school. He could tell himself that he was saving the world and at the same time develop a social network and go out with different girls and watch the older protest leaders operate. He was especially taken by Soglin. "He wasn't a Marxist, but he was kind of like a beatnik, and I liked that part of Paul," Kaplan said later. "I didn't like the Marxists. I wanted to be a beatnik rather than a Marxist. He was cooler, a little more hip. And I liked that side of him."

Soglin "picked up a girl" one night during the siege and faced a con-

flict that only a budding politician, not a true beatnik, could fall into—
and solve. He wanted to take her back to his apartment on Dayton
Street, only five blocks away, but worried that it would be embarrassing
if anything dramatic happened while he was gone. If authorities came in
and cleared the place out, it was important for him to be able to say that
he was there. So he found Ralph Hanson, the campus police chief, a
friendly adversary, and quietly got reassurance that there was nothing in
the works. Sometime after midnight, Soglin and his newfound friend
"slinked out a back alley."

A few days into the sit-in, in the brilliant sunlight of a springtime
noon, several thousand protesters marched up Bascom Hill. They
flooded the wide lawn from the Abe Lincoln statue halfway down to
Park Street a few hundred yards below and cheered thunderously when
Williams called them "the conscience of the university." Then Harrington and Fleming announced that a faculty meeting would reconsider the
school's draft policy. Word of the reconciliation infuriated many members of the Wisconsin legislature, none more than Republican legislator
Gordon Roseleip of Darlington, who had denounced the sit-in as "a
great help to our enemies and communism all around the world."
Equally upset were hard-line members of SDS who had stayed behind
in the administration building. They complained that the students had
been "out-finessed" by Chancellor Fleming, a veteran labor negotiator.
Fleming was indeed proud of the way he handled the potentially explosive situation, and later, in a private letter, described his "pillow" strategy: "Students can punch the pillow but it moves over without greatly
observable changes." But one of those most heartened by the protest and
its resolution was Paul Soglin. On May 19 he ripped a page from his
notebook and wrote a letter bursting with optimism.

President Harrington,

Please excuse the way in which I am writing you this note (the
notebook paper and pencil) but it is all I have with me at this time
and I felt that it was important to express my feelings to you at this
very moment.

As I was walking up the Hill just now I recalled what happened twenty-four hours ago and the whole series of events since
last Friday. All of us are so very critical of what we call the 'multiversity' and the resulting alienation that is felt by the student.

No matter how this draft question is resolved I think this last week will be one that will most vividly remain in my mind when in the future I recall my four years as an undergraduate at the University of Wisconsin.

Perhaps thrilling would be the best way of describing my feelings—thrilled at seeing so many people discuss, debate and resolve a difficult problem. Thrilled at being part of thousands who have taken part in the attempt to reach a consensus. And thrilled most of all at seeing an administration, a faculty and a student body—which according to myth are never supposed to agree on anything—working together so that the views and interests of all may be accommodated.

For the first time I am able to say that I am proud to be a student at the University of Wisconsin.

I feel that you and your administration are the ones who have created the atmosphere in which I have obtained this feeling— and I have an obligation to notify you of it.

Thank you,

Paul R. Soglin

The next day came the reply, spare and ironic.

Dear Paul:

Thank you for your warm note. I want to keep it and share it with one or two others.

Since you may later want to recall your feelings of May 19, 1966, I am sending you a copy of your letter.

Cordially,

Fred Harvey Harrington
President

The promising spirit of that exchange was soon lost. During the next school year, as the war in Vietnam persisted, the tone of demonstrations at Wisconsin took on a more confrontational edge. It was Soglin's first year in graduate school. When the Dow Chemical Company visited the campus in February 1967, activists decided to stage protests and surround the corporate recruiters inside the Chemistry, Engineering, and

Commerce buildings, where placement interviews were being held. SDS president Henry Haslach, a teaching assistant in mathematics, led a group to the Chemistry Building. They carried picket signs bearing the color photographs of napalmed Vietnamese children that had been published in *Ramparts* magazine a few months earlier. A campus policy, newly imposed for that event, banned the use of signs on sticks inside the building. When Haslach reached the front door, a police officer stopped him, declaring that the signs were too large and dangerous to be taken inside. Haslach was infuriated and argued with the officer, saying it was a question of free speech. The officer pinned Haslach against the wall and placed him under arrest for disorderly conduct. At the Commerce Building two more protest leaders, Robert Zwicker and Robert Cohen, the then-bearded but eventually shorn philosopher, were being arrested on similar charges. The three were bailed out that night and organized another protest the next day at which sixteen more students were arrested.

In the midst of the action that second day, a band of demonstrators marched up to Bascom Hall and blockaded the offices of Chancellor Fleming and Dean of Student Affairs Joseph Kauffman, demanding that all charges be dropped and that Dow Chemical be barred from interviewing on campus as long as it made napalm. Kauffman found himself face-to-face with a crowd screaming "Joe must go! Joe must go!" One demonstrator came up to him and said earnestly that it was "nothing personal, but the chancellor is LBJ and you're McNamara."

The siege lasted several hours, with more surreal twists. Kauffman's wife kept calling, but the students who were sitting on his desk answered the phone and would not let him talk to her, until finally she threatened to call the police. When Kauffman lamented aloud that he felt like he was in a Shelley Berman sketch, one radical leader pounced on the cultural reference, declaring that Berman's neuroses were too bourgeois and that it was "just typical that someone like Berman lives and Lenny Bruce dies." The denunciations of "fascistic" university administrators at one point became too much for Kauffman, who sharply reminded the students that there were "only two people in the room"— the old guys, Kauffman and Fleming—"who had actually fought fascists."

Fleming warned the students that if he tried to leave the room and anyone touched him, they would face the far more serious charge of aggravated assault. "And I would just suggest to you that if any one of us starts to walk out of this room, you take very, very seriously whether you even put a hand on us."

"I would suggest that what the chancellor says is absolutely correct, both under criminal and civil law," responded Robert Cohen, speaking as "one of the leaders" of the action. Cohen urged someone to get word to the large crowd blocking the hallway outside that "if either of these gentlemen at any time wish to leave they certainly are free to do so." Fleming, acting cool, and Kauffman, clearly agitated, waited them out, and eventually the whole show—students and administrators— adjourned for an hour and reconvened, minus the siege atmosphere, in Bascom's auditorium, where the discussion continued. During the break, at Kauffman's suggestion, Fleming found a novel way to employ his "pillow" strategy again. In a decidedly un-LBJ-like act, he signed a blank check from his own bank account and directed one of his assistants to take it to the county jail and use it to post bail for the arrested students. The bail total was $1,260. When he announced his action to the crowd in the auditorium, some in the audience rose to give him a standing ovation, but the protest leaders, cemented to their seats up front, looked around with displeasure, feeling they had been co-opted.

"I furnished my personal funds because if I am going to have to disagree with students I don't want to do it with some of them in jail," Fleming later explained to the faculty. He expanded on that explanation in a letter to Robert E. Howard of Beloit College, a fellow administrator. "My reasons for putting up the bail bond were mixed. In part, they were tactical. I knew that unless I could persuade the students to change their position and refrain from blocking the Dow Chemical interviews . . . we were in for a major siege in which perhaps two hundred students would have to be arrested. I thought I could talk them out of it that night if I could gain their good will. I have been on campuses long enough to know that rightly or wrongly students do not like the police on campus. From a tactical standpoint, therefore, I thought that if I could gain their good will by an immediate stroke I perhaps could spend the rest of the evening vigorously disagreeing with them and talking them out of their position." His action, in any case, at once defused the tension, frustrated the protest leaders, and widened the split between the UW administration and the state legislature in the Capitol building on the other end of State Street.

Soglin missed the arrests, but he was among those jamming the corridors at Bascom Hall, where, he later said, he found himself "suddenly thrust in this position of leadership." The intention was to block the doors and not let the administrators out until the matter was resolved. "And one of the assistant deans starts to walk out of the office, and the crowd which is sitting in is making a path for him, everyone moving out of the way." Soglin said he called down from the opposite end of the corridor, "'Why is everyone doing that?' And somebody yells back, 'He's got to go to the bathroom. He says he'll come back when he's done.' And, wait a minute, this is a sit-in! We're holding them until this thing is resolved. If he wants to, he can go piss out the window, and the ranks closed up and he suddenly found himself stranded in the middle of the crowd and had no choice but to go back into the office. And this was the kind of momentary lapses that we had. It also showed our humanity."

According to Soglin, perhaps, but not according to the *Daily Cardinal,* which strongly criticized the physical tactics this time. "We are taken aback by the baiting and insults showered upon University administrators who were willing to consider the protesters' points," the student paper's lead editorial stated. "A threat of confinement to men willing to cooperate turned the demonstration into a mockery of freedom rather than a fight for it. Discussion must be two-sided, not a one-way harangue."

Along with taking part in the protests, Soglin studied them as sociological cases. He was particularly interested in the way people lost their sense of proportion when they became members of a crowd, and why some people emerged as leaders. The leaders tended to be older, usually graduate students, and had a way with words; but not everyone who spoke was considered a leader, and not all the leaders were the most respected members of the group. Cohen and Evan Stark, a graduate student in sociology, tended to be at the center of the action even though many considered them caricatures of radicals. University administrators were awed by Cohen's oratorical skills and exasperated by his mood swings. One minute he might be sitting in the dean's office, bumming cigarettes and bemoaning how bad things were going for the left, then later he would target the same dean as first on the list to be hanged when the revolution came. Stark proudly called himself the "resident demagogue." He and Cohen were out front, Soglin decided, because they were articulate, but more than that they had a psychological need to be there.

During that spring of 1967 a woman student was seriously injured when she was struck by a city bus driving in a divided single lane that urban transportation planners foolishly had decided to run the opposite way down one-way University Avenue as it cut through the campus. The incident sparked a massive student protest, including a sit-in on the avenue and a march the wrong way down the bus lane. Soglin would never forget Cohen's attitude that day. "After the thing had kind of broke down after about three or four hours that afternoon, there were about a hundred, hundred fifty people who were finally left after everybody was scattered between being arrested and going to various corners and tying up the city . . . and Cohen comes up to me just as the crowd's breaking up and people are scattering and says . . . 'Where's everyone going?' I said, 'I don't know, they're going.' He said, 'How could you let them go?' 'What?' He said, 'You never let a crowd go. Always keep a crowd. Never let it go.' And that was Bob Cohen. I remember him at the Union; he would start talking with one person, a little louder voice, a little louder voice, then there'd be three people, twenty people, and eventually forty people, and the larger the crowd would grow, the more he would go on."

To SOGLIN and his political cohorts Vietnam had become the dominant organizing issue of their lives, but to many students at Wisconsin it was merely a distraction. They might be mildly for the war, but more than that they wanted nothing to do with it. Richard B. Cheney counted himself in that group. He was not a naïve freshman but a seasoned graduate student who had turned twenty-six in 1967 and was already a husband and father. This was his second year in Madison, and he felt that he still had some catching up to do. He called himself a "slow starter" academically, so slow that he had been kicked out of Yale twice before going through his home state school, the University of Wyoming, on the six-year plan. Now he was working toward his Ph.D. in political science and serving as a research assistant for professor Aage Clausen, whose specialty was studying voting patterns in the U.S. House and Senate. His wife, Lynne, was teaching composition to UW freshmen while studying for a doctorate in English literature, writing her thesis on the poetry of Matthew Arnold.

> And we are here as on a darkling plain
> Swept with confused alarms of struggle and flight
> Where ignorant armies clash by night.

From Arnold's most famous poem, "Dover Beach," the novelist and antiwar activist Norman Mailer could take the title of his book—*The Armies of the Night*—about the antiwar March on the Pentagon later that October.

Politics brought the Cheneys to Madison. In his final year at Wyoming, Dick Cheney had written a paper on the handling of right-to-work legislation in the Wyoming legislature, which for a rare, brief moment in that conservative state had one chamber controlled by Democrats. The paper won a contest run by the National Center for Education and Politics. Another of the center's programs offered young scholars six-month fellowships in a governor's office. Cheney's adviser urged him to try for it, noting that no one from Wyoming had ever applied. He received a fellowship and was directed to Madison to serve his internship under Wisconsin governor Warren P. Knowles, a moderate Republican who was running for reelection by the time Cheney arrived in early 1966.

As the lowest staff aide, Cheney traveled the state with the governor, serving as gofer and valet, cruising in "the right front seat, riding shotgun" in a black sedan driven by a state trooper, with Knowles and the chief of staff in back. His main duties were to pass out "We Like It Here" buttons (economic development buttons with the slogan printed inside an outline sketch of Wisconsin) and to carry a Polaroid camera. They would "go through the county fairs and up and down the Main Streets of the towns," Cheney recalled, and he would "snap pictures of everybody" the governor shook hands with "and rip off—Polaroid was fairly new—rip off that paper and leave it with whoever it was and they'd have a picture." Knowles also was big on barbershops. His reasoning, according to Cheney, was that "everybody had to get a haircut, and when they got haircuts they talked politics. So he worked every barbershop in the state of Wisconsin." This was the old culture, small town, traditional, a world apart from the change blowing into Madison.

Vietnam was barely a part of the political discussion, at least from Cheney's perspective, except for one memorable night in the fall of 1966. Knowles, after attending a political dinner upstate, had offered to give Melvin Laird, then the Republican congressman from Marshfield, a lift down to O'Hare International Airport so that Laird could catch the first flight to Washington the next morning. Knowles and Laird were old friends who had served in the state legislature together. There sat young Cheney in the cramped cabin of a small plane, saying nothing, hearing everything, as the two pols talked through the night. He would never forget how Laird kept warning Knowles not to be "too enthusiastic" about the Vietnam war. Be careful about that damn war, Laird kept saying. "Not that Laird was antiwar at all, he wasn't," Cheney said later. "But he had doubts about whether the Johnson administration had its act together and understood what was going on." (Since the introduction of ground troops in 1965, Laird had been pushing Johnson to expand the air war and diminish the vulnerability of infantrymen on the ground, and his harping on the subject inevitably irritated the sensitive president. "Take care of your boy," LBJ once groused to Laird's House Republican colleague, Gerald R. Ford of Michigan, even proposing a political horsetrade—Laird for the antiwar senator Wayne Morse.)

Mel Laird muttering about "that damn war" was an image that would flash back to Cheney many times in later years. He would recall it for the first time less than three years later when the Wisconsin congressman was put in charge of the war as President Nixon's defense secretary. But back in 1966 Cheney was the unmoved observer. He recorded the scene but was not changed by it. He thought of himself as "a reasonably conservative Republican, generally supportive of the Johnson administration at that stage." He was "not by any means an antiwar activist or even a critic." America was engaged, troops were committed, and he supported the war.

Supported it, but had no intention of fighting in it. His draft board in Casper, Wyoming, where he and Lynne had gone to high school, reclassified him often over the years. He carried student deferments three times and was switched to 1-A draftable twice, briefly, during the periods when he dropped out of school and worked for a power company building transmission lines. But those moments of vulnerability came in the early sixties, before the war heated up and the draft call intensified with it, and he managed to get through without being drafted. By the time he reached Wisconsin, he had three conditions helping him steer clear of military service: his age (they had stopped drafting from oldest to youngest by then), his school situation (graduate students were still protected; the policy did not change until 1968), and his status as husband and father (daughter Liz was born in Madison), which shifted him to 3-A until he was no longer of draft age.

If Cheney had no "moral or philosophical objections" to the draft, neither did he feel the slightest tinge of guilt about not serving. He was, as he put it later, "working my buns off" as a political aide and then full-time graduate student. He and Lynne lived in Eagle Heights, the housing for married graduate students up in the hills hugging Lake Mendota on the far western rim of the campus. They were young and "trying to get ahead in the world." They had one problem with the established order, or at least Lynne did. She found it impossible to land a mentor on the English faculty, which she considered sexist; even the noted scholar Madeline Doran seemed interested only in helping male graduate students, she thought. That frustrated her, but she did not rebel against the system. Their friends were other young married students trying to make it in academia: one couple from Quebec, another from Ohio, a third from Georgia. The wife of the Canadian couple was a nurse who babysat the Cheneys' infant daughter on the days Lynne taught. Vietnam and the draft were "not the most important things" in their lives, Cheney said later. "There's a tendency now to look back on it, those periods of the sixties, especially on a campus at a place like Wisconsin, to think of it as the centerpiece, the most important thing going on, but it just wasn't. Not for all of us."

Dick Cheney walked around campus carrying boxes of IBM punch cards, each one holding eighty fields of data concerning the voting patterns of congressmen and senators. Computer time at the UW computer center was cheaper and more readily available at night, so he spent many midnights waiting for his computer runs, in which he and Professor Clausen used multiple regression analysis to determine why legislators voted the way they did. He thought of life as "good but very full and very intense," and the last thing he wanted was for his studies to be interrupted by the war. Not by the draft and certainly not by protests on campus. "They were a distraction. They were disruptive," he said later. "You didn't get caught up in the issue that people were protesting or demonstrating against. There were a lot of us who felt, 'This is a pain in the neck. I've got to get to class.'"

PAUL SOGLIN was more dabbler than zealot. He considered himself part of the left (perhaps more than some on the left considered him part of it), but he was interested in everything the times had to offer and moved easily between various interests and groups. That spring of 1967 he was the only self-described radical among six Wisconsin delegates elected to the National Student Association. During the run-up to the election he and other delegate candidates traveled from dorm to dorm debating one another, and after one presentation at the Lakeshore dorms he continued the debate with Cathy Dietrich, a striking young woman who had grown up in Madison and represented a relatively conservative, Greek-oriented party. She and Soglin had what Dietrich later described as "a feisty back-and-forth, a sort of one-upmanship to see who could get in the last word" that was charged with politics and sexual tension.

Soon after the election, in which both Dietrich and Soglin were elected, there was a regional NSA meeting at the University of Illinois in Champaign-Urbana. Soglin rented a car for the drive, and when the other delegates piled in, he secretly hoped that Dietrich would sit in the middle seat next to the driver, which she did. In Champaign, after the first session of the convention, out-of-state delegates spread their sleeping bags in the spacious upper floor of a university building. Again Soglin hoped that Dietrich would be next to him, and again she was. After the others were asleep, the odd couple, the dark-haired radical and the lissome sorority girl, undid their sleeping bags and zipped them up as one and crawled inside together. Soglin was shocked that she would share a sleeping bag, and the night, with him. He thought it was luck; later he learned it was the design of a young woman who was unafraid to act on her desire. The student movement might be utterly sexist, young women might constantly complain that activist men had an exasperating tendency not to listen when they had something serious to say, but in sexual matters women had more power and were learning to use it.

His male contemporaries often wondered, with a shade of envy, what it was about Soglin that made him so successful with the opposite sex. He seemed unkempt, hardly the classic model of attractiveness. But there was about him, Dietrich said, an "impishness and charisma" that "really attracted women." She described him as playful, openly affectionate, flirtatious, and a bit dangerous. The crowd he moved with was especially edgy to Dietrich, unlike anything she saw over at Pi Beta Phi. Soglin and his roommates that summer were deeply into drugs, mostly marijuana, but also peyote and various synthetic concoctions. There were parties several nights a week at various student flats in what later became known as the counterculture's Mifflin Street neighborhood, and at every party, Dietrich noticed, there was a "drug room" with a closed door. She never wanted to go in. Soglin always wanted to get high. It bothered her, but her discomfort was eased by the fact that dope seemed to make him happy, not hostile or depressed, and though he obviously enjoyed it, he showed no signs of addiction and appeared less beholden to the drug culture than some of his friends. Dietrich's mother was a nurse who had access to free pharmaceutical samples. One night Dietrich brought a sample pack of Dexedrine over to Soglin's apartment and watched in amazement as two of his friends meticulously took apart each pill to separate the stimulant from the downer.

Soglin and Dietrich spent the rest of the summer together. He worked with underprivileged boys at a recreation center on the south side. She served as a waitress at the Madison Club, an exclusive hangout for legislators, business executives, and lobbyists housed in a dark-brick building overlooking Lake Monona two blocks south of the Capitol square. She came home at ten every night with presents—"a piece of pie, a good sandwich, maybe tenderloin, half a pint of chocolate milk, sometimes silverware." Most of his meals were leftovers of the city's elite. One night she slipped him into the Madison Club's cellar and let him clean out the fridge. He never had any money, she noticed, yet was proud of his possessions. He drove around town in a 1959 TR-3 convertible, red with a black top, though it was always in need of repairs and usually on empty. He also had an extensive record collection that he kept in shelves made of boards on cinderblocks next to the mattress on the floor. Junior Wells, Otis Redding, Sam and Dave, Eddie Floyd, Irma Thomas, Sonny Terry and Brownie McGhee, the Paul Butterfield Blues Band, Jefferson Airplane, Jimi Hendrix, and all the Beatles. The *Sgt. Pepper* album seemed to be playing day and night.

In August they headed off together to the NSA's annual congress, this one in College Park, Maryland, where they heard Allard Lowenstein, a former NSA president, talk about ending the war by dumping LBJ. They also participated in an encounter group, listened to an obscure new band called Wind in the Willows featuring an unknown singer named Deborah Harry, and watched a film about the liberation of Algeria. Soglin was not yet a known player on the national scene, but he seemed to be in the middle of the action. He was in one strategy huddle after another, talking not only about how to oppose the Vietnam war but also about the dominant internal issue of the year, a revelation that the CIA had been funding NSA activities for more than a decade, violating its charter not to get involved in domestic matters.

Rank and file delegates like Soglin knew nothing beforehand about the agency's involvement. Only the NSA's elected officers knew, and they passed the closely held but dirty little secret down through the years as though it were a password to one of Yale's select societies. In the argot of the clandestine operation, those student officers in the know were identified as "witty." When reports of the connection went public in 1967, and the students realized that they were being manipulated by the CIA in its fight against Marxist organizations, the effect was explosive. Some national student leaders tried to minimize the importance of the relationship, arguing that the CIA officers who ran the operation were open-minded and were not trying to redirect the NSA from its liberal-to-radical course on issues of race and war. But for Soglin and others, the disclosure widened the generational and ideological gap. Here was "conclusive proof that the CIA was not to be trusted," Soglin said. The student activists were "not pure, sweet innocents," and the radicals among them for some time had accused their national officers of being so closely aligned with the establishment that they seemed to be "running a little State Department" in Washington, "but we also had this naïve belief that while we were subject to overt government pressures, we never imagined covert activities." Now they had evidence that the establishment was cynically manipulating them and trying to co-opt them, and it served only to push them leftward and leave them further disillusioned with old-line liberals.

Asserting its rebelliousness and newfound freedom, the student congress passed a resolution embracing the "by any means necessary" rhetoric of the black power movement, and delegates erupted in cheers when a television commentator labeled the NSA "a left-wing radical outfit."

Soglin and Dietrich had slept in separate dorms in College Park, and when they got back to Madison, she went over to his apartment and he jumped at her from behind his door. They spent more time in his world than hers, but she did take him up to her parents' cottage in northern Wisconsin for a weekend. Her family was Catholic, and the fact that she was dating a Jewish guy, and a radical no less, did not sit well with her father, who worked in the Madison post office. She also got him out on a tennis court and was surprised by his athleticism, and she took him sailing on Lake Mendota. It was, she would say later, an "idyllic summer, the sort you wish would go on forever, but they don't." At summer's end she was looking for a commitment, and that frightened him. It was the last thing on his mind. He started pulling away. Having to find new housing for the school year, he settled on a first-floor flat at 123 Bassett Street, which he would share with two new roommates and two dogs, Che and Kafka. And there were other distractions: women, the *Cardinal* column, graduate school, opposing the war.

WHEN THE NEW school year began in September, Soglin and his political associates gathered each day outside on the Union Terrace, a splash of Paris set down in the American Midwest, with its vibrantly colored green and orange metal tables and chairs stretching from the back door of the Rathskeller down to the edge of Lake Mendota. They carried on a perpetual discussion, and one of the topics involved their personal histories: how their teachers in junior high school and high school had often been men who were veterans of World War II, and how the schools had preached to them about the nobility of the American fight against the Nazis and of standing up against evil. The patriotic message pounded into them during their teenage years had led them not to fight in Vietnam against the Viet Cong, but rather the opposite, to stand up against a war they considered immoral. "We had grown up on a steady diet of World War II issues," said Bob Swacker, another activist affiliated with the University Community Action party. Swacker came from Kenosha, Wisconsin, the son of a tombstone merchant. "There was always that message of the 'good Germans.' Now we weren't going to be the good Germans. It was the stock line in all of our speeches. We did not want to be the good Germans who would go along with brutality and war crimes. We had to be different. It was our turn."

One afternoon, someone in the group was leafing through the registration issue of the *Cardinal* and came across a page that listed the corporations that would be recruiting on campus that semester. There was Dow Chemical Company, makers of napalm, scheduled to arrive on October 17 for three days of interviews at the Engineering, Agriculture, Chemistry, and Commerce buildings. The dates were circled and the beginnings of a plan started to form. Dow brought home the theme of the good German. This would be the fall event around which they would organize. The word went out. Soglin wrote about it in his "Hi there, Badger!" column:

> The Placement Office has brought back one of the longest running road shows, the Dow Chemical Company. We are promised that the October 17–20 show, back for a second

performance, will not simply be a rerun of last spring's spectacle. To start with, the University has agreed to tell the Left where the show will *be held*. To give Dow an equal chance, the University will supply more police protection. The four day festival will be highlighted by an obstructive sit-in . . .

The dramaturgy of protest, with the script already written. But the second coming of Dow would differ from the first in one other respect, Soglin understood. The cast of characters had changed over the summer. Robben Fleming, creator of the "pillow" strategy, had left to preside at the University of Michigan and had been replaced by William H. Sewell, a noted sociologist with no administrative experience.

How would the new chancellor take to his role? That was a topic of considerable speculation. The student activists knew that Sewell opposed the war. They considered him generally sympathetic to their cause but still in a sense unknown and untested. "Unfortunately, he has never been in a position of power, forced to make split second decisions," Soglin wrote in his column, adding a note of foreboding: "Sewell's liberal rhetoric may fail him when the pressure's on or he may simply become an administration tool, exercising no independent power; in either case, the pot is going to blow up in his face."

CHAPTER 8

SEWELL'S PREDICAMENT

ELOW, TO THE EAST AND WEST, a luxuriance of treetop green shrouded the campus in midday sleepiness. To the north the slender peninsula of Picnic Point poked out into the waters of Lake Mendota, sailboats speckled the soft blue surface, white triangles flitting silently from here to there, and at the shoreline barefoot waders slipped along rocks slimed with squishy algae. Few scenes could be more reassuring than the one William H. Sewell took in on a summer's day in 1967 as he gazed out the wide windows of Room 1820 atop Van Hise Hall. It was a vista of serenity that seemed appropriate for such a notable moment in his distinguished academic career, when he was introduced at the boardroom of the UW Board of Regents as the new chancellor of the university. But no sooner had Sewell reached the hallway on his way out of the room than a local newspaperman sidled up and posed a question about the reality of what teemed below. *Well, what are you going to do about the student problem?*

Student problem? Sewell's mind revolved back to something he thought Winston Churchill had once said, that he hadn't become prime minister to preside over the demise of the British empire. Out came an uncensored wisecrack. "I didn't become chancellor of this university to be dean of students!"

For some reason the reporter chose not to use the quote in his story about the event, much to Sewell's relief. It would have made him sound elitist and contemptuous of the young people without whom a university would be little more than a think tank and research institute, which is what many critical students complained it was becoming in any case.

But the truth was, even though Sewell felt in no way dismissive of students, he meant what he said in that moment when he was caught off guard. He took the job of chancellor with no intention whatsoever of being dean of students, and in fact with a promise that he would not have to deal with daily student concerns, especially not the *problem* to which the journalist referred, which meant protest and disruption. The men who had recruited him for the job, including president Harrington and Robben Fleming, the chancellor he was replacing, had all tried to erase his doubts with variations on the same theme. Troubled times were ending, they said. Student protests had peaked. They knew how to deal with them now. No problem.

And if anything did come up, they said, Joe could handle it. Joseph F. Kauffman was the dean of student affairs, and though he had suffered through a rough spell with protesters the previous spring, when they had blockaded him in his office, he too thought the worst was behind them. People tended to take his word on the subject. He had a national reputation in higher education circles for understanding the psychological needs and motivations of college students. Sewell heard it over and over: *Joe can handle it.*

The stress of dealing with rebellious and hostile students was not something Sewell needed. He was fifty-six years old and had high blood pressure, occasional angina, and a leaky heart valve that had plagued him since he had been struck by rheumatic fever in college. His wife, Elizabeth Shogren Sewell, a painter and superb athlete, feared that the burden of running the university would exacerbate his heart problems, and she advised him not to do it. But when Sewell checked in with his cardiologist at the UW Medical School, he received a more encouraging judgment: the job should not be debilitating as long as he kept it in perspective and did not work day and night. That was all he needed to hear to take a post that he was eager to try, even though he had no administrative experience beyond the faculty level as chairman of the sociology department and president of the university committee. He believed deeply in the concept of the academy. A university was defined by its faculty, he often said, and should be governed by the faculty as collegially as possible. What most excited him was the prospect of overseeing that faculty governance, and subtly manipulating it just as he had in the sociology department, all in the cause of shaping a great university in a bright new age.

Sewell was not the sort of academic to get lost in his own make-believe ivy-covered cloister, but like many professors his sense of the world around him could be off a notch. He might be years ahead of popular culture or years behind, but rarely perfectly in step. In 1967 he was still looking at the world, and at his university, with the optimism that had infused Lyndon Johnson's Great Society vision in Washington a few years earlier. There was a sense in the social sciences during those middle years of the sixties that solutions to the problems of American society were within reach, that the racial dilemma was being solved, that there was enough money, brainpower, and momentum to eliminate poverty and its attendant afflictions (Wisconsin had its own Poverty Institute at work on it), and to move on from there to the ills of the world. It was with this sensibility, with what sociology department demographer Hal Winsborough described as "a kind of euphoria," that Sewell grabbed at his chance to run things. He became enthralled with the idea that he and the Wisconsin faculty could create a liberal pragmatist ideal—just when the tide was turning in another direction, when liberalism was facing its greatest vulnerability, attacked from right and left, and when the notion of an all-encompassing super-school was being disparaged by student critics for its corporate entanglements and the impersonal nature of what they called a "multiversity."

Some of his colleagues thought that Sewell, in his euphoria, underestimated the ways in which the war would affect everything, especially his university, but he was not unmindful of the raging debate over Vietnam and on the contrary had long participated in it. He had been the chief organizer of a Vietnam teach-in on campus on April 1, 1965, one week after a first-in-the-nation teach-in was held at the University of Michigan in Ann Arbor. One of his many friends at Michigan had called him and said, "Why don't you guys have one too?" and Sewell agreed. This was less than a month after the U.S. Ninth Marine Expeditionary Force had landed at Da Nang, starting the rapid buildup of American troops in Vietnam. Sewell had already concluded that he "didn't think we had any business over there" and that "we shouldn't be invading a country because we had some political differences; we weren't going to stop communism there, anyway." As chairman of the sociology department he arranged for the large lecture halls in the Social Sciences Building to be used for the teach-in that day and helped schedule an array of speakers from the faculty, including ten from history and four from sociology. With topics ranging from U.S. foreign policy to French existential philosophy, the discussion was intellectual but rather one-sided, against the war. Posters lined the walls: "Out of Vietnam By Easter." "End Gas Warfare." "In Your Heart You Know It's Wrong." Crowds grew from three hundred in the afternoon to a thousand at night. The audience was roused to a standing ovation at one point when a professor proclaimed that this was not a teach-in but Wisconsin's first "freedom school."

The memory of Sewell's role in that event, more than anything else, prompted some student activists, including Paul Soglin, to respond with at least mild enthusiasm to his appointment as chancellor. As Sewell reflected decades later, looking back on that era, his reputation "may have made the students feel . . . that I would turn the war over to them, turn the university over to them, and go along with anything they wanted." His style in the classroom certainly would not have encouraged that assumption. He had no interest in entering the pantheon of hero-professors and "didn't teach the kinds of courses or teach in a way that the kids liked." He had none of George Mosse's spellbinding eloquence and certainly not Harvey Goldberg's dramatic radical flair. He never inflated his lectures with the hot rhetoric of the day. Rather he believed in the hard, dry science of social science, in numbers, methodology, the meticulous work of analyzing statistics and testing hypotheses against results. He was a stickler for process. The first responsibility of people seeking to improve the human condition, he maintained, was to get the facts right. Here was the living definition of a rational and orderly man.

Few students who encountered him at Wisconsin in 1967 realized how intricately the threads of Sewell's life story wove through themes they considered the exclusive domain of their generation. Economic disenfranchisement, inequities of the military draft, the effects of massive aerial bombing on civilian populations, the role of early childhood parenting in shaping human behavior—these disparate interests were the stuff of William Hamilton Sewell's career long before they became totems of the sixties.

ONE OF THE unforgettable figures of generational tension during the Vietnam era was General Lewis Blaine Hershey, the crew-cut, bespectacled director of the Selective Service System, an agency that through its military draft had near godlike powers, making decisions about who would be called to military service and who would not, determining the lives and potential deaths of millions of young men. Hershey was a relic of another era, his reign at the draft agency going back to the dawn of the U.S. involvement in World War II. At his side in those early days was none other than Bill Sewell, who came to Washington as a navy lieutenant during the war to serve as assistant director of research for the Selective Service. Sewell, born in 1909, had grown up in the small town of Perrinton, Michigan, the son of a well-to-do Republican pharmacist, and had been a jock as a young man. He was recruited to play football at Michigan State University by Jim Crowley, one of the famed Four Horsemen of Notre Dame. Sleepy Jim, as he was known, later went on to coach Vince Lombardi and the Seven Blocks of Granite at Fordham. A broken ankle in his freshman year ended Sewell's football career and set him on the scholar's path that took him to a Ph.D. in sociology at the University of Minnesota and a professorship at Oklahoma A&M, where he made his first mark developing a farm family socioeconomic scale to determine living standards in rural homes during the Depression. It was that work that attracted the attention of Hershey's top statistician, who persuaded the boss to call the young social scientist to Washington.

Sewell's specialty at the Selective Service was manpower statistics. He analyzed the number of young men being drafted each month from every state and how various occupational exemptions affected the call-up. In his statistical breakdown of the deferments, Sewell reached the conclusion that farm states were benefiting from deferments far more than industrial states. In a state like Wisconsin, for example, the point system was based on a ratio of persons to cows. "Let's say you were up for the draft and your father had a herd of a hundred cows; he could get two sons deferred on that basis," Sewell explained later. "And there were probably more people deferred in Wisconsin taking care of cows than there were machinists in all of the United States. In the South it was bales of cotton, the same way." When Hershey testified before a Senate committee, Wisconsin Senator Robert M. LaFollette Jr., the mastermind of the cow-ratio deferment, saw Sewell sitting next to Hershey at the witness table passing the director notes containing statistics that accentuated Wisconsin's deferment break. Later, infuriated, LaFollette called the young statistician into his office, closed the door, and thundered, "The committee on manpower is now in session!"—and proceeded to "grill the hell" out of Sewell. Fighting Bob LaFollette might have been the voice of Midwestern Progressivism and the force behind the Wisconsin Idea, but his son Young Bob was never a particular favorite of one future university chancellor. By contrast, Sewell considered General

Hershey "one of the nicest men" he ever met, although eventually he would disagree with his former boss's draft pronouncements.

Days after Japan surrendered, Sewell was dispatched to Tokyo with a team of social scientists to study the effects of the air war on Japanese morale, part of the larger United States Strategic Bombing Survey. Relentless U.S. bombing raids from June 1944 to August 1945 killed hundreds of thousands of Japanese civilians and destroyed nearly two-thirds of the buildings in the nation's sixty-six largest cities, according to the survey. Sewell spent four months in Tokyo, Nagoya, Osaka, and Hiroshima as a research team leader, constructing a probability sample for the morale study and conducting interviews with civilians. "What bombing experience have you personally had?" Sewell and his cohorts would ask, using Japanese-Americans from Hawaii as interpreters.

Sewell learned that, even taking into account the atomic tolls of Hiroshima and Nagasaki, by far the most civilian deaths and injuries were caused by incendiary bombs—forerunners of the napalm bombs that two decades later would incite Vietnam war protests. Fleets of B-29s loaded with napalm bombs had burned out almost 60 percent of Tokyo. More than half of the Japanese civilians who had survived bombing raids said the attacks came at night and involved incendiary bombs.

Then came the follow-up question: "Can you tell me more about your personal bombing experience? Tell me what happened, what you did and how you felt." The survey revealed that "fright was by far the most common emotional reaction to the bombing experience. Many thought that they would be killed. Others (10 percent) were so paralyzed that they could neither think nor act. Few claimed that they were not frightened and practically none indicated that their experience heightened their desire to carry on the war against the United States."

Notwithstanding the methodological precision of the social scientists, the final report of the United States Strategic Bombing Survey could not—or chose not to—avoid the most political and subjective debate of that time and place. It concluded that even before the atomic bombs were dropped, the strategic air war had achieved its purpose, effectively destroying both Japanese morale and its war machine, and that the Japanese were ready to surrender and were suing for peace through third parties. The implication of this finding seemed to contradict the prevailing rationale that the nuclear attacks on Hiroshima and Nagasaki were horrors necessary to preclude a land invasion in which countless more American soldiers would be killed.

When he finished his assignment in Japan and arrived at the sociology department at the University of Wisconsin in 1946, Sewell brought with him lasting memories of both the horrors and complexities of modern war. Margaret Bright, among his first graduate assistants in Madison, recalled that he talked constantly about the morale survey and the devastation of what he saw in Japan. She described him as a "man of great conscience" tormented by the vision of Hiroshima—people living in tents in public parks, buildings leveled everywhere, phantasmal shadows of lost human existence. And yet many of his graduate students were married veterans attending school on the GI Bill and living in trailers near campus, good young men with their own awful stories of buddies killed by the Japanese. Was the bomb necessary? Sewell concluded yes, as Bright remembered it, but still seemed haunted by "that torturing feeling of whether or not it was."

Sewell soon turned from one twentieth-century trauma to another, from the atomic bomb to the Freudian theory on the effects of breast feeding and toilet training on human personality. Employing many of the probability methods that he learned or refined in Japan, he decided to lift Freud's theory from the analyst's couch and put it to the test in the field. First he studied the demographic maps of Wisconsin until he found a setting, Richland County, in the rolling hills northwest of Madison toward the Mississippi River, where he could have a controlled sample— 162 children ages five and six, all from farm families and all of what he called "old American stock," which in this case meant white and Anglo-American. Then he conducted a study over a five-year period with the assistance of four women graduate students who compiled personality test data and conducted interviews with the children's mothers.

His conclusions: the personality adjustments of children did not differ significantly whether they were breast-fed or bottle-fed, nursed on self-demand or regular schedule, weaned gradually or abruptly, had bowel and bladder training early or late (though those with late training were less likely to bite their nails), punished for toilet-training accidents or not punished, or slept with their mothers during infancy or did not. It was more likely that other factors, including the general attitude of the mother, had greater influence. "Consequently," Sewell wrote in the abstract of his paper, "Infant Training and the Personality of the Child," "considerable doubt is cast upon the general validity of the Freudian claims and the efficacy of the prescriptions based on them."

The findings created an international stir. "I got letters from all over

Europe, especially from Jewish mothers, who would say, 'My family has been blaming me for Irving's troubles and his psychiatric symptoms. Now you have freed me!'" Sewell recalled. "And of course I was condemned by the Freudians as a charlatan. But the Freudians never had a course in statistics, so they couldn't really attack."

SINCE THE 1950S in America, the word *liberal* had rarely come unattached. In Madison the common phrase was *west side liberal*. Madison was an east side–west side town, with the Capitol Square downtown serving as the line of demarcation. East and West were the rival high schools, symbols of two very different ways of life. The east side was grittier, more working-class, home to the meatpackers of Oscar Mayer and the machinists of Gisholt. Aside from the village of Maple Bluff, an enclave of country club wealth hugging Lake Mendota, the east side was a land of aluminum siding and corner bars. The west side had the university and its professors, along with high-level supervisors of the state government and other professionals, who lived in comfortable neighborhoods moving out from old homes near Vilas Park to modern split-levels made of redwood and stone in the former corn fields of University Hill Farms. The east side sent more of its sons into the military and offered the strongest support for the war in Vietnam, an issue that by 1967 was tearing apart long-standing political alliances between working-class unionists and white-collar liberals.

One small measure of that tension in Madison was the diminishing circulation of the liberal afternoon newspaper, the *Capital Times,* which, along with the subscription decline that all evening papers faced, was losing even more subscribers on the east side, traditionally its strongest base of support, because of its early and unequivocal editorials against the war. Since its founding in 1917 by William T. Evjue, a leading figure in the Wisconsin Progressive movement, and during the 1950s and '60s under Evjue's disciple, Miles McMillin, the newspaper had developed a reputation for taking strong liberal stands on controversial issues—most notably in standing up to Wisconsin's red-baiting senator, Joseph R. McCarthy—and the Vietnam war was part of that progressive continuum. On February 12, 1965, a month before the marines landed in Da Nang, the paper ran a headline reading "Negotiate in Viet Nam Before It's Too Late." "The fighting in Viet Nam is escalating to a point of serious danger," the paper wrote:

President Johnson, we hope, is finding out that the Goldwater policy leads to the dangers predicted. The President should go back and look at the election returns again. Before it is too late, the Johnson administration should move toward the negotiations that should have been initiated long ago.

We are heading into a war that we can't win. Even now, as Sec. McNamara has said, we cannot defend against the type of fighting being carried out against us. We are losing not only the military engagements. But we are losing prestige in Asia even faster. It is bad enough that we are looked upon as an intruder. We are looked upon as a bumbling intruder that can't even match the fighting prowess of the Viet Cong guerrillas.

The antiwar editorials continued incessantly from there, month after month: "The Only Way to Save Face Is to Get Out of Viet Nam." "Why Are We Bombing When It Has No Military Significance?" "A Cynical Rationalization of Broken Promises on Viet Nam." "Time for Congress to Reassert War Making Authority." "Viet Nam Bombing Strains Credibility Gap Again."

On the west side of Madison, the epicenter of Wisconsin liberalism, people and institutions were judged not only by what they said about Vietnam but when they said it. Antiwar credentials were determined by the month and year one came out against the war: before or after the Gulf of Tonkin, before or after the marines landed, and so on through the Tet Offensive and other benchmark events of the sixties. By national standards Democratic senator Gaylord Nelson was regarded as an antiwar stalwart, but in his own retrospective accounting he did not enter the fray early enough. He had trouble excusing himself for voting for the Gulf of Tonkin resolution on August 7, 1964, a congressional acquiescence that LBJ used as authority to widen the war. Nelson had been skeptical during floor debate before the vote. He had been reassured, wrongly, that the resolution would not be used as congressional authorization for a full-scale war and had authored an amendment limiting the authority of the president to wage war, yet he thereafter regretted not having joined the two lone senators who voted against the resolution, Wayne Morse of Oregon (who was born in Madison and a graduate of the University of Wisconsin) and Ernest Gruening of Alaska.

The divide in Madison then was chronological as well as geographic. A defining point on the timeline was the grassroots Hearing on the War in Vietnam conducted by Democrat Robert W. Kastenmeier, the liberal Second District congressman, on Friday and Saturday, July 30 and 31, 1965. It was one thing to organize a teach-in on the war on a college campus, as Sewell had done a few months earlier, and quite another to bring the debate into the larger civic realm. Kastenmeier's was the first such congressional hearing in the country. The issue was so controversial that he was denied use of the City-County Building and instead held the hearing in a downtown Methodist church. Opposition to the hearing was orchestrated by the local hard-hat boss, city alderman Harold (Babe) Rohr, a World War II veteran and leader of the building trades labor council who supported LBJ's war policy, explaining that "building trades is a big part in any war."

In contrast to the UW teach-in, this was not an overwhelmingly one-sided hearing but reflected the fuller range of the Vietnam debate. In this civilized forum there was no jeering, but partisans applauded speakers on both sides of the argument. Among those testifying in support of the Johnson administration's war effort were representatives of the American Legion, Young Americans for Freedom, the Military Order of the World Wars, UW political scientists Fred Von Der Mehden and David W. Tarr (with some reservations), and the chairmen of both the local Young Democrats and Young Republicans. The latter was a second-year law student named Tom Thompson from Elroy, Wisconsin, who testified despite having qualms about "the wisdom, advisability, and intent" of the gathering. "If this hearing is to take up that question of abandonment—if it is only to hear the cries of appeasement from people who cannot find enough distaste for communism to fight it— then this hearing does not serve a purpose, that is, no other purpose than to weaken dangerously the determination of our country and its people at a time when great determination and strong moral courage are demanded as fitting examples of democracy."

The YAF spokesman at the hearing, David A. Keene, focused his testimony on Viet Cong atrocities encouraged by the government of Ho Chi Minh as part of its strategy of destabilizing the South. Starting in 1957, Keene said, Ho Chi Minh "began a campaign of terror in South Vietnam designed to isolate the people from their government. Principal targets included teachers, doctors, nurses and village officials. The late President John F. Kennedy, in May of 1961, revealed that between May 1960 and May 1961 more than 4,000 low level officials were killed by the Viet Cong." That number had grown to thirteen thousand by 1965, Keene added, and the only way to stop it was to defeat the Vietnamese Communists. American withdrawal, Keene said,

> would abandon fourteen million people to Communist enslavement. . . . More than a million of those people voted with their feet against Communism when they fled from North Vietnam following the Geneva Agreements of 1954. They have trusted our word and they have fought Ho Chi Minh. The South Vietnamese population has suffered more than we can possibly imagine to keep their country out of the hands of the Communist regime to their north. Communism, and this is too often ignored, is evil. It is a pseudo-religion which justifies a ruthless dictatorship. Since 1917 its disciples have been responsible for the planned deaths of many millions of innocent men, women and children. It is a system of government that destroys its opponents without mercy, controls the minds of those who live under it, and ambitiously boasts that it will one day dominate the world.

Both Thompson and Keene would emerge decades later as players on the national political stage, Tommy Thompson as Wisconsin's governor and as secretary of health and human services in the administration of George W. Bush, Keene as an aide to Vice President Spiro T. Agnew and longtime chairman of the American Conservative Union. Thompson joined the Wisconsin National Guard and did not serve in Vietnam. Keene, who opposed the draft even as he supported the war, was protected from the draft by deferments.

The oldest speaker supporting the war was retired Captain Joseph Bollenbeck, representing the Military Order of the World Wars, whose service in the military went back to the First World War. "The Vietnam affair is not, as some falsely allege, a revolt against the government, but an invasion by the North Vietnamese Communist forces," Bollenbeck said. "It is another incident of Communist violation of the 1954 Geneva Agreement and the basic principles of the United Nations which oppose the use of force. It is conclusive proof of the hypocrisy of Communists who talk peace but blatantly violate it as they arrogantly announce they will support "wars of liberation and popular insurrections." He had little doubt, Bollenbeck added, that "American and foreign demonstrations . . . are largely Communist inspired. Leaders of college groups demanding our withdrawal have a long record of pro-Communist activities, and this is particularly true in Madison."

William Appleman Williams, the academic critic of American empire, appeared among the antiwar speakers and dealt first with Bollenbeck's charge. "I should like, at the outset, to speak to three charges made against the critics of American policy in Vietnam," Williams began.

First: that some critics are Communists. This is true as fact. It is also true as fact that some extreme reactionaries are also critics of American policy in Vietnam. Both facts are incidental to the substantive issues. Criticism is properly judged by its relevance, by its evidence, and by its internal coherence and logic. If Communists offer a better critique than non-Communists, which I deny, then the effective non-Communist response is to do better homework on the issues instead of forwarding fantasy and hearsay to Washington.

Second: that the critics lack the necessary information. I deny this to be the case. I deny it on the basis of my experience as a naval officer cleared for secret documents. I next deny it as an historian who has seen such data after the fact of failure. I finally deny it on the basis of several extended conversations with officials who have served, or are serving, in Vietnam. The information that some critics lack does not destroy the validity of their criticism.

Third: that, whatever mistakes we have made, we are caught in a situation of fact, and we have seen it through on the road we have chosen. This argument is part of a broader pattern of evasion. We humans are very prone, when we make a major mistake, to begin lying to ourselves. We go on indefinitely—until we pay the wrenching cost of the mistake, or until we muster the courage and the will to stop lying to ourselves. I am here to suggest that it is long past time to stop lying to ourselves about Vietnam.

James P. Hawley, chairman of the UW Student-Faculty Committee to End the War in Vietnam, said the Johnson administration was leading the nation into a war "which remains not only undeclared, but tragically undebated." It was a war, he said, "that violates the ideals and the heritage of American democracy and freedom. The support of a series of unpopular dictatorships in the name of protecting the independence and freedom of the South Vietnamese people is not only hypocritical and morally wrong, but is utterly self-defeating. The administration says it wishes to protect the freedom and democracy of the South Vietnamese people from the aggression from the North. But in the place of protecting freedom, democracy, and independence, we have supported, aided, and when it was convenient, overthrown, a series of brutal dictatorships, all of which have come to power not by any means even vaguely representing democratic elections, but by a series of coups d'etat." Hawley was one of several speakers who argued that the United States was intervening in a civil war and that the National Liberation Front in the South was not controlled by Hanoi. As Stuart Ewen, a history graduate student, told the hearing, "The assumption that the NLF is a direct and connected arm of the Hanoi regime is, I think, a fatal error." The argument would be undone by later events but was an accepted part of antiwar rhetoric in the mid-1960s.

If there was a featured speaker at the hearing, it was R. W. Smail, a history professor at Wisconsin who specialized in Southeast Asian studies. Even more than Williams and the better known historians at Wisconsin, it was Smail whose informed lectures on Vietnam served as the foundation of the Madison debate. "I imagine that there is going to be a good deal of preaching in this room before this day is over," Smail began his testimony. "For my part, I am going to try to confine myself to what I think is the plain power politics of the situation confronting the United States in Vietnam today. I do this not because I think that morality has no place in foreign policy but because I believe that neither the critics nor the supporters of our Vietnamese policy have been able to develop a moral position which is strong enough and clear enough and unambiguous enough to bear the weight of the extremely important decisions which must be made in Vietnam." Smail's analysis of the military and political situation in Vietnam led him to the conclusion that there was no prospect of a viable noncommunist government that could survive without a substantial American force to sustain it. "It is probably more accurate to say that such a government will never be possible," Smail said. "In any case, it would be necessary . . . in order to create the conditions in which such a force could grow, to more or less completely clear the Viet Cong out of South Vietnam. On the conventional 10 to 1 basis, this would require over a million American soldiers for an indefinite period.

I doubt if anyone would consider paying this price for the even-then un-certain chance of creating a stable independent non-Communist South Vietnam."

Invading North Vietnam was not an option, Smail said, because even if it did not lure China further into the war (and he was already among those believing that Chinese assistance to the Viet Cong was consider-able), it "would simply double the area to be garrisoned in the face of guerrilla resistance." The strategy of the Johnson administration, he said, seemed to be to introduce enough troops into Vietnam to produce a stalemate and then negotiate a compromise settlement, which he ar-gued was "theoretically possible" but "not very likely to achieve a per-manent solution." The remaining possibilities were to have a unilateral withdrawal or a negotiated withdrawal. The most practical course, in Smail's assessment, was to have a negotiated settlement that would lead to a united Vietnam under Communist control. He acknowledged that this "may not seem a very attractive proposition to Americans," but that it was at once the most likely eventual outcome in any case and also the resolution that would be best for the United States in the long run be-cause, he argued, the interests of the Vietnamese and the Chinese in-evitably would diverge, and the "long run goal of the United States in mainland Southeast Asia should be to split rather than to drive together China and Vietnam."

Here, in 1965, from a liberal opponent of the war in Wisconsin, was an argument that seemed almost Kissingerian in its realpolitik formula-tion while at the same time challenging the prevailing government ar-gument that if Vietnam fell, other countries would fall to the communists in domino succession. And in juxtaposition to Thompson's rhetoric, it contradicted the notion that opposition to the war was shaped by foggy idealism and support by hard-headed pragmatism.

BILL SEWELL LIVED ON the west side, and in some ways he seemed like an archetype of the west side liberal. He was an outwardly conven-tional man who would never want to be categorized as conventional. He collected cool jazz records, belonged to the Blackhawk Country Club, where he could shoot in the low nineties, voted Democratic, attended the Frank Lloyd Wright–designed Unitarian church, wore corny sport coats and a spiffy touring cap, tooled around town in a red convertible, played poker twice a month in a faculty game called the Probability

Seminar, grew a mustache, exercised in a morning regimen of push-ups, sit-ups, touch-toes, and running in place, began the evening with a two-mile walk in the woods near his home on Countryside Lane, chewed on a pipe, and stayed up reading monographs and abstracts from the *American Sociological Journal* until he fell asleep in his favorite blue leather easy chair. He could be impatient at times yet had the soul of a committeeman, able to persevere through endless convention sessions, academic panels, and departmental meetings, a trait that proved essential to his administrative rise. He was an institution man through and through, his academic career threaded with interconnections as a consultant to the Ford Foundation, the Division of Behavioral Sciences, the U.S. Department of Agriculture, the Fulbright Selection Committee, the National Institutes of Health, the U.S. Office of Education. Some colleagues thought of him as a public democrat but a private elitist, meaning that people he considered the most talented got the most attention, yet he also was known for effectively pushing his department and the larger field of sociology to be more inclusive of women and minorities.

He was an inveterate pedagogue, constantly looking for ways to inform the world around him and at the same time, as one colleague said, "always seeking relief from monotony and trying to add spice to the mundane." His three children learned sampling theory during long car rides from Madison to northern Wisconsin for summer holidays. To keep them occupied, he would have them count license plates to determine whether there were more vacationers from Wisconsin or Illinois, but he instructed them not to count the plates of cars passing them in the same direction because those cars were speeding and speeders invariably came from Illinois, thereby skewing the sample.

Sharp humor was Sewell's favorite spice. In a methods class once, he was discussing the role of the interviewer in conducting a survey. Margaret Bright was seated near him at the seminar table. "And he mentioned one should beware of hiring women interviewers who were too good-looking," Bright recalled. "They made people uncomfortable. And without changing the tone of his voice in his inimitable way he added: 'This is generally not a problem with women in sociology. They don't usually come that good-looking.'" Bright refused to look up or show any sign that this bothered her. She kept taking notes. Finally, demanding a reaction, Sewell gave her "a good hard kick under the table." His humor had a sarcastic twist that gave added weight to a political message. Mary, his daughter, would take into adulthood the lasting memory of her father driving her and two friends home from elementary school when she was ten or eleven and the girls in the back seat talking about what they wanted to do when they grew up. One said she wanted to be a teacher. The other said she wanted to be a nurse. From the driver's seat Sewell blurted out, "Why don't you be a doctor? All nurses do is clean up other people's shit!"

Cleaning up for other people was a task Sewell seemed determined not to take on as he became chancellor. Joe could handle it. Joseph Kauffman, the forty-six-year-old dean of student affairs, took pride in being called "soft on students and a bleeding-heart type." He had been recruited to Wisconsin after burnishing his liberal credentials with the Peace Corps during the Kennedy administration, as a dean of students at Brandeis University, and as a consultant for the American Council on Education in Washington, where he was known as "an advocate for students." Kauffman's arrival at Wisconsin in June 1965 coincided with the early stirrings of change on campus, starting with the Berkeley Free Speech Movement. Having seen the change coming before many others of his generation, he had warned the academic establishment. One of his reports for the education council stated that students who came back from Mississippi Freedom Summer civil rights work, after violating unjust laws in the South, would be willing to violate bad rules on campus.

Kauffman's insights into student behavior made him much in demand. The National Student Association regularly scheduled him to speak at its yearly conventions, and a speech he had given on the depersonalization of students and the need for universities to get more involved with them served as the basis for an editorial in the *New York Times*. Most of his early work in Madison in 1965 and 1966 was directed toward giving students more control over their lives: changing parietal curfew rules, pushing to place students on faculty committees, encouraging students to express themselves in peaceful protest if they saw fit. When Tom Pettit of *NBC News* came to the university in 1966 to do a piece about student protest, Kauffman was asked whether the antiwar movement was communist. "To my knowledge, no," he responded. And not only that, he added, but in his opinion "not enough young people are protesting."

"Say that again?" Pettit said, and the dean repeated his statement.

Kauffman's liberal philosophy was not the product of a bookish life of leisure and affluence. He was an immigrant grocer's son, his early years in Norwood, Massachusetts, shaped by the family's work ethic and the darkening world outside the store: the anti-Semitic radio rants of Father Coughlin, the reports from Germany of Hitler's destructive rise. When Joe finished high school, there was no money for college. He helped at the grocery and practiced his first love, singing. His ambition to succeed as a professional jazz singer was within reach—he had made it to New York City as a featured crooner at the Roseland Ballroom— when he enlisted in the army in 1942 to fight the Nazis. The army trained him as a radioman with the light artillery of the Eighty-fifth Infantry Division and sent him to Italy, where they slogged away on the Cassino line, an experience that left him with more questions than answers. Fighting through Italy inch by inch, hill after hill, struck Sergeant Kauffman as unnecessary. They could have landed in the north and cut off the rest of the country, he thought. "War is stupid," he concluded. "We were stupid. The only reason we won is they were more stupid than we were."

When the war ended, he went through Denver University on the GI bill and earned graduate degrees at Northwestern and Boston universities, then returned west to open an office of the Anti-Defamation League in Omaha. His two closest allies in Nebraska were Whitney Young, director of the Urban League in Omaha, and Ted Sorensen, then in his final year of law school in Lincoln and editor of the *Nebraska Law Review.* He and Young worked on equal employment and open accommodations issues together, and a letter of recommendation from Kauffman was among those going out when young Sorensen, eager to go east and join the political world, applied for a job with Congressman John F. Kennedy of Massachusetts.

A decade later Kennedy and Sorensen were in the White House, president and wordsmith, and Kauffman was brought to Washington as an original officer of the Peace Corps. In his role as director of training, he lobbied to make the Peace Corps an alternative to the military draft, borrowing a phrase from William James—"the moral equivalent of war"—to describe its purpose. Peace Corps director R. Sargent Shriver Jr. held the same view, but they could not persuade a skeptical Congress. One result became evident to Kauffman as the sixties decade progressed: young men who did not want to be in school but faced only the military as an alternative and opposed the Vietnam war, flooded into the universities to avoid the draft. Kauffman was an early opponent of the war himself, speaking against it in 1964. He was particularly critical of student deferments, arguing that only the poor and unrepresented would be drafted. "If the sons of congressmen had to go," he said, "we wouldn't be having this war." He also worried about the long-term psychological effects deferments would have on those who used them to avoid the war. The day would come, he told friends, "when these young men will feel guilty that they didn't go and someone went in their place, and they will wonder if they had the courage and the ability to go through something like that."

Joe Kauffman loved nothing more than a campus. He had a tendency, he once said, to "romanticize and idealize universities." Higher education had made his life, and he saw it as a defense against the narrow-mindedness of the world. He brought all his life experiences to the job at Wisconsin, but by 1967 he was facing the startling realization that, to some activist students, who he was and what he had done in his life made no difference and in fact only enraged them more. McNamara to the chancellor's LBJ, indeed. "You know the worst thing you can do with a New Left radical is to tell them how you sat at restaurants with Whitney Young and how you helped start the Peace Corps and how you were against the war in Vietnam—but you weren't for revolution. You were a despised liberal."

JOE KAUFFMAN AND BILL SEWELL wore the same label in that sense: west side liberals. Throughout Sewell's rise in academia, from sociology chairman to chairman of the humanities and social sciences committee to chairman of the university committee, which served as the voice of the faculty at large, his natural tendency was to confront people and issues head-on when necessary, but until then to do all he could to find reasonable ways to avoid confrontation. The most heated moments of his tenure as chairman of the university committee came near the end, at special faculty meetings in late February and early March 1967. The university was dealing with the aftermath of the unsettling protests against Dow Chemical Company at which city policemen had arrested a band of nineteen obstructing students and Chancellor Fleming had posted the bail that sprung them from jail. There was intense pressure from the public and state officials to crack down on disruptive students. Governor Knowles, a moderate Republican generally friendly to the university, had turned into a rhetorical hard-liner on the issue of protests. The napalm demonstrators, Knowles said, went "far beyond the area of reasonable conduct." He demanded that administrators expel misbehaving students "if this should ever occur again in Wisconsin." Mail to his office was running twenty to one in favor of his tough stance. Newspapers from Saint Louis to Sheboygan took up the call. The *Sheboygan Press* editorialized against "long-haired protesters who are so convinced that their ways are the only ways."

At the first special faculty meeting after the protests, on February 23, Chancellor Fleming said that he would not refrain from calling in the police the next time under similar circumstances, although with specific precautions. "Given the traditions of this campus," he said, "it is fair to assume that the faculty wants to preserve dissent, but without anarchy, and that it wants order, but without repression." The faculty overwhelmingly approved Faculty Document 122, which reaffirmed Chapter 11.02 of university regulations, prohibiting student protesters from disrupting university functions or the operations of corporations (such as Dow Chemical) that had been invited to use university facilities. In setting out guidelines for student demonstrators to follow, Fleming also thought it was important to give them advance warning. "Insofar as potential violations of Chapter 11 are known in advance, protest groups will be advised of the rules which will apply and will be cautioned that they must take any disagreements which they may have with the rules through orderly channels."

The faculty then took up the related issue of the university's relationship to private corporations. Maurice Zeitlin, an assistant professor in Sewell's sociology department, introduced a proposal to prohibit firms that make war materials from interviewing and recruiting on campus, a measure aimed directly at Dow. Many professors who opposed the war, west side liberals, said that they nonetheless opposed Zeitlin's proposal because they considered the issue a matter of free speech. The vote was 62 to 249 to allow Dow to continue to recruit on campus.

One of those sixty-two faculty members voting to move Dow's recruitment interviews off campus was Bill Sewell. He considered it a practical matter, something not worth turning into a question of principle. He had noticed from advertisements in the *New York Times* that Dow set up student interviews at off-campus hotels when it was in New York City and other large eastern cities. "I didn't see why they couldn't have the interviews off campus since they had done that elsewhere," he explained later. "But all the engineers, all the people in business, in agriculture, all with placement problems, they were all in favor of being accommodating. They thought moving it off campus was being unfriendly. We wanted the corporations to take our people and to make it as easy for our students and them as possible."

Once the faculty voted not to change the corporate interview policy, Sewell accepted the decision as the reasoned will of the majority. He believed deeply in the sanctity of faculty decisions. Later that year, when Fred Harvey Harrington asked him to become chancellor, the specific question of whether Dow should recruit on campus did not come up, nor did Sewell dwell on it. He did not become chancellor to be the dean of students.

BOOK THREE

Into sunlight they marched,
into dog day, into no saints day,
and were cut down.
They marched without knowing
how the air would be sucked from their lungs,
how their lungs would collapse,
how the world would twist itself, would
bend into the cruel angles.

Into the black understanding they marched
until the angels came
calling their names,
until they rose, one by one from the blood.
The light blasted down on them.
The bullets sliced through the razor grass
so there was not even time to speak.
The words would not let themselves be spoken.
Some of them died.
Some of them were not allowed to.

—Bruce Weigl, "Elegy"

CHAPTER 9

"WHAT A FUNNY WAR!"

CLARK WELCH WAS in a spirited mood as he sat in his small hideaway office at the Delta base camp in Lai Khe and wrote a letter home to Florida. His natural tendency was to share virtually every experience with his wife, Lacy, good or bad, trivial or exciting, but this was something special. It was the first day of the second week of training for his new rifle company, and he was exuberant about the budding esprit de corps. "This is going to be one hell of a fine combat rifle company," he wrote. "I talked to the whole company yesterday and when I said—we had a new company and could make it what we wanted to, and what I *wanted* and would *have* would be the best damned company in the Big Red One—the company that would be the first in and the last out, the company that would be called on when any other company needed help, the first combat rifle company in the 1st Infantry Division—all the men started yelling and cheering. It sounds kind of silly written down here, but if you could have seen them, you'd know why I'm here and what this is all about. These are good men, Lacy. Sometimes I don't like to have to think about what must happen to some of them before the year is over, but to see these men now—this is America at its finest."

Life is all in the perspective. Greg Landon, one of Welch's new men, wanted to be a good soldier and for his platoon to function effectively, but he also expressed hope that his company commander would not be too "gung-ho." The road to glory might lead instead to trouble, he feared. The question of whether Delta was going to be the best damn company in Vietnam seemed less relevant to him than the fortitude of the enemy. On the same day that Welch wrote Lacy about his spirited ambitions, Landon sounded a note of concern. "The possibility of the war ending before my time is up, although present, is not very large on the horizon," he wrote to his parents. "The determined V.C. counter every new strategy with a new one of their own. His monumental patience leads me to believe that he actually likes living in his tunnel reading his newspapers and occasionally going out to tend his manioc or set up an ambush."

At the *New York Times* bureau in Saigon on that very day, correspondent R. W. Apple was filing a dispatch that offered a perspective close to Private Landon's. After interviewing dozens of military experts and "disinterested observers," Apple presented a grim assessment of U.S. military prospects in Vietnam as of August 6, 1967. His conclusion was neatly summarized by the headline that would appear over the front-page article—"Vietnam: The Signs of Stalemate." The number of American troops in Vietnam had increased from 50,000 to nearly a half million in two years, Apple wrote, yet there was a growing sense that "the war is not going well. Victory is not close at hand. It may be beyond reach. It is clearly unlikely in the next year or even the next two years, and American officers talk somberly about fighting here for decades." The war was now draining the federal treasury of $2 billion a month, Apple noted, and there was a far larger human cost—74,818 American wounded and 12,269 dead.

Three reports to America on the same day: one bursting with pride, one cautious, one skeptical. Welch, the optimist of the three, was not naïve. He was often frustrated by the way the war was being run and strongly disapproved of constant attempts by army brass to make it sound as though things were going better than they were. His language was a mix of the blunt and the romantic. In one letter to Lacy, he longed for the sort of world that Hemingway might describe on his most optimistic day, one that was "clean, and clear, and real, and solid and good." But he nonetheless had a subtle grasp of his Vietnam experience and was flexible enough to balance seeming contradictions. He was unflinching in his belief that he was fighting the good fight with the good guys. "There's no doubt about whether or not we should be here," he wrote home. "The VC are murderers and assassins and just plain thieves. The Vietnamese people want us here because for the first time in 20-30 years they are protected by someone who is not taking advantage of them." Yet at the same time Welch worried about what war was doing to this beautiful, alien land and to its people. He could be angry and heroic, sardonic and reflective.

As for his own troops, he knew that if they were all still living their past lives as civilians in the States, he might not care too much for some of them. They were "hoods and kids just off the block." But here in Vietnam they were his boys, and as he led them through an intense training schedule to ready them for combat, he declared that he would rather have one of his young draftees than a hundred "of those poor bastards carrying picket signs and burning their draft cards" on college campuses. There was nothing disengaged about commander Welch. It could not enter his mind that he was preparing his soldiers to fight to a stalemate.

FROM THE DAY he started training Delta out in the rubber trees on the northeast rim of Lai Khe, Welch received a daily round of visitors. Some were welcome, none more than the friendly general who followed through on a promise of sheets and pillowcases for all the men of this new company. Others were barely tolerated. One day in mid-August, a colonel and his staff from First Division headquarters stopped by to watch explosives practice. The training was going fine, Welch thought, until "some assistant flunky came running over" and asked to have a word with him alone. This flunky was in fact a captain—Lieutenant Welch's superior officer. Welch had little use for staff captains and majors. He assumed that some of them were jealous because he had his own company, and he feared that sooner or later one of them might actually snatch it away from him. Lieutenant Colonel Terry Allen Jr., the new battalion commander, had reassured Welch that he was doing a first-rate job but also warned him that if all other positions normally held by captains were filled and a new captain joined the battalion, Allen might be compelled to give that captain Delta and find some other job for his talented but outranked lieutenant. So far five captains had entered the battalion and Welch still had his command, but it was uncertain that his luck would hold.

On this day the captain from division staff seemed to take pleasure in chewing out Welch for not following safety regulations in the way he conducted explosives training. Then the officer "sidled up" to the colonel and complained that he had "tried to convince Welch of the importance of the safety regulations but that he just didn't pay attention."

The colonel asked Welch if he knew he was violating the minimum safety distances. "You're damn right I know," he responded, as he related the incident later that day in a letter to his wife. "I'm training these men for combat, not for practice maneuvers, and they have to get close to it to get any benefit from it." To which the colonel replied, "You're right, Welch—that's the way we all ought to be thinking!" Another captain forestalled.

But again, life is all in the perspective. Greg Landon, writing home about that day's training regimen, recalled dryly: "We set off a few explosions today. No sweat, except the C-4 that we had didn't go off because the match was too wet."

Late on the afternoon of August 19 a call came from brigade headquarters with word that there was a special guest waiting to be picked up and hosted for dinner at Delta's mess hall. Miss South Carolina. When news spread through camp that the southern beauty queen was coming, the number of men claiming to be from South Carolina increased considerably. Authentic or not, a band of soldiers became South-Carolinians-for-a-day. First Sergeant Bud Barrow, who had been a drill sergeant at Fort Jackson, ran a quick tutorial, and four of the self-styled South Carolinians piled into a jeep to escort the visitor up to their place. It was apparent upon her arrival that the young woman had already accomplished one unlikely feat. "For the first time," Welch wrote afterward, "everyone took a shower, and my whole company smelled of deodorant, after shave and soap! What a funny war!" Welch led the welcoming party, then showed Miss South Carolina around camp so that she could pose for pictures. She was brave and generous just to be there, yet the episode was almost unavoidably odd. Here she was standing in front of the bunkers. Here she was patting the company dog (which urinated on her outfit). Here she was serving food in the mess hall. After dinner Welch showed her the machine gun placements. *Oh, that's nice.* And the mortars. *Oh, that's nice.* And took her up to the perimeter and pointed into the distance across the north bridge and said the enemy was out there somewhere. *Oh, that's nice.*

The original plan called for two months of training for the new company, but the contingencies of war changed everything. First Welch was given a combat readiness date of October 12. Then it was late September. By the last week in August, his company was being yanked from its training schedule to protect the Lai Khe perimeter. "Right now I could take this company into just about anything and we would come out on top," he wrote to Lacy one night that week. "I'm really proud of these Americans. They want to do a job and we are ready for anything. I hope I can give them what they need so that we can be 'successful in combat.' That phrase is in all the manuals and books I've been looking at for over 10 years—now it really has meaning."

And these soldiers of whom Welch was so proud, were they as determined as their commander to achieve "success in combat"? It depended, for many, on one's definition of success. If it meant staying alive and getting back home, certainly.

"Right now I am back in the tower" guarding the perimeter, Mike Taylor wrote home to his parents in Alaska. "I am getting tired of this crap. I should jump out of the tower and break my leg. It's worth a six-month profile, which means easy work. Christ, I'll probably break my neck. I do the same crap every day & night. I can see now why you got out of the %*#% Army, dad. Anybody that stays in the outfit has to be crazy."

Greg Landon, with characteristic sarcasm, told his parents that he was "hoping for a slow-healing, painless wound in a couple of months that will clean up around springtime of next year."

Jackie E. Bolen Jr., the oldest of six children who grew up hunting and fishing in rural West Virginia, wrote home with increasing concern. He had arrived in Vietnam a few months before the C Packet men. His comrades respected him as a skilled soldier, and Lieutenant Welch had already made him a squad leader, but Bolen wanted to leave. Vietnam was nothing like he expected, and war was worse than he could have imagined. "You don't know what it is to have to kill men or to watch your friends die," Bolen said in a letter to his grandmother. "It's even worse to have to carry them off the battlefield when you can't even find a part of a body. Grandma, I don't know what I ever done to deserve the hell that I am in."

It was "just a Chicken Shit War," Mike Troyer wrote home to his parents in Ohio. "The V.C. have everything in their favor, why should they resign to a peace treaty?" In his next letter Troyer presented an enlisted man's brief against the army:

You asked about the Army and how things are over here. Well if I really got down to the nitty-gritty I'd use a lot of cuss words because that is the language fitting to use when discussing the army. . . .

You wouldn't know who you were fighting over here if it wasn't for Charlies shooting at you. The sergeant fu-ks with you and the generals do. For instance you've been in the field a long time and you go out on patrols all day long. Now you got a nice perimeter set up with your foxholes and overhead cover on them. Well you are hot and tired and just plain pissed off. You come in and here some S.B. general comes in his bubble top chopper and looks over your perimeter in the boonies. Well he's got out his ruler and decided your firing points are a half inch too far to the left. Then you have to tear the top off and move the firing point over. This takes hours when you work like hell. In our case it's 6 P.M., you are tired and could work like hell to save your soul. Then you get maybe 3 hours sleep if you get out of pulling guard. So there's two hours sleep and you're back up and ready to go after Charlies before the sun even thinks about coming up. . . . Now you're out all day long and what happens, another general comes in and says that very same about firing points are too far to the right by a half inch. Now I've really got a case of the ass because it has to be done all over again and you're twice as tired as the night before. This goes on all day long and every day.

Now what really gives me a case of the ass is that for one thing I am going to be fighting from that foxhole not that S.B. of a general. And in the second case the damn thing was perfect to start with. I had a perfect field of fire I could cover my buddy and cover myself. But it wasn't exactly by the book so it was wrong and do it again.

The whole damn war is run by the book and Charlie can't read English so he gets all the breaks and we usually get killed.

Now after you've went through this routine just once your morale has went so far down it will never come back.

Now if the facts were known over here there would be real heartbreak. For the simple reason a man can only take so much and after a while he goes through the jungle pissed off at the army for so many reasons that I haven't enough paper for. Also, he's had sleep, according to the army, 2 hours a night. Everything is done in double time in the army, if you get 2 hours sleep they call it four. That goes except for the paycheck.

Now you take said GI walking through the jungle with his head up his ass pissed off at the world. First thing you know Charlie has blown him in little pieces with a claymore or else put a bullet between his eyes. Now don't let no one tell you Charlie can't shoot because there have been a hell of a lot of men killed with a bullet right between the eyes over here. Now then you got one American boy, soul sounds listening, average protester against the war in Vietnam (if he had a chance) killed. Why? Because the army would not leave him alone to fight a war with the knowledge he learned to fight with. They keep fu-king with him and making the whole damn thing a Disneyland war fought by a book with some S.B. in the sky in a chopper with no more intention of getting shot at as the man in the moon. He's up there looking and waiting for a chance to bitch at something.

I've got three words for the army and I'll tell LBJ himself or Westmoreland, makes no difference. "F——K The Army."

CLARK WELCH, the soldier's soldier, was driven by his vision of an ideal, but he was not unaware of war's chaotic effects. One night, as he was writing Lacy a letter, a call came in about a reckless shooting on the perimeter. "You won't believe what happened," he reported later. Two men from the battalion's communications section, who had been assigned for that night to Delta company, got in a fight. One hit the other, "so naturally the second loaded his M16 and shot the first thru the heart." *Dead man in front of Bunker fourteen.* By the time Welch arrived, all he could do was fill out forms, answer questions, and ruminate on why it happened. "I just don't understand. No, I guess I do understand. Both men, I just found out, were pending discharge for being unsuitable for military service. They both had jail records and have IQ's under 100. All this shooting and dying just got to be too much for some people and they react in odd ways. I guess it will be called 'murder'—but it's not as simple as that. A war is really something, Lacy. Some people can take it and others can't."

Snafu—situation normal, all fucked up—was coined in the American army and followed it to Vietnam. Most things went right, but there was always something screwed up in Lai Khe. An air force pilot accidentally killed by Big Red One artillery, his wing struck by an eight-inch shell as he banked overhead to make the next pass with his napalm bombs. An infantryman wounding himself in the leg with his M-16. A radio operator shooting his buddy in the arm with his .45, mistakenly thinking a VC was sneaking up on him. Two patrols running into each other in the jungle and wounding five of their own men. Three soldiers hospitalized when a claymore mine exploded as they set it up. And now another call from the perimeter: this time a soldier on ambush patrol had taken too many pills. He was slapped awake and "dusted off"—taken by helicopter—back to camp, where his stomach was pumped, his life saved. Welch interviewed him there. "When I talked to him then, he said he wanted to kill himself and had taken 10-20 Darvon. He had gotten a letter from his fiancée that she was pregnant and was marrying another guy. He said he didn't realize he was endangering the other guys on the patrol and he sure didn't want to do that," Welch recounted. "I asked if he was ready to come back to the company and be part of a team again. He said he'd come back if I ordered him to and he sure didn't want to cause any trouble, but if he ever got his weapon back he'd shoot himself! Well, the Division psychiatrist and Division chaplains are taking turns with him now."

Dealing with the local Vietnamese—sorting out the friendly, the benign, and the dangerous—was more difficult. When Delta Company was sent to a village near Lai Khe to practice what was called search and seal—surrounding a village and searching it for VC—the practice session immediately became real. The first troops on the scene encountered four men scampering out of a dilapidated hut. To Welch's relief, his men "handled it real well—no shooting—they just grabbed the old men. By the time we'd finished we had 35 people. They were supposed to have been resettled in a refugee village about two miles away, but there wasn't room so these 35 had just moved out and no one knew where they had gone to. Well, Delta 2/28 found them. The whole thing came off real well. These are the types of operations that can really help over here. So often on something like this—4-5 civilians are needlessly killed. Then we have to fight their friends and relatives for years afterwards."

Who was who? It was a question that never went away. One night that same week Welch stopped an old man driving a truck down Highway 13 after the curfew. "I had to go out and explain to him that the road was closed at 1800 and no vehicles are supposed to move after that, and that he was lucky he hadn't been shot, etc. etc. After seeing the old guy who really doesn't know anything about curfews, road blocks, or anything—he just wants to bring the wood he's cut down to Ben Cat and sell it—I really wonder about WARS and things. I'm so damn tired I can't think right, but it sure is confusing."

In his encounters with the Vietnamese as commander of Delta Company, Welch was haunted by one incident from his days running the recon platoon. Most of the time he could not afford to think about the people he was shooting at. In a sense he had tried to dehumanize the essential act of his job—killing human beings—by using descriptive lingo that was almost light-hearted: putting "little holes" in the enemy and "killing them real dead." But early on the morning of May 16, for one brief moment, the hard walls he had built up to stave off empathetic emotion and perform his job collapsed. His platoon had been assigned to conduct a night ambush patrol about six miles west of Lai Khe in a joint mission with a Civilian Irregular Defense Group, the South Vietnamese equivalent of the National Guard. Big Red One intelligence reports indicated that the VC were using a certain trail late at night and early in the morning to move supplies. At noon on the fifteenth Welch and his men took their gun jeeps to a nearby village where they hooked up with the irregulars and rehearsed the action, plotting their moves on a pictograph map and a sand table, with Welch using his rudimentary Vietnamese when necessary. They planned an L-shaped ambush where the trail made a sharp bend as it paralleled a creek.

At midnight on a pitch-black night, they moved into position. Claymore mines lined the side of the trail. One machine gun was placed to fire straight down the trail, and two machine guns were hidden in locations down the long side of the L.

Welch, with his Car-15, a .45 pistol, and night vision scope, waited at the bend of the trail. The irregulars, serving as advance scouts, were to alert him by radio when they saw the VC coming, and he would trigger the ambush by firing a long burst from his semiautomatic. They waited through the night; every other man could sleep, according to Welch's order, though he stayed awake. Just before first light the irregulars called quietly on the radio to report a squad of bicycles on the trail. Welch whispered to his men to get ready and pass the word down the line through short tugs on a string. Through his scope he saw the enemy coming into view—one soldier in front, followed by heavily loaded bicycles pushed by more troops. The first soldier was illuminated by a dim light; the others were nothing more than shadows. As the lead soldier reached the bend in the trail, Welch let loose, emptying the magazine of his Car-15. The claymore mines blew and his entire platoon started firing. It was over in a few minutes. "The noise, light and concussion of the claymores was incredible," Welch recalled. The sounds and smells were overpowering. What moments before had been dense jungle was now leveled, only smoke and dust remaining. The Americans started yelling to each other that they were okay.

In front of Welch there was no sound or movement. The enemy seemed slumped in crumpled mounds on the trail. One bicycle remained upright, wedged against the wreckage. After calling in artillery to the left and right, Welch gave the signal for some of his men to go to the trail. He went with them, flashlight shining. The lead enemy soldier was sprawled on the far side of the trail, dressed in the black work clothes of a farmer, still holding his AK-47. Welch rolled him over on his back, took the rifle from his mangled hands, handed it to one of his men, and moved on to the next fallen enemy in line. This soldier, also carrying an AK-47 and dressed in the traditional work clothes of black pajamas, was lying in a heap of rice spilled from the bicycle load. Welch, on his knees, again pulled out the rifle and handed it to one of his soldiers. Then he ripped open the dead enemy's shirt, looking for more ammunition. A flash of awareness washed over him, making him nauseous. The face had been hit and the body was badly shot up, but there were no wounds or blood on the chest, and there was no mistaking the white breasts, glistening in the darkness.

"It's a girl," a soldier standing above Welch shouted.

"No. God damn it, no!" Welch said.

But he knew it was a girl. He pulled her shirt over her and stepped back, his mind reeling. He could not search any more bodies himself. He stood and looked down at the young woman, this Viet Cong soldier in her black pajamas, her faced bloodied and ripped open, her legs crumpled under her, still partly covered by the bicycle and the rice, her conical hat torn and lying on the ground under her head, a ribbon tied under her chin—and he turned away and could not look again. The mission was called a "success." Welch eventually was awarded a Bronze Star with "V" for his "heroism" in the ambush. But that one horrible sight, a quick and deep pang of awful recognition, stayed with him for the rest of his life, and it had nothing to do with success or heroism. From then on, as he trained soldiers for battle, starting with the new men of Delta

Company, he made sure the training included role-playing in which soldiers dealt with enemies who happened to be women.

FOR MUCH OF THE PERIOD that Welch was training Delta Company, the rest of Terry Allen's Black Lions battalion were detached from the Big Red One and sent down to the Bien Hoa area where, under the temporary command of another division, they pulled relatively safe duty as part of Operation Uniontown. The assignment was to patrol the villages on the northern outskirts of Saigon and try to keep Viet Cong activities to a minimum just before and after the September 4 elections that would seek to legitimize the power of Nguyen Van Thieu and Marshal Nguyen Cao Ky. The elections were heavy with symbolism. South Vietnam was being pushed by its sponsor, the Johnson administration, into at least the appearance of a new democratic society, with a freshly minted constitution and nationally elected officials; all of that might make it easier for the United States to draw clearer lines of distinction between the government it was supporting and the communist totalitarian regime against which it was sending American soldiers into battle.

Along with persistent reports that Thieu and Ky were bribing and manipulating their way to election victory, there were also fears that the Viet Cong would undermine the election process and its aftermath. Keeping matters relatively quiet during that period, if not entirely clean, was one of the tasks given the Black Lions. Big Jim Shelton, Allen's operations officer, was anticipating action from the local VC guerrillas, but it never happened, and the turnout for the elections surprised him. "I don't know if they beat them or what, but people came out and voted." It was quiet enough that Michael Arias's platoon in Alpha Company spent some time guarding an engineering crew that was carving out a new golf course for officers and businessmen.

During their three weeks together in the comparative calm of Bien Hoa, Shelton and Allen stayed up late many nights talking about their lives, frustrations, and hopes. They were thousands of miles from their families. (Shelton had six children, on his way to eight, and Allen his three little daughters.) Shelton knew about Allen's marital troubles and his failed mission back to El Paso to try to repair the relationship with Jean. It was obvious that Allen was disheartened by the mess, but he did not appear entirely undone by it. "I might say that he was never despondent nor did he ever let his concern for his personal problems interfere with his duties as a battalion commander," Shelton wrote later. "I think I was the only one, with the exception of the chaplain, who knew about the problem within the battalion." Allen still functioned, as a leader and a person. He still seemed to love a good cigar, a long story, a shot of whisky, and anything from Texas, especially the Las Palmas picante sauce that his mother, Mary Fran, would send to him by the pack. Shelton was a history buff, drawn especially to military history, and was awed by the fact that his boss was the son of the famous General Terrible Terry Allen. Twice during his own military career Shelton had heard senior officers say that Terry Allen Sr. was the best officer they had ever known. Eager to learn everything he could about the general, he pumped Terry Jr. for stories.

Allen was not the boasting type; he did not go around pretending that he was his old man, "punching guys in the chin and grabbing butts and bullshitting with the guys," as Shelton later put it. He lived in his father's shadow but did not seem overwhelmed by it. He loved his father and was not put off by requests to talk about him. He had some of his father's traits but not all. General Allen believed that a good infantryman always wore his web gear, and that was something Terry Jr. was religious about; the belt and suspenders with the hooks were part of his uniform every day in the field. The general slept on the ground with a bedroll during wartime; Terry preferred a cot. He was more reserved than his father, less boisterous in showing that he was one of the guys. The father didn't mind looking like he had been roughing it. The son was insistent about appearing clean shaven. Every morning, wherever he was, he shaved with a straight razor. If all he had was his helmet, he filled the steel pot with cold water, washed his face, lathered with a brush, and shaved slowly and carefully while looking into a little stainless steel mirror. According to Shelton's recollections, if the son once aspired to reach or surpass his father's rank, he had abandoned that dream by the time of their late-night chats. "I'll never make general," Shelton remembered Allen saying to him.

Shelton sensed, much as the estranged wife Jean Allen had during Terry's emergency leave in El Paso, that the realization that he would not make general was accompanied by, or perhaps caused by, a certain disillusionment with the military and a desire to do something else when he finished his war tour. Allen and Shelton talked about setting up a deluxe concierge service: businesses that needed something done would come to them and they would find the right subcontractor for the job. "Terry thought it was a great idea," Shelton recalled. He also talked about going into financial management.

At his home on Cumberland Circle in El Paso, Terry's father knew nothing about his son's apparent turn away from the life they had so carefully plotted together. The general, though suffering from mental deterioration, was not altogether gone. He understood when Mary Fran told him that Terry's marriage had gone to hell. He still had hundreds of contacts spread across the military world, friends from the officer corps and former soldiers who had fought for him with the Big Red One and the Timberwolves, and he recruited one of them to check on his son. James A. Snow was in Vietnam working for Pacific Architects and Engineers, one of the large contractors employed by the U.S. military in its massive effort to pave and build over much of South Vietnam. At the general's request Snow tracked down Terry Jr. during the Uniontown assignment at Bien Hoa. "It was a highlight of my life," Snow wrote later of the meeting. He saw no signs of trouble. Terry seemed to be performing his duties well and "filling the 'Allen Boots' to the letter." After taking over the Second of the Twenty-eighth under "adverse conditions," replacing a fired commander, he had made his battalion "the first of the First." It appeared obvious to Snow that Lieutenant Colonel Allen had won the "respect and high regard" of his men. "We talked long that night," Snow recounted. "I must say that, short of being with his loved ones, he was doing what he wanted to do; what he was trained for; and doing it outstandingly!" At the end of the night Terry Jr. gave Snow a certificate naming him an honorary "Black Lion Extraordinaire—*Vincit Amor Patriae*." Love of Country Conquers.

Nothing to worry about in this report. It could not have been rosier had it been written by the publicists at MACV headquarters or in Lai Khe.

The combat readiness test for Delta Company, its final exam of sorts, was supposed to take place on September 25, less than a week after Allen, Shelton, and most of the rest of the battalion returned to Lai Khe from the Uniontown operation, but it never really happened. Midway through the test, Delta was sent off to seal a nearby village where First Division engineers were repairing a bridge. They stayed at the village two days, and when they returned to Lai Khe, the brigade commander told Welch his company had done enough to pass the readiness test. At the end of a short critique Welch got an operation order. "We go out tomorrow as part of the battalion on a real hot operation," he wrote to his wife that night. "This time we're acting on real reliable recent information. We should be able to get something. Everyone's really up for it. . . . I can't say that I've done all I can—I can always do a little more right up to the time some of mine get into it. And then I can really help—once I know where Charlie is, I'm sure I can get him. I shouldn't even say that—it's silly. But if we are 'successful in combat,' that's all and everything I can ask for over here."

FOR THE U.S. Army rifle companies in Vietnam, combat usually took place during what were known as search-and-destroy missions. In later years this terminology would evoke images of soldiers searching Vietnamese villages and destroying them, thatched roofs set aflame with Zippo lighters or napalm. The original concept, when the phrase was coined by General Westmoreland and his aides at MACV headquarters, was no less violent but more precise in its military connotation. Search and destroy meant sending infantrymen into the jungle and countryside in search of enemy units and base areas, finding them and fixing them in place, engaging them if possible, and destroying them with massive firepower, preferably from a distance through artillery and air. Even though the larger American military objective in Vietnam was essentially defensive—to stop the North from overrunning the South—the search-and-destroy mission reflected an offensive strategy designed to reach that objective. Westmoreland and his staff believed that they could prevail through a campaign of attrition, much like General Grant won the Civil War. If they could pile up body counts in their favor, they thought, sooner or later North Vietnam would relent and pull back.

Major General DePuy, one of Westmoreland's top infantry strategists, and himself commander of the Big Red One from March 1966 to February 1967, had been the godfather of search-and-destroy missions as the best way to fight a war with no front lines against an enemy whose favorite tactic was the ambush. DePuy often used Thunder Road as an example. If U.S. troops remained defensive and merely tried to protect supply lines along Route 13, they could be subjected endlessly to ambushes unless they lined twenty battalions up and down the road. Mere defensive protection was a "forlorn strategy," he told Associated Press correspondent Malcolm W. Browne. "The only way to keep the road open is to attack the Viet Cong units which in turn have been attacking the road." This same military theory was applied to the larger war. But the problem was in finding the enemy forces and getting them to stand and fight. In a moment of frustration DePuy once said that while the VC were skilled at staging ambushes, "that was kind of a coward's way of fighting the war." He could not have meant this literally, for if he did he was calling every American company cowardly. They sent out ambush patrols every night—and was it not an ambush when Clark Welch's recon patrol staged its surprise attack on the L-shaped trail in the predawn darkness? What he meant was that the VC were not making it easy for American forces.

At their First Division base camp in Lai Khe, the 2/28 Black Lions sat smack in the middle of the Big Red One's 5,700-square-mile area of operations. It was prime search-and-destroy territory. To the east was War Zone D, to the west War Zone C, to the southwest the Iron Triangle, to the north the Long Nguyen Secret Zone. Enemy forces operated in all of them, part of a region known to the war planners in Hanoi as the B2 Front. Along with several indigenous Viet Cong guerrilla units, the three regiments of the regular army Ninth Viet Cong Division, starting with Vo Minh Triet's First Regiment, had been roaming the fields and jungles of the B2 Front for several years, joined later by other regiments and the Seventh Division of the North Vietnamese Army, all supported by a string of logistical units. As disparate as these elements seemed, they were thought of as one seamless operation, controlled by political and military leadership from Hanoi, which had set up mobile forward command posts run by the Central Office for South Viet Nam (COSVN) and its military affairs department in the dense jungles of the Fishhook area near the Cambodian border north of Tay Ninh.

By the time Terry Allen Jr., Jim Shelton, Jim George, and Clark Welch reached their respective positions with the Black Lions battalion, the First Division had been searching for these units for more than eighteen months, since early 1966, undertaking two massive operations, Junction City and Cedar Falls, and a score of lesser ones. The enemy had not been destroyed, not even by the most optimistic American account, but there had been claims of victories large and small. Three hundred and eighty-nine Viet Cong killed in Operation Cedar Falls. Seventeen hundred tons of rice captured in Operation Tucson. A cache of 350 weapons and 450 rounds of ammunition found in Operation Manhattan. Nearly eight thousand acres of jungle cleared by the huge Rome plows in Operation Paul Bunyan. In all, they killed (or claimed to have counted the bodies of) more than four thousand enemy soldiers, captured thousands more documents, and unearthed dozens of base camps and vast tunnel complexes with underground hospitals, sewing rooms, and mine factories. Every body count, every cache of war materiel, every enemy document, was used by MACV as proof of progress and evidence in the case against the claims of stalemate. If the war in Vietnam could be decided by statistics, no doubt the Americans would win.

THE OTHER SIDE was fully aware of the American search-and-destroy strategy, according to Vo Minh Triet, deputy commander of the First Regiment of the VC's Ninth Infantry Division. His response was: *If they can't find us, how can they destroy us?*

There was a touch of bravado to his boast, for his First Regiment had been roughed up in several major battles with the Americans over the previous two years, but it was valid in one sense. The Viet Cong had a far easier time finding the Americans than the other way around. Their advantage was obvious long before the moment of combat. Among the Vietnamese living inside the village of Lai Khe were people who secretly worked for the Viet Cong and regularly provided information. One such informant, whose loyalties were misjudged by the Americans until they killed him in an ambush firefight, was the man who had served as the barber for Jim George's Alpha Company. Some VC supporters inside Lai Khe communicated with the Ninth Division by leaving messages in a bottle at a pickup point in the jungle nearby. There was also a special reconnaissance team from the VC Ninth Division that worked stealthily around the perimeter of the Lai Khe base camp. Soldiers on this team climbed trees to observe the Big Red One's daily operations and relayed reports over hard-line telephones hidden in the dense brush. They counted precisely how many soldiers were leaving camp every day. "They saw them and let us know," said Triet.

If the early warning system failed, the Americans in any case were easy to follow once they were on the move. The First Division was vastly superior to the Ninth VC in terms of airpower and military hardware, but its reliance on technology and heavy equipment also made it easily detectable. What Triet and his men feared most, even more than the heavy pounding from B-52s, were airborne squads that swooped down on them in helicopter raids. They considered speed more disruptive and dangerous than power, because with speed the Americans could confront them before they were ready to fight, or escape, or go underground. They respected the Big Red Brothers for power and ferocity but not speed. First Division maneuvers seemed predictable, cautious, and slow to develop. "If we saw an observation plane, we knew the American ground forces were coming in," Triet recalled. Soon would follow artillery and air strikes and napalm-grazed landing zones and a squadron of supply helicopters, all in a familiar routine. "So," Triet said, "unexpected attacks were not many."

Just as General DePuy disparaged the Viet Cong for relying on "cowardly" ambushes, the military rhetoric from Hanoi sounded harshly critical of American combat methods. "Their basic fighting methods are the following: Seek ways to quickly get away from liberation troops and determine enemy and friendly lines in order to call for help from air and artillery units," wrote Brigadier General Vuong Thua Vu that fall, according to a Hanoi Domestic Service report translated by the CIA. "This is a very monotonous and outmoded fighting method of a cowardly but aggressive army." By Vu's account this method virtually emasculated the infantrymen of the Big Red One. While air force and artillery units seized the primary offensive role, infantry forces were "given the secondary role of searching and pinning down enemy troops"—a task at which "they are not efficient."

There were two keys to success for communist forces facing American search-and-destroy missions, Vu wrote. The first was to get so close to the enemy during battle that artillery and air power could not be effective. In the metaphorical language of the Vietnamese, this tactic was popularized by a saying: "Grab the enemy by the belt and hang on." The second element was surprise. "The side which is caught by surprise will be embarrassed and unable to capture the initiative. The side which is caught by surprise will be at a loss and be quickly annihilated." In several recent battles, Vu wrote, the other side seemed surprised. "When he believed we attacked from the east, we attacked from the west. When he believed we stopped, we attacked again. When he believed we advanced, we stopped. Truth and falsehood, falsehood and truth. This completely confused the enemy."

During the same week that Clark Welch was concluding his training of Delta Company, liberation forces were holding their Second Congress of Emulatory Heroic Combatants at a base camp deep in the jungle north of Tay Ninh. More than two hundred delegates arrived from all fronts. Tran Quoc Vinh, deputy political commissar of the People's

Army of Vietnam forces in the South, gave a speech stressing "seven manifestations of revolutionary heroism." The heroic soldier, he said, must be staunch, be absolutely loyal, have a firm grasp of the revolutionary offensive, ardently love his fellow fighters, associate his personal interest with the revolution's by "adequately resolving the problems of life and death, happiness and hardship, and individual and collective welfare," scrupulously implement orders, and be self-reliant and creative "in finding every ways and means of fighting the enemy."

The military exploits of the VC Ninth Division (whose slogan was "To be victorious everywhere and completely wipe out enemy forces in every attack") were extolled, and particular honor was given to its oldest unit, the First Regiment. Three members of the regiment, Ta Guang Ty, Doan Hoang Minh, and Nguyen Duc Nghia, were named Hero of the People's Armed Forces, and the regiment itself was cited as "the best regiment of the Eastern Nam Bo's main-force contingent." Vo Minh Triet's men were given a banner with sixteen words embroidered in gold:

> With loyalty and bravery
> Overcoming all difficulties
> Continually recording achievements
> Destroying the puppets, defeating the Americans

In reality the storied VC regiment had not so much prevailed as survived. It had been the target of American searches for two long years, and though it was not destroyed, even its own glorifying historians acknowledged that it had been subject to "fierce American attacks" during the 1966–67 dry season (roughly November through March). Documents captured by a unit of the Fifth U.S. Special Forces Group indicated that there was some "friction . . . in relations between officers and men" in the aftermath of the battles, and an accompanying "loss of revolutionary pride" that was exhibited through "escapism and demoralization . . . lack of determination to seek and fight the enemy . . . weariness and the inclination to enjoy some rest . . . lack of a sense of responsibility and lack of a sense of discipline." Regular army soldiers who became casualties during that season had been replaced by fresh recruits from the provinces and filler troops marching down from the north along the Ho Chi Minh trail.

The supply system, less easy to replace, was a mess. "A number of rice and ammunition depots had to be scattered or evacuated to evade enemy mopping up operations," Ninth Division historians later wrote, and the rainy season of 1967 made "the transportation of material and logistical supplies even more difficult." As a way to recover from the earlier battles and to help with the resupply effort, the First Regiment had been given a new mission in the summer and early fall of 1967. It was put in charge of moving supplies and defending the transportation corridor that cut across from War Zone D to War Zone C.

Truth and falsehood, falsehood and truth. As much as the VC First Regiment prided itself on confusing its foes, this did not mean that the Americans were unaware of what Triet's unit was doing. From documents recovered in battle and information gleaned from Chieu Hoi (a former VC who went over to the other side), the Big Red One had detailed and basically accurate intelligence on the enemy unit. In the special intelligence estimates for September and October 1967 seen by First Division commanders at Lai Khe, the First Regiment (or 271st, as the Americans called it), was listed with a battle strength of fifteen hundred soldiers, bolstered by three hundred men from a rear services supply group, three hundred guerrilla fighters from the Phu Loi battalion, and another two to three hundred local VC forces. The latest evidence also showed that the regiment was well armed, with heavy machine guns and 82-millimeter mortar ammo, but desperately hungry, suffering from a lack of rice, and always on the move. It was said to have marched from War Zone D into a new supply area in the Long Nguyen Secret Zone north of Lai Khe along the southern border of Binh Long province. It was a sparsely populated area (Binh Long was the sixth-least populous of South Vietnam's forty-three provinces) of scrubby, rolling terrain and moderate-growth jungles. From their interpretation of captured documents, American intelligence officers concluded that soldiers in the Viet Cong regiment were "becoming increasingly disoriented and vulnerable."

Everything seemed in place for a successful search-and-destroy operation. When First Division troops went after the regiment in Long Nguyen, the VC unit would face the choice of leaving or being destroyed. "Even if it moves, the significant quantities of supplies in the area will be destroyed. So the conclusion is: Both the [First regiment] and its supporting logistical structure can be simultaneously destroyed or seriously incapacitated." There was one final word of caution: because of all those conditions, the report noted, "the probability of chance encounters with sizeable enemy forces will be appreciably heightened."

It was with such great expectations that Operation Shenandoah II began.

THE YOUNG SOLDIERS of Delta Company sensed that they would be seeing a lot of combat from late September into October. It was the talk of their camp: something's coming. "In the months ahead we're really going after the V.C.," Greg Landon reported in a letter home. "No let up. Should be interesting for me since the company has been decimated by health problems, transfers etc. The CO [Welch] is a gung-ho lieu-tenant who . . . emphasizes close-in combat. Whew! Looks like lots and lots of jungle tramping after the little men."

That was the word: they were heading into the jungle north of Lai Khe. "The gooks up there have got their shit together," Mike Troyer wrote to his parents. "The last time a company went up it took ten chop-pers to take them up and about four to bring back those that were left." But Troyer was the sort of young soldier who thought he was invincible. "I am not too worried because there hasn't been a gook born yet that is going to get me. Not as long as I have anything at all to do with it."

Jack Schroder was less confident. One night, after cleaning his M-60, he wrote a letter to his mother with more details about the mission ahead. "We're supposed to be going up to Operation Shenandoah II for a ten-day operation," he noted. "It doesn't sound good. It kind of wor-ries me. All hard core VC. So I don't know what to expect." A few days later he urged his wife, Eleanor, to send him a .38-caliber revolver. He had been pushing her on the subject for a few weeks, with no success. She had said that she might be able to send him a .22, but he worried that it "just won't have enough to stop Charlie," and furthermore he would have a hard time getting ammunition for it. "My buddy Bob Nagy from Ohio, his father bought and sent him the exact .38 revolver like I need and 100 rounds ammo," Jack told his wife. "All they did is wrap it in newspaper and aluminum foil and put it in a coffee can with some cook-ies and mailed the package. . . . I know 5 different guys that have got these." They were loading up on weapons for battles to come.

The first few days in the field there was much searching, some find-ing, but little combat. "We found a base camp with 20 bunkers but no VC," Clark Welch wrote of his company's maneuvers on September 28. They destroyed the bunkers and brought back "all sorts of odds and ends"—land mines, booby traps, gunpowder, bicycles, clothes, fifty sets of chopsticks, thirty-two baby chickens, and a bag of documents. Welch's company was the only one to find anything, so they were sent back the next day and found twenty more bunkers about a half mile from the first. They just missed the enemy troops; still-wet toothpaste remained on one of the low tables, and in the bunkers they found a map, dated the day before, that showed the Black Lions' night defensive position and had several key marks on it, a prized document for the intelligence staff. On the way out one of Welch's squads came across a small unit of VC setting up their version of claymore mines, pointing them straight up in the air, apparently to be used as antihelicopter weapons. There was a brief firefight and one Delta soldier was wounded. The casualty left Welch distraught. "I know we're going to have them—but it really hit me when I saw him and knew he was mine . . . and there wasn't anything I could do. A rifle company has a lot of people and some are certain to get hurt. I wish I could be right there each time to help."

These were still sporadic operations. During the last week of September the Black Lions were in the field a few days at a time, but they were called back on the third of October to serve as the division's ready reaction force, which meant they spent most of their time in Lai Khe, waiting for action. Welch, who felt that he had not done much yet, was stunned to hear how Delta's modest exploits were being exaggerated by the publicists of the First Division.

Truth and falsehood in another context. "I don't know sometimes what I should say about our actions—the 1st Infantry Division has got quite a reputation for 'slightly distorting' what actually happens," Welch confided in his letter to Lacy. "Most of the time I guess they really bend things around so it seems like we always come out on top. Lately we've been taking quite a beating—my recon platoon killed more VC in the first two months than the entire battalion has killed, or even seen, since then. But the stories that come out of this don't show that at all. I saw some of the stories being prepared for this last operation—and they're just plain not true. They're really building up Delta company. We were pretty successful in this operation . . . and they're making Delta company into the shot in the arm to get the Bn going again. The end result is good—I hope we can bring success to the battalion—but I don't like being a part of 'lying.' Maybe I don't know enough about this whole thing to make any statements about it, but somehow I just don't like to be part of it."

On the night of October 4 the Black Lions were placed on one-hour alert. Delta Company had to be able to pack its gear and get to the heli-copter assault pads two miles away within sixty minutes of being called. Welch plotted how his troops could do it, taking trucks instead of marching, then went to sleep after midnight. At five the next morning he got the alert to be at the strip by six. At ten minutes to six Welch and the first truck arrived. "We were met there by evaluators from Divi-sion—they were just checking our reaction time," he reported to his wife. "What a funny war!" Only two days earlier Welch's company had been yanked back and forth in the field as division officers twice changed their minds on where they should go; now this. He would be "pretty disgusted with this sort of thing," Welch said, but he was trying hard to look on the positive side. "My men do just about exactly what I tell them to and even after what we've had to tell them to do the last few days they're still working and putting out for me. I know I've got a good company—even during these screwed up affairs—and they know they're good so it comes out all right. All we have left to do now is find some Charlie."

Four days later, not practice but the real thing. On the morning of October 8 the entire battalion, minus C Company, which was assigned to protect an artillery fire base along Thunder Road, got the alert to be at the helipads in thirty minutes. George Burrows, a member of the recon team, would forever remember his squad's quick trip to the heli-copters. They were sitting in the back of a deuce-and-a-half, rolling through camp, when they passed the Red Cross station, and there, stand-ing outside in the early morning light, stood a group of American women volunteers—"donut dollies," they were called—singing softly: *Shenan-doah, I long to hear you. Away, you rolling river.* Burrows loved the tradi-tional folk song, and its hauntingly beautiful melody stayed with him as they boarded the choppers and were taken to the field. Official reports later said that 450 troops were moved by twenty-five airships making three round-trips each. The numbers were fictitious, based on the mis-taken assumption that Terry Allen's battalion was at full force. A more accurate count would have found about a hundred fewer men.

Their landing zone was in the jungle of the Long Nguyen Secret Zone, about twelve miles to the northwest of Lai Khe near the Cam Xe stream and a Michelin rubber plantation. It was in this same region, eight months earlier, on February 12, 1967, that the First Infantry's chemical division conducted what its commanding officer later called "the largest CS [tear gas] attack of the Vietnamese war, and possibly of any war." They had flown a fleet of Chinooks over the Long Nguyen jungles that February day and dumped 25,000 pounds of powdered CS gas on Viet Cong targets. The gas, actually a fine powder, almost like talc, was expelled from fifty-five-gallon drums, 80 pounds of agent per drum. The choppers held fifteen drums on each side, thirty in all, for about 2,400 pounds per helicopter. Bombardiers on either side fed the drums out at a rate of one every three seconds. This massive use of CS gas, said Lieutenant Colonel Alvin Hylton, was an effective way to harass the enemy by contaminating base camps, rice storage facilities, supply routes, and road crossings. But what had the largest gas attack of the war accomplished? Reports now indicated that the Long Nguyen was thick with base camps and enemy forces. Triet's First Regiment was said to be in that jungle, somewhere.

It was expected to be a "hot LZ," meaning a landing zone where the enemy might be lurking, but there was only one spray of gunfire and the rest of the day was quiet. So quiet, in fact, that a crew of print and television journalists (including a striking woman in a flamboyant black jumpsuit—could it be Oriana Fallaci?) who had come along to chronicle the action, left before nightfall, bored and disappointed. The battalion had spent most of the day trying to find a place to dig bunkers—a task made more difficult by the soggy ground—and preparing the night defensive position for what was expected to be a long stretch in the field.

On the morning of October 9 two companies left camp on a search-and-destroy mission, Delta in the lead, Bravo behind. Battalion commander Allen monitored the scene in an observation helicopter. They moved slowly and kept coming across fresh tracks and trails. At 12:35 Sergeant Mike Stubbs, leader of the point platoon, quietly called back to Welch on his radio and reported that he saw three Viet Cong and was certain they had not seen him. As Welch moved forward, an enemy soldier popped his head above a large anthill. Stubbs shot and killed him, and an intense firefight began. It seemed to the soldiers that it lasted two hours. In fact, according to radio logs, it was thirteen minutes.

"I have never been in anything like that before. I thought for a moment that somehow we had gotten in the middle of an air strike!" Welch wrote in a letter the next day. "The bullets were knocking down leaves and bark off the trees and kicking up dust so much there was just a cloud of dust and dirt all around. There were about 50 VC in trenches right in front of us and about 10 VC tied up in trees right above us. In the initial burst of fire 4 men were hurt, but the whole company kept firing.

We expended our entire basic load before it was over." Once again Welch struggled to explain precisely what it felt like in the heat of the battle. "I just can't describe what it was like—I've been in firefights and other battles but this was 10 times any of those. There was so much noise we couldn't use the radios. The VC in the trenches were shooting low through the grass—you could hear those shots kicking through the grass and ricocheting off the ground. Some VC were hiding behind ant hills and trees—their fire was mostly going over our heads. You could hear them cracking and snapping and breaking off branches and leaves. But the worst was the firing coming from the trees. That was just driving down on top of us and thudding into the ground."

Welch yelled for the men behind him to fire up into the trees. "And right then 3 VC fell down dead about 25 feet in front" of him. They had been tied into the trees, and "when they were shot, they just fell down the length of the rope and hung there in mid air." When the battle ended, Welch counted 13 dead Viet Cong, all apparently members not of Triet's regiment but of a rear services group in the region. One of Welch's Vietnamese scouts was hit in the leg, and six Delta soldiers were wounded, including Sergeant Stubbs, one of Welch's best fighters. Stubbs had been shot in the neck near the beginning of the firefight, yet had continued to direct his battered troops until they made their way to safety. He carried some of his wounded himself, ignoring his own more serious condition. The wounded were evacuated swiftly. They seemed to be in relatively good shape as they were dusted off. Stubbs, despite his wound, snapped a salute to Welch as the helicopter lifted; Welch made a note to himself that his sergeant's actions were worthy of a medal. He was overwhelmed by how well not only Stubbs but the whole company had responded. "They did everything I wanted or asked of them, and then more. When I'd call to one of the platoons to move up on the flank, they'd just say, 'Already moving, sir.'"

It had been two months since Welch, at the beginning of training in Lai Khe, had roused his men to shouts and cheers when he told them they would be the best damn company in the Big Red One. Now they had endured their first battle, and they had not disappointed. They had found some measure of "success in combat." They had come away with a sack of enemy weapons while leaving nothing behind except the boots of Private Cook; medics had cut them off to work on his wounded feet. A day that had begun in surprise ended in victory. "We ran into Charlie," Jack Schroder wrote home to Eleanor afterward. In his rhetoric he had been chasing Charlie since the day he got off the USNS *Pope*. But the reality of the battle, as opposed to his earlier boasting about hunting down the VC to gain revenge for fallen buddies, left him with a different feeling. "For a lot of the men, this was their first firefight, they hope the last, too," he wrote.

On new stationery handed out to the men in the field after the battle, another Delta soldier, Ray Albin, a member of the mortar platoon, wrote home to his girlfriend Rhonda Sue Ruick at Principia College in Elsah, Illinois. He told her where he thought they were ("About 10 miles east of the Cambodian border. If you have a Vietnam map and know a little about maps, I'll give you the coordinates of our location and then you can see where we are. The coordinates are 658-557") and the name of the operation ("Oh, the name of this operation is Shenandoah II. In case you read about it in the papers you can tell your friends that PFC RR Albin, a fan, sincere admirer, and close friend of yours is or was there.") He also told her that they had "paid the price" for finding a VC base camp, with six men wounded. "But that's the way this war and all wars are, Rhon."

The soldiers of Delta knew more was ahead. Word came down that they would stay in the field for seven more days of search-and-destroy patrols. Their commander, at least, felt they were ready for anything. "They're some good men, Lacy," Clark Welch wrote that night, recalling in his mind's eye the scene of his tired troops trudging out of the jungle after the battle on their way back to the night defensive position. "I wish you could have seen them. Every one—whether they were walking or being carried—saluted me and said 'Black Lions, sir' as they came by."

CHAPTER 10

GUERRILLA THEATER

IT WAS ON the very next day, the tenth of October, thousands of miles away in a markedly different world, that the San Francisco Mime Troupe hit the road for a national tour through the universities of the Midwest and on toward New York. First stop, Minneapolis, then down to Madison, retracing a route they had followed the year before. Few institutions were more evocative of the counterculture than this spirited ensemble, yet by that fall, in the effusive wake of the Summer of Love, the troupe and its director, Ronald Guy Davis, seemed eager to get away from the hippie ambience of the Bay Area and focus on political action.

Davis, who founded the troupe in 1962, became a noted figure in the Berkeley Free Speech Movement when he was arrested in a San Francisco park in August 1965 for performing what the park commission deemed to be an obscene version of an Italian farce. By the summer of 1967, as young people around the country were getting their first heady whiff of the counterculture, Davis had been through it all and was becoming concerned about contradictions he saw emerging. He felt the tension between free and easy do-your-own-thing egalitarianism, which was the attitude of the moment, especially in San Francisco, and artistic excellence. His political seriousness, as he later wrote, "made no headway against a tide of long hair, electronic music" and "the democratic notion of amateuristic total participation." He was also struggling to keep the San Francisco Mime Troupe afloat financially, with more and more people hanging around, calling themselves members, and pushing their version of freedom, which was free everything. As a way of easing his artistic frustrations and money problems, he purged the troupe of thirty-five actors and stagehands that summer. Those cut loose tended to be more social than political, and they were eager to transform the troupe into a leaderless commune.

That attitude, as Davis saw it, was a threat to effective guerrilla theater. While he kept a few superior actors who happened to be more into the Haight-Ashbury scene than he was, including Peter Cohon, who later made it in Hollywood as Peter Coyote, he worried about a valueless aspect to hippiedom that he considered as inane in its own way as the larger American entertainment culture. "The greatest error of the hippie movement is its amateurism, its innocence, and its ignorance," he argued in a statement of purpose that he wrote to himself. "The result I presume of allowing everyone a creative soul. A good assumption under a strict artistic rule—but a bad one where all rules are discarded and all discipline, art, creation or tension are thrust away. The hippie generation with its acceptance of all with no values, no judgments, is impossible, nay stupid. To attempt to make no judgments is to deface oneself into a mere potato—just as the style of culture called entertainment does. The object is to produce mashed potatoes for mashed potato heads. All soft, thickly packed, soft gooey and heavy. Where there are no standards or comparisons or judgments we achieve no style, we receive trash called art, superficiality called inspiration."

The issues Davis contemplated in 1967 were philosophical questions that in various forms stayed at the center of the sixties debate for decades thereafter. Where did the unfettered individualism of the hippie movement take you? Davis from the Marxist left and conservatives on the right might agree that it led to a seeming lack of values. But while conservatives would call it a rejection of the American way, Davis saw it as the opposite; he considered it just another byway wending through that insipid land of "capitalistic middle America," differentiated in this case only by hip language. Most of society operated in a dull haze, he believed, so in that sense merely dropping out was different only in style, not substance. He believed it was necessary to "step away" from bourgeois society, not drop out. To transcend mediocrity, he wanted to act as "a great man," and he wanted his actors to be in the same mold. Only then, with will and talent, could they change the world. If this called for a certain elitism that ran counter to the democratic rhetoric of the movement, so be it.

He was driven by an ideal—no stars in the ensemble, but each actor a total performer. Ronald Davis wanted the San Francisco Mime Troupe to be the best damn company in alternative theater no less than Clark Welch wanted his men of Delta to be the best damn company in Vietnam.

Audiences who had never seen the mime troupe perform often assumed that they would be watching variations of the silent white-face routines made famous by Marcel Marceau. But this mime was something else entirely, an extremely verbal mode of acting that was also overtly physical and broadly comic. The signature method of the San Francisco Mime Troupe was to reconfigure old commedia dell'arte plays and stage them as modern farces laced with political commentary about racism, capitalism, authoritarianism, and the Vietnam war.

The main play for the Midwest tour in October 1967 was a revision by Joan Holden of Carlo Goldoni's eighteenth-century melodrama *L'Amant Militaire*. In its barest outline the plot involved a Spanish army that was occupying Italy to protect Italians from their own rebellion. From that alone it was obvious how the material could be transformed into a tragicomic story of Vietnam. Davis played the role of Generale Jesús Maria José Álvaro Diego Garcia y Vega, an amalgam of MACV commander William C. Westmoreland and President Johnson, and Peter Cohon took the role of Pantalone, the greedy mayor of Spinachola, a sort of Nguyen Van Thieu character who profited from the war. Sandra Archer, regarded by critics as the best actor in the ensemble, played the dual role of maidservant and pope. Darryl Henriques, a comic talent who also later went to Hollywood, played both the servant Arlecchino (backflipping his way onstage) and the puppet Punch, who operated inside a cardboard box, offstage and apart from the script, a sarcastic commentator and cheerleader for the audience. The rest of the cast included the stock characters of farce, a beautiful daughter played by Marilyn Sydney, and three soldiers from the Spanish army: Alonso, a lieutenant played by Arthur Holden, Sergeant Brighelle, played by Charles Degelman, and Corporal Espada played by Kent Minault. It was a wild and talented cast playing around with a rollicking script.

"You're looking good, José, but what's going on with the war?" Pantalone asks in the opening scene.

"The tide of the war has definitely turned," responds Generale Garcia, echoing some of the optimistic words of General Westmoreland that October. "Allied forces have seized the initiative. We now control most of the cities and towns, and our pacification teams are sweeping the countryside. The rebels are being rolled back, they're scattered, they're on the defensive, as is proved by the growing number of attacks."

The Vietnam analogy was obvious throughout the script, designed to draw whoops of recognition from antiwar audiences. Davis played the *generale* with a heavy Spanish accent, except for the end of one scene, where he rode off stage on a mock horse, wearing a Texas cowboy hat and mimicking LBJ's Hill Country twang.

"The government I work for is crazy," Sergeant Brighelle says at one point. "Ten years we have been fighting in this stinking country, and we got to stay here till we win. Then we go fight in another stinking country. We could move now: there's nothing left to steal, and Italian food makes us all sick. But without victory the generals get no satisfaction. . . . With the weapons we got now, they may finally get it. Blast you full of holes, melt your flesh off—pretty soon somebody's going to get hurt."

When the puppet appears, the historical analogy often vanishes altogether and the story becomes the present and Vietnam. There is even a moment where the puppet leads the audience in shouting the familiar protest, "Hell no, we won't go!"

"Stupid clod," the puppet says to the audience, referring to a perplexed soldier. "He didn't have to go into the army. This is becoming a pro war play. Who put this on, the Voice of America? There are still a few ways out of the army, one is to psyche out. Shoot yourself full of methedrine, stay up for three nights and go down to your Draft Board, write with your left hand (if you can still see the paper), let them know you are a leading pervert . . ."

Later, when Pantalone considers selling off his daughter in an effort to keep the Spanish military in Italy, the puppet confides in the audience again:

"The thing to do is to hire the Generale and put him on your board of directors. General Dynamics has 52 ex-generals on its board of directors and they get over 2 billion a year from the government. Eisenhower warned the country about the Military and Industry having a complex, but JFK went right ahead with his New Frontier. JFK said, 'Go West, Get More Land.' So who do you think's in Saigon? You're right. General Westmoreland. Not bad for a puppet, huh?"

Before leaving for the Midwest, Davis wrote an essay that appeared in *Quixote,* a radical alternative literary magazine in Madison run by Betsy and Morris Edelson, who sponsored his visit to Wisconsin. The object of the mime troupe, he said in that piece, was "to work at a presentation that talks to a community of people that expresses what you (as a community) all know but what no one is saying: thoughts, images, observations, discoveries that are not printed in newspapers nor made into movies: truth that may be shocking and honesty that is vulgar to the aesthete." He also presented his rules for guerrilla theater, a term that his troupe coined: "Prepare to go out of business at any moment; prepare to give up your house, your theatre or your troupe, and even your ideas if something more essential comes along; travel light and keep in shape; Ideas like property cannot be private; nothing is sacred—only sometimes tenderness."

Most of the cast and crew drove from San Francisco to Minneapolis. Davis and Archer, his girlfriend, traveled by airplane. The director was thirty-four, but in order to get a half-price student fare ticket, he later acknowledged, he wrapped bandages around his head to cover his graying hair, put a stocking cap over the bandages, wrapped another fake wound on his left hand, and hobbled onto the plane as though he had been in a severe accident, with Archer nursing him aboard; playful deceit was an unwritten rule of guerrilla theater. Members of the cast had salaries of eighty dollars a week and lived off the land in the underground circuit. In Minneapolis they received five hundred dollars from the University of Minnesota and were put up by the Firehouse Theater. In Madison the Edelsons, both teaching assistants in the English department, arranged a five-hundred-dollar advance and promised Davis a percentage of the gate. It was a safe proposition since the ensemble had drawn a packed house at the fifteen-hundred-seat Memorial Union theater when the Edelsons had brought them to Madison for the first time the year before. Each cast member had a "complete list of names, addresses, and tel. numbers of the people who will provide accom" and were told to "arrange among yourselves and contact the people upon arrival." (Davis and Archer would stay with the Edelsons at their first-floor pad on Charter Street, a few blocks from the Union.) They were also given the name and address of the local American Civil Liberties Union lawyer, just in case.

THE FALL'S ANTIWAR DRAMA in Madison had already begun, though the guerrilla theater in this case was unrehearsed and it was not always clear who the actors would be.

William Sewell, the new chancellor, took the stage reluctantly. He had wanted to concentrate exclusively on academic concerns, but that was a naïve hope. It would be impossible for him to ignore the challenges of student activists. The antiwar tensions that had been building the previous school year had not lessened, as some colleagues had predicted, but only increased. The formation of an Ad Hoc Committee to Protest Dow Chemical; Paul Soglin's columns in the *Cardinal* predicting a blowup at the mid-October Dow demonstrations; the time-for-resistance rhetoric now common in the refrains of radical orators at the Memorial Union and on the Library Mall—all conspired to force the issue on Sewell from the moment he took over his new desk in Bascom Hall.

In his first appearance before the faculty, on the afternoon of October 2, the question of student protest and how the chancellor would handle it was unavoidably the most anticipated and dissected aspect of his speech. What he said that day reflected his liberal sentiments as well as the conflicted feelings he struggled with in such contentious times. He began by saying that the outspokenness of today's students, even that of the rabble-rousers so reviled inside the Capitol building on the other end of State Street, was part of Wisconsin's time-honored tradition of sifting and winnowing. The students, he said, were "greatly concerned with what they perceive to be injustices and some are very active in mounting protests and demonstrations against them, both on the campus and in the larger community." Great universities had always been places of "energetic contention and dispute," he argued, and the disputatiousness so evident now only showed how seriously these students took ideas and issues. "Would we have it otherwise?"

Then, gently, Sewell made the turn. "We have, however, held that support of causes must be by lawful means which do not disrupt the operations of the university, even as we are prepared to examine and to discuss with students the purposes of university operations which they question. My predecessor laid down general guidelines for the enforcement of this principle which this faculty accepted and I believe are fair to all. Until such time as the faculty acts to change these guidelines they will be followed. We will continue to protect the integrity of the university as an educational institution in an open, democratic society." If it took the Madison police to ensure that protection, then, as Robben Fleming before him had promised, the university would call them in.

With his position articulated, Sewell again tried to turn the matter over to Joe Kauffman, as he had planned all along. *Let Joe handle it.*

The dean of student affairs began meeting daily with Ralph Hanson, the campus security chief, and several assistant deans, including Peter Bunn, Jack Cipperly, and Joel Skornicka. Discussing the policing issue, they decided that a group of off-duty Madison officers would be requested to supplement the campus force for the Dow demonstrations, with more on call if needed. All the officers, from both the university and city forces, would work under Hanson's command and respond to different situations based on a detailed plan he was drafting. The group also prepared what was called an "abstract" of building guidelines, detailing in a friendly and conciliatory tone precisely what sort of protest behavior would be allowed in each of the various university buildings that might be targeted for demonstrations, almost in the manner of a formal invitation prescribing proper attire for a social event. In the Commerce Building, for instance, demonstrators would be permitted "in reasonable numbers" but would not be allowed to block classrooms or otherwise disrupt the classes. They could carry signs of paper or cloth inside, as long as they were not attached to sticks. And if any questions remained, "staff of the Graduate School of Business, together with representatives of Protection and Security and Student Affairs, will be available to consult with demonstration leaders on questions of procedure."

All of this sounded sensible enough, but who was listening? One frustration for Kauffman's team was attempting to find an effective way to communicate with the anti-Dow activists, who operated in an ad hoc alliance that appeared leaderless or burdened with too many leaders. One student who seemed approachable was Robert Swacker, a senior history major who was Soglin's cochair in the University Community Action party. Swacker's rhetoric was to the left of Soglin's (associates remembered him rhapsodizing about the Marxist government of Albania), but by temperament he was a moderate who believed in process and procedures, not freewheeling anarchy. As a high school student in Kenosha, an automobile town south of Milwaukee where American Motors made the Rambler, Swacker had served as chairman of Young Democrats for three years and had even led the First Congressional District Young Dems for LBJ in 1964 before heading up to Madison. During his first two years at the university, he had worked part-time as a Capitol page for a liberal Democratic assemblyman from Kenosha. Though the experience had left him disillusioned with mainstream politics, he knew how to operate within that world and how to deal with his elders. He developed friendly relationships with both Chief Hanson and Peter Bunn, the director of student organizations.

When Hanson sought to find out what was going on with the students, he often went to the Union and tracked down Swacker, an early riser who could be found in his blue jeans and work shirt, long hair and goatee, reading the newspaper in the Rathskeller by seven every morning, hours before most other activists got there. For some measure of privacy, Hanson and Swacker would head back to the Paul Bunyan room, a less frequented meeting place in an obscure corner of the first floor. Swacker was not a police informant, he gave away no secrets and in fact rarely knew any, but he liked Hanson—as did most of the students—and enjoyed their exchanges, in which both men tried to figure out what the other side was intending. He had more formal meetings with Bunn, an earnest young assistant dean who wore a crew cut and preppie sport coats and was invariably direct and polite. Swacker first appeared at Bunn's office inside the Memorial Union early on the afternoon of Monday, October 9. As Bunn later recorded in his log, Swacker requested and was granted a temporary permit for the Anti-Dow Coordinating Committee to hold a predemonstration strategy session in room 5208 of the Social Science Building that Friday night. For the next thirty to forty-five minutes Bunn and Swacker talked about the "activities and plans" of the anti-Dow group, but Swacker, Bunn wrote, "could make no representations to me concerning the exact nature of their planned activities since he was acting only as registrant and temporary chairman."

Swacker's approaches to the administration were in fact barely tolerated by the more confrontational groups in the ad hoc coalition, who thought that asking the university for permission to do anything was a form of capitulation. He would "catch flak," Swacker said later, from comrades who told him, "This is bullshit, the streets belong to the people." But along with his sense that the demonstrators should at least get permits for their meetings, Swacker was also performing a bit of guerrilla theater himself, by vaguely misleading the authorities. "What this entailed was me constantly reassuring them that we wouldn't do anything that would embarrass them or be illegal or get them in trouble with the legislature. We knew we would do all of those things, but we wanted to be able at least to meet without being arrested."

After Bunn's first two meetings with Swacker, the administration realized that sending messages solely through him was not sufficient and that a stronger statement needed to be made apprising students of the consequences if they broke university rules. The warning was a matter of due notice, Joe Kauffman believed. In the aftermath of the first Dow protest the previous spring, they had even put it in writing. If potential violations of university rules were known in advance, they had declared, "protest groups will be advised of the rules which will apply and will be cautioned that they must take any disagreements which they may have with the rules through orderly channels." There was no legal counsel's office in the administration in 1967, but when Kauffman took the issue informally to leading professors at the law school, they reinforced his thinking. Don't just go arresting people, they told him. Warn them first about what would constitute a violation of the law. Give them due warning and the opportunity to act accordingly.

Who would issue the warning? Fleming had made all major pronouncements when he was chancellor, but Sewell was new, he was sympathetic to antiwar sentiment, and he was not eager to look like the hard guy so soon. *Let Joe handle it.* A bit of tension was developing between Kauffman and Sewell, the two quintessential liberals. Bill worried that Joe was burning out, Joe wondered whether Bill had the fortitude and savvy his job demanded, but at that point they were keeping their concerns to themselves. If Sewell did not want to issue the warning, Kauffman would do it. He would, as he said later, volunteer to make himself expendable as "the guy to run over if you were a revolutionary." Kauffman drafted the statement, showed it to Sewell, who "approved every word," then had it delivered to the *Cardinal,* which printed it October 11. What became known as the Kauffman statement, after reiterating university guidelines, ended with a clear warning. "If any student obstructs scheduled placement interviews, or otherwise disrupts the operations of the University or organizations accorded the use of university facilities, the University will not hesitate to invoke university discipline, including disciplinary probation, suspension or expulsion whether or not arrests are made."

Although Kauffman described his statement as something issued for the benefit of the protestors—a fair warning—it was interpreted far differently by those to whom it was directed. When Paul Soglin read it in the *Cardinal,* he saw a free speech issue, a subject that had been of special interest to him since he had sent away for the HUAC transcripts when he was fourteen. This was not due notice, he thought, but prior restraint. He scrambled out to his red TR-3 and drove around the square to the near east side law office of a young black lawyer named Percy Julian. Julian was *the* lawyer for student demonstrators, one of the few attorneys in town who would take up their cause. There were two hip lawyers in town who counseled young men on how to avoid the draft, but Julian, with the help of Michael Reiter, an activist law school graduate who was doing doctoral work in philosophy, carried the legal load for almost everything else. Julian already represented Robert Cohen and the students arrested in the first Dow protest seven months earlier. He agreed with Soglin's argument that Kauffman's statement was not due warning but an attempt at prior restraint. The university, he said, was trying to intimidate protest leaders and find any excuse to kick them out of school.

Before drafting a lawsuit, Reiter and Julian asked Soglin to write an affidavit explaining how Kauffman's words coerced him and prevented him from exercising his rights of free speech. It was a difficult assignment, Soglin acknowledged later, because he knew that he "was going to demonstrate regardless of what had been said," so in that sense his speech was not stifled. But he also felt in danger of being arrested and expelled and felt that Kauffman's statement had a chilling effect on people before they had done anything, and to that extent it was impinging on their rights.

Soglin rounded up signatures and affidavits from nine other students—Swacker, Henry Haslach, Robert Cohen, William Kaplan, David Goldman, Richard Scheidenhelm, James McFadden, Daniel Bernstein, and William Simons—and borrowed enough money from a woman friend for the filing fee necessary when Julian would take the lawsuit to federal court seeking a restraining order against Kauffman and the university. Also to be named as defendants were the officials who might prosecute the demonstrators, Dane County District Attorney James Boll and Wisconsin Attorney General Bronson LaFollette, as well as the law enforcers who might order their arrests, UW chief Hanson and Madison's chief of police, Wilbur Emery.

LATE ON THE SATURDAY MORNING of October 14, as Soglin finished rounding up cosigners for the lawsuit, Wilbur Emery received a detailed report from an undercover detective who had been on special assignment monitoring antiwar activists at the university and had spent Friday night at a meeting on campus. The report was a remarkable document of its time, an interpretation of one world by another, written in a language with which Emery was intimately familiar, the formal and convoluted lexicon of policedom, about a student political scene that could not have been more alien to him.

"On 13 Oct between the hours of 7:00 and 12 midnight, I attended a special meeting of an Ad Hoc Committee to Protest Dow Chemical," the detective's report began. What followed was a deadpan account of the endless doings in room 5208 of the Social Sciences Building, the meeting for which Peter Bunn had given Bob Swacker the permit. It was a typically intense gathering of student leftists and liberals who agreed about the biggest thing—their opposition to the war in Vietnam—but could talk and quarrel forever about the strategy and tactics of their movement. The Friday night meeting was open to anyone, theoretically, since it was on campus property and the large lecture room had been secured with a temporary permit from the university. But the detective was allowed in and stayed throughout because he was not recognized as a cop. Chief Hanson and Peter Bunn had been invited to the meeting by Swacker, but then disinvited by others once they arrived. They left after dropping off 250 copies of the abstract Kauffman's team had put together on guidelines for protests in the university buildings. A reporter from the *Daily Cardinal* was also there and remained to the end, taking notes for an article that told essentially the same story as the police account, with more quotes and less chronology.

The officer's report began by explaining why the ad hoc committee existed. It was a defensive tactic, the agent explained, aimed at averting Kauffman's preemptive discipline threat. "A number of organization heads—such as the Committee to End the War in Viet Nam, Draft Resistance Union, Young Soc. Alliance etc.—were told by the person in charge of organizations at the Memorial Union that, in lieu of [Kauffman's] declaration that anyone involved in breaches of UNIV. regulations whether arrested or not would be subject to disciplinary action, it would be advisable for established organizations to *not* carry out any protest actions in the name of any established organizations; rather it was suggested that they form an ad hoc committee en masse to protect their individual organizations from disciplinary action." So far, understandable enough.

From what the undercover officer "could make out," the meeting was organized by a leader of Students for a Democratic Society, not someone from YSA (Young Socialist Alliance), as he had previously assumed. There were also representatives from the Committee for Direct Action, the alternative newspaper *Connections,* and three other organizations with which the detective was not familiar. (In fact the largest contingent there was from Paul Soglin's University Community Action party.) With little contention the group elected a chairman (the vote seemed to be "prearranged," the detective thought) and agreed on an agenda that called for a four-stage process of presenting and discussing various motions on how to deal with the Dow protest.

When the rules were set, the show began. "The first phase of the meeting boiled down to a confrontation between *P* of SDS and *F* of YSA. (Names in the police report, as in an FBI file, had been blanked out.) *P* made an elaborate speech for the protest against Dow to be OB-STRUCTIVE as well as merely educational. *F,* on the other hand, stated that, although he too had once been in favor of OBSTRUCTIVE picketing of Dow, he had changed his mind since Concerned Black People pulled out of the Dow protest action and now he was in favor of peaceful and educative type demonstrations anti-Dow."

The second phase of the meeting brought an even more intense debate over obstructive versus peaceful protest. Four young men familiar to the undercover cop dominated the discussion. All four "were in favor of the obstructive method of protesting and while they were haranguing some members it certainly appeared that they would have no trouble getting those members to rapidly pass a motion favoring obstruction." But it was not that easy. "Had this been the case the meeting might well have been over at 9:30; such was not the case. Sometime between 9 P.M. and 9:30 P.M. discussion was cut off and the chairman began the reading of 6 motions which had been written up and handed to him during the preceding discussion period." The undercover officer explained the motions as best he could.

Motion 1 was from SDS: "The protest against Dow should be obstructive and it should not be limited to Dow but protest should be maintained against any organization which comes to the UNIV. to recruit personnel and which is involved in any way in the war effort."

Motion 2 came from an unidentified party: "A tribunal should be organized to try Dow for war crimes in the manner in which the Nuremberg Trials tried and condemned [the German industrialist] Krupp. This was not to exclude an acceptance also of obstructive protests against Dow or any other firm."

Motion 3 was submitted by the fellow named F and his roommate:

"1) TUES. October 17, mass unobstructive picketing of Dow, 2) WED. Oct. 18, block all access to the Dow interviewers and act in any way possible to get them off the campus, 3) FRI Oct. 20, everyone go to Washington D.C. and march, 4) have a meeting next week at which time this large group be broken up into cadres of smaller groups which really get to work on organizing radicals."

Motion 4 was "submitted by *P* and was eventually combined with Motion 1. Its only distinctive mark was the vehemence with which it attacked AMERICA as it now exists. This is probably not new to anyone, but both *F* and *P* are obsessed with eventually leading a Castro type revolution in AMERICA."

Motion 5 was submitted by "a party unknown and called for both obstructive and non-obstructive picketing not only of Dow but also of Oscar Mayer simultaneously."

Motion 6 was submitted by the Young Socialist Alliance and called for "a peaceful and educational type demonstration anti-Dow, not because the Young Socialist Alliance is against obstructive methods but merely because, at this time, it was felt more practical to employ non-obstructive methods so as to avoid arrests which might take the wind out of the protest sails."

If the sextet of motions was confounding to the officer, what happened next was more so. The motions were amended, combined, rejected, tabled, amended again. There was a walkout by some aggrieved parties after a motion was changed by what the policeman agreed seemed to be "devious and sinister means," then more debate, and finally, when the dust cleared, the group voted to accept motion 3, which was defended by a student so articulate that even the cop was buying into him now, describing him as "a most effective rabble rouser and even a delightful person to listen to." So here was the plan: No obstruction the first day, obstruction the second, take the buses to Washington for the March on the Pentagon, and then come back and organize. A few minutes before midnight the group elected ten representatives to implement the plan and set up another meeting for Monday evening, October 16.

Five hours earlier, when the meeting had begun, there were about three hundred people present. By the end only a hundred or so remained. "The tenor of this meeting started out very militant, then switched to a rather restrained pitch, but ended on a very militant note," the officer's report concluded. "I would suspect, on the basis of what I saw and heard tonight, that some of those involved in the protests on

TUES and WED will get themselves arrested and that a number of them intend to go in the building. They are confident that they will have some very large crowds, and it would not take an extremely large crowd to really get the area around the Commerce Building atop Bascom Hill congested."

WILBUR EMERY, the recipient of this report, was from another Madison. He was a straight-arrow retired U.S. Marine Corps major who fought in the Pacific during the Second World War, all spit and polish and shining brass. One of his habits was to order about-faces during random inspections to see if officers had shined the heels of their shoes. Anyone who didn't shine his heels didn't wipe his ass, he would say. His men—and they were all men in 1967, all white men—shined their heels. This anal bit of Emery-style logic was perhaps the foulest thing he ever uttered. For a cop and a leatherneck, he had an unusually chaste vocabulary. Smoking was his only obvious vice, but most cops smoked then, and so did the secretaries, the dispatchers, and the police reporters. If his men strayed, he called them in for counseling. Anyone who wanted to get divorced had to explain it to him first. He belonged to Masonic Lodge no. 5 and the Madison Scottish Rite Bodies; he was also a Rotarian, an Elk, recorder of the Zor Shrine, and a trustee of Bethel Lutheran. He was known among his troops as "the pope of the Lutheran Church."

Like most of his men, Emery was a Madison townie. He came out of the Central High district that encompassed the old ethnic working-class neighborhoods around the Capitol Square and stretched southwest toward the Italian-American Greenbush neighborhood (known as "the Bush") and beyond to the small black community on the far south side and straight west toward little Lake Wingra and the edge of the west side. There was a Central High connection at the top, an old buddies' club of captains, lieutenants, and detectives. Most of them, Emery included, went straight from high school into the military, lacking the money or interest to attend the great university nearby. They knew Madison from the street level. One question on the police entrance exam was to name every street that intersected State as it ran from the Capitol down to the university. With so many Central High grads among the brass, it was important for cops working the territory to understand the lifelong connections, which taverns to work and which ones to avoid. If it was owned by Phil Imordino, stay out. Imordino was a pal of Captain

George Schiro. Or if the DiSalvos owned it, don't mess with it. They were "friends of the force."

That was intuitive for most Madison beat cops. If they grew up there, they knew. But the university subculture was foreign to them. In 1967 the department only recently had begun trying to crack the new worlds of radical politics and free-flowing drugs. One of the first detectives working the campus drug beat was Tom McCarthy, who was thirty-seven that year. He had come onto the force out of East High and the navy with an aggressive attitude and a blunt way of talking that was at once effective and controversial. He prided himself on being "a busy type who did a lot of arresting and pissed people off." Things "were different then," he would say of his early years on the force, recalling how he carried a blackjack in a side pocket of his pants, how he once unpinned his badge to get into a street brawl with a man he thought was "intimidating people" in the Bush, and how he and a group of cops once "dealt with a guy accused of abusing his wife" by heaving the miscreant off a bridge into the Yahara River. A law-and-order version of guerrilla theater.

Word of these off-the-books operations invariably filtered back to Wilbur Emery. Eventually he became so concerned about how McCarthy was "wearing out the rug" on the way to the chief's office that he arranged to meet with his fiery officer in a police car away from headquarters in the City-County Building. McCarthy's loose mouth would land him in trouble long before the era of political correctness. When he started the drug beat, he said later, he "didn't know shit from shinola" about the drug culture and thought it was "the most important thing in the world" to arrest a student for pot possession. One day he was invited to a meeting on campus with Ralph Hanson and Joe Kauffman, who expressed concern about the increasing use of drugs among students.

How do you find the drug crowd? Kauffman asked.

Easy, McCarthy said. *You take the student directory, go down to the first Jewish name from New York, and start there.*

This comment did not go over well with Joe Kauffman, who responded angrily and later complained to Emery. McCarthy "got in all kinds of trouble," he said later, even though he was only "being facetious." Or was he? "To be honest with you, that *was* just about the way it went. Because we had no idea. Most of the kids from New York, to them it was an everyday occurrence. To us it was brand-new." McCarthy did not work undercover, so he became a known figure around the student haunts, especially the Rathskeller. He came across most of the characters of the student subculture and became especially friendly with Kenny Mate, a rhetorical firebrand who delivered carry-out orders for Ella's Deli on State Street, and Edward Ben Elson, a brilliant iconoclast who strutted around in bellbottoms and an admiral's hat and whose own Kafkaesque worldview set him apart from any crowd. Once when a student taunted McCarthy by calling him a pig, Eddie Elson, a former boxer, "coldcocked the guy."

With McCarthy, as with most people, there was a difference between how he dealt with individuals and how he viewed groups. Even as he joked and grew oddly attached to Elson and Mate, he hated the campus and detested long-haired students as a type, especially antiwar radicals or "outside agitators." To "ninety percent of the guys in the department," he estimated, the flag and the military "were two things that meant the most to us. To see somebody put the flag on the seat of their pants, or even drag it down the street or cut it down, it was like, you would almost die to keep the flag from hitting the ground. And 'one, two, three, four, we don't want your fucking war' . . . well, we had very strong feelings about the war. Right or wrong, my country. Yeah, I hated them. They hated me and I hated them."

How much did he hate them? Once as he was riding a city bus from his home over near East High down to headquarters, he saw a long-haired antiwar student come aboard and was so agitated by the sight that he barked aloud, for the entire bus to hear, "If they want to practice dropping the bomb, they should drop it right on the top of Bascom Hill and let it go off!" It wasn't right to feel that way, McCarthy knew, but that's the way he felt.

McCarthy might have been correct in his assumption that students, at least the ones who called him a pig, hated him as much as he hated them, but their feelings were more complicated about Ralph Hanson, the cop they knew best.

Hanson took over as the campus police chief in the spring of 1965, just after the marines landed in Da Nang. As the intensity of the war in Vietnam increased, so too did the tensions on campus and the pressures of his job. He had started his law enforcement career as a trooper for the Maine State Police, and back then he could drive for hours along the highways near Houlton, his hometown up near the Canadian border, without seeing anything but stands of tall pines and maybe a deer or two. When he arrived on the UW campus, he would joke, the most hostility he faced was if one of his officers issued a parking ticket. Within two years even those days seemed ancient, as buried in the past as the tranquillity of northern Maine. But Hanson was an inveterate diplomat with a ready sense of humor and what his wife, Lucille, called "a knack for socializing" that helped him talk his way through most difficult situations. He was six foot and stocky with a big, open, heavy-browed face and receding hairline that he covered with a Badger-red baseball cap in good weather or a Russian fur hat in winter.

Seasoned antiwar activists on campus got to know him during the weeklong antidraft sit-in at the Peterson Administration Building in the spring of 1966, when he spent as much time inside the building as most of the student occupiers. At one point when they took a vote on whether to seize another room, Hanson loudly recorded his own "No!" eliciting some sneers but more laughs. It was that year, after the release of the movie *Alfie,* starring Michael Caine, that they began greeting him at demonstrations by singing a variation of Burt Bacharach's title tune: "What's it all about, Ralphie?" (Hanson secretly appreciated this so much that he later borrowed the line for the title for his unpublished, and unfinished, memoir.)

Hanson was a student of human nature. His father, a house painter, was an alcoholic who had been away from the family for long stretches and was finally gone for good when Ralph was eighteen. Early on during his stint with the Maine State Police, Hanson realized that if he did not further himself through more training, "the inevitable would happen—marriage, family, and living in the Houlton area" for the rest of his life, a future that he did not want. He trained at the Northwestern Traffic Institute in Evanston, Illinois, and when he returned to Maine was eventually promoted to run the state police traffic bureau in Augusta, the capital, where one of his assignments was chauffeuring the governor, Edmund Muskie, whom he greatly admired. After ten years with the state police, he headed out for Madison, first taking a job as security chief at Truax Air Force Base. The university recruited him three years later.

The week Hanson was hired, Wilbur Emery sent a congratulatory note, chief to chief. "May your new position be replete with pleasantries," Emery wrote, "and each challenge you confront an instance where the state university and our community benefit from your administrative ability." Though he did not have a college degree, Hanson took UW extension courses all through the 1960s and was studying sociology and constitutional law as the world was cracking around him in 1967. He read David Riesman's *The Lonely Crowd* and Paul Goodman's *Growing Up Absurd,* looking for lessons on alienation and the reasons for youth rebellion. His instructor gave him a B, but his ability to deal with confrontational students won him even higher marks from the administration. After the 1966 sit-in at the administration building, then-chancellor Fleming sent him a note of praise: "Not only did you keep hours which must have pushed you close to exhaustion, but you remained good humored throughout and managed to maintain rapport with students." After the first Dow protest in February 1967, which was decidedly more confrontational, Joe Kauffman wrote to him: "In the past year we have all come to realize how sensitive a position such as yours can be in calming or irritating highly emotional situations. We have all learned a great deal from our confrontations, including the fact that some cannot be prevented from being disruptive. But your reactions illustrate our reasonableness, as well as firmness, and this makes all the difference in maintaining the respect of the entire campus community."

As the second coming of Dow approached in October, Hanson understood that his skills would be put to their toughest test. Although few at the university knew it, he was also dealing with a career distraction. He had driven down to the University of Chicago early that month and interviewed for its chief of security job. Along with an expense report—twenty-four dollars for gas at eight cents a mile, three ten for tolls, twelve dollars for lodging, and a buck and a quarter for breakfast—he also sent word back to UC that he found his discussions there "inspiring" and that he had "no doubt that whoever gets the appointment will have plenty of challenge, but he will also have plenty of backing, which is most essential." Hanson's wife was from Chicago, they had just had their second child that August, a son, and the job at the private school paid better. The decision would take several weeks. In the meantime there were preparations to be made for Dow.

At meetings with Kauffman's team in the dean's office, Hanson was noted for both his humor and his endearing way of mangling words. His favorite phrase, when presenting a plan, was "Okay, here's the scene-a-rio." "The what?" Kauffman might say. "The scenario?" "Yeah, the scene-a-rio." The scene-a-rio after Kauffman's October 11 statement was not so bright. A collision of wills now seemed likely, especially since the student activists voted at that October 13 meeting of their ad hoc committee (the one Hanson was asked to leave but that the undercover

Madison cop attended) to go ahead nonetheless with plans to sit in and obstruct the Dow interviews. Hanson's officers, and the off-duty city cops who would supplement them, had no riot training. There had been no physical confrontations at previous demonstrations, aside from a few minor shoves between individual officers and activist leaders. He did not expect violence this time, but it was possible, and he wanted to make sure that at least the men under his command knew what they should and should not do, so he prepared a six-point plan on police guidelines and another five-point memorandum explaining the "limitations" of police action.

Every instruction Hanson put on paper seemed aimed at avoiding violence. Police would "exercise patience, tolerance and restraint, as well as good judgment," he wrote. If established rules were violated, the first response would be for university officials to talk to student leaders. If violations persisted and police had to act, first they would inform the students of the violations and again ask them to conform. If that didn't work, the students would be asked to identify themselves. If they did and the problem stopped, no further action would be taken. If the violators refused to identify themselves and kept breaking the rules, they would be subject to arrest. But arrest was the last resort, and if "in attempting to implement an arrest" there were "significant physical efforts of other students" to thwart it, the police would not force the issue but instead back away "to preclude further physical violence." In that case they could prepare arrest warrants to be issued later. "Mass noisemaking, chanting, and other disruptive tactics, short of blocking, obstruction or physical harm" would not be reason for arrests. And mass obstruction that was "beyond the control of police manpower at the scene" would be "tolerated" until a decision was made "to involve further police manpower or cancel the interviews."

CHAPTER 11

JOHNSON'S DILEMMA

FOREIGN CORRESPONDENTS WHO STROLLED over to the Rex Hotel in the hot, leaking heart of Saigon wanted numbers at the daily five o'clock military briefings, if only to question them. The Pentagon needed numbers, if only to bolster believers back home. So numbers in endless procession are what U.S. public affairs officers in Saigon provided. In the late afternoon of October 15, the numbers of war seemed imposing even at the end of a quiet Sunday.

American and allied forces were in the field on sixty operations of battalion size or larger that day in South Vietnam. The Ninth Infantry Division had seized nearly five hundred weapons in Viet Cong tunnel complexes east of Saigon. Although cloudy weather over Hanoi forestalled bombing near the northern capital, U.S. air power pounded the lower panhandle of North Vietnam, with marine, navy, and air force pilots flying 125 missions. In the South, U.S. aircraft made almost five hundred tactical air strikes, and helicopter and fixed-wing support aircraft flew nearly eleven thousand sorties. Three U.S. marines died near Con Thien when an American bomb fell short of its mark, but an estimated forty enemy troops were killed, placing the "kill ratio," as it was known at the Pentagon, comfortably above General Westmoreland's preferred rate of four to one.

What was the sum of all the numbers? Progress or no? Winning or losing? If only there were an easy formula that could provide the answer, the military equivalent of the Dow Jones average. Twelve mid-level Vietnam experts from the CIA, Pentagon, and other intelligence units were meeting in isolation at Vint Hill Farms in northern Virginia that week with the assignment of concocting an equation that would define American progress in Vietnam. Stay out there until you figure it out, they were told, but it would be a doomed mission. The war was beyond mathematical expression. Anecdotes and hunches came more readily, if with less precision. What did the numbers add up to? Readers of the *New York Times Magazine* would awake that Sunday morning to one old soldier's confident answer. General Maxwell D. Taylor had made a grand tour of Vietnam in late summer, and now the former chairman of the Joint Chiefs of Staff and former ambassador to South Vietnam had his byline on an article asserting that "the cause in Vietnam is being won."

At the White House, military aides in the situation room kept vigilant watch on statistics flowing out of Saigon, and Lyndon Johnson himself pressed constantly for more reports like the one from General Taylor. He was in never-ending search for evidence to disprove, or discredit, the pessimists who had pronounced the war an unwinnable stalemate. He hungered for numbers and good news, and many members of his staff were now reassuring him with confidential memos brimming with positive interpretations. From aide William Leonhart, who helped run the pacification effort and had once served in the U.S. embassy in Japan, came a report on "A Japanese View of the War" based on a dinner conversation he had that week with General Sugita, retired chief of staff of Japanese self-defense forces. Sugita had arrived in Washington after visiting Vietnam, where he spent time with the First Infantry Division at Lai Khe. The general came away convinced that "Hanoi and the VC have lost the war," Leonhart wrote to the president. "Much hard fighting may be ahead, but the NVA and VC can only lose more the longer they hold out. In Sugita's view, Hanoi's military may already understand this." That had been the word spreading through Lai Khe. Even Clark Welch had heard it, and in one letter home to Lacy he expressed surprise about a rumor that the North would stop fighting before the end of the year.

If Hanoi understood, why couldn't the press corps and the American public? Along with the drumbeat of skeptical news reports from Vietnam, there were also increasing signs of uncertainty about the war at home. Every few months in 1967, the Gallup Poll asked the same question: "In view of developments since we entered the fighting in Vietnam, do you think the U.S. made a mistake sending troops to fight in Vietnam?" In May half the respondents said no. By July the figure had dipped to 48 percent, and by October only 44 percent of those polled thought American involvement in Vietnam was not a mistake.

For war managers in the Johnson administration, the art of persuasion now seemed as important as the art of war. "We are losing support in this country. The people just do not understand the war," the president had lamented weeks earlier at a meeting of his war council. After that meeting a cable had gone from the White House to the embassy in Saigon urging officials there to "search urgently" for ways to show progress. Ellsworth Bunker, the ambassador in Saigon who had succeeded Henry Cabot Lodge in April, was on his way to see his wife in Katmandu when the cable arrived. ("Avast, belay, I am on the way," the patrician Bunker announced joyously in a telegram. "Great day yesterday. Assembly validated election just before midnight . . . and Boston Red Sox won the pennant.") First things first with the ambassador, so his deputy, Eugene M. Locke, took up the progress assignment.

Locke responded to the urgent plea from Washington with a long memorandum that was circulating through the White House in mid October. The embassy had stepped up its public relations effort, he said, and had developed a plan to "demonstrate to the press and the public that we are making solid progress and are not in a stalemate." There would, Locke promised, be more comparisons of where they stood militarily compared with two years earlier, more use of captured documents to make the case, concerted efforts to brief the press in detail about pacification progress in specific villages, encouragement of "selected pressmen" to visit those areas for in-depth stories, and "hard-hitting briefings" on subjects about which the press had expressed doubt.

Locke's central argument, echoed by General Taylor in his magazine piece, was that the Americans were "winning where it counts, that is, in the minds of the people." Not the American people, perhaps, but the Vietnamese, or at least some Vietnamese. Newspaper accounts from Saigon that week reported "an intensifying anti-American mood" in the South Vietnamese capital, especially among students, professors, local journalists, and Buddhists who believed that the United States had rigged the election of General Thieu. But Locke's countervailing argument that the Americans were in fact winning Vietnamese minds was based on signs of disarray within the Viet Cong and North Vietnamese ranks. There was ample evidence, Locke argued, that "the enemy is losing control of the people for his side. His recruitment has dropped off sharply, he is having food shortages, and he is having serious problems collecting

Viet Cong taxes. Furthermore, he admits losing control over the people (see captured documents). This is a much more significant measurement of who is winning than territory gained."

The enemy documents Locke cited included a captured letter dated August 8, 1967, that described a meeting that day attended by twenty-eight Viet Cong cadres. According to a CIA translation it noted seven problems:

1. The majority of the Viet Cong soldiers in Giong Trom district are tired of the length of the war.
2. They are afraid of air strikes, artillery and M-113 armored personnel carriers.
3. Leadership cadres do not want to work harder to indoctrinate guerrillas.
4. Many Viet Cong soldiers robbed or oppressed the people.
5. Many Viet Cong soldiers were undisciplined, used weapons to kill each other or have caused dissension among various units.
6. Many Viet Cong cadres were not dedicated politically.
7. Many Viet Cong soldiers were tired of warfare and did not think they would defeat the government of Vietnam or the Allies.

A second document, captured April 22, 1967, was addressed to all district committees and party chapters in the southern provinces. According to the CIA translation, it "expressed concern over the number of persons who rallied to the Government of Vietnam [meaning deserted from the Viet Cong to the allied forces] following Operation Cedar Falls in January, 1967, when a large number of cadres [approximately 530, by U.S. military estimates] took the opportunity to surrender . . . some because of personal dissatisfaction with the Viet Cong."

Truth and falsehood, falsehood and truth. On that same Sunday at the midpoint of October, the Viet Cong were telling another story entirely through their propaganda channels. "President Johnson is now in a dilemma," declared a broadcast on Liberation Radio, as translated by the CIA. "The Vietnamese problem is like an ox bone stuck in his throat. He can get this piece of bone out of his throat only if he agrees to undergo the pain of a surgical operation. But instead of doing this, he is trying to swallow another bone."

Colorful metaphors were part of LBJ's Texas storytelling tradition, but the ox bone analogy was not one the president could appreciate then, even if in its own way it came as close to the truth as most memos reaching his Oval Office desk.

THE DAYS OF OCTOBER had been one hard swallow after another for LBJ. He had closed September by traveling to San Antonio on the twenty-ninth and delivering a speech that was described as an "upbeat" account of the war but was aimed primarily at negotiating a way out. The United States would begin a bombing pause, he said, if Hanoi indicated it would enter into "productive discussions" leading toward a negotiated settlement. "Why not negotiate now? so many ask me," Johnson had said in that speech. "The answer is that we and our South Vietnamese allies are wholly prepared to negotiate tonight. I am ready to talk with Ho Chi Minh, and other chiefs of state concerned, tomorrow. I am ready to have Secretary Rusk meet with their Foreign Minister tomorrow. I am ready to send a trusted representative of America to any spot on this earth to talk in public or private with a spokesman of Hanoi."

The most promising back channel to peace talks was already under way and involved Dr. Henry Kissinger, a Harvard professor who was serving as an informal consultant and middleman for the White House. Since midsummer Kissinger had been orchestrating contacts between a North Vietnamese diplomat named Mai Van Bo and two French civilians, Herbert Marcovich, a biologist, and Raymond Aubrac, an old friend of Ho Chi Minh. The Kissinger contacts and what was known as the San Antonio formula became linked, and discussions about negotiating a bombing pause dominated White House deliberations during the first half of October, even as the president and his aides expressed doubts that a pause would have any beneficial effect. Johnson was uncertain but leaning toward a pause, though in darker moments he suspected that the North Vietnamese were "playing us for suckers" and had "no more intention of talking than we have of surrendering." Day after day the full measure of LBJ's dilemma came into view.

On the evening of October 3, the president met from 6:10 to 9:32 with Secretary of State Dean Rusk, Defense Secretary Robert S. McNamara, CIA Director Richard Helms, National Security Adviser Walter W. Rostow, and Press Secretary George Christian. Aide Tom Johnson was in the room taking notes. At LBJ's request, Rusk began with a report on his recent trip to the United Nations in New York, where the General Assembly had opened a new session. Rusk said he held "forty-seven bilateral meetings and one hundred in various groups" and could not find anybody who could tell him "what will happen if we were to stop the bombing." Even the Russian foreign minister, Andrei Gromyko, was no help, claiming that the Soviets had "given up any attempt to try to influence Hanoi." When Johnson brought up the back channel negotiations, he was told there might be an answer in two days. "Kissinger told them that we are against waiting any longer, that we are getting impatient," Rusk said. "Bo wrote a message which is on the way by air mail special delivery. In his phone call with Kissinger, Bo said something like talks will start after the cessation of bombing."

Rostow jumped in, pointing out a semantic discrepancy, as well as revealing his own skepticism: "To correct that, it was that talks *could* start but no other assurances were given."

Helms, the spy chief, then noted the vagaries of communications, even when they involved an issue of grave importance to people who usually had the most sophisticated technology in the world at their command. "There were some great difficulties," he said of a conversation between Kissinger and his French contacts, "because we had an American who does not understand much French talking to a Frenchman who does not understand much English over a trans-Atlantic phone call. It is important that we wait and see what the written message actually says."

LBJ rambled into a monologue about the deficiencies of his South Vietnamese allies. He said President Thieu had to be pressured to bring more progressive civilians into the government. He compared it to the situation when home rule was established in the District of Columbia and he had told the new mayor, Walter Washington, that there was "a need to 'get with it' out there." South Vietnam needed programs for health and education and land reform. They had to show they knew what they were doing. And Westmoreland had to snap the South Vietnamese army into line. "They have got to get in where the fighting is," Johnson said. "We cannot have our fatalities running higher than are on the [South] Vietnamese side. I want to know it first if this is a white man's war, as so many people are charging."

According to Tom Johnson's notes, LBJ then turned his attention from the war to the antiwar. He had met with congressional leaders the night before, he said, and they had brought up the subject of a massive antiwar rally being planned for Washington on the weekend of October 21–22. The word from Capitol Hill was that the leadership "would not tolerate" the large demonstration, Johnson said. He had instructed Mc-

Namara to "get going on plans to protect the White House, the Pentagon, and the Capitol."

McNamara reported that Warren Christopher, a deputy attorney general, was leading an interdepartmental task force on the October demonstrations. There were several key questions to be answered, McNamara added. "They would include whether the president should be in Washington or not."

"Yes, I will be there," Johnson responded. "They are not going to run me out of town."

Certainly not, McNamara said, but nonetheless "the president's presence in Washington may do more to stimulate than to calm it." And there were other matters related to the protest that needed answers, McNamara added. "We have got to train the Washington police and the National Guard to handle this job. We also have to figure out how to arrest thousands and put them in jail if it is justified. The jails won't hold the numbers that could be arrested."

The conversation eventually circled back to the war.

LBJ brought up a captured document written by a North Vietnamese professor that "showed that the Gallup Poll in this country sustained them in Hanoi." In the document the professor asked, "'How can we believe anything Johnson says if his own people do not believe him?'"

McNamara said the Kissinger formula seemed the appropriate way to go if they stopped the bombing.

The president said he would not stop the bombing unless the North agreed "one, to meet promptly, and two, to push for a settlement."

As they deliberated the bombing pause, McNamara said, it was important that they "know the facts" about the impact of Rolling Thunder, the operational name of the aerial bombardment of North Vietnam. It was a strategy about which McNamara now had grave doubts. As far back as February 1966, according to Vietnam historian Stanley Karnow, the defense secretary had shared those doubts privately with journalists, telling Karnow and other correspondents during a meeting in his hotel room in Honolulu that he believed "no amount of bombing" could end the war. In August 1967 he had testified at hearings on the air war conducted by the Senate's Preparedness Investigative Subcommittee, chaired by Mississippi senator John C. Stennis and dominated by like-minded hawks who wanted to give the military the freedom to bomb at will in the North. At those hearings, which were closed to the press and public, McNamara had asserted that no amount of bombing could stop the enemy "short, that is, of the virtual annihilation of North Vietnam and its people."

American planes had dropped nearly 1.5 million tons on the two Vietnams, more than they had dropped in the European theater during World War II—and some 864,000 tons on the North alone. Yet all through 1967 the effect of the bombing runs had been questioned in American intelligence reports. "The NV transport system has emerged from more than 30 months of bombing with greater capacity and flexibility than it had when Rolling Thunder started," a CIA intelligence memorandum reported in September 1967. "The inventory of freight cars has been maintained and its carrying capacity increased; the number of trucks has also increased despite the high rate of destruction."

Rusk was less dismissive of the impact. "If the bombing isn't having that much effect," he said, referring to the North Vietnamese, "why do they want to stop the bombing so much?"

Rostow, seeking to "sum up" from his perspective, said the bombing had cut industrial and agricultural production in the North and diverted nearly a half million men from other tasks. "If we stop the bombing, it will bring their economy back up and permit them to increase their commitment in the South," Rostow said.

"I do not agree with that," McNamara said.

Johnson shifted the conversation back to politics. He brought up the latest polls and said there seemed to be movement away from the administration position in recent weeks. "We need to get answers to all of these slogans which everybody is making up," he said. "We need a few slogans of our own." Then he framed the dilemma in a way that alarmed his advisers. They were hearing something they had not heard before.

"The president said he did not want any of the information which he was about to discuss to go outside of the room," Tom Johnson wrote in his notes. "The president asked what effect it would have on the war if he announced he was not going to run for another term. He said if it were set either way today, the decision would be that he would not run." He was "already in the goldfish bowl," LBJ said, so it might be "good for all of those who want to have the job" to "come out with the programs and policies and let the American people decide who they believe should be their next president."

Rusk was in no mood for such musings. "You must not go down," he said. "You are the commander in chief and we are in a war. This would have a very serious effect on the country."

"If I were to run again, I would be the first president to do it," Johnson responded. "That is, no other president who has served for part of a term, then for a full term, has ever succeeded himself for another full term."

"I don't think you should appear too cute on this," said McNamara. It was an interesting comment from a defense secretary who himself was burning out that October, privately losing confidence in the war he had prosecuted with such mathematic assuredness in earlier years. It was now obvious to his colleagues and the president that the defense secretary's nerves were raw, even if he could hide the private sadness that overtook him occasionally in the privacy of his Pentagon office. While telling LBJ not to appear too cute, McNamara was already assessing his own way out, from his position, not the war—a job offer from the World Bank.

"What I am asking is: What would this do to the war?" Johnson continued.

"Hanoi would think they have got it made," said Rusk.

"Our people will not hold out four more years," Johnson said. "I want to get rid of every major target. Between now and the election, I am going to work my guts out. I would be sixty-one when I came back in, and I just don't know if I want four more years of this. I would consider telling the American people that it is an awfully long period. But I am afraid it would be interpreted as walking out on our men. We are very divisive. We don't have the press, the newspapers, or the polls with us, although when I get out into the country, it seems different than it is here."

"Victor Riesel, a labor columnist, said you would win by a bigger margin next year than you did before," Rusk noted.

"What I really want to know," Johnson said, "is the effect of the announcement—what we say if we do decide that way, and the timing of it."

"Of course, there would be no worry about money and men," McNamara said. "We could get support for that. I do not know about the psychology in the country, the effect on the morale of the men, and the effect on Hanoi. I do think that they would not negotiate under any circumstances and they would wait for the 1968 elections."

The same group, minus Helms, met again on October 4. There was no talk about Johnson's future this time, only hard words about North Vietnam and negotiations and bombs. Two messages had come in from the Kissinger contact, generating confusion about Hanoi's intentions. The first message quoted Mai Van Bo as saying that a cessation of bombing would elicit "a solemn engagement to talk." That line was missing from the second message. "They are still weaseling on us," Rusk concluded.

Johnson was in a bombs-away mood. He wanted to bomb everything right up to the edge of Hanoi, he said. "I know this bombing must be hurting them. Despite any reports to the contrary. I can feel it in my bones. . . . We need to pour the steel on. Let's hit them every day and go every place except Hanoi."

DOUGLASS CATER, another White House aide, had what he called his "bi-monthly clash" at lunch with James (Scotty) Reston of the *New York Times* that day. He began by reading from Reston's latest column, which accused LBJ of addressing "the politics rather than the policy of the problems" in Vietnam. This was "bad history and bad analysis," Cater lectured Reston. He said the columnist might understand how wayward his thinking was if he read Bruce Catton's *Terrible Swift Sword*. That book, as Cater described it in a memorandum to President Johnson, "recounts the misguided criticisms of Horace Greeley, the Scotty Reston of his day, against Lincoln during the awful middle years of the Civil War."

Reston "lamented the spectacle we were creating throughout the world of an idealistic nation that was coming more and more to rely on pure power." Cater answered that there was a "certain amount of hypocrisy in the public position of foreign political leaders," who for the most part were "not really so critical in private." Reston then took "a different turn in the argument by asking what we really hoped to accomplish in Vietnam. We were committed to get out within six months of a settlement. Obviously, we would never go back in if trouble flared again. What would all the death and suffering have accomplished?"

A few days later White House officials picked up early word of another development in the journalism world more problematic than a Scotty Reston column. *Life* magazine, once a pillar of establishment support for the war, was preparing an October editorial calling on the Johnson administration to stop bombing North Vietnam and negotiate a peace settlement. Henry Luce, founding editor of Time-Life, had died earlier in 1967, and his death had coincided with a significant shift in his magazine empire's view of the world in general and Vietnam in particular. Hedley Donovan, the new editor of Time-Life publications, had returned from Vietnam that year rethinking his support and talking about journalists who ought to consider "saying out loud that they were wrong about the war." That is precisely what the editorial would do. In *Life*'s revised view, the United States had gone into Vietnam "for honorable and sensible purposes," but the task "proved to be harder, longer, and more complicated than had been foreseen" and it was no longer vital enough "to ask young Americans to die for."

The liberal *Times* was one thing, a dovish *Life* quite another. News of the imminent antiwar editorial heightened the siege atmosphere at the White House.

During that second week in October, newspapers in New York and Washington were presenting the latest analysis from General Giap, which stirred more controversy. Americans tended to think that Vo Nguyen Giap was the unchallenged voice of the North Vietnamese military, but that was a misreading. Sick for much of the summer and early fall of 1967, he had spent weeks at a time in Hungary, recovering from a heart ailment. Hanoi's military planning for the next year was being done largely without him and even at times against his advice. But what he had to say, internally or for world consumption, still carried great weight. Giap too was now declaring the war a stalemate, according to a CIA translation of a lengthy assessment he wrote for the North Vietnamese Armed Forces newspaper. And a stalemate meant that eventually his side would win. No matter how many troops the United States sent to Vietnam, the stalemate would persist. The Americans were unlikely to invade the North, he suggested, because that would only further dilute their forces and run the risk of bringing China into the conflict. His side would outlast the Americans in a protracted war. America did not have the stomach for it, he said, especially with so many people in the United States already opposed to the military intervention in Vietnam. In the second-to-last paragraph of the *New York Times* story, Giap was said to have called the antiwar movement in the United States "a valuable mark of sympathy."

This last comment did not signify anything new. The antiwar movement had been praised in Liberation Radio broadcasts and propaganda from Hanoi since the troop buildup began in 1965. As the war continued, the peace movement in the United States became an increasingly important factor in the strategy of the National Liberation Front and the politicians in Hanoi. At provincial meetings during the summer of 1967, local Viet Cong officials had been lectured on the details of Resolution 13, a measure adopted by the North Vietnamese Communist party (Lao Dong) that "mentioned antiwar sentiment in the U.S." and "dissension between hawks and doves and between negroes and whites." According to an American intelligence report based on captured documents and prisoner interrogations, "the stated VC policy was that the longer the war continued, the stronger the U.S. doves would become and the Viet Cong were therefore dedicated to fight at least until the 1968 presidential election." The prevailing view in Hanoi was that the Johnson administration was "losing prestige" and that LBJ might "lose to a dove candidate."

All of this, but especially Giap's assertion that the antiwar movement was valuable to his side, provoked a vitriolic congressional debate about the meaning of wartime dissent. Speaker John W. McCormack, an old-line Johnson loyalist, strode to the well of the House on October 11 with a copy of the *Times* rolled in his hand and angrily pounded the table with it as he denounced critics of the American war effort. "If I was one of those, my conscience would disturb me the rest of my life," McCormack said. He followed with an obligatory homage to freedom of speech that served as a rhetorical bridge to further denunciation of outspoken doves: "Nobody argues with the right to dissent. But if I had an opinion that I thought would be adverse to the interests of my country, I would withhold it." A hundred congressmen rose to a standing ovation in the House chamber and bathed their old speaker in thunderous applause. His attack was seconded by another party loyalist, Emanuel Celler of New York, who said that Johnson's detractors "wear their criticism as if it was a badge of intellectual superiority."

In the Senate, Republican minority leader Everett McKinley Dirksen had launched a vigorous bipartisan defense of President Johnson a few days earlier. "He has a little stronger chemical in his system than others," explained Dean Rusk, when Johnson wondered aloud at a meeting of his war council how the hoarse-throated septuagenarian Illinois senator could "stand up and be my defender the way he has been." The first line of Dirksen's defense was to challenge the president's critics, saying they had gone beyond "due bounds." Dirksen was talking primarily not about liberal Democrats, and certainly not about activist students, but rather was aiming at moderate members of his own party who had turned against the war, senators like Charles Percy, his Illinois colleague, Thurston B. Morton of Kentucky, and Clifford P. Case of New Jersey.

Dissent, Case responded, was not only within due bounds, it was vital to democracy. "Just as it was proper for the Senator from Illinois to call to the attention of us our responsibility not to weaken the cause of our nation, the cause of freedom in the world, so I think it is equally important for all of us to meet our responsibility, when we disagree with the conduct of affairs by our government, to state that disagreement as clearly and distinctly as possible, whether in time of peace or in time of war." One of the lead critics on the Democratic side, Senator J. W. Fulbright of Arkansas, chairman of the Senate Foreign Relations Committee, said the hostile atmosphere was not caused by the war's opponents but by the war itself, which had created "an unhealthy atmosphere of suspicion and recrimination." And it was the war, Fulbright argued, that was threatening to turn LBJ's Great Society into a sick society.

Vietnam consumed Congress no less than the White House in those days of October. Senate Majority Leader Mike Mansfield of Montana, a moderate Democrat who was universally respected as he operated in the space between his president and antiwar liberals in his party, was now pushing hard for a United Nations role in peace negotiations, a concept that had the support of at least thirty senators. Senator George McGovern of South Dakota (whose daughter Susan was in Madison, a senior at the University of Wisconsin) sent a memorandum to the White House on October 12 in which he urged the president to halt the bombing of North Vietnam indefinitely and tell Saigon that "we now expect them to assume a greater burden of responsibility for the conduct of this war and for securing negotiations to end it." McGovern also offered some military advice that related directly to what Terry Allen and Clark Welch and their soldiers were doing in the Long Nguyen Secret Zone that week. "Recognizing that this is a struggle for people rather than territory," McGovern wrote, "we should quietly replace the search and destroy operations with clear and hold operations in the South."

The next day thirty members of the House sent an open letter to Johnson expressing alarm "at the increasing escalation of bombings by American planes over North Vietnam." The bombing campaign "has been tried and has failed to accomplish its objectives," the congressmen argued, so "the time has come" to stop it and open the way for "a reasonable and peaceful settlement of this tragic conflict." Among those signing the letter was Robert W. Kastenmeier, whose district included Madison.

ALL WAS AFLAME THAT OCTOBER. The war, the antiwar, the fields and jungles of Vietnam, the halls of Congress, the campuses of America. *Pour the steel on,* Lyndon Johnson said.

But his battle was more than bombs and statistics. It also involved trying to make the hardest case against his enemies, real and perceived. Who were these people in the antiwar movement? What were their connections? Who was funding them? Why were they organizing a nationwide week of protests against the draft and the war, preparing to spread a fire of dissent from the recruiting station in Oakland to Bascom Hill in Madison to the mall in Washington? How could they march on the Pentagon and dare to think they could run the president out of town? Were Communists behind all this?

Some in the Johnson White House suspected they were, and the CIA had been given the clandestine mission to find out. Two months earlier, in the heat of August, the agency's counterintelligence staff had set up a special operations group to monitor "radical students and U.S. Negro expatriates as well as travelers passing through certain select areas abroad." Its goal was to determine the extent to which the Soviets, Chinese, and Cubans were "exploiting our domestic problems in terms of espionage and subversion." The operation would soon take on a presumptuously descriptive code name, CHAOS. By the middle of October, the CIA had collected enough surveillance data to begin preparing a report about the international connections of the U.S. peace movement.

There was, it turned out, not much substance to the argument that antiwar groups were part of—or unwitting dupes of—a worldwide red conspiracy, though a few antiwar leaders had "close Communist associations," and contacts between some leaders of the movement and Hanoi were "almost continuous," the CIA determined. That September, in a well-publicized event, a group of forty American activists had met with representatives from North Vietnam and the National Liberation Front at Bratislava, Czechoslovakia. The U.S. delegation was leaderless and diverse, including academics and magazine editors along with such better-known leftist figures as old-line radical David Dellinger and SDS leader Tom Hayden. The Vietnamese representatives made it clear that they were not interested in negotiating with the U.S. government, at least not before American troops were withdrawn and the bombing of North Vietnam was permanently halted.

Phom Van Chuong, who three and a half decades later would be serving as the deputy director of the foreign relations commission of the party central committee in Hanoi, was then stationed in Prague as a youth and student representative of the NLF and attended the Bratislava meeting. He remembered that the antiwar activists gave a briefing on what "they were planning to do in America against the war—the mass mobilization and march on Washington [planned for October]." The Americans, he said, "asked a lot of questions" about the intentions of the Vietnamese and NLF, citing reports in the western press and asking "for verification." It was clear to him that his visitors were more willing to believe the Vietnamese than what they read in their own newspapers. "The U.S. administration had talked a lot about peace and negotiations and from the Vietnam side there had been no positive response," Chuong recalled. "So the Americans present in Bratislava asked what was the position of the NLF to a peaceful solution, and we explained our position based on national independence." At the time, preparations were already under way for the massive Tet Offensive that would come little more than four months later, but those plans were still a fairly tightly held secret in the top echelons in Hanoi and unknown to Chuong and his comrades who dealt with the American activists.

News of the Bratislava gathering—including Tom Hayden's bravado comment that "now we are all Viet Cong"—was a source of tension within the larger antiwar community back home. The mainstream peace movement, including such groups as Americans for Democratic Action and SANE, believed that the way to end the war was through negotiations, not by openly supporting the other side. But even the contacts with the NLF and North Vietnamese by some American radicals did not, in the CIA's analysis, mean that the antiwar movement was part of a worldwide communist conspiracy. There were very few contacts between antiwar groups and the Soviet or Chinese governments, and the peace movement was too diverse and freewheeling to be under anyone's control. With or without Communist support, "most of the Vietnam protest activity" would go on in any case, the CIA noted. "Diversity is the most striking single characteristic of the peace movement at home and abroad," the agency concluded. "Indeed it is this very diversity which makes it impossible to attach specific political or ideological labels to any significant section of the movement."

In their intensive investigation of "the peace umbrella," the CIA analysts wrote, they found "pacifists and fighters, idealists and materialists, internationalists and isolationists, democrats and totalitarians, conservatives and revolutionaries, capitalists and socialists, patriots and subversives, lawyers and anarchists, Stalinists and Trotskyites, Muscovites and Pekingese, racists and universalists, zealots and nonbelievers, puritans and hippies, do-gooders and evildoers, nonviolent and very violent." What brought them all together was not outside money or manipulation but "their opposition to US actions in Vietnam." They did not join for a single reason—"there are as many motives as there are groups"—and they operated on different levels, some driven by political impulses, some by more personal motivations. "Out of such diversity comes much confusion and more than a little disagreement." A few key activists had found ways to move between the various groups and coordinate the action to some degree, but the movement was "too big and too amorphous to be controlled by any one political faction." And some of the factions, especially among students on the New Left, seemed to exert as much energy "countering each other" as dealing with anyone else.

The CIA assessment painted a realistic picture of the antiwar movement in all of its messy urgency, the broad colorful splash of American dissent, nothing simplistic in black and white, though CHAOS was also churning up just enough gossipy morsels about individual activist leaders to hold Johnson's attention. But there was a corollary of sorts to the question of who controlled the antiwar movement: who controlled the war? That is, specifically, who controlled the war being fought by the liberation forces in Vietnam?

One theme often used by the American peace movement was that the National Liberation Front was an indigenous and autonomous entity and that the war in the South was driven by nationalism more than revolutionary ideology. There were, to be sure, antiwar radicals, many of them at universities such as Wisconsin, who rhetorically at least supported the North Vietnamese Communists and hoped that they would win the war. The argument made by some, refuted by later events, was that Ho or his successors would not impose a doctrinaire totalitarian state. But the primary focus of the antiwar movement was more benign and focused on the NLF, not the North Vietnamese. The liberation front, established in 1960 at the dawn of the war, was presented as a broad-based organization that could accommodate progressive non-communists and anyone else who opposed the Saigon regime. It was maintained that the NLF would run the South if the liberation forces prevailed, or be part of a coalition government if negotiations succeeded. One of the most popular chants on campuses in the United States was "Ho, Ho, Ho Chi Minh, the NLF is gonna win!" The slogan said NLF, not North Vietnam.

Nationalism and patriotism were definitely part of the mix, but history would show that the North, not the NLF, was stirring the bowl. Some antiwar activists were as naïve and mistaken about the lines of power in Vietnam as some supporters of the war were cynical and mistaken about the lines of power in the American antiwar movement. But who controlled whom in Vietnam was still an open question in 1967. For two years the Johnson administration had been trying to prove that North Vietnam controlled the NLF and the Viet Cong and virtually all the key decisions of war and peace, and in October 1967 the State Department had accumulated enough captured documents—"several million pages"—to make a strong case. As part of the larger public relations battle, it prepared a footnoted, seventy-four-page white paper entitled "The North Vietnamese Role in the War in South Vietnam."

"While the insurgency has been in part South Vietnamese from the start, the North Vietnamese involvement has been determining at every stage," the white paper asserted. "The scope of this northern involvement is all-encompassing. It extends from the power of decision to make war, which the Lao Dong Party Politburo exercised in 1959, to the power of decision to make peace, which the Politburo has so far chosen not to exert. It includes the definition of strategy, and the provision of the indispensable means—human as well as material. In both the political and military sphere, the authority of Hanoi is final." Captured documents showed that the North Vietnamese were astute about how they would present a less threatening public face. Great care was taken to scrub revolutionary rhetoric from directives that the people of the South might see and to replace it with patriotic messages. A captured party letter in 1966 criticized the movement's Liberation News Agency for referring openly to "Uncle Ho, party leadership, class struggle, etc." and said revealing propaganda of that sort was "not appropriate." Provincial committees were told they could hang party flags and portraits of Ho "only in conferences held by party chapters"; at any conferences attended by noncommunists they should hang the NLF flag and a portrait of the chairman of the front, Nguyen Huu Tho.

The organizational structure North Vietnam set up to control the war in the South was complex, but all flow charts pointed north to south. The main link—"the one to which all others are ultimately subordinate"—ran from the Central Committee and Politburo of the Lao Dong Party in Hanoi to its southern branch, known as the Central Committee of the People's Revolutionary Party, which was said to comprise "30 to 40 high-ranking Communists," although its size and composition varied. The real power to make decisions within that committee fell to an elite group of its highest-ranking members, known as COSVN, the Central Office for South Viet Nam. COSVN itself had "two major arms"—military and political, and the military arm was the equivalent of MACV under General Westmoreland, overseeing both the Viet Cong and North Vietnamese troops, with the general staff "heavily weighted with prominent North Vietnamese officers." North Vietnamese General Nguyen Chi Thanh had been the chief officer of COSVN, with both military and political status, until July 1967, when he died of a heart attack while attending a party function in Hanoi.

Although some antiwar members of Congress and leaders of the peace movement were calling on the Johnson administration to negotiate with the NLF, the Lao Dong Party in Hanoi in fact had full authority in that realm. Ho Chi Minh, the symbolic link between the nationalist and socialist impulses, was ailing. He had turned seventy-seven in May of that year and spent much of the summer and fall convalescing in a mountain retreat outside Beijing. Most of the key letters and communiqués from Hanoi regarding negotiations were coming from Le Duan, the party's chief executive under Ho. "There are those who hold the view that the political struggle is of major importance, but such a view is different from ours as to degree and time to use this strategy," Le Duan wrote in one party letter. "At present the U.S. imperialists . . . are trying to force us to the negotiation table for some concessions," but the time for negotiations had not come yet, he added. Another document from Lieutenant General Nguyen Van Vinh, who was both a military man and a political leader, appraised the negotiating climate from various perspectives. The Americans, he said, "find it necessary to negotiate." A number of other countries, including East European socialist countries, "hold the view that conditions for negotiations do prevail, and are ripe for achieving success. (The Americans would withdraw their troops, and we will continue the struggle to achieve total success.)" China, on the other hand, "holds the view that conditions for negotiations are not yet ripe, not until a few years from now, and even worse, seven years from now. In the meantime, we should continue fighting."

The decision, in any case, would rest with the Lao Dong politburo, Vinh wrote. The future "may lead to negotiations," he said, but even while negotiating his side would "continue fighting the enemy more vigorously."

"DEAN, I WANT TO KNOW all you know and think about Pennsylvania," President Johnson said to Dean Rusk at a meeting of his war council on October 16. *Pennsylvania* was the code name for Henry Kissinger's back channel operation.

"We haven't seen any serious response from Hanoi," Rusk replied. "They are not in the business of talking about negotiations at this stage. It has been a one-way conversation." It was Rusk's hunch that Bo wanted the talks about the talks to continue, and not just because that meant the United States would maintain its ten-mile limit on bombing around Hanoi.

McNamara agreed. He said he expected nothing to develop in the next few weeks. "What does matter is what we do in the next three to four months."

LBJ wanted to know about the joint chiefs. "What was General Wheeler's reaction to all this?" he asked. Earle G. Wheeler, chairman of the Joint Chiefs of Staff, was just returning to action full time after recovering from a heart attack. His staff was finishing a long report on how the military wanted to fight the war that would be presented to Johnson the next day.

McNamara said, "General Wheeler's reaction was one of concern if we pause and the North Vietnamese take advantage of it. He is not concerned if they do not take military advantage, although he does not believe it will bring about negotiations. General Wheeler was tolerant of our views given the domestic situation we have."

"What damage would we suffer with a pause?" Johnson asked.

"There is a possibility we will suffer no damage. We could develop our own talk-and-fight strategy," McNamara said. "I would recommend a pause because of the domestic plus it would be."

"How long a pause?" Rusk asked.

"You will never have a long enough pause to satisfy Fulbright and others," said McNamara. "A pause of at least a month would be necessary."

Rusk said he had just talked with Hedley Donovan of Time-Life. "As you know, they are coming out with an editorial next week in *Life* which calls for a halt in the bombing." (In fact the issue was hitting the newsstands that day.) Donovan, Rusk said, "thinks a lot of people will have their minds changed with a pause. We would not get much out of a short pause with international public opinion."

What if the enemy resumes military operations? Johnson wondered.

"We would resume military operations if they did," McNamara said.

The CIA's Richard Helms joined the discussion. "I do not think anything will come out of the Pennsylvania channel," he said. "It will get information back to Hanoi. But I do not expect to get anything out of it."

"The proposal we made to them was almost too reasonable," Rusk said.

IN MADISON AT THAT HOUR antiwar leaders were positioned outside the Memorial Union and along the paths leading up Bascom Hill, passing out leaflets with the bold headline: "Dow: The Predictable Explosion."

In Vietnam, twelve time zones ahead, October 17 had already arrived, and in the predawn darkness at the Black Lions' night defensive position, Clark Welch was restless, upset that he had lost a tactical argument with his battalion commander, Terry Allen.

In Washington President Johnson looked around the room at his war council and asked, "How are we ever going to win?"

CHAPTER 12

NO MISSION TOO DIFFICULT

THE FOURTEENTH HAD BEEN A MISERABLE DAY out there. No men were killed, no search-and-destroy patrols went awry, no ambushes were set up, barely any ammunition was expended, nothing more than a few random M-16 sprays into the menacing jungle. Still, things seemed relentlessly difficult from morning to night. It was moving day for Terry Allen and his 2/28 Black Lions, who had been working the Long Nguyen Secret Zone for six days when the decision came to relocate their field camp several kilometers to the north and east along the Ong Thanh stream.

First they had to close the night defensive position they were abandoning. That meant burying the battalion's junk to prevent industrious Viet Cong from putting every recovered scrap of tin and plastic to productive use, filling in the bunker holes, smoothing the ground, and emptying the canvas sand bags so they could be carried to the next spot, twenty to forty per man. The ground was muddy, the bags were soaked, and the cleanup took more time and muscle than usual. When they finally went out, Bill Erwin's scout platoon led the way, followed by Jim George's Alpha, Jim Kasik's Bravo, and Clark Welch's Delta. (Charlie Company was breaking in a new commander and not yet in the field.) They walked with the stream on their left and the jungle to their right. It was what Erwin described as "a ball buster" of a march. He was constantly rotating his point man, who often had to use a machete to clear the way through heavy, entangling brush—"wait-a-minute brush," some infantrymen called it—wielding the sword two-handed as the next man in formation carried his M-16.

The October sun pounded down on them and the temperature shot to ninety-four. Many of the soldiers moved sockless through the soggy marshland. Their boots were wet and itchy, the black shine long since washed to gray, but at least the boots could crack-dry in the sun; nothing seemed more uncomfortable than soggy socks that never fully dried. Now and then someone slipped waist-deep into a buffalo hole filled with monsoon rainwater. Their shirts were drenched with sweat from the stifling humidity. One man collapsed from heat exhaustion and had to be helped the rest of the way. Lieutenant Colonel Allen, hobbled by an ankle sore, observed the march from his little command-and-control bubble helicopter circling overhead. Travel on the ground looked so deceptively easy from that airborne perspective. He thought his battalion was moving too slowly and radioed down to Erwin to pick up the pace.

Walk two steps, stand around for half a minute, move ten yards, wait five minutes, the companies now stacking up, breathing heavily, now spreading out. It took all day to negotiate a curved and uneven route that ended up only six kilometers from where they started. Gerald Thompson of Maryville, Tennessee, a squad leader in Delta Company, was in agony the entire time, his boots waterlogged, both his big toes swollen and black and blue, sharp pain streaking up his body whenever an ingrown toenail scraped against boot leather. They walked along the earthen dikes of fallow rice paddies and found traces of old enemy camps on the edges of their route but no stores of food or ammunition. Every hour or so, from his company's position in the rear, Clark Welch sent out small squads on cloverleaf patterns to scout the nearby jungle and make sure no one was following them. A few times his men thought they saw flashes of movement and fired into the trees. No contact, so they kept going, cautiously following the stream as it meandered up and across the uneven terrain of lower Binh Long Province.

The new night defensive position was being set up when the rear forces of Delta arrived. Welch was disappointed by the location. The ground was low, swampy and exposed. The site was as bad as the last one, which none of the men had liked—or worse. To build fighting position bunkers here was no easy task. Many of the holes started filling with water as they were being dug. There were ants everywhere, even falling from the trees like nasty little bombers. Private Frank McMeel was miserable from ant bites; he had misplaced his towel, which he usually draped around his neck to ward off the falling ants. Darkness coming in a rush, exhausted men shoveling in the gloaming drizzle of the open field, sometimes having to use C-4 explosives to blast open hard laterite soil, not enough time to bring in resupply helicopters for a hot meal, C-rations for dinner instead, guard duty after all that, two hours on, two hours off—the fourteenth was a long day that did not end well.

The command readjusted the perimeter the next morning, moving some troops a hundred meters to ground that was higher and half-protected by bamboo and trees. They were now near the intersection of two intermittent streams, the Ong Thanh and Ba Gia. The coordinates were noted in the daily log and radioed back to Lai Khe—XT684586. This is where the First Division operations center wanted Allen's Black Lions to be—on the northern rim of the Long Nguyen Secret Zone, 12.3 miles north of Lai Khe, blocking the path north toward Cambodia, within striking distance of where the latest U.S. intelligence put their long-sought quarry. By whatever name—Q761 or First Regiment to the Vietnamese liberation forces, the 271st to the Americans—elements of the elusive unit were now thought to be closer than ever in the jungle to the south.

Erwin's recon platoon and Kasik's Bravo Company were sent on the first search-and-destroy patrol from the new location while Alpha and Delta stayed back. They marched due south toward an area that had been targeted for B-52 bomb strikes the day before. Not far into the dense jungle, they discovered "a kind of trail that was really spooky," as Kasik later reported. The trail "consisted of broken saplings to your left and right as you walked down it. If you were not directly between the broken small trees, you would totally miss it." Kasik assumed they had found "a marker system used by the V.C. to move at night." The Americans followed the markers carefully and reached a larger trail, where recon spotted a rucksack placed at the trunk of a tree. Erwin set up an ambush, and soon three Viet Cong soldiers came into view, walking north. One was shot in the surprise attack, but his two comrades pulled him along as they made their escape, leaving behind the wounded man's canteen and a pair of blood-stained sandals. Kasik took the canteen, Erwin the sandals—mementoes of war.

The mission that day and the spoils the officers brought back added to the cocksure sensibility of the battalion leadership. Yes, the long march of the day before had been trying, but overall the experience in the fields of the secret zone that month had built their confidence. They were the Black Lions, feared unit of the powerful Big Red One. It seemed apparent to Allen and some of his aides that they had the enemy on the run, that the Viet Cong did not want to stand and fight, and that an American victory inevitably would result when and if a battle developed.

A few days earlier, during a search-and-destroy operation out of their first NDP (night defensive position), Bravo and Delta had wandered into the largest VC base camp they had ever seen, larger than three football fields, in "good repair but otherwise unoccupied," according to Kasik. When they had reported their find back to Allen, he had responded with the bold order, "Each bunker gets a grenade." Kasik had joked with Welch that they would have to "put in a rail line and haul box cars of grenades in" to carry out the command, but they tossed as many grenades as they had with them. There was little voiced concern that a base camp of that size, though empty, might portend danger. On another patrol that first week, Alpha Company had chased after a lone Viet Cong soldier at dusk. They had wounded him and picked up his AK-47, which he dropped while escaping. Jim George double-timed his troops back to the defensive perimeter as the sun fell and brought the captured souvenir to the nightly meeting of the Black Lions command group, where the other officers "had some good laughs" about it. George went along with it, but he was not feeling invulnerable himself. As he rushed his men back to the safety of their protective bunkers, an eerie sensation had washed over him. He wrote in a letter to his wife, Jackie, that he had "a very bad feeling" about the mission in the secret zone.

FOR PROSAIC, OBVIOUS, AND ODD REASONS, or for no discernible reason at all, soldiers came and went, even when the battalion was in the middle of an operation. Joe Costello, the grenadier in Alpha's second platoon, rejoined his company on the morning of the fifteenth after spending a week in the infirmary at Lai Khe, where he was treated for a huge abscess on his ankle. Someone snapped a photograph of Costello as he waited for the Huey that ferried him back to the field. He was sitting in the scruffy grass near a helicopter pad, a lanky, dark-haired private of only eighteen, knees drawn toward his chest, arms tucked under his legs, helmet and rifle to the side, eyes squinting into the sunlight.

What was Costello thinking as he sat there? *If only I had said I could type.* When word had gone out that the company was looking for a clerk, Costello had thought about applying for the job but decided not to because the clerk was supposed to have minimum typing skills, which he lacked. Now, looking forward to another round of grunt work in the field, he thought, *Damn, I could have volunteered for the thing. How much typing could there be? They wouldn't have given me a test. What a jerk!* He was confident by nature, not afraid, but still he wanted to make sure that he got back home to his high school sweetheart on Long Island. Behind him were piles of supplies headed for the field with him—ammo boxes, weapons, food, clothes, including a new pair of pants for Michael (Peewee) Gallagher and a fresh web vest for Allan V. Reilly, two members of his platoon. Peewee and Reilly would be "feeling all spiffy about their clean, new clothes" when the shipment arrived. Their reaction, such a simple pleasure, stuck in Costello's mind's eye as a grain of unsullied memory.

The same Huey that brought him in might have taken Gerald Thompson out on the return flight. As Costello's ankle healed, Thompson's toes worsened. The long march had aggravated his ingrown toenails so much that he now was rendered virtually immobile, and a medic recommended that he go back to Lai Khe for treatment, which entailed wearing flip-flops and soaking his feet three times a day. The point man in Thompson's squad, Fred Kirkpatrick of Stow, Ohio, also left that morning on a helicopter that took him down to Bien Hoa. He was yanked from the field for a welcome but unexpected week of R and R in Japan. Kirkpatrick had put in for the vacation with his squadmate and good friend Ronnie Reece. He expected Reece to get the break but not him, since he already had taken five days off in June. Military bureaucracies work in mysterious ways: Kirkpatrick was approved, Reece denied. Kirkpatrick did not complain; he was exhausted from the daily grind and glad to be getting away. In the morning stillness, before leaving the NDP, he had a brief talk with his buddy Reece, who confided that he was nervous about going out on another mission. Kirkpatrick tried to ease his mind by borrowing ten dollars from him, promising to repay it when he returned. In Bien Hoa later that day, as he awaited his flight to Japan, Kirkpatrick scribbled a lighthearted letter to Gerald Thompson, the "Baddest Squad Leader in Delta" Company.

"Hello Dude, how's the infantry life going?" he began, as though he had been away from that life so long that he could barely remember. "I've been in the NCO club most of today and the rest of the time in the EM [enlisted men's] club. I'm about half drunk now. Hope you guys are staying out of trouble; I'd sure hate to come back and find no squad."

The letter was postmarked the next day, October 16, from Japan.

Kirkpatrick, a battle-tested rifleman who took pride in walking point for his squad, was one of nine Delta soldiers on R and R that week. Another seven had contracted malaria during the rainy season and were recovering in the medical wards of the Ninety-third and Twenty-fourth evacuation hospitals at Long Binh. Ten more were being treated for wounds suffered in the battalion's skirmishes during the first half of October. And at least that number were back in Lai Khe with various problems ranging from swollen feet to combat fatigue. The unit that Clark Welch had in the field was a thin shadow of a company. By the book he might have had 185 men, and at least 140. According to the personnel roster for October 1967 he had 92, including cooks, supply staff, and a mortar platoon that did not leave the NDP. Jim George's Alpha Company was equally shorthanded. There were almost half a million American military personnel in Vietnam, and General Westmoreland was clamoring for more, but only one in eight was going to infantry units that did most of the fighting and were being further depleted every week.

Nothing to be done about it; most vacancies just sat there, ghosts of men left behind. Only a few positions were considered essential and filled quickly. Every company had a forward artillery liaison team, usually a lieutenant and sergeant detached from an artillery battery who walked with infantry commanders and called in artillery strikes during search-and-destroy missions. Clark Welch had been working with a new team since the start of Operation Shenandoah II, but he had an uneasy feeling about the lieutenant, who "thought he was hot shit." Late one afternoon, after a long day in the field, Welch watched the lieutenant and sergeant as they sat side by side cleaning their .45s. When the sergeant finished with his weapon, the lieutenant said, "Let me see that!" and grabbed the gun. The gun was turned toward the sergeant. It went off; a bullet ripped into his abdomen an inch above the navel. "Mama! Mama! Mama!" the sergeant shouted.

There was no blood and no bullet; it had lodged in the sergeant's midsection, expending all its energy inside. Before the battalion surgeon arrived, the sergeant was dead. Welch, disgusted, ordered the lieutenant to leave on the same helicopter that carried away the lifeless soldier. The next incoming Huey brought in Delta's new forward artillery liaison officer, a young second lieutenant with a bright smile who had eagerly volunteered for the job. He was Harold Bascom Durham Jr. of Tifton, Georgia, who had answered to one nickname since the day he was born in a hospital that had run out of blue blankets. A random act, reckless gunplay by his predecessor, is what brought Pinky Durham out to march with the Black Lions along the bamboo-shaded edge of the Ong Thanh.

The thinness of their ranks drained bravado from the men. So did daily contact, or near contact, with the enemy. Many of the officers might be exuding confidence, but more soldiers were feeling that they were being used, or misused, as pawns in the larger search-and-destroy strategy. During the long march, the man in front of Alpha Company radioman Ernest Buentiempo turned back to him as they slogged through the brush and muttered, "Ernie, we ain't nothin' but a chain of fools."

Back at Lai Khe, Lieutenant Tom Grady, now Jim George's executive officer at Alpha Company, was spending more time as a psychological counselor, the same role he had played during the July voyage to Vietnam aboard the troopship. A private balked at an order to rejoin the company in the field. Grady was given the job of "getting him straight," as he recounted later. "I talked to the kid and he was a nice kid and I sat him down and said, 'Look, you gotta go. You gotta go. We gotta go.'

"He said, 'Sir, I'm scared.'

"'We're all scared,' I said. 'If you think I'm less scared than you are, you're nuts.' He said, 'I'm just too scared to go.' I said, 'But you've got to go, because what'll happen is when you refuse, when I say, "Private, get your gear, get on the helicopter, go to the forward area," if you refuse it's disobedience of a direct and lawful order. I'll then have to put charge sheets together. You'll be court-martialed. The normal sentence is six months confinement, reduced to lowest enlisted rank and forfeiture of two-thirds pay'—it's called Six and Two-Thirds—'You'll go to Long Binh Jail for six months and the bad part is that's bad time. You still have to do your full year. You're scared? We're all scared. You just gotta go. We'll get through this together. Just stick with me. Stick with somebody and we'll all get through this.' And he was a good kid." Reluctantly, the private joined his buddies in the field.

AT A QUARTER AFTER SEVEN on the evening of the fifteenth, General Westmoreland took leave of his family at Clark Field in the Philippines and flew back to Saigon to prepare for another week as commander of American forces in Vietnam. In his wallet he carried a slip of paper on which he had scribbled a few words to remind him of what he considered most important for his soldiers: Food, mail, and medical care.

The scorecard in those areas was not perfect but mostly good.

The lives of wounded American soldiers were being saved at unparalleled rates by skilled doctors, nurses, and medical evacuation teams that could get wounded men to field hospitals within a half hour of a battle. There were complaints about mail service, to be sure, and a hot rumor spreading from base to base, according to army intelligence reports, that "pacifists employed in the San Francisco Post Office" were "deliberately delaying the mail in order to undermine the morale of troops in Vietnam." Army postal authorities were said to have documented a deterioration in mail service and were investigating the cause. There were periods when the men got shut out for a week or more, then a whole delayed batch came in, but at other times the letters that Danny Sikorski received from his sister Diane in Milwaukee, for instance, came almost as dependably as if they were being sent to Green Bay instead of Lai Khe.

As for Westmoreland's third necessity, if wars were decided by food alone, this one would have been an overwhelming victory for the United States. In an effort to make GIs feel at home, the military built more than forty ice cream plants in Vietnam. One was at the base in Lai Khe. In the First Division every effort was made to fly in at least one hot meal a day to troops in the field, often including gravy and mashed potatoes, with even a garnish of parsley—and pastries for the morning. When Alpha Company soldiers returned to base camp, they walked past barrels filled with Coke and beer on ice. Steve Goodman, a Black Lions armorer who also served as the unofficial acquisitions expert for his battalion, traveled down to Long Binh twice a month and was amazed by what he could find in the huge warehouses there—"everything from soup to nuts . . . Coke, Pepsi, piled as far as the eye could see, mountains of stuff."

The list of basics was in Westmoreland's wallet, but there were more pressing matters on his mind when his plane touched down at Tan Son Nhut Air Base that autumn Sunday night and he was chauffeured to his villa in a black Chrysler Newport that had four silver stars above the front bumper. For more than a week he had been exchanging telex messages with Major General Robert G. Fergusson, his former classmate (class of 1936) at West Point, now the American military commander in Berlin. Fergusson's son Bob had been critically wounded, shot in the head, while serving as a forward observer for the 101st Airborne Division during a search-and-destroy mission in Vietnam on October 8. Young Bob was now at the Ninety-seventh Evacuation Hospital in Qui Nhon, slipping in and out of consciousness, his brain damaged, fighting for his life. Westmoreland could not possibly know the personal story of every wounded soldier under his command, so in a sense Fergusson's struggle became representative of them all. He received hospital reports daily and passed them along to General and Mrs. Fergusson in Germany. Would medical care make any difference for this twenty-four-year-old lieutenant? The latest report from the hospital showed slow improvement, vital signs stable.

Westmoreland also had to deal with the fallout from a report from Vietnam that had appeared on the *CBS Evening News* with Walter Cronkite six days earlier. The story involved a company of the First Division at Lai Khe, in this case not the Black Lions but the First Battalion of the Eighteenth Infantry Regiment. Correspondent Don Webster and a cameraman had gone out with the battalion on a search-and-destroy mission and witnessed soldiers cutting ears from enemy bodies. Here is how it played:

> **Cronkite:** Ambush, surprise attacks, terrorism, brutality, all are part of the character of the Vietnamese conflict. It remains a basically guerrilla war defying the normal conventions of warfare. As such, it can produce savage responses, even among American GIs. CBS newsman Don Webster came across one example at a U.S. Army base camp thirty miles north of Saigon.
>
> **Webster:** This is not a pretty story. In fact, it's a rather appalling one, but there are situations in this war which are appalling, when perfectly normal Americans under the intense pressure of combat do things they'll later be ashamed of.
>
> Last night this base camp, a unit of the First Infantry Division, had a sneak mortar attack. The VC fired hundreds of rounds of mortar into the camp, but the Americans fought back valiantly, and, as dawn came, their own mortars were still firing back. Many air strikes were also called in, pounding the jungle growth where the enemy was believed hiding. All in all, there was little doubt the Americans took more enemy lives than they gave up.
>
> The Viet Cong like to drag away the bodies of their dead to confuse the Americans about how many casualties they took. In

this case the Americans turned the trick, dragged Viet Cong out of the nearby jungle and into the camp. The main reason this was done was to get intelligence, to search the papers on the bodies and find out what unit they were with.

A base camp like this is an eerie sight the morning after a big battle. These men have brushed close to death, and death has passed them by. In a situation like this, nothing is treated more gingerly and more lovingly than the body of a dead companion. Many of these men are still in their teens, impressionable and emotional. They've lost a good friend. They also know it might have been them.

When the battle is over, some of the men keep souvenirs. This Russian-made Viet Cong rifle, and this light machine gun, both taken off dead VC. Sitting in a comfortable living room in the United States this will seem shocking, but you must understand the emotional state of some of these young men and their anger and sorrow at the loss of their buddies. A few of the Americans, as souvenirs of the battle, cut off the ears of the dead Viet Cong to keep as mementos. Of the three dead VC we saw, all three had one or both ears lopped off.

A few days from now these soldiers will probably be as aghast as anyone at what they've done, and the so-called mementos will be quietly thrown away or buried, but for now it's a sort of revenge for lost buddies in a war in which dead enemy are found but no one knows exactly who killed them. It's an emotional outlet.

There were no officers or noncommissioned officers present when this took place. They probably would have stopped this, and, if one must rationalize, we have no indication of what happens to the bodies of American dead which fall into Viet Cong hands.

Don Webster, *CBS News,* with units of the First Division near Lai Khe, South Vietnam.

Short of not running the piece at all, Webster seemed to do everything possible to place the barbarous act in a sympathetic, or at least understandable, context. But his words were lost in this case, overwhelmed by the visual presentation of disembodied ears. Army Chief of Staff Harold K. Johnson heard immediately from congressmen and senators, and he passed his concern along to Westmoreland, who passed it along to his aides, who went looking for answers in Lai Khe. The word came back that the ear-cutting incident did happen, though at first soldiers blamed it on the cameraman, saying that he encouraged them to cut off another ear after noticing an earless head. Westmoreland told Johnson he would supply a complete report as soon as the First division investigation was completed.

"I regret very much this incident," Westmoreland said in a cable to Johnson. "It is, of course, absolutely contrary to all policy and cannot be defended. . . . A reminder relative to policy on this matter is being issued to the entire command."

In addition to the wounded son of a fellow general and ears being knifed off near Lai Khe, Westmoreland was also preoccupied with two impending visits. Retired Lieutenant General James M. Gavin, his former boss at the Eighty-second Airborne Division, had accepted an invitation to take a firsthand look at the war zone, and Vice President Hubert H. Humphrey was also coming at the end of the month to represent the Johnson administration at the inauguration ceremonies for South Vietnamese president Thieu. Humphrey could be counted on to show the flag. From Westmoreland's perspective, Gavin's visit was by far the more ticklish of the two. This was not just another obliging old general desperate to relive his glory days by reviewing the troops one more time. Gavin was a mature star in the American military constellation, the heroic "Jumping General" of World War II who had led his airborne troops into battle at Sicily and Normandy and across the Elbe. Rather than fade away in retirement, he had served as ambassador to France under President Kennedy and had become an increasingly outspoken and independent voice on matters of foreign policy and military strategy. Once long ago, a year after the end of the Second World War, Gavin had taken Westmoreland under his wing, recruiting him to run his 504th Parachute Regiment at Fort Bragg. Now the two men were at odds over Vietnam.

In his public writings and speeches Gavin had denounced Westmoreland's search-and-destroy policy, saying it was a grave mistake to believe that the war could be won through attrition. Even if the United States brought in massive numbers of men and firepower, enough to win on the battlefield, the strategy would only backfire, Gavin argued, by drawing the Chinese further into the war. For similar reasons he considered it a mistake to bomb North Vietnam. He suggested instead that the United States develop an "enclave" policy in which U.S. troops withdrew from the jungles and set up protective cordons around the population centers of the South. In the meantime they should halt the bombing of the North and push for a negotiated settlement. Westmoreland thought Gavin was mistaken in all respects, that he was too removed from the conflict to form an accurate assessment, and that a visit to Vietnam might soften his public posture if not change his mind. But once the invitation was accepted, Gavin loomed as a problem. Telexes from the Pentagon apprised Westmoreland of Gavin's latest public utterances and made it clear that the White House—meaning President Johnson himself—was "quite concerned about what may eventuate" from the visit.

Gavin would be given the complete tour, Westmoreland assured Washington, with one full day in each corps and a final day in Saigon. It was important, he said, that the retired general spend at least five days in country. With that amount of time they could make the case that the war was being won. (In this, as in many things, Westmoreland was overly confident. After the tour Gavin would return to the United States and declare of Vietnam: "We are in a tragedy.")

In Westmoreland's victory scenario, which although optimistic still envisioned the war lasting at least two more years, the First Infantry Division played a central role. The Big Red One had to come through for him. Westmoreland had been insisting all summer and fall that the war of attrition was gaining momentum. The military situation, he maintained, had finally reached what he called the "cross-over" point—which meant that the number of enemy soldiers lost in battle exceeded the number being added through infiltration or local recruitment. His argument was partly a matter of political mathematics—who would be counted in the enemy order of battle and who would not be counted. (He agreed with his new intelligence chief's decision to drop 120,000 Viet Cong self-defense militia from official estimates that fall, a controversial move that infuriated some analysts at the CIA, created a major internal dispute for months, and remained at the center of the Vietnam debate for decades thereafter.) But it was also a matter of offensive warfare. Westmoreland needed his generals to apply constant pressure, to stay on the offensive, search and destroy. And that meant he had to keep pushing the commander of the First Division, Major General Hay.

"Handsome John" Hay was by all outward appearances the very model of a modern major general. He rose from the Rocky Mountain West, a hunter, horseman, and skier from Montana with the rugged good looks that his nickname conveyed. He was six foot three with a sharp, clean face and perpetual tan. He had commanded a platoon and then a company of the famed Tenth Mountain Division in Italy during World War II and later served under Westmoreland as a battle-group commander with the 101st Airborne Division. But from the time he took over the Big Red One in Vietnam in February 1967, there had been a slightly uncomfortable rub in his relationship with the war managers at MACV headquarters.

Westmoreland and the III Corps commander, Major General Frederick C. Weyand, thought Hay was too slow, deliberate, and cautious. They went through the same routine after almost every battle. His superiors would bury Hay with faint praise, congratulating the Big Red One for its performance and then ask, pointedly, why Hay's troops had failed to pursue the enemy at battle's end and allowed it to slip away. Hay's answer to Westmoreland, as he later recounted, was usually the same. "I told him that we pursued by fire (artillery and air) and that risk to troops pursuing overland into territory more familiar to the Viet Cong was not worth it unless we knew where they were." Hay assumed that Westmoreland, who would have preferred "an aggressive overland pursuit World War II–style," nonetheless understood and accepted his reasoning at least to the extent that he was not relieved of command. That was, in fact, a bit of self-deception: in correspondence with the Pentagon that October, Westmoreland had been plotting a rearrangement of his generals in which Hay would be shifted from command to a staff position, to be replaced by someone with "flexibility." According to the transcript of a private discussion between Westmoreland and Weyand about the generals commanding their divisions, Weyand also wanted to have Hay moved.

"Hay has done a tremendous job with that division, but I can't tolerate this business of walking away from a fight just because it gets dark," Weyand said. "We have to hit these people when we have them, not just worry about night defensive positions."

"The enemy isn't attacking night defensive positions anymore anyway," Westmoreland said. "You should have a heart-to-heart with John. I got the impression talking to him that he's planning aggressive tactics."

Hay felt the pressure and thought that he was being unfairly criticized, even conceding his naturally deliberate nature. The enemy main force units in his tactical area of operations had been only intermittently active during that rainy season of 1967 and were "hard to find." The other side could strike and then move across the Cambodian border in a few hours. Also, the weather made it difficult, as did a shortage of helicopters for offensive operations.

Like most commanding officers of his generation, Hay was steeped in the history of the Big Red One, and an unavoidable character in that military story was General Terry Allen. Hay knew all about Terrible Terry and his days leading the Fighting First in North Africa. Alpha Company's Jim George once overheard a radio conversation between Hay and Terry Allen Jr. during which Hay called him Terry (instead of Allen or "Dauntless Six," the code name for a 2/28 Black Lions commander) and said, "Terry, your dad was a great soldier!" In their command styles Hay and the elder Allen could not have been more different. Hay was a man of routine who went by the book, slow and steady, fond of distributing long "Commander Notes" on subjects like how to clean a .45, how to brief your troops, how to cross a river, and how to prevent malaria. Members of his staff knew that if they asked him a question, they were likely to get a lecture. General Allen had been a stickler mostly about one thing: fighting. When he wrote, he wrote about fighting. The rest of it was less important to him. He was a doer, not a talker.

Terry Jr. was somewhere in the middle, not as bold as his father nor as pedantic as Hay. He was personally selected for the job, like all of Hay's battalion commanders, and had to undergo an "audition," showing the general how he would conduct a combat assault. "I demanded perfection and insisted they follow our division SOP [standard operating procedure] to the letter," Hay explained later. Being a battalion commander under him "was not an easy job," he acknowledged, because he "perhaps oversupervised . . . not allowing them very much leeway in a fight, particularly new commanders," lest they "do something stupid" and get a lot of men "killed needlessly."

But now they had a Viet Cong regiment in their sights. The 2/28 Black Lions were moving and preparing to strike. They had a chance to search and *pursue* and destroy. Pressure flows downhill, and here it came thundering down in a molten flood. Down from Lyndon Johnson to William Westmoreland to John Hay. And down from there, down to William Coleman, Hay's deputy; down to George (Buck) Newman, who ran Operation Shenandoah II for the First Brigade; and then down to Terry Allen. *Pour the steel on.*

Yet even then, unknown to the public, and out of sight of Terry Allen and his Black Lions and the other men who did the fighting, a dispute was roiling among the war managers in Washington about whether Westmoreland's strategy of attrition through search-and-destroy missions could ever succeed. General Gavin's grave skepticism on the subject was shared privately by many of McNamara's top analysts at the Pentagon, led by Alain Enthoven and his so-called whiz kids in the Office of Systems Analysis, who had been pointing out the weaknesses in the concept for months in private memos and studies related to Westmoreland's request for more troops. The essence of Westmoreland's strategy was that if the war had reached the mystical crossover point where more enemy troops were being killed than North Vietnam could provide or the Viet Cong could recruit in the South, then the United States, with an even larger force, could search and destroy more of them and improve the crossover ratio to the point of eliminating the enemy army in ten years and debilitating it long before that.

Enthoven's analysts tested this thesis in a study of fifty-six pitched battles fought in Vietnam during the previous year, and they found it illogical. Their central conclusion, in fact, was that "the size of the force we deploy has little effect on the rate of attrition of enemy forces." The determining factor was not battlefield superiority, which usually went to the Americans, but the choice of battles. In a vast majority of cases, the Viet Cong and North Vietnamese controlled whether they would stand and fight. And when they did, according to the study, it was usually because they had initiated the battle. Some 66.2 percent of the battles began with an enemy attack on U.S. troops: the enemy attacked as U.S. troops landed to deploy on the battlefield (12.5 percent), or attacked a static U.S. defensive perimeter (30.4 percent), or ambushed a moving U.S. unit in a preconceived battle plan (23.3 percent). When another category was included—attacks on a moving U.S. unit by the enemy in a dug-in or fortified position in which the engagement came as a virtual surprise to the American tactical commander (12.5 percent)—the percentage of battles involving some element of enemy initiative rose to 78.7 percent. This meant that even though U.S. forces had vastly superior kill ratios on the battlefield, the enemy, at almost any time, could limit losses—and frustrate Westmoreland's attrition strategy—by simply refusing to stand and fight.

On the morning of the sixteenth, Clark Welch's Delta led the way for the Black Lions, with Kasik's Bravo following. They headed out on a search-and-destroy mission at two minutes before eight, marching in a southeasterly direction through an open stretch of heavy bamboo and then moderate-growth jungle. They stayed south of the Ong Thanh but crossed to the far side, or east, of what the Americans called a draw and the Vietnamese identified as the lower extension of a stream. The trees in the jungle beyond the draw were about 120 feet tall at the highest and at places formed a complete canopy overhead. The marshy soil underfoot, littered with deadfall brush and trees, made for slow moving.

Welch felt most comfortable when his company was placed in the lead, as it was that morning. In two-company patrols, the lead company commander had substantial control of the operation, while the rear company commander was there mostly for backup work. The lead commander could set the pace of the march. He could decide how and when to cloverleaf to assess where the enemy might be. Even while taking orders from the battalion commander and others above him, he could make instinctive judgments on where to place his men and whether to diverge slightly from the planned route. And he could control artillery support from the big guns located at fire bases a few miles away.

Welch and his new artillery forward observer, Pinky Durham, had melded into a smooth team in their few days together. They shared a philosophy of using artillery aggressively and proactively. Welch would order what was known as marching fire as soon as he left camp, directing mortar and artillery rounds in front of him, and sometimes to the sides, as his platoons moved forward. This had a dual purpose. The obvious one was to discourage the enemy from setting up an ambush. The less obvious but to Welch more important purpose was to establish an early and continuous dialogue with the artillery officers on the other end of the radio (in this case at a Thirty-third Artillery fire base camp, Caisson V, near the village of Chon Thanh on Route 13), so that when real trouble arose, they would have the bureaucratic procedures authorizing the use of artillery already out of the way, the coordinates established, enough rounds of 105-millimeter shells broken down, and everything ready to aim and fire.

Walking point in front of Delta's troops that morning was a little squad that Welch liked to bring along for patrols through unknown territory. It was a provincial reconnaissance unit comprised of Vietnamese scouts from nearby Ben Cat. Some were former Viet Cong, some were thrill seekers, most were local men who signed up for the money. They were paid as independent contractors—cold cash handed out at the end of a day's work—and they worked only when they felt like it. Their numbers on any given day ranged from two to six men from a pool of twenty. Army Captain Bernard Francis Jones of Coalton, West Virginia, served as their adviser. Jones could speak Vietnamese fluently and implicitly trusted his little squad of irregulars. They looked out for each other, Jones said, and performed important work that went largely unappreciated.

"Important work" in this case meant killing people, an estimated four to five suspected Viet Cong a week. Welch, who understood Vietnamese but was not fluent, was among the few who appreciated them. He believed that the closer the Americans worked with the Vietnamese, the more they understood about Vietnamese behavior patterns, and the more they tapped into local knowledge of the geography, the better they could fight the war. Nonetheless many American soldiers viewed the scouts—Kit Carsons, they were informally called—with skepticism. To them Vietnam was a forbidding and alien place, its people difficult to read. They felt they could trust nothing. A persistent rumor rustling through the enlisted ranks was that some Kit Carsons were surreptitiously working for the other side.

Welch walked near the front of his second platoon, accompanied by his dependable first sergeant, Bud Barrow, and his two radiotelephone operators, both Scotts from Michigan, Jimmy Scott from Detroit and Paul D. Scott from Flint. Scott Up and Scott Down, he called them, Up carrying a radio for contact with battalion headquarters, and Down on a frequency with the platoon leaders. They were both experienced soldiers, and Paul D. Scott had been through several major operations before, including Junction City and Billings. Also in the group was the medic, Joe Lovato Jr., a large and friendly man who knew Welch's fighting tendencies all too well. Lovato carried two stretchers with him that morning, each weighing twenty pounds, along with his oversized medical bag.

What are you carrying two stretchers for? Welch asked.

God damn, Lieutenant Welch, Lovato answered. *Whenever you go out, guys get hurt.*

Welch could not argue; he knew it was true. He had a way of finding the action. His men might get hurt, he conceded, but not killed.

He moved his company south and east with extreme caution. Late in the morning they were a mile from the NDP. At 11:17 they reported back to the operations center that they had located an oxcart trail running through the high brush. An hour later they were in the canopied jungle when a Vietnamese scout scooted back to the command group and reported that they had spotted a few enemy soldiers in what appeared to be a base camp. They could hear them and smell them.

Welch came forward to look for himself. A Viet Cong soldier was sitting on a bunker, facing the other direction, smoking a hand-rolled cigarette or dope. The bunkers hugged the ground, hard to see unless you knew what you were looking for, barely distant cousins of the "Hay hole" bunkers of the First Division, which could be seen from far away. The firing points were only a few inches above ground level. But this soldier was atop the bunker, not in one, and he seemed unconcerned with the possibility that an American patrol was on the search. A Delta soldier standing near Welch said that he had always wanted to make a "silent kill." A macho thing, Welch thought, but he said okay, try it. The soldier took off his shirt and brought out his knife and began crawling forward silently. "And then the Vietnamese started to turn around," Welch later reported. "So I shot and killed him, and that's what started the fight."

The skirmish over the next few hours in some ways seemed easy, as if it had been choreographed, although there was one significant tactical argument near the start. Terry Allen, monitoring the action by radio, wanted to bring in close air support, but Welch said continued artillery would be more helpful because the enemy was hugging so close to him. Okay, Allen said, he would hold off air support for now. By the time Delta soldiers began taking small arms fire, Welch had directed his three platoons into position and set up his M-60 machine guns where he wanted them. He was able to employ fire and maneuver tactics to maintain the offensive, moving one platoon forward in a left hook while another was firing. His platoon leaders were close enough that he could direct them by yelling loudly. Amid all the clatter the voice of the lieutenant, Big Rock, could almost always be heard. He moved his first platoon toward unoccupied enemy bunkers ten yards in front so they could use the low berms for protection. Although there was a tunnel network in the base camp, Welch and his men were not disoriented and had a fairly easy time establishing fire superiority. Mike Troyer even found time to eat a can of peaches. A few enemy soldiers were shot as their heads popped up like prairie dogs from their tunnel holes. Welch and Pinky Durham were in constant touch about how closely to call in the artillery support, which came quickly. Welch also called in mortar rounds from his weapons platoon stationed back at the NDP.

When the shooting began, Kasik positioned the lead Bravo platoon ten yards from Delta's rear position to maintain a connecting file between the two companies. The Bravo soldiers formed a rough oval perimeter behind Delta, stayed low, and held their fire until one of Kasik's platoon leaders spotted another group of fifteen to twenty enemy soldiers moving toward them from the right side about twenty yards away. They caught only fleeting glimpses in the jungle darkness; Kasik watched one Viet Cong soldier throw a grenade that hit a tree and bounced back toward him. *Dumb shit,* he thought. After a brief firefight, those enemy troops vanished as quickly as they had appeared.

As the shooting slowed, Lieutenant Colonel Allen directed Welch to start pulling back. No sharp disagreement. It was already a clear victory. They had caught the enemy by surprise and never lost control. They had killed at least seventeen and lost none, though four Americans were wounded. They knew more now about where the Viet Cong were. Now napalm bombs could set the jungle ablaze and later the B-52s could come in and level the place.

Welch rested on his knees, calling in a final situation report. Captain Jones was at his side. Welch got off the radio and turned to the adviser.

God damn, we did it again, he said. *This has been a good day.*

Helluva day, Jones agreed. But he was thirsty and his canteen was empty. *Here,* Welch said, handing Jones his canteen. They were good friends, both trained in Special Forces, both at home in dangerous places, both instinctive soldiers. The captain stood up and tipped the canteen and took a swig. Then he said he hadn't killed any Viet Cong in two weeks and ran up toward the front. Before he could fire, he was killed by a burst of machine gun fire from a bunker.

Peter Miller was a few yards away, and as Captain Jones was dragged back from the point where he was shot, his lifeless body brushed against the rifleman who had been drafted out of the soap factory in Quincy, Massachusetts. For weeks Miller had been telling himself that he was ready for action. He burned to get into a firefight and be the John Wayne character that he imagined he could be. But then the captain's dead leg brushed against him in the jungle, and he never thought of war the same way again. *Holy shit,* he said to himself. *This is a freaking war.*

When they reversed directions, Bravo led the way back with Delta trailing. Bud Barrow, the first sergeant, was the last man out. He heard one of the platoon leaders, Lieutenant David Stroup, call out from behind an anthill, "Hey, Sarge, move back," so he jumped up and started to run toward the anthill and halfway there tripped over a root and fell flat on this face. His first thought was that he had been hit. When he realized what had happened, he was embarrassed but relieved, and he pulled himself up again to run for safety.

What a strange and macabre procession back to camp that was. Medic Lovato had been right. He needed the two stretchers to carry the wounded. The Vietnamese irregulars, shaken by the loss of the American captain, walked two by two, hoisting their fallen leader on their shoulders. Clark Welch asked to carry him part of the way. It was the first man he had lost in battle in Vietnam, although Jones technically was not one of his. He had never carried a dead man before. He was shocked to realize that there was next to nothing to Jones now. When he threw the body over his shoulder, the waist virtually disappeared. It was like toting a saddlebag.

Further down the line some of Welch's men, at his order, were bringing back two dead enemy soldiers, hauling them by their feet. Welch was not bloodthirsty. He did not cut off ears, nor did he allow his men to mutilate bodies in any way. It was uncharacteristic of him to bring back these bodies; something out of the ordinary had to compel him to do it, and that something was the uncertainty of his relationship with his boss, Terry Allen.

At the end of an earlier patrol in the secret zone, Welch had reported to Allen that his men had killed three enemy soldiers. *Are you sure?* Allen had responded, offhandedly. Welch had taken it as a challenge to his integrity. If he said they killed three, they killed three. What he heard Allen saying, in effect, was, *I don't believe you. Why don't you bring them back?* Now he was returning with two, their dead heads dragging against the undergrowth.

A QUARTER CENTURY EARLIER, Terry Allen was the boy of thirteen in El Paso, darting through the neighborhood near Fort Bliss with his pals, pretending they were fighting the Nazis in North Africa, just as his dad was fighting them for real, the Old Top who wrote home to his beloved Sonny and sent him tennis shoes, a battle flag, and the words to the First Division Song: "No mission too difficult, no sacrifice too great / Our duty to the nation is first, we're here to state." Now, no matter how earnestly he tried to be his own man, he could not avoid the pressure of measuring up to a famous father. Ten years earlier he was that debonair bachelor officer dashing about Colorado Springs in his T-bird convertible with polo boots and mallet in back. Now how could he push the agony of his collapsing marriage out of his consciousness, his wife living with some rodeo clown in the same house with the three little Allen daughters, Consuelo and Bebe and baby Mary Frances, back in El Paso on Timberwolf Drive? Seven months earlier he had arrived in Vietnam with much to prove, a rising officer with dreams of making general. Now his ambitions had changed, but the pressure still flooded over him.

Welch and the other officers in his battalion respected Allen. He was not a martinet. He seemed neither timid nor foolhardily macho. He cared about his men and did not convey the impression that he was there only to get his ticket punched. Alpha's Jim George thought "he was a good leader." Bill Erwin of the recon platoon said there was no doubt that Allen "commanded, he was in charge." But the tension Allen had been absorbing during that operation in the secret zone was sometimes apparent to his officers. Tom Reese, a fellow West Point graduate who had just taken over Charlie Company, had a long discussion with Allen before his unit was sent to guard the artillery base near the village of Chon Thanh. Reese, struck by how preoccupied the lieutenant colonel seemed, speculated that perhaps his job was on the line. Gerard Grosso, the S-3 air (forward air operations officer) for the battalion, who was monitoring radio transmissions that week, heard a dissonant symphony of terse and difficult conversations, some between Allen and his superiors at the brigade and division level, others between Allen and his own company commanders. For most of those communications, Allen was airborne in his little command-and-control helicopter.

Helicopters were an enormous boon to the American army in Vietnam, but they could be a mixed blessing when commanders used them to direct search-and-destroy operations; helicopters gave them a better perspective but also made it easier for them to cross the fine line between helping and interfering. The technology, in Grosso's opinion, gave senior officers "a sense of personal presence, influence, and accountability that was both false and disruptive" in a setting where, even though they might be only a few hundred feet above the fight, the dense terrain cut them off "from the real points of decisive action." In the secret zone it often appeared to Grosso that the command situation from air to ground

had "some of the earmarks of a Chinese fire drill." Not long after the patrols went out in the morning and entered the dense jungle, Allen began
calling down at regular intervals ordering his company commanders to
pop smoke grenades so he could know precisely where they were. This
was a minor but constant irritation to Welch and the others, who had
more pressing concerns and worried that the smoke might reveal their
positions to the enemy.

When the shooting started, Grosso noticed, Allen's requests for situation reports became more frequent and he had "a tendency to sound a
little overwrought, particularly when he started to get the same sort of
treatment" from his superiors at brigade and division level—Colonel
Newman and Brigadier General Coleman—who were also monitoring
the action. The tension was particularly evident to Grosso on the sixteenth, even as Welch and Kasik and their companies had a successful
day in the field. At one point during the firefight Grosso served as a "radio middleman," relaying messages between Welch and Allen, and then
between Allen and Newman and Coleman, who were second-guessing
his decisions. When the Black Lions began pulling back after the fight,
Grosso was riveted as Newman and Coleman "blew up at Allen on the
radio and ordered him to meet at the NDP." Helicopters touched down
and the big brass walked into camp to meet with the battalion commander at his command post.

Newman barely knew Allen and had never before dealt with the
2/28 Black Lions. He ran the First Brigade, stationed in Phuoc Vinh,
and Allen's outfit was normally attached to the Third Brigade in Lai
Khe. But ass chewing was the Big Red One's specialty, and Allen got his
chewed now. The words are forgotten, but the message was clear: *Get
out of that helicopter, get down on the ground with your men, and go back in
there and find 'em and fix 'em and kill 'em. Do what your old man would
have done. Tomorrow, walk.*

AND NOW HERE CAME THE TROOPS in from patrol, first Bravo,
then Delta, trudging back to the night defensive position, out of the jungle and into the late afternoon haze, bullets still snapping behind them,
not close enough to worry about, but enough to keep them moving, the
Vietnamese irregulars carrying Captain Jones, other soldiers dragging
the two Viet Cong. One horrible loss of his officer friend, but otherwise
"a wonderful day," Clark Welch was thinking. In war it was possible for

someone to hold those impossibly contradictory thoughts at the same time. When they reached the perimeter, Lieutenant Colonel Allen was there.

"Well, Welch, how many are you going to claim today?" he asked.

Welch burned inside. "Sir, I think I killed twenty"—seventeen confirmed—"and I brought two of them back to show you." His soldiers walked up with the two bodies and dropped them near the lieutenant's feet.

Allen was unimpressed. Battalion commanders by then had received the policy reminder Westmoreland's office had sent out after the October 9 CBS report. Troops were not to cut off ears or mutilate enemy dead in any way. "You take care of these bodies," he told Welch.

Welch led a small party across the draw again, some two hundred yards east of the perimeter, and buried the enemy soldiers in a shallow grave. Not six feet deep, because the diggers would hit water well before that.

When he returned, Welch walked from bunker to bunker in the Delta area, debriefing his men. Then he was called to a meeting with the visiting brass: Coleman and Newman and Donald Holleder, who was the brigade S-3, Newman's operations officer. Holleder was a strapping crew-cut bull of a major, a former All-America end and quarterback for Red Blaik at West Point. Maps were taken out and the group talked briefly about what had happened. Verland Gilbertson, a military photographer for the division who came along to record the Black Lions' missions that week, stood a few yards away, capturing the scene.

Click: They are in the clearing, a few scattered trees in the scrubland behind them, the rotary blades of a command-and-control helicopter visible above their heads, a few shirtless Delta boys seated in the background to the right, resting in the brush. Welch, with his characteristic forward lean, stands at the right edge of the huddle, his pictograph map stashed in his side pants pocket, gesturing now with his hands. Coleman is next to him, listening intently, followed by Holleder, Allen, and Newman. The bespectacled Allen's helmet is off. His hair is thinning and gray. His arms are at his hips, and on his left wrist one can see his Omega Seamaster watch. (On the watch's back, etched in gold plate, an engraving reads "J.P. to T.A." on top and "Oct. 2 1961" below—a wedding present from the wife who has left him, Jean Ponder Allen.)

"Tell me about today," Coleman said to Welch at one point. The division's deputy commander had been keenly interested in the new Delta companies of the First Division since they had been formed during the summer. He had visited Welch's base area in the rubber trees of Lai Khe several times and had developed a warm relationship with him.

Welch responded in his clipped style. These were not local guerrillas, he said. They were regulars. He saw the shoulderboards on the uniform of an officer. *God damn, sir. We got 'em. We got 'em. We know where they are now. I saw where they ran. I saw where they carried off their wounded. Jesus Christ.*

As the huddle broke up, Coleman took Welch aside. An aide handed him a piece of cardboard with a Silver Star attached to it. The general plucked the medal off the cardboard and pinned it on Welch. Another little side drama of pride and tension. Coleman had chewed out Allen, and Allen had dealt coolly with Welch, and now here was Coleman pinning a medal on Welch's chest.

"We lost Captain Jones today," Welch told Coleman. "My friend."

"Yes, yes, my friend too," Coleman said. An aide came running and told the general that it was time to leave. Coleman started walking toward the helicopter, then turned and saluted and Welch saluted back.

The Vietnamese scouts approached Welch to say good-bye. They were leaving. They had paid final respects to Captain Jones by digging a hole and burying his equipment, except a pistol, which they gave to Welch. The body was gone, on its way to Graves Registration in Lai Khe, first stop on the lonesome journey down to the morgue at Long Binh and across the ocean and over the mountains and all the way back to Coalton, West Virginia, and now the Vietnamese irregulars intended to vanish as well. No way they were staying without Jones. "Beaucoup VC out there," they kept saying before they left. "Beaucoup VC." One of Jim Kasik's lieutenants heard them muttering and approached his commander and said, "Damn, sir, those guys are scared shitless and glad to be leaving. They say there's a shitload of VC all over the place."

Welch had time to clean up and take a catnap, then he reported to Terry Allen's tent, the field headquarters, for the battalion command briefing. These were the last moments of sunlight. It was a small white tent, with room enough for three rows of chairs. Allen sat in front, facing the others, and at his side was Major John F. Sloan, the battalion's new operations officer. Less than two weeks earlier, Sloan had come in to replace the previous S-3, Big Jim Shelton, who had been moved up to serve as deputy operations man at division headquarters. His promotion was a huge loss for Allen. Shelton, who had been Allen's closest friend in the battalion, had a fluid conversational style that kept the lines of communications going in every direction. Now he was gone, and through no fault of Sloan's, issues of command seemed harder. In the first row sat the battalion captains, all Jims—Jim George, Jim Kasik, and Jim Blackwell, the intelligence officer. Behind them were lieutenants Welch and Erwin and Sergeant Major Francis Dowling.

One of Terry Allen's habits was to take off his glasses and rub his eyes with his knuckles. When he did, Jim George could see the fatigue. But his voice and words held steady. He gave a brief summary of what had happened that day. No soldiers lost except Captain Jones, who didn't count against the battalion. *We've got them where we want them,* he said. *Tomorrow is going to be a great day for the Black Lions.*

Then he unveiled a map and let Sloan run the briefing. Sloan wanted Erwin's reconnaissance platoon to walk due south to scout the area where they thought the enemy base camp was. Two companies would patrol to the west. Allen interrupted. No, they weren't going to do it that way. The main two-company patrol would march south toward the base camp and recon would go in another direction. Erwin looked at Sergeant Major Dowling. It was the second time in a week that Allen had changed his route.

A frontal attack? Welch looked at the map in disbelief. *Man, it can't be. I have very good eyes and very good hearing and it can't be. I must be misunderstanding that. That's just a fucking arrow showing us going south. Where's Shelton? Jesus Christ! That is crazy. We're going to attack right into them?* It made little sense to Welch. They knew where the enemy troops were; why not bomb them for a day with B-52s and napalm and then tiptoe in with a small force to see what effect they had had, then tiptoe out again and bomb them again?

But here are the orders. Alpha and Delta go south. Delta leads. They leave at eight thirty. Make sure everyone has enough water. Looks like another long day.

Major Sloan sat down and Allen stood up. Any questions?

"Sir, I . . . ," Welch said. That was as far as he got.

Allen stared him down. "If you're not ready to lead, we'll get Alpha to lead."

"Sir," Welch said.

"We'll talk about it later," Allen responded.

It was a shorthand argument that was so brief and loaded with unstated meaning that some officers in the room missed it completely.

One more thing. The command group was coming on the ground. Allen would walk with them. Here was another sensitive issue, another contradiction. The company commanders groused when Allen was in the air asking them to throw smoke to show where they were, yet in some ways they preferred his being up there to his being on the ground. Now they might be more defensive and worry too much about protecting the command group in their midst. In the jungle a commander could only see as far as the next tree. During a firefight, George thought, Allen could do them "more good from the air, from the standpoint of directing our artillery, bringing in the air, asking our headquarters for additional troops if there was a need for it, assessing the situation." But this was not a debatable issue. Alpha would now lead. The command group would walk with Delta. Allen did not tell his commanders that he had been ordered to walk by Newman and Coleman.

When the meeting broke up, Welch and George met outside the tent. Welch told George that he would have his hands full the next morning. George questioned too the plan to walk straight south but thought he could handle it. As Welch turned to leave, Major Sloan emerged from the tent. "The colonel wants to see you," he said. It was dark now; a Coleman lantern illuminated Allen's face as he sat on the edge of his cot. He looked at Welch. *You wanted to say something?*

The tension between the two men did not arise from disrespect. Allen thought the world of Welch as a soldier. "First Lieutenant Albert C. Welch is one of the most outstanding officers with whom I have had the pleasure to serve," Allen had written in Welch's last U.S. Army Officer Efficiency Report. "Due to his exemplary performance of duty he was one of the few First Lieutenants selected to serve as a company commander in the First Infantry Division. His performance was characterized by the highest standards of leadership, aggressiveness, determination, maturity and sound judgment. He organized, trained and led a fourth rifle company of his battalion. . . . He is mature, cool and courageous in combat and has the ability to simultaneously look after the welfare of his men without sacrificing his mission." If Allen was dismissive of Welch now, it was a reflection of the pressure he felt from above.

Welch did not have his own Plan B but made it clear that he did not like Plan A. "Jesus Christ, sir," he said to Allen. "We're going to get our ass kicked, sir. I was right there. I believe that's the base camp. And we're going to sneak up on them?" Allen listened but said nothing.

At the same hour in Lai Khe there was a nightly briefing of the division staff at the operations center. Charts, grease pencils, map overlays, all nice and neat and direct, *bing, bing, bing*. The room was juiced, everyone eager. It had been a good day, and the plan for the morning looked solid. There were three battalions out there on the move. Dauntless—shorthand for Terry Allen's 2/28 Black Lions—was closest to the elusive Viet Cong regiment and had its marching orders. The artillery fire bases were ready. Finding the enemy was the name of the game. *Hope Dauntless has good hunting,* they said.

WELCH RETURNED TO DELTA'S POSITION inside the perimeter. He pulled out his pocket-sized flip-up spiral notebook, dark green with MEMORANDUM embossed in gold on the cover, and wrote out orders that he would give to his platoon and squad leaders. Five straightforward paragraphs: the general situation, the mission, the concept of the mission, the logistics, and command and signal. He presented it the same way every day to maintain a sense of order and stability—even if, as in this case, parts of the larger order made little sense to him. He spent the next few hours pacing the camp, talking to his men. Tomorrow they would be in a big fight, he said. They were in a fight today, but tomorrow would be big. He went over to his weapons platoon to set up a plan, figuring that as rear company he would have no control of artillery, so it was important to have his mortars ready. He tried to remain outwardly positive, but some of his boys sensed that he was upset. *The man is steamed,* Santiago Griego said to Faustin Sena.

Big fight, is the most Welch would say. *Bring all the ammunition you can carry.* No mention of water, nothing about food. *Just bring all the ammunition you can carry.* George spread a similar message to his leaders in Alpha.

In their bunkers the troops were apprehensive. Michael Arias wrote a letter to his mother, Julia H. Arias, on Sixth Street in Douglas, Arizona, saying that Shenandoah II "might make the headlines back home." He and his buddies stayed up most of the night. No one could sleep. Carl Woodard, an Alpha squad leader, walked the perimeter and noticed that his men were "talking about the bad things." Nobody was drinking beer. Resupply had brought Coke and beer, and the beer sat there. Sometimes they drank because they were scared. Now they were too scared to drink. Peter Miller sat near a fellow draftee, a kid from Alabama who "never should have been in the army in the first place,"

Miller thought. When they were eating dinner, the kid had been "shaking so bad he couldn't hold a spoon"—and he was still shaking in the bunker hours later. *Jeez, this is terrible,* Miller thought. *This just isn't right.* Joe Costello, a Catholic, but not particularly religious, said "a couple of extra prayers." He prayed for his girlfriend and his family.

There was a lot of chatter among the guys. *There's big time stuff going on out there. There's a lot of enemy and we're going out and A company's into it and the shit's gonna fly.* Rumors raced from bunker to bunker among the enlisted men. Costello was next to Michael Gallagher and Allan V. Reilly, the squadmates feeling spiffy in their clean new clothes. Reilly was older, street savvy, an operator who liked to talk about women and gambling and who would somehow disappear when the company was back at Lai Khe. The guys respected him as the toughest fighter in his platoon, someone who actually wanted to walk point, but they were "a little scared of him" and they were all ears now as he declared that "if the shit hits the fan," he was "going to get gone."

Ray Albin of the Delta weapons platoon had a brief conversation with "a guy named Schroder" that night. It was Jack Schroder, the would-be dental technician who had sailed across the Pacific with C Packet.

"How'd it go today?" Albin asked.

"Well, we ran into some stuff," Schroder said. "Lot of lead flying."

"Good you got out," Albin said.

Schroder showed him his M-16. "One took it right there," he said, pointing to where an enemy bullet had struck the rifle. "Man, I was lucky." His weapon, he said, had saved his life.

CHAPTER 13

MICHIGAN MEN

O N THE SIXTEENTH OF OCTOBER, in time for dinner and his customary pair of after-meal manhattans, the recruiter from Dow Chemical Company arrived in Madison and checked in at the Ivy Inn, a two-story red brick motor hotel and restaurant ten blocks west of the Wisconsin campus along University Avenue. He registered under the name Robert Miller. It was an alias that Dow representatives had begun using in potentially hostile situations, in case antiwar protesters came looking. In this instance, in case they came looking for a recruiter named William L. Hendershot, known to his friends as Curly.

Curly Hendershot at age fifty-five was new to the recruiting game but old to Dow. He had worked for the headquarters in Midland, Michigan, since 1942, most of his adult life. Dow was that sort of place, a paternalistic company in a company town. One needed only to examine the listed occupations of forty-eight citizens on a typical page—page 521—of the 1960 *Midland City Directory* to see how deeply the chemical company had saturated the community. Fifteen, nearly a third, were Dow employees: Heindel the patent attorney, Heintsill the technician, Heisman the supervisor, Helmreich the chemist, Helt the welder, Hembree the products manager, Heminger the electrician, Henderson the building superintendent, Henderson the utilityman, Hendrickson and Henninger the office secretaries, Hennis the chemist, Henry the machinist, Henry the supervisor, and Hendershot, William L., the department supervisor.

During most of his tenure at Dow, Hendershot had supervised communications services. He became so identified with the department that company telephone operators were often referred to by Dow's male executives as "Hendershot's Harem." The connotation was more sexist than sexual: Curly was a God-fearing married man, conservative, but not without his own flair. He was a precise dresser, his row of business suits always lined up facing the same way on hangers in his closet. He wore white shirts, cufflinks, and black-rimmed glasses; smoked Camels; played golf; exercised three times a week; and drank those two cocktails after supper. He was about five foot eight and wiry, and clinging tenuously to the sides of his balding head were the last thin remnants of the curly black hair that had inspired his nickname.

Hendershot had worked his way up at Dow without a college degree. Management kept giving him chances and he took advantage of each one. They sent him to Europe to set up their communications office in Rotterdam for a few years, then brought him back and made him a recruiter, a job for which Curly had a natural aptitude. His daughter, Sherlynn Hendershot, who was in college at Michigan State during those years, described him as the classic "hail-fellow-well-met" who exuded positive feelings. In that he exemplified the Dow corporate personality. "Everything at Dow was positive superlative," the wife of one executive explained. Curly also excelled at secondary relationships. When his daughter went with him to the grocery, gas station, or drugstore, strangers seemed to know him and would call him by his nickname. He was happy among like-minded folks but had no use for taxes, welfare, liberals, long hair, or dissent. Sherlynn, who was growing to distrust the government and dislike the war in Vietnam, tried to avoid those issues when she was with him, but there was a strain in the father-daughter relationship nonetheless. It would not enter his mind that there were parts of society that needed to be changed, she said. To him, the antiwar movement was nothing more than "kids who don't know how to behave and needed discipline."

This was not Hendershot's first trip to Madison. He and fellow recruiter A. K. Prince had been on campus during the demonstrations against Dow the previous February, when then-Chancellor Fleming bailed out the arrested students. The Dow men were caught in the middle of the action then, confronted by angry, jeering students who called them "baby killers" and "good Germans." Their job placement interviews persisted despite the hubbub, and they even had more appointments than usual, though it was often difficult for them to carry on conversations above the hallway din outside the interview rooms. It had been an unsettling experience for accentuate-the-positive Curly, and he returned to Midland complaining that he didn't see why the authorities "couldn't just throw those people in jail and keep them there."

Shortly after that episode Hendershot's boss in the recruiting department, Ramon F. Rolf, was summoned to the office of Dow's president and chief operating officer, Herbert Dow (Ted) Doan, grandson of the company's founder, Herbert Henry Dow. "Sit down, Ray, let's talk about this," Rolf later remembered Doan saying to him, referring to the campus protests. "What is your position? How do you intend to handle this?" Rolf responded that he had talked to the recruiters and developed a position. "We go back year after year," he said. "We know the placement director, we know the faculty, and we have job opportunities for the students, and I think we ought to continue to go and hold a hard line and do that until we are not welcome. We are going to go and behave as gentlemen. If they tell us not to come, we don't want to go if we are not welcome."

Doan smiled and said, "That's great. You've got the whole problem in your hands. Let me know if you need me."

It was a familiar response, similar to what Doan had said to Ned Brandt, his director of publicity, when Brandt had suggested that Dow send a delegation to the Pentagon to discuss the anti-Dow protests and how the chemical company, rather than the military, was taking most of the heat over the war. *Good idea, go do it,* Doan had said then. In both instances this seemed to be more a reflection of the corporation's delegate-to-the-troops management philosophy than of any effort by Doan to avoid the napalm controversy.

From the outside Dow appeared narrow and inbred, a stunningly homogeneous institution run since the turn of the century by conservative midwestern, Anglo-Saxon Protestant men, all carefully molded in the personality of the original old man Dow, an inventive chemist who first settled in central Michigan because of the area's rich deposits of ancient brine. The board of directors was made up solely of Dow executives, with no outsiders to infuse it with differing perspectives. It began as a curious college of chemical cardinals with H. H. Dow as pope. In the old days you knew when a debate had ended and a disagreement had been resolved, at least in Dow's mind, when he would break into song. "I'm coming, I'm coming, for my head is bending low," he would croon, and soon the entire board of white Michigan men would be singing along, their gentle voices calling to "Old Black Joe" as they filtered out of the board room in capitalist harmony.

Even as Dow developed into a multinational corporation in the 1960s under the stewardship of what became known as the Troika, consisting of Ted Doan, chairman Carl A. Gerstacker, and chief operating officer Ben Branch, the corporate personality carried the imprint of its isolationist past. Gerstacker had come from a family of America Firsters who opposed U.S. entry into World War II. His father, he once said, "had no use for foreigners, and he included people from the west coast and east coast as foreigners." Doan's father, Lee Doan, who had married H. H. Dow's daughter Ruth, was of the same view. He ran a postwar Dow management team that wanted nothing to do with the Japanese and little to do with the Germans or British either. "Those guys came out of the war mad at the world and they had a chemical company that was damned good, the envy of the world, and they didn't need anything and they thought, 'To hell with those guys,'" Ted Doan later explained. As a young turk in the corporation, he said, he got into many arguments with the old-timers as he pushed the idea of finally "getting with the world."

The board of directors in 1967 was still an inside operation of white Anglo-Saxon Protestant men, but within that limited realm debate was encouraged and dissent tolerated, to a degree. Doan had overseen a two-day discussion of the napalm issue at the board meeting that year. At the end of the first day, as he later described it, "with nothing decided but with three or four members looking as if they might take a stand against napalm, everyone went home and must have had a very troubled sleep." The next morning many of the doubters came to Doan individually and said they had decided that Dow should continue producing napalm. A lone dissenter, marketing director Bill Dixon, held firm. "There was no equivocation in his mind that we should get out of that business, and not because we couldn't stand the pressure, but because it was wrong, just wrong to be producing that product," Doan recalled. "A very sensitive man. One of the best marketing guys Dow ever had. He was the kind of guy to worry about this more than the average fellow. Everybody respected Bill Dixon for his stance on napalm. Nobody said, 'Bill, you're out of your mind. You shouldn't do that.' Instead it was, 'All you have to do is get eight more of them [votes, for a majority on the sixteen-member board] and we're out of this thing." Dixon never could get eight more votes.

The most difficult ethical issue for Doan and the board was whether

Dow, by arguing that it was fulfilling a government request, was essentially falling back on the just-following-orders rationalization that German manufacturers used to defend their support of the Nazi war effort. Doan considered this "an excellent point," but he eventually prepared a formal answer that evolved from the board's discussions: "We reject the validity of comparing our present form of government with Hitler's Nazi Germany. In our mind our government is still responsive to the will of the people. Further, we as a company have made a moral judgment on the long range goals of our government and we support those. We may not agree as individuals with every decision of every military or governmental leader but we regard those leaders as men trying honestly and relentlessly to find the best possible solutions to very complex international problems. As long as we so regard them we would find it impossible not to support them. This is not saying as the critics imply that we will follow blindly and without fail no matter where our government leads. While I think it highly unlikely under our form of government, should despotic leaders attempt to lead our nation away from its historic national purposes, we would cease to support the government. Our critics ask if we are willing to stand judgment for our choice to support our government if history should prove us wrong. Our answer is yes."

Doan later translated that last point into more graphic prose. "If we're found wrong after the war," he said, "we'll be glad to be hung for it."

As the anti-Dow protests continued throughout that year, the napalm issue came to dominate Doan's working days. Memos from the recruiting department, phone calls from Ned Brandt at public relations, letters from university administrators—"it was a topic of conversation every day," Doan said. It also became a topic of conversation many nights when he got home to his wife and four children. The Doan family lived amid the old Dow apple orchards on Valley Drive in a modernist house designed by an uncle who had studied at Taliesin, Frank Lloyd Wright's studio in the Wisconsin countryside west of Madison. For all its seeming inwardness, Midland also had a progressive streak that was never more evident than in the Wright-inspired architecture of Alden Dow, whose homes and other buildings could be seen throughout town. That progressive sensibility had filtered into the mind of Donalda Doan, Ted Doan's wife, who by the fall of 1967 was turning against the war in Vietnam.

She came from "the patriotic generation," Donalda Doan would say, but to her "there wasn't any real reason to get into that mess" in Vietnam. She viewed the defense of the war as "kind of the knee-jerk response of big businessmen"—including her husband. One of her close friends in Midland, a clinical psychologist, had been antiwar from the start, and Ted Doan complained that the woman was putting ideas in Donalda's head. Donalda said she could think for herself. And if the dinner table conversation got a bit heated, at least there was conversation. Her husband, from Donalda's perspective, was usually "very much closed, like most of the Dow men." They were not talkers, and particularly not about what they were doing at work. The tension of the war was starting to change that, for better or worse. Ted Doan found the new family dynamics frustrating. "My wife, in addition to being a very, very good, sound person, also got quite liberal," he recalled. "One of the difficult things was that she was never sure herself that napalm thing was a good thing. I used to go home and have to talk this over—why were we doing what we were doing?—and I don't think she believed me worth a damn. I think that was my hardest sell." It was not exactly a family revolt, Doan said, but his views were no longer going unquestioned. He had to defend himself.

The reverberations of that family disagreement went on for years. The oldest Doan son dropped out of Pomona College in Southern California and was drafted into the army, but happened to be in the stockade when his unit was sent to Vietnam. "That bad boy was saved," Donalda Doan later declared when describing the "wonderful story" that kept her son from going to Vietnam. The oldest daughter also headed west to California and turned away from the family history by marching with Cesar Chavez and the farmworkers during the grape boycotts. The youngest son became a conscientious objector. And so it went with one upper-middle-class midwestern family whose children were coming of age in the sixties and whose father happened to be president of Dow Chemical Company. Ted Doan was not alone. As he would later say, "There were a lot of guys in Midland who had a lot of trouble with their families."

As CURLY HENDERSHOT settled in at the Ivy Inn, a young son of Michigan sat among a group of 350 antiwar protesters who had gathered in Great Hall in the Memorial Union on that Monday night of October 16. There could never be enough meetings in the student movement, it seemed, and here was one more, a final tactical briefing and debate

1

2

3

Terry Allen Jr. and his mother, Mary Frances, welcome home General Terry Allen Sr. after World War II. Deep affection, not intimidation, funneled "Sonny" through the narrow chute of his family's military tradition.

4

5

Second-to-last in his West Point class, Allen rose quickly in the army. In Vietnam, he commanded a Big Red One battalion at Lai Khe. Studying this photograph decades later, his daughters saw a proud, haunted look in their father's gaze.

Jean Ponder Allen, the Texas beauty queen. While Terry fought in Vietnam, Jean hosted a local television show and felt alienated from her husband and the military.

Lieutenant Colonel Terry Allen (center) and his 2/28 Black Lions commanders before the battle. Delta's Clark Welch is second from right, Alpha's Jim George second from left.

Jack Schroder studied to be a dental technician in Milwaukee. "They're not playing games over here," he wrote to his wife after arriving in Lai Khe.

7

Mike Troyer was drafted out of a truck plant in Ohio. In a letter home he wrote, "The whole damn war is run by the book and Charlie can't read English so he gets all the breaks and we usually get killed."

8

"Sad to think that a certain percentage of people here are sure to die in Vietnam," Greg Landon wrote before leaving Fort Lewis. The Amherst dropout known as "the professor" sensed who would survive and who would die.

Michael Arias, drafted out of Douglas, Arizona, said later that to avoid Vietnam he could have walked six blocks south into Mexico and disappeared. With Alpha company during the battle, he read the compass and found the way out.

10

Captain Jim George of South Carolina, commander of Alpha company. "I'll do what I can and pray that God will lead me," he wrote during the voyage to Vung Tau. "I've already started to dream of killing and am already tired of the smell of death."

11

13

If there was a prototype of the young men from Wisconsin who fought in Vietnam, it was Danny Sikorski, son of a brewery worker from Milwaukee's heavily Polish south side. Boys from his neighborhood went into the military, not to college.

12

Willie C. Johnson, staff sergeant, took Alpha's lead platoon into the jungle that October morning. He marched as fourth man back in the right file, singing his rhythm and blues anthem of good luck, "Knock on Wood."

Danny on home leave with sister Diane in February 1967. Diane dreamed about him the night before the battle. In her vision, he appeared with a hole where his stomach should have been.

14

Tom Hinger, a medic from Pennsylvania, was a walking skeleton by mid-October, down to a hundred pounds, but carried seventy pounds of supplies, an antlike ratio of load to body mass.

15

Joe Costello of Long Island, grenadier in Alpha's second platoon, waits to rejoin his company in the field on the morning of October 15. As men retreated during the battle, Costello returned to the front to help stranded comrades.

16

Delta commander Clark Welch. Long and sinewy, his frame always tilting forward slightly, ready to move, the first lieutenant from New Hampshire was a soldier's soldier in the most elemental sense. His boys called him Big Rock.

17

Lieutenant Welch and his trusted top aide, First Sergeant Clarence (Bud) Barrow, who came with him to pick up their new Delta company troops at Vung Tau. Barrow was the only one brave enough to wake Welch in the morning.

18

For Operation Shenandoah II, soldiers from 2/28 Black Lions gather at the helicopter pads at Lai Khe for the mission into the Long Nguyen Secret Zone. "It kind of worries me," Jack Schroder wrote. "All hard core VC. I don't know what to expect."

20

The evening before the battle, Clark Welch (*right*) returned to the field camp and described skirmishing to senior officers. Behind bespectacled and helmetless Terry Allen stands the former West Point All-America football player Major Donald Holleder.

View from a medic's tent the morning of the battle. October 17 opened in a bright haze, with temperatures already in the eighties. "It was just a very muggy dog day," said Joe Costello. "It was just kind of aaaggghhh."

22

The morning after the battle, survivors from Alpha and Delta were shipped back to Lai Khe. It usually took twenty helicopters to move a complete rifle company; now, with so many casualties, it required only five.

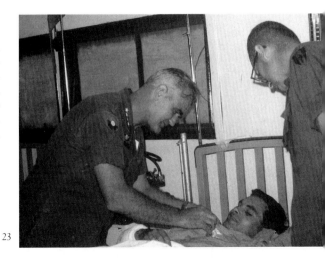

Five days after the battle, General William C. Westmoreland visited the 93rd Evacuation Hospital and pinned the Purple Heart on wounded Black Lions. He disagreed with soldiers who told him they had been ambushed.

Some of them died. Some of them were not allowed to. A memorial service at Lai Khe for the fallen Black Lions soldiers.

23

The Union Terrace, epicenter of the University of Wisconsin, with its vibrantly colored green and orange metal tables and chairs stretching back from the Rathskeller down to the edge of Lake Mendota.

Jane Brotman followed a well-worn path to Madison. She was one of 124 New Jersey residents, seven from her high school, to enter Wisconsin that fall of 1967. She had a favorite table at the Rathskeller.

When Betty Menacher of Green Bay said she wanted to go to school in Madison, her father, a lumber salesman, muttered that the state capital was "a cesspool of queers."

27

History professor George Mosse, an expert on the rise of fascism, nationalism, and Nazism, took the New Left seriously but criticized radical students for suppressing the speech of others.

When his hair was shorn in jail, protest leader Robert Cohen, a philosophy graduate student, said his jailers failed "to comprehend the historical alternatives to their present non-qualitative existence."

Evan Stark, graduate student in sociology, the entrancingly fluent orator of the movement. His return to Madison in fall 1967 elicited a round of concerned letters among campus officials.

Minutes before the confrontation in the Commerce Building, Percy Julian, an attorney for the protesters, placed a call to U.S. District Judge James Doyle, who said it was not within his power to stop the police.

31

32

"Down with Dow! Down with Dow!" the marchers chanted on their way to the Commerce Building. As they rounded Bascom Hall, local television newsman Blake Kellogg (*in white trench coat*), filmed the protest.

33

The gray-speckled granite floor virtually disappeared from view as the hall-way flooded with demonstrators. The hallway was narrow, a mere ten feet across. This was no place for a claustrophobic.

Students recoil as Madison police make their charge. The tall student on far left is Jonathan Stielstra; in the sheepskin coat on the right, starting to cover his neck, is Paul Soglin. Within seconds, Soglin was on the floor being pummelled by club-wielding officers.

36

As the police moved into the foyer, there was no space to gain footing, just a wall of people. The officers started flailing with their nightsticks.

37

After the hallway was cleared, officers huddled in a protective semicircle at the front of Commerce. The confrontation had enraged the crowd. "*Sieg heil! Sieg heil!*" came the shouts.

Jonathan Stielstra scrambling off the Bascom Hall roof after cutting the flag lanyard and setting off firecrackers. This photograph by Norm Lenburg started a manhunt for the flag-cutter.

39

The arrest of Vicki Gabriner, Miss Sifting and Winnowing, was pure guerrilla theater. She went limp, then resisted vociferously as two policemen dragged her away. One of the defining pictures of the day was of Gabriner's painted face staring out the back window of a paddy wagon.

40

There were messy scrums on the Commerce plaza, with students surging forward and policemen responding with billy clubs. "Everyone in the pile was swearing, 'God damn, get off me!'"

Most of the students treated at nearby UW Hospital had scalp wounds that gushed with blood but looked more serious than they were.

In the aftermath of the Dow riot, Paul Soglin (*standing in sheepskin coat*) emerged as a student leader. Within six months he was elected to the city council, and within six years he was mayor of Madison.

William Sewell, the UW chancellor, testifies at a legislative hearing after the Dow riot. A renowned sociologist, Sewell was the classic liberal of that era, caught between radical students and conservative state politicians.

A connection that defies all odds, bringing together the worlds of war and peace. Dave Wagner (*left*) was at the Dow demonstration at Wisconsin while Michael Arias (*right*) was at the battle of October 17. Wagner's son, Ben (*second from left*), married Arias's daughter, Theresa.

45

Thirty-five years after the battle, Vo Minh Triet (*right*), commander of the First Regiment, greets Nguyen Van Lam, an officer with the local rear service group, at Lam's house near the battlefield. "Oh my God," Lam said. "You are still alive?"

46

Clark Welch and Vo Minh Triet retrace their steps on the battlefield. "We once fought against each other; now we are becoming old soldiers together," Welch said. "We together grieve for the terrible losses."

47

concerning the anti-Dow demonstrations that were to unfold over the following two days. The young Michigander was Jonathan Stielstra, identical twin of Phil Stielstra, the sons of William Stielstra, descendants of the Dutch-Calvinist Stielstras who settled in Holland, Michigan, in the mid-nineteenth century as part of a wave of religious immigrants fleeing the Netherlands. William Stielstra, who served as a lieutenant in the U.S. Army Signal Corps in the Pacific theater during the Second World War, was a highly respected college administrator who had been hired recently to serve as the dean of students at the Wisconsin State University system's campus in Stevens Point, one hundred miles north of Madison. Clarence "Stiely" Stielstra, William's brother and Jonathan and Phil's uncle, worked as an executive at Dow Chemical Company. All in the family, again.

Jonathan Star Stielstra was a transfer student from Calvin College in Grand Rapids. He had arrived in Madison the previous spring term as a second-semester junior and philosophy major, and it would be hard to imagine a more dramatic cultural transition than the one he made that year, though in broad outline his journey resembled ones made by countless college students coming out of America's suburbs and small towns and plunging headlong into the abundant new world of freedom. Calvin College was affiliated with the Christian Reformed Church, which based its faith on the Scriptures as "God's holy, inspired, infallible Word." It housed the largest collection of scholarly works on John Calvin in North America. Its students attended mandatory chapel services. There was no dancing on campus. The student body was largely conservative. In his sophomore year Stielstra ran for class president and reached the office through a series of accidents, when the favorite dropped out and the subsequent winner was stripped of the title. He was regarded by some as an unconventional class leader, largely for bringing the New Christy Minstrels to campus to sing folk songs.

How did a young Calvinist get to Madison? For Stielstra part of the impetus was that he could attend Wisconsin as an in-state student since his parents had moved to Stevens Point (from Lafayette, Indiana, where William Stielstra had been an administrator at Purdue University), and part of it was a compulsion to escape, to find a place with a more free-wheeling atmosphere. At Madison there was no infallible Word; everything was up for grabs; they sold beer to eighteen-year-olds; students smoked in classrooms; marijuana was available. Stielstra came into town a gangly, blond, six-foot-three Dutchman, and took spontaneously to the open life. His cultural and political interests bloomed. He grew out his hair, smoked dope, and began attending leftist student meetings. He bunked at a bohemian rooming house on North Frances near the corner of University Avenue, then found a house at 1215 Drake Street in the old neighborhood down by Henry Vilas Park that he rented with his brother Phil, who came at the end of the summer, and two other students, including Mark Knops, an antiwar activist and graduate student in history.

Only nine months after he got to Madison, the transformation of Jonathan Stielstra was complete: He and Knops were churning out antiwar leaflets in the dank basement on Drake Street on a mimeograph machine they called the Clandestine Bolshevik Press. He was a regular at SDS meetings and was on the periphery of the planning for the protests against the napalm-producing corporation where his uncle Stiely worked. The latest missive denounced the alliance between the university and the corporation: "Dow Chemical Corporation manufactures napalm that burns and maims the people of Vietnam. The university is furnishing the technicians who create the tools of destruction as well as the facilities for hiring these technicians. But war and violence have no place in an institution of learning. By permitting this recruitment to occur here the university in fact works for the war effort, in this case for the burning of children. The student can no more allow this university to facilitate this recruitment than he can excuse himself for seeking employment with Dow."

The crowd in Great Hall was larger than that for the previous planning meeting three nights earlier at Social Sciences, and less contentious. There was less political posturing now among the various groups that had joined together to form the ad hoc anti-Dow committee. Evan Stark and Robert Cohen stood up front but did not try to dominate the session. Paul Soglin was there but did not speak. He and his lawyers, Percy Julian and Michael Reiter, had just filed papers in federal court— *Soglin et al. v. Kauffman et al.*—seeking to prevent university officials from usurping the free speech rights of the protesters. U.S. District Judge James J. Doyle had issued a temporary restraining order, Reiter announced, but this did not give the students "free reign to obstruct or be violent." The court action, another law student explained, was "primarily for the newspapers" and probably would not be of much help. A group of law students would wear armbands to the demonstrations and provide legal advice as well as bring cameras to document the scene.

Students were told that they did not have to give their names or show their fee cards unless they were placed under arrest. They were advised to come to the obstructive rally empty-handed, with nothing more than a fee card and draft card in their pockets, leaving their wallets, purses, and books at home. Women were told not to wear pierced earrings, rings, clips, chains, or contact lenses.

The same undercover agent from the Madison Police Department who had attended the previous meeting was there again, gathering information for another report to Chief Emery. He estimated the crowd at three hundred, and it seemed to him that "a majority of them seemed to be looking forward to the following two or three days of protesting in an especially militant fashion." He paid particular attention to the final plans for Wednesday's obstructive protest. The demonstrators would gather at 9:10 at the bottom of Bascom Hill and be told there which of the three buildings where Dow interviews were taking place they would target for the sit-in. Then they would march to the chosen site en masse. (In his report to Emery, the agent offered a suggestion on how to counter this tactic: "It would probably be advantageous for us to divide and disperse them by only allowing a certain number into whatever building they pick, locking the door behind them and not letting any more in until those who go in come out. This would prevent them from getting their number concentrated in a small area, which would be to their advantage. It would also mean that they would have to subdivide several times in order to cover all the entrances to that building by which those legitimately wishing to interview with Dow might enter, and it would give our police more room to maneuver in." An interesting idea, but apparently not one that the police leaders later considered.)

There would be monitors leading the way to the demonstrations, instructing participants on when to walk and when to sit, and Evan Stark would be in overall charge. No professors were joining the protests, one speaker noted, because "the rally was far too radical for them." Maurice Zeitlin, the leftist sociologist, was mentioned specifically as a professor who opposed the obstruction tactic. As the meeting neared an end, Evan Stark rose to speak. He said there was no reason to be too defensive. "You can bet the university will not be brutal by bringing in the police," he said. If things did get violent, there was "no reason at all that if you are hit by the police that you can't hit back," he added, but he did not expect that to happen. As another note taker at the meeting, an assistant dean, recorded it, Stark "felt very strongly that the University would not even drag people out of the building"—a prediction that he based on the experience of the antidraft sit-in at the administration building in 1966, when there were so many people taking part that the Madison police reacted cautiously. As Stark recalled it, when Chief Emery was asked during that earlier protest whether he intended to impose mass arrests, he responded by saying, "Are you crazy?" There would be no bloodshed, Stark said.

That is the impression that Jonathan Stielstra took away from the Great Hall meeting, as did many others in attendance that night. Over at the Ivy Inn, Curly Hendershot girded for what he figured might be a trying couple of days, though the worst the Dow men anticipated was that they might be trapped inside an interview room for a few hours. Hendershot had his own contingency plan. In his briefcase he was packing a ham sandwich so that no matter what happened on campus, he would not miss lunch.

CHAPTER 14

FOR WANT OF RICE

THE TOUGH LITTLE PIECE OF VIETNAM known as the Long Nguyen Secret Zone held no secrets from Nguyen Van Lam. This was his home territory. He knew the hamlets, the rice paddies, the buffalo trails through the tall grass and secret paths through the jungles. He was at home in the forest, and forest is how his name, Lam, translated into English. He was born in the nearby village of Long Nguyen in 1946, the year of the dog. His parents worked a small plot of rice and like many farmers in that area supported the liberation forces, first against the French, then against the Americans. Some families did this because they wanted to, some because they felt they had no choice. Lam was not coerced. He fought alongside the local guerrillas when he was in his middle teens and at nineteen joined the communist-led forces of the People's Army of Vietnam, preferring it to the other side, the Army of South Vietnam, which had just drafted him.

Now, at age twenty-one, Lam was company commander of C1, a security unit that protected the perimeter of a base camp for Rear Service Group 83. He had no uniform to speak of, just the traditional lightweight pants and shirt, usually black, sometimes blue, and homemade rubber-tire sandals. He carried a Thompson submachine gun. Over the course of two years he had seen the big-nosed Americans only occasionally. There were two battles during that period, and every month or so a patrol might come near. He had become intimately familiar with the hardware of the U.S. military. He knew how to time the bombing runs of the massive B-52s, which circled round again with metronomic precision thirty or forty minutes apart. He had witnessed the destructive power of cluster bombs, napalm, and 105-millimeter howitzers. Trouble arrived in a swarm of helicopters. There was nothing fun about his youth, he once said, smiling and gesticulating, his high, cackling voice like that of an excited rooster. It was all work, all war.

A military doctor from Hanoi once told oral historian James Zumwalt that working in the southern jungles during the war of resistance against the Americans was "like being Robinson Crusoe on the island." Everything had to be foraged and improvised; success depended on sweat and ingenuity. The quintessential example was of a soldier pedaling vigorously on a stationary bicycle in the tunnel complex of an underground hospital to power a generator that kept the lights flickering in the operating room. The Crusoe analogy aptly conveyed the need for adaptive skills, but in this case there were hundreds of thousands of Crusoes functioning inside South Vietnam, all supported by an intricate logistical network, of which Rear Service Group 83 was a small but integral part. The conditions demanded improvisation on the ground, but at least on paper it was all part of an elaborate bureaucratic plan.

Like other aspects of the war, the logistical command flowed from Hanoi, overseen by the General Directorate for Rear Services. As one of three main directorates in the National Ministry of Defense, Rear Services was responsible for moving men and materiel south and sustaining the war effort there. Its functional arm was the famed Group 559, which created and operated what became known as the Ho Chi Minh Trail. From the time Group 559 was formed at the dawn of the war in May 1959 (hence its name), it had grown into a massive logistical unit of nearly fifty thousand men who ran twenty-five military stations along the trail and were divided into six departments and twenty-three regiments: six engineering regiments, six antiaircraft artillery regiments, one surface-to-air missile regiment, three vehicle transportation regiments, two regiments for maintaining the POL line (petroleum, oil, and lubricants), two for assisting the Pathet Lao (for the trail's path through Laos), one communications regiment, one for driver training, and one for rest and recuperation.

The Ho Chi Minh Trail, which started as a scraggy walking path wending south along the spine of the Truong Son range, had evolved over the years into a veritable interstate system of jungle-shrouded trails and roads (some, by the fall of 1967, allowing motorized transport) that snaked down through North Vietnam, Laos, and Cambodia, with several arteries slicing west to east at entry points for B4, B3, and B2, the

military fronts in the combat zones of South Vietnam. Each front in turn
had its own rear service department. The rear service headquarters for
B2 Front had offices for plans, political affairs, quartermaster, arma-
ments, military medicine, finance, administration, and supply purchasing, in addition to a medical technician school, a pharmaceutical
production unit, a drug storage site, the 320th hospital, three makeshift
armories, and three units responsible for recruiting and managing
people to grow and harvest rice and raise pigs and chickens. Finally, hidden deep in the jungles of B2 Front, there were five rear service groups
that maintained their own base camps and were responsible for providing food, clothing, and supplies to the mobile regular army units in the
area. Rear Service Group 83, with most of its operations in the Long
Nguyen Secret Zone, served a strategically vital function, located as it
was in the vortex of the southern action, halfway between War Zone D
and War Zone C on an east-west axis, and between the Cambodian border and Saigon running north-south.

Food, mail, and medical care, read the list in General Westmoreland's
wallet, reminding him of what made an army function well, and it was
no different with the other side. The communist forces did not build
forty ice cream plants, and they did not have resupply helicopters to
ferry hot meals and pastries to troops in the field, but they placed the
same emphasis on feeding soldiers.

The results were mixed, but the effort was enormous. There were a
variety of means for getting food to Rear Service Group 83 base camps
and then on to the fighting units. Less than one percent of the rice and
other food was produced by military agricultural teams or civilians
working directly for the Viet Cong in combat hamlets. More rice could
be obtained from local farmers. This involved coercion at times, but
more often the motivation was neither political nor physical but financial. If a food broker was paying a farmer X amount for fifty kilograms
of rice, and the broker then sold it to a processor for X plus two, who in
turn sold it to a retailer for X plus three, an agent for the Viet Cong
would cut out the middlemen and offer the farmer X plus two or three.
"The reasoning process involved was, 'I can make more money selling it
to the agent. Why should I not sell it to him?'" said Robert DeStatte, a
former U.S. Army interrogator who became expert on the methods of
the enemy after conducting hundreds of prisoner of war interviews.
There were also purchasing networks in several local villages that
helped the rear service group acquire other foodstuffs. An agent would

approach a woman and ask her to purchase ten cans of sweetened condensed milk for him the next time she went to market. He would give her enough money to buy fifteen cans. In doing that small service she also helped her family. The modest amount was less likely to come to the attention of local authorities, but if the agent had fifty people in the area willing to make the same deal, he could buy a substantial supply of food and other necessities, including antibiotics, bandages, and vitamin supplements.

Along with materiel, nearly half the food was supplied by Hanoi and came from outside the region into B2 Front through transshipment points along the Cambodian border. From there rice would be hauled to Rear Service Group 83 base camps on old one-speed bicycles that were double-tired and reconfigured with wooden poles so that each could carry up to four 220-pound bags, or a total of 880 pounds of rice per bike. The task required men and women of uncommon strength and stamina. They traveled long distances over jungle paths less than a meter wide, fording rivers and crossing streams on creaking monkey bridges made of bamboo. Group 83 held elections every year to honor the best bicycle rice transporter. Nguyen Van Lam was not strong enough for the job. It would have killed him, he said later. He weighed less than 110 pounds.

There were no temperature-controlled warehouses to store rice once it reached the jungle base camps. Some was amassed underground, most in thatch-roofed huts, protected from the soggy ground by nylon stretched over ropes and poles. Depending on the weather and storage conditions, the rice might rot after a few months, and it was constantly being destroyed by American bombing attacks and infantry patrols. According to mandates of the Rear Services Directorate, Group 83 was never to allow the storage level of rice to fall below fifty tons and also was supposed to receive three days' advance notice that a fighting unit was coming in for food and resupply.

In practice things were different. When the First Regiment of the Ninth Division came traipsing into the Long Nguyen Secret Zone, there was no warning and no rice. October had been a difficult month for the First Regiment, as had all of 1967. The proud First had been badly hurt during the year's early fighting in Operation Junction City (Gian-xon Xity, the Vietnamese called it, using the phonetic spelling for Junction that was similar to that used for Johnson, as in President Gian-xon). After that battle the unit had moved east to the jungles north of Phuoc Vinh in

War Zone D, where its responsibility was to defend a logistics supply route that ran diagonally from central headquarters near the Cambodian border north of Tay Ninh across and down to the South China Sea above Vung Tau. It was also directed to recuperate, rearm, replenish its manpower, and prepare for the next offensive. But there were more problems in War Zone D. Some villagers had rallied to the Americans and gave away the regiment's location, resulting in another fierce battle with elements of the Big Red One near Bau Chua in September. Equally troublesome, Rear Service Group 81, which was in charge of that sector, by October had run out of rice. The complex logistical network was of no use: there was no rice to be bought, no rice to be harvested, and no rice in storage.

Twelve hundred soldiers in the First Regiment had virtually no food. They avoided starvation by eating baby bamboo shoots and boiling a plant known as stink grass, a distasteful weed that in the north was used as fertilizer.

The regimental commander, whose revolutionary name was Sau Hung, had already left for central headquarters near Cambodia to take part in planning for the next offensive, leaving the hungry regiment under the command of Vo Minh Triet, his deputy. Triet was given orders to move the unit from War Zone D west and then north to a staging area along the Ba Chiem stream, where they would prepare for a massive, multiunit attack on the city of Loc Ninh. It was not part of the plan to stop halfway on the march west and spend several days in the Long Nguyen Secret Zone. Triet took his regiment there for one reason only, to search for rice. He was disappointed to discover that Rear Service Group 83 had no rice either. After meeting with the logistics commander, he set up temporary quarters there to await the next shipment of rice, which was said to be imminent. His engineers dug a water hole near the draw and they boiled more stink grass.

Triet's purpose was to get the food and move on, but now something else was in the way. On his first night American high-performance jets screeched overhead and dropped an assortment of cluster bombs and napalm bombs on the jungle. Helicopters were sighted, and it appeared obvious to Triet that an American battalion was nearby, looking for him and his men. There had been two minor scrapes since his regiment had arrived. He had no food, but firepower was not a problem. His three battalions were fully armed with AK-47s, along with DK-2 antitank weapons, Chinese- and Soviet-produced recoilless rifles, mortars, howitzers, rocket-propelled grenades, the Chinese equivalent of M-60 ma-chine guns, heavier .50-caliber machine guns, and DH-10s, a variation of the claymore mine that was three times larger than an American-made claymore and had two hundred fragments packed inside. He had several local security units, including Nguyen Van Lam's C-1 Company, and local guerrillas who knew every foot of the territory. He placed two battalions of his First Regiment in the jungle on the west side of the draw and one battalion on the east side. He set up a communications network with hardwire telephone lines and placed radiomen high in trees along various paths leading into his camp. Then he waited for the Americans. He did not know who they were. It was not his job to know. His job was to get to the Ba Chiem stream.

This was not part of the plan; no battle was intended here. It was rather only an annoyance to Vo Minh Triet that Terry Allen's 2/28 Black Lions kept marching out from their night defensive position a kilometer to the north.

CHAPTER 15

"THE TREES ARE MOVING"

T HE NIGHT BEFORE, under a full moon, the last thing Clark Welch had talked about was the coming of the B-52s. The huge Stratofortress jet bombers flew so high in their missions over South Vietnam that they usually went unseen even in daylight, but they would soar overhead hauling payloads of up to sixty thousand pounds in their big bellies, and the falling bombs made a sound all their own, and there were violent flashes of light, and then "the fucking world erupted." It would be that way all night, Welch had predicted to Sergeant Barrow. The eight-engine swept-wing monsters would fly in from the U-Tapao Royal Navy Air Field in Thailand and make the world erupt in the jungle of the secret zone where the Viet Cong tried to hide.

In the soggy earth next to his sleeping mattress, Welch placed two small sticks and pointed them in the direction that he expected to hear the overnight rumble. The B-52s, he thought, would be only the loudest instruments in a percussive symphony of devastation that might also include the boom of howitzers from 105- and 155-millimeter artillery batteries at the fire base on Route 13 as well as the *thwoop* of rocket grenades from the night defensive position and the eruption of claymore mines beyond the concertina wire. Noise was good, the more racket the better. The Viet Cong had even coined a phrase to describe the cacophony of fire they usually received from the Big Red Brothers. They called it "New Zealand music," a poetic allusion to the atonal sounds of the Maori people, some of whom were in Vietnam fighting in alliance with the Americans.

There was no New Zealand music from midnight to dawn on the morning of October 17. There were no sounds of war at all, only stillness.

Welch woke up realizing that he had missed the artillery and the B-52s. The big bombers had made preplanned strikes earlier in the week a few miles away but had not returned. They were assigned elsewhere in MACV's countrywide B-52 strike plan, a tightly controlled operation run by the Strategic Air Command and not always tied directly to specific ground missions at specific times. Some First Division officers would say later that B-52 strikes preceded the march that day, that in fact the mission was designed specifically for the 2/28 Black Lions to go in and see what damage the bombs had done, but it did not happen that way. An air force captain later signed an affidavit certifying that "no B-52 strikes were placed in the area" until five days later. Instead, as Welch put it, "the big thing that happened all night was nothing. Silence. Silent night."

They woke at six, then roll call, and with coffee the buzz started, same as the night before. The resupply helicopter arrived with more ammo. Men were moving faster, with more determination, though not all of them reacted to pressure the same way. Some soldiers, by training or instinct, focused only on what was in front of them. This was another day, another search-and-destroy mission, and they would handle whatever came their way, when and if it came. They knew little about the orders and had no desire to learn more. They survived in the moment; anything else was extraneous and probably dangerous. Other men, sensitive to the slightest portent of trouble, felt an unusual stir that morning. They would later describe an eerie sensation in camp, as though an ominous smell or a smog were hanging over the Ong Thanh stream.

Private Melesso Garcia of Delta told his buddies that he had a feeling he shouldn't go out that day.

Jim George, the Alpha commander, awoke with a sense that if ever he was going to be shot, it would be that day. He gave his executive officer the addresses of people to write to just in case.

Ernie (Goodtimes) Buentiempo, a radioman in Alpha, conducted his morning ritual, placing his hands in front of his chest in a healing motion, as though he were divining the future.

Hey, man, what is it? asked his fellow RTO, Michael Arias. *Something,* Goodtimes responded. *I feel it in my bones.*

IT WAS EARLY EVENING in Washington, twelve hours behind Vietnam time, and LBJ and McNamara at that very moment were meeting with the White House economic team, including Charles L. Schultze, director of the Bureau of the Budget, and Gardner Ackley, chairman of the Council of Economic Advisers. Johnson too felt something bad in his bones. With growing desperation he was searching for ways to sustain the war effort without sacrificing his domestic agenda.

The notion that the U.S. economy was so powerful that it could support "guns and butter" simultaneously was collapsing. There were projections of a ballooning budget deficit. Johnson wondered how he could "fight the war, send children to school, and meet all our other responsibilities." Although he did not want the press or public to know the details yet, he was considering asking Congress for another $4-billion supplemental appropriation to fund the war. His prized Great Society initiatives, especially the War on Poverty, were in jeopardy. A test vote in the House had just slashed $1.2 billion from the poverty programs. Schultze and Ackley suggested that McNamara could restructure his budget to make it appear that he was cutting non-Vietnam expenditures. They advised Johnson to co-opt Congress by proposing modest cuts in some of his favorite programs along with a tax increase—"even if in your judgment there is no chance of getting a tax increase passed." Without it, they said, interest rates and inflation would soar in 1968, and "responsibility for those conditions [could not] help but be a major election issue."

At the same approximate time, in Hanoi, a communiqué was being released announcing the formation of the Committee of Solidarity with the American People, a group intended to "provide favorable conditions for understanding between Vietnamese and American" citizens. In its first pronouncement the committee urged Americans "to demand that the U.S. government stop its aggression, bombing raids and other military actions against the People's Republic of Vietnam, withdraw U.S. troops, and recognize the National Liberation Front as the only true representative of the South Vietnamese people." American intelligence officers in Vietnam and Washington immediately interpreted the communiqué and related it to events at home. "The announcement was obviously timed for the antiwar demonstrations scheduled this week in the United States," the State Department intelligence and research office reported to Secretary Rusk. "Within a few hours of the initial announcement, Hanoi radio reported that the Front committee had sent a message to the U.S. National Mobilization Committee and the Students Mobilization Committee applauding their October 21 'struggle to end the war in Vietnam.' The message added that 'our struggle . . . in coordination with your struggle' will compel the U.S. government to end the war in Vietnam."

In Moscow, it was "Hanoi Day." The mayor of Hanoi had arrived the night before, and preparations were under way for a daylong "soiree" at the Central House of Culture of Railway Workers. The mayor spoke in praise of the "two hero cities" and the "immense help" the Soviets had provided liberation forces in Vietnam.

THE BLACK LIONS began gathering at twenty to eight. Kasik's Bravo Company would stay back to guard the NDP, along with the mortar platoons. Reese's Charlie Company was stationed at the artillery fire base, Caisson V, a few kilometers away. Erwin's reconnaissance platoon had its separate marching orders, to head west later in the morning. For the two-company search-and-destroy mission, George's Alpha would lead, followed by Welch's Delta. Major Sloan, the battalion's operations officer, would stay at the field camp's tactical operations center, but Lieutenant Colonel Allen was bringing most of the rest of his headquarters staff on the ground with him, including his intelligence officer, Captain Blackwell; Sergeant Major Dowling; operations sergeant Eugene Plier; and his new radioman, Pasquale Tizzio. The battalion's air operations officer, Captain Grosso, would stay back and then go overhead in an observation helicopter. The mission was of enough significance to the division's commanders—especially General Coleman, Colonel Newman, and his operations officer, Major Holleder—that they intended to pay special attention to it when they went up in command-and-control helicopters that day. General Hay would not be around; he had a meeting at MACV headquarters near Saigon.

As the battalion gathered to leave, Blackwell came running back toward the operations tent and asked Grosso to lend him his K-Bar knife. "I'll bring you back an ear," he said. It was a moment of mindless bravado that at least reflected some confidence from the command team. They were going hunting for VC.

The morning opened in a bright haze, with temperatures already in the eighties. It was "just a very muggy dog day, with no air movement," thought Joe Costello, the Alpha grenadier. "It was just kind of *aaaggghhh*." At two minutes after eight, out from the perimeter they marched, into the sunlight, into the dog day, through the tall grass, toward the wood line to the south. They were loaded. Each rifleman carried fifteen magazines of ammo, with eighteen rounds per magazine. Don Koch, a platoon sergeant from Bravo who had been up all night guarding the perimeter, stood silently watching the companies march away. He had never bothered to study a departing patrol before, and never would again, but he watched that morning and the image stayed with him.

Alpha came out in left and right files ten to fifteen yards apart, with small teams protecting the flanks. To call this a company would be generous. Captain George had only sixty-five men with him, half a full complement. The acting platoon leader of his first platoon was a staff sergeant, Willie Johnson, who had two squads of eleven men each. The second platoon was similarly undersized. Second Lieutenant Peter J. Edwards had been in charge of the platoon for only ten days and had not had time to work with his men on fire and maneuver drills before leading them into the field. The third platoon, known as the hillbilly platoon because many of its men came from Appalachia, was under Second Lieutenant Thomas V. Mullen Jr. It was not a platoon at all, only eleven men total, including a machine-gun team. Its other eleven members had served on ambush patrol overnight and remained in the perimeter to rest. Still, with two platoons in front and another company behind him, Mullen thought it would be "a walk in the park" for his little outfit. In the shirt pocket of his fatigues he carried a wallet that a soldier had given him when he went out on ambush patrol the night before and had forgotten to retrieve.

Jim George, carrying a Car-15 semiautomatic and a .45, marched in the right file behind the first platoon along with his forward observer team and two RTOs, big Lee Price and Michael Farrell, the kid from New Orleans who had come over with George on the *General John Pope*. Willie Johnson was the fourth man back in the right file ahead of George, followed by his radioman, Buentiempo. Johnson had a favorite song, the 1966 rhythm-and-blues hit "Knock on Wood" by Eddie Floyd, that he sang every day as an expression of soulful superstition. "It's like thunder, lightning, the way you love me is frightening. . . . Think I better knock, knock, knock on wood." Buentiempo, his own superstition giving him bad vibes that morning, could only hope that Johnson's wood knocking would get them through.

At the front was a point team led by Ray Gribble, who had left Alpha briefly to work as an aide to Big Jim Shelton in the First Division's operations shop in Lai Khe but had returned a few days earlier, saying that he wanted to be in the field and that his men needed him. Reluctantly, Shelton had let him go. On the left file, platoon sergeant Donald Pipkin was the ninth man back, followed by his RTO, Michael Arias, who lugged a twenty-five-pound PRC-25 radio on his back. Along with six smoke grenades to mark his platoon's positions, Arias also had a Chinese hand grenade, a souvenir that he had found during Alpha's operations on the fifteenth. Behind them was the company's tough first sergeant, José Valdez, a professional soldier with fifteen years in the army, who by standard operating procedure always marched on the file opposite George.

Private Costello was positioned as the second-to-last man on the right file of the second platoon. As a grenadier, he seemed especially vulnerable, yet he felt comfortable with his unusual weapon. The M-79 grenade launcher, known variously as the bloop gun, blooper, or thumper, was shaped liked a large-bore sawed-off shotgun. It was fired from the shoulder and sent out a single 40-millimeter high-explosive grenade spiraling on an arc toward a target thirty to a few hundred yards away, thereby covering a middle distance farther than a tossed grenade's and closer than a mortar's. The spiral rotation caused the grenade, after thirty yards of spinning, to arm itself for detonation on impact. The grenade's flight path was fairly steady, but grenadiers in Vietnam, where the M-79 was first used, learned to take into account that it tended to drift right. It was a light weapon, weighing only 6.6 pounds, so Costello moved free and easy compared to the man walking behind him, his buddy Tom Hinger, the platoon medic.

Doc Hinger was a walking skeleton by mid-October, down to barely a hundred pounds on his five-eight frame. His pants were twenty-six at the waist. On most days he armed himself only with a .45 pistol, but today he switched to an M-16 and two bandoliers of ammunition because of the high probability of action. He also carried his C-rations for the day (spicy beef), extra water (three canteens holding a quart each), along with his medical aid bag, which contained field dressings, morphine syrettes, IV tubing, a small surgical kit with scalpel, blades, and sutures, antibiotics, salt pills, pain relievers, and other drugs and ointments. Taped to the side of his aid bag were several heavy cans of blood volume expander, each about the size of a can of tennis balls, containing a ready-made IV kit of serum albumen, a clear, nonperishable liquid that was used to replace massive blood loss in the field until a wounded man could receive a transfusion. In all, it was a seventy-pound burden for the gaunt medic, an almost antlike ratio of load to body mass.

Fifteen minutes after Alpha's march began, Welch's Delta started moving. Sergeant Barrow had counted sixty-eight men at formation before they left—another severely depleted company. At the start there was a break of seventy meters between the two companies, but Alpha had already slowed and the distance separating them narrowed. Delta's third platoon led the way, marching in a three-squad wedge formation so that Lieutenant Stroup, the platoon leader, could more easily keep visual contact with the rear of Alpha. Doc Taylor, the platoon medic, also known as the Preacher, was praying, softly but audibly, on the way out. Private Peter Miller, the Massachusetts rifleman, walked at the front of the right flank. He was wary now, questioning, his gung-ho attitude shaken by the brush of death he had experienced the day before when Captain Jones's lifeless body fell against him. Welch and Barrow, the inseparable pair, marched at the rear of Stroup's platoon, Welch leaning forward, sensitive to every broken twig, Barrow nervously clicking his M-16 from semiautomatic to automatic. The habit annoyed Welch, who would shoot Barrow a smiling glance with every click. Walking with them were Welch's two radiotelephone operators, Scott Up and Scott Down. Barrow had his own radioman, Raymond Phillips, nearby as well.

Behind them marched Terry Allen and the battalion command group, which moved in a protective pocket in Delta's second platoon. Allen wore a pair of binoculars around his neck. Blackwell had his borrowed knife. Then came Pinky Durham, the forward artillery observer, and his radioman, Jim Gilliam, who had just taken the job that morning because Durham's first RTO had been hit in the leg during the brief firefight the day before.

Like Alpha's first platoon, Delta's second was led by a sergeant, in this case Dwayne Byrd, a sharpshooter from Texas who took over in the field when a young second lieutenant left for Lai Khe with an ailment. Byrd had been shocked that morning when "all the big brass" assembled with his platoon. He had never seen the battalion commander on the ground before, and considered it "strange," especially since both companies were short of men. Many of the soldiers in his second platoon were among those who had arrived at Vung Tau less than three months earlier aboard the USNS *Pope*. Mike Troyer was an acting squad leader. On the way across the Pacific he had worried about whether he could kill another human being, but he had long since resolved that question. As he now told new recruits, if you can't do it, you end up in a body bag. Doug Cron marched in the file across from Troyer, carrying ammo for the M-60 machine gun. Thomas Colburn, recovering from a slight elbow wound, was carrying a rifle instead of his usual grenade launcher. The rifle was less burdensome for Baby-san, as his buddies called him, a kid so thin that it was said he could hide behind a bamboo pole and never get hit. Faustin Sena carried the flamethrower, walking security in the center flank about twenty meters behind the command group. It was a new weapon for him; the only living thing he had killed with it so far was a chicken that popped out of a tunnel. It had surprised him, so he had "toasted it."

Fred Kirkpatrick, the skilled rifleman, would have walked point, but he was on R and R, hanging out with a prostitute at the Club Bohemian in Shibuya, Japan, where women took American names and altered their eyes to look more western.

The rear platoon, led by Second Lieutenant Andrew Luberda, also included many former C Packet men. Jack Schroder was back there, marching in the left file. The nickname Machine Gun Red no longer fit. "I got off the M-60 and now carry an M-16 rifle, which is a lot lighter, too," he had written to his wife, Eleanor, in his last letter from the field. A minor injury had made it hard for him to carry the machine gun. He was still waiting for someone from home to ship him a .38 revolver like the one that Bob Nagy carried, but so far the switch from the machine gun had seemed propitious, as that life-saving bullet notch in his rifle from the previous day's battle testified. Schroder had something else new—a bold tattoo on his arm with the insignia of the 101st Airborne, which provoked his latest nickname, Airborne Schroder.

His team leader was the soldier who had taught him how to use the M-60, Danny Sikorski. Just a few more months for Ski and he would be back in Milwaukee, carrying his cue to Mazo's on the south side for a game of pool. His little sister, Diane, was thinking about him all the time, wondering where he was. That night, in her blue bedroom, she would dream about him. Not far from Sikorski, also marching in the left file, was Steve Ostroff, a Jewish kid from Sun Valley, California. "See you later," his buddy Steve Goodman, the battalion armorer, had said to him as Ostroff left the perimeter. A few weeks earlier Ostroff and Goodman had been given special leave to go into Saigon, usually off-limits for the troops at Lai Khe, to celebrate Yom Kippur.

On the right file Greg Landon, the Professor, was hauling a PRC-25 radio for his squad leader, Sergeant Dewey Lester. Landon was a hardened soldier now, ready for battle, eagerly asking his folks to send him a big knife, talking body counts. A copy of an Amherst student magazine had reached him in the field, and he reflected that it seemed surreal to him "to read that stuff now," when he was "so disoriented" from college life. But even as he adjusted to the infantry, Landon maintained his in-

quisitive, skeptical nature. On the way out that morning he was grous-
ing about how the battalion command seemed so eager to get in a fight.
What are we doing this for? he asked. Behind Landon, holding the rear
position, came the first squad, led by Jackie Bolen Jr., the skilled young
soldier from Appalachia, homesick and tired of war.

What are we doing this for? Clark Welch was thinking the same thing,
though he would never tell that to his men. There were many aspects of
this patrol that concerned him. He didn't like the direction they were
going, or the fact that the battalion command group was on the ground
with them. He wished that they had shelled and bombed the target area
more beforehand. And even though Terry Allen had virtually accused
him of being afraid, and yanked him from the lead position, Big Rock
would rather have had Delta out front. In the rear he could only respond, not decide.

Along with his compass and pictograph map, which superimposed
positions over an aerial photograph of the area, Welch constantly recal-
culated his location in the field by counting paces. It was a way for him
to tell reliably how far his company had moved, where it was, and how
long it might take to get back. He knew at all times how many paces he
had stepped off from the perimeter. His normal pace was thirty-four
inches. This morning, with Alpha in front, it was slow moving, and his
step was shorter. When his men started to bunch up, he shouted,
"Spread out! One peanut butter can would get you all. Spread out!" It
was one of his favorite phrases; better peanut butter than some deadlier
allusion. Among their field rations were peanut butter cans that the men
liked to throw into the fire to watch them explode in a messy effusion.

With every step southward, the vegetation grew denser and the field
of vision narrowed. They moved through tall grass and shrubbery, then
edged into the woods. At 8:45 Captain George reported Alpha's position
to the NDP. Forty-five minutes out and they had traveled less than 250
meters. Before proceeding further, George sent teams out to cloverleaf
the territory to his southeast and southwest. The rest of the troops
stopped and waited fifteen minutes for the teams to come back. While
they were standing around, an F-100 screeched overhead for the first air
strike. It was Yellow Bird II, on its way to dropping eight 750-pound
napalm bombs and six 500-pound cluster bombs on a preplanned target
far to the southeast, beyond where Welch's Delta company had made
contact the day before. The cloverleaf teams came back and reported no
movement, no smells, nothing. At 9:10 there was another F-100 over-

head, this time Devil II with six 750-pound napalm bombs heading for a target area even further south. Three more F-100s and two B-57s were also on their way to that same target area.

Big Red One officers were reasonably sure that they knew where the enemy base camp was, but in the end it was only a guess, just as their depth of knowledge about who was out there, and how many, was only a rough estimate. In fact, the napalm bombs were being dropped too far south. The preplanned strikes had been called in by the air liaison officer for the Big Red One's First Brigade, who was supporting the mission even though it was outside his normal tactical area of operations. The forward air controllers working under him were also new to the area and had not had time over the previous week to conduct visual reconnaissance of the territory. They were relying on intelligence provided by people on the ground. The air force had its own team of forward air controllers, part of an overlapping network of army and air force bureaucracies that required great coordination and often led to confusion. Starting at eight that morning, just as the 2/28 Black Lions were leaving their NDP, the only air force forward air controller in the area "was busy for several hours putting in eight preplanned missions on suspected base camps and bunkers several miles away," according to a combat evaluation report later prepared by the air force.

On the ground George's men were humping the jungle. Their noise discipline up front was excellent, he thought. They seemed focused, not distracted. Some of them had cut grass and bamboo and used it around their helmets as camouflage. After another three hundred meters, the growth thickened. Doc Hinger, in the second platoon, could see only ten meters in front of him. It seemed like triple canopy jungle overhead, with "towering trees and vines." Moving up behind Hinger was an RTO from the third platoon, who came close enough that Hinger could overhear a conversation on the company radio, or "push"—something about a trail. Word came back that there would be another cloverleaf. Costello took a few furtive puffs on a cupped cigarette, swigs from the canteen. A guy near him took a piss. The same all the way back to the rear of Delta. Smokes for Jackie Bolen and Mike Troyer. Doug Cron snuck a bite of pound cake. And they waited some more.

The trail ahead was discovered by Alpha's first platoon at 9:56. It was a well-used path running southeast to northwest. Fresh sandal tracks—the Americans called them Ho Chi Minh sandals—led in both directions. Trees nearby seemed newly cut. Willie Johnson radioed the sighting to Captain George and requested permission for his platoon to investigate further. George said okay. Johnson sent cloverleafs to the left and right within sight of the trail. At fifty yards out, the point man on the right cloverleaf team reported seeing several Viet Cong moving through the jungle toward the southwest. George got on the battalion frequency and conferred with Terry Allen. They agreed on a plan. They would stop the cloverleafs and have the point squad set up a hasty ambush at the side of the trail.

From his position with Delta, Clark Welch received word that Alpha had spotted "seven to ten" Viet Cong. By counting paces, he estimated that the lead elements of the battalion were now about two hundred meters short of the point where the day's marching orders called for them to turn east. Welch sent word to his platoon leaders. "Alpha's seen seven," he reported up to Stroup and back to Luberda. "Seven means seventy. Let's get ready. It's going to start." From the platoons the heads-up went down to the squads and teams. By the time it reached Paul Giannico, a team leader in Delta's rear platoon, the message was reduced to its rawest form: *Gooks on the trail. We're setting a hasty ambush.* Many of Welch's men, along with Allen and the command group, had come to a stop in a hazardous zone in the jungle, an oblong stretch of smaller trees and thick shrubs surrounded by bigger trees, some a hundred feet tall, that flanked them on the east and west. The platoon leaders pushed their security flanks out another twenty-five meters toward the tall trees.

Rifleman Peter Miller, in Delta's lead platoon, was puzzled when he got word about the plans. *Ambush? Who the hell are we gonna surprise? More than a hundred guys crashing through the jungle here, and we're gonna sneak up on somebody?*

Ray Gribble led his lead Alpha squad across the trail and began setting up the ambush. Willie Johnson nudged forward with his right file, and Top Valdez brought the left file up and angled it to the right, or west. The troops behind them held in place. Time seemed to stop. Nothing, silence, for a minute, two, three, five. The jungle air was heavy. There was no breeze.

Finally, in Alpha's second platoon, Doc Hinger heard a rapid *click-click-click* above him. Other men up and down the columns were startled by the same sound. Private Arias saw something flash above him. Sergeant Johnson got on the radio with an urgent message to his company commander.

"The trees are moving," he said. "And I think someone's in them."

CHAPTER 16

AMBUSH

THE FRESH TRACKS along the trail, the sighting of enemy soldiers in the distance—these were lures designed to draw the Black Lions deeper into a trap. Scouts from Vo Minh Triet's First Regiment and Rear Service Group 83 had been watching the American soldiers for two days. From Jim George's point patrol all the way to the last man in Clark Welch's rear platoon, every step the Americans took from the perimeter through the tall grass and into the ever-denser jungle had been noticed. Triet was back in his command post a few hundred meters south of the point where Alpha's lead platoon saw the trees move. He was receiving constant updates on the approaching force over a telephone line. Through hand signals, scouts stationed high in trees sent word down to camouflaged comrades below, who then reported the American positions to the command post.

The tree scouts armed with AK-47s and captured American radios, some of them tied into position with ropes and vines, were instructed to look and listen only. They were not to use their radios until Triet told his communications officer to flip the switch so everyone could talk. That order came simultaneously with the signal to attack. When the trap was set, when the American soldiers were just where Triet wanted them to be, moving down and to the right, on a line facing his camouflaged bunkers and the machine guns and preset claymore mines, two of his battalions ready on the west and the third moving into position from the east—at that moment he gave the signal.

Three knocks on a block of wood.

Life absurdly mocking art: How could Sergeant Willie Johnson's favorite song, his superstitious incantation, *knock, knock, knock on wood,* carry such lethal meaning?

PRIVATE FIRST CLASS BREEDEN was the first to die. Clifford Lynn Breeden Jr., aged twenty-two, from Hillsdale, Michigan. He was point man in Gribble's squad on the front right file and the first to cross the trail. A burst of enemy fire struck him as he was setting up his own hasty ambush. Six bullets ripped open his chest and guts. He fired a clip from his M-16 and slumped to the jungle floor.

The opening spray slanted down from trees to the right, or west, followed by a thrum of machine-gun fire coming in low from the front. Jerry Lancaster fell next, and Leon East, and Gribble was losing his squad. He called to Sergeant Johnson that his men had been hit—Ray Neal Gribble's last transmission. Johnson moved the remainder of the right file forward, directing his troops to get down and face the front and right. The point squad from his platoon's left file cut across toward the right, and Captain George called his second platoon forward to reinforce the first.

The opening fusillade echoed back through the woods to the rear platoon of Delta. What was it? Some soldiers in the rear assumed it was Alpha springing its ambush. It sounded like the sort of skirmish the Black Lions had been getting in day after day that October. Contact, a quick firefight, the Americans pulling back to call in artillery and air, the Vietnamese disappearing as suddenly as they came. But this time, up and down the line, sniper fire started pinging down from the trees.

Terry Allen called Alpha and asked the company commander for a situation report. Jim George relayed what he heard and saw in front of him, but he could not say much about the first platoon because he was having trouble raising anyone on the radio. He yelled for Sergeant Johnson. No reply. It sounded bad, but was it? Allen told George to move forward to survey the scene. George crawled through heavy brush with the five-man Alpha command group. It was slow moving, but they eventually found Johnson and the point troops pinned down by machine-gun fire. The machine gun was hidden behind a low bunker protected by a dirt-covered log. It was about fifteen meters away, pointing east and detectable only by the trace of bullets. George pulled a hand grenade and flipped it over his shoulder in the direction of the fire, and in so doing revealed his position. The enemy gun turned on him, but the bullets

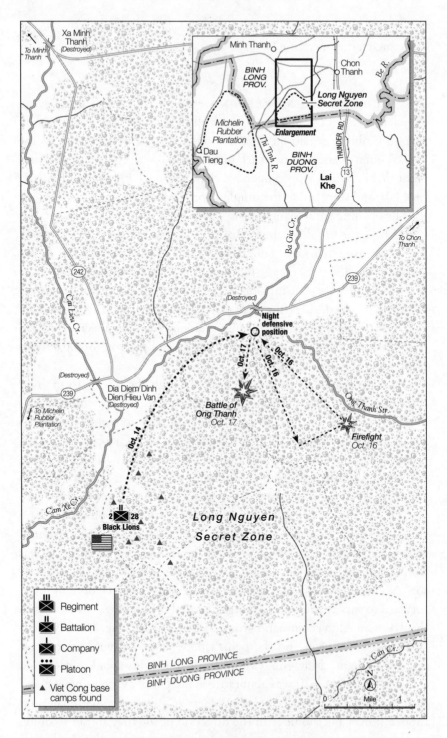

Movements of 2/28 Black Lions

missed and George could see the muzzle flash. He opened up with his Car-15 and silenced the machine gunner.

Moments later one of Triet's men sprang from the thicket with a thirty-six-inch handmade claymore mine and faced it toward the Alpha soldiers. It popped prematurely, killing the man who carried it and ripping out a tree, tearing it to pieces, yet the detonation was so close and powerful that it lacerated George's command group and soldiers nearby. The blast zone was littered with blood and body parts. His company radioman, Michael Farrell, was dead. Others were wounded, including Alpha's artillery forward observer. Men screamed for medics. "I'm hit, Top!" Willie Johnson yelled to Top Valdez. Welts were forming along his arms from the hot, flying shrapnel.

Captain George was struck in the face. The sharpest gash was at his left cheekbone, near his eye. His vision was poor already (he had needed glasses but had not been able to get them in Vietnam), and now in the aftermath of the claymore blast his sight was reduced to a blur of silhouettes. The concussion also ruptured an eardrum. He was supposed to be in command, but he was going deaf and nearly blind. On the ship across the Pacific, George had dreamed of killing fields and had grown weary of what he imagined to be the smell of death. Illusion and reality now merged in this jungle south of the Ong Thanh stream. In a fog he crawled back and to the east, away from the dead zone. He tried to stay low, but also told himself to keep his shattered face above the dirt. He yelled for Top Valdez, but his voice was not loud enough, so he sent an aide out to find the first sergeant. He radioed the battalion commander that he had been hit and was trying to break contact and that he had already lost a radiotelephone operator. "I understand," said Allen, who had been driven by sniper fire to take cover behind a four-foot anthill.

No sooner had Willie Johnson regained his equilibrium than he was hit again, this time in the leg by AK-47 fire. Valdez reached Johnson and tied a handkerchief around his bleeding leg, then heard George's shout and moved toward the captain. *Take over,* George said to him.

From his position near Alpha's rear, Lieutenant Mullen, leader of the third platoon, responded instinctively when he heard a radio squawk that Willie Johnson had been hit. Before being promoted to command the first platoon, Johnson had been Mullen's platoon sergeant in the third, and more than that, his mentor in the field, teaching him much of what he knew about jungle fighting. Mullen rushed toward the point to see if he could help, bringing along one soldier and his radiotelephone operator. They had moved no more than a few dozen meters when they saw Johnson being carried back down the column behind them. Mullen stopped momentarily, then was hit by "a tremendous volume of fire" along the flank that knocked him to the ground, unconscious. Only a few minutes into the fight and Alpha's command was shattered: the company commander and two of his platoon leaders already were casualties.

Alpha's remaining platoon leader, Lieutenant Edwards of the second platoon, had also moved up to help. His intention was to merge his two files into one and link his unit with the right flank of the first platoon. On the way his troops started receiving fire from both sides, left and right, with the heaviest fire now coming from the left flank. It was becoming clear that the Viet Cong had Alpha enclosed on three sides. Edwards was pinned down by tree snipers, then took machine-gun fire from the front. He had brought up a machine-gun team of his own, but the M-60 quickly broke. A grenadier came on line to support, but the cocking lever on his M-79 "got out of position somehow and couldn't be fired." Most of Edwards's men were twenty meters behind him, virtually out of sight. His firepower situation was deteriorating rapidly— broken machine gun, broken grenade launcher, and soon two M-16s were rendered useless by jammed bullets. All Edwards and his party had left were "one M-16 that worked, one grenade, a knife, and a .45-caliber pistol."

Privates Costello and Hinger, the last two men in Edwards's right file, had responded swiftly to the action at the front. Doc Hinger spotted movement in the trees at the exact moment that Michael Arias and Willie Johnson noticed it further to the front, and pointed it out to Costello, who aimed his M-79 at the treetops and lobbed a few grenades in that direction. The movement stopped. A call for medics could be heard in the distance, and with that Hinger scooted forward. Costello asked his squad leader if he should follow the medic forward and give him cover. *Do it,* came the reply, but by the time Costello turned around, Hinger was at least fifteen yards in front and lost from sight.

Dodging sniper fire, moving toward the "Medic!" shouts, Hinger made his way to George and the others wounded by the claymore blast. He began working on the first man he encountered, a private who had two massive tissue wounds, one on the leg, another on the elbow. Top Valdez was there, trying to organize the company amid the chaos. Ernie Buentiempo was nearby. After his ominous morning vibes, Goodtimes was already without his radio, which he had thrown off, and his M-16 was jammed by blood. George, barely functioning, struggled to get on the battalion net again with Terry Allen, giving him a situation report. Allen wanted a body count. George thought it was an odd time to ask for a body count. It was hard enough for him to give a reasonably accurate accounting of his own men. He had Alpha soldiers still fifty meters to the front of him, he reported, and about ten casualties in his vicinity, five of whom had to be carried. And he was still receiving fire. Allen told him to mark his position with smoke and move back. They would bring in the artillery. Breaking contact was slow, George told Allen. After that he could hear no more.

Hinger moved from one wounded man to the next. The artillery forward observer, Lieutenant Kay, was a mess: his face bloody, his leg mashed, a big chunk gone from his wrist, two gashes in his shoulder. As Hinger worked on him, the fire was so heavy that he "could almost taste the cordite." He had tunnel vision now, the commotion around him blocked out, concentrating only on what was in front of him. Someone had taken his M-16, or he had given it away, he could not remember and it didn't matter. Weapons were moving from one soldier to another and being left and recovered. He took Lieutenant Kay's .45 and a clip of ammo and moved on to another soldier wounded in the kneecap. He heard someone yell, "Fall back! Fall back!" but it barely registered and he could not leave a wounded man. Riflemen Paul Fitzgerald and Olin Hargrove, along with Private first class James C. Jones, an aide to Lieutenant Kay, stayed with Hinger while the others pulled back.

Jones emptied the ammunition belt for his .45, then picked up the M-16 of a fallen soldier and fired until it jammed, and finally grabbed a discarded grenade launcher. He saw bushes moving and flashes from rifles but never spotted a single enemy soldier, though he knew they were all around. When he tried to rise up, an AK-47 shot the strap off his radio. His boss, Lieutenant Kay, was unable to call in the fire missions, so Jones would do it himself, even though he was "too scared to think clearly." He made contact with the First Division's artillery batteries at Caisson V, who fired 105-millimeter shells within fifty meters of his location.

Costello had been looking for Doc Hinger. As he moved toward Alpha's front, the gunfight reminded him of "an extraordinarily good fireworks show." Time was distorted; a minute seemed like an hour. Men were returning fire, but in the distance behind him he could hear periodic shouts of "Hold your fire! Cease fire!" Were they shooting their own men? Toward the front he was pinned to the jungle floor, hugging the ground, pressing down, anything to get a millimeter lower, his head sideways with the big steel helmet sticking up. There was no brush to cover him, only dirt and smoke. He heard rounds go overhead and felt dizzy, certain one would hit. From the sound he determined that the VC were using a big, .50-caliber machine gun, more of a *boom-boom* than a *brrrr.* He looked down and saw ants crawling on his arm. They were biting him, and he knew from experience that it should hurt, but his adrenaline was running so strong that he said to himself, *I can't feel these suckers.* From nearby came a yell for help. He looked over at a wounded soldier. The man's insides had come out, hanging there, suspended. Costello's first instinct was to stuff them in, but from training films he remembered that was wrong. Cover them and apply pressure, he thought to himself, and that is what he did.

Another explosion went off behind him. Costello felt a shrapnel sting in his back. He could do no more for the wounded soldier, who was going into shock and probably dying. Try as he might, he could not call up the man's name. He remembered that the guy had a candy-apple-red '62 Chevy that he was proud of and a young wife he loved very much and that he didn't care for Costello at all and Costello wished that he had. With bullets zinging overhead, there was the young grenadier, taking one last look at a dying comrade and thinking strangely, *I wish we had been nicer to each other.* In the din he could hear Top Valdez yelling, "Fall back! Fall back!"

Valdez, in command of Alpha now, had radioed Allen with another situation report. Move north, Allen had told him. He was calling in the artillery. Valdez and the soldiers with him moved seven wounded men north and east about seventy meters and formed a makeshift assembly area. He had Captain George there, and Lieutenant Kay. There was Sergeant Pipkin, who had been shot in the leg as he tried to move the first platoon's left file over toward Gribble's decimated right squad. Specialist 4 Carl Woodard, a squad leader at age nineteen, brought his men from the second platoon over to provide security on the right flank. Pipkin's radiotelephone operator, Michael Arias, and rifleman Fitzgerald came stumbling back carrying a wounded comrade, Charles Morrisette. Arias had tried to get two other men to help carry Morrisette, but they were taking cover behind a shrub, pinned down by machine-gun fire; they waited for a lull in the shooting before they too crawled back. "Come to the fire!" Valdez shouted, shooting his .45 twice into the air.

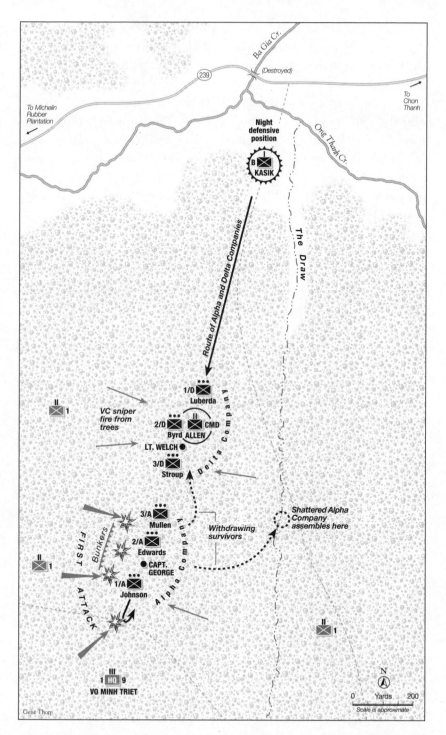

Ba Gia Cr.

239   (Destroyed)

To Chon Thanh

To Michelin Rubber Plantation

Night defensive position
B KASIK

Ong Thanh Cr.

The Draw

Route of Alpha and Delta Companies

1/D Luberda Delta Company

VC sniper fire from trees

2/D Byrd   CMD ALLEN

LT. WELCH

3/D Stroup

3/A Mullen   Alpha Company

Shattered Alpha Company assembles here

Withdrawing survivors

2/A Edwards

CAPT. GEORGE

FIRST ATTACK

Bunkers

1/A Johnson

1 HQ 9
VO MINH TRIET

N

0   Yards   200
Scale is approximate

Gene Thorp

Moving into the Ambush

Lieutenant Edwards, who had been separated from his platoon near the front, with two of his men and a useless armory of malfunctioning weapons, could sense that the American artillery was coming in closer and closer to their position and that they would have to move north. They crawled fifty meters, then got up and ran in a crouch. He could hear the artillery but not much enemy fire. The shots he heard seemed spaced and deliberate, as though they were "taking careful shots at the wounded." They finally reached Valdez and the assembly area, joining the band of Alpha soldiers there who had formed a circle and were taking cover where they could, behind shrubs, anthills, logs. It was a few minutes before eleven.

AT THAT MOMENT in the American Midwest, the clock read thirteen hours earlier, half past nine on the evening of October 16. The San Francisco Mime Troupe was just reaching the climax of its final performance of *L'Amant Militaire* at the Firehouse Theater in Minneapolis. Sandra Archer, wearing a miter, appeared suspended in air above the stage and brought the house down with the announcement "I'm a da Pope!" Before the play ended and the troupe packed up for the next stop on its college tour, the University of Wisconsin in Madison, all issues of war and peace were swiftly and neatly resolved from on high. "The war is over. Peace is declared," the pope said. "Pacem in terris. Now, my children, we want to hear no more lies and we want to see no more destruction."

But the war in Vietnam was not over, not even close. It would not be over until another forty-five thousand American soldiers were dead. Young infantrymen were dying in the Long Nguyen Secret Zone right then, as the curtain fell at the Firehouse.

THE BLACK LIONS certainly had found what they were searching for. Now what? Was this an offensive operation or defensive? Would they destroy or be destroyed? How many Viet Cong were out there? Would the enemy stand and fight? That George's lead company had walked into an ambush became apparent to Clark Welch as soon as he heard reports over the radio that machine-gun fire at the point was coming from enemy bunkers. This signified more than a sniper attack; it meant the Viet Cong had been ready and waiting. But Welch did not yet feel that his own Delta Company at the rear was hopelessly outmanned. Though the enemy fire began simultaneously up and down the line, with Triet's knocks on the wood block, the opening minutes of the battle had been somewhat less intense in Delta's area. Only a few men had been wounded in the initial volley, including the battalion's S-2 intelligence officer, Captain Blackwell. Welch figured that he was dealing primarily with some well-placed machine guns and a squad of snipers high in the trees to his right. He shot the first one himself. "I got that sonofabitch!" Big Rock yelled to a platoon sergeant who had pointed toward the tree. Private Garcia, a rifleman on the right flank, took out another sniper, who fell ten feet and dangled in midair, his legs tied in ropes and vines. In Delta's lead platoon Peter Miller watched a squadmate fire high above him and was splattered by debris, including a magazine of ammo and what Miller thought was a sack of rice balls. One by one, Delta was quieting the trees, but for every sniper killed it seemed three others appeared.

Welch's role commanding the rear company was to serve as a backing force for Alpha, and that is how he now concentrated his efforts. He passed the word to his men to hold fire unless they had a definite target. He called his lead platoon and directed Lieutenant Stroup to link up with the rear element of Alpha. Prepare to take Alpha's wounded back through your ranks, Stroup was told. And be ready for an about-face on a 360-degree azimuth. The azimuth was the angle of deviation from a fixed direction, which in this case was due north, the location of the NDP. As the first trickle of dazed and wounded Alpha men staggered back, Peter Miller and several other Delta soldiers ran forward to help, crossing the same trail that Gribble had first discovered. There was machine-gun fire ripping straight down the trail. The Delta soldiers tore branches from trees and took off their shirts to form makeshift stretchers. Welch closed his second platoon around Terry Allen to provide security for the lieutenant colonel, who remained behind the anthill as his battlefield command post.

Stroup and his first Delta platoon waited for the main force of Alpha to withdraw through them. After the first battered group, only a few others came back in a haphazard retreat. Top Valdez had set up his makeshift perimeter to the left of Stroup's point troops. In the dense forest, it was like being in another world, and they never connected. Valdez and his men thought they heard the Delta troops but could not see them. Stroup wondered what was taking so long, why they were just sitting there. The battlefield slowly quieted. It was by no means silent; the Viet

Cong were still firing away, but the volume had diminished considerably. What was happening? The First Division artillery had been stopped, check-fired in army terminology, so that air support could come in. Most of the soldiers lost track of time. The lull seemed like a few minutes to some, forever to others. It was at least a half hour.

The second wave of the enemy attack, when it finally came, started near the front and moved back through the battalion columns with awful fury. Delta was hit from both sides and even some from the rear, but this time the worst was coming from the left, or east. Triet had taken advantage of the pause to bring more elements of his third backing battalion across the draw from the east. He also had moved more men on line from the south and west. The U ambush was complete. With fire pouring in from three sides, it became difficult to distinguish enemy fire from friendly fire. A machine gun pounding at the battalion command area from the east sounded like an American gun and further confused the situation. First Sergeant Barrow heard Terry Allen and other officers shout, "Cease fire! Cease fire! You're shooting your own men." Welch thought differently and began yelling "Fire! Fire!" Confused soldiers decided for themselves. Most returned fire. More Alpha soldiers made their way through the crossfire and reached what became a makeshift aid station for wounded men near the battalion command perimeter. Welch, with his familiar forward lean, lurched up toward Stroup's platoon and back toward the rear, trying to hold his company together, firing his .45 as he went. He calculated on the run that he was now dealing with four machine guns on the east, six to ten from the southeast, and four from the west. The machine-gun fire came at them in fifty- to one-hundred-round bursts, six inches off the ground.

There was no longer any question as to who held fire superiority. The Black Lions' lone advantage was artillery support, but that was minimized by close fighting—the enemy's trademark tactic of hugging the Americans by the belt and holding tight—and by confusion over when and where to stop the artillery to bring in air power, which never came close to the actual battle site in any case. The Viet Cong stayed within fifty meters at all times and often came within ten meters. They were blowing claymore mines, sending in rocket-propelled grenades, and firing down from the trees with AK-47s.

Welch tried to call in mortar support. *Fire the last targets,* he radioed back to Sergeant Terry Warner at the mortar station inside the night defensive position. He could not remember the "last targets" (the coordinates he had arranged with his mortar team during the march south), but he intended to adjust the mortars once he knew where they were landing. *Wilco! Wilco! Wilco!* Warner replied affirmatively. But nothing happened. The orders were countermanded by a battalion officer at the NDP who said it was against First Division policy to fire mortars into thick canopy jungle.

In the din of war Welch could hear enemy soldiers "yelling, scream-ing, and laughing back and forth," especially from the east. Trying to eliminate the enemy machine guns became a task of great courage but Sisyphean frustration. Welch would fix the location of a machine gun and point it out to his men. Two or three would rise up and go after the gun, often taking out the Viet Cong but getting shot in the effort. All those letters home to Lacy about building the best damn company in the First Division, the best damn unit in all of Vietnam, had come down to this—one after another, his kids sacrificing themselves to silence ma-chine guns, if only for a minute. Not long after each enemy gunner was hit, replacements from Triet's regiment filled the void and the firing started again.

Though the machine-gun charges proved futile in the face of such a large enemy force, they at least involved clear action with a defined goal. For most Delta men most of the time, the battle was undefined and the enemy unseen. They were pinned down, confused, woozy with fright, fighting to save themselves and their buddies. Dwayne Byrd, the young Texan leading the second platoon, had a sharpshooter's eyes, but could never find the face of the enemy. He saw only flashes that seemed to be coming out of the ground.

Jack Schroder was one of the first men wounded when the second round of shooting started. "Airborne Schroder's hit in the leg," platoon sergeant Luther Smith shouted, and members of his squad crawled over to help, dragging him toward the battalion command area, which they assumed was secure. "I'll be all right, I can make it," Schroder said. A few meters away a rocket grenade hit Sergeant Smith, blowing off much of his left leg. He was still conscious when Faustin Sena reached him. Sena took out his first aid kit and lit a cigarette and gave it to Smith, then moved back when a bullet pinged off his helmet and he heard his squad leader tell him to take over the radio. Machine-gun fire struck Sena in the wrist, making it difficult for him to work the radio and painful for him to crawl.

Radioman Frank McMeel, another of the former C Packet troops, got stuck behind a clump of bushes that offered less protection by the minute, the once-leafy branches pruned by withering enemy fire. Every time he moved, the wood-chipped ground in front of him was sprayed by fire from brush to his right. His uniform became covered with sawdust. The first thump McMeel felt was a joke; a bullet had gone through his C-rations and sent spiced beef flying. "Someone shot my fuckin' lunch," he said to his buddy, Donnie Hodges. Then McMeel looked down at his T-shirt and saw blood and realized that he had been hit too, though he was too numb to feel it. He was shot again. And a third time. All became a blur around him. He fell back against his heavy radio and thought to himself, *Three strikes so far and I'm lucky I'm still here. Better not get hit a fourth time.*

Specialist Four Mike Troyer had been lighting a cigarette when the firefight intensified. He was near the battalion command post, where he had just undertaken an unfinished effort to evacuate the wounded Captain Blackwell. He and Joe Lovato, the company medic, had placed Blackwell on a stretcher and had started to move out when an officer said they should bring Blackwell back to the command area. The fighting might be over; the captain could be evacuated later, they were told. After leaving the prone Blackwell north of Allen and the anthill, Troyer took his position on the flank, lit his cigarette, and came under fire. He found cover behind another anthill, sharing it with a humble private with the august military name of Colonel Fett. Troyer crouched on the left side of the anthill, in the shade. Private Colonel Fett was on the right side, in the sunlight. Troyer avoided enemy fire. Fett took a bullet in the shoulder. Most of the men getting hit were in the sunlight, Troyer noticed. He rose to his knees and ripped open Fett's shirt. He had a hard time finding the hole. It wasn't where it was supposed to be, Troyer thought, because the bullet had entered but never come out. He finally found the wound, started to patch it, and yelled for a medic. Here came Doc Gomez, the second platoon's aidman. Gomez jumped on Troyer and pushed him facedown into the mulched earth. "You damn fool! What are you trying to do, get killed?" Gomez said, worried that Troyer had made himself an easy target. Then he pulled Fett into the shade and began working on him.

To his left Troyer saw Melesso Garcia behind a log, gesturing. It seemed that Garcia wanted to say something. He turned on his side and pushed his body up with one hand—and at that moment was shot. A look came over his face that Troyer had not seen before. For two days

Garcia had been haunted by premonitions that he should not be out there, and now the realization of his foreboding registered on his face. Troyer had never been hit. He wondered what it would feel like. He could only imagine from Melesso Garcia's silent expression of horror.

Tom Colburn was also on the right flank, taking cover behind an anthill, where he had been hiding since the shooting began. He had been "scared shitless" the entire time. His buddies joked that Baby-san was so thin he could disappear behind a bamboo reed, and the anthill seemed to be doing the job now, but his fortunate position brought its own measure of psychological torment. Only a few meters away on the jungle floor another Delta soldier was caught in the sunlight, exposed to a tree sniper. "Colburn! Colburn!" the man yelled when he was hit. Then he was hit again and their eyes met and Colburn could see the look of desperation. The soldier, crying for help, tried to crawl from the line of fire. Each time he moved, he was shot. Five shots. Six. What should Colburn do? The noble response, he thought, would be to leave the anthill and try to pull his comrade to safety. But he could not force himself do it. It would only lead to his own death, he thought. "Charlie wanted you to go out there so he could kill you too." So Colburn stayed behind the anthill, haunted, as the wounded buddy called his name. He felt helpless, guilty, protecting his own ass, guys dying all around him. He was only eighteen, but he "got old real quick."

To the rear on the right flank Greg Landon, the Professor, had taken off his PRC-25 radio and was trying to unjam his squad leader's faulty M-16 when he got shot in the back. Like Troyer and most Delta infantrymen who had come to Vietnam on the USNS *Pope* three months earlier, Landon had never been shot before and did not know how it would feel. It was just a thud, and he remained conscious and kept moving. A machine-gun bullet from the south had grazed his back, cutting through his skin in a long, ugly, but superficial slice. Reynolds Lonefight crawled over and tried to patch him with bandages, but it was "like trying to put a hamburger bun over a plate of spaghetti." Lonefight had discarded two faulty weapons already, first his M-79 and then an M-16 that jammed on his fourth magazine, and now he took Landon's rifle and started covering the right flank. A claymore mine went off and sent shrapnel flying into his wrist, hip, and leg. Nearby, another grenadier, Robert Jensen, saw a soldier from Alpha running toward them with no weapon, no shirt, and no helmet, screaming, "Get me out of here!" It appeared as though medics had worked on this soldier's wound-ravaged body once already. He had been hit in the groin, chest, arms, testicles, and right leg and was bleeding badly. Jensen jumped up, stopped the man, placed him against a tree, gave him water, and started to bandage him. Landon crawled over to help.

At their makeshift assembly point to the southeast, Top Valdez and his weary band of Alpha survivors decided to withdraw. Captain George had wanted to hold there until he had collected all of his men, but with machine guns spraying around him and with friendly fire coming closer every minute, it became clear that if they stayed any longer, casualties would only increase. In the turmoil of the moment, rank mattered little, and it fell to Michael Arias, a private, to calculate the way out. They had come down on a 180 and so they would return on a 360-degree azimuth, he said. He read the compass and pointed the way. The order spread around the perimeter and through the woods: *Three sixty! Three sixty!* Valdez, afraid of being overrun, had sent security teams to his left and right flanks; he now tried to call them in for the withdrawal. Privates Fitzgerald and Hargrove, who had been sent to the east flank, had not come back when the Alpha group started moving. Doc Hinger could not find them. Ernie Buentiempo saw a claymore mine exploding over where they might have been, but no one knew for sure. Goodtimes took Arias's machete and started hacking a trail back, and the ragged line of withdrawal began, slowly, with two fit soldiers needed to carry each wounded one.

Pinky Durham, Delta's artillery forward observer, had been stationed near the battalion commander, where the firefight was most intense. His radiotelephone operator, Jim Gilliam, saw a rocket grenade explode nearby, knocking Durham down. Durham's glasses dangled from his left ear. He tried to hook them on and they dangled from his right ear. Someone on the other end of the radio wanted to stop the artillery fire again to bring in more air, but Durham, with Welch on his side, vehemently disagreed. "No," he said. "Hold that air strike. Keep sending us artillery. It's what I need. I know what I need." Then Durham took off, heading for the Alpha front, where he thought he could be more effective since the Alpha observer was wounded. He left without his radioman, telling Gilliam to stay near the battalion command. Durham moved the artillery fire to the eastern edge of the battlefield for a brief spell, hoping the Black Lions could use the time to gather up their wounded. Then he started moving back toward Delta and was hit again.

On the other end of the radio Sergeant Calvin Moore, an artillery liaison man at the fire base near Chon Thanh, noticed that Durham's transmissions were growing weaker. His voice "no longer sounded natural" and sometimes faded away altogether. High above the battlefield, an airborne observer in a helicopter urged Durham on by his call sign. *Please, ninety-three, old boy, just tell me right or left. I know where you are.* Durham kept calling in the fire closer to his own position. Shell fragments were now splattering over the Black Lions, but bringing the artillery in that close was the only way to deal with an enemy that was hugging them by the belt. "I can't see it, but it sounds good, bring it closer," Durham told Sergeant Moore. Delta's first sergeant, Bud Barrow, stationed near a tree a few meters away, had been knocked out by a rocket-propelled grenade. When he came to, he saw Durham straining to lift himself slightly and get a message to Barrow. "Top!" Durham shouted to him, using the nickname for any first sergeant. He pointed toward two enemy soldiers advancing with AK-47s. As Durham fell, mortally wounded, Barrow turned and fired. Pinky's last word had saved his life.

While many around him were ducking for cover, Clark Welch remained on his feet. Since Alpha's command was knocked out early in the fight, he had been working with Durham to call in artillery fire. He had wanted more artillery support from the beginning, and now he was calling in all that he could. He was also "shooting like a madman." He killed one rocket-propelled grenade gunner with his .45 and shot another sniper out of a tree. The body didn't fall this time, just a waterfall of blood. At first Welch stood up so that he could see the action. With his men taking cover behind anthills, tree stumps, and bushes, he felt that he should maintain a wider view of the battle as it unfolded and redistribute ammunition and weapons to men in need. For a brief time the battle seemed like Clark Welch against an entire regiment. It was not long before he was hit. The first bullet pierced his back and cut between two ribs, causing a sucking chest wound. If he leaned over, he could not breathe. If he stood straight, he could breathe. So he stood during the battle, his uniform drenched in blood. Men were moaning all around him. He estimated that fifty percent of his company was down by then, dead or wounded. He made his way through the clutter of fallen soldiers inside the battalion command area and checked on Captain Blackwell, still prone and woozy on the abandoned stretcher. Blackwell said something and Welch tried to lean over, and as soon as he moved, the bullets came in, ripping into Blackwell, killing him.

A battle is riddled with inexplicable events, odd twists of fate determining who will live and who will die. Blackwell might have lived had he been evacuated earlier, and now, at the moment he was killed, Welch was by far the easier target, standing there with his chest wound, stiff and dazed. Yet the shooter for some reason aimed down at Blackwell.

People passed through the forest as if in a dream. There were Captain George and Top Valdez and the Alpha command group, stumbling in and out of the shadows, hacking their way back toward the NDP. Other soldiers filtered north in ones and twos. *A helluva lot fewer going back than came out,* Joe Costello thought to himself as he joined the rag-tag line. He was perhaps halfway out when he heard someone say that there were still many soldiers huddling near the battle front who needed help. The news stopped him. He had to go back. He had to turn around and find the soldiers left behind. He did not feel careless or daring. He wanted nothing more than to get home to his parents and girlfriend waiting on Long Island. But something told him to return to the battlefield. Later he would dismiss his decision as guilt avoidance, a way to prevent "having bad feelings for a long time." It was self-serving, he would say. It was Catholic, he would say. But mostly it was the instinctive response of one of many brave men on both sides of the battlefield that day. As soon as Private Costello turned around, another feeling washed over him. He felt numb, confident. He was overcome by a sensation that he would live and that this moment would shape how he felt about himself the rest of his life.

Another soldier joined Costello for the return trip. As they passed men going the other way, eyes met, but there was no conversation. Nothing to be said. Most of those retreating north were wounded. Even though Costello felt protected, his trip to the front was perilous. Fire was still coming from both flanks. And he was without a weapon. He had gone through four already during the battle and figured he could find another along the way. The jungle floor was strewn with discarded rifles. On his return trip he passed the battalion command area and encountered Lieutenant Colonel Allen. The commander was seated near the anthill. Captain Blackwell was dead. One of the radiotelephone operators was dead. Sergeant Major Dowling was wounded. There was chatter on the radio. Allen seemed to be in control, though his face looked shell-shocked. *Where's your weapon?* Costello was asked. *Don't have one now. I'll get one,* he said. Someone gave him a short, snazzy Car-15, and Costello tucked it under his arm and moved on.

Raymond Phillips was behind another anthill nearby, watching. He was Sergeant Barrow's radiotelephone operator but had been separated from the Delta first sergeant in the every-man-for-himself moments after the Viet Cong unleashed their second attack. He saw Lieutenant Welch get hit in the shoulder. Then he saw a round of antitank rocket-propelled grenades explode near the battalion command post, killing the already wounded Sergeant Dowling and striking Terry Allen in the face. Phillips saw "blood everywhere." Allen stared at the dead sergeant major, then gazed silently at Phillips. He "looked numb." From his position on the battalion command's right flank, Mike Troyer also noticed blood streaming down the side of Allen's face. But it seemed to Troyer that "there was still a lot of fight in him." Pasquale Tizzio, one of Allen's radiotelephone operators, was sprawled facedown with part of his shoulder ripped off. "I want to get this radio off him," Allen said. He stepped around Tizzio and straddled him with the body between his legs and started to pull the radio off. At that moment Troyer heard an AK-47 and saw Allen hit the ground.

Welch passed through again on his way north to his rear Delta platoon. He glanced over and saw that Dowling was dead, battalion operations sergeant Eugene Plier was dead, the radioman was dead. Allen was "covered with blood," working the radio, talking to officers in the air above. Allen saw Welch and yelled out orders: *Start getting your company out of here. Move back on a 360!*

Welch found his medic, Doc Lovato, and instructed him to come forward and assist the battalion commander. Lovato said, "Yes, sir," started crawling toward Allen with his big aid bag, and was killed. "Heavy machine-gun fire killed him," Welch would remember. *"Boom, boom, boom."* "God damn, lieutenant, whenever you go out, guys get hurt," Lovato had said the morning before, explaining why he was heading into the jungle with two stretchers. The medic had meant it as a rugged compliment. Hurt, yes, but not killed. Men wanted to fight for Welch because they knew they would see action but return alive. He had tried to keep them out of this mess but had not prevailed, and now they were dying—*boom, boom, boom*—and Lovato himself was gone.

Upright and hurting, Welch kept moving. He found Lieutenant Luberda near the rear. *We're moving back on a 360,* he said. *If nothing else, don't let them get around to the north of us.* It was a few minutes after noon now, the battle almost two hours old. Welch found shelter behind another anthill. There was a ten-yard clearing that he wanted to cross.

Halfway to the other side, he was hit, this time in the arm. Machine-gun fire ripped through him with such power a biceps flew out and fell to the ground, a piece of muscle wriggling like a hooked fish. He looked down and thought, *what the hell is that?* He assumed a biceps muscle would be red, but it was blue. Scott Down—company radioman Paul D. Scott—came up, removed C-ration tins from a sock, and used the sock as a tourniquet on Welch's arm. Blood was still gushing out of the bullet hole. Welch was beyond pain now, just numb. He was having difficulty breathing. It helped to stand erect, but he was too tired to stand any longer. He slumped down behind a tree and passed out briefly. *I'm not going to die,* he told himself as he drifted in and out of consciousness. At one point he came to and in the haze thought he saw Sergeant Barrow pointing a machine gun directly at him and firing. In fact Barrow aimed slightly above Welch and killed a Viet Cong soldier who was trying to remove the lieutenant's shoulder strap. *I know I'm not going to die.*

At the Delta front Peter Miller's M-16 jammed. He "hated the damn rifle," especially compared to the M-14 that he had trained with at Fort Polk. But in this situation he was not sure what good the weapon was doing him anyway, even when it worked. He had been firing away at his flank since the second round of the firefight began, yet in all that time he had not seen a single enemy soldier. He could sense movement, but that was all. As the battle wore on, he experienced a sensation common to many soldiers that day. He knew that there were other men out there, yet he felt "absolutely totally alone and hopeless in the whole freaking world." At some point he looked around and it seemed that everyone was gone, so he started moving back. There were dead bodies to his left and right as he crawled north. He found a wounded machine gunner from his platoon and started to take out his aid pack to treat him, but an explosion knocked him to the ground and tore the machine gunner in half. This was friendly fire, he determined; they were being shelled by the American artillery. Miller crawled forward and found an abandoned radio and started pushing it until he found the battalion frequency. He hugged the ground, his arms outstretched in front of him toward the radio. Another explosion, and Miller was hit, a hunk of shrapnel ripping through the earth and into his right arm.

Miller's platoon leader, Lieutenant Stroup, at that time estimated that he had only five to eight men who were not casualties. From radio reports he had heard that his battalion commander was wounded and his company commander had been shot. Welch, struggling to keep conscious, had called and told Stroup to leave on a 360. "We're getting the hell out of here," Stroup said to his platoon sergeant, George A. Smith, and his radiotelephone operator, David Laub. They started moving back, every soldier "crawling more or less on his own," a few inches at a time. On the way, as he encountered more soldiers, Stroup passed the word about the 360. He came to an area where many of the wounded had been treated, just in front of the battalion command area. The machine-gun fire seemed fiercest there. The Viet Cong were zeroing in on the wounded. Unarmed and unconscious soldiers were being hit a second, third, fourth time. Sergeant Barrow witnessed it and could not clear his mind of the savage tableau—the bodies "bouncing up and down" as rounds hit them.

Terry Allen was still conscious when Stroup reached him on the way out. He "sounded very calm, but he looked weak." His glasses were off, and blood was running down his face. Clouds of colored smoke fogged the anthill. Some was noxious black smoke from an enemy rocket grenade; some brightly colored friendly smoke identifying the area for the helicopters and planes above. Allen asked Stroup what he intended to do. No orders, just the question. Stroup replied that he intended to get as many people together as he could and leave. George Smith joined Stroup at the anthill.

Allen waved them away. "This is death right here," he said.

He looked at Smith and told him to take the radio off his dead radioman and call in more artillery. As Smith reached for the radio, automatic fire thrummed in and nicked the commander. One bullet glanced from Allen's helmet and hit Smith's. Another round of machine-gun fire knocked Allen down. He was losing consciousness now, slumped behind the anthill. Raymond Phillips was afraid to look up, but when he did, he saw bullet holes in Allen's head. One of his eyes was shot out. Private Santiago Griego came over and cradled the dying battalion commander in his arms.

Terry Allen Jr. died at twenty minutes after twelve. "The battle is the payoff," his father, the great general, had once declared in his booklet on combat leadership.

The Black Lions were pulling out. Peter Miller reached the battalion command area a few minutes later and saw Jack Schroder there, in the middle of the mess, on his knees, praying. Miller yelled at Schroder to get going, then lifted a canteen from one of the dead officers and crawled away. Frank McMeel, his leafy protection behind a bush now

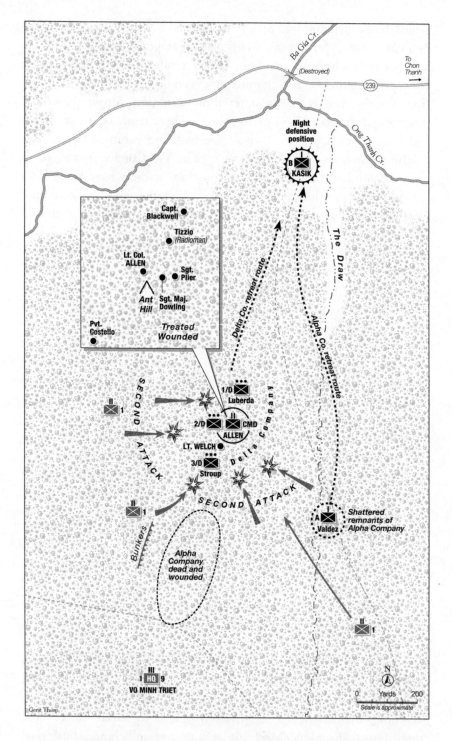

Attack on Delta and Black Lions Command

completely stripped away by the unceasing fire, was nearby, crawling through the sprawl of dead bodies. He noticed Griego on the ground, motionless but breathing. "Come on, we're getting out of here," McMeel said to him. Griego shook his head no. A bullet sliced a chain off his neck. Griego was persuaded that it was time to leave. Viet Cong rocket grenades were falling two and three at a time. Stroup had his helmet blown off twice as he crawled through the death zone. He got separated from platoon sergeant Smith, who was up ahead. Smith reached Clark Welch first. Welch told him to take everyone he could and get out of there. Smith grabbed Welch and tried to take him along, but the Delta commander resisted. "I'll make it. I'm in good shape," Welch said. Smith crawled twenty yards further, then got up and ran.

Stroup was the next to reach Welch, who was being cared for by his radioman, Paul D. Scott. He seemed so weak now that Stroup thought he was dying.

"Lieutenant Stroup, please get my company out of here," Welch said.

"Yes, sir. And I'm also going to get you out of here," Stroup responded.

Welch's tourniquet was soaked in blood. He told Stroup and his men to leave without him. He would keep fighting from there and try to cover their retreat. Not a chance. Private first class Scott attempted to lift Welch and carry him on his back, but Big Rock's wounded arm made that impossible. He would have to crawl and crouch as best he could with one good arm and a chest wound stifling his breathing. Fire came in from both flanks. The Viet Cong seemed to be toying with the weary American troops. They would wait for an infantryman to move and then pour bullets directly in front of his path.

Jack Schroder, with his severe wounds, had been picked up by the Delta group on their way through the battalion command zone and was now following behind radioman Laub, who carried the compass. After inching north fifty meters, they reached a small clearing in the dense jungle. Never crawl through a clearing, they had been taught in jungle training school. Get up and run. Schroder, last in line, didn't make it. He had been lucky the day before, when an enemy bullet lodged in his M-16, but not this time. That final night at Fort Lewis before the Fourth of July, he had told his young wife, Eleanor, that he would not return a cripple. He was coming home dead.

The soldiers of Delta's rear platoon were the last ones into the jungle but faced the heaviest fire near the end. Lieutenant Luberda had started to retreat, then turned around and said that he had to find more of his soldiers before he left. He was running in a low crouch from man to man, telling them the way out, when he was killed. Jackie Bolen, leader of the third squad, was nearby, already wounded by a sniper but shouting in the smoke, trying to gather his men. Private Jensen approached. "Let's go," Jensen said. Bolen wanted nothing more than to leave this jungle and all of Vietnam—"to get out of this godforsaken place," as he had described it in a letter to his grandmother in West Virginia. But in his last letter he worried that he would never get out of "this hell on earth" alive. And now he was sprawled on the jungle floor, wounded but still firing his M-16, Jensen looking down at him, and just when Bolen looked up, "a sniper with an AK-47 stitched him across the back," and Bolen was dead. "No! No!" yelled another soldier nearby who saw Bolen die. The sniper turned on him next.

On the left file virtually an entire squad had been decimated. With his platoon leaders falling one after another, Danny Sikorski, the young squad leader from Milwaukee, took charge, organizing a small perimeter where casualties could be treated. He had heard Luberda's final call to withdraw on a 360. For several hours Ski had been fighting to save the lives of his buddies. Now they were leaving, and he was killed as he started to bring them out. In Wisconsin, on the other side of the world, asleep in her bedroom, Diane Sikorski struggled with a nightmare. She could hear her brother Danny calling her name. *Diane! Diane!* And then his image came to her and he had a huge hole in his stomach. The vision jolted Diane awake. Only a dream. She reminded herself to write her brother in the morning. Jim Gilliam, who had been in Sikorski's team until the day before, when he was recruited to carry Pinky Durham's radio, came across Ski's body as he was withdrawing. It looked as though he had been killed by a claymore mine explosion. There was a hole in his stomach.

Greg Landon had seen too many friends die already. He had crawled away from the killing zone near Lieutenant Colonel Allen just in time, as rocket grenades were exploding. He had "watched helplessly as one of our shells tore up the side of one of our men." He had seen "uncountable acts of heroism" all around, most by soldiers who would not live to tell their stories. One image haunted him—a bullet slicing through the head of the company medic, Joe Lovato. At Fort Lewis back in April, as C Packet was being formed, Landon thought he was smart enough to tell which soldiers would live and which would die. No more. During his first weeks at Lai Khe, he had written home sarcastically saying that he was hoping to get a "slow healing, painless wound" that would take him out of action until the next spring. Now the Professor thought there was no way he would get out alive. He joined the ragged stream of soldiers moving north.

Mike Troyer was just ahead. This is taking forever, Troyer thought as he crawled away from the field of death near Allen's anthill. His last vision had been of a rocket whistling in and black smoke rising from the battalion command post and pieces of bodies landing in different places. He withdrew with radioman Jimmy Scott and Doc Taylor, the third platoon medic and Preacher. Taylor was praying aloud. His booming voice penetrated the chaos. *Stand up with me. God is with us. We'll make it.*

Through the darkness of the jungle floor they crouched and limped and ran. Troyer and Jimmy Scott and the preacher Taylor. Griego and Miller and Lonefight and McMeel and his buddy Donnie Hodges. One couldn't crawl, the other couldn't walk. Stroup and Laub and Paul D. Scott and Lieutenant Welch, struggling to breathe, feeling stronger. *I'm not going to die. I know I'm not going to die.* Jim Gilliam and Greg Landon and Jensen and Giannico and sergeants Smith and Byrd. Faustin Sena, collapsed, on a stretcher. John Fowler, overcome by fear, breaking down. *He maketh me to lie down in green pastures.* Lieutenants Edwards and Kay and Sergeant Pipkin and Private Jones. Top Valdez and Michael Arias and Goodtimes Buentiempo. Woodard and Morrisette and Doc Hinger and Captain George, half blind and deaf, his face swollen, his left eye shut. *He leadeth me beside the still waters. He restoreth my soul.*

One by one and in loose bunches the Black Lions stumbled out from the trees into the sunlight of a marshy clearing near the draw cutting along the eastern edge of the jungle. Fresh troops in clean uniforms were moving toward them, on the way to help.

CHAPTER 17

HOLLEDER'S RUN

OF THE AMERICAN SOLDIERS remaining on the battle-field, most were dead. Lieutenant Colonel Terry Allen Jr. was dead. Captain Blackwell was dead. Sergeant Major Dowling was dead. Forward Observer Pinky Durham was dead. Lieutenant Luberda was dead. Sergeant Luther Smith, Sergeant Plier, and Sergeant Larson were dead. Radiomen Tizzio and Farrell were dead. Medics Lovato and Jagielo were dead. Gilbertson, the division photographer, was dead. Danny Sikorski and Jack Schroder, the Milwaukee connection, both dead. Squad and team leaders Bolen, Barker, Chaney, Lancaster, Sarsfield, and Ostroff were dead. Specialists Cook, East, Miller, and Wilson were dead. Ralph Carrasco, the two-hundredth Arizonan killed in Vietnam, was dead. Ammo bearers Crutcher, Lincoln, and Thomas were dead. Riflemen Adkins, Anderson, Camero, Dodson, Miller, Gilbert, Randall, and Dye were dead. Anthony Familiare, one day after his twenty-first birthday, was dead. The Garcias, Arturo and Melesso, both dead. Jones, MeGiveron, Moultrie, Platosz, Shubert, Ellis, Fuqua, Crites, Gilbert, and Breeden were dead. Ohioan Bob Nagy, who wanted his parents to meet him in Hawaii when he got a break from the war, was dead. Reilly and Gallagher, in new uniforms brought in by supply chopper the day before, were dead. Ray Gribble, who left a safe job at division headquarters to come back to lead his squad, was dead. Ronnie Reece, denied R and R while his pal Kirkpatrick was granted a second vacation in Japan, was dead. Fitzgerald and Hargrove were missing and presumed dead. Half regular army, half draftees, white, black, and brown—all dead.

Joe Costello was alive, one of a small band of Black Lions who had not made it out. After turning around and walking back into the battle to help his stranded buddies, Costello ended up amid a group of twelve to fifteen soldiers who had been cut off from the withdrawing forces late in the firefight. They had formed their own desperate perimeter. Most were wounded, some barely aware of their surroundings, some unconscious, some dying. Anyone who could hold a rifle was given one. Costello was among the few who could move around and perform lifesaving functions. It was a mix of Alpha and Delta soldiers with no distinction between companies and little regard for rank. Lieutenant Mullen was there from Alpha's third platoon, along with Randy Brown, a young squad leader from the first platoon, and First Sergeant Barrow from Delta, all seriously wounded. Barrow had been hit in both legs and could barely walk. His M-16 was down to its last magazine, only a few bullets left, but he found a machine gun and a supply of ammo nearby and pulled it into the circle, then crawled from man to man offering encouragement. To treat one wounded man, he unbuckled his belt and used it as a tourniquet. Another soldier, near death, asked him whether multiple wounds merited two purple hearts. The waterfall of enemy fire had slowed to a persistent drip, with occasional sniper shots from the flanks, but other sounds of war now haunted the battlefield—the moans of mangled men. Private Costello noticed that the dying cried out for their mothers, not for their wives.

Even the heartiest among them felt trapped and doomed. Something was coming, they were certain, but nothing good. They would be overrun, they feared. The Viet Cong only had to come and get them. Though much of the dense brush had been trimmed by gunfire, smoke hung over them like a fog, cutting visibility to a few meters. The surviving Black Lions could barely see one another, which made them more jittery. Rustling noises . . . *Who's that? Sergeant Barrow. How the fuck do I know it's you? Could be an enemy who speaks English. Prove it.* Costello heard the nervous exchanges, back and forth, and he understood. The fear was overwhelming and constant.

Randy Brown, wounded in the leg, foot, and back, swore he heard enemy soldiers calling out mockingly, "Hey, GI, where are you? Where are you, GI?"

Barrow had decided not to let the Viet Cong take him alive. He was prepared to kill himself if it came to that.

Doug Cron, wounded in the left leg and shoulder, heard Barrow's voice and crawled toward him, reaching an anthill, where he played dead, his face yellowed by a smoke grenade that discharged when he was hit.

These last, lost men kept going with adrenaline and cigarettes, whoever had them. When Costello ran out, he turned to the soldier next to him, shoulder to shoulder. *You got a smoke?* he asked. No answer. Costello shook John D. Krische until he realized "the poor guy was dead." That spooked him even more. He had been talking to Krische earlier but never heard a cry for help and did not hear him die.

Three radios were strewn on the ground nearby. Costello gathered one to his side and tried to operate it, but he was a grenadier and had never used a PRC-25 before. "Does anyone know the battalion frequency?" he shouted, and from one of the wounded men, Private Edward J. Grider of Chicago, came the answer. *Grider?* Costello thought. *That's great. Grider was always in and out of trouble, on the fringe. Yet this guy, of all guys, knows the frequency?*

Costello got on the radio.

"This is Unknown Station. Please help. We need help. This is Unknown Station. We are out here by ourselves. We need help. This is Unknown Station. Please . . ."

He kept pushing: ten minutes, fifteen. Finally . . .

"Unknown Station, this is Seven-niner. Who is this?"

"This is Private Costello."

Although he had no idea who Seven-niner was, Costello was fluent enough in military jargon to know it was brass. Seven-niner meant the deputy division commander. It was Brigadier General Coleman, flying overhead in a command-and-control helicopter with the division chemical officer, the division chaplain, and a general staff aide. Coleman had been in the air, with several long breaks for refueling, since a quarter after ten, a few minutes after the shooting started. He had spent most of that time on the radio with Buck Newman, the brigade commander, who was also circling overhead in another helicopter with his operations officer, Donald Holleder, and all of them had been talking to Terry Allen on the ground. But Allen was dead, and there had been no contact with soldiers on the ground since.

"What do you have down there, soldier?" Coleman asked.

"A bunch of wounded guys. And we're worried they're going to overrun us," Costello answered.

"Well, can you see my chopper?"

Costello could hear it but not see it, until he realized that he had not been looking high enough. It was "way the hell up there."

Coleman told Costello to throw green smoke to mark his position so artillery could be directed to the flanks, which might prevent the group from being overrun. Newman got on the frequency and fixed Costello's precise location so rescue troops would know where to look, then he and Holleder headed toward the NDP. Coleman asked Costello about the condition of the soldiers. One guy had a sucking chest wound, Costello said. This was Grider, the buddy who knew the battalion frequency. Coleman told Costello to tear off Grider's shirt, take out a cigarette wrapper, and place it on the wet wound. It would stick like Saran Wrap, he said. There was a commotion about the green smoke. Some of the guys yelled at Costello for throwing it. They were afraid the smoke would just show the Viet Cong where they were. They had a point, Costello thought. It was "kind of like putting up a flag." But Coleman reassured him. He would drop medical supplies. Just hang in there, the general said. Help is on the way.

The artillery, as it turned out, came in closer than the supply drop. Rounds started landing within meters of the stranded group. Bill Mc-Gath, who like Costello had decided to turn around during the retreat, noticed that friendly artillery was "coming in on the wounded." When the medical supplies were dropped, McGath headed out to retrieve them until he realized they were too far to the rear.

FOR THE BLACK LIONS who had remained inside the defensive perimeter that morning, the deadly hours brought a kind of horror once removed. They could hear the battle unfolding, and stage by stage it gradually became apparent to them that it was turning into a disaster, yet they felt helpless to prevent it. Ray Albin, a member of Delta Company's mortar platoon, spent the morning in the fire direction center reading coordinates and making calculations on a plotting board. He was just learning the job, which carried a grave burden; if you made a mistake, you could end up killing your own guys. As the morning began, Albin could hear various Delta radiotelephone operators checking and cross-checking with other platoons to make sure they could communicate as they marched into the jungle. This was the daily background noise of infantry units in the field, and it was easy to tune out. Then came a clattering, and a violent counterburst, and suddenly a

crescendo of sound. Albin and the soldiers around him could hear it all
on the radio, followed by the distant echoes of rifles, machine guns, and
claymore mines from the battle site. It was like listening to a recording
and a live symphony performance at the same time, playing the same
discordant notes a few seconds off, an eerie modernist syncopation of
war. The radios would go silent and there was only the sound of live fire.
Then the radiomen would squeeze their handsets and the static rataplan
of weapons fire could be heard over the air, juxtaposed against the
sounds reverberating from the jungle. All the while the calls became
more desperate.

The key point for Albin's platoon came when Welch, with a sense of
urgency, called for his mortars, but Major Sloan, citing division policy,
countermanded the request. The Delta mortar men, in the gun holes,
eager to support their company, were ordered to hold fire. At the time,
in the heat of the moment, Sloan did not elaborate. He explained later
that he was acting on previous standing orders from above, coming all
the way down from Major General Hay, the division commander.
There had been "some bad luck" with mortars—"several misfortunes of
mortars firing on our own troops," Sloan said, and this made the ever-
cautious Hay "reluctant to use mortar support" when soldiers were maneuvering in the jungle. Several months earlier, when Lieutenant Welch
was teaching his new soldiers how to maneuver in a firefight with mortar and claymore explosions going off to their front and sides, he had
been chewed out by an officious staff officer for ignoring division safety
regulations. Welch had responded that he was trying to prepare his men
for the realities of battle. He had won the argument that time, but now,
when it counted, he could not get the mortars. As it turned out, Sloan in
fact sympathized with Welch and disagreed with division policy, believing that mortars were "much more responsive than close artillery support," but he upheld the order as it came down to him.

The mortar dispute at the time seemed minor to Sloan. Of greater
concern, early in the battle, were the conversations he was overhearing
on the radio of Lieutenant Colonel Allen on the ground talking to
Colonel Newman in the air.

The relationship between the brigade and battalion commanders had
been somewhat uncomfortable from the time the Black Lions headed
out to the Long Nguyen Secret Zone for the start of Operation Shenandoah II. As Sloan saw it, Allen preferred deploying smaller and lighter
units, usually single companies, on search-and-destroy missions, with

the battalion commander in the air coordinating artillery support, while Newman believed in sending out two companies at a time with the battalion commander on the ground. Now Sloan could sense a tension between Newman and Allen over the use of air strikes. He heard Newman tell Allen that he was check-firing the artillery and wanted to put in six air strikes. Allen did not like the idea and tried to disagree. He wanted the artillery support to continue. As Sloan interpreted the discussion, he sensed that Allen "was forced into . . . I shouldn't say forced, but his better judgment told him not to accept the decision. However, he was told by a superior officer and without agreeing, he accepted it."

First Lieutenant Lester T. Scott Jr., an aerial observer for First Division artillery, was also witness to the check-fire dispute. His version corroborated Sloan's, with additional detail. Scott, who maintained contact during the battle with Pinky Durham, Delta Company's artillery observer on the ground, said that he was ordered by the brigade commander, Colonel Newman, to check-fire artillery for an air strike. He heard Terry Allen try to cancel the check-fire, but "the answer was negative." Pinky Durham was "begging for artillery because the VC rate of fire was increasing," Scott reported, but "the check-fire was in effect for more than thirty minutes before the air got there. Then the air went in about six hundred meters to Durham's west." The battalion made another request to bring in artillery, but again they were denied. Finally, according to Scott, Durham and the Black Lions were "being hit so hard there was no alternative but to fire the artillery." But by then, he said, the check-fire had "lasted long enough for the VC to regroup for an overwhelming attack." It was indeed during that crucial period that Vo Minh Triet brought up his reserve battalion to seal the three-sided attack.

It was also during that period that many of the Delta and Alpha soldiers on the ground wondered why they were not pulling back to the NDP. Perhaps only Allen could answer that question definitively, and he took his reasoning to the grave with him. There would be conflicting arguments about whether that was a tactical error on his part, but it reflected something larger in any case. His determination to stay on the battlefield was a manifestation of the pressure coming down, all the way down, from President Johnson, who wanted good news and enemy body counts, to General Westmoreland, who wanted more troops and believed the war could be won through search-and-destroy missions in which the First Division pursued the enemy overland relentlessly, to

Major General Hay, who was feeling the heat for being too cautious, to Colonel Newman, who wanted the Black Lions and their commander out there on the ground, not just searching but destroying, to Lieutenant Colonel Allen, who wanted to prove that he could do it.

As the battlefield situation grew bleaker in the hour after the artillery pause, the soldiers stationed at the NDP could not believe what they were hearing. Craig Watson, a rifleman in Bravo Company, had been assigned to a listening post just outside the perimeter. By the middle of the battle, when it "almost sounded as one loud roar," his group was called back in and deployed in bunkers circling the perimeter. There was great fear that the camp would be overrun. Don Koch, a Bravo sergeant, "never felt so helpless" in his life. There were snipers shooting at them. They could not leave the bunkers they were guarding. Their battalion buddies, the soldiers he had watched so carefully as they marched away that sunlit morning, "were getting hit, and they were not that far away, but they might as well have been on the moon. There was nothing we could do for them." Albin and a few others left the mortar gun hole and walked south of the perimeter about fifty meters, and "here comes this GI running towards us with nothing on, no web gear, no helmet, no weapon, no ammo clips, just him." Before that, they knew the horror of the battle only secondhand, from the radio and the roar echoing back through the woods. Here was the real thing, the first survivor, a soldier "who got the shit scared out of him and took off."

Along with Bravo Company, Lieutenant Erwin's scout platoon had been stationed as a protective force around the perimeter after being called back from their morning march to the west of the battle site. At 1:15 that afternoon Erwin was in the NDP's tactical operations center and encountered Colonel Newman and Major Holleder, who had just landed. The full extent of the calamity on the ground was becoming clear to them. With Allen dead, Newman had decided to take personal command of the battalion and organize the rescue. He had wanted Holleder, his right-hand man, to stay airborne in the helicopter and help run things from there, but Holleder talked him out of that plan. Since his days at West Point, Holly, as his classmates called him, had been a man of action. If soldiers were fighting and dying and in need of help, he wanted to be on the ground to help them.

During the brief discussion at the battalion operations center, the brigade officers said they intended to march toward the draw, a third of the way to the battlefield past the southeastern edge of the perimeter,

where they could set up an evacuation area. Colonel Newman needed a
radio operator, and Erwin, who knew the call signs, was pressed into
service. As they moved beyond the perimeter, Major Holleder seemed to
be pulsating with an adrenaline rush, as if he were leading a squad onto
the field at Michie Stadium. "We've got to get in there and help them!
They're in trouble and need help!" he kept saying. Newman repeatedly
told him to calm down until they had assessed the situation.

As they neared the marshy clearing, a weary band of soldiers ap-
proached from the wood line, some without shirts, helmets, or weapons.
It was the Alpha contingent that included Captain George, Michael
Arias, Top Valdez, and Doc Hinger.

Valdez looked up at Erwin and said, "It's a massacre out there, sir."

Newman was finishing his plans. He would send the recon platoon
in first, bolstered by Bravo Company, which was marching down from
the NDP, and Charlie Company, now being called in from the fire support station at Chon Thon, plus any fresh men available from Alpha,
Delta, and the headquarters unit. Holleder was an untamed mustang,
pawing the turf, urging Newman to let him run. He had to get in there.
The colonel reluctantly relented, again, and Holleder swiftly recruited
his little advance team. He rounded up a handful of medics and riflemen
from Bravo who had made it to the draw. Erwin gave him a .45 and two
magazines of ammunition. As Holleder headed out, he saw Doc Hinger,
without either weapon or helmet, trudging toward them and told him to
get a steel pot on his head and come along. Then Holly accelerated into
the soggy marshland, breaking away from his soldiers, his legs churning
high, just like he ran as the fearsome end and valiant quarterback at
West Point, a hardheaded bruiser, all knees and elbows, bone and muscle, hurtling hell-bent down the field.

When Holleder arrived in Vietnam in late July, a few days before the
shipload of C Packet soldiers, the glow from his years of athletic glory at
the U.S. Military Academy a decade earlier had barely dimmed. He had
washed out of flight school at San Marcos, Texas, after graduation, but
then rose through the infantry, commanding a company in the Seventh
Infantry Division in Korea, serving as aide-de-camp at the Continental
Army Command at Fort Monroe, Virginia, and attending Command
and General Staff College at Fort Leavenworth, Kansas. During much
of that time he also played football or coached, including a stint during
the early sixties as an assistant at his alma mater. Still and always he was
a winner and golden boy, and his celebrity not only made him the young

officer every general wanted nearby, but it also could have kept him safely away from Vietnam had he wanted to skip the war. The same characteristics that sent him rushing down the draw in the Long Nguyen Secret Zone pushed him to get sent to Vietnam, even though by then he had a wife and four young daughters. He burned to go places. Some of his superior officers thought he was on the path to becoming a four-star general, much like another hard-charging member of the cadet class of 1956, H. Norman Schwarzkopf.

Holleder had the instincts of a leader, if not refined intellect. He fared only slightly better in his West Point studies than Terry Allen Jr., who had graduated second-to-last in the class of 1952. In the order of merit, Holleder ranked 444th out of a graduating class of 480, and did that well only because of the nightly tutoring of his scholarly roommate, Perry Smith, a future Air Force general. But in that regard Holleder would be only another in the long gray line of officers who proved that there was not necessarily a correlation between class rank and military achievement. This duality was apparent all through his cadet years. "His uphill battle for tenths left him with two turnout stars," the 1956 *Howitzer* yearbook noted, using academy jargon to convey that he nearly flunked out twice and had to take special exams to avert dismissal. Yet his leadership skills were so evident that he was appointed a cadet captain and commander of his company, M-2, the Mighty Deuce, comprising the tallest cadets in the corps.

With some men the gap between performance on a football field and how they live the rest of their lives is so vast that not much can be learned about one from the other. Holleder played the way he lived, and his football career at Army went a long way toward explaining him. He had been a schoolboy star at Aquinas Institute in Rochester, New York, and was recruited to West Point by Doc Blanchard, the great former Army star, and an assistant coach named Vince Lombardi. By his junior year he was regarded as one of the elite ends in the country, a six-two, hundred-and-eighty-seven-pound All-American who made devastating tackles on defense and was a cunning receiver who could outjump defensive backs for the ball. He and his quarterback that season, Pete Vann, working on pass routes seven days a week, became so attuned to one another that when Holleder flicked an eye, Vann knew precisely where he was going. They hooked up on nine touchdowns and nearly eight hundred yards of completions, even though Holleder had to sit out two games because of the minor infraction of leaving his post to call his girlfriend.

Though he had a body that seemed sculpted in iron, it was not athleticism that set Holleder apart but his presence. In a culture of toughness, he was toughest. Vann remembered "a look in his eye, this look of 'Don't screw with me, baby, and you better do it right.'" People either loved or hated Holly. If he was not on their side, they might consider him a bully, another one of Blaik's thugs. But he made the men around him believe that they were going to win. Even as an underclassman, from his position on the flank, he was the undisputed leader of the team. Vann, who began West Point a year ahead of Holleder, flunked a semester and ended up graduating in the same class, but he had exhausted his eligibility by the 1955 season, forcing Red Blaik to find another quarterback. Not satisfied with the apparent choices, the coach decided to try to turn a leader into a quarterback rather than a quarterback into a leader. Just before spring practice he asked Holleder if he would make the switch. "Colonel, I have never played in the backfield in my life," Holleder responded, but he did what his coach wanted, turning in his old jersey for a new one—number sixteen. "I knew he could learn to handle the ball well and to call the plays properly," Blaik later wrote in his autobiography, *You Have to Pay the Price.* "Most important, I knew he would provide the bright, aggressive, inspirational leadership at the key position of the game."

If this was a daring move, its wisdom was not universally accepted. Old Army mules groused that Blaik had stripped the team of its best player by moving him out of position. Why make him start all over again at something unfamiliar? The pessimists were fortified by a weakness that became obvious from the first day of practice: Holleder passed like a misfired howitzer. Vann tutored him as best he could in the mechanics of throwing a football, but the spiral was not in his repertoire. "He had trouble throwing anything but a kickoff, if you know what that looks like," Vann would joke later. Distance, no problem. Holleder could wind up and heave the thing seventy yards. Velocity, he had it. Even without a spiral, his ball had juice. But timing the pattern, judging the proper arc, using the right touch—those quarterback skills were slow in coming. Before the season started, even Blaik's closest pals in the New York press corps thought he had made a grave mistake. The second-guessing intensified during the season when Army lost to Michigan,

Syracuse, and Yale. The quarterback switch became known as "Blaik's folly."

After the Michigan game, in which Holleder had completed only one of eight passes, the coach and his quarterback met privately. Holleder approached Blaik's office prepared to end the experiment even though he secretly hoped to get another chance. "It doesn't matter what anybody else thinks or says around this place," Blaik told him. "I am coaching this Army team, and you are my quarterback." As the coach later recounted the scene, Holleder's hard eyes glistened with tears.

Blaik's reasoning all along was to have his quarterback ready for the most important game of the year, against archrival Navy, played at the end of the season in Philadelphia. The best Army season could be ruined by a loss to Navy, and the worst season salvaged by a win. Army had lost in 1954, and Blaik did not intend to lose again. He was a coach who believed in traditions. One of his annual rituals came the night before the big game, when he would take his squad out for a walk and tell them a motivational story. He concluded this time by saying that he had "grown weary of walking across the field" after games to offer congratulations to winning coaches on the other side. "Now, I'm not as young as I used to be, and that walk tomorrow, before one hundred thousand people . . . would be the longest walk I've ever taken in my coaching life."

There was a long silence, finally broken by Holleder.

"Colonel," he said, "you are not going to take that walk tomorrow."

The next day the big lefty completed no passes, but it did not matter. Running sweeps and sneaks, handing off, blocking, pushing his teammates, he was the point man in a ferocious infantry attack that leveled Navy fourteen to six. He was the leader Blaik needed.

Now, twelve years later, another autumn afternoon, and here came Holly rushing down the draw, through the tall grass, water splashing left and right, losing his balance and regaining it, lunging on with his long stride and big thighs, his knees pumping high, breaking away from his men, filling the breach.

Doc Hinger was far behind, watching this officer, a man he had never met before, lead the way toward the jungle and the fallen Black Lions. He saw Holleder reach a point near a large tree where the draw narrowed, and he heard the AK-47 shots ring out and he saw the major go down. The other soldiers edged to the sides of the draw, looking for cover, keeping low as they moved forward to reach him. Hinger, protected by a sergeant who sprayed overhead with a machine gun, tried to drag Holleder to the safer side of the big tree, but he was too heavy. It took two men to pull him. He had been hit twice, once in the chest, once in the thigh. He was ashen gray, unconscious, his eyes closed, but still breathing when Hinger went to work on him. As the first bandage was being applied, he died.

Jim Kasik of Bravo Company reached the clearing at the front of the draw a few minutes later. A small helicopter was idling there, and as Kasik approached, he saw three soldiers loading a mud-splattered body into the passenger side. "Who the hell is that?" he asked. "Some major," one of the men replied. "Some major who just landed here and told us to go running into the jungle with him. And when we told him that there were VC out there, he just said, 'Come on!' He got some yards on the rest of us and they nailed him."

Soon after the helicopter lifted off, Colonel Newman came by and asked if Major Holleder was in the area. He was told the story about the big officer running down the middle of the draw ahead of his men and getting shot by a sniper. Newman twice had tried to hold Holleder back, keep him in the helicopter, station him at the NDP, but there was no way, and now the bull-rushing quarterback was stone dead at age thirty-two. "You gotta watch out for these young ones," Newman said, taking in the news.

IN THE ANTI-U.S. war of resistance for national salvation, the actions of Vo Minh Triet's regiment that October morning were by the book, right out of the combat manuals of the People's Army of Vietnam. Plan the operation in detail. Conduct reconnaissance. Rehearse in detail. Use the three-pronged attack. Maintain complete security during move-ment. Conduct a sudden assault with maximum firepower. Retain a re-serve element. When the enemy believes you are attacking from the west, attack from the east. When he believes you have stopped, attack again. When he believes you are advancing, stop. Plug the ears and blind the eyes of the enemy, the generals in Hanoi would say. Create surprises. Walking in the middle of the night, a man is deadly frightened if he is struck from behind. It is the same in the military field. The side which is caught by surprise will be embarrassed and be unable to capture the ini-tiative. The side which is caught by surprise will be at a loss and be quickly annihilated.

Truth and falsehood. Falsehood and truth. To the individual Viet

Cong soldier, this battle, like any battle, was a blur of chaotic moments. Nguyen Van Lam, the company commander attached to Rear Service Group 83, who grew up near the battlefield, could remember only moving from one entrenched bunker to another with his comrades that morning, shooting at Americans, listening to the helicopters and high-performance jets, trying to predict where artillery and air strikes would come in, so they could stay away from those places. He felt little threat from the Big Red Brothers on the ground.

Some American soldiers withdrew from the battle wondering how, with the trap so deadly, with the firepower so massive, the Viet Cong commanders could let even one of them get out alive. But Triet had concerns other than killing every enemy soldier. His men were tired and starving—they still had no rice—and, more important, this fight had not been planned by his superiors and was of little interest to them. For all the ingenuity and agility that Viet Cong soldiers showed on the battlefield, there was an equal and opposite rigidity in their military bureaucracy. A quick ambush was one thing, but a full-blown battle with an entire regiment engaged was quite another. Triet's superiors were expecting him to get across the east-west corridor and meet them to prepare for the attack on Loc Ninh, a battle that had been in the planning stages for some time, part of a larger high-stakes strategy that eventually would lead to a massive attack on the cities of the South.

Triet's reasoning, as he later explained, went like this: His regiment, in its search for rice, was already behind schedule as it moved across the corridor to its next assignment. The fact that the battle was being fought in mature jungle made it easy for him to spring the ambush but difficult to sustain a prolonged fight. The longer the battle went on, the greater the possibility that his unit would take significant casualties, especially from American artillery and air power. His regiment had been badly bruised all year, starting with Operation Junction City, and had only recently been replenished with new recruits. The last thing he needed was to bring a depleted force into the next campaign. When his scouts, observing the action from trees, told him the American forces were withdrawing, he considered the battle over and pulled back most of his troops.

It would take several hours to sweep the battlefield, dress the wounded, bury the dead, and hole up in bunkers and underground tunnels as protection against late-arriving American air strikes. Much of that work would have to be done at night, when the Americans would cede the jungle. Triet filed a report by Morse code to Ninth Division headquarters, located in what was known as the Fishhook region up near the Cambodian border. They had annihilated an American battalion. The regiment would resume its march the next morning. "We had to get where we were going," he later explained.

LIEUTENANT GRADY was in Lai Khe during the battle. As Captain George's executive officer, he monitored the radios in Alpha Company's communications center, known as the commo bunker. Protected by sandbags and concrete, he listened to the distant sounds of war on the battalion frequency as the firefight grew more intense and the American position more desperate. Allen was dead. George was being evacuated. Grady's company and battalion were in disarray in the jungle to the north. At approximately the time that Vo Minh Triet considered the fight over, Grady wheeled a quarter-ton jeep down to the 2/28 Black Lions headquarters at the sprawling base camp. On the way there he encountered the battalion's executive officer, Robert Gillard. "Get your stuff, you're going out," Gillard said. Grady turned around and gathered his combat gear. He stopped at brigade headquarters on the way to the helicopter pad, and just then they were bringing in his boss, Jim George, who had been medevaced directly to Lai Khe.

The captain was a bloody mess, conscious, but deaf in one ear and barely able to see. Grady, with his light-hearted nature, could not grasp the horror, or perhaps could not yet accept it. He looked at George and blurted out, "You big dummy, what'd you do?"

During the voyage across the Pacific three months earlier, Grady had tried to ease the concerns of young recruits destined for the Vietnam battlefields. Just one year and you're home, he would say. And the three weeks aboard the *General John Pope* counted toward that year. Only a week earlier he had persuaded one of the former C Packet soldiers, frightened and certain that he would die, to overcome his fright and return to the field. "You're scared? We're all scared. You just gotta go," Grady had said then. Now, as he reached the resupply pad and loaded case after case of ammo in the chopper and then climbed in himself, the same fear that he had tried to ease in others washed over him. *What the hell . . . what am I . . . what the hell am I doing here?* he muttered. The helicopter hovered over the treetops and clattered north toward the trouble near the Ong Thanh stream. The rescue mission was under way when he arrived at the perimeter.

Back toward the jungle, with Sergeant Mark Smith in the lead, marched most of Erwin's recon platoon, followed by Kasik's Bravo Company, Reese's Charlie, plus Lieutenant Grady and fresh soldiers from Alpha, Delta, and Headquarters, including Ray Albin, the mortar plotter, Steve Goodman, the armorer, and Rick Calef, a senior medic, along with survivors like Private Hinger and Sergeant Valdez who wanted to find their buddies. The force that marched south to extract the wounded and the dead was larger than the force that Terry Allen had taken into battle. Albin borrowed an M-16 from someone in the Alpha weapons platoon, then started worrying whether it would fire properly or if the soldier had forgotten to clean it. Hinger, shaken by Holleder's death atop everything he had seen earlier, had "broken down pretty bad" at the battalion aid station, where his friend Dave Berry, a fellow medic, tried to tranquilize him by giving him a shot of muscle relaxant, but he could not relax and could not stay in the NDP; he had to get back to find more wounded men, so here he was in the long line heading out again, following almost the same path he had taken seven hours earlier.

On the way Hinger passed the battalion surgeon and some other medics and noticed that they had four volume blood expanders going into a wounded man, one in each arm, one in each leg. Jim Kasik came across another scene he would long remember. He saw, passing the other way, a black soldier, short and slight, weighing not much over 110 pounds, limping out of the jungle carrying a wounded white soldier over his shoulders who seemed to weigh at least 80 pounds more. Steve Goodman, nearby, helped a platoon sergeant who weaved toward him, weakened by two gunshot wounds. Goodman held the sergeant and started carrying him back. The weight, the heat, the sun pounding down once they emerged from the wood line, the uneven footing through the tall grass and the mushy swamp along the draw—it was a difficult journey for Goodman. He fell flat on his face, the sergeant collapsing in a heap over him. Then he gathered himself, picked up his load, and moved on. Finally reaching the same huge tree under which Major Holleder died, Goodman placed the sergeant down in a dry spot in the sun and collapsed. He needed a short rest before going in for more.

There was still fire coming at them; snipers from Rear Service Group 83 and the local Phu Loi battalion harassed the Americans after Triet withdrew his battalions. The Black Lions rescue forces maneuvered

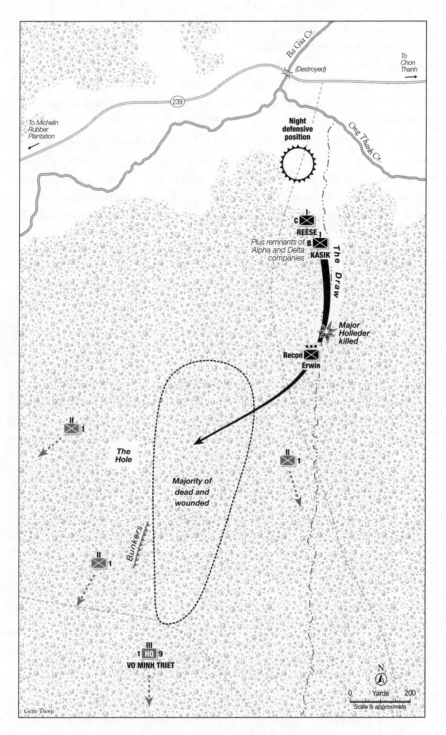

Return to the Battlefield

with great caution as they moved through the jungle, protecting their flanks, sending point squads forward before bringing up the rest of the men, platoon by platoon. Captain Reese, whose company was airlifted to the NDP from the artillery fire support station along Highway 13, considered it his first priority to get his own men in and out safely and not lead them into a second enemy attack. They had heard there would be "Cong on the ground" near the perimeter, and were relieved to find that wasn't so, but now, as they neared the battle site, they took automatic fire from the right flank. Reese had his soldiers hit the ground and stay prone for fifteen minutes, not moving until the threat diminished.

Recon reached the death zone first, followed eventually by men from the other units. They knew it would be an awful sight, but that expectation could not diminish the shock. There were bodies everywhere. Lieutenant Erwin radioed back to Colonel Newman to "report how bad things were, in terms of the numbers" and to request more medical personnel and supplies. The first identifiable casualty was Captain Blackwell. He was prone on the stretcher, his battle wounds neatly dressed. How did he die? During the battle Clark Welch, hovering above Blackwell, had seen several rounds come in and kill him. At least that is what Welch remembered. But when Erwin and Jim Kasik now looked down at him, it appeared that he had been murdered. There was, Kasik noted, a single bullet hole in the captain's forehead.

Another fifteen yards to the south, they came to the anthill. There was Terry Allen, a bullet wound through his left temple, his body curled into a fetal position. Sergeant Dowling was off to his left side. From the way their bodies were situated, it appeared to Kasik that Dowling had died trying to shield his commander, but in fact Dowling died first. There was a map in Allen's pocket, and Kasik removed it, "lest it be left for the VC." Captain Reese, the third commander in the recovery party, was given the assignment of formally identifying Allen's body. Arrangements were made for it to be carried back to the perimeter. Nearby Erwin saw Pasquale Tizzio. Guys had been kidding Tizzio about becoming the commander's radiotelephone operator a few days earlier. Erwin had recommended him for the job. Now he was dead. And there were the bodies of Verland Gilbertson, out on his first photography shoot with the battalion, and Sergeant Plier, also new to the battalion.

It was hard to look at the dead and not think about fate.

Lieutenant Grady found the body of the soldier he had persuaded to go to the field. By the positioning of his rifle, it looked as though the kid might have shot himself before the Viet Cong could.

Ray Albin came across the remains of Melesso Garcia, the rifleman who had had a bad feeling about going on patrol. Thousands of red ants had fallen from a tree and were crawling across his face and body.

Steve Goodman found the body of his friend Steve Ostroff. Horror has so many faces. Here was a freakish one. Ostroff's smoke grenades had exploded on him and "he was all different colors; he was yellow and red and green from the smoke grenades." Goodman was numb. He couldn't believe this had happened. He could not help thinking, *Most of these soldiers were drafted. Were they drafted to get killed?*

It happened more than once, this death-stain of colored smoke. George Burrows, a radiotelephone operator for Bravo Company, got down on his stomach to talk on the radio and found himself right next to a dead soldier. What he saw was his one "clear, hard memory" of the battle's aftermath. The soldier's right shoulder was gone, along with the right side of his head. His nose was angled to the left, and a smoke grenade that had rolled next to him had burned a bright yellow slash into the remaining left side of his face.

Sergeant Mark Smith showed Lieutenant Erwin seven more soldiers stacked up a few yards from a drum-fed Chicom long machine gun. All the Americans were oriented toward the gun, as though they had been trying to silence it. Behind the gun Erwin found a dead enemy soldier, one of the few he saw. He remembered the man's eyes. They were open. Erwin "looked right into them." Ray Albin saw the body of another enemy solider, turned it over, and realized that he was looking at an adolescent. He searched the pockets and found some documents, including an identification card with a date on it, 1953. A kid from the north, only fourteen years old. Doug Tallent, another member of Delta's mortar platoon, saw one dead enemy soldier during the recovery. He was wearing a black uniform, and his orangish face had a single bullet hole in the middle of the forehead. *Looks like a jack o' lantern,* Tallent thought.

Farther back and to the right they started finding the wounded. Private Costello was there with his lost delegation. Doc Hinger spotted him. They hadn't seen each other since the first seconds of the battle, when they had been walking together in the back of the second platoon and Doc had noticed movement in the trees. Now here was Costello, "somewhat in a state of shock at this time, because everything had wound down," Hinger thought. Nearby were two medics, Archie Porter and Joe Booker, both seriously wounded. Booker had been shot in the stomach. Someone held his hand and said, "Hey, guy, you're still alive. You have a chance."

On the way into the jungle Sergeant George Smith had been told by a retreating soldier that Delta's first sergeant, Bud Barrow, was sitting on a log, waiting for them. Where was he? Barrow could hear the recovery forces before they spotted him. Shouts: "Who's there?" Then, staring down at him, there stood George Smith, and next to Smith was Ray Albin.

"Thank God, Top!" Albin shouted, seeing that Barrow was alive. There had been reports back at the NDP that he was dead.

Another soldier called out, "Hey, first sergeant! How ya doin'?"

Barrow broke down, his relief at being saved overwhelmed by the travail of the bloodbath. He had been shot through both legs and had ninety-two pieces of shrapnel in his knees, back, and buttocks, and more than that, his nostrils were aflame with a smell that he would never forget, the strong, rotten smell of dead bodies.

"I ain't doin' worth a damn," he said, weeping. "They killed all my boys."

IT WAS EASIER to find the fallen Black Lions than to get them out. Triet's harassing units kept up enough fire to make the Americans uneasy. General Coleman, circling above the battlefield, spotted a point in the denseness where they might clear enough space to bring in evacuation helicopters. A small squad arrived from the NDP with chainsaws and was assigned the task of cutting down four trees. In comparison with all else that day, it seemed a simple task, yet it turned into a mess. The chainsaws were heavy and old and kept breaking. ("The U.S. Army has the sorriest chainsaws in the world," Colonel Newman reported.) It took almost an hour to cut what became known as the Hole. The helicopter evacuation effort was led by Lieutenant Colonel Paul B. Malone, commander of the Big Red One's First Aviation Battalion, who had been in the air with his operations officer, Larry E. Lowe, when they were called to the scene. They got on the 2/28 Black Lions' radio frequencies and quickly analyzed what could be done with the Hole. Lowe estimated that the trees around it were 100 to 110 feet high. At first they thought of using big UH-1s, the transport-and-attack helicopters, and dropping a hoist and harness down into the Hole. But this process was too slow, so they brought in the little OH-13 bubble helicopters that could descend straight down to the stamp-sized landing area.

Except for Allen and Blackwell, whose bodies were carried back by stretcher to the clearing near the opening of the draw, priority in the jungle was given to the wounded. A form of triage was set up: wounded before dead. Sergeant Barrow, his pain dulled by morphine, was lifted in and sent away. Private Costello came soon thereafter, and as the chopper rose straight up above the trees and headed north, he was struck by how detached the pilot seemed. *This hump isn't even asking what happened, for God's sake,* Costello thought to himself. *What's the matter with him? You've got to be at least curious about what's happened here.* This was a common feeling among the survivors, but of course those who had not been there could not feel what Costello was experiencing at that moment, and even he would be hard put to describe it.

Lieutenant Mullen, who had been unconscious, awakened to find someone bandaging his wounds. It was an old supply sergeant who had no business being in the field, Mullen thought, but had come because of the emergency. In a matter-of-fact way the supply sergeant told Mullen that he had found a couple of pairs of rolled-up socks to stuff in the hole in his left leg and that he had placed the lieutenant's left index finger in the lieutenant's shirt pocket. He also gave Mullen some morphine. The next thing Mullen remembered, they were loading people into the chopper and he heard someone yell, "This is the last one in good-enough shape to fly out." Mullen, in his semiconscious state, shouted "Bullshit! There's no reason I can't be flown out." So he was next.

They placed him on the passenger side of the bubble. It was "awash with blood from the previous occupants"—pools of blood that sloshed around every time the chopper moved. That was the least of the pilot's worries. His blades had been striking the jungle canopy every time he came in and out. The "vibration was frightful" to Mullen, who was both concerned and amazed. This brave pilot, this young warrant officer, he thought, must have needed a wheelbarrow to carry his balls around.

The evacuation was going well but seemed excruciatingly slow. Four helicopters received enemy fire as they dropped into the Hole, but they escaped damage. There was room for only one or two wounded men on each little chopper. At one point the recovery team on the ground used explosives to expand the hole so that a big UH-1 might be able to land. The wounded were all evacuated by then, but there were still dozens of dead. The medevac pilots, who were not attached to Malone's aviation unit, told him they were done for the day. If there was still enemy fire, they would not risk going in to take out the dead. Malone decided that he and Lowe would start that process themselves, but as they hovered over the Hole, six rounds of enemy fire poured in. Malone was wounded in the foot. Lowe abandoned the mission and headed away to assess the damage.

Darkness comes fast and early in the jungles of Vietnam. It was now quarter after six, and Colonel Newman had a crucial decision to make. General Coleman had asked him to try to get the dead out before nightfall, but the task seemed impossible. The last thing he needed was a helicopter crash at the end of this awful day. With enemy snipers still active and the light fading, he called off the aviation rescue. But he also realized that "transporting the dead by litter back to the NDP was not feasible considering the number to be evacuated, the exhaustion of the troops and the problems this might cause if necessary to fight en route." Newman saw only one solution, unpalatable as it seemed. He would stack the dead in a concentrated area near the Hole, box the area with artillery fire overnight, and come back to pick them up the next morning. He discussed the decision with Coleman, who agreed with him even though it violated the Big Red One policy of never leaving a dead comrade on the battlefield.

The First Division indeed prided itself on always going back for its men, even if it meant more soldiers would be wounded or killed in the process. So ingrained was this conduct in division lore that General Hay had flaunted it as a matter of honor against the enemy. Earlier that year he had distributed a propaganda leaflet to the commanding general of the Viet Cong's Ninth Division. "Dear General," the leaflet began. "This is to advise you that during the battle at Ap Bau Ban on 20 March, the Regimental Commander of Q763 [the Ninth's Third Regiment] and his battalion commanders disgraced themselves by performing in an unsoldierly manner. During this battle with elements of this Division and attached units your officers failed to accomplish their mission and left the battlefield covered with dead and wounded from their units. We have buried your dead and taken care of your wounded from this battle. Sincerely, J. H. Hay, Major General, USA, Commanding." And now this.

Lieutenant Grady ignored Newman's order for a brief period, pretending that he did not hear it, but eventually even he and his Alpha group gave up. The recovery team stacked all the bodies they could find, one atop the next, in six neat piles.

Then the weary soldiers retraced their steps. Moonlight filtered down through the trees, illuminating the way. The last man made it inside the perimeter a few minutes before eight. It had been twelve hours—a lifetime ago—since Jim George's point squad had marched out on that sunlit morning.

AT LAI KHE late that night General Hay gathered his staff. The division commander had been at a meeting in Saigon all morning, away from the action, and by the time he was called out of the meeting and informed of the battle, it was already a disaster, unrecoverable. He had little to do with it, for better and worse, except as his policies shaped the decisions of those under him. He wanted to believe, or at least would say later, that if he had been there it would not have happened. There were other officers who told themselves the same thing. Details were still coming in, not all accurate, and what Hay knew was secondhand information from official logs and the best-face descriptions of his aides. He seemed shocked but was making an extra effort to calm those around him. "We've had a very tough day in this division," Hay said. There was one point he wanted to emphasize above all else. This was not an ambush. This was a meeting engagement.

Big Jim Shelton was in the room, a deputy operations officer, numbed by the day's events. Terry Allen was his closest friend in Vietnam. Through the long summer they had spent night after night together in the tent they shared, talking about everything. Shelton knew the intimate details of Allen's life, including the trouble Terry had at home with his wife, Jean. Big Jim had been gone from the battalion for nearly two weeks, but he still considered himself a Black Lion. Only ten days earlier, on the night of October 7, before the battalion headed out to the field, Allen and the other officers had thrown a farewell party for him at the club in Lai Khe. It was a merry night of steaks and beer and bullshitting. Captain Blackwell announced that he was giving Shelton, who already had six kids, a condom—and pulled out a huge plastic bag. They gave him a Zippo lighter with a Black Lion on it. Shelton tried to speak, but he was half-drunk and a born romantic and for once the first-class talker could not get through a sentence. And now Allen and Blackwell were dead and General Hay was saying it wasn't an ambush.

And Holleder. His death was beyond Shelton's imagination. He knew Holleder as a tough sonofabitch. They fought often during their brief time together in Vietnam, two strong-willed staff officers swearing and fuming at each other. Holleder, as the operations officer for the First Brigade, would bring in a plan, and Shelton, as the division deputy, would say, "That's just dumb, Don," and the fulminating would begin. Shelton figured that the only way to deal with someone as overpowering as Holleder was to stand up to him. Holleder's whole approach was that he was going to whip your ass, whether you were an enemy soldier, or a staff officer in his way, or a defender trying to tackle him. Shelton had tried that once too. It was the fall of 1955, Big Jim's junior year at Delaware, Holleder's final year at Army. The Fightin' Blue Hens went up to West Point for a scrimmage against Blaik's nationally renowned squad. Shelton, a linebacker on defense, had worked up a series of red dog blitzes, but it was preseason and "no one could remember what the hell to do," and anyway Army was bigger and better. They ran through Delaware, Shelton remembered, "like shit through a goose, like piss through a tin horn." Holleder was the new quarterback. It was obvious to Shelton that "he couldn't pass worth a shit," but he could run, and when he ran, no one wanted to tackle him, not with his arms flailing and his knees bucking high. He was nasty, Shelton thought. And when you tackled him, he was even nastier; he'd kick you on the way up. But he was damn near indomitable, and even when you fought with him, he was a good guy to have on your side, as tough as the Big Red One itself. Holleder was dead, and General Hay was up there saying it was not an ambush.

This was a hard one for the brass to accept and explain: Terry Allen, the son of the famous general, and Don Holleder, the great All-American, both dead. Shelton had typed out the telegram notifying General Westmoreland's office at MACV himself, but even he couldn't believe it. One thing he was sure of was that this was not a meeting engagement, a case of two opposing units just happening to bump into each other. But it was hard for Hay to acknowledge anything else. The division's special intelligence reports for October had revealed in fairly accurate detail where the enemy forces were, how heavily armed they were, and predicted that there was a heightened probability that American units would encounter them in sizeable numbers. It was all on paper, hard intelligence, ahead of time.

To say that a prized battalion of the First Division had been wiped out in an ambush would be "a mark on the escutcheon of the division," Shelton concluded. "A First Division unit ambushed? Never. We clover-leaf patrol, we do this, we do that, how the hell could we get ambushed? It's all part of the aura of the Big Red One." Hay talked for a long time. No one asked any questions. More reports came in about body counts. The latest estimate was that the Black Lions had killed at least sixty-seven Viet Cong. They could say they won a difficult fight. No one both-ered to figure out where the numbers came from, at least not yet.

Colonel Newman was still in charge at the Black Lions' NDP. He spent much of the night talking to Hay and other division officers back at Lai Khe. A company from the 1/16 Battalion had come in to help, and he placed them around the perimeter. His artillery liaison officer said that all of the division's artillery was available to fire overnight to help seal the area around the stacked bodies that would remain in the jungle until morning. He asked his units to muster and account for personnel. It was a pathetic sight when Alpha and Delta fell into line. Grady was now in charge of Alpha. He thought he could account for everyone but Hargrove and Fitzgerald, but there was great confusion about where everybody was, who was injured, and who had been taken where, and he could not be sure. Clark Welch was gone. Lieutenant Stroup had put him on a helicopter and they had snapped salutes at one another and it was over—Welch was on his way to the Ninety-third Evacuation Hos-pital near Bien Hoa, the same place that Sergeant Barrow and Private Landon and many of the old C Packet survivors were being taken. What was left of Welch's proud new company, the unit he had hoped to make the best damn company in Vietnam, was now in the hands of Captain Grosso, who had been the battalion's air officer.

The camp was full of dazed men, drained of feeling, shaken by what they had been through and frightened by what yet might come. Rumors swept through camp that the Viet Cong stopped the battle so that they could overrun the entire battalion in the middle of the night. Michael Arias, the radiotelephone operator who used his compass to find the way out for Jim George and his Alpha group, felt more afraid in his bunker than he had during the battle. He shivered involuntarily and tears rolled down his face as he thought to himself, *Those motherfuckers are coming back tonight to finish the job.* The place was all jitters. Lieutenant Grady tried to light a cigarette. He had managed to keep calm on the recovery mission, but now his hands trembled. He could not hold a match. He just took a deep breath, said, *Oh, man,* and leaned up against a bunker all night.

No silent night this time. The artillery pounded away, and the men inside the perimeter were sending out a constant barrage of nervous fire. A soldier on the perimeter mishandled a claymore mine and it went off in the wrong direction, injuring him. One final evacuation. Stories flew from one bunker to the next. Word spread that Terry Allen's body had been evacuated before the wounded were taken out. Much of the anger among the privates went toward their fallen commander. He had messed up, and then they took his body out first. Was it the right thing to do? Yes, probably, some of them said, but that did not lessen the us-versus-them anger. There were more stories about who lived and who died. In Alpha they talked about Randy Brown, who had come back into camp saying that his foot was killing him. His buddies had noticed that there was still a bullet in Brown's foot; they took the boot off and Michael Arias kept it as a souvenir. The C Packet guys talked about Ronnie Reece. He and three other soldiers on the USNS *Pope* had cut a dollar bill in fourths and were going to match all the pieces at the end of the war. It would not be a full dollar.

Noise all around, yet the camp was enveloped by quiet despair. Some of the medics were hurting most. George Burrows of Charlie Company watched silently as the medic next to him washed and rewashed his hands. No matter how hard he scrubbed, he could not get the blood from his fingernails.

Doc Hinger was disoriented from the moment he returned to the NDP. The normal routine would be to get something to eat, then do a radio watch or an ambush patrol or a listening post. But now he and the other Alpha survivors had nothing to do. They were unimportant and almost invisible. Hinger's uniform was an unspeakable mess. Blood and body parts stained his pants and shirt. Hot chow came in plastic foam cups. Macaroni and beef. He looked at it and couldn't touch it.

His bunker had been taken over by one of the new companies, so he went to the mortar pits. He found a spot in a trench where they kept the ammunition, but there was no way he could sleep. The adrenaline was gone. The reality of the day was setting in. Hinger felt deeply alone. Now and then someone came by, patted him on the back, and said, "Well done," but that was the last thing he was feeling. He had performed acts of bravery in an impossible situation, yet he felt like a failure. His job was to save men, but too many men had died. He had gone through twelve weeks of training at Fort Sam Houston and after that had performed medical tasks on a daily basis that interns in the states had never done. He was a humble person, but sometimes in the field, when he was working the volume blood expander or doing an emergency tracheotomy or tightening a tourniquet, he felt almost godlike. Now he was aching with guilt. He was saying to himself again and again, *If I am alive, I must have really done something wrong. Did I run? What did I do?* He knew better, but he almost convinced himself that he had turned and fled. He took out a pistol and thought of killing himself. The urge passed, but the guilt did not. As midnight came and the dreadful day slipped into history, Tom Hinger could not find a logical explanation for why in the world he was still alive.

CHAPTER 18

"THE NEWS IS ALL BAD"

THE DEEPEST DARKNESS in Vietnam, forty minutes after one, and Doc Hinger was still awake in the mortar pit, suffering through the bleakest night of his life. In Washington at that moment, twelve time zones earlier, President Johnson had just left a meeting with Lee Kuan Yew, the prime minister of Singapore, and walked into the weekly Tuesday lunch of his war advisers.

The meeting was in the second-floor dining room of the White House residence, the same intimate room where LBJ and Lady Bird and their daughters, Lynda Bird and Luci, took their meals. As historian Henry Graff once described the weekly scene, Johnson and his men were surrounded by "brilliant panels of wallpaper depicting American soldiers of the Revolutionary War in the glorious moments of victory at Yorktown and elsewhere—as if to mock the subject of their own war counsels." They gathered around a formal Sheraton dining table, with LBJ at the head in a high-backed black swivel chair. Secretary of Defense McNamara sat to his left. Secretary of State Rusk sat to his right. Presidential assistant Walt Rostow was at the other end, with CIA director Helms, General Wheeler of the Joint Chiefs, and Press Secretary George Christian in between. Aide Tom Johnson, as usual, was the note taker.

As he entered the room, Johnson mentioned that he was impressed with Prime Minister Lee.

"We need to get him with Reston and Joe Kraft," Rostow said, referring to two nationally syndicated correspondents, skeptics on Vietnam whose opinions carried great weight.

"He would be good," said Helms.

Washingtonians who drove to work that morning listening to the 6:55 "Front Line" radio report of CBS correspondent Dan Rather on WTOP had been given a heads-up on the way things might go from there. Rather devoted his entire five-minute report to explaining the rituals of the Tuesday lunches and what to expect this time. "Lunch begins, so does the serious conversation. There is an occasional pause, punctuated by the whirl of Mr. Johnson's battery-powered pepper grinder. He likes pepper and he likes the gadget." Rather called the session "Target Tuesday" and noted that McNamara would come with a list of potential targets to bomb in North Vietnam. The site selection would be preceded by the usual debate about whether to reduce the bombing, intensify it, or invoke a bombing pause. McNamara, by Rather's estimation, was the strongest proponent of a reduction, with Wheeler the hawk pushing a dramatic increase of bombing targets around Hanoi, and Rusk in between. "In thinking about Target Tuesday and the White House luncheon where so many decisions are on the menu," Rather concluded, "you may want to consider the words of nineteenthth-century writer F. W. Borum: 'We make our decisions, and then our decisions turn around and make us.'"

The debate at the Tuesday lunch was framed by two top-secret memoranda that reached Johnson's desk that day, both at the president's request.

The first, from Wheeler and his Joint Chiefs, represented a wish list of everything they wanted to do to win the war. "The Joint Chiefs of Staff consider that NVN is paying heavily for its aggression and has lost the initiative in the South," the memo began, making an argument that was the conventional wisdom of military brass that month, though of little comfort to the Black Lions ambushed in the Long Nguyen Secret Zone. The chiefs went on to argue that, although they believed progress was being made on all fronts, "pace of progress indicates that, if acceleration is to be achieved, an appropriate increase in military pressure is required."

In their wish list they asked the president to let them unleash American military might in ten more ways, everything short of an invasion of North Vietnam: remove restrictions on the air campaign over the North, known as Rolling Thunder; mine the deepwater ports in the North; mine inland waterways and estuaries in the North above the twentieth parallel; conduct naval surface operations against targets north of the twentieth parallel; use sea-based surface-to-air missiles against northern aircraft; increase bombing along the Ho Chi Minh Trail and along Laotian waterways; eliminate the need to pretend they were striking South Vietnam when conducting B-52 strikes in Laos; increase the "exploitation force" in Laos; expand the secret military program in Cambodia, known as Operation Daniel Boone, from a reconnaissance mission to a sabotage and destruction mission; and expand covert operations in North Vietnam.

The second October 17 memo came from McGeorge Bundy, the former national security adviser who had left the administration to run the Ford Foundation. Along with McNamara, Bundy had been a central figure in the expansion of the war a few years earlier, providing the rationales for Johnson to launch the Rolling Thunder bombing campaign and to send U.S. ground troops to Vietnam. He was the quintessential representation of what writer David Halberstam would describe with the ironic phrase "the best and the brightest," his arguments always nuanced and carefully calibrated, as though the war could be won by following a precise intellectual construct. A White House correspondent had spotted Bundy roaming the corridors that morning and had asked Press Secretary Christian about it at the eleven o'clock press briefing. "Mr. Bundy does come down from New York occasionally," Christian said, adding that he did not know why Bundy was there that day. In fact Bundy was a houseguest at the White House residence and had been making the rounds—talking to McNamara, his brother William Bundy, CIA director Helms, Rostow, Clark Clifford, Vice President Humphrey, and "a knowledgeable junior interdepartmental staff team"—in preparation for the "Memorandum for the President" entitled "Vietnam—October 1967."

"Basically, I think your policy is as right as ever and that the weight of the evidence from the field is encouraging," Bundy began. "I also believe that we are in a long, slow business in which we cannot expect decisive results soon."

Where the Joint Chiefs gave Johnson a to-do list, Bundy, noting that his "most important preliminary conclusions are negative," proffered his own not-to-do list. It was neither militantly hawkish nor dovish but typically Bundyish. He said he was "strongly against" any unconditional pause in the bombing, any extended pause "for the sake of appearances," any "major headline-making intensification of the bombing," any large-scale reinforcement of troops for General Westmoreland beyond what had already been agreed to, any change in LBJ's public posture, and any "elaborate effort to show by facts and figures that we are 'winning.'" This seemed to be nothing more than a nuanced explication of the status quo, but Bundy ended with a series of recommendations for subtle action that nudged the argument further away from the wish list of the generals. He suggested, for example, that through "careful study" they could maintain continuous bombing in the North that avoided "startling targets" and "had the public effect of de-escalation without seriously lightening the burden on the North Vietnamese." As to the battle in the South, he urged Johnson to "expand the visibility" of South Vietnamese military forces and to persuade the U.S. military command to place more emphasis on pacification programs. One way to do this, he said, was by rewarding officers involved in pacifying the hamlets as much as battalion commanders leading search-and-destroy missions.

While the Joint Chiefs and McGeorge Bundy were presenting their grand cases that day on what should and should not be done about Vietnam, LBJ arrived in the dining room preoccupied with two lesser documents, single pieces of paper that informed him of the real-life consequences of his decisions. He read both of these short notes before leaving his office for the war council lunch.

The first was from presidential aide Joseph Califano and came to Johnson's desk at 12:50. Califano had just received an urgent call from Warren Christopher, a deputy attorney general in the Justice Department, concerning a mass demonstration under way outside the U.S. Army induction center in Oakland, California. The day before, at five in the morning, there had been a peaceful sit-in at the induction center, ending with the arrest of 123 demonstrators, including Joan Baez, the movement folk singer. It was the first act in a weeklong series of protests against the draft and the war machine that would roll across the country from the Bay Area to Madison to Washington. By Tuesday morning the crowd in Oakland had become larger and less passive, and the police had responded with clubs and gas, news that was swiftly relayed back to the president of the United States. In his note Califano informed his boss that the U.S. Attorney in Oakland had contacted the Department of Justice with word that "there are two to four thousand people outside the Induction Center milling around, that the situation is tense, and the police had to use mace, a debilitating chemical or gas, which makes an individual lethargic, in order to clear the streets immediately adjacent to the Induction Center." The federal attorney, Califano added, was inside the building and "will keep us up-to-date."

Johnson hungered for reports of this sort. He had become nearly as obsessed with the targets of protest as with the bombing targets around Hanoi. Since the beginning of October he had been receiving nightly memos laced with the latest intelligence on antiwar activities around the country, with a special focus on the huge national mobilization rally planned for Washington at the end of that week. Now, before heading down the hall and upstairs to the dining room for his Tuesday lunch, Johnson dictated his response to the news from Oakland: "Tell Joe to tell them to put their best men on it—be adequately firm—I want no pussyfooting on the part of the Department of Justice."

The second note came from Arthur McCafferty, the briefing officer in the White House Situation Room, a windowless nerve center in the White House basement where the latest worldwide intelligence was monitored around the clock for the president and his national security staff. Every morning, apart from other intelligence, the Situation Room staff provided LBJ with a one-sheet summary of the previous day's military actions in Vietnam. This included enemy and U.S. body counts, totaled by the day, week, year, two years, and duration of the war. Much like Califano's update, McCafferty's memo now provided Johnson with the latest urgent news. It reached the Oval Office at 1:15, and the president carried it, along with Califano's note, into the Tuesday lunch. The latest accounts from the battlefields of war and peace.

Johnson sat down in his swivel chair and the meeting began. "It looks as though the news is all bad," the president said.

He took out the two notes and read them. Califano's first. Then McCafferty's: "A battalion of US Army troops taking part in Operation Shenandoah II, 35 miles northwest of Saïgon, fought a fierce four and a half hour battle yesterday in which heavy casualties were inflicted on both sides. Among the US killed was Col. Terry Allen, the battalion commander. US casualties in the engagement were 58 killed and 31 wounded compared with 67 enemy killed. The US battalion is still operational and is conducting a sweep of the battlefield area."

Not accurate, but devastating nonetheless. No amount of pepper from the battery-powered grinder could make this taste better.

General Wheeler tried anyway, throwing more wildly false statistics at his commander in chief. The battalion "had about one hundred casualties out of a battalion of nine hundred," Wheeler said. "Of course the battalion is still operational."

IT LOOKS AS THOUGH the news is all bad, the president had said.

That afternoon in El Paso, Jean Ponder Allen was in the car with her live-in boyfriend, the rodeo clown, pulling into the driveway at the house on Timberwolf Drive. She saw a white government car come to a stop behind them. A man in uniform got out, and Jean immediately sensed what had brought him there. She turned to her boyfriend and said firmly, "Just leave!" He drove off and never returned, such was the depth of that relationship. The officer was nervous but tried to go ahead with his horrible assignment. He told Jean that her husband, Terry Allen Jr., was missing in action in Vietnam.

"He's not missing in action, he's dead!" she said.

"Ma'am, all I know . . ."

"Don't tell me that. I know."

"Ma'am . . ."

"For God's sake, stop telling me he's missing! I know he's dead!"

Her husband was not missing, she was the one who was missing, emotionally, she thought. How could she possibly be allowed to grieve for a husband she had so publicly betrayed?

Another high-ranking officer was sent to General Allen's house on Cumberland Circle. Their son was missing in action, Terry Sr. and Mary Fran were told. The old man was suffering from dementia, but he understood this news only too well. He sprang into action one last time. He called friends who knew people at the Pentagon and ordered them to find out what really happened to his dear Sonny.

CHAPTER 19

THE SPECTACLE

J IM ROWEN AND SUSAN McGOVERN returned to Madison for the 1967 fall semester so late that they had no luck finding a place to rent near the university. They settled for a prefabricated garden apartment on Femrite Drive seven miles away in the town of Monona, a world apart from the sixties bohemia of the downtown off-campus streets. The Beltline was nearby, with its constant thrum of heavy traffic leading out to the interstate and beyond to nowhere, and the ambience was deathly dull. The lone signs of life within walking distance were a pizza parlor and a musty old go-go joint called the Satellite Lounge. For Rowen and McGovern, it was merely a place to sleep and to keep their dog, Schnapps, a mixed terrier that they had bought out of the window of Fur, Fin, and Feather on State Street.

They had been married almost two months, a merger of two families of the liberal Washington establishment, though such a description, while perhaps unavoidable, was not how the young couple defined themselves. Susan McGovern, the daughter of Eleanor and Senator George McGovern of South Dakota, was a senior in sociology. Jim Rowen, the son of Alice and Hobart Rowen, an economics writer at the *Washington Post,* was in his first year of graduate school in English. They were a compact and tight-wired pair who shared a love of books and movies and had two preoccupations: their studies and Vietnam. As "liberal Democratic kids, raised to be tolerant and respectful of other cultures," the war to them seemed both unnecessary and indefensible. Whether the United States was fighting in Southeast Asia "on behalf of some half-baked imperialist extension of power or this outdated notion of anticommunism . . . it just seemed so ridiculous," Rowen thought. On a date two years earlier, he and Susan had gone to see Bob Hope at Homecoming and had listened in disbelief as Hope interspersed his stand-up routine with an enunciation of the domino theory, saying "If we don't stop them in Vietnam, we are going to be fighting them in the streets of Lodi"—a small farm town north of Madison.

When the audience applauded, Rowen looked at McGovern and thought, *We are in the wrong crowd.*

Rowen's first political stirrings, like those of many antiwar activists who came of age in the fifties and first half of the sixties, before Vietnam and the cultural revolution, involved civil rights. His parents had taught him to respect other races and to avoid or challenge people and institutions that did not. When he was ten and his elementary school in Bethesda was being integrated, a teacher screamed at Joe High, a black classmate Rowen had befriended, and the incident upset Rowen and helped fix his sense of self as "an enemy of people who treated blacks badly." When a bowling alley in the community, Hiser Lanes, was reluctant to allow "negro" patrons, Rowen's parents would not allow him to go there.

In the spring of 1963, a few months before Martin Luther King Jr.'s "I Have a Dream" speech, Rowen was finishing his senior year at Bethesda–Chevy Chase High School in suburban Washington, where he had joined a group of classmates in challenging the genteel racist order. As a self-described "goody two-shoes," he belonged to the Junior Civitan Club, a service club for teenagers. They met every few weeks with their parent organization, the Civitan Club of Bethesda, whose motto was "Builders of Good Citizenship." Rowen and some friends questioned why an outfit promoting good citizenship met at Kenwood Country Club, a racially segregated institution. When they had started raising the issue a year earlier, their adult sponsors ignored them or told them to mind their own business. But the young men refused to back down, and finally Rowen and fourteen others quit the club in protest and wrote a letter, published in the April 26, 1963, *Washington Post,* that denounced the adult Civitans for not living up to their motto and "violating a trust with the community of Bethesda." Standing on principle was "heady stuff" for young Rowen; he felt morally virtuous, yet it was not without consequences. One childhood pal declared that the fuss would destroy the Junior Civitans and promised that if Rowen persisted, their friendship would end and he would never talk to Rowen again.

And he never did. The activists from then on were regarded by former clubmates as "pariahs." From that small incident Rowen learned a larger lesson on what can happen when you act on your beliefs.

The transition from civil rights to the antiwar movement seemed natural and seamless, but by 1967, with Vietnam now dominant, Rowen found that opposing the war intellectually was easier than figuring out how to respond to it physically. Along with many classmates, he spent a considerable amount of time during his senior year at the University of Wisconsin debating what to do if he got drafted, and he viewed the draft dilemma, among other things, as another manifestation of racism. He saw the war "as a reflection of domestic racism," both in how "the draft was taking minority kids not in college" and in how "the government, in our name, was making war on Asians with dark skins, the endless talk about gooks and slopes, our technological military destruction of life and culture across Southeast Asia—it all went hand in hand."

Rowen eventually joined the Wisconsin Draft Resistance Union and signed a petition saying that he would not serve if drafted, but how exactly he would not serve was something that he and Susan "talked about endlessly" with no resolution. He knew that he was "going to beat the thing one way or another," but he was also "overwhelmed with guilt" for his privileged status. McGovern broached the idea of escaping to Canada, but he never felt comfortable with that alternative, nor could he see himself going to prison as a draft resister. He was five foot seven and 135 pounds—at his heaviest. His size was considered substantial for a coxswain when he led the UW freshman crew to the 1964 national championship at Lake Onondaga, New York, but it would be of no use in prison, where he feared that he would "last about ten seconds." In the summer between his junior and senior years, he and Howard Dratch, a friend who followed the same path from Bethesda–Chevy Chase High to Wisconsin, had nearly talked themselves into joining the U.S. Coast Guard, a way to fulfill their service obligation while probably—or so they thought—avoiding Vietnam. At the last moment, though, as they were heading to downtown Washington for the final paperwork, they decided that they were not sailors, that they were not fit for the Coast Guard, and that they were only doing it to beat the draft, so they turned around and came home.

By the fall of 1967 Rowen was waking up every day "angry that the war was still going on" and determined to do something to stop it. At the time, he said later, the "anger seemed so reasonable" that he never "slowed down to analyze it. It was just wake up, feel that anger, get dressed, get to a meeting, get in the streets." That was his frame of mind early on the morning of October 17 as he and McGovern got into their little red Opal Kadett and drove to campus to participate in the first day of protests against Dow. They had attended many of the organizational meetings of the Ad Hoc Committee to Protest Dow Chemical and had talked about Dow with their friends at night around one of the heavy wooden tables in the Union Rathskeller. These were the two days they had been waiting for all fall. The war was escalating, the draft was escalating, the level of violence was escalating, in America and Vietnam, Dow had been on campus once before, the previous February, and Dow was coming back, and Dow made napalm. Dow and its napalm were not just symbolic targets, Rowen felt, but rather were directly responsible for some of the worst violence of the war.

The issue was not whether they would protest Dow's presence on campus but how much they were willing to risk in that protest. They argued about whether civil disobedience was "a correct or legitimate tactic," whether people had the right to obstruct other people's free access into a building. Some of their friends contended that napalm "wasn't the right issue" around which to make such a large personal commitment, which might lead to arrest, jail, and possibly expulsion. But finally they decided that they had talked enough, that "the university should not permit itself and its facilities to be used for war-employment recruiting," and that they would try to stop the process. But not yet, not on this day of peaceful picketing; the civil disobedience could wait one more day.

Paul Soglin, who had run through the same debate with his circle of friends, made his way toward the first day of Dow demonstrations that morning on a far shorter and easier route. From the front bedroom of the apartment he shared with two friends at 123 North Bassett Street, he said good-bye to Che, his reddish mutt, named for the revolutionary guerrilla leader who had been hunted down and killed by the Bolivian Army earlier that month, and walked out the door and down the street toward campus. He followed his daily route, which included a shortcut through the back parking lot of Kroger's, where a free improvisational breakfast awaited. Every morning between eight and eight thirty the grocery replaced its day-old doughnuts with fresh ones and placed the old doughnuts on a rack in the parking lot. Soglin, a creature of habit, pocketed a few chocolate and honey glazes and moved on, down University Avenue and right across Lake to State, then left toward the Library Mall, the Memorial Union, and up the shaded slope of Bascom Hill, where he would join other antiwar activists picketing outside the Commerce Building.

University officials, having had weeks to prepare, were going over their final plans. William Sewell, the chancellor, had arrived at his office at sunrise and after studying the day's agenda, decided to survey the protest site before the action. Out the back door of Bascom Hall, down a few steps, right twenty yards, hang a left, and there he was, entering the glass double doors at the front plaza of Commerce at eight o'clock sharp. When he reached the first-floor hallway, an assistant dean of students was already there, reassuring Erwin A. Gaumnitz, an expert in risk management who had been dean of the business school since the Commerce Building opened in 1956, that there would be little risk to manage on this first day. Joe Kauffman, dean of student affairs, was in his Bascom Hall office, reiterating the assignments he had given his task force: Dean Clingan was to serve as negotiator during the demonstrations; Peter Bunn was to be on hand to clarify university rules; Jack Cipperly, known for his rapport with students, would also try to "establish communication" with the protesters; and Ralph Hanson, the university police chief, was responsible for "preventing injury to persons and damage to property."

Hanson had been up since four, when the alarm went off in his house on Chapel Hill Road off Whitney Way, four blocks from the Beltline on the far west side. The early morning was his time to read poetry and paint. He liked outdoor scenes, favoring birch trees, lilacs, and forest streams, but also tried his hand at portraiture. One of his proudest works was a portrait he had given to Robben Fleming before the former chancellor left Wisconsin for Michigan. "Oil painting is a hobby of mine and I find it relaxing after every demonstration to splash a little paint on canvas," he wrote to Fleming in a note accompanying the gift. "It keeps me cool! About a year ago, after the kids had taken over the administration building and Bascom, I started this portrait in your likeness. I did not complete it, however, until this spring, as we always seem to have a demonstration, so my painting got interrupted."

"What's it all about, Ralphie?" the students would sing. The activists thought of him as a congenial boob, or as a tool of the establishment, certainly not as an artist.

By six in the morning he was shaved, showered, and dressed, in civilian clothes as usual, white shirt, dark suit and tie, a cardinal red baseball

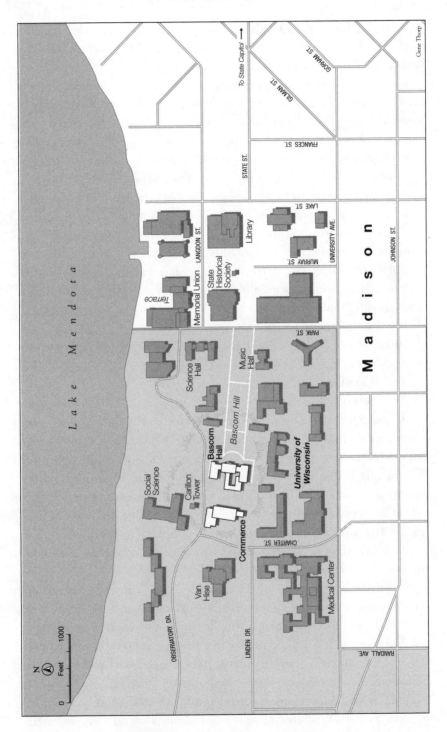

University of Wisconsin Campus

cap covering his balding head, no gun, never a gun. He steered his gray unmarked Ford down to the campus cop shop at the corner of Mills and Spring, a dilapidated hut that housed his department, Hanson joked, "because they couldn't find anything worse." By eight he was meeting with his twenty officers and ten off-duty cops recruited from the city of Madison, going over the elaborate guidelines he had established for the two days of demonstrations. Since the protest leaders had telegraphed their plans, with an obstructive sit-in scheduled for the second day, this first day of peaceful picketing was viewed as a dress rehearsal of sorts.

The demonstration began at nine thirty at the front of Commerce with twenty "well-groomed picketers," as the *Capital Times* described them, then grew to a hundred or so and "got progressively rowdier and gruffer." The number of participants waxed and waned over the next several hours, with late arrivals and people leaving for class. They marched in the autumn sunlight, in a loose loop, chanting rhythmically, "Down with Dow! Down with Dow!" and holding handmade signs.

"Dow's Malignant, Cut It Out," read one.

"Who Would Make A Bomb for a Buck? Dow," read another.

And "Vietnam for the Vietnamese."

And "Let's Get Out."

And "Stop the Bombing."

A few signs had no words, only pictures of napalm-ravaged Vietnamese civilians. One young man marched holding not a protest sign but his infant son. There was a table where students could sign up to ride the bus to Washington later in the week for the big national protest against the war. No effort was made to prevent students from going inside to be interviewed by Dow. Curly Hendershot, having arrived from the Ivy Inn with the precautionary ham sandwich in his briefcase, was never in danger of being trapped inside room 104, where the placement interviews were conducted.

Shortly before a change of classes at eleven, a squad of picketers entered the front doors of Commerce, turned right, or west, in the east-west hallway, and marched halfway down the corridor until they reached room 104. They did not try to go in, nor did they sit down to obstruct entry, but rather circled quietly inside the narrow hallway. The six police officers who had been stationed inside watched nervously but, in keeping with Chief Hanson's guidelines, did not interfere with the peaceful protest. With the change of classes the plaza outside Commerce filled with students. Most glanced at the protest and moved on, some paused to watch, some joined in, and others stopped to heckle. There was one minor scuffle, when a few football players "deliberately tore part of a rather long sign held by some of the picketers."

This caught the attention of protest leader Evan Stark, the entrancingly fluent orator of the movement, who came to the protest conservatively dressed in coat and tie. Stark approached Hanson, who had been monitoring the event from a ridge between Bascom and Commerce, and asked the chief to pull a few of his officers from inside the building to protect the larger group of protesters outside. Hanson knew Stark well from previous episodes, as did all the university officials, and especially Chancellor Sewell. Stark had studied in Sewell's department, sociology, and had been in one of Sewell's graduate seminars (which he stopped attending to organize a boycott of the local Sears). Sewell thought of Stark as "the genius behind the whole thing, the planner, the master strategist." And while he never doubted the authenticity of Stark's opposition to the Vietnam war, and agreed with him wholeheartedly on that issue, he also thought of him as "the kind of guy that takes advantage of any situation that he can to promote whatever aims he may have at the moment." When Stark had left Madison earlier that year, the administration had hoped it was for good, only to learn that he had been accepted back for another year of graduate school. A bustle of letters between administrators and deans had accompanied word of his return. "I feel compelled to say," lamented Dean Kauffman in one note about Stark, "that it is unfair to inflict on some of us the additional burdens of coping with disruptive and destructive behavior for which the admitting departments and the Graduate School accept no burden of responsibility."

But Stark was back, to be sure. He had come up to Bascom Hall to visit Sewell privately several times in the weeks before the protest, informing the chancellor that there was going to be trouble, that he would do everything he could to prevent it, but that the real problem was Joe Kauffman and the cops, who were conspiring to confront the demonstrators. Whatever reservations Sewell had about his dean of students, they were nothing compared to his skepticism about Evan Stark, of whom he once said, "I wouldn't trust him any farther than I could throw him." Stark had his own mixed feelings about Sewell. From a professional standpoint, he considered Sewell "one of the most decent men" in the sociology department, a scholar who made a serious attempt to address big issues but was a "second-rate methodologist." In political terms he admired Sewell's "instinctive pacifism" but thought he was over-matched as chancellor.

Chief Hanson responded coyly at first to Stark's plea for help, saying that Stark would have to be patient, that they "didn't have a large army of police officers here." When the break between classes ended, Hanson went inside Commerce, noticed that all was quiet, brought out two officers, and stationed them near the picketers.

Shortly before noon, the demonstrators gathered for an hour of speeches. The audience stood on the cement plaza outside Commerce, looking up at a collection of campus speakers on the ridge to the east who were angling for position in front of a bullhorn. Someone held a sign above their heads: From Protest to Resistance. More students stopped to listen, and the throng grew to about four hundred. Soglin, Bob Swacker, Rowen and McGovern, and the Stielstra twins were there, drawn not by the leaders but by the cause, determined to do what they could to end the war. Stark and Bob Cohen claimed their familiar posts among the self-designated speakers, along with their acolytes William Simons and Robert Weiland.

Three poems were read in honor of the fallen Che Guevara. Up stepped sociology professor Maurice Zeitlin, a charismatic young social-ist, his hair neatly trimmed, wearing a coat and tie and cool dark shades. It was Zeitlin who had presented the losing motion to the faculty senate the previous spring that attempted to ban corporations with military ties from recruiting on campus. With Stark at his side holding the bullhorn, and with his rhythms mimicking Bobby Kennedy, Zeitlin now said that "we live in a sad time, because it is a time in which as Americans the transparency of our government's attempts to contain and to crush the aspirations for democracy and social revolution abroad have become so clear. That's why we meet here. It is the United States government, under Democratic and Republican administrations alike, which has inter-vened, interfered, toppled democratic governments, destroyed demo-cratic and reform administrations and prevented their fulfillment."

Next came a few brief denunciations of Dow and napalm, followed by an existentialist rap from Cohen. "Now we have the corporate struc-ture," he said. "We have uni-processed students. You go work for them. You bring home your bacon. Nine to five every day. Pay the mortgage. Let yourself up. You're a lawyer, doctor, teacher, what have you, and are now set to accept this society. What I'm saying is we've got to understand that society, we've got to analyze it, and indeed we've got to negate it. That society is keeping two-thirds of the people in the world in the Stone Age. It's keeping us from relating to one another as human beings. It's alienated us from ourselves. It's gotten to the point where we can't even think in terms of what this reality is. Where we can accept expressions like 'clean bombs.' How can a bomb be clean? Luxurious fallout shelters. Comfortable poverty. Escalation is peace. All the contradictions. They're all contained right there within our language, right within the modes of our thought, and they just slip right past us. We think of things statically, not in process. We think in value neutral terms. We don't evaluate. We don't criticize. The role of the intellectual should be critical. We are so dominated by these modes of thought, by this system, that we become totally receptive and we walk along like sheep."

And then Stark delivered what he later called "one of the best speeches of my short career as a student leader." He even had a title for it: "Why the Wisconsin Football Team Is Losing." The Badgers were losing football games week after week, Stark said, just like the peace movement seemed to be losing in its struggle to stop the war in Vietnam. "It might have to do with the same thing, the fact that we were all accepting the rules of the game as they were dictated to us. In the case of the football team, through mechanical means out on the field, in the case of students, through the mechanical rhetoric of our faculty." The time had come, Stark argued, "to really burst this spectacle that had been created for us. . . . Everyone talks about the revolt of youth. Sociologists and psychologists study it. It is a spectacle like a football game or a movie. Soon there will be so much talk about the revolt of youth that people will forget to participate in it. We must stop looking at events as pictures on a wall and enter the arena of action to make the kind of history we want." In his use of the word *spectacle,* Stark drew on a new vocabulary that was becoming popular in New Left intellectual circles. In France the cultural philosopher Guy Debord was just publishing *The Society of the Spectacle,* in which his first postulate was that "the whole life of those societies in which modern conditions of production prevail presents itself as an immense accumulation of *spectacles.* All that once was directly lived has become mere representation."

Assistant Dean Cipperly was in the crowd, looking around and occasionally listening. "Mr. Cohen and Mr. Stark spoke at great length regarding their personal philosophies related to the nature of present day American society," he later wrote in a memo to Dean Kauffman. "Since

I had heard both of them expound their maxims before, I must truthfully say that I did not pay particular attention to the specific contents of their statements." Cipperly did perk up near the end, however, when Stark announced that the time of the Wednesday demonstration had been pushed back an hour from 9:30 to 10:30.

People were handing out the latest anti-Dow leaflet during the speech, a sheet that was distributed not only outside Commerce but across the campus and all the way up State Street to the Capitol Square, where Republican State Senator Walter Chilsen had one stuffed in his palm as he strolled to lunch. It was a call to physical resistance that could serve as a time capsule of radical sensibility in the fall of 1967. The influence of feminists was not yet evident, as demonstrated by the use of the word *men*. Any signs that the antiwar movement had entered the mainstream meant not that it was on the verge of ultimate success but that it had sold out and was ineffective. And counterbalancing the anger was the dream of a revolutionary socialist ideal.

> Like other large corporations, Dow is a political institution. 75% of its business is with the military. [The statistic was exaggerated; Dow records indicated that 5 percent of its total sales were to the government.] Dow makes the napalm used in Vietnam. Recruiting for Dow is recruiting for the war. Being against the war is not enough. Last year 61% of the students on this campus indicated they opposed the war. National polls show more than 50% of the American public oppose the war. But opposition is not enough. Even on this campus, opposition has become 'in.' Not one faculty member in a hundred will defend the government. But the war effort has not even slowed down. Opposition must move against the forces which underlie the war.... On Wednesday morning, we will meet on Bascom Hill, enter a building in which Dow is recruiting and stop them. We will not beg the Administration or Faculty to do our work for us. Corporations do not disappear upon request. Neither will the war. If Dow is to be removed from this campus and if the war is to be ended, all of us must do it.... Let us break through the spectacle and become people who act!
>
> Stopping Dow will not end corporate imperialism. It is merely a first step in that direction. Like those fighting tyranny throughout the world, we must build as we resist.... To those who plead

neutrality, we say there are no neutrals. We are not neutral. Not only do we oppose the war and the corporations that make it and the university that feeds it, we are also for a society in which men control their own products and in which men make themselves and are not designed by other men.

Three in the afternoon brought a spectacle of another form, an absurdist scene that might have been scripted by Samuel Beckett. In room 105 of Commerce, next to where the Dow interviews had been taking place, twelve students from the ad hoc protest committee sat down with Chief Hanson and the task force of assistant deans, including Bunn, Clingan, and Cipperly. Hanson was under the impression that the meeting had been arranged by Evan Stark, since Stark had approached him earlier in the day and suggested it. Bob Swacker, who had served as the student intermediary for weeks, was there, along with Bob Cohen and William Simons, who had been the bearer of the bullhorn most of the morning, and a few students connected to the alternative newspaper *Connections*. But Stark was notably absent. The administrators wondered why the students had asked for the meeting. The students thought the university had called the meeting and wondered what the administrators wanted. Had Dow agreed to leave? Had someone told the cops to back away? Had the students decided not to force the issue? Could there be a compromise concerning the next day's protest?

These questions were not on the agenda. There was no agenda. It was not a case of miscommunication so much as no communication. "Bunn made a few friendly overtures," as *Connections* reported later, and then there was silence. "Complete silence," according to Chief Hanson. Silence for "approximately five minutes, but it seemed much longer." Finally the students got up and left, having uttered not a solitary word.

When his task force reported the strange nonevent to Dean Kauffman, there was some discussion about sending a delegation down to the Union again to try to find some of the students and determine what had happened. But Kauffman decided not to press the issue. Hanson, taking note of the communications breakdown and the forceful rhetoric in the noon speeches and leaflets, said he would need to bolster his police corps for the planned obstruction the next day. Kauffman agreed, and Hanson placed a call to Chief Emery downtown. He told the Madison chief that he wanted twenty off-duty officers, double the number he had used that first day, and suggested what Emery and officials at city hall already knew—that the rest of the police force should be ready just in case.

INTO THIS UNSETTLED PLACE rumbled the San Francisco Mime Troupe. Having bought another cheap used car in Minneapolis, they drove down from the Twin Cities that afternoon in a three-vehicle caravan led by a blue-paneled truck carrying the stage, sets, equipment, and costumes. The performances at the Firehouse had gone well—packed houses, throatily supportive audiences that were in on all the inside jokes of this ribald Vietnamized version of *L'Amant Militaire*. Ron Davis, the troupe's director, was feeling better than ever about his "rambling wild and talented" ensemble. On the theatrical side, he considered this the best commedia dell'arte his group had ever performed, with five first-rate actors out of the seven on stage. And on the political side, the traveling show was precisely the "stimulant" that he had hoped it would be. Free and easy, determined to raise hell and move on. "We are now outside agitators," he wrote in one of his frequent notes to the troupe. "This is what we are supposed to be doing."

The atmosphere on the way down State Street to the Union reminded actor Peter Cohon, aka Peter Coyote, of "a crammed Telegraph Avenue in Berkeley." In Madison, he later wrote, describing that trip, "there was music in the air and revolution in the air. You could crash, get weed, meet great girls who would talk with you about books, music and politics, and sleep with you if they felt like it. . . . The student radical cafeteria, the Rathskeller, was full of old army jackets, long hair, beards, levis, and fur coats. It was dark, the food was bad, the crowd was intense." All interesting, but not a place to relax or prepare after a long day on the road, so the troupe escaped to the second-floor rear balcony, with its serene view of blue-green Lake Mendota and the surrounding canopy of elms and birches splashed by the autumn paint box in deep reds, oranges, and yellows. Then they made their way to the fifteen-hundred-seat Union theater and began setting up in preparation for that night's performance.

The rehearsal was interrupted once by the appearance of "a few curly-haired, old army jacketed kids," as Coyote described them, who asked if the mime troupe might be so accommodating as to conclude the show with a general announcement from the stage about the demonstration against Dow Chemical the next morning.

No problem, said Davis. Not only would they make the announcement, they might participate in the protest themselves.

When the curtain rose at eight, the theater was full. Morris Edelson, the *Quixote* editor and campus impresario, moved around like an expectant father, whispering invitations to an after-party at his pad on Charter Street. Paul Soglin decided not to go. He reasoned that the next day would be hectic and he should take this time to study. Also he had an uneasy feeling about the outsiders, preferring to think that "local agitators could get the job done." Jim Rowen and Susan McGovern were there. Rowen felt the electricity of the moment, a connection to the West Coast, to San Francisco, to the larger movement, a sense that right then, right there, was where it was happening. The atmosphere lifted the spirits of protest planners, who had trudged down Bascom Hill that afternoon in an anxious mood, fearful that the obstructive sit-in the next day would fizzle, with only a few dozen participants. This crowd, buzzing, pulsating, ready for action, gave them hope. Maybe they could burst the spectacle.

The performance was full of knowing references to LBJ, Westmoreland, Dow, even Joe Kauffman. (The troupe made a point of finding out who the local villains were and inserting their names into the script.) The audience delighted in the irreverence, all the way to the end, when Sandra Archer declared, "If you want something done, do it yourself." The ensemble then took off its commedia masks and "marched in a line, cast of seven, stamping and clapping together downstage, full phalanx," and Davis addressed the troops. "We are from another area, but would like to help you all here," he said. "We were told there will be a demonstration against the Dow recruiters tomorrow and we thought that you and we might all be there. We have learned through our experience that, after all, this country is our country and if we don't like it, then we should try to change it. This is your school, and if you don't like it, you should try to change it. And, if you can't change it, then you should destroy it. See you at the demonstration."

And that was it, the way the seventeenth came to a close at the University of Wisconsin, with an audacious call to rebellion and the echoes of a standing ovation lingering in the sweet, dark October air.

CHAPTER 20

"That's All There Is?"

T HE MORNING AFTER THE BATTLE, Vo Minh Triet and his
aides in the First Regiment awoke early to survey the damage
and prepare for the march east and north toward Cambodia,
away from the Long Nguyen Secret Zone. Big Red One howitzers had
pounded the jungle and American high-performance jets had swept
overhead late into the night, leveling trees and rearranging the landscape with napalm and fragmentation bombs, but most of the Vietnamese soldiers by then had withdrawn into deep bunkers and tunnels.
Near Triet's command post, all the tall trees but one had been destroyed.
High in that tree, clinging to a branch, was a monkey, the kind that lives
in the treetops and never touches the ground. When Triet noticed the
solitary monkey atop the lone standing tree, it reminded him of himself
and the existential isolation of a single living thing. When his soldiers
saw the monkey, they thought of something more basic, food. They
were still famished. They asked Triet to give the command to shoot the
monkey for a meal.

Triet declined. "Forgive it," he said of the monkey. "His life is miserable enough already. Let him live."

Soldiers from Rear Service Group 83 were also active early that
morning. Nguyen Van Lam, the local farmer who commanded C-1
Company, took some of his men to the northeastern edge of the battlefield. They had constructed a concealed water hole within yards of the
biggest tree in the area, likely the same tree that American troops remembered so vividly, the one under which Major Holleder had died. As
they approached the water hole, Lam came upon an American corpse. It

was torn in several pieces, shredded, it appeared, by a fragmentation bomb. The largest section was a white torso with arms attached. There was a shattered watch on the wrist of one hand. The flesh was raw and freshly ripped. Wild pigs, Lam realized, had found the body before he did.

There was no reason to stay another day, that much was obvious. The Vietnamese troops left shortly after dawn, both the First Regiment and the local logistical forces, following narrow oxcart paths through dense woods and skirting the edge of an old Michelin rubber plantation. Lam and his service group would return in a few days, when they felt safe from American bombs. Triet and his men would keep moving east and north, fording three waterways, including the Saigon River, using branches and cloth tarps to float across. There was rice, at last, at a base camp of Rear Service Group 82, but the regiment would stop only long enough to eat. They were late for their next mission. They were supposed to be the lead force in the attack on Loc Ninh, but because of the weeklong search for rice and the unexpected battle with the American battalion near the Ong Thanh stream, plans had changed. The VC Ninth Division's Third Regiment, or Q763, would lead the attack, with Triet's force held in ready reserve.

WHEN MEN FROM Bravo and Charlie companies returned to the battle scene later that morning, the bodies of dead Black Lions were exactly where the recovery team had left them the night before, stacked like cordwood in six tight piles at the side of the Hole. The surrounding terrain had been leveled by artillery fire—an overnight shelling, in a box pattern around the body pile, that was designed to deter the Viet Cong. It seemed to have served that purpose. Nothing was touched. Major Sloan, the battalion operations officer, who accompanied his two remaining companies on the morning trip back into the jungle, reported that "the US bodies were lying in the same place." Bravo's Kasik noticed that "large quantities of weapons, gear, and radios" were also still there, neatly stacked, though such things were coveted by the Viet Cong. The Americans approached the body pile cautiously, fearful of enemy booby traps. None had been set, but the recovery was chilling nonetheless. "That is a sight I can close my eyes and see to this day," Sergeant Koch of Bravo Company said later. "My fellow Black Lions laying there with dirt all over them from the mortar rounds and artillery that was fired all

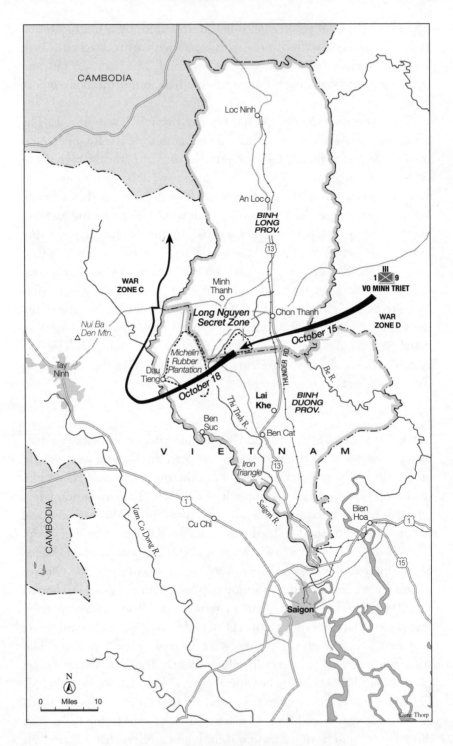

Movements of Triet's VC First Regiment

night to keep the VC away from their bodies." Dirt all over them, and an infestation of maggots.

And that was not the worst of it. When they swept the battlefield in the morning light to see what else was out there, they came across an unaccounted-for body, then another, and more, until they found seventeen dead comrades who had not been protected in the pile. Two of these, unlike the rigid bodies in the stack, had not yet stiffened with rigor mortis, leading Kasik and his recovery team to an awful conclusion: "there may have been people alive down there overnight." The task of removing the dead men was easier this time, since there was no enemy fire and the Hole was enlarged. But it was still a ghastly endeavor. They ran out of body bags, officially known as "human remains pouches." A few body bags in the inadequate supply had been ruined by heat and humidity. As a result, some uncovered bodies and body parts were loaded onto the helicopter nets. The sight of them lumped together at the bottom of a net—an indignity, though perhaps a practical necessity—stuck sourly in the memory of some of the surviving soldiers.

Major Sloan, studying the scene, reported that they found three weapons that had not been fired and three M-16s that had jammed. From looking at the radios and helmets, it appeared that "generally speaking the equipment showed more evidence of being hit by shrapnel than anything else." Other troops reported finding four helmets "with holes in them, obviously fired from close range," and a flamethrower that had large, .50-caliber holes through both tanks.

THE REMOVAL OF the bodies was well under way by ten that morning, when Lieutenant Grady held muster for Alpha Company back at the defensive perimeter. Alpha and Delta were of no use now, most of their men either dead or hospitalized, so those who remained were being shipped back to Lai Khe to await reorganization. Doc Hinger was in the same helicopter as Grady. It was, he reported, a "very somber" trip. "Very quiet. Normally, when you get extracted out of an NDP, you're going home, you're upbeat. It was a very quiet ride." No one talked. The men were lost to themselves.

The standard operating procedure for Alpha was for the company commander to ride the first lift into the field and the last lift out. Grady, in temporary command, was on the last chopper out. He carried his own radio. When the last ship landed, he hopped out and started walking with Hinger and Top Valdez toward the wood line on the way across to the road that led to Alpha headquarters. They were greeted by Charles Bivins, an old supply sergeant, who would make sure everything was ready in the rear when the company returned to camp. Bivins knew by routine that if he saw the commander, that was the end of it, no men behind him. It took twenty helicopters to move a complete rifle company with supplies, but Grady had come in on the fifth chopper. There stood Bivins, here came Grady, bringing up the rear of this weary band of Alpha soldiers. Their eyes met. In disbelief the old sergeant asked, "That's all there is?" He was weeping.

The only job to be done at Lai Khe was a distasteful one. Soldiers with any connection to the 2/28 Black Lions were asked to identify corpses at a makeshift morgue that had been set up by Graves Registration near B Med, the base medical facilities. It was brutally hot by late morning, near one hundred degrees. The bodies were arrayed in two long rows inside a tent. They were on their backs, in black bags, most of the faces uncovered, head first toward a center viewing aisle. The tent, even with open sides, reeked with an overpowering stench of death and decomposition. ID-ing dead buddies was something no soldier wanted to do. Some flatly refused. Some got drunk first. None of those who went ever forgot what they saw or how they felt.

Gerald Thompson, the Delta squad leader who missed the battle because of his ingrown toenail, was the first soldier brought in to look at the dead. He went reluctantly, under pressure from a brigadier general who had said to him, "I can't order you, sergeant, but I'd rather you do it." It was an experience that Thompson had not recovered from more than three and a half decades later. He had dealt with corpses before, but nothing like this. "God, it was nauseating," he said, not only the smell but the realization that he was looking at his own men. There was Gary Lincoln, good kid—Thompson called him Abe, of course—dead without a scratch on him. And Luther Smith, platoon sergeant, a big black guy who loved to gamble. You never knew whether Sergeant Smith was winning or losing. Once he won a big pot with a pair of deuces. Thompson ID'd him by his ring, "a big old diamond on a gold setting." And here was Richard Jones, a little guy who had come over on the ship, and next was Ronnie Reece.

When Mike Troyer got to the morgue, they unzipped a body bag and he detected an airborne tattoo and said, "If that arm belongs to that body, that's Jack Schroder."

Tom Colburn was overwhelmed by the smell as soon as he entered the tent. At the sight of the first body part in an unzipped bag, he vomited. "I can't do this anymore," he said.

Larry McDevitt from headquarters company went in "half drunk . . . it was such a terrible thing to do." He noticed that some corpses seemed peaceful, untouched, others were torn and broken or burnt by napalm.

Lieutenant Grady walked down the aisle of death with Doc Hinger. They could recognize most of the Alpha faces. Peewee Gallagher was identifiable by a tattoo on his forearm. Allen Jagielo was a medic who came in with the resupply helicopter on the sixteenth, the night before the battle, and no one in the battalion knew him, but Hinger could pick him out now by his brilliant white hair. Then Grady came upon the face of the kid he had grown so close to on the voyage across the Pacific. It was handsome Michael Farrell of New Orleans, with his olive skin and perpetual smile. One week short of his twentieth birthday, Farrell was dead. His lifeless face would haunt Grady in nightmares for years.

Major Shelton also visited the morgue. Big Jim recognized Captain Blackwell and Pasquale Tizzio, who had been his radiotelephone operator before Shelton left the Black Lions for the division operations shop. A New York City kid, Tizzio had Shelton's style—not an ass-kisser. And there was Donald Holleder. Shelton "absolutely recognized" Holleder as soon as he saw him. "He was gray. He looked like he had been totally drained of blood. And he was like stone. It was like marble. He looked like a statue laying there."

"God damn it, Don! How the hell!" Shelton said, looking down at the impassive face of the once-great Holly. He could not believe that "a guy so powerful was laying there dead as a doornail and there was not a mark on him."

Nearby was another dead soldier, a sergeant. *Who is this?* they kept asking. *Who is this?* Shelton could not place him. He thought he knew everybody. Knowing everybody was his trademark, but he was drawing a blank.

Who is this? McDevitt would have the answer, after Shelton had left. It was Eugene Plier, sergeant first class, from Sheboygan, Wisconsin, an older guy with thinning hair. Plier, the battalion's assistant operations sergeant, had been new to the company, arriving only six days before Shelton left for division. Later, when he heard that it was Plier, Shelton felt terrible. In the few days they were together, he had been too busy to find out anything about the sergeant: whether he was married, what his first name was, where he had served before coming to the Black Lions. Shelton had "never said a god damn thing to him except to tell him to do something," so he had no memory hook. From then on, wherever he went, Shelton would engage people until he had a way to remember them, haunted by the day he drew a blank on Sergeant Plier.

THIS IS NOT VIETNAM, Joe Costello said to himself when he awoke. He was at the Twenty-fourth Evacuation Hospital at Long Binh, recovering from surgery. Doctors had taken a long piece of shrapnel out of his back. The bed was comfortable, and had a knob he could turn to adjust the angle of recline. The room was well lit. Cool, maybe air-conditioned. There were women around from the U.S. Army Nurse Corps, wearing fresh outfits. The environment seemed neat and clean. What time was it? Day or night? He didn't know and couldn't tell. He got out of bed and walked to the nurses station and looked around "at all these soldiers in various conditions." Who was that across from him? "Grider, is that you?" Yes, it was Grider, cursing about how lousy he felt and how he had to get in touch with his grandmother.

Morrisette was in the next bed, and then Jenkins, and down the line eight more enlisted men from Alpha.

Officers were recovering in the next room. Lieutenant Tom Mullen awoke to find an X-ray technician digging into his chest with needle-nosed pliers. "He said he collected bullets and shrapnel, and if I didn't mind, he'd collect a bit more," Mullen reported. "The bullets pinged into a gallon size mayo jar that was three-quarters full."

Jim George was nearby, unable to sleep. The Alpha commander, with a patch over his eye, was sweating, running a fever, haunted by visions of men dying. The nursing captain told him to get up and make his bed and shave, and he did.

The Twenty-fourth, which specialized in neurosurgery, was considered the "downtown" hospital in the region, meaning not that it served downtown Saigon, since it was in the far northern suburbs near the sprawling U.S. bases, but that it tended to be favored by dignitaries and high-ranking officers. Most of the wounded Black Lions had been taken to the Ninety-third Evacuation Hospital two miles away, the primary support hospital for the First Infantry Division. The Ninety-third had more of the atmosphere of a big-city general hospital, with four hundred beds in wings for surgery, regular medical care (mostly malaria patients), and psychiatry. One wing treated Vietnamese, including Viet Cong prisoners of war. The physical plant consisted of a series of thirteen buildings, each created by connecting four quonset huts in an X configuration. The fourteenth building, the operating room, was made of three quonset huts shaped in an H. Covered walkways connected most of the buildings. The place was an amalgam of the old, the new, and the improvised. Much of the X-ray equipment was left over from the French, but when it broke down, the staff could not replace the parts and instead brought in portable field units. Outdoor showers were constructed from fifty-five-gallon drums. Only the operating room and mess hall had reliable running water. Eight operating tables were so rusty they could not be moved. Dust blowing into the emergency room created a constant sanitation problem. But the doctors, most of them young draftees just out of medical school, were first-rate, as were the army nurses. The skilled medical teams, the speed with which dust-off helicopters ferried wounded soldiers from the field to the hospital, and the youthful vigor of the wounded young men—all of these elements combined for a remarkably low death rate at the Ninety-third. In all of 1967, 12,723 soldiers were brought in, three-fifths of whom required surgery, and there were only 67 deaths.

Clark Welch was taken to the Ninety-third unconscious and did not come to until that morning after surgery, when he noticed a nurse looking down at him. The last thing the Delta commander had remembered was Lieutenant Stroup putting him on the helicopter and saluting. Did that even happen? He had some vague memory of it, as vague as anything that took place after he had collapsed near a tree and started drifting in and out of consciousness.

Bud Barrow was nearby. "Well, there's a typical first sergeant!" Barrow heard a doctor proclaim as he emerged from an anesthetic fog.

What was that supposed to mean?

"The first thing that came out of your mouth was, 'What the fuck am I doing here?'"

They had removed forty-two pieces of shrapnel from Barrow's legs, but at least he was alive. Clark Welch had been under the impression that Barrow was dead. And the last Welch had seen of his trusty first sergeant, Barrow was shooting directly at him.

No, lieutenant, Barrow would say. *Not at you, at the Viet Cong right behind you.*

Greg Landon was there, his back wound treated but the skin not yet sewn in place. And Dwayne Byrd, Santiago Griego, and Reynolds Lone-fight. Frank McMeel had been groggy since they operated on both of his wrists. When they first wheeled him out of surgery the night before, he started to sit up, and a nurse put a hand on his chest and pushed him back down and said, "You're safe. You're in Long Binh." And he fell asleep. But now, the day after, he was afraid to sleep, because when he did "it started all over again" in his mind: he was pinned down by enemy fire, metal flying, bushes turning into wood chips, men crying out in pain. He woke up, startled, and said, "I can't go back to that again."

John Fowler, from Delta's third platoon, another draftee who came over on the USNS *Pope,* was taken to the psychiatric wing. It would mark the beginning of a long period of mental distress for him. His last cogent memory before the hospital had been seeing his commander, Clark Welch, being lifted onto the dust-off helicopter and giving the thumbs-up sign. He had collapsed then, from utter exhaustion, and started crying, and had been crying ever since. "Couldn't take no more," he said later. "That was the end of me."

The Ninety-third evac was a world unto itself, with its own rhythms and rituals, attempts at normal life twisted by the realities of the war. One minute they would be watching a movie in the open-air theater, the next they would be scrambling to prepare for the arrival of broken young men. On the morning of October 17, according to the duty offi-cer's log, the hospital flag football team "played its ninth game of the sea-son beating the 185th Maintenance Battalion 14–6." Next item on the log: "Received an influx of 35 casualties from the 1st Infantry Division."

The dust-off choppers from Lai Khe had come in from midafter-noon until after dark, each one landing at the heliport with the large READY NOW sign painted on the ground. Most of the wounded men were carried to the emergency room on litters. Some walked. Those who were conscious looked around anxiously to see who else was there. For the first time since the battle, they could start to piece together who was dead and who was alive. The entire medical staff had been called in for the mass casualty situation. Internists, nurses, and medics manned the emergency room, recording vital signs on the "skinny sheet," perform-ing tracheotomies, controlling bleeding, binding up sucking chest wounds, getting X-rays, preparing patients for surgery. The chief of sur-gery performed the most critical function, triage. The worst were not treated first. He triaged for survival. The very worst were categorized as "expectant," expected to die, and operated on last. The critical ones who could be saved and operated on fastest were taken first.

Thirty-four of the thirty-five Black Lions who arrived at the Ninety-third required surgery. There was one unfortunate but understandable hitch at the beginning. One of the first patients to be anesthetized started vomiting internally because he had been given too much water before he reached the hospital. This "alerted the anesthesiologist to the possibility of recent fluid ingestion by the other 34 patients," according to a hospital report. Time was precious. They had to pump thirty-four stomachs before the operations began. Nine men underwent laporatomies, meaning their abdomens were opened for exploratory surgery; one underwent a right hepatic lobectomy: surgeons removed part of a bleeding liver. Most of the wounds were caused by shrapnel, the doctors noted, relatively few by gunshots. Within eight and a half hours, all the wounded were treated and taken to the postoperative recovery room.

Private Joseph Otis Booker, a medic from Richmond, Virginia, died there, in the middle of the night, of septic shock. He was twenty-two.

Willie C. Johnson was nearby, alive but in critical condition. Knock on wood, trying to hang on.

Faustin Sena opened his eyes the day after and thought he saw a priest hovering over him. Last rites? *No way I'm gonna die,* Sena said to himself. *No way.*

IT HAD BEEN A typical morning for General Westmoreland. Up at six for a soft-boiled egg, two slices of toast, and ginseng tea on the veranda of his villa. To the MACV office at Tan Son Nhut by 7:30. A telephone conversation with Ambassador Bunker, then a stream of aides and visitors. He heard news of the latest discontent in Washington. And he talked about his trip the previous afternoon to the prison on Con Son Island in the South China Sea, where he had asked John Paul Vann, an official at CORDS (Civil Operations and Revolutionary Development Support), whether they could "take advantage of the abundance of rock" on the island by using prison labor and "then transporting the crushed rock by barge to the Delta where it is sorely needed" for roads and other paving projects. One of Westmoreland's favorite phrases for describing how to defeat the insurgent Viet Cong was "to pulverize the boulder." Here, literally, was another way to do it. At 12:15 the general left for his regular Wednesday tennis match at the Cercle Sportif Country Club, the elegant French colonial retreat in the shadows of the Presidential Palace. It was de rigueur for the American and Vietnamese elite to practice lobs and backhands in the noonday sun.

Then back into his green fatigues, four stars on the left collar, four stars on the baseball cap, and over to Tan Son Nhut airfield, where at 2:10 his white-and-blue command helicopter flew him to First Division headquarters at Lai Khe. The purpose, he wrote in his diary, was "to get a firsthand report on the severe engagement by the 1st [he meant 2nd] Battalion, 28th Infantry, in which the Battalion Commander, LTC Terry Allen, and the Brigade S-3, Major Donald Holleder, were killed." He first had been told of the battle while contemplating the pulverization of boulders on Con Son Island. He immediately realized the implications of a battle with so many casualties and two well-known officers dead. It was exactly the kind of story that he did not want to be dealing with then, not while he was pushing LBJ and McNamara for more troops and arguing that the search-and-destroy strategy of attrition was prevailing. And not while he was preparing for the impending visit of the most respected military skeptic of his search-and-destroy policy, the retired General James M. Gavin. This was the kind of story that would be hard to contain. A pack of correspondents and cameramen from the Saigon press corps were even now tailing him to Lai Khe.

Lieutenant Grady was just leaving battalion headquarters, where he had responded to an "officers' call" to meet the new battalion commander, the replacement for Terry Allen. It was Louis Menetrey, new to the First Division, having arrived only two days earlier from the First Cavalry. Menetrey, who would go on to be a four-star general, was still a major then but on the list for promotion to lieutenant colonel, and he had jumped at the chance to run his own battalion. He was there, waiting in the wings, when Allen was killed. Vietnam, he thought, would now become his war. "Brigades and divisions had a place, but it was really a battalion commander's war. You had a great deal of latitude in what you did or did not do as long as you didn't screw it up too bad."

As he took command of the 2/28 Black Lions, Menetrey set to work reconstituting the two lost companies and bolstering the spirits of those who had been through the worst of war. He was that rare commander who washed his men in a feeling of security and good sense, exuding what one of his officers called "a wonderful air about him," including a sense of calm that many young officers lacked. In that first meeting

Menetrey seemed to know exactly what to say. He searched out Grady and told him that he had heard that the lieutenant "had done a lot of good things" in the hours after the battle. When Gerry Grosso introduced himself as the "acting commander" of Delta Company, Menetrey quickly responded, "No, not acting anymore; you're permanent." He took it as his mission to study the October 17 battle and make sure the battalion would never be put in that position again.

The division commanders, led by General Hay, were coming out to greet Westmoreland just as Grady and Grosso were going back to company quarters. There was chewing out to be done, all the way down the line, but first Westmoreland and Hay had to figure out how to explain this to the rest of the world. The generals retreated into a back room and did not come out until they were ready to brief the press. Bert Quint was there from CBS, and Joseph Fried from the *New York Daily News,* and reporters from the wire services and magazine newsweeklies and radio networks. The buzz had already started about this being an ambush. Hay insisted that it was not an ambush but rather a meeting engagement, and that mistakes had been made by the battalion command but, despite the mass casualties, the battle had been won. "After I received a briefing I made a brief statement to the press and then turned them over to General Hay for further details," Westmoreland noted in his diary. In his statement he attempted to diminish the battle by saying it was "among many that are going on throughout the country on a day-to-day basis." The American military, he stressed, was not stumbling around unprepared in the jungle darkness. "We know, we have a pretty good idea of the enemy troops in this area. We have quite a bit of intelligence on this particular regiment."

"What happens now, sir?" Quint asked General Hay.

"What happens now? What happens now is we continue to work on him until we destroy him," Hay said. He sounded aggressive and determined to pursue the enemy. Westmoreland could not accuse him of being too cautious now. "This is what I've hoped we could do for a long time, is to get him to stay in one place. For the past two months I've been chasing units all over my area—we just get a hold of 'em and they break contact and run. And he's finally gotten into an area here where it appears he's going to stay. And I hope he does stay because we'll destroy him."

When the briefing was over, Westmoreland got in touch with the III Corps commander, Major General Frederick C. Weyand, and asked him to attend the five o'clock follies in Saigon to "put the engagement in better perspective." The battle, they would say, "was a severe engagement which was fought on the enemy's terms, since the Second of the Twenty-eighth was moving into a well-established enemy base area." But they did not want the press calling it an ambush, and they wanted it to be considered not on its own but as part of a larger operation that was overwhelmingly successful. Weyand told the Saigon press corps that the battle "did not have the flavor" of an ambush. Fortified with a new body count from the division staff, he said that by "conservative estimate" 103 Viet Cong were killed. The enemy regiment, he asserted, was "as close to destruction as it has ever been." By the time Operation Shenandoah II was done, he concluded, "we will have removed the closest main base area to the north of Saigon from which they had attempted to launch major attacks."

Hay and Westmoreland were airborne by then, flying in Westmoreland's helicopter north to Chon Thanh and west into the Long Nguyen Secret Zone, where they hovered briefly, at high altitude, over the deserted battlefield.

The correspondents and camera crews were ordered to stay back in Lai Khe. They were led around by "a very scared colonel who didn't like to have us there," as CBS cameraman Kurt Volkert described him. Alpha soldiers who had survived the battle and wanted to talk were set up on folding chairs outside the orderly room at the company area, and the "fruit flies," as soldiers called the press, descended. Top Valdez and James Schultze talked about the opening moments of the battle at the Alpha front and of unseen enemy snipers shooting down from trees. Doc Hinger was asked about the death of Major Holleder. It was from the correspondents that he learned who Holleder was. All he had known when he cradled the dying officer in his hands was that he was holding a brigade major. He had never met Holleder before and knew nothing of his glory years of Army football. Hinger felt "extremely wary" of saying the wrong thing. He knew that every soldier's version of the truth would differ somewhat, because "a battle wasn't a single battle but a hundred individual battles." He was also nervous about saying anything that would disturb the families of dead soldiers.

But in describing what they had walked into, Hinger and other survivors were more interested in the truth than in cautious military semantics. They said it was an ambush. As Top Valdez told a correspondent from the Associated Press: "They were set up and waiting just like a cat getting ready to jump, and that's what they did."

• • •

THAT NIGHT Lieutenant Grady gathered the remnants of Alpha, a to-tal of twenty-seven men who had not been killed or wounded. This is going to hit big, he said. "I want every man right now to write a letter home and you tell your wife, sister, brother, mom, dad, whoever, that you're okay. I want to see a letter from every man." They all followed Grady's advice—all, that is, except Grady himself, who got too busy dealing with replacement troops and forgot to write to his wife, Mary Helen, who was staying with her parents in Reading, Pennsylvania.

Michael Arias wrote a one-page note to his mother on First Infantry Division stationery. "Dear Mom, I don't know where to begin. But I must tell you that I'm O.K. thanks to God. Remember I told you about Operation Shenandoah II, well the 17th of Oct. we lost 2 companies against a Viet cong regiment. . . . Mom, it was the most terrible 2 hrs I have ever spent in my life. Men were dying right and left and there wasn't anything anyone could do. Out of my platoon—4 made it back to our perimeter without a scratch—I was one of the 4—I don't know how I did it but God was with me. . . . P.S. Mom—I lost a lot of good buddies. Love, Your Son, Michael."

Doc Hinger had never told his parents back in Latrobe that he was in a rifle company. They thought he worked in a hospital in the safety of downtown Saigon. He wrote instead to his fiancée, Jane, and told her that he was okay and that she might see an account of the battle in *Newsweek*.

Delta Company survivors received the same instructions. Ray Albin, of the Delta mortar platoon, wrote to his mother, Geraldine Albin, in Detroit. "Dear Mom, Hi, how are you doing? Got your letter yesterday and I was glad to hear from you. Hope to receive those flicks from you soon." He eased into the story of the battle, talking about lost friends and "dead gooks," and then closed: "I still can't believe it happened. The company area is deserted now and no replacements are due for a week. As you might have guessed D company won't be going to the field for a while. Well, mom, guess I'll sign off for now. Write soon and take care. Love, Ray."

In his letter home to Alaska, Mike Taylor let his parents know that he had made it out of the jungle somehow, then said everything about the battle in three sentences. "I'll never forget the screams out there. The way my buddies were being killed. One minute they were there, the next they weren't."

Mike Troyer scribbled a quick note to his parents in Urbana, Ohio ("I am alive and unhurt. I survived that massacre"), then turned on his tape recorder and began preparing another three-inch reel-to-reel tape to send home. Troyer was not one to hold things back. During his three months in Vietnam, his messages home had become increasingly hard-edged. In one letter—the one with a long riff about officers that ended with the refrain "Fu-k the Army!"—he had said sarcastically that any-one stupid enough to volunteer for Vietnam should be shot "to save the gooks the trouble." But now the workaday complaints of military life seemed trivial in comparison with what he had endured, the worst of war. His oral report on the battle was typically graphic, but more philo-sophical: "People had faces blown off, legs blown off. Charlie just run-ning up and setting claymores and running back and blowing them. He really had things going for him that day. I don't know that we killed that many of them because I didn't see but one. Somebody else shot him. They were staying in trees. I was scared to death. . . . It was hell, you know. The worst I've ever been through. I hope I never get it like that again. Some-thing was with me. I told you my helmet came off. Charlie knocked it off with a round. I ask myself why I made it out. . . . That was suicide out there. Charlie really put it on us. Couldn't have got much worse."

The wounded too were sending word home that night from the hos-pitals. Jim George, recovering at the Twenty-fourth, wrote to his wife in Spartanburg.

> Dear Jackie,
>
> I don't know where to begin, but the kid finally got hit. I want you to let Mom and the Georges know. We got into a hell of a fight yesterday. I was the lead company. All of my platoon leaders were hit and I think two are dead. My F.O., Lt. Kay, was also hit. The Bn CO & Sgt. Maj were both killed.
> I got hit in the face and had my left sinus hit with a piece of metal. I'll enclose it for the boys. I got hit in the arms, legs & back with fragments also. They operated on me last night and I believe I'll be fine. I must really

look funny. My whole face is swelled and
my left eye is swelled shut.

A little more about the battle, and then George closed: "So much for the
details. I don't want to talk about it any more for right now. Darling,
please don't worry about me, as I am in good shape. I walked all the way
out of the jungle with part of my company." They were taking good care
of him in the hospital, George said. They told him he would hardly even
have a scar.

Over at the Ninety-third, Frank McMeel couldn't use his arms, so he
dictated a letter to an army nurse. Nearby, Greg Landon wrote a long
letter to his parents on American Red Cross stationery. "Dear Folks," he
began,

I'm O.K. I just got a bullet run across my
back. They'll sew me up in a couple days
and soon I'll be back up and around.
Yesterday's battle was one of Vietnam's
worst. Two companies were very nearly
destroyed by North Vietnamese regulars in a
gigantic ambush in the jungle. Alpha and
Delta companies left the N.D.P. south for
about a mile with no sign of the enemy. Day
before we were caught in a firefight with
several wounded, but only one death—an attached captain. It was a well-executed ambush.
Yesterday's was a regular Little Big Horn.

A reference to Custer's Last Stand was not in the minds of the army
press officers who at that hour were churning out the MACV news for
morning release. The battle was mentioned on the fifth page of release
No. 291-67. The description would not have been recognizable to any
soldier who had fought in it. It began:

OPERATION SHENANDOAH II
(Binh Long Province)—Elements of the
U.S. Army's 1st Brigade, 1st Infantry
Division killed 103 enemy yesterday . . .

At Westmoreland's direction, his aides kept massaging the story, pressing the argument that the battle was a victory. The effort had mixed results. In the United States, on the next evening broadcast of *ABC News,* the young anchor Peter Jennings, an experienced Vietnam hand, analyzed the battle in great depth. He accepted some of the new military spin but placed it in his own skeptical perspective. Within hours of the battle, Jennings noted, correspondents in Saigon were being told that "this disaster was really a big victory." This, Jennings said, was "not merely because the enemy lost more than one hundred men, but because the same VC unit was planning an assault on Saigon, less than forty miles away. Because of losses incurred in yesterday's battle and the discovery last week of an enemy supply depot, also not far from Saigon, the assault presumably did not take place." Jennings went on:

> There is no reason to doubt that the VC were planning an assault on Saigon. Apparently, the American military learned of it from a communist defector and troops were sent into the area of yesterday's battle in order to smash the plot. This they have now done, even though we must recognize a fearful price was paid—fifty-eight Americans killed.
>
> Nevertheless, even if it is accepted that yesterday's fight was a victory, the battle raises some very disturbing questions about the overall state of the war. First, this was not just a few guerrillas making a hit-and-run attack. This was a full regiment, two thousand five hundred men. This large unit was able to position itself to ambush the American battalion—two thousand five hundred men so well concealed that the Americans literally walked into a trap. A force of this size cannot move through the countryside or the jungle, no matter how thick it may be, without Vietnamese civilians knowing about it, and there's the heart of the matter, because there is good reason to believe the very people who staged the ambush yesterday are back tending their fields in the same area today.
>
> Not long ago, a high-ranking American officer told an ABC correspondent that the VC in that region were so weak, they could fight as a unit only one day a month; the rest of the time they had to work as farmers. Well, that may well be true, but it is not very encouraging to reflect on the fact that while they are farming, they are preparing for fighting. There seems to be little prog-

ress in winning their hearts and minds, as the saying goes. There
are officials in Washington who insist enemy morale is very low;
maybe it is, but the people who took the lives of fifty-eight young
Americans yesterday, obviously, do not believe their cause is hopeless. And if they are so weak they can fight only one day a month,
but on that one day they are strong enough to do so much terrible
damage.

In fact Triet's unit was not planning an assault on Saigon. That attack
was months away. Triet was headed the other direction, toward an attack on Loc Ninh. And though it was not quite accurate that some of the
Viet Cong who fought in the battle were back farming the local fields
the next day, here Jennings was close to the truth. Farmers in that isolated area of the Long Nguyen Secret Zone who supported the South
Vietnamese had fled by then to the protected hamlets of Chon Thanh or
Ben Cat. The farmers who remained were Viet Cong or sympathetic to
the Viet Cong. One was Nguyen Van Lam, commander of one of the
Rear Service Group 83 security companies. Lam was not yet back working the fields because he and his men had gone into hiding to avoid the
intense American bombing that followed the battle. But the land he
farmed was indeed close to the battle site along the Ong Thanh stream.
His house of bamboo, mud, and tin was even visible in a pictograph map
that Clark Welch had carried in his pocket.

CHAPTER 21

DOWN WITH DOW

T HE MORNING SKY hung low and gray over Madison on the morning of the eighteenth. An unsettling wind slapped across Lake Mendota and ripped the first dying leaves from the canopy of American elms, foretelling winter's approach. The darkening atmosphere felt like dusk even though it was only twenty after ten. At the base of Bascom Hill, on the vast lawn between Science Hall on the north and Music Hall on the south, a battalion of students who wanted to challenge the Dow Chemical Company's presence on campus was now taking rough shape.

Paul Soglin had done his daily doughnut run in the Kroger's parking lot on the walk over from North Bassett. Jonathan Stielstra had bicycled to campus from his Drake Street rental house on his old English three-speed, which he left on the sidewalk without a lock. Phil Stielstra was there too, though the twin brothers were intent on going their own ways. Jim Rowen and Susan McGovern had made it in from their apartment in Monona. Evan Stark and Robert Cohen were there, though they had delegated the task of organizing the two hundred or so troops on hand to a few younger students who were called "marshals" and wore red cloth armbands on their left sleeves and took turns shouting instructions into a battery-powered bullhorn. Most of the crew from the underground paper *Connections* was on hand, including Michael Oberdorfer, the photographer, who wore an army fatigue jacket and wool ski cap and carried a Nikon.

Stuart Brandes, a doctoral student in history, had descended from his fourth-floor carrel at the State Historical Society library across the street and joined the crowd as something between participant and curiosity seeker, a straddling position that was not uncommon. Like many people who opposed the Vietnam war, he considered it a tragic waste of human life and a misuse of American military power—the wrong place at the wrong time—but he was also unmoved by leftist rhetoric and interested only in peaceful protest. With a poor sound system and swirling wind, no one could hear much of anything, but Brandes, who recorded his observations that day, noted that one marshal cautioned participants "not to give their identification until they were arrested" and told them they should be prepared for "fisticuffs" at the site of the demonstration. *Fisticuffs,* Brandes noted, was "not a term people generally use, and that sticks in my mind." He also heard someone welcome "our brothers from San Francisco." It was not hard to pick out the interlopers from the West Coast. Brandes described them as "very unkempt, more outlandish even than our most wildly dressed hippie in Madison. One had a drum, another a bugle, and there were also a couple of marimbas."

That would be the San Francisco Mime Troupe, following through on the promise director Ron Davis had made the night before at the end of the performance at the Union Theater. "See you at the demonstration," he had told the audience, and here they were, all but Peter (Coyote) Cohon, who missed it, as he explained later, "having overslept after a bawdy night with an undergraduate Valkyrie who was not about to let me go until I had decimated every ideological misconception and physical tension she had accumulated since birth." But Davis, Arthur Holden, Darryl Henriques, Kent Minault, and Charles Degelman had roused themselves in time and came with a collection of instruments they had brought along in the blue-paneled truck. Now they were not mimes but mummer agitators, an early configuration of what Davis would later call the Guerrilla Marching Band. Brandes had it about right, except for the marimbas; they were tambourines. Filling out the band on this morning were a few members of the local guerrilla theater group Uprising painted in whiteface and dressed as symbols of the university and the military-industrial complex, including an LBJ and an Uncle Sam on stilts. Vicki Gabriner, a veteran activist from Brooklyn, came as Miss "Sifting and Winnowing"—the singular phrase evoking the UW's proud tradition of vigor and tolerance in the pursuit of knowledge and truth.

In keeping with a compromise that had been reached at the final organizing meeting of the protesters, the crowd was divided between those who intended to sit in and obstruct Dow interviews that day and those who did not want to obstruct but would participate in supportive picketing. As these delineations were being explained, a young man walked through the crowd with a bag of firecrackers. Stielstra stuck out his hand and pocketed a few and then "forgot about them, completely" for the next several hours. Enough with the instructions. The mime troupe grew tired of milling about and decided to move out. "A bugle call, blat, blat, blaaa . . . a drum roll . . . and the whole crowd followed the incipient marching band up the hill," Davis wrote later. The obstructionists were supposed to march up one side of the hill and the supporters the other, but less than halfway up they joined forces again and moved forward as one high-spirited crew. Behind the bugle and drum corps and the whiteface mimes and the stilted Uncle Sam followed a ragged but diversely attired line of students, with as many sport coats, ties, and skirts as army jackets, blue jeans, and beards.

Paul Soglin, wearing jeans and his trademark coat with sheepskin collar, marched up the hill with certain expectations. The students would obstruct. They might get arrested and carried off to jail. But the university would respect the tradition of civil disobedience and not further punish demonstrators, despite Dean Kauffman's threat to expel students who broke the law. Those were the "unwritten rules of engagement," Soglin thought. The day before, U.S. District Court Judge James Doyle had refused to issue a temporary restraining order in *Soglin v. Kauffman,* but in doing so the federal judge had kept the case open and directed both sides to make their cases on the question of whether university regulations regarding disruptive protests were unconstitutionally vague and broad. Soglin and his lawyers had considered the ruling a partial victory that might compel the authorities to handle the Dow demonstration with extra caution. There would be no violence, Soglin assumed.

Jim Rowen, dressed in traditional English grad student attire, dark green turtleneck and sports coat, marched up the hill with his wife and a few friends, feeling "excited and energized, but a little scared." *Okay,* he said to himself, *later in the day you might be in the pokey, and then see what happens.* He was afraid of being arrested and made more vulnerable to the draft and having to explain to his family that he was not in grad school after all. But he also remembered the great history of civil disobedience and the heroes of the civil rights movement who had been willing to make sacrifices for a good cause. He hated the war in Vietnam above all, and he was outraged by the hideous effects of napalm, and he told himself that if enough people did enough things to stop the war, maybe it would stop.

Stielstra, wearing dark tennis shoes, a cotton sweater, and a hip-length tan coat, had never experienced anything like this at Calvin College. He felt alive with "that full-bodied feeling." It had been a decisive week for him already. Two days earlier, in keeping with the Stop the Draft movement throughout the nation that week, he had sent his draft card back to his draft board, Indiana Local Board no. 266 in West Lafayette (where he had finished high school), along with a letter withdrawing his request for a student deferment. He was uncertain about the next step but determined to show that he opposed the war and the draft. Now, walking up the hill to oppose Dow Chemical, he was also unsure of what awaited, but he knew he was "walking into the face of it." The mime troupe added to the sense of adventure and helped "light up the charge." He and his fellow marchers "had no idea really where this was going. It was on some level an understanding that we were going to step over the line into the unknown. And with a lot of energy. A lot of good fellow feeling. You didn't necessarily know the person next to you. You didn't know how committed they were. But it was sufficient that they were marching up the hill, too."

"Down with Dow! Down with Dow!" the marchers chanted. From his office window at the top of the hill, Chancellor Sewell watched them advance. Their destination was supposed to be a tactical surprise. Dow interviews were being held in two buildings, Engineering and Commerce. But every student seemed to be in on the secret. They were on their way to the Commerce Building. Up the left side of the hill, gathering more marchers along the way, around the south side of Bascom Hall, where Sewell lost sight of them, partway down the long set of stairs toward Van Hise, a sharp right turn and there they were, at the side of Commerce. The mime troupe marching band stayed outside, leading the line of a hundred or so supportive picketers in a thrumming, blaring, rhythmic procession along the wide sidewalk on the east side of the building and over to the cement plaza on the northeast front. Chancellor Sewell had moved to Dean Kauffman's office in the back of Bascom Hall, where the rear window provided a clear view of the events unfolding on the plaza below. At 10:50 the protesters who had decided to obstruct filtered inside and took their places in the east-west corridor. Soglin, Rowen, McGovern, and Stielstra were bodies in this crowd.

Soon the gray-speckled granite floor virtually disappeared from view as the hallway brimmed with demonstrators sitting cross-legged side by side and leaning against the walls. This was no place for a claustrophobic. The hallway was narrow, a mere ten feet across, and no more than fifty yards from end to end. The ceiling hung low, eight feet high. The walls, lined with salmon-colored institutional tile, were nearly as hard and slick as the floor, creating a cacophonous echo effect when the protesters began chanting and singing. Because there were classrooms on either side, behind closed wooden doors, the only natural light barely glanced in from stairwells at either end. It felt like being in an overcrowded basement or submarine.

Curly Hendershot, the Dow Chemical Company recruiter, had set up shop behind the closed door of room 104, about halfway down the east-west corridor. The protest marshals, supplied with an intelligence report from scouts who had come by hours earlier, moved their strongest and most determined demonstrators to the floor just outside this room, space they considered the epicenter of the obstructive sit-in.

FRED HARVEY HARRINGTON, the university president, left Madison at eight that morning. Like General Hay on the seventeenth in Vietnam, he was preoccupied elsewhere on the pivotal day. He had "left Madison reluctantly," a report later stated, "realizing that it would be a difficult day on the Madison campus" but drawn away by regular appointments in Milwaukee. Harrington in the past year had extended his administrative vision far beyond Madison, to the burgeoning UW system statewide, and was leaving matters at home to Chancellor Sewell, whom he had talked to the previous day, and to Dean Kauffman. "Joe can handle it" was a phrase first uttered by President Harrington.

At about the time Harrington rode out of town in the back of a dark chauffer-driven Cadillac, Ralph Hanson assembled his troops. He began with forty men, including all twenty from his own Protection and Security force on campus and twenty off-duty Madison officers, ten more than he had had available the day before. After reiterating the guidelines he had drawn up for handling protesters, which seemed designed to minimize the possibility of violence, he told his combined force that they were "not facing a hostile group," despite exhortations of resistance coming from some radical student leaders. The chief felt that he had come to understand Wisconsin's antiwar students and did not believe that physical confrontation was in their repertoire. "The kids," he said, "are too sophisticated for this sort of thing." As a measure of Hanson's confidence, his initial group of forty were dispatched without riot gear helmets or batons. The Madison off-duty cops carried .38-caliber pistols but removed the bullets and put them in their pockets.

Hanson was less certain about where the action would be, so he deployed his troops in several places. A handful went to Engineering, another group to Bascom Hall, protecting the offices of Sewell and Kauffman, a small reserve force roamed in squad cars, and the largest number, fourteen, were stationed inside the Commerce Building.

The ranking officer inside Commerce, aside from Hanson, was Captain George Schiro of the Madison Police Department, who placed two or three officers outside the door of each room on the east-west corridor. Schiro and his men observed quietly and did nothing to stop the protesters when they came in at 10:50 and began their obstructive sit-in. Almost immediately a young woman tried to enter room 104 to see Curly Hendershot for a job interview. Schiro was pinned against the wall by the mass of humanity, which made it difficult for him to help her. He found himself in the odd position of asking her, rather than the protesters, to calm down. "I asked the young lady please not to make any trouble because this was just impossible," Schiro reported later. "She told me she had her rights and she wanted to exercise them. I said, 'I agree with you, but these students evidently feel that their rights are a little better than others.' I advised her to write to Dow Chemical and ask for an application and to set up an interview at a later date and she got to arguing back and forth with the other students. The students told her that she didn't have any rights. She had no rights to be interviewed by Dow. Dow had no right to be on campus, and so forth. And the girl, you could see the girl was getting emotionally upset and I tried to reason with her and tell her to leave but she wanted to stay there."

Stuart Brandes, the doctoral student in history, was standing atop the wooden base of a portable bulletin board in the foyer to get a better view. With that small boost, and with his imposing six-foot-five height, he was able to see clearly down the hall, and he watched the prospective Dow applicants get stopped at the door to room 104. Students who tried to weave through were pushed away, he reported. "A campus mailman didn't even make the effort." One of those turned away was Leonidas Doty, a Vietnam veteran, who was already familiar with napalm. "I unloaded napalm because it was on my plane," he told a *Daily Cardinal* reporter. "It's not more deadly than any other weapon." Warren R. Wade, a graduate student in political science, entered the building as a sort of test, to determine whether he could get an interview with Dow if he wanted one, which he did not. It was "jammed," he reported later, but with great effort he was able to force his way in and out.

A few minutes later Professor Charles Center descended from his office on a higher floor and headed toward room 108, about halfway down the corridor, where he was to hold an eleven o'clock class on life insurance. The route was blocked, and he could get no further than the school of business's administrative office in room 102, a larger room close to the main entrance that Chief Hanson and several officers and deans were using as their tactical headquarters. Center told Hanson that he had to teach a class, and Hanson decided to escort him down the hall. "Professor Center has to go to class! Professor Center has to go to class!" Hanson shouted as they inched along, accompanied by three of Center's students. Another three students made it in after that group, and Center started his class. Six of his seventeen registered students were there.

Hanson maneuvered his way back to room 102 and called Joe Kauffman's office at Bascom Hall. Chancellor Sewell was there, along with one of Harrington's top aides. Hanson reported that the corridors were filling up with more protesters, who were now "willfully" obstructing the Dow interviews, thus breaking university rules. He also suggested that Chancellor Sewell remain in Bascom and not attempt to visit Commerce because it was not safe. "Down with Dow! Dow Must Go!" resounded in the hallway.

Professor Center, at the other end of the hall, began teaching. "A real futile effort to conduct class was made. We could scarcely hear each other and the distraction outside the door made concentration most difficult," Center recounted in a memorandum to authorities later that day. "There was in the corridor immediately outside upwards of a hundred in the protest group, their enthusiasm stirred by their leadership by use of bullhorn, to lead singing, to chant slogans and by means of stamping of feet. It is noted that the corridor has a terrazzo floor and hard tile walls. The din can be imagined." After a few minutes Center went to the door and asked the police officer outside if anything could be done to quiet the protesters. The officer returned moments later with Jack Cipperly, an assistant dean, one of four members of Joe Kauffman's task force who had been monitoring the scene all morning.

"We can only carry them out," Cipperly told the professor, referring to the noisy demonstrators. "Do you wish to enter a complaint?"

Yes, he did. Center and his students drafted a formal complaint. Cipperly was unable to quiet the crowd or dislodge the protesters from their doorway roost, but he persuaded a protest marshal to clear a narrow aisle through which people might leave the building at the northwest stairwell. It took Cipperly five minutes to make his way down the hall to room 102, where he presented the complaint to the other deans and Chief Hanson. Center by then had given up trying to teach his insurance class. A police officer escorted him to the northwest exit, and from there he walked to the parking lot, found his car, and drove downtown to the weekly luncheon of the Madison Rotary.

While Hanson and the assistant deans huddled inside room 102, the crowd's mood in the hallway outside ran from righteous to confrontational. Spirited renditions of the civil rights anthem "We Shall Overcome" were followed by shouts of "Where are you going? Stop him! Stop him!" Hanson tried to exit, and his path was blocked. Robert Cohen "directed rather excited verbal responses" toward Hanson, as one dean later described it, but the chief "showed a great deal of composure and even a sense of humor in the face of these rather pointed remarks." At 11:20 the first arrests were attempted. Hanson targeted three student leaders who had refused to move away from the door where he was trapped. A campus police sergeant grabbed the arm of one of the three, Robert Weiland, and tried to pull him into room 102, which had also been designated the "detention room," but several students held onto Weiland's legs and made the apprehension impossible. Hanson aborted the arrests, applying rule no. 4 of his guidelines on the limitations of police actions: "If in attempting to implement the arrest or removal action, significant physical efforts of other students thwart the arrest attempt, the police action will terminate to preclude further physical violence." Instead, arrest warrants would be issued later.

For several minutes more Hanson was stuck at the door. When he asked, once again, to be let out, Cohen told him that he was "part of the society this movement is going to negate" and that if he wanted to leave he should jump out the window. Hanson went to a desk inside and called Kauffman's office. Sewell got on the line. Things were getting difficult, Hanson said. He needed more officers to keep order. Chief Emery had told him the night before that more Madison policemen would be ready to help out if Hanson needed them, and now he needed them. After talking it over with Kauffman and other aides in the room, Sewell agreed to authorize Hanson's request for more city cops.

Emery took the call in his office at the City-County Building at 11:30. He had been expecting it. He had thirty officers ready and waiting; some brought in from days off, others yanked from the traffic bureau. Outfitted in riot helmets and cowhide-strapped billy clubs, they shuttled to campus in squad cars. A paddy wagon came along. After finishing his conversation with Emery, Hanson called James Boll, the district attorney for Dane County. Boll, on his way to lunch, suggested that the university chief come downtown and talk to him when he got back, perhaps at 1:30. "I'd like to, but I can't," Hanson said, explaining the situation at Commerce. Boll said he would skip lunch and come right up.

THE OFFICIAL WORD, which confirmed Jean Ponder Allen's intuition the day before, reached El Paso at about that time. Terry Allen was not missing, he was dead. The *Herald-Post* got the news in time to change the lead story in the October 18 city edition. A banner headline declared:

Col. Terry Allen Jr. Killed in Vietnam Battle
AMBUSH MAULS U.S. BATTALION
1st Infantry Officer on Casualty List. Son of
Famous General Decorated for Heroic Deeds

Conseulo Allen and her two sisters were at their grandmother's house when the car pulled to the curb at Cumberland Circle. The precocious five-year-old, oldest of the three daughters, saw a man walking toward her in dress uniform and thought it was her father. She pushed open the screen door and skipped down the front walk, squealing "Daddy! Daddy!"

The commanding general from Fort Bliss paused, horrified, at the gleeful approach of the unsuspecting girl.

General Allen knew what was coming. His friends had been working the story all night and had already told him that his son was dead. He had gone for a long walk through the streets between his house and Fort Bliss, asking a variation of the question that all parents in that situation ask. *Why my son? Why not me?* And now, as he received formal notification, the old soldier steeled himself one more time.

"The Lord giveth and the Lord taketh away," he said, rising from his chair in the living room and walking toward the front hall. "This is the house of an infantryman. There will be no tears."

THE MASS OF PEOPLE outside Commerce was growing larger by the minute. Some were students who opposed the war and wanted to lend support; many were curious bystanders like Jane Brotman, who made her way east down the sidewalk along Observatory Drive just as the protesters arrived. Brotman, the freshman from New Jersey, thought of herself as "a real anxious person, a worrier," and now she had reason to be anxious. She was preparing for the first six-weeks exam of her college career, scheduled for the next day, and was heading toward Van Hise for a review session. The subject was French literature, mostly the philosopher Pascal. "Pensées 10: People are generally better persuaded by the reasons which they have themselves discovered than by those which have come into the mind of others."

With schoolbooks clutched to her chest, Brotman was between the rear of Bascom Hall and the front of Commerce when the sights and sounds of the demonstration brought her to a halt. The drums, the bugles, the whiteface mimes, the Uncle Sam on stilts, the Miss Sifting and Winnowing, the chanting, the tambourines, the scruffy jeans and beards—she had never seen anything like this in her life. As she would put it, this stuff blew her mind. *What is going on here?* she thought to herself. There was nothing like this in South Orange. She was amazed by what she called "the spectacle." At first she found the whole scene repellent. Yet there was "something compelling and captivating" that kept her there, watching and listening. She decided to stay ten minutes before heading on to class. Ten minutes came and went. She moved around, from the knoll below Bascom to the sidewalk under the Carillon Tower and back across the street to the cement plaza in front of Commerce, and when her review class started, she was still there, watching.

It was an internal struggle, but her will to leave weakened with every passing minute. She rationalized her decision, saying to herself: "I'm going to stay here. I'm not going to class. I've been studying all semester. I know this material. I'll study hard tonight. I'm a good student. I know I'll do well on the test. I don't have to go to a review session. I gotta watch this. I can't leave. It'll be okay. It'll be okay." She was still standing on the knoll when the squad cars and a paddy wagon arrived in the parking lot behind her.

Just then a platoon of sociology professors gathered on the eighth floor of the Social Science Building, rode the elevator together down to the lobby, and trooped outside toward the Carillon Tower and Observatory Drive on their way to the Union for their daily communal lunch. Hal Winsborough, the demographer, took one look at the crowd of protesters gathered on the Commerce plaza and said to a colleague, "By God, I'm glad I'm at a well-run university for a change, where people will have the good sense to just leave it alone." Nothing to worry about, their man Sewell was in charge. The men of methods did not break stride on their way to midday nourishment.

Warren Wade, the curious political science graduate student, decided at about that time to conduct his experiment again by walking into Commerce as if he had an appointment with the Dow recruiter. The east-west hallway was now crammed wall to wall, and many of the protesters had linked arms to form a seemingly impenetrable bulwark. Wade could not get past the front foyer. One of the red-armbanded marshals told him that if he did not want to get involved, he should leave the building.

Paul Soglin and one of his friends then decided to get up, stretch their legs, and take a break from the sit-in. They slipped inside room 103, next to the Dow recruitment room, and found it empty, so they went to the window and stood there talking casually as they took in the scene outside. They were surprised by how the crowd had grown on the plaza; it now numbered over a thousand. And there, in the far right corner of their vision, they noticed a unit of police in riot helmets gathering in the rear parking lot of Bascom Hall. Word quickly filtered out to the corridor. A student marshal started screaming, "The cops are here! The cops are here!"

Jack Cipperly was standing in the hallway shortly after noon as word spread about cops in riot equipment. "With the advent of this news, the attitude of the group appeared to change perceptibly," the assistant dean later reported. "The women were asked to remove their jewelry and glasses, pull their knees up and lift their coats over the back of their heads." And the men, Cipperly noted, were instructed to congregate closer to the doorways. One protest leader, Billy Simons, asked Cipperly what was going to happen. Cipperly said he was not sure but would try to find out. He squeezed his way into the business office again to make some phone calls. When he reached a colleague at Kauffman's office, he offered his opinion that there were "three types of people in the hallway:

persons who were trapped between classes, casual observers, and students who clearly intended to demonstrate and obstruct." An attempt should be made, he said, to "allow those students who did not wish to demonstrate the opportunity to leave the building."

When he finished this firsthand report, Cipperly turned to one of Hanson's lieutenants and asked what procedure he expected authorities to use to clear the building. The additional city police who had been called in would probably form a wedge, the lieutenant said, and force the students in the hallway to move outside. *Would nightsticks be used?* Cipperly asked. The officer said he did not think that would be necessary.

Sergeant Kenneth Buss, an eighteen-year Madison police veteran, had been in one of the last squad cars to pull into the Bascom parking lot. The lot was full when Buss's group arrived, so they ended up parking behind another squad car in an end space. As Buss and his four patrolmen were unloading their helmets and billy clubs from the trunk, Percy Julian, the attorney representing Soglin and other antiwar activists, came by carrying a camera and inquired, "What's the matter, fellows? You expecting trouble?"

Buss grunted a noncommittal response and marched his troops to the staging area under the Carillon Tower on the far side of Observatory Drive. He and the others carried sidearms and were dressed in their midnight blue uniforms with heavy blouses. They all took off their badges, arguing later that it was for safety purposes, though students suspected that it was so that they could not be identified. Buss had unloaded his pistol and tucked it in his pocket. There were thirty officers gathered under the bell tower, waiting for orders. Most of them were military veterans who came out of the working-class east side, like Buss, or the small towns surrounding Madison, like traffic bureau investigator Al Roehling, a Korean conflict–era veteran who had moved to Madison from Reedsburg. Roehling's view of Vietnam was uncomplicated: "It was a war and men were getting killed and everybody does their part." But he wasn't thinking about the war that day. He was focused on his mission as a cop, preparing himself to do whatever his bosses directed him to do. Who would give the orders?

Chief Emery was on his way to the scene by then, and though Ralph Hanson ostensibly was to be in charge of the combined force, Emery's men were more inclined to listen to him than to the campus chief. And neither chief was to act without going up the chain of command to Dean Kauffman and Chancellor Sewell, who were huddling nearby in Kauffman's office. There were already tensions evident within that foursome. When Hanson saw the Madison cops assemble in full riot gear, he walked over and asked whether the helmets and billy clubs were necessary. The riot gear was only for defensive purposes, he was told. As further reassurance, a Madison lieutenant suggested that when and if the police entered the Commerce Building, Hanson could lead the way with his unarmed and unhelmeted university squad. This left Hanson with an uneasy feeling, but he did not press the issue.

Kauffman and Sewell were reacting in very different ways to the pressure as the protest wore on. Sewell was becoming increasingly remote, uncertain, almost paralyzed by a situation from which he saw no decent way out. He could not believe what was happening. Here he was, a man of peace and goodwill, a sociologist who during World War II had studied the effects of incendiary bombs in Japan, and who hated war and had helped set up the first UW teach-in on Vietnam, and who had voted as a faculty member against allowing Dow Chemical Company to recruit on campus, and now his students were obstructing inside Commerce and cops were assembling to go in and clear them out and he was alarmed by the prospect but had no idea how to change the course of events. Kauffman was becoming increasingly strident and hawkish. He was an old JFK man who had first spoken out against the war in 1965, who encouraged students to question authority, who indeed had built his reputation as a college guru who understood the students of the sixties, but this was too much. These students, he now thought, had gone too far. He had always believed in reasonable compromise, but he sensed that the radicals were contemptuous of his very reasonableness. No more accommodation.

"We have to let them go in! " he kept insisting to Sewell, referring to the police. "We have got to let them go in!" Sewell was less eager. He was willing to give the students every last chance to leave.

Hanson shared Sewell's caution. At one o'clock he entered Commerce again with a cordon of unarmed university officers, leaving the larger Madison contingent outside. He made it as far as the foyer and stood facing the jammed east-west hallway. Stuart Brandes, the tall doctoral student standing atop the bulletin board platform, said that Hanson still presented a "cheerful" demeanor, though when he first tried to speak he was "shouted down" by some of the students. As Hanson stood there, smiling, according to Brandes's account, the demonstrators broke into a sarcastic round of "For He's a Jolly Good Fellow." Hanson's voice was soft, he was suffering from a bad head cold, but he finally got a few words in, using his bullhorn. Marshall Shapiro, the news director of WKOW radio, was standing nearby. He heard Hanson declare, again, that the students were breaking university regulations, that this was an unlawful assembly, and that they should leave. But this time Hanson went further. He seemed willing to negotiate. He said he wanted to go down the corridor with his officers to room 104 and escort the Dow recruiter out of the building. Would the students leave if Dow left?

One student, unidentified then and later but heard on tape, started negotiating with the chief. "Hanson, for God's sake, get the cops out of here," he said. "You get the cops out of here and stop the Dow interviews and I'll clear this corridor." He then put the question to the protesters nearby, those who could hear him. If Dow left and was not allowed back, should the protesters leave? Newsman Shapiro, who tape-recorded the encounter, heard the crowd respond with a resounding "Yes!" He assumed at that moment that the confrontation had been resolved, that "it would all be over." But other protest leaders were less trusting. Evan Stark, who had been standing further down the corridor, made his way to Hanson and took over the discussion. He said there were two problems. First, Hanson did not have the power to unilaterally cancel the interviews. And second, the goal of the protest was to have Dow barred permanently from campus, not just for that day. Only Sewell and Kauffman had the power to make those decisions, Stark said. He said he would lead a delegation to Kauffman's office to discuss the issue if Hanson would take his officers out of the building. Hanson agreed, and directed the men who were with him to join the other officers under the Carillon Tower until he returned. Stuart Brandes, the history doctoral student, noted that the effect on the protesters of this possible last-minute resolution was "electrifying."

With their threats of expelling students who took part in the demonstration, Brandes thought, Kauffman and Sewell had "rather stupidly dared the students and limited their alternatives." But now he saw some hope that the confrontation could be resolved without violence.

Stark and three escorts accompanied Hanson to Bascom Hall, where Sewell, Kauffman, and several assistant deans awaited. Percy Julian, the protest lawyer, was in the hallway outside Kauffman's office. Julian had already made a private plea to Kauffman and Sewell to send away the riot police, fearing they would only trigger violence. He had seen riot police in action before, he argued, during civil rights sit-ins in Nashville and Cincinnati, with ugly results. Kauffman, with his own civil rights background, found the comparison unconvincing. Sewell sat there with his hand over his mouth, saying nothing. When Stark entered the room, he said he wanted Julian at his side as legal counsel. Sewell and Kauffman rejected this request. It was an informal meeting, they said, and there were no lawyers on hand representing the university. Stark then went outside to confer briefly with Julian, who left the building and found a phone booth outside, where he placed a call to Judge Doyle, the federal judge whose court was hearing the challenge to the university's demonstration policies. "I told him I was speaking only as a citizen and as an alumnus of the university and asked him if he could do anything," Julian recounted later. "Doyle replied that it was not within his power to stop the police, since nobody could offer any proof that they would be excessively brutal. I reluctantly agreed."

Stark was back in Kauffman's office, where he spoke directly to the chancellor. Here was a final offer, he said. If Sewell signed a statement directing Dow to leave the UW campus and never return, they would try to get the obstructive sit-in to end.

No deal, Sewell responded. It was his duty to enforce university regulations. He would not capitulate to an illegal action. The student leaders had no right to tell him what to do. If Bob Cohen and Evan Stark and their associates could dictate to him, he thought, that would be the end of his administration anyway. "You guys better get out of that building," Sewell told them, "because people are going to come in and get you out if you don't."

As Stark left, he warned of a possible "bloodbath." Only the administration could prevent it, he said. On the way out he walked by Chief Emery, who was coming in.

This was now a police matter, Sewell told the two chiefs after Emery joined the meeting. From Bascom's rear window, they could see the hive of students around the front door of Commerce. Hanson turned to Emery and asked, "Do we have enough troops, do you think, to get them out?"

Chapter 22

Moments of Decision

I T WAS TEN AFTER ONE and Miss Sifting and Winnowing pranced on the edge of the crowd, teasing cops under the Carillon Tower and entertaining curious students who gaped nearby. There was something about assuming this alternative persona in costume and mime face that made Vicki Gabriner feel bold and uninhibited. Fraternity boys and policemen in riot gear were people she usually avoided, but now she tried to engage them in her extemporaneous show. "Glad to see you're supporting us, boys!" she sang out to Richard Swearingen, a sophomore from Milwaukee, among a group of hallmates from Tripp Hall who had stopped briefly on the way to class. Swearingen and friends had no interest in joining the protest, but it was hard to walk by without melding into the audience for a minute or two. Though few bystanders could see what was going on inside Commerce, the performance on the plaza was curious enough, with local and visiting mimes doing their thing. Ronnie Davis, ever the director, had instructed his San Francisco ensemble to be provocative without getting "trapped in the action" or arrested. They had "other colleges to stir up," he said, and could not afford to be delayed in Madison. As for himself, Davis had errands to run; he now headed down the hill to the university library, intent on stealing *The Art of War* by Sun Tzu.

William Bablitch, a third-year law student from Stevens Point, was just then returning to the front of Commerce after taking an hour's leave to attend Evidence class. The crowd, he noticed, had greatly increased in number and intensity since he was last there. Decades later Bablitch would serve as a justice on the Wisconsin Supreme Court, a position reflecting a propensity to mediate that he satisfied at this early age by serving as self-designated neutral observer at the demonstration. He nudged his way in Commerce's front entrance but "could proceed no further than about five feet inside the door because people inside were packed, standing like sardines, and there was no room to move." He went out again and headed left down the sloping sidewalk to the far west entrance. After reaching the main floor east-west corridor from that end, he worked his way down the jammed hallway to a room with open windows overlooking the front of the building. Taking in the sights and sounds, the determined crowd inside, the police formation under the Carillon Tower across the street, the swirl of antiwar protesters and by-standers on the plaza, Bablitch made the observation that this was "quite obviously a stalemate." If the "police did not move, the students obvi-ously were not going to move." They were not going to attack the police. "If nobody does anything stupid, the status quo is going to remain," he reasoned. "These students will get hungry some time and will go home."

Some students even now, two hours into the demonstration, with everything bubbling around them, were focused not on the protest but on getting to class, even a class on the main floor of Commerce. Betty Menacher, the freshman from Green Bay, took basic English composi-tion there twice a week on Mondays and Wednesdays at 1:20, and she had not missed a class since the fall term began. As she rounded Bascom Hall and walked down toward Commerce, she noticed students carry-ing signs and chanting slogans about napalm and Dow. She still did not know what napalm was or how it was used in Vietnam. Her reaction to the protesters was not as instinctively negative as that of her fellow freshman, Jane Brotman of New Jersey, who was standing in the crowd outside. Menacher considered herself mildly intrigued but politically uninformed and certainly not ready to participate, but nor did she want to cross a picket line. She circled the building once and finally came in through an entrance on the rear or south side. Her classroom was on the main floor's north-south corridor, with street-level windows facing east toward Bascom Hall. This corridor was a secondary hallway in the protest, away from the Dow interview room, but by the time Menacher got there, it was teeming with supportive picketers and observers who could see directly down to the main entrance.

Only a handful of students were in the classroom when Menacher ar-rived, among them Jerilyn Goodman, a sprightly seventeen-year-old freshman from Springfield, New Jersey, who had pushed her way through the crowd without stopping to talk to anyone. The hallway scene, like much of what she saw during her first few weeks on campus, was wholly alien to her. Goodman was not into politics, nor into sex, drugs, and rock and roll. Her intentions, as she later described them, were to "go to class, make my parents happy, get good grades, and do what I was supposed to do." What she was supposed to do now was be in freshman comp, so she climbed over people to get into the room. But shortly after arriving, she determined that class would not be held. She had no interest in what was occurring outside the door or how it would be resolved, so she climbed out the window, circumnavigated the crowd between Commerce and Bascom Hall, and walked down to the Union to study for an hour before her 2:25 French class.

Soon after Goodman slipped out the window, her teacher, Michael Krasny, arrived in the classroom. Krasny, an English department graduate student, had been straddling different worlds since his arrival in Madison that fall. He came to Wisconsin from Ohio University already opposed to the war and quickly immersed himself in the movement culture, hanging out at the familiar haunts, Ella's Deli on State, the Plaza Tavern on North Henry, and the Union Rathskeller. He had adopted the prevailing teaching assistant attitude of the day, making his classroom less structured, more student-centered. There was a handbook for the teaching assistants detailing how to teach freshman composition, with the students assigned to write an essay a week while reading the essays of Emerson, Thoreau, and Camus, among others, but many of the young teachers found ways to circumvent the curriculum or make it more relevant (the essential word of the times) to the happenings of the sixties. Krasny was part of this movement, yet also "appalled by part of it"—repelled especially by the hostility he saw on campus toward police and soldiers. He had grown up in a working-class neighborhood in Cleveland, the son of a dairy worker, and many of his childhood friends were second-generation Poles, Italians, and Slavs who had gone into the service and were fighting now in Vietnam. Others had become cops. Krasny winced whenever he heard his college contemporaries refer to officers as pigs, as some of them had been doing inside the Commerce hallway when he made his way to class. When protesters in the north-south corridor challenged him for holding class at all that day, he satisfied them by saying that he intended to turn the hour into a teach-in on the war, and that is what he did when class started at 1:20, though "relating *Tess of the D'Urbervilles* to Dow was a bit of a stretch."

Menacher took in the scene with bewilderment. For a few minutes the open side windows in Krasny's classroom seemed like the main portal of Commerce. She looked over and saw a ragtag team of students climbing in and striding confidently across the room as though this were a routine passageway. The door to the outside hallway opened for a split second, letting in the ever-louder hum of protest, then closed again, until another round of interlopers appeared. Krasny tried to lead a discussion about "what was going on," linking obstruction outside the door to destruction in Vietnam, but it was a disjointed conversation in which "nobody was totally articulate," Menacher thought. At about 1:28 the door opened and someone in the hallway shouted, "It's going to get wild!"

In the crowd outside Krasny's door stood John Pickart and Everett Goodwin, two students in the UW School of Music. Pickart, a cellist from Madison, was trying intensely to convince Goodwin, a violinist from Wausau, to leave the building. Although Pickart opposed the war, he did not believe in obstruction, and he was worried that Goodwin would get arrested and suspended from school. They were best friends and roommates, part of a trio sharing an east-side apartment on Sherman Avenue near the Oscar Mayer plant. They called themselves "the Berlioz Society." Goodwin considered himself a follower, not a leader, and a "nonreligious peaceful guy, influenced by Albert Schweitzer and Gandhi." He thought he was following the teachings of those two great men in his actions now. He and Pickart were deep into a philosophical discussion about civil disobedience and pacifism when they heard rumblings down the hall that protest leaders had returned from a meeting with Sewell and Kauffman at which "the results of the discussion were negative."

IT WAS A POLICE MATTER, Chancellor Sewell had said, and now the two chiefs placed in charge of the situation stood outside Commerce making final plans. Bill Emery and Ralph Hanson believed that the protesters would use the common civil disobedience tactic of going limp upon arrest, forcing officers to carry them out by their arms and legs. To make the detention process easier, Emery said he would have the Madison Police Department paddy wagon back up to the edge of the Bascom parking lot so that arresting officers would have to drag demonstrators no more than forty feet. When the paddy wagon was filled, they would take the arrested students downtown to the Dane County jail, then return for another load. It would be like a shuttle service, Emery said. He then walked across Observatory Drive toward his band of city officers, assembled under the Carillon Tower, and prepared them for the imminent confrontation. Hanson returned to the front of Commerce alone and pushed his way through the crowd into the foyer, reaching the opening to the east-west corridor where protesters were sitting with their arms linked together.

Marshall Shapiro of radio station WKOW positioned himself near Hanson and turned on his tape recorder. "This is an unlawful assembly," Hanson said into a bullhorn, his voice weakened by his persistent cold. "We are going to clear the place out." Only those students closest to him could hear him clearly, but the response was vociferous nonetheless. His words, Hanson testified later, were greeted with "jeers, curses, insults, and tumultuous noises." Someone standing nearby could be heard saying, "You want to bring in your cops, bring them in, baby!"

Stuart Brandes, looming over the crowd in the back of the foyer no more than fifteen feet from Hanson, strained to hear, but could pick up only part of the message. Brandes did not want to get arrested, so he decided it was time to leave, but that was easier said than done. He found himself "completely hemmed in" by the mass of humanity, unable to escape. Down the east-west corridor, toward the epicenter of the protest where the Dow interviews were being held, Hanson's warning went largely unheard. Paul Soglin and Jonathan Stielstra, Bob Swacker and Billy Kaplan, Jim Rowen and Susan McGovern—all were down there in the sit-down crowd, expecting something to come but unsure what it would be. Even if they had wanted to, which they did not, they would not have been able to escape. The hallway was impassable. Stielstra was "not planning to get into a fight with the cops." He had been in a fight only once in his life, back in fifth grade. But did he have some other prank in mind? "You want to see something?" he said to Rowen, revealing the firecrackers in his pocket.

Rowen had no idea who Steilstra was, but the incident worried him. This stranger with the firecrackers seemed to him to be "an impressionable kid." Now Rowen looked down the corridor toward the foyer and the front of the crowd and saw something else that startled him—a protester taking off his belt and wrapping it around his fist as a makeshift brass-knuckle weapon. *Uh-oh,* Rowen thought to himself. *There are some people here who are going to fight.* He hoped otherwise, that protesters would hold the moral high ground and resist through civil disobedience, and that the police would carry them out without violence.

Protest leaders spread the word to get "the beef" up front, near the foyer and back by the interview room. It was at that moment that Michael Oberdorfer made the transition from sympathetic *Connections* photographer to full-fledged protest participant. He took off his army jacket, placed his Nikon camera in the large front pocket, and sat down right outside the interview room. The time had come for resistance, he believed. The war rolled on and on, the university seemed more beholden to corporate interests, hiding behind its cover story of impartiality. The only thing left was to stop business as usual at the university, Oberdorfer thought, even if only for that one day.

Lock arms, one marshal instructed. Hold your ground. Someone could be heard urging women to kick the officers in the balls.

Hanson found his way out and walked across the street to the police formation under the tower. He had given a final warning to the students, to no avail, he said. William Bablitch, the law student observer, had by then slipped outside to monitor the action and was standing near Hanson. He thought he heard Hanson say, "Let's take a crack at 'em." Emery turned to his men and said, "All right, let's go and carry it out." Hanson, in civilian clothes and without a helmet, led the way back toward the front of Commerce, followed by Sergeant Buss and his men. Jane Brotman gasped as she watched the sea of students on the plaza open a lane for the wedge of policemen who strode forward with a quickening gait, badges off, elbows out, nightsticks at the ready. The crowd fell in behind the officers, virtually engulfing them. Bablitch was in the group hovering just behind the last man in blue. Emery moved to the side and found a lookout on the rise above the plaza, between Commerce and Bascom, not far from where Brotman stood. He thought of it as "a command position" where he could "see what was going to transpire," though in fact he could see nothing inside the building.

No more than two minutes after Hanson issued his final plea for the students to leave, here came Sergeant Buss and the wedge of cops, marching through the first set of glass doors. Al Roehling, at Buss's flank, thought his state of mind was typical of the officers at that moment. He was, he would say later, "full of piss and vinegar and ready to go." They reached the narrow vestibule, then moved through the second set of doors into the foyer. There was no space to gain footing, just a wall of people, and the human wall surged forward, pushing up against the oncoming force. The officers started flailing with their nightsticks but fell backwards into the vestibule. Chief Hanson was propelled "over and around bodies" and found himself "spilled outside the double doors." He could not get back inside and was unable to lead or control the police force for the next several minutes. Sergeant Buss braced himself with his feet and arms against the corner of a door in the vestibule and remained there. One officer stumbled against a floor-to-ceiling plate glass window, accidentally breaking it into jagged shards with his nightstick, a frightening sound that added to the panic of the moment. As people around him backed away, the officer kept swinging his club at the window frame, now apparently attempting to clear it of sharp edges of glass. Some in the crowd saw only the raised nightstick, assumed police were on the attack, and started another surge forward in an attempt to keep them away. One officer who had been pushed out of the building caught sight of Emery standing on the slope and ran up to him and said, "Chief, we can't do it."

Chancellor Sewell was looking out the back window of Kauffman's Bascom office with a clean sightline to the front of Commerce. He watched in horror as the first wave of officers marched in and stumbled back out. *This cannot be happening at our great university,* he thought to himself. His son Chip Sewell, a graduate student at Wisconsin, came bursting into the room.

"Dad!" he shouted. "Look at those cops going into the building. They're going to beat the hell out of those kids!"

Sewell was lost, haunted, the well-intentioned man immobilized by events beyond his imagination. "Well, it's out of my hands now, you know," he said to his son. "They weren't listening to me."

Inside, in the few moments after the glass broke, there was an eerie silence. Then the police regrouped and reentered the foyer, this time without Hanson and with nightsticks raised. Once inside, they felt pressed against a wall, according to Buss, and then "really started using clubs." John Lederer noticed that the officers "had a very set look on their faces." Evan Stark, who had led the students to that moment, whose rhetoric resounded with calls for resistance, quickly decided when the time came that physical resistance "was not worth it" and managed to slip around the police and out the double doors, disappearing into the protective embrace of the gathering crowd. He said later that he had ordered everyone to leave when the police began their charge, but if so, fewer people heard this utterance than had heard Chief Hanson's final declaration of an unlawful assembly.

Stuart Brandes, adrenaline flowing, found himself only a few yards from the police and about to become caught up in the human push against them. Here was his moment of decision, he thought. He could lend his considerable strength to the surge, probably without getting caught, and in so doing participate in what he considered a violent act against police. In that split second, with the cops moving toward him and the students pushing back, he had to decide whether he was willing to resort to force. The answer was no. He was a liberal, not a radical. Although against the war, he was not confrontational and was not going to fight the police. He found an opening and made his way partway up the eastern stairwell, standing amid a group of business school students who were there jeering the protesters and cheering the cops. That is what they were doing, that is, until a few officers rushed the stairs, billy clubs flashing, unwittingly going after their own supporters.

Near the front door police were able to grab a few demonstrators and drag them outside and up the knoll toward the waiting paddy wagon. One of the first to be arrested was Vicki Gabriner, Miss Sifting and Winnowing, who darted in front of the cops as they arrived at the entryway and went limp and started shouting at them as they hauled her away. Her arrest was pure guerrilla theater, and she made the most of it, resisting vociferously as two policemen dragged her by the arms, slowing them down enough so that every movement was captured on film. One of the defining pictures of the day was of Gabriner's painted face staring out the back window of the paddy wagon.

Lynne Cheney, the English doctoral student who also taught freshman composition, and her husband, Dick Cheney, the political science graduate student, could not recall later precisely where they were as the Dow protest unfolded that day, but they retained a strong memory of seeing, and being revolted by, the antics of the mimes. In an interview with *The New Yorker* three and a half decades later, when her husband was vice president of the United States, Lynne Cheney said that she distinctly remembered "going to class and having to walk through people in whiteface, conducting guerrilla theater, often swinging animal entrails over their heads, as part of a protest against Dow Chemical." What surprised her most, she said, "was that you would enter the classroom and here would be all these nice young people who honestly wanted to learn to write an essay. That, in a sense, was the real university, but this other was what was attracting so much attention."

The breaking of the glass had "scared the hell" out of Officer Roehling, who was afraid that one of his fellow officers would be

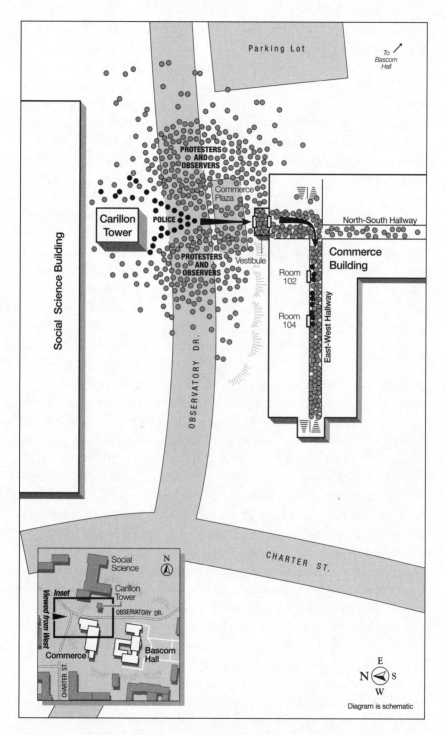

Parking Lot

To Bascom Hall

PROTESTERS AND OBSERVERS

Commerce Plaza

Carillon Tower

POLICE

North-South Hallway

Commerce Building

Social Science Building

PROTESTERS AND OBSERVERS

Vestibule

Room 102

Room 104

East-West Hallway

OBSERVATORY DR.

CHARTER ST.

Social Science

N

Carillon Tower

OBSERVATORY DR.

Inset

Viewed from West

Commerce

Bascom Hall

CHARTER ST.

E
N — S
W

Diagram is schematic

Confrontation at UW Commerce Building

wounded by the shards. He also felt overmatched by the crowd, and he started swinging his nightstick with abandon. Roehling knew nothing about the proper way to use a baton in a hostile crowd, he would admit later. Madison police had not been trained in that yet, aside from four who had taken a brief riot control course in Chicago. What they should have done, and would be taught to do in later confrontations, was to keep their batons in front of them, using them two-handed to poke and jab and protect. Instead they lifted the clubs above their heads and started swinging. There was, Roehling recalled, "a lot of overhead swinging."

Eric Nathan, a junior from Manhattan, was in the surging mass just inside the front doors when the pushing and swinging began. He and his friend Donald Lipski had debated whether to take part in the demonstration at all, wondering about the worthiness of the linkage between Dow Chemical Company and Vietnam. Even during the march up the hill they had debated whether to be supportive pickets or obstructionists but finally decided to go inside and "take our stand." They sat cross-legged in the corridor at first and experimented with interlocking their legs, before deciding that was too dangerous. Lipski felt "an adrenaline rush like pregame in a locker room" as the police approached. He and Nathan were part of the shoving match at the front door, with police trying to force their way in and students attempting to keep them out. When nightsticks went up, Nathan, feeling a sense of shock and outrage, decided that he did not want to "mess around" with the police. He raised his hands above his head in a "don't hit me" gesture and managed to snake his way through the melee untouched, stumbling into the roiling crowd outside. John Lederer got out of harm's way by rushing up to the stairwell, near Brandes and the gaggle of business student bystanders. He watched the melee near the entrance as police started swinging. "Some of the people were grabbing onto their clubs, mostly to keep them from being shoved in their stomach," he reported. "They were pushing with their hands and the police officers would yank their clubs back to get them free of the hands, and the next thing they were hitting people and seemed to be very indiscriminately hitting people. They were definitely hitting people on the head."

Some protesters were resisting the police, Lederer noted, and some were not. He counted himself among those not resisting. An officer stomped toward him and jabbed him in the stomach. Lederer put his hands to his head for protection. *Don't get clubbed, and don't look like you're resisting,* he said to himself. He tried to walk out the double doors under his own power. Another policeman shoved him forward and he fell to the ground and was hit across the back of the neck. He got up and "was sort of half-shoved and half moved myself out of the building." Stuart Brandes, from his position on the stairs, saw an opening through the foyer and vestibule and decided to make a run for it. He was afraid of being collared by the police, thinking that he might be "going out the door and right out to a paddy wagon and right out of school." He made his way, shouting all the while that he was leaving as fast as he could, and though he was jostled, he managed to avoid the nightsticks. Brandes reached the second set of glass doors and stepped out to the plaza and saw a ring of officers in front of him and the swirling crowd behind them. He decided to turn sharply to the left, following the side of the building a few yards until he looked down and faced a sudden ten-foot drop-off.

Below him cut into the earth was a cement walkway leading to a basement utility room, and standing down there looking up at him, urging him not to jump, was Maurice Zeitlin, the assistant professor of sociology. Zeitlin did not support the obstructive protest and had not participated in the demonstration but felt connected to the demonstrators. He had sponsored the faculty resolution the previous spring that had sought to ban Dow and other military contractors from recruiting on campus, and only the day before he had been a featured speaker at the noontime rally on the Commerce plaza against Dow. Shortly before the confrontation now, he had attempted, with no luck, to persuade the police not to enter Commerce. When all else failed, he noticed the dangerous precipice to the side of the front doors and decided to station himself down at the bottom, thinking that he might catch anyone who jumped or fell.

Within a few minutes the first wall of protesters inside had vanished. Police had gained control of the foyer and started to move down the east-west corridor toward the obstructionist students in front of the Dow interview room. It was "kind of close quarters" in the hallway, Sergeant Buss later recalled, and protesters "laid on the floor, kicked at you, spat at you, cursed you—but it wasn't the violent type where we met the swinging fists and trying to choke you and so on." Buss said he and his fellow officers "did manage to use" their clubs "and a couple of students were knocked to the floor and we then started taking them by the arms or any way we could get them. We kind of broke their resistance and started . . . pushing them back through the door and there were enough policemen so that one guy would get hold of him, the next guy would take him, the next guy, and out the door they would go, so finally we just had them out of the way."

Captain George Schiro, in charge of the fourteen Madison and campus officers who had been stationed inside the building all morning, started moving away from room 104, where the Dow interviews were supposed to have taken place. Curly Hendershot had given up any pretense of conducting interviews by then and had retreated through an interior doorway into the business school's administrative office, where a few secretaries and faculty members remained. Schiro edged down the hallway with his back pressed against the wall, as soon as he heard the commotion at the front. As he neared the foyer, he started grabbing students, trying to eject them. He was without a nightstick himself, but he saw the other officers wielding their batons. It was only in self-defense, he thought. Bob Hartwig, a sergeant in Hanson's university force, had been standing near Schiro outside the Dow interview room when the police wedge entered the building and the glass started breaking, "sending a jolt through everybody." He tried to usher students out the far western stairwell, but many would not, or could not, leave. Utter chaos, he thought.

Jim Rowen and Susan McGovern, two-thirds of the way down the corridor, could see and hear the commotion at the other end. It was an eerie phenomenon, Rowen recalled, all noise and light moving their way, the screams of students and the lights of television cameras. And on top of this a sound Rowen had never heard before, one that he could not immediately place. Then, perhaps ten seconds later, he realized what it was—"the sound of people having their heads hit. It was like a basketball bouncing on the floor. Or hitting a watermelon with a baseball bat. It makes a sort of *thunk*." It all became clear to Rowen at that moment. "Civil disobedience wasn't working on our terms. They weren't arresting people, they were beating people. That's how they were clearing the hallway. Just going through like a machine and beating people." Tom Beckmann, a business student from Whitefish Bay, was taking a pop quiz at that moment in a classroom one floor above the melee. The door to the room was closed, but still Beckmann and his classmates could hear it all. "We could hear kids being hit on the head with nightsticks. It was gut-wrenching. It sounded like somebody taking a two-by-four and slamming it on a table."

From his place amid the students halfway down the hallway, Jack Cipperly, the assistant dean of students, saw police helmets bobbing above the heads of the crowd and "nightsticks rising and falling, rising and falling." He heard "a series of cries emanate from the group" and tried to move forward toward the police to warn them that they were approaching an area occupied by many young women protesters. Cipperly pleaded with the first officers to refrain from using their clubs. "At this point it must be explained that a certain amount of hysteria and panic was apparent within the group," he reported later. "In many cases the officers and the students appeared to be acting independently. Several curses were reciprocally exchanged between the police and the demonstrators. . . . In my direct observation I witnessed many policemen who pulled students to their feet without using their nightsticks; at the same time, I witnessed individual policemen who struck students who were on the ground." Some cops were restrained, Cipperly said, but some were not. When he saw one officer wind up as though he were going to strike a young woman, Cipperly "grabbed him, like hockey players do." It turned out to be Jerry Gritsmacher, with whom Cipperly had gone to Catholic grade school and high school.

"Jerry, what are you doing?" Cipperly asked.

"Jack, what are *you* doing?" the officer responded.

As people in the hallway retreated, Michael Oberdorfer, who had been sitting outside the interview room, moved forward. He heard a woman screaming "Stop! Stop! I'm hurt! I'm hurt!" and moved toward the screams, finally reaching a young woman who was bent over, clutching her knees, sobbing. She had been clubbed in the abdomen and uterus. Oberdorfer picked her up and carried her toward the foyer and the front entrance. He was enraged, acting on reflex, shouting madly as he moved through a phalanx of police clubs. *What the hell's wrong with you guys! Can't you see I'm trying to help someone who's hurt!* He brought the young woman out the double doors, swinging his elbows furiously as he went, knocking an officer to the ground.

Paul Soglin and Jonathan Stielstra had been in the line of protesters standing not far from Cipperly, outside the Dow interview room. Suddenly the crowd in front of them disappeared and there was nothing between them and the bull-rushing police. Soglin saw five officers coming toward him. He and Stielstra and the others started backpedaling very slowly, trying not to start a stampede, shouting at the police as they retreated. Soglin pulled the collar of his sheepskin coat over his neck and the back of his head. Then, as he later described the moment, "they just came right at me. It was almost like, 'We'll get that one next.' And they grabbed me and started beating me, and I ended up right on the floor. I don't know how long it lasted. . . . But I know I was holding my own and they were getting frustrated. Because the jacket was doing its job. The jacket was doing its job in protecting my head and my back pretty much. One of them hit me right on the base of the spine. I was on my side, and instinctively my arms went out and my legs went out, my limbs just shot out. And at that point everything was exposed. And then they started working on my legs and my head."

The students behind Soglin were scrambling. After watching the police go through the demonstrators "like a hot knife through butter," Billy Kaplan, the junior from Wilmette, decided that he would save himself from that fate. He heard people "crying and screaming, and it was real crazy, real chaotic," he recalled. He had "never seen police beat anybody at that point except on newsreels from down South, beating blacks. And it had all happened so fast." As he remembered it, "all of a sudden the doors just blew open and there was this big noise and people were falling down left and right, and you could see these big things coming down on people, and I got the shit scared out of me. I was really frightened. And I ran. I just ran. And having just been near the bathroom, I went inside. There were maybe a half dozen of us." A policeman followed Kaplan into the bathroom. He thought he and the others would "be beaten to within an inch of our lives." And what a way, what a place to get beaten, he thought, "in a damn bathroom." But the officer did not touch them. "Out! Out! Get your asses out!" he yelled, pushing them back into the hallway.

Rowen and McGovern, who had been positioned a few yards behind Soglin, were trying to escape toward the stairwell at the western end of the corridor but found their way blocked. Rowen turned around in time to see Soglin being beaten. Less than a decade later the two would run the city of Madison together, Soglin as mayor and Rowen as his chief of staff, but at the time they barely knew each other. Rowen recognized Soglin by "his hair and his jacket. The trademark jacket with sheepskin lining." The image that would stick in his mind was of Soglin "in a ball, a little fetal position ball. And a cop beating him on his back and making this tremendous sort of whacking sound."

Finally, as Soglin recounted, "one of the officers said, 'Have you had enough?'—as though it had been asked several times before. And they picked me up and threw me forward, and I am now on my own, on my feet. And they are moving on to whoever is behind me. And they are now escorting me out. Sort of like running the gauntlet, because there are more officers. And they had no real further interest in me except getting me out of the building, which was a surprise." Soglin made his way to the foyer and through the vestibule, past the broken glass, out to the plaza. "And there is a mammoth crowd out there. And I come out and another officer just kind of throws me by the collar beyond the ring of officers into the crowd." Swacker and Stielstra were right behind him. Swacker made it through untouched. Stielstra had been whacked a few times on the way out, but was able to remain standing and avoid serious blows. "I probably covered my head," he recounted later. "Or maybe they just thought, 'This guy doesn't look robust enough, let's not hurt him too bad.'"

The scene in the north-south hallway, where the nonobstructive supportive picketers were gathered, was much the same. John Pickart and Everett Goodwin watched the approaching wedge of officers with disbelief. Pickart was standing on a chair outside the door to Krasny's classroom. He saw "a Quaker girl" with whom he had argued philosophy just moments earlier, "still sitting there and getting hit so hard by a police nightstick." And "a boy lying across a girl and obviously just trying to shield her, getting kicked and struck by two policemen." Much as in the scene in the east-west corridor, students who wanted to escape found themselves trapped: police coming at them from one direction, an immobile jam of people behind them in the other direction.

Betty Menacher was in the north-south hallway when the police charge began. She had heard the ruckus outside her classroom and opened the door, which locked behind her. Soon the crowd was backing up in her direction.

A woman pushed her against the wall and said, "What's wrong with you? You're not ready at all. Pull your hair back and take your earrings off!" Then the corridor resounded with shouts and shrieks and it seemed to Menacher that "an army was coming down the hallway." She watched as two policemen grabbed a young woman by her long blond hair and yanked her down the hall. Then she saw "a policeman hit a kid over the head and the blood just gushed out." It was time to flee, Menacher thought. She started moving backwards down the hallway, trying to enter each classroom door she passed. Finally she banged on a door and heard voices inside. A woman opened the door just as a policeman grabbed one of Menacher's arms.

"You fucking pig, let go!" the woman inside screamed at the officer. A young man came up and grabbed Menacher's other arm. The officer let go and shoved Menacher into the room. Pickart made it into the room as well, and they all climbed out the window and ran toward the front of Commerce. Krasny and his handful of freshmen students joined them out the window. On the way toward the plaza Pickart saw several students running by, covered with blood. "Those damn bastards can't do this to us," one girl screamed.

In the heat of the confrontation, cops versus students, individual human beings tended to be seen only as representatives of a type, and the intense hatred of one type for the other now was overwhelming. But John Pickart felt conflicting emotions. He was furious about the police attack, by their use of nightsticks, by the fact that the administration had allowed the confrontation to take place, yet he was also disturbed by the mass psychology of the angry crowd. "In the general confusion I made my way to a point where I could get a fairly good view of the front doorway," he reported in a letter he wrote later that night to Pam Crane, a high school friend who attended Oberlin College. "It was a terrible sight. . . . Then the students by the door started spitting on the police and screaming at them. The policemen charged with their clubs. I left again. This time for good. I couldn't stand to see 2,000 people acting like animals. I still can't believe it, in my home town! On my university! It was terrible. I have never seen such hysteria and hatred in so large a group of people. On my way out, I looked back to see the whole crowd screaming 'Dirty Fascist Honky' at the police."

CHIEF HANSON had been out of the action since that initial foray when he had been pushed back through the vestibule. He saw only the first few seconds of the confrontation inside. From the front plaza he had walked down the slope to enter the building from the western side, a floor below the main level, and was walking up the stairwell when he encountered a band of students rushing down toward the exit. He heard someone shout, "They're coming, they're coming," and presumed this referred to the police. Hanson decided to leave with this group and went back across the street to the original police assembly area near the Carillon Tower, where he found his bullhorn. Looking across Observatory Drive at the front entrance of Commerce, he saw students spilling out the double doors, the police forming a semicircle in front of the doors, and an enormous crowd now stirring behind the ring of officers. "This was a growing or escalating crowd of people," Hanson later testified. "Some of the people coming out, they were holding their hands on their head, some of the girls were crying hysterically, some of these people came over to me and for the next few minutes they were in front of me. The students who had formed around him, Hanson said, were "verbally abusing me, in other words subjecting me to insults and spitting on me and this type of thing."

Michael Reiter, an attorney for the student protest leaders, approached the chief and urged him to do something about the bloody confrontation inside. The police were using clubs, Reiter said, and Hanson should go in an attempt to stop them. Hanson said that things were beyond his control, that he could not get back inside. Reiter persisted. He said that he and a few other students would form a cordon and clear the way for him through the mass of students. "I indicated to them that I didn't think I could get in there but I was willing to try," Hanson recalled. "This they did then. They did form a wedge for me through this—now I am calling it a hostile and belligerent, defiant, mad, frenzied crowd."

"Let him through! Let him through!" Reiter shouted to the students as he led Hanson across the plaza toward the front doors of Commerce. As Hanson recalled the difficult procession, he got "a couple punches in the face and one in the back." He saw some people charging at him, but they were blocked, and he made it to the perimeter and had the bullhorn up and was yelling "Stop! Stop! Stop it! Stop it!" But when he reached the vestibule and stepped into the foyer, he looked down the corridors and there was nobody there—nobody, that is, except police officers.

Chancellor Sewell had not moved from the back window of the Bascom office. He saw the students staggering out of Commerce, heads bloodied, disappearing into a thunderous crowd that now numbered nearly five thousand. *My God, I've just screwed everything up.*

Jonathan Stielstra, now a face in that angry mob, looked up toward Bascom Hall, his gaze moving above Sewell at the window, up to the peaked roof of the old building, where he noticed the Wisconsin and American flags flapping in the breeze. *How incongruous,* he thought. How could the flags fly above this mess? *This is not right,* he thought. *This is not what the flags stand for.* At that moment, acting on impulse, the young philosopher from Michigan, the earnest transfer student from Calvin College, the son of a university administrator and nephew of a Dow executive, came up with a brazen plan.

CHAPTER 23

STARS AND STRIPES

OWNTOWN AT police headquarters, Tom McCarthy was
trying to dictate a report to the secretary of the detective
squad, but he kept being distracted by anxious squawks coming over the scanner in the captain's office. It was obvious that something
had gone terribly wrong on campus—that "the shit was hitting the fan
down there." McCarthy stopped to listen, then dictated again, then listened to the radio some more. He was not altogether unhappy to be
away from the action at Commerce. When Chief Emery had called for
volunteers for riot-control duty, McCarthy had not volunteered. He
wanted nothing to do with the long-haired kids and was content to dislike them from afar. That time on the city bus when he told a hippie-
looking student that someone should drop a nuclear bomb on top of
Bascom Hall, he was only half joking. He was a detective, not a riot-
control cop. He worked in street clothes, tracking down thugs and rob-
bers. It was best, he thought, to stay away from the demonstration.

Before McCarthy could finish dictating his report, Jack Harrington,
the chief inspector, came by and barked, "C'mon, Tom, you and I are going down there." It was an order, not a request. On the way out the door,
they picked up Lieutenant Jim McNally. The three officers headed
toward campus in an unmarked Dodge: Harrington driving, McNally
riding shotgun, McCarthy in the back seat. Only McNally was in uniform. The radio reports sounded more dire by the minute as they
wheeled down Langdon Street, past the Union, right at Park, and then
a quick left and up the incline of Observatory Drive as it curved above

Lake Mendota. They had reached the crest of Bascom Hill and were heading down toward Commerce and Social Science when a rock came hurtling toward them and cracked the windshield.

A squad of students, their emotions let loose by the confrontation at Commerce, spilled into the street, preparing to surround the car. One young man jumped on the hood and began smashing the windshield with his boot. Another officer who happened to be nearby chased the culprit toward Bascom Hall. Perry Pierre, a first-year law student from tiny Seymour, Wisconsin, had been standing on the grass in front of Bascom and witnessed the scene. "Here comes this kid running through the crowd, running towards us, and the police officer is chasing," he reported later. "We trip the kid, and stop him, and the police officer gets there and jumps on top of him. And we say, 'Hey, wait a minute! We didn't trip him for you to beat the crap out of him.'" Detective McCarthy, in the meantime, had slipped out the back door of the Dodge and crawled on his hands and knees through the vast throng of students, trying to go unrecognized. When he saw a clearing, he rose and made a run for it toward the front of Commerce, where he joined his fellow officers at the main entrance.

The last demonstrators were being cleared from the building as McCarthy arrived. He saw students with bloody heads being treated on the lawn. He stood there without a helmet or nightstick, protected only by his trenchcoat, as thousands of students screamed obscenities and chanted, *"Sieg heil! Sieg heil!"* An hour earlier many of them had been curious bystanders; now the vast majority seemed at least temporarily radicalized and hostile to authorities. McCarthy went inside and encountered his longtime colleague, Captain George Schiro, who had been stationed in the east-west corridor all day.

"What the fuck happened?" McCarthy asked.

"Don't ask me," Schiro responded.

He directed McCarthy and the others to go back outside and push the crowd further from the door. If they formed another wedge, he said, perhaps they could clear the plaza all the way back to the Carillon Tower across the street. McCarthy and five other officers attempted to clear the plaza, but were able to move forward only a few feet when the huge crowd surged back at them. As they started to retreat, Officer Bert Hoffman was struck in the throat, perhaps by someone who had grabbed his baton. McCarthy, at that point, was thinking of only one thing: survival.

· · ·

PAUL SOGLIN by then had staggered through the crowd to Observatory Drive, where a station wagon awaited, a makeshift ambulance that would ferry him and several other wounded students two blocks down Charter Street to the University of Wisconsin Medical Center. *Where did this driver come from? How did he have the foresight to know he might be needed? Why are they letting him drive on campus through this chaos?* In moments of crisis, odd little questions can run through the mind, and those are the questions that obsessed Soglin at that moment. He had no answers. The sheepskin coat had done its job, he said to himself again. There was no blood on it; the nightsticks had never made it to his scalp. There was a small cut on his forehead and a larger gash on his shin. He was brought to the emergency room through the back entrance of the hospital.

Word of mass casualties had reached the hospital only a few minutes before the first students arrived. After emerging from Commerce with the injured young woman, Michael Oberdorfer had raced down the hill to the emergency room exit. "You've got to get up there," he shouted to the hospital staff. "People are being seriously injured by the police!" At about the same time, Dr. Robert Samp had been walking across Charter Street from his office to the hospital when "a kid with a handkerchief wrapped around his head, covered with blood," approached and asked whether he was a doctor. The student said he was among dozens of students inside Commerce who had been injured. Samp told the student how to get to the emergency room, then found a telephone and asked the hospital operator to make the calls that would set in motion the disaster plan. The medical center had been rehearsing how to handle "catastrophic occurrences," and here was the first opportunity to put the plan in action. They were ready by the time "a stream of students began pouring in," as Dr. Robert Hickey, the chairman of surgery described the scene. The university's medical staff had not expected the disaster but had prepared for it in any case.

Still, the atmosphere in the emergency room at first reflected the chaos of the events that preceded it. Some students were distraught, even hysterical, and lashed out at any figures of authority, even doctors who would treat them. "The initial response was one of agitation and aggressiveness toward the physicians," Dr. Hickey noted in his report on the treatment of injured students. "And the companions of those injured were more prone to this emotional outlook." The doctors tried to remain cool, Hickey said, and "followed an agreed-upon position not to offer an expression of judgment." Soon enough, he noted, "order was established and maintained." Hickey was in charge of triage, making the first cursory examination of patients before sending them along to X-rays and treatment. Each student was also given a tetanus shot. Forty-seven students were treated, half of them with head wounds. "In interpreting the trauma, the students were mainly injured with nightsticks, a weapon which produces a cutting injury to the scalp," Hickey reported. "A scalp wound is vascular, bleeds profusely, and is alarming. These facts are consistent with our observations."

While he was being treated for a leg gash, which required stitches, Soglin asked about the head wounds. They looked horrendous, a doctor told him, because of all the blood dripping down, but were not as damaging as they appeared. None of the students with broken scalps required surgery. The confrontation had been awful enough, but some apparently felt an urge to make it look worse. Journalists noticed some students playing to the cameras, moaning until photographers turned away, then smiling in private. Two students who were taken to the emergency room had smeared the blood of others onto their heads to make it look as though they had been injured. But most of the agony was real. William Bablitch, the law student observer, escorted a group to the hospital; he reported that "there was no doubt that these students were seriously injured. One fellow that I helped carry had a slash in his head and he was bleeding profusely and he was semiconscious. I lifted him up and we commandeered a car that was able to get through and I carried him into the back seat of the car and at that point he was just crying, 'My hand! My hand!' and I looked at his hand and it was just swelled completely out of proportion."

Jim Rowen and Susan McGovern, after avoiding injury inside Commerce, had made their way to the front row of the crowd on the plaza. They were "just livid, outraged" by what they had witnessed, Rowen said, and wanted to express that outrage now to the police who had formed a protective semicircle in front of the main entrance. They joined in the curses and chants of *"Sieg heil."* Rowen noticed that a hailstorm of debris was coming over his head, aimed at the officers—"shoes, textbooks, rocks, people throwing anything they could." The crowd surged forward and knocked him and a few other students toward the cops, causing a messy scrum. Officer Roehling's helmet got ripped and the band fell over his eyes, temporarily blinding him as he fell. He felt a kick in the head but had so many people on top of him that he was protected from any more blows. Rowen was struck by a baton, a glancing blow in the back of the head, as he fell. "We all just wanted to get up, but we couldn't," he recalled. "Everyone in the pile was swearing. 'God damn, get off me! I can't! Someone's on me!'" He finally wriggled out of the pile and resumed his place at the front of the enraged crowd.

Oberdorfer, having returned from his run to the hospital, was near the front of the throng. He grabbed a badgeless Madison policeman and screamed in his face, "You got kids? You got kids?"

The officer did not respond. "How come you won't tell me who you are?" Oberdorfer stormed. "I'll tell you who I am. I'm Michael Oberdorfer. That's O-b-e-r-d-o-r-f-e-r. Five forty-eight West Main Street." Someone wrote it down.

Jonathan Stielstra was nearby, and after catching sight of the flags waving above Bascom Hall, he noticed that a crowd had formed on the northwest balcony off the top floor, just below the midsection of the Bascom roof where the flagpole stood. It seemed easy enough to get to the balcony, just climb the middle stairs of the old building to the top and walk out the side door, so he went up to "reconnoiter." From there he assessed what it would take to reach the flagpole on the gently slanted roof. It looked "doable enough," he thought. A steam vent offered a foothold from which he could shimmy up. His tennis shoes would give him good traction. But to finish the deed, he needed wire cutters to snap the steel cable. Where could he get wire cutters? He remembered that one of his roommates on Drake Street had a toolbox.

Stielstra scrambled down the stairs and out the front door of Bascom, skirting past the Abe Lincoln statue to the bottom of the hill, where he found his old English three-speed sprawled sideways on the ground, unlocked, near where the demonstrators had assembled that morning. Down Park Street he pedaled, then right on Regent and left on Mills, all the way to the little house at 1215 Drake. The toolbox was on the first floor, in the utility room next to the kitchen, and the wirecutters were in the toolbox. They could be used one-handed, Stielstra noticed. On another shelf he saw a book of matches. Another bold notion. He remembered the firecrackers that someone had given him and that he had stuffed into his pocket that morning. He grabbed the matches, raced out the door, and biked furiously back to campus, standing up as he rounded the corners and churned uphill, this time heading directly to Bascom Hall.

JIM BOLL, the district attorney, was horrified by the scene he encountered when he reached the Commerce Building shortly before two o'clock. The violent confrontation inside the building was over by then. The police had formed a protective cordon at the main entrance, holding off the massive throng of screaming students. Boll made his way through the police line, was given a goofy-looking white riot helmet with a football-style chin strap by one of the cops, and climbed the stairs to the flat roof of Commerce to survey the chaos from there. It was only three stories above the plaza, and as he stood in full view of demonstrators below, he was shocked to realize that many recognized him. When he was a student in Madison in the 1950s, having come down from the northern Wisconsin town of Antigo, he had no idea who the Dane County district attorney was, nor did he care. Now the students were shouting his name, bracketing it with obscenities. *Boll, you son of a bitch! Hey, Boll, you bastard. Fascist!* Sieg heil, *Boll!* He decided to leave the roof and went out behind the police line, where he stood next to John Patrick Hunter, a respected political reporter for the *Capital Times*.

A young woman rushed toward them and snapped, "Boll, you suck cock!"

"No, I deny that," Boll responded. Hunter broke into a laugh.

Radio newsman Marshall Shapiro, who had been standing nearby, realized the demonstration-turned-riot was big enough for the national news. He scurried across the street to the lobby of Social Science and gathered his notes to file a report as a stringer for CBS radio. The WKOW radio news director had seen much of the action, inside and out. The students packed in the hallway "like sardines." Hanson declaring the assembly unlawful. Police marching in. Demonstrators trapped inside, nowhere to go, arms locked, some resisting, some being clubbed. Students stumbling out, bloody and shrieking. The huge, angry crowd. Officers being pelted by debris. As he thought back on it later, Shapiro would conclude that the police had "overreacted," but at the time he was "just there to report the story," not to make judgments. He was a townie himself who had grown up with many of the cops in the old Greenbush neighborhood, and if anything, his sentiments were with them. He was not sympathetic to the antiwar cause, because he "didn't understand it."

Aside from editors at the *Capital Times* there were, he believed, "very few in the media at that time who did understand it, at least speaking for the local radio and television media. Almost all of us believed that the government, the establishment—that you just don't question them, that they know what is right for the country and you just follow along like sheep."

Still, the confrontation came as "a total shock, something that was unexpected by everybody," and it left Shapiro with contradictory feelings. On the one hand he was thinking, "God damn, they deserved that. They took over classes. If they got whacked it was their own fault." Yet the day's events also shook him up and forced him to consider the war in a way he never had before—"at least a little bit." Shapiro's sixty-second piece, including audio and a you-are-there extemporaneous style, led the two o'clock national news report. His only regret was that broadcaster Douglas Edwards transposed the call letters, introducing him as a reporter for WOKW. Not long after filing the report, Shapiro left campus and drove out to the WKOW television station on the far west side. He was a man of many hats, serving as both radio news director and television substitute sports anchor, but now he had to change clothes for the role for which he was best known. A preposterous transition, but such was life then: he would go from covering the Dow riot to putting on a cowboy suit and hat and badge to entertain a group of five-year-olds on the afternoon cartoon show he hosted as "Marshall the Marshal."

Dave Wagner, a senior in comparative literature, was arriving at the scene about the time Shapiro was leaving. Wagner's wife, Grace, who had been translating German documents at the State Historical Society, followed the demonstration from the beginning that day. She called him at their third-floor apartment at 105 State Street up near the square. He had been home studying for a test when the violence erupted inside Commerce. "You've got to get down here," Grace told him. "They're beating the shit out of everybody." Wagner hopped on a city bus and rode down to State and Park, then walked up Bascom Hill and into the "sea of people screaming at the cops."

As the literary editor of *Connections,* the alternative newspaper that had been formed in response to the first Dow protest the previous February, Wagner was looking for his *Connections* compatriots, who were ubiquitous this day. Bob Gabriner, the editor, was there, the intellectual force quietly observing the action. As soon as Gabriner saw Wagner, he gave him an assignment. They were going to put out a special edition of the paper, Gabriner said. *The Great Dow War. Start interviewing people and gathering information.* Wagner went to work—and never attended another class that semester. The journalists at *Connections* had no use for mainstream notions of objectivity. Objectivity, Wagner would argue, "was no more than a literary device, like any other literary device." In any case, the connections of *Connections* to the Dow demonstration were anything but neutral. Gabriner's wife, Miss Sifting and Winnowing, was in the paddy wagon, looking out in her whiteface. Stuart Ewen, a cofounder and feature writer, had been one of the lead organizers of the protest, a righthand man to Evan Stark, as was Richard Samson, the news editor. Michael Oberdorfer, the art director and photographer, had been in the middle of the action. Stark and Bob Cohen, the movement orators, were on the fringe of the *Connections* crowd and listed as contributors to the newspaper.

The students who took part in the protest acted from their own convictions, with individual motivations and expectations, sharing the one overriding common principle of being opposed to the war in Vietnam. But they walked into a situation that was shaped nonetheless by self-selected leaders, and in that respect the Dow demonstration was in many respects a *Connections* production, with an assist from *Quixote,* the literary magazine. It was *Quixote*'s editor, Morris Edelson, after all, who had brought the San Francisco Mime Troupe to town in the first place. Edelson also had marched up the hill that morning with the protesters but declined to go inside Commerce, fearing that violence would erupt. Instead he found a perch on the northwest balcony of Bascom Hall and watched from there. After the halls of Commerce had been cleared and the action turned to the plaza outside, Edelson heaved loose concrete and pipes and other debris onto the roofs of police cars and the paddy wagon parked in the lot directly below him. His philosophy, he explained, was that he "didn't want to destroy the whole place, just dent it, throw some sand in the machinery."

Edelson was not alone. In the heat of the moment people responded in ways they never had before. David Westley, a sophomore dropout from Madison who worked at the Wisconsin Draft Resistance Union, found himself going "from a pacifist to a militant" as he stood in the plaza watching students emerge from Commerce with bloody heads. He became so enraged that he picked up some paving bricks and started throwing them toward the police line. Others nearby were doing the same.

Detective McCarthy was standing down there, in his light tan trenchcoat, without a helmet or baton, surrounded by angry students, trying to dodge the incoming debris, feeling hopeless. The police had "done everything wrong you could think of," he thought. The students had managed to let the air out of the tires of two squad cars up in the Bascom lot. They had surrounded the paddy wagon and rocked it so much that the authorities felt compelled to release Miss Sifting and Winnowing and the others. As McCarthy saw it, no one "knew what the hell to do." And then an object—he was never sure what it was, a brick or a heavy shoe, most likely—came hurtling down and struck him flush in the nose. McCarthy did not see it. He slumped to the cement, unconscious. Jack Cipperly, the assistant dean, had been standing next to McCarthy, and in his periphery vision had noticed an object (he thought it was a brick) coming and had ducked just in time, only to see it strike McCarthy. With McCarthy's blood dripping on his face, Cipperly helped two officers carry the detective inside to the nearest classroom.

Captain Schiro took him from there, cradling McCarthy in his lap. Still dazed but slowly regaining consciousness, McCarthy noticed that Schiro was rummaging through his trenchcoat. "Where's your gun?" Schiro asked. McCarthy said he didn't have one; no way he was going to bring a gun down to that mess, he said. Blood was still streaming down his face. The pain became intense. A bone in his nose had been pushed close to his eyeball. The bridge in his teeth was knocked out. Every time Schiro touched him, it hurt more. Chief Emery came into the room, then Ralph Hanson. It was not a happy place.

"Who the hell gave the order?" Emery asked.

Schiro said it wasn't him. He had been inside, down the hallway, when all hell broke loose. Hanson said it wasn't him. He had been concerned about the nightsticks all along, he said, and had been reassured by the Madison police that they would not use them. Jack Cipperly, standing next to Hanson, wiped "some spittum" off his coat. McCarthy was drifting in and out of consciousness, listening in disbelief, as the three senior cops argued about who gave what orders. It seemed, McCarthy thought, that they didn't know any more about it than he did.

Bob Hartwig, a sergeant on Hanson's university force, helped load McCarthy onto a stretcher and carry him out the western exit, away from the main entrance, to a waiting ambulance. The emergency room was buzzing with students when they brought him in. A doctor asked whether he was a police officer. The conversation was overheard by someone who shouted, "He's a cop!" A friend of an injured student, in a rage, lunged toward McCarthy and "gobbed" on him. The spitter was shoved away by a doctor, who then placed McCarthy in a private room. Hickey came by to examine him. It looked serious, he said. The detective would need surgery.

Chief Emery had long considered McCarthy a handful, an officer who took his police mission to the edge of what was permissible, occasionally crossing the line, but whatever had happened on this chaotic afternoon could not be blamed on McCarthy. He had come to the assistance of his buddies and stood there and got hit in the nose and knocked unconscious. Not long after McCarthy was carried out the side door of Commerce, Emery decided that he could not let the boisterous crowd remain assembled on the plaza any longer. He walked up to the Bascom parking lot and called for a supply of tear gas. When the canisters were delivered from downtown a few minutes later, Emery directed Captain Schiro and a few of his men to disperse the crowd.

Tear gas had never been released on the Wisconsin campus before. Soon enough, the noxious, burning scent would become as familiar on Bascom Hill as the pungent odor of algae blooming in Lake Mendota on a midsummer's day. But in the use of tear gas, as in many other respects, this demonstration was a first, a prelude to all that was to come at Wisconsin and other campuses over the next four years. The police had no practice using tear gas; the students had no experience dealing with it. One canister was accidentally dropped next to a huddle of professors standing near the Carillon Tower. Another was picked up by a student and thrown back at the policemen. The wind was swirling. "We had a very poor day for the use of tear gas because it was so windy it wouldn't stay," Chief Emery later noted. "The crowd would move out immediately from downwind of the gas, but lieutenants"—here he was talking about demonstration marshals—"would muster forces back into the area again to close the gap."

That is not to say that the tear gas had no effect. Stuart Brandes, the history doctoral student, reported that he "saw many students crying and vomiting"—among them curious bystanders who had nothing to do with the protest. Warren Wade, the political science graduate student who hours earlier had pretended that he wanted to be interviewed by Dow, and who thought the students, not the police, had provoked the violence, was now on the Commerce plaza. He heard the pop of a tear gas canister going off about twenty feet away and, unable to see, he stumbled back toward the Social Science Building, where he was blinded for about ten minutes, he estimated. Tom Beckmann, the business student from Whitefish Bay who had been taking a class inside Commerce, was also out there, watching, and was alarmed when the tear gas wafted toward him and his eyes started burning. He and a cluster of students scrambled up a fire escape on the side of Bascom Hall and barged into the back of a huge lecture hall where a professor was holding forth on art history, oblivious, until then, of the chaos outside. Another canister exploded at the feet of Eric Nathan, the junior from Manhattan. He stumbled away, tearing and temporarily blinded, until he collapsed on the sidewalk at the side of Bascom Hall. A young woman rushed to him, treated him with water—the wrong treatment for tear gas, but no one knew it then—and walked him back to his apartment on West Johnson.

Jane Brotman, the freshman from New Jersey, who had watched the entire protest after skipping her French literature review, had no idea what tear gas was or how to react when a canister landed near her. Given her "anxiety and fearful nature," as she put it later, she started thinking, "What if you breathe this in and you die?" She was terrified. "Does this make you blind?" She started running and didn't stop until she had reached the safety of her familiar table in the back of the Rathskeller, where she began to take stock of everything she had seen that day. Betty Menacher, who had been watching the action after climbing out the window of her freshman composition classroom, heard someone shout "Tear gas! Look out!" The people around her dashed away, but she stood still, "watching this thing come through the air." It hit the cement "and this huge cloud of tear gas" floated right at her. That was enough excitement, Menacher decided. She walked back to Sellery Hall, barely able to see through her contacts.

When the tear gas floated toward Evan Stark, he ducked into the Social Science Building and found a bathroom where he could wash his eyes. An odd thought popped into his mind—"Why not check the mail?"—so he went upstairs to the sociology department. The hallway was empty, he noted, but "faculty members were clustered at the windows in the offices overlooking the melee, occasionally cheering a student they recognized." Stark "slipped in next to them for a few minutes, realizing the irony of this 'participant observation,'" before heading back downstairs and out into the crowd. His days as a radical leader on the Wisconsin campus were over. He visited the hospital, briefly, then left the campus and the city, resigning from school before he could be suspended.

Jonathan Stielstra had returned from his homeward errand and was now heading toward his mission atop Bascom Hall. When he reached the northwest balcony, Stielstra was single-minded; he felt no concern about whether he would be caught and in fact wanted to be seen. He went to the wall, found a foothold on the vent, pulled himself up to the roof, and strode to the flagpole. Holding the wire cutters with one hand, he snapped the lanyard on the flagpole, holding the cable at the same time so that the flags would not fall until he had put the wire cutters back in his coat pocket and lit the firecrackers with his free hand. He did not want this to be a tree crashing in the forest unseen and unheard. This was to be a public statement, a visible, political act of defiance. He did not consider it a desecration of the Stars and Stripes. He considered himself an idealist who was disgusted by what he thought was a contradiction—"the idea of what the flag stood for, flying free over what had just happened on the plaza and in the building."

It was windy, and it took a few strikes before the firecrackers lit. *Pop! Pop! Pop!* Stielstra opened his fist and released the cut cable, and the American and Wisconsin flags started to fall.

Rowen heard the loud pops, remembered someone flashing firecrackers in the crowded corridor, and looked up at the top of Bascom in time to see the same guy scrambling on the roof. Norman Lenburg, a photographer for the *Wisconsin State Journal,* had spotted him even before the firecrackers made their public announcement. After the first volley of tear gas, Lenburg had decided to position himself on Bascom's northwest balcony so that he could take better pictures if the police fired another round. He had been standing up there for about fifteen minutes, amid a group of a few dozen people, when out of the corner of his eye he noticed someone walking up the slanted roof toward the flagpole. *What's he doing?* Lenburg wondered. "And all of a sudden the guy's kind of kneeling at the base of the flagpole and I don't have a clue what he's trying to do." Just as Lenburg swung his camera around to shoot a picture, the student set off firecrackers and ran. *Click.* Lenburg got one vertical shot of the flag coming down and the perpetrator dashing away. It was not much of a picture, he thought at the time, too much flagpole and dull gray sky, but it certainly told a story.

Bob Rennebohm and Don Thayer, two UW freshman townies from

Madison West High, also stationed on the northwest balcony, had seen someone climbing the roof toward the flagpole but had thought nothing of it at first. Their attention was drawn in the other direction, past Commerce toward the parking lot beyond Social Science, where they noticed a busload of riot-equipped reinforcements, Dane County sheriff's deputies, disembarking and starting to march down Charter Street toward the rear doors of Commerce. Then the firecrackers went off and Rennebohm and Thayer turned again and saw the American flag fluttering down. The entire scene had been shocking to the two freshmen, who had gone to the rooftop balcony to watch the demonstration after finding the way back to their dorm at Tripp Hall blocked by thousands of people. They had never seen authority figures challenged so angrily before, but this, cutting down the flag, was the ultimate shock. "Once his mission was complete," Rennebohm remembered, "this guy coolly ran down the inclined roof and walked within several feet of us to the door . . . and he was gone."

Not quite that easily, as it turned out. Someone in the crowd yelled "Get him!" as Stielstra clambered down from the roof, and the chase began. A few students were running toward him as he jumped off the incline. He beat them to the door. Although he never looked back at his pursuers, in his imagination, and from the sounds, he thought three or four people were behind him.

During Stielstra's teenaged years in West Lafayette, his family had lived in an old converted farmhouse where he and his twin brother, Phil, shared a room on the third floor. They often held races to see who could get to the first floor first, so Jonathan had become "pretty adroit at getting down stairs." Now he was taking full advantage of his long-striding six-foot-two frame, descending several steps at a time. By the third floor he was already outpacing the pack. "Which way did he go?" he heard someone shout. He had never experienced an adrenaline rush like this before. No way they were going to catch him. He kept racing all the way down to the basement, where he fled down the hallway to the south end, turned a corner, ducked into an empty classroom, closed the door, and slumped to the floor. He was winded; his heart was thumping wildly. He stayed in hiding for several minutes, until he regained his breath and was certain that the posse had given up. Then he walked up to the first floor and out the side door, slipping unobtrusively into the crowd outside Commerce. He found his twin brother, the one person he knew he could count on, and felt more secure standing next to Phil the rest of the afternoon.

THERE WAS MORE TEAR GAS, more scrambling, more regrouping, more shouting, more chaos. The original focus of the protest, Vietnam and the Dow Chemical Company's role in the manufacture of napalm, now seemed incidental, if not forgotten. Now it was kids against cops. Curly Hendershot, the Dow recruiter, was long gone from the scene, escorted out a back exit after the corridors had been cleared. At one point a faculty member approached Emery and Hanson and offered his theory that if the police disappeared, the students would leave soon enough. It was worth a try, the chiefs thought. They pulled their men off the plaza and stationed them out of sight inside Commerce. No one left, so the officers reemerged ten minutes later, and this time managed to take control of more territory, forming a cordon on the outer perimeter of the plaza, forcing the students back to the sidewalk near Observatory Drive or up on the ridge between Commerce and Bascom. With the next volley of tear gas, Jim Rowen and Susan McGovern moved away from the plaza toward the back of Commerce above Van Vleck Hall. They came across a Madison police officer who looked disheveled, his helmet gone, his shirt covered with spittle. He did not look injured, Rowen thought, "just sort of in a daze. And he was talking to himself. And he was saying, 'I've never seen anything like this. This is terrible. I've never seen anything like this.'"

The officer marched in one direction, back toward the front of Commerce, and Rowen and McGovern in the other, down the hill toward the Union. They too were "in a state of shock, dumbfounded" by what had happened. Only hours earlier they had marched up Bascom Hill as "naïve, vaguely pacifistic liberals expecting to engage in some civil disobedience that at worst would get us arrested or expelled," as McGovern later put it, with "no expectation of violence being used by the police, no sense that we would become outraged and radicalized in ways we could not have known prior to the events." But now here they were, walking back down the hill feeling a deep and irreversible transformation. Rowen had always thought the notion of having a "radicalizing experience" was jargon, but now he felt it. He felt like an outsider—"outside American society, outside American culture." He had tried to follow the tradition of civil disobedience, he thought, and had been rewarded for it by being clubbed and tear gassed. "Everything had changed," he thought. The rules had changed. His goals had changed. The outsider—it was a feeling he had never had before that day, October 18, 1967, and one that he would never entirely shake thereafter, even during later decades when he worked within the system as a city official.

By the time Paul Soglin was stitched up and released from the hospital, the demonstration was just about over. He walked back to Commerce to recover his schoolbooks—he had left a notebook and a history book inside—but the police would not let him in. They had control of the building, but a diehard band of demonstrators remained outside, "taunting from the edges." The sharp odor of tear gas lingered in the air. Soglin walked all the way around Bascom Hall and entered through the front door, walking past a metal Sifting and Winnowing plaque on the way inside. Students were bounding through the foyer and hallway, most of them participants in the protest, some still seeking targets for their rage. One young man grabbed a metal *Daily Cardinal* news box, lifted it above his head, and heaved it at the wall, breaking the glass enclosing an ornate portrait of John Bascom. Soglin kept moving down the hallway toward the administrative offices and found whom he was looking for—Joe Kauffman.

"You lied to us! You lied to us!" Soglin screamed at the dean of students, his antagonist in the legal case *Soglin v. Kauffman*. He was overcome by the rage of a generation, or part of a generation, that was feeling the betrayal of the young by the old. The way he saw it, the protesters were supposed to follow certain rules and the authorities would follow certain rules, but "we did and they didn't." Kauffman turned away, and Soglin followed him down the corridor, so angry that he started crying.

It had been four years exactly, to the day, since Soglin had attended his first Vietnam protest, which also happened to be the first ever Vietnam demonstration on the Wisconsin campus. He was a sophomore then, on October 18, 1963, when he was photographed as a face in the crowd of a few hundred students who rallied on the Union steps to denounce the regime of soon-to-be-assassinated Ngo Dinh Diem. Four years: as long as the Civil War, as long as Americans fought in World War II, as long as an undergraduate education—a seeming lifetime during which nothing had changed and everything had changed. As the Vietnam war had deepened and become more complicated, so too had the antiwar movement at Wisconsin. The warm note that Soglin had written to President Harrington on May 19, 1966, the one in which he had said that he was "thrilled" about the way students and university officials handled the sit-in at the administration building, the handwritten note that had surprised Harrington so much that he made a typed copy of it and sent it back to Soglin so he might remember how he once felt— that seemed like ancient history now, gone forever. Instead, the metaphorical prediction that Soglin had made in his recent "Hi There, Badger!" column in the *Daily Cardinal* had come all too true. The pot had blown up in Chancellor Sewell's face.

HERE THEY WERE, side by side, on the front page of the final edition of the *Milwaukee Journal* that afternoon, both above the fold, early reports from the battlefields of war and peace. First, on the upper left, an understated dispatch from Madison: "Club swinging policemen and hundreds of angry, yelling University of Wisconsin students clashed Wednesday afternoon in a battle that left at least 12 students injured. At least one ambulance was called. The policemen waded into the Commerce building where about 150 demonstrators were protesting job recruiting by Dow Chemical Co., makers of napalm for Vietnam."

Then, tucked beside it, with a Saigon dateline: "A veteran Communist regiment ambushed two companies of the United States 1st infantry division in canopied jungles 41 miles north of Saigon Tuesday. After a day of fierce fighting, 58 Americans and at least 103 Communists had been killed and 61 Americans wounded. The battle took a costly toll of American officers. Among them were Maj. Donald W. Holleder, a quarterback voted the most valuable player of Army's 1955 football team, and Lt. Col. Terry Allen Jr., whose father commanded the 1st division in Tunisia and Sicily in World War II."

Allen and Holleder were still the only identified casualties in the account from Vietnam. Even with the front-page story in the local paper, his family had no idea yet that Danny Sikorski had been in the battle.

AT QUARTER TO FIVE, six hours after the first protesters entered Commerce, as the action appeared to be winding down at last, Chief Emery left campus to attend a Police and Fire Commission meeting back at the City-County Building. He let John Patrick Hunter of the *Capital Times* hitch a ride, and as they rolled through the October darkness away from campus, Emery sighed and muttered to himself, "It was just awful. It was terrible. How did they ever let things get down to this?"

By half past five the last students had left the plaza outside Commerce, and the battalion of city and campus officers, along with the late-arriving sheriff's deputies, finally withdrew from their battle stations. The Dow protest was over, but its effects were not. Nineteen officers, in addition to the forty-seven students, had been taken to the hospital, and three of them, including Detective McCarthy, were the most seriously injured of anyone. Sewell, after conferring with President Harrington, released a statement to the press. He reiterated the university regulations that led him to call in the police, an action that he had not wanted to take. "I deeply regret that it was necessary to bring police onto the campus to maintain the operations of the university. This was done only after our officers and staff found it impossible to maintain order," he said. "I regret that students and police were injured. This must not be repeated." In hopes of cooling things down, he added, he was temporarily suspending the Dow interviews pending a special faculty meeting that he was calling for three thirty the next day. Sometime after the statement went out, some angry students returned to Dean Kauffman's office and tried to start a fire outside his door. The damages were minimal, the perpetrators never caught.

News of the calamitous events had reached the other end of State Street and sent the state legislature into full fury. Before adjourning that evening, the assembly passed a resolution calling the demonstration "a flagrant abuse and perversion of the treasured traditions of academic freedom." Disruptive students, the resolution declared, should be expelled from the university. Milwaukee assemblyman Edward Mertz issued a familiar refrain, that the legislature should "take over" the university, which he said was in danger of being seized by "long-haired, greasy pigs." On the senate side, conservative lions were roaring. "Communism is on that campus and it's operating today," declared Senator Gordon Roseleip of Darlington. Leland McParland of Cudahy was in an executioner's mood. "We should shoot them if necessary," he said of protesting students. "I would. I would. Because it's insurrection."

AFTER EATING AND REGROUPING in the Rathskeller, Soglin marched up the hill one more time and returned to the Commerce Building to get his books. It was an eerie sight, the place empty, shards of broken glass still in the vestibule, the east-west hallway a mess of papers, plastic cups, clothing, debris. Soglin found his books, right where he had left them, and moved on to a seven o'clock meeting where protest leaders would talk about what to do next. Everything had indeed changed. A young woman walked into the meeting and declared, "I'm a radical! I'm a radical! I don't know what it means, but will someone please explain it to me. I've just become a radical."

There was a mass meeting at the Great Hall in the Union at nine that night, and the crowd was so vast, more than three thousand students, that they moved it outside to the Library Mall. Ron Davis and his San Francisco Mime Troupe, who originally had been scheduled to hold a seminar on guerrilla theater, instead helped serve as meeting facilitators. "The meeting was hectic, but instructive," Davis wrote later. "There was no clear line, many of the students, as usual, didn't know about Dow's involvement in the war or the complicity of the university. But many were disturbed that their fellow students had been bashed by clubs, gassed, and dragged off. . . . Personal assault was more important than any of the protest factors. We stood by, watching and listening. It was instructive to us as well. What would the organizers come up with?" Percy Julian, attorney for the students, took the bullhorn and asked people who had been inside or outside Commerce to provide eyewitness accounts that could be used in court. Several dozen sympathetic faculty members, alarmed that police had invaded their academic sanctuary, attended the open-air rally and formed a symbolic protective ring around the students, who finally voted to strike classes until the faculty permanently barred city police from campus and the administration agreed not to punish leaders of the Dow sit-in.

Soglin had begun the day as just another person in the ranks of the protesters, but here was his opportunity to take a leading role. Stark was gone, and many of the protest lieutenants had gone into hiding, fearful that they would be suspended or expelled. Soglin and his University Community Action Party, which had supported the protest all along, were ready to assert leadership. He gave one of his first public speeches that night; countless more would follow. And along with his emergence, the ranks of the antiwar movement on campus seemed to have grown exponentially in that single day, or at least the ranks of people agitated by what they had seen or experienced. Davis was right in that respect; many in the crowd knew little about Vietnam, the distant war, but were reacting viscerally to the sight of the police clubs.

John Pickart, the music major from Madison, who had witnessed the violence inside Commerce while trying to talk his friend Everett Goodwin out of participating in the sit-down protest, felt torn by competing impulses once again. He did not think a strike was the best way to protest the situation, but "decided to go along with it for one day" to show his sympathy for the strikers. "Obviously, a mistake or a series of them had been made somewhere," he explained in a letter to his friend, Pam Crane. "When you see something like that you feel that somehow you have to do something actively."

Betty Menacher, the freshman from Green Bay, who had stepped out of her classroom to witness the police charge, walked over to the rally from Sellery Hall that night, the memory of what she had seen inside Commerce fresh in her mind. For eighteen years she had "gone with the program," but now, for the first time, she felt an urge to reconsider her basic assumptions and think about the world around her. October 18 was "a turning point."

Jane Brotman was also in the crowd. The freshman from New Jersey had not changed her politics. She had only the vaguest comprehension of napalm, and she still thought the protest leaders were strange and frighteningly unlike her. But she felt she had "a personal responsibility" to go to the rally and make a statement about what she had witnessed. She found herself part of "a huge mass" of people who seemed as "personally upset" as she was. The issue, for her, was police brutality. "That's what I felt I had to take a stand on," she said later. "I did not like the protesters. I didn't feel like I was supporting the people. But I had witnessed something and I felt I had to take some action. I kept thinking, if my parents were here, they would do the same thing. I had no doubt in my mind." After the students had voted to stage a protest strike, Brotman called her parents from her room at the Towers and told them that she was not going to take her French exam the next day. She was anxious about her decision and felt she had to tell her parents about it, desperately hoping for their support. She knew that her mother was against the war, and that her father, while supporting the war, was a man of deep moral principles. He would understand, she thought. Instead her parents "freaked out" at the news. They could not believe that she would miss an exam. And Brotman found herself struggling again, just as she had hours earlier when she had to choose between watching the protest and going to her review class. Now what should she do?

That night, while students debated whether to strike, President Harrington, Chancellor Sewell, Dean Kauffman, and Chief Hanson gathered at Kauffman's house on Celia Court on the far west side. Kauffman's wife and teenaged son drove to Kentucky Fried Chicken and brought back dinner. Harrington constantly worked the phone, dealing with legislators, the governor's office, faculty members, and regents. With frequent interruptions the four men huddled late into the night, discussing how they should deal with the faculty, the legislature, and the press. It was difficult for them to understand or accept the reality of violence that had erupted on their campus, on their watch. The police had overreacted, they thought, and the students had turned on them with a vengeance. It was a mess and would only get messier, they knew. Now the university would be portrayed as an out-of-control institution and there would be more pressure from state legislators and the public to crack down on radical students.

William Sewell was the most traumatized. He said little that night, then retreated to his house on Countryside Lane and slumped down in the blue leather easy chair that usually gave him so much comfort as he dug into his copies of the *American Sociological Journal*. Now he was overcome by dread. Feeling drained and defeated, he thought to himself, "My God, I've just screwed everything up. It's my fault. I let those police go in there and I shouldn't have. I've bollixed it up. I've just ruined my career. I've never been involved in anything in my life before where anyone was hurt. People won't remember me for anything but the Dow riot."

CHAPTER 24

"BOMBING WASHINGTON"

THE RELENTLESS DIFFICULTIES of war and peace had consumed Lyndon Johnson that Wednesday. At a midday Cabinet meeting, while the Dow protest inside the Commerce Building in Madison was devolving into chaos, the president and his department secretaries gathered in the White House Cabinet Room, where they received a detailed briefing from Attorney General Ramsey Clark on the massive peace demonstrations to be held in Washington a few days later under the sponsorship of the National Mobilization Committee to End the War in Vietnam.

It was still "undeterminable" how many citizens would travel to the capital to protest over the weekend, Clark said, but FBI agents and informants had picked up signs that the crowds might be less substantial than antiwar leaders were predicting. While "they sincerely believe they will get 100,000," Clark reported, the government's "best count at the moment" was less than a third of that number. Clark then recited statistics that could be gleaned from any newspaper or wire service report. A four-hundred-car train was conveying an antiwar battalion from New York. There were 243 buses scheduled to bring protesters down from Connecticut and New Jersey, but only a hundred had been filled. Philadelphia was "down from fifty to thirty-six buses," but Baltimore had three hundred buses making the trip.

The Department of Justice itself would be the first protest target Friday afternoon, Clark reported. He expected a few hundred demonstrators "to seek access to the building to turn in their draft cards." Two days earlier, as part of Stop the Draft Week, young men who opposed the war had turned in draft cards at rallies around the country. At the largest rally, an interfaith peace service at Arlington Street Church in Boston, eighty-seven men had burned their draft cards and another two hundred handed theirs to the Reverend William Sloane Coffin, chaplain at Yale. Coffin was now coming to Washington as part of a team of antiwar luminaries, including Dr. Benjamin Spock and writer Norman Mailer, to take part in the demonstration and deliver the card collection to government officials. Clark told the president and his Cabinet colleagues that the full group of antidraft protesters would be denied entrance to the Justice building, but a delegation led by Coffin would be received. Since Selective Service regulations required that draft cards "be in the registrant's possession," they would not be accepted by government officials during the protest, although, to be sure, FBI agents would be hovering in the shadows to gather "abandoned" cards from which they might launch investigations.

The large demonstrations were scheduled for Saturday, October 21, with speeches on the mall, picketing outside the White House, and a mass march to the Pentagon. The "risk of unplanned incidents remains," Clark said, but "police and military manpower have been marshaled in anticipation of unexpected outbreaks." In addition to the D.C. metropolitan police force and federal security guards, three thousand army troops were on standby and fifteen thousand in "deeper reserve," some from as far away as Fort Bragg in North Carolina, Fort Hood in Texas, and the Presidio in San Francisco.

"Above all," Clark said, without apparent irony, "we want to maintain the appearance of business as usual."

According to notes of the meeting, Vice President Humphrey inquired about protecting the Capitol, two other department secretaries discussed security plans for their buildings, but LBJ himself remained silent. That was uncharacteristic of Johnson, who had been obsessed with the protest for most of the month and had been pushing Clark and other administration officials to let friendly journalists know about any and all communist affiliations of left-wing demonstration leaders. "The fact of communist involvement and encouragement has been given to some columnists," Clark had reported at an earlier Cabinet session. "Let's see it some more," Johnson had replied. He always wanted more of it for himself. The bundle of papers his secretaries prepared "for the President's night reading" often included documents about the protesters. One aide saw Johnson perusing a list of "antiwar leaders and their communist connections" as he got his hair cut at the White House barbershop.

The administration's campaign questioning the allegiances of protesters was now leaking its way into newspapers across the country. In Madison, editors at the *State Journal* were laying out their Page of Opinion for October 19, choosing the headline "Reds Publicize Peacenik March" for a piece by conservative columnist David Lawrence. His column, datelined Washington, quoted at length from a promotion of the antiwar rally in the latest issue of the U.S. Communist Party newspaper, *The Worker*. Detailed instructions were given in the party organ, Lawrence reported, "as to the exact time and location" participants could catch buses to Washington. There was even a local angle to the list, and hence Lawrence's column, with the revelation that "In Madison, Wis., several campus and community groups have joined to charter buses for Washington." Lawrence cited *The Worker*'s interest in the rally to make LBJ's point. He charged that "there are influences at work in this country and abroad which are trying to break down the spirit of America's armed forces and to mobilize public opinion, if possible, in the U.S. to bring about a withdrawal of American troops from Vietnam."

When the Cabinet adjourned, Johnson slipped out the White House's southwest gate and rode up Pennsylvania Avenue to his old hangout on the Senate side of the Capitol where the luncheon host, Senator Allen Ellender, Democrat of Louisiana, was serving his signature dish, succulent shrimp and crab gumbo.

THAT NIGHT, while antiwar students in Madison planned a class boycott and University of Wisconsin administrators huddled at Dean Kauffman's house, trying to figure out how to respond to that day's violent turn of events on campus, President Johnson reconvened his war council. The session this time was expanded to include—along with the regulars Rusk, McNamara, and Rostow—Associate Supreme Court Justice Abe Fortas, an old LBJ confidant who moonlighted as a presidential adviser; Undersecretary of State Nicholas Katzenbach, General Maxwell Taylor, and unofficial White House counselor Clark Clifford. There was one other special guest. It was not McGeorge Bundy, who had slipped LBJ a memo urging him to maintain his gradualist course and then retreated to New York, but Dr. Henry Kissinger, the Harvard professor and national security consultant who had been overseeing back channel negotiations with the North Vietnamese through two French scientists. Kissinger's improvised effort revolved around a question that had dominated White House discussions about Vietnam all fall—when and whether to implement a bombing pause in an effort to bring Hanoi to the bargaining table.

Secretary of State Rusk opened the meeting by hailing Kissinger. "I am sure I speak for all of us in expressing appreciation and admiration of Professor Kissinger," Rusk said. "He handled a very delicate matter in a very professional manner. I think we may wish to begin this discussion with Professor Kissinger's explanation of M and A." (M and A were the initials and code names of the two Frenchmen: Herbert Marcovich and Raymond Aubrac.)

The professor offered his hard assessment of the two men: "M is a biologist with very little political judgment. He is similar to many American scientists who are carrying placards. His primary motive is to bring the war in Vietnam to an end. A is probably a Communist. He is very aware politically. He has close relations with Ho. In 1946, Ho stayed at his home in Paris. I have little confidence in M's judgment. I have greater confidence in A's judgment." However, Kissinger added, "if it served his purpose, A might color his report."

Since late August, with the Frenchmen as intermediaries and Kissinger overseeing them, the White House had exchanged three sets of messages with the North Vietnamese. As soon as the process began, the Americans decided not to bomb within a ten-mile circle of central Hanoi. This was regarded by the White House as a gesture of goodwill. There had been no reciprocal gesture by the North Vietnamese, Rusk said, and no indication that they would not take military advantage during an American bombing pause.

Now he read aloud the key paragraph of the most recent message to Hanoi:

The United States Government understands the position of the Democratic Republic of Vietnam to be as follows: That upon the cessation by the United States of all forms of bombardment of the DRV, the DRV would enter promptly into productive discussions with the United States. The purpose of these discussions would be to resolve the issues between the United States and the DRV. Assuming the correctness of this understanding of the position of the DRV, the United States Government is prepared, in accordance with its proposal of August 25, to transmit in advance to the DRV the precise date upon which bombardment of the DRV would cease and to suggest a date and a place for the commencement of discussions.

The response from Hanoi seemed unpromising. Rusk read it to LBJ:

At the present time the United States is continuing the escalation of the war in an extremely grave manner. In these conditions words of peace are only trickery. At a time when the United States continues the escalation we can neither receive Mr. Kissinger nor comment on the American views transmitted through this channel. The position of the Government of the Democratic Republic of Vietnam is perfectly clear. It is only when the United States has ceased without condition the bombardments that negotiations can take place.

Nothing constructive had come from the exchange, Rusk concluded. The North Vietnamese said talks *can* start with a cessation of bombing, but not that they *will* start. And they were silent on the request not to press forward militarily in the South during a bombing pause. This indicated to Rusk that they were planning a "negotiate and fight" strategy.

Kissinger said he detected "slight movement" in Hanoi's position since the exchanges began. There were signs, he said, that the North Vietnamese wanted "to keep this going."

President Johnson listened to the debate for a few minutes before offering his opinion. "My judgment is that they are keeping this channel going just *because* we are not bombing Hanoi," he said. "I know if they were bombing Washington, hitting my bridges and highways, I would be delighted to trade off discussions through an intermediary for a restriction on the bombing. It hasn't cost him one bit. The net of it is that he has a sanctuary in Hanoi in return for having his consul talk with two scientists who talked with an American citizen."

Katzenbach disagreed with the president. A bombing pause made sense, he said. It would "bring together the ranks in this country and abroad." He favored a pause beginning in mid-November or early December.

"Just pause, period?" Johnson asked.

"Yes," Katzenbach answered. "I would say very loud and clear that we are ready. I would make clear through private channels that the assumption that they would not take advantage of the bombing still holds. If they attacked us along the DMZ, I would respond immediately. If they were to begin a major resupply, we should deal with that immediately."

Johnson turned to Defense Secretary McNamara. "Bob, how effective can you be in dealing out resupply?"

McNamara, who had become a disbeliever when it came to bombing North Vietnam, used this opening to press his point again. "Mr. President, I believe I can show beyond a shadow of a doubt that bombing in Hanoi and Haiphong will not affect resupply in the South one bit." If the North took military advantage of a pause, he added, "we should counter with military reciprocal action."

General Taylor now entered the debate. The former ambassador to South Vietnam and former chairman of the Joint Chiefs of Staff had recently returned from a trip through South Vietnam and much of Asia with Clark Clifford. Fresh in everyone's mind was the article Taylor had written for the previous Sunday's *New York Times Magazine* in which he argued assuredly that the war was being won. "Any indication of weakness is viewed with contempt," Taylor said now. It would be weak, he argued, to initiate a bombing pause without any signs of reciprocity from Hanoi. "If we have a pause, let Thieu request it," he said, referring to the South Vietnamese president, who was to be inaugurated at the end of the month. "This would give us a better position and would not make it appear as another Washington proposal to Hanoi. We cannot afford to be weak."

Clifford, in lawyerly fashion, parsed the message from Hanoi. "As I see it, there are five parts to their response," he said. "One, they charge the U.S. with escalation. Two, they charge the U.S. with trickery. Three, they will not receive Mr. Kissinger. Four, the position of their government is clear. Five, it is only when bombing ceases that negotiations—or discussion—can take place."

To Clifford this seemed like old stuff. "We should say that we assume from the language you have used that you feel there is nothing to be gained from a continuation of this dialogue. If you have a different view, we would be glad to hear it," he argued. The exchanges with the Frenchmen were probably not viewed by the North Vietnamese as anything more than a way to stay informed, he said. "I do not believe they will use this type of channel when they are serious about really doing something." There was, then, "no basis for suspension or cessation" of the bombing, he concluded, agreeing with his traveling companion, Taylor. "I think it would be misinterpreted in Hanoi. It would be utilized to build up their supplies, just as they did during the four-day Tet holiday." If there was to be a suspension of bombing, he said, it should not come until "after the formation and shake-down of the new government" in South Vietnam. In conclusion, Clifford said, he would recommend ending "Henry's effort" and doing three simple things: "One, watch; two, wait; and three, see how the situation develops."

Abe Fortas agreed with Clifford. The unofficial channel should be closed, he said. "Professor Kissinger should say, 'Thanks, it's too bad. You know you could have gotten somewhere if you had really wanted to.'"

The next time the president made a public statement about suspending bombing, Fortas argued, he should be prepared to stop bombing altogether, not merely pause. "The bombing pauses have intensified criticism in this country. I cannot see why they will not negotiate with the bombing but say they will talk without the bombing. This has always been incomprehensible to me." In any case, given the circumstances, Fortas thought it "would be sad" if Johnson were to cease the bombing now.

"I see no ray of hope out of this," Justice Fortas said.

Rostow, the national security adviser, had the last word. The enemy's military situation in the South was weak, he declared. The major field of battle now was "no longer in the South [of Vietnam] . . . but in American politics." The White House was slow to come to that realization he said, but it was obvious. "The question is, would a pause destroy our strength with the hawks and the doves? Domestic politics is the active front now." A bombing pause, he argued, "would be no more than an exercise of domestic politics and international politics." He recommended sending word back to Hanoi that they interpreted the last North Vietnamese message as "a dignified rejection" of the American proposal. But he also thought they should keep the Kissinger channel open. "After that, then we could see about a pause which would unite the country rather than divide it."

Johnson agreed with Rostow. The back channel discussions might be a failure to that point, but he saw no reason to stop them. He doubted that a pause would work, but he still held out hope.

The president and his aides, with the world's most sophisticated military hardware and intelligence gathering apparatus at their disposal, had no idea that another mass gathering scheduled for that weekend would have far more bearing on the course of the war than the peace demonstration in Washington. The Politburo in Hanoi was convening for five days of meetings at which back channel talks with a pair of French scientists over a possible bombing pause seemed inconsequential. The agenda was to "finalize the bold plan" for an all-out military attack against the cities of the South, what would become known as the Tet Mau Than event, or Tet Offensive. As the evening of October 18 drew to an end, LBJ and his men seemed to be stumbling through the fog of war and peace.

CHAPTER 25

BODY COUNT

O N THE MORNING OF October 19 Jim Shelton visited the 2/28 Black Lions officers quarters in Lai Khe. It had been only a few weeks since he had last lived and worked there as the battalion operations chief, but that posting, in a more literal way than he could have imagined, was many lifetimes ago. The surroundings were familiar but empty-feeling now, every mundane object transformed into a relic of the dead. As he looked around, a Vietnamese woman approached and pulled on his sleeve. Big Jim recognized her from the old days; she was the woman from Ben Cat who washed their laundry. She motioned for him to follow her into a quonset hut, where she showed him stack upon stack of folded clothes. *This is all the dead guys, all their laundry. Those are Terry Allen's pants and shirts,* Shelton realized. He paid and tipped the laundrywoman, then asked some enlisted men to take away the stacks of clean clothes and burn them.

At Alpha Company's camp nearby, Tom Grady, the highest-ranking company officer now that Captain George was in the hospital, began taking inventory of the personal effects of soldiers killed in the battle. It was an uncomfortable task, and in the rush to get it dispensed with, someone said they should just dump each dead man's belongings into a box and ship them home. To Grady that seemed thoughtless. Check every item first, he said. He did not want incriminating items going back to the families. There could be letters to married men from girl-friends or pictures of the wrong woman. Life was always complicated, and it seemed more so for young soldiers. The families had enough heartache already, Grady said. There was no reason to make it worse. It was also Grady's responsibility to write letters to the families, and for that he used the same cautious philosophy of benign censorship. He found no compelling reason, for instance, to tell grieving parents that their son had put an M-16 to his head and killed himself in the heat of battle. In death all the soldiers were heroes.

On the other side of Lai Khe, up at the Delta Company base camp amid the rubber trees on the northeastern perimeter, a helicopter flew overhead at midmorning and hovered above the company street, a dirt road where Clark Welch and Bud Barrow once held formations. Big Rock and his trusty first sergeant were gone now, recovering from wounds at the hospital in Long Binh, and the new company commander, Captain Gerry Grosso, was just beginning to rebuild the devastated unit. Ray Albin, the plotter for the mortar platoon, looked up and noticed "this huge net hanging from" the helicopter. "And they dropped the net and the helicopter took off." Albin and a few other soldiers walked over to see what was inside the net and were appalled by the sight. "It contained all the web gear and weapons of guys who had been killed and wounded," Albin reported. "It was the most classless thing I had ever seen, to just plop that stuff down like that. We were still mourning. It couldn't have been a worse place and a worse time. There it all lay—web gear, helmets, weapons, aid kits, radios—all with the scars of battle."

The pile was at once awful and mesmerizing, and curious Delta survivors combed through the mess. David Laub, the third platoon radioman who had made it out of the battle unscarred, rummaged through the strewn gear and found a roll of film stuffed into some web gear. The photos, when he later had them developed, were not combat shots but more the stuff of a tourist travelogue. Several showed a group of soldiers posing around a Vietnamese cart. Laub also picked up an M-16 that had the cleaning rod welded into the barrel. A broken weapon was no surprise to him or any of the men who combed through the debris. In accounts given to military historians, at least ten surviving riflemen claimed that their M-16s jammed and became worthless and two grenadiers said that their M-79s broke during the battle. Taking into account the dead men and others who were not interviewed, it is reasonable to assume that many more weapons malfunctioned.

Coincidentally, only hours before Laub and his buddies examined the broken rifles in the battle pile, a House Armed Services subcommittee in Washington had released a scathing report accusing the army of "unbelievable" mismanagement of the M-16 rifle program. The M-16, which became the regular combat rifle for troops in Vietnam earlier that year after a long phase-in, was now a controversial symbol of a troubled war. When it replaced the M-14, the Colt-made M-16 was thought to be a superior weapon and the answer to the problems of fighting in the hot jungles of Southeast Asia. It was five inches shorter and nearly four pounds lighter than the M-14, was easier to hold, aim, and shoot, and could fire more rounds per minute when switched to fully automatic. As the rifle was originally designed, when it was known as the AR-15, it was considered reliable. But with its use in Vietnam came persistent newspaper articles and network television reports detailing instances where it jammed in combat. One NBC news account, in which the correspondent described several men throwing the M-16 away (as Black Lions did in the October 17 battle), drew the attention of congressional investigators. So did a letter that a soldier wrote home to his mother lamenting that several buddies had been killed when their rifles failed.

The congressional subcommittee, chaired by Democrat Richard H. Ichord of Missouri, held hearings throughout the summer, visited two camps where the M-16 was tested, and traveled to Vietnam for ten days in July. At the start of the investigation Ichord defended the weapon, accepting the military's argument that any problems were the fault of soldiers who did not properly clean their rifles. As the hearings progressed, Ichord changed his mind. The final report asserted that the M-16 had malfunctioned "seriously and excessively." Most of the malfunctions involved jamming, and the jamming was caused primarily not by inept soldiers, although there were problems with training, but by a change in the gunpowder used in the rifle. The original IMR powder, recommended by the inventor of the M-16, Eugene Stoner, was clear burning and sent a minimal amount of residue down the gas-tube recoil system to the bolt. The replacement Ball powder created more residue but was considered easier to make and safer to manufacture because it was less combustible. The powder change, according to the congressional report, was done without adequate testing and reflected a decision for which the safety of soldiers was a secondary consideration. In fact most testing of the M-16 was done with the original powder, even though the army had already switched powders, a sloppiness that, in the words of the subcommittee, "borders on criminal negligence."

The guns found on the Ong Thanh battlefield eventually made their way to Steve Goodman, the unofficial battalion armorer, who examined them to see if any could be repaired. Of most interest to Goodman were not the M-16s, whose problems were familiar, but the larger M-60 machine guns. There were eight M-60s recovered from the battlefield, and when Goodman started pulling them apart, he discovered that in five the gas pistons had been turned backward. "When the gas piston in the M-60 is turned backwards that means it only fires one round at a time; it's not a machine gun anymore, because there's nothing to collect the gas to perform the recoil of the bolt which makes it an automatic weapon," Goodman reported. He thought back to the battle and to the possibility of soldiers being killed and wounded or fleeing because they lacked the firepower they should have had. What happened? Could five machine gun teams make the same mistake? Goodman did not have answers. When he raised the question with higher-ups, he never heard another word about it. The thought of the backward pistons haunted him for years.

They had a dual meaning, these weapons recovered from battle, signifying not only possible mechanical malfunctions, but human ones as well. In the horror of the ambush, with enemy soldiers on three sides and firing down from the trees, with the Black Lions outnumbered almost eight to one, some men froze, some threw away their weapons and fled, some hid without firing back, and most struggled to reconcile what the eminent military historian S. L. A. Marshall, in his seminal work *Men Against Fire,* described as the competing impulses of fear and honor, the instinct of self-preservation versus the desire to be respected by comrades. In his study of combat in World War II, Marshall concluded that as few as 15 to 25 percent of soldiers on the front line fired their weapons during combat. For various reasons most did not fire. Using a smaller sample, Russell Glenn examined the combat instincts of infantrymen in Vietnam and arrived at different results. While a majority acknowledged at least one instance where they did not fire, Glenn concluded that in a normal firefight in Vietnam about 80 percent of the soldiers would use their weapons.

From research conducted by military historians after the battle, it appeared that the percentage of riflemen who engaged the enemy in the jungle of the Long Nguyen Secret Zone on the morning of October 17 was somewhere in the middle, above Marshall's estimates but below Glenn's.

JOHN A. CASH, an army historian, happened to be in Saigon that week when the 2/28 Black Lions marched into battle near the Ong Thanh stream. Cash was there to conduct research for the Office of the Chief of Military History, which by 1967 had begun to document the history of the U.S. Army in Vietnam. To call him a military historian defined Cash no more adequately than to say that he was an army captain. He was a soldier of uncommon qualities. He had a master's degree from Rutgers, was fluent in Spanish, helped train Cuban nationals for the abortive Bay of Pigs invasion, commanded his own rifle company in Vietnam, served as an assistant brigade operations chief for the Seventh Cavalry during the famous early battle of Ia Drang, and then temporarily turned his attention to history and writing. It was hard to miss John Cash when he strode down the creaky wooden floors of Tempo C at Fort McNair in Washington, D.C., where the army historians were quartered. He was an imposing presence, nearly six foot three, 205 pounds—and black. He was the only black officer there, as in most places he had served since joining the army in 1960. It was said that he bore a resemblance to the magnetic young boxer, Muhammad Ali, with smooth coffee-colored skin and a handsome face, and while Ali would refuse induction into the army and Cash was fiercely loyal to the institution, the two shared a strong sensibility about race. When colleagues asked Cash how he preferred his coffee, he invariably responded, "I want it beautiful." Beautiful, they came to learn, meant black.

On the afternoon of the nineteenth, when he was at the military quarters at Long Binh, Cash received a message that his orders had changed, at least for the next few weeks. The brass in Saigon and Honolulu, where the Pacific command was located, wanted him to conduct a special investigation of the battle in which Terry Allen Jr. and Donald Holleder were killed. Cash was to quietly prepare his own confidential report while working in concert with Major William E. Daniel Jr. of the First Division's Seventeenth Military History Detachment, who had begun gathering information for the standard after action report. Military history detachments in Vietnam were in the regular chain of command, responsible to brigade and division commanders, and because of that their reports sometimes could be shaped to satisfy superiors, consciously or unconsciously. The Office of the Chief of Military History, by contrast, had an ethic of academic freedom and a fierce pride in not being a mouthpiece for the army. That independence was not always prized by the generals running the war, but in this case it might come in handy. General Westmoreland in particular, Cash was told, "was not satisfied" with early reports he was getting on the battle from the First Division. It was a terrible firefight by any definition but became especially delicate because of the deaths of the famed West Point football star and the son of the former division commander. Old man Allen was said to be working his network already, trying to find out what in hell really happened to his only son.

Cash was picked up by a driver at Long Binh and taken to the Big Red One rear headquarters in Di An, where he caught a flight to Lai Khe. When he arrived, Major Daniel was in the field conducting interviews, and no one else seemed particularly eager to see him. It became apparent to Cash that he had walked into a sensitive situation. The First Division was "very uptight," he later reported, and at first refused to make the daily staff journals and duty officer's logs available to him. The journals and logs recorded the times and brief summaries of communications between officers in the field and at the base camp. When he finally received the files for October 17, Cash suspected but could not prove that some entries had been altered.

What happens in a battle? The "fog of war" is the classic cliché of military jargon. It means that when the fighting starts, the objective truth or reality of what is happening unavoidably becomes clouded by the chaos of the event. There is no omniscient observer hovering overhead, looking down at the battlefield with all-seeing eyes (down through a canopy of trees, in the case of jungle warfare), understanding every move on each side, chronicling who fired when and precisely where they were located and what the response was, as though it were a ballet that had been carefully choreographed. There are, to start with, several different levels of awareness within the experience of the battle. The reality of the average infantryman is shaped by what he does and sees, a hectic little narrative that presents a world in itself and yet often seems absurdly infinitesimal and haphazard in contrast to the comprehensive story. The radiotelephone operator might have a more nuanced slice of reality—what he sees augmented by what he hears. A medic tends to move around more and so might see things from several angles. Among officers, there are two competing conditions that shape their version of reality: the higher up they are, the more they might understand how the mission objectives compare with the mission as it is being carried out, how different units in the battle are performing, and how it all fits into a larger picture, but the less likely they are to be near the heat of the action. Who had a better grasp of a battle's reality, the brigade colonel monitoring the fight from an observation helicopter or the company commander down maneuvering among his men?

Captain Cash wanted to talk to them all. Armed with a notebook and a small cassette tape recorder, he began methodically piecing together the narrative of the battle. Moving back and forth between Lai Khe and the two hospitals in Long Binh, he interviewed thirty soldiers and officers who had been in the battle, and reinterviewed several who had talked to Daniel or his assistant. He built his own timeline of October 17, piecing together the official logs and interviews, and from that timeline drafted his report. His job was to present a precise account of the battle, not to draw conclusions about it, but some themes came through in his interviews. Soldier after soldier raised questions about the half-hour period early in the battle when Lieutenant Colonel Allen had his troops hold their positions in the jungle instead of withdraw, with the artillery check-fired and no air support yet. Cash, from his interviews, was uncertain whether that decision not to withdraw rested entirely with Allen or with the higher-ups, but he was certain that the decision to check-fire the artillery came from above. He also developed some opinions that he kept out of his report. While Westmoreland and the generals persisted in calling the battle a meeting engagement, not an ambush, Cash's oral interviews with soldiers made it obvious that they had walked into an ambush. His reporting also made it clear to him that the body count of Vietnamese was false. The body count had been concocted, sloppily if not intentionally, through a sort of battlefield confidence scheme.

Hours after the battle, at the night defensive perimeter, a brigade intelligence officer had canvassed each company of the 2/28 Black Lions for a body count. The reconnaissance platoon reported 22 dead enemy soldiers. Delta reported 21. Alpha reported 43, Bravo 6, and Charlie 9. Total—101.

But the companies reached their totals by adding up the numbers provided by various soldiers. If a sergeant reported seeing 11 dead Viet Cong and a private saw 12, that became 23, with no consideration that the two might have seen—and probably did see—the same bodies. The brigade reached its 101 total using the same flawed methodology, again assuming the same bodies were not being reported by more than one company. When he interviewed the brigade intelligence officer, Captain Cash pointed out that the body count was "obviously duplicative." The officer, he noted, "had no comment." Major Sloan, the battalion's operations officer, told Cash that he believed "101 bodies was a grossly exaggerated figure . . . the same bodies were counted two or three times." The most reliable number, Sloan and others said, might have been the 22 seen by the reconnaissance platoon, which was the first unit to reach the battlefield after the firefight.

The false body count would become part of the legend of October 17, and a source of bitterness for the soldiers from Delta and Alpha who marched into the jungle that day. If it was not quite the Little Big Horn massacre that Greg Landon compared it to, it was undeniably a lopsided fight. The enlisted men wanted no part of an official effort to sugarcoat what had happened. They knew what they had endured, and to deny the reality, however horrible, or perhaps because it was so horrible, was, in a sense, to strip them of their battlefield honor.

At the time of the October 17 battle the military was undergoing an intense internal debate over body counts and the larger issue of battlefield numbers. Statistical experts at the Pentagon's Office of Systems Analysis had concluded that the official body counts from Vietnam were greatly exaggerated. The tendency to exaggerate was most pronounced, they determined, in instances where American troops were ambushed. "In the opinion of systems analysts, American field commanders were inevitably embarrassed by [their] losses, believing themselves rather than their tactics at fault. To protect both their own careers and those of their superiors, they compensated by padding their claims of enemy killed," William M. Hammond noted in his detailed study *The Military and the Media.* In "case after case," the analysts noted, body counts were inflated at the company level and then subject to "almost universal doubling" at the battalion and brigade levels. Although the military in Vietnam conducted its own study that disputed assertions that body counts were being inflated, Winant Sidle, the brigadier general in charge of information at MACV, worried about credibility problems with correspondents in Saigon and decided to play down the numbers, inflated or not.

The body count debate that month was not only about enemy dead. On October 15, two days before the Black Lions battle, General Westmoreland had received a telex from his nominal boss, U. S. Grant Sharp, commander in chief of the Pacific Command, urging military spokesmen in Vietnam to obfuscate the numbers of American casualties. "I note that reports of action in the vicinity of Con Thien continue to cite exact numbers of enemy artillery and mortar rounds and to recount precisely U.S. casualties," Sharp wrote, referring to fighting near the Demilitarized Zone. "It is difficult to see any advantage to releasing such information to the press regarding an engagement and certainly there are disadvantages to telling the enemy how he is doing. Request you review press release procedures at all echelons to assure precise statistics are not made available during the general time frame of an action."

The attention that the deaths of Allen and Holleder brought to the October 17 battle made it difficult to misrepresent the number of American casualties even if the army had wanted to do so. It was far easier in this case to inflate enemy numbers.

THE BATTLE WAS ONLY a few days gone, but at the Alpha and Delta camps it seemed ancient and distant. Things were defined by whether they happened before or after October 17. The men who survived without serious wounds felt out of sorts in Lai Khe, like lingering ghosts. By what right could replacement officers in fresh new uniforms tell them what to do? A new lieutenant came in and found Ernie Buentiempo sprawled on his bunk. He would not get up and would not salute, and the lieutenant, incensed, tried to challenge him until Buentiempo said that he had been in the battle and that his M-16 had jammed with blood and that he had carried the radio for platoon leader Willie C. Johnson, who was in a hospital bed down in Long Binh, dying, his body riddled with bullets, and that Buentiempo himself had just returned from being sewn up for minor wounds. Some of his old card-playing, pot-smoking buddies in Alpha were dead or wounded, but those few still around headed out to the farthest bunk to smoke some joints, which the laundry woman still provided, neatly rolled, in a plastic carton. It was always "for medicinal purposes," Goodtimes said, and those purposes had never been more urgent than they were now.

Nothing could be worse than what he had experienced already, so he was unconcerned about the consequences of getting caught smoking marijuana. "What are they gonna do?" he asked, in the familiar grunt soldier's refrain. "Send me to Vietnam? We're already in hell. Put me in jail? Thanks!"

Who were these new soldiers moving into the old hooches? "They didn't wait to build our company back up," Mike Taylor wrote to his parents in Alaska. "We got about 75 new guys already. It isn't the same around here anymore. The guys who made it are a helluva lot closer, but you sure miss the rest of the guys." Captain Grosso, the new commander of Delta Company, was sensitive to the complicated feelings of the battle survivors and spent much of his time that first week in conversations with small groups of them, trying to draw them out. One platoon leader, watching Grosso in action, joked sarcastically that he was "doing an S. L. A. Marshall on them"—referring to the military historian who had based his findings on men in combat from conducting thousands of after-battle interviews.

Among the new Black Lions was Phil Duncan, a dropout from the University of Missouri at Kansas City who had signed up for a four-year stint in the army believing that he might avoid Vietnam by enlisting rather than waiting to get drafted. No such luck. He ended up in Lai Khe and was in his second week of jungle training when the Black Lions were devastated and he was called in as a replacement. If he was not already anxious enough about Vietnam, his introduction to the battalion was sufficiently traumatizing. In every tent were bunks where men now dead had slept. Duncan had managed to convince himself when he arrived in Vietnam that if he "kept his head down and obeyed orders" he would survive. Now that confidence was shattered. He felt as though he had "been operating under a myth. Anything could happen to you, and probably would. It was paralyzing that your fate was the luck of the draw."

At night, in the tent or down at the enlisted men's club, soldiers who had survived the battle recounted the experience. They were seething men, angry that they had been led into an ambush. Their buddies died, they told Duncan and other replacements, because of Lyndon Johnson, General Westmoreland, General Hay, and Lieutenant Colonel Allen. They had seen the worst of battle and felt that only those who went through it with them could understand. The ambush might have been an unmitigated disaster, but nothing upset them more than to hear outsiders question the battlefield effort of those who fought. Carl Woodard, who had marched into the jungle that day as a nineteen-year-old sergeant in Alpha and come out alive, was at the club drinking a beer and watching a John Wayne movie when he heard a new second lieutenant behind him "running off his mouth" about how the Black Lions would have lived if they'd had "their heads out of their fuckin' asses" on the seventeenth. Woodard turned around and asked him to stop, but the new lieutenant only grew bolder. "And all you fuckin' guys, if you don't listen to me, you'll get killed just like the dumbass fucks on the seventeenth!" he ranted. Woodard rose from his chair and slugged the lieu-tenant twice, then chased him out of the club into the darkness.

What he had done, Woodard realized, striking a commissioned offi-cer, could be grounds for court-martial. He was not certain that the sec-ond lieutenant would report him, but he took no chances. He went to Alpha headquarters, found Lieutenant Grady, and essentially turned himself in, telling Grady what offense he had committed and why. "Woody, what the fuck have you done?" Grady said to him, after hear-ing the story. He told Woodard to go to his bunk and stay there until he was called. Grady stayed up late into the night pondering how to handle the case. His friend and leader, Captain George, was in the hospital. The kid he had become close to during the voyage across the Pacific on the USNS *Pope,* Private Farrell, was dead, along with so many other of his soldiers. Woody's punch was a blow for them all, but it was also against regulations. He had to be punished. In the end, after conferring with the new battalion commander, Lou Menetrey, Woodard's officers gave the young sergeant a slap on the wrist, an Article 15, confined him to base camp for a thirty-day suspension, two weeks without pay. Decades later, fondly recalling the incident, his Black Lions buddies would label Woody "the battalion disciplinarian."

"TODAY IS THE nineteenth of October," Delta survivor Mike Troyer drawled into his tape recorder that evening, preparing another reel for his parents in western Ohio. "Got one letter. Tell everybody I'm still kicking. I want to get off line. Drive a truck or something. Some easy job. The tape's pretty short. Don't have much more to say. I'm still alive and all. You can tell everybody. If you get anything in the papers about Shenandoah II, you can send it to me. I want to see the papers and how they're gonna lie about it. See what they're gonna say. 'Cause I know what happened out there. I wanna see what they'll say about it. They'll say things we really didn't do."

At the Ninety-third Evacuation Hospital in Long Binh, Greg Lan-don was still waiting for his back to be resewn, and since he was in bet-ter shape than the other wounded, he had spent most of that Friday assisting the staff. As he moved from bed to bed, the Professor tried to learn more about who had died in the battle. "I have very little informa-tion yet as to just who was hit," he wrote home to his family in New York State. What he had learned was horrifying enough. The other two squads in his platoon had been wiped out, including the lieutenant and his sergeants. By the luck of where they were positioned, the men in his squad were the only ones to all survive. "It really can unnerve a person to go through that mess," he wrote. "October 17—I'll remember that day."

Nearby, at the Twenty-fourth Evacuation Hospital, Jim George took out his American Red Cross stationery and wrote another letter home to his wife, Jackie, in Spartanburg. "Feel about the same today," the wounded Alpha commander reported. "My right eye is almost swelled shut, but I can see a little out of it. Gen. Hay (Div. Co.) came by to see me today. He said we did a good job. . . . The psychology of all of it hasn't registered yet. I keep having nightmares of men dying and yelling out, but hope that will all pass with time."

CHAPTER 26

"TRAGEDY BEYOND OUR WORDS"

ILL SEWELL AWOKE to a shattered world. He had begun his job as chancellor at the University of Wisconsin only a few months earlier with a euphoric sense that he and a collegial academy could construct a liberal pragmatist ideal in Madison. Now that grand notion lay in ruins, broken amid the blood and chaos of the Commerce Building. He was angry and depressed and could not bring himself to place the blame entirely on others. He could not fault only a faculty that, against his advice, had voted to allow the Dow Chemical Company to recruit on campus; nor the police who, to his horror, had marched into the swarm of demonstrators with nightclubs raised high; nor the students who, to his dismay, had rejected pleas to end their unlawful assembly. This was the worst of situations, where he could find no single scapegoat upon whom to focus his wrath. Sewell felt badly served by everyone, including himself. Bascom Hall was the last place he wanted to be now, so he spent the morning of October 19 holed up at his house, dodging phone calls, taking only a few from his closest faculty friends, wondering how he would be received at the three thirty faculty meeting, and preparing his own defense.

Paul Soglin had run through a range of emotions since that moment inside Commerce when he curled into the fetal position to protect his body against police clubs. First fear washed over him, then anger, then sadness, but by the end of that day, with the mass rally in the darkness on the library mall, it struck him that the violent confrontation—shorthanded into police brutality—had sparked a combustive reaction in the larger student body that years of speeches about Vietnam had not. Now, on the morning after, he was invigorated by the sudden prospect of a mass audience and his enhanced role as cochairman of the Committee on Student Rights, an ad hoc group that had been formed the night before to lead the strike.

Madison had made the evening news. The networks and big city papers were sending correspondents to town. There was a stirring sensation of being part of something larger, of Madison making its mark on the national movement as it swept across the country that week. Antiwar leaders in New York and Washington would take notice of the scrappy little band of demonstrators on the midwestern campus who had stood up to the war machine and had their heads bashed. Soglin made his way up Bascom Hill at the unlikely hour of eight thirty for the first rally of the day, attended by nearly two thousand students. It was held on the steps near the statue of Lincoln, whose noble face was covered with a gas mask.

This was not Old Abe's sort of day. The prevailing mood was malice toward all and charity for none. Several speakers, including Soglin, who wore his sheepskin coat unbuttoned in the bright morning sun, attacked the university for sending police into the Commerce Building and urged students to express their disapproval by boycotting classes. The circus atmosphere of the morning before was gone, along with the San Francisco Mime Troupe, whose members had packed their costumes and instruments into the blue-paneled truck and were driving their raucous caravan out of town, traveling southwest on Route 151 toward Iowa City, where, as Ron Davis put it, they would "see what mischief we might stir up" at the University of Iowa.

In place of the mime agitators, the morning crowd was now filled with unexpected faces. Much as the night before on the library mall, some people were attending their first demonstration. James Hadden, a freshman from Madison, came to the rally displaying a visual statement of his changing sensibility, a "nonconformist jean jacket." For Hadden, who still lived at home, on the west side, with a father who was a veteran of World War II, this was all new. He listened to Soglin connect the university to the "war machine" and denounce Sewell and Kauffman for lying to the students. He heard rumors rippling through the crowd about how police had clubbed girls in the midsection and had ruptured the uterus of one. *Look up there,* someone said, and Hadden noticed men in trenchcoats perched on the roofs of nearby buildings, focusing down on the scene with binoculars and cameras. He thought he might be put on "some subversive list by the FBI and considered a commie sympathizer." Should he be there or not? He found no easy answer. It made him uncomfortable to think that he was among "the students who could afford to go to school, protesting against the establishment, while poor kids who couldn't afford to go were fighting for the establishment" in Vietnam. Just standing there with the activists made him feel guilty, yet he was also thinking, "I'm a student and I've got to break the home ties and I don't like the war."

When the rally ended, picket lines were set up in front of major buildings on campus. The most boisterous picketing took place outside Bascom Hall and Commerce, where several dozen students chanted and carried homemade signs and banners that had been constructed overnight. "Stop Administration Brutality." "Cops OFF!" "Strike against Police Brutality." "Support Strike." "Get Out of Vietnam." "Police Brutality—Kill It Before It Multiplies!" Several students entered Bascom and stood outside Sewell's office holding a sign that read "*J'accuse* William Sewell—Student Blood Is on Your Hands." As another measure of how things had changed in twenty-four hours, the strike now had the blessing of Wisconsin Student Association leaders, who had opposed the obstructive sit-in the day before. Steve Richter, the WSA vice president, said that police brutality, not the war or Dow, was now the issue. The president of the National Student Association, Ed Schwartz, was on his way to Madison from Washington, D.C., arriving at Bascom Hill in time for the second rally of the day there, where he would say that the country was being "ripped apart at the seams" and that the actions at Wisconsin marked "the beginning of a long, hard struggle for politicization of American students."

The strike was also supported by movement-oriented graduate teaching assistants who had begun organizing themselves that year in the Teaching Assistants Association (TAA). About 150 teaching assistants had met as an ad hoc group late Wednesday night, after the rally on the library mall, and had decided to support the student strike. Bob Muehlenkamp, then a leader of the Wisconsin TAA, who went on to become a reform organizer for the Teamsters, explained the group's decision in a pamphlet about the strike and its aftermath. "Like everyone else on campus, the TAs had been deeply troubled by the day's events and were carried along by their emotion," Muehlenkamp wrote. "Certainly some response seemed necessary—and a particular form was already available: to strike. Also, TAs consider themselves as teachers to sympathize with and represent the student point of view. We thus felt impelled to join the strike because the students had already decided on it, and because TAs were expected to and indeed wanted to unite with the students in the protest. It now seems clear that these forces were strong enough to cause us, even before we met, to make up our minds to participate in the strike." Since the decision seemed obvious, Muehlenkamp wrote, there was no discussion of issues, only tactics. They settled on three: first, that they would wear armbands reading "TA on strike"; second, that they would "depart from the normal academic routine by bringing their students outside the classroom to join the strike and to discuss the issues"; and third, that they would circulate a petition supporting teaching assistants and other graduate students and faculty against administrative reprisals.

In the end 302 TAs signed the petition, about one-seventh of the two thousand teaching assistants on the Wisconsin campus. Lynne Cheney was among those in the English department who rejected the petition and continued teaching. Her husband, Dick Cheney, the political science graduate assistant, found the picketers "a minor hassle" as he made his way through campus with his stacks of computer data cards.

The first picketers stationed outside Music Hall on the bottom of Bascom Hill were not teaching assistants but John Pickart and Everett Goodwin, the strings section pacifists who had witnessed the events inside Commerce. The music school "in its typical manner kept right on rolling along, oblivious to the real world," Pickart reported in a letter he wrote later to his friend and fellow cellist, Pam Crane. "Even so, we really shook it up some." Before class they walked inside and talked to students and professors, explaining why they were striking, then walked out and picketed the entrance. The music school held its weekly all-school convocation that day, a one-hour session that music majors were required to attend every Thursday, and Pickart and Goodwin and several allies marched in and stood in the aisles holding signs. "Music students are inventive, and we had some good signs, although somewhat irrelevant to the question," Pickart reported to Crane. "Johannes Brahms Not Tear Gas Bombs," "Mahler Not Mauler," "Hammerklavier Not Well-Tempered Students," and "Music Strikes Keys and Classes" were mixed in with signs deploring police brutality.

"Of course, being a radical in the music school is not without its dangers," Pickart noted, citing several ugly incidents. A professor, he said, "threatened to beat up" one student picket, and the school secretary angrily ripped apart a picket sign, and Pickart was accused of being "a dirty communist pig," and several musicians who played in the university band were called in for a lecture "on the evils of the New York Commies etc. who organized the strike." Pickart also told Crane of a teaching assistant "who is being brought before a committee" for refusing to take class attendance that day. Pickart himself refused to take attendance in orchestra (he was the orchestra manager, a work-study job for which he was paid), though he did play his cello in that class.

In a university of more than thirty thousand students, the strike call that first day was in numerical terms only minimally successful. There were virtually no pickets and no noticeably greater absentee rates at the engineering and agriculture schools. The boycott was more keenly felt at the College of Letters and Sciences, home to about seventeen thousand students. Statistics kept that day by the office of Dean Leon Epstein indicated that history, philosophy, and sociology—Chancellor Sewell's old department—were the heaviest hit, and that in all perhaps four thousand students were reported absent, compared to the usual thousand.

Jane Brotman, although she did not carry a picket sign, supported the strike and stayed away from her French literature class, which meant that she was absent for the six-weeks exam. It had been only one day since she had taken her position as a curious bystander outside the Commerce Building and watched the police march in, but it seemed to her that she was now on the way to becoming a different person. She felt a great awakening. There was still something about the way the student leaders looked and presented themselves that turned her off, but she felt open, for the first time, to hearing the antiwar point of view. Before she had trusted in authority and believed that her government and her university would never lie to her. The possibility that her trust had been misplaced now roiled her mind. She "wanted to know more and more and more and couldn't get enough," she would say later. Her hunger to learn about politics, power, and foreign policy became insatiable. Dow had "opened the world" to her. Rather than take the French literature exam, Brotman instead sat at her favorite table in the back of the Union Rathskeller and wrote a long letter to her father the dentist in Maplewood, New Jersey. It was, in a sense, her six-weeks essay test. "You tell me that I'm here to STUDY—to stick my head in big fat books but to ignore the world around me," she began.

Well, there's a basic principle which you have overlooked, and that is there is more to an education than learning from books.

College is a big investment. For quite a lot less money I could have easily gone to the University of Maryland or another school close to home. I could have read the same books I read here, and for all practical purposes, I could have gotten a decent education there, too. So why did I have to go all the way to the U. of Wisconsin?

One of the major reasons for coming to this campus was due to the great diversification of the student body, and thus to the variations of existing ideas. In other words, I want to learn, I want to weigh every idea, I want to open my eyes to everything so I can make the best possible judgments.

As for today's incident—I won't be able to respect myself for not standing up for what I believe in. Would you be able to respect yourself? I know what I saw, and I can't allow that to happen again. I know you don't want me to get hurt or involved (I'm not going to get hurt), but I must take a stand. And in this case, my stand coincides with the students involved in the protest. . . .

I want to make something clear: today's student strike had nothing to do with the left, the right, or the conservatives. It was merely a general consensus of a great deal of the student body in reaction to the police brutality which took place on this campus yesterday. I honestly feel that if you had seen the unwarranted brutality that I witnessed, there would be no doubt in your mind as to the only possible action to take.

There is something else you must realize objectively. I respect your ideas and opinions very highly, for I realize that you have experienced many things during your lifetime. Yet I cannot possibly accept every one of your ideas, goals, or whatever, simply because you feel they are right. I must think about your ideas along with other ideas and evaluate them to the best of my ability. Then, and only then, can I accept or reject an idea (be it yours or someone else's). For I am a human being, too; I have a head and I want to make use of it. You can't possibly ask me, or demand, that I believe in something that I don't. That lies with me. Can you understand what I'm saying, or am I lacking clarity?

In order to operate as a functioning citizen in society, one must question and, if necessary, one must stand up for what he believes in and make himself heard. According to what you believe in, the Germans under Hitler acted in a justifiable manner—they didn't question and they didn't stand up to make themselves heard. They accepted something without thinking about it.

Does this mean that I am a liberal? A communist? A left winger? I don't think so. I would rather think that I am a responsible individual who is ready to grow up, and trying to do so.

> I miss you a lot and love you,
> Jane

At about the time that Jane Brotman was writing home instead of attending her French literature exam, President Johnson began an hourlong conversation in the Oval Office with Robert Manning, a former State Department public affairs officer who edited *The Atlantic Monthly*. Press Secretary George Christian sat in and took notes.

Manning said his magazine had decided to devote an entire issue to "what's happening in this country because of Vietnam."

The president, as recorded in Christian's notes, said that he could guess the results. "He mentioned a 1951 poll showing that while 81% of the people favored our entry in Korea in June, 66% said in January that we should pull out and only 20% said stay in. The president said this has been the pattern throughout American history, mentioning difficulties in the Revolutionary War, the Mexican War and the Civil War, and the 202 to 202 vote which extended the draft in 1941."

The thought of an entire magazine issue devoted to the war sent Johnson's mind spinning in several directions.

He thought about his critics from the left and said: "One of our weaknesses is that every hippie tells us of the evils of war, but we won't let those who have been there say anything about it."

He thought about his critics from the right and said they had to be careful not "to get the country on an anti-communist binge" because it would undermine the gains being made in relations with the Soviet Union.

People become inflamed during wartime, LBJ said. As examples, according to Christian's notes, "he related incidents in World War I involving his father, who helped defend against an oppressive anti-German bill in the Texas legislature, and his uncle, Judge Martin, who was indicted for speaking up for a German in Fredericksburg [Texas] who got drunk and said he hoped that the Kaiser would win.

Manning, picking up on Johnson's comments about the press's not listening to "those who have been there," said his magazine planned to look at "what happens to veterans who come back after being in Vietnam."

Even that comment took Johnson down a pessimist's road. He recalled talking to a university administrator who told him that his school "had 21 Marines, 20 of whom were sound men and one was a sorehead. The sorehead got all the attention."

THAT THURSDAY WAS Norman Lenburg's second-to-last day of work as a photographer at the *Wisconsin State Journal*. He planned to move from Madison on Saturday to run his father-in-law's camera shop in Milwaukee. The pictures he had taken of the riot at the Commerce Building would be his last on the job. Two were displayed on the front page of the morning paper: a five-column shot, above the fold, of Madison police officers wading into the crowd on the Commerce plaza, nightsticks held high; and a four-column shot on the bottom left corner that ran with the caption: "Several Students Carry One of Their Injured from Scene of Clash with Police." Still, Lenburg was "very disappointed" about the play that morning. When he had returned to the office Wednesday night to develop his pictures, he had told the editors the story of being up on the northwest balcony of Bascom Hall late in the day and seeing a young man climb to the roof and cut down the American flag. It was quite a story, Lenburg thought, and he knew he was the only photographer who got the picture.

Now where was it? Not on the front page, nor on page six, where there was almost a full page of pictures. Instead it was back in Section Four, the Madison and Suburban section, displayed in a narrow format. The cutline read: "'So Proudly It Falls'—An unidentified protester runs from the flagpole atop Bascom Hall Wednesday after cutting down the American flag during the height of the demonstration at the nearby Commerce building on the University campus." In truth, despite Lenburg's immediate disappointment about the photo's position, it mattered little where the picture ran; it was going to be noticed. It was not a great picture by artistic standards; dozens of others more vividly captured the trauma of the confrontation between police and students, but none of those pictures published in the *State Journal, Capital Times,* and *Daily Cardinal* was more noticed than the little two-column shot of the unidentified flag cutter. Soon enough that morning the flood of calls would start pouring in from outraged readers, and the growing fervor would leave Lenburg almost wishing that he had never taken the shot.

At least one reader of the morning paper could identify the flag cutter, of course. Jonathan Stielstra that morning had gone over to *Connections* headquarters at 22 North Henry Street, an old house near campus that had become the epicenter of the New Left in Madison. Someone at the alternative newspaper showed him the picture. Until then he had had no idea that a photographer had caught him in the act. He had assumed that the danger had passed when he had melted into the crowd on the Commerce plaza after that frantic chase down four flights of stairs in Bascom Hall. Now he realized there was a permanent and indisputable record of what he had done. Was he recognizable? Probably. Although the shot was taken from some distance, his face was pointed almost directly at the camera, and his black tennis shoes, mid-length coat, and long blond hair were distinguishing characteristics. *You gotta cut your hair!* someone in the *Connections* office quickly advised him. Vicki Gabriner—the whiteface Miss Sifting and Winnowing and wife of *Connections* editor Bob Gabriner—found a pair of scissors and gave Stielstra a trim. He did not know if the police were looking for him, but in case they were, the haircut might confuse them. He also had a natural ruse. The authorities eventually might determine that the flag cutter was a student named Stielstra, but how would they prove which Stielstra—Jonathan or his identical twin brother, Phil?

The *Connections* office was humming that day. Half the staff had been inside Commerce when the police arrived, and most of the rest had been outside watching. As with all political issues, the reaction to Dow provoked heated debates within the *Connections* crowd. Some supported the strike and saw it as a way to radicalize the student body, but a larger number thought the strike was an ill-conceived and emotional reaction that distracted from the larger issues of the war and the power structure and that it only further separated the campus from the rest of society, where the real battle had to be waged. On one matter the young radicals were unified—their growing anger, edging into hatred, for their liberal elders. The fiercest anger was directed not at LBJ types, domestic liberals who were foreign policy hawks, but at the liberals closer to home, most of whom were against the war themselves, the group represented by Sewell, Harrington, and Kauffman at the university and by the editors of the city's old progressive paper, the *Capital Times*. These liberals tended to rile the New Left even more than cops with nightsticks or conservative state legislators harrumphing that student demonstrators should be shot. "We were just intolerant of the liberals as they sought to deal with Dow and the war," Bob Gabriner said later. "They were the enemy. We didn't spend any time at all on the right wing in Wisconsin. It was the liberals."

Liberal university administrators, as Gabriner and other *Connections* radicals saw it, were timid and defensive, and their response to the Dow protest was motivated by their need to preserve their own status and power. They were said to be afraid of the legislature, afraid of state industrialists, afraid of wealthy alumni, and were accused of using the notion of academic neutrality to avoid making a moral judgment on the war. "Sifting and winnowing" was nothing more than a hollow phrase that allowed the university to give equal weight to right and wrong. Sewell and Kauffman and liberal faculty members might be against the war, according to a *Connections* editorial, "but they were not ready to resist, and they think they have less to lose by discrediting the antiwar movement itself." The *Capital Times* was the other target for the radicals. "The *Capital Times* prides itself on being one of the last of the great progressive fearless newspapers in the nation. This is bullshit," Gabriner wrote in an essay about the press in Madison. Instead, he argued, the paper had become "venomous and confused" by the events of the sixties.

It was all part of what Gabriner portrayed as the liberal fallacy of Madison. "The city of Madison prides itself on its liberality, tolerance and cleanliness. To those middle-aged liberals living in beleaguered little communities surrounded by reaction, Madison appears to be a utopia. Madisonians and the *Capital Times* uphold this image. They like it here. They enjoy battling the forces of the evil right. They can't do without them, because it reinforces their image of themselves. They are cosmopolitan, moral, and open-minded. The University of Wisconsin is the cornerstone upon which the progressive image was built." But with the university in crisis because of the Dow events, Gabriner wrote, the *Capital Times* felt "threatened and insecure" and unable to grasp the situation, because "to understand would be to admit that the progressive image is hollow and irrelevant to the crisis which we are confronting."

It was not a pretty fight, this side struggle between radicals and liberals, and it had many unfortunate reverberations for years and decades to come. But it was not one that Miles McMillin, the fifty-four-year-old editor and chief editorial writer of the *Capital Times,* was afraid to confront. Mac, as he was known, part native American from the Menominee tribe, grew up in Green Bay. He was partial to gentlemanly dress, seersucker suits and bowties, yet had a striking presence, bulldog and Hemingwayesque, his shock of graying hair brushed back from a huge forehead, his massive jaws obliterating an ever-present crackling wad of gum, his eyes ablaze, his face set in a scowling smile. He was not a defensive liberal but a fearless one, his positions honed by decades of arguments with critics from left and right. When he arrived in Madison to attend law school in the thirties, after graduating from St. Norbert in DePere, he found himself debating radical organizers on campus and taking his stand with anticommunist progressives. As a reporter and editorial writer in the late forties and early fifties, he led the *Capital Times*'s fight against the red-baiting Wisconsin senator, Joe McCarthy. Long before McCarthy had emerged as a national figure, McMillin had pegged him as a political charlatan, breaking a story that he had failed to pay taxes on stock income he had earned during World War II.

The hypocrisy of self-righteous ideologues was McMillin's favorite target. He hated the dogma of received wisdom, whether it came from McCarthy or Stalin or his Catholic church. It was through that historical lens that he filtered the recent events on campus. As Gabriner and the *Connections* writers prepared their next round of antiliberal salvos that day after the Dow protest, McMillin was banging out an editorial that would appear on the top left front of the afternoon paper's October 19 three-star edition. Appropriating a favorite word of the New Left for his own use, he titled his editorial "The Spectacle of Violence." His brief was not primarily a lament about police brutality, nor about the Dow Chemical Company, but focused instead on the rights of individuals and groups and the rule of law in a democratic society. It was a classic expression of the liberal dilemma of that era. "The horrible spectacle of violence and brutality on the campus of the University yesterday is the continuing price this country is paying for the reckless deception by which we were thrust into the war in Vietnam," it began.

It is not easy for students, who are aware of the promises
made to this country in the 1964 campaign, to honor the

regulations of the University regarding their very natural and laudatory protests at what is going on in Vietnam.

Chancellor Sewell, who deplores the tragic venture in Vietnam as much as any of the protesting students, has outlined this situation as well as it can be done and has warned that the unrest will continue as long as the war does.

But he has also made clear what the University must do to keep operating. The lines for legitimate protest have been carefully delineated. While those lines were observed during the protest on Tuesday there was no serious trouble. The trouble came yesterday when the protesters disrupted the functioning of the University and interfered with the right of the overwhelming majority of the students to pursue their education.

There was no acceptable alternative for the University to the course it took in ordering the disruptive students cleared from the building.

If it had acceded to the demands of this small minority, it would have faced continuing disruption. If Dow can be stopped from interviewing on the campus, Procter and Gamble can because it makes soap for the armed forces.

Could students who object to Negroes or Jews being allowed in the University be permitted to interfere with the functioning of the University to gain their ends?

In a democratic society there are rules—written and unwritten—which must be followed if the free institutions of that society are to endure. They include the right to protest—even against the freedoms which allow those protests. But they do not include the right to interfere with the rights of others without due process of law.

The story of man is the story of the continuing struggle to establish that principle of freedom. It was only recently that the world was engulfed in war to end the challenge of the Nazis to that principle. They believed they had the ultimate truth and could use whatever means available to those ends. The Communists believe that Marx' holy scripture gives them the same license.

When the principle that the end justifies the means prevails freedom is destroyed.

When it is attempted, as it was by a handful of students yesterday, it results in the kind of violence we all deplore.

When this kind of extremism is resorted to the only winner can be the opposite extremists. The anti-white bigots in the black power movement only strengthen the anti-black bigots in the white power movement. The anti-war extremists only strengthen the pro-war extremists. If there is any doubt about it, observe the strutting self-righteousness of Sen. Roseleip and his breed since the events of yesterday.

The University has no alternative but to follow the course it has taken if the protesting students do not stay within the rules designed to protect the rights of all.

If there are those either in the student body or faculty who cannot live with those rules, they are free to leave, of course, and seek their education and livelihood elsewhere.

But above all, the University administration must be held accountable to the people of this state to keep the University functioning for the great majority who are here for an education. This requires order. Order should be maintained, whether it is in downtown Madison with the American Legion creating chaos or students on the campus protesting the war.

If it takes the National Guard to do it, let it be the National Guard.

Next to the front-page portion of the editorial was a five-column picture of two riot-helmeted police officers pulling on the arms of Bob Gabriner's wife, Miss Sifting and Winnowing, as they began dragging her to the paddy wagon.

WHEN THE SPECIAL MEETING of the University of Wisconsin faculty began at three thirty that afternoon, the Memorial Union theater was filled to the highest row of the balcony. Professors who could not find seats spilled onto the stage and into a nearby reading room and lobby, where the proceedings were piped over a loudspeaker. According to the minutes, 1,350 of the 1,800 faculty members were present at the start, about the maximum for any meeting where attendance was not mandatory. The lobby and hallway and outside terrace were bubbling with hundreds of students inflamed by the events inside Commerce the day before and the administration's later announcement that it was suspending thirteen leaders of the Dow demonstration.

Sewell, reentering the fray after hours of isolation at his house, made his way through the unfriendly gauntlet toward the stage. He chose not to preside, giving that job to James Cleary, a vice chancellor, but first opened the meeting with his version of the events that brought them together. He reviewed the chronology of the first Dow protest the previous February, when Robben Fleming was chancellor. Students had blocked the entrance to a building and been arrested. After bailing them out of jail, Fleming had gone to the faculty and gotten a reaffirmation of Chapter 11.02 of the university rules and regulations, prohibiting student protesters from disrupting student functions. Fleming had then declared that the rules would be enforced thereafter even if it took the massive force of outside police. A few weeks later, Faculty Document 122 was approved, reaffirming the right of Dow or any other corporation to use the placement services of the university to interview students seeking jobs. Sewell had voted against that measure, but when he took over as chancellor, he felt obliged to enforce it. He believed above all in following the rules.

Then came Dow II: students announced that they would obstruct, then followed through and obstructed. Sewell's moment of decision, he said, was when Evan Stark and three protest marshals met with him in Bascom Hall as the sit-down protest was under way next door at Commerce and said that they would try to get the demonstrators to stop if the administration removed Dow from campus and promised in writing that the company would never return. Sewell would not be coerced. "I regret more than I can possibly tell you that it was necessary to bring in outside police," he explained to the faculty. "At the time, I saw no alternative—other than to surrender. I was given an ultimatum to make a statement in writing. Even so, no assurance was given to me that the demonstrators would leave."

Everything that followed, Sewell said, filled him with deep remorse—the resistance by the students, the club swinging by the police, the injuries to both students and police, the blood and screaming and tear gas. "Things like this should never happen on this great campus where we have so long had freedom of speech, freedom of peaceful protest." In his heart Sewell pounded on himself for letting things get out of hand. But in his head, by the logical reasoning of cause and effect, he blamed the protest leaders. "It is my firm conviction that the fault lies with those that refused to cease and desist," he said, fingering in particular the thirteen students who were being informed that day of their suspensions, pending "full due process" before a university conduct committee. Although the identities of the thirteen had not been released, two names, the most prominent ones, had leaked already at the state capitol. Stark and Cohen were on the list.

Sewell concluded his opening statement by saying that despite the difficulties of the job and his ambivalent feelings about leadership, he would not resign. "I did not seek this office," he said. "I have no great desire for administrative roles nor for power. I love and respect students. My actions yesterday were taken reluctantly and only to preserve the integrity of the university which I love."

Eugene Cameron, a professor of geology and Sewell's successor as chairman of the University Committee, was recognized next, in prearranged sequence, to present a defense of the chancellor. "During the past twenty-four hours we have reached a crisis that is shocking to us all," Cameron began. "Yet this crisis is no chance, no isolated event. It is a crisis that we should all have expected out of the developments of the past two years. The University Committee has studied the progression toward this crisis, in its various manifestations, since the spring of 1966." The statement he was about to read, Cameron said, was based on that study and had the unanimous support of his committee.

It was the McMillin thesis, in essence, using some of the editor's words. "Every human community must have its rules and regulations," the statement began. The rules can change, slowly, over time, but they must be followed or chaos results. The rules on student obstruction were "not designed to infringe upon the rights of any member of our community, but rather to protect the freedoms of all members, and specifically to protect them from the actions of ruthless minorities who are unconcerned with the rights of others and who attempt to justify their violations of those rights by the specious argument that the end can somehow justify the means. This argument is as old as history, and in perspective history has judged it to be false." The statement went on to argue that the organizers of the demonstration had to know that they were creating a situation that could turn violent, and because of that they "must bear the onus of the consequences." These consequences included not only the physical injuries to students and policemen, but also a deeper injury to the dedicated effort of other students and faculty members who had been meeting for several months to work out new policies giving students more power and more meaningful roles in the life of the university. "At a time when these efforts are approaching their culmination, a carefully planned, willful flouting of accepted rules such as yesterday's affair is a tragedy that is beyond our words."

Cameron ended by introducing a motion of support for Sewell: "Be it resolved that the faculty upholds the Chancellor's action in recognizing his obligations to enforce the mandate of the faculty as expressed in Chapter 11 of the University regulations."

And the debate began. The atmosphere in the theater was electric, tense, heavy with rhetoric and things implicit but unsaid. There were blocs of professors on the right and left who thought Sewell was either too lenient with the students or too easy on the police, but most were somewhere in the middle. They were shaken equally by the sight of riot helmets and nightsticks on campus and by the way that protest leaders had radicalized the academic atmosphere, upsetting the quiet pursuit of knowledge by making everything political. It was as though these faculty members simply wanted the whole unpleasant scene to disappear. Part of the record of what happened at Dow was on film, and several minutes of that film had been provided to the faculty by Blake Kellogg, news director of Channel 27. Should they watch it before taking any substantive votes? The decision was yes, but barely: while 633 voted to see the film, 522 professors opposed the idea, either because their minds were settled already or because they could not bear to revisit the violence. After the film was shown, they took a two-hour dinner break.

IN JAPAN BY THEN it was morning of the next day. Fred Kirkpatrick, the Delta Company point man, was nearing the end of his week's break from fighting in Vietnam. He left the Club Bohemian in the Shibuya district and checked into the USO club in Tokyo, where he happened to pick up that day's edition of *Pacific Stars & Stripes*.

The front-page headline ran in boldface type: **103 Reds Killed in Triple Attack on U.S. Battalion.** That was enough to grab Kirkpatrick's attention, and he kept reading. "A communist regiment, heavily manned by North Vietnamese replacements . . . flare-up of fighting . . . northwest of Saigon . . . conservative estimate of 103 Communists killed . . . eight-hour battle . . . U.S. losses . . . 56 killed and 63 wounded . . ."

Then the connections started coming, and Kirkpatrick's head began spinning. "Among the dead were Lt. Col. Terry Allen Jr. . . . Allen was killed when the battalion he commanded was hard hit by the enemy . . . fighting broke out around 10 a.m. when a squad from the 1st Inf. Div.'s A Co., 2nd Bn, 28th Infantry . . ."

"That's my battalion!" Kirkpatrick shouted. He called over to his buddy, Roy Key, another Delta rifleman on R and R who was standing nearby. They read the story together, stunned. They knew that their Black Lions were going on search-and-destroy missions two depleted companies at a time. Fifty-six killed and sixty-three wounded meant a complete disaster. "My God, they're wiped out," Kirkpatrick said. "Wiped out!" He left the club with his Japanese girlfriend, Keiko Kinoshita, who took him to a local market, but Kirkpatrick was overwhelmed by the horror he had escaped. What would he have done as a point man? Would he have been killed too? He was agitated, all nerves. He encountered a Japanese man who bothered him for some reason, Kirkpatrick didn't even know why, and he cocked his fist and was about to strike the man in the face when Keiko grabbed his arm and stopped him.

THE RANKS INSIDE the Memorial Union Theater in Madison thinned a bit for the evening session, down a hundred professors from the afternoon, but the student audience on the other side of the doors and out on the terrace had swelled in numbers and energy. As the faculty debated the Cameron motion and a counterproposal—the one acknowledging Sewell's "good faith" but strongly condemning the "indiscriminate violence" of the police—the students reacted like a raucous sporting crowd jeering and cheering every pitch. In this crowd, as in most student protest gatherings, the range of alienation and willingness to rabble-rouse was wide.

Jim Rowen listened to the faculty debate with dismay, shaken by the violence of the day before and furious that the faculty seemed more interested in faulting students than police. Jane Brotman stopped by to show her solidarity with the cause, if not the people of that cause, still sorting out the feelings she had expressed in the letter to her father and worrying about her French literature grade. Betty Menacher, taking an interest in politics for the first time after being unexpectedly caught in the melee inside Commerce, came over from Sellery Hall, curious to learn more about the issues of the day. Paul Soglin was with the crowd on the Union Terrace. Even though he had been lead plaintiff in the legal brief against the university and had been among those obstructing inside Commerce, he was not picked out as a ringleader facing suspension and possible criminal action because he had not led the resistance against the police. If anything, as a student who had been pounded by nightsticks without responding, he was a poster boy for police overreaction. He was angry with the administration now but determined to avoid further violence.

Robert Barnett, a senior in history from Waukegan, Illinois, with moderate antiwar leanings, had not participated in the Dow protest but came to listen to the faculty debate out of political curiosity. His focus that week was less on the war and more on a sophomore named Rita Braver, a reporter at the *Daily Cardinal* whom he had taken out the previous weekend and brazenly asked to marry him on their first date. Now as he stood amid the hubbub outside the theater, Barnett was stunned by a scene that would remain vividly in his memory decades later (when he was a Washington lawyer, agent for Bill Clinton, and Braver was his wife and a *CBS News* correspondent). That night in the Memorial Union theater hallway Barnett "saw a guy stand up above the crowd" and shriek, "Let's kill the faculty!" A few bravado shouts followed, but the would-be revolutionary was largely ignored. Kenneth W. Thompson, a visiting professor of obstetrics and gynecology, was positioned nearby and observed a similar scene. There were, he said, "a few very evident belligerent male students who blusteringly talked of 'taking the auditorium.' All they needed was a spark of encouragement and they would have attempted something."

Dr. Thompson spent the evening mingling with the students in the lobby, because he was not a voting member of the faculty and not allowed inside. The group dynamics of the students struck him as so interesting that he later recorded his observations in a four-page memo. It was immediately apparent to him that these several hundred students "were vitally interested" in the faculty debate and that their focus was almost entirely on the issue of police brutality. "No concern was felt that students were in any way to blame," he wrote. In his conversations with them, he had heard students say that they had expected a hundred or more of them to be "dragged off to jail" during the Commerce sit-in, that "the charging by the police was unwarranted," and that no warning had been given for the tear gas outside. Thompson noticed that "there was good discipline" among the students and that certain leaders were obeyed with "excellent attention." It seemed to him that the speeches of certain faculty members were "directed to the students and encouraging their obstructionism and disrespect for authority." Although the causes were diametrically different, Thompson said the behavior patterns in some ways reminded him of when he was a foreign student at the University of Freiburg "in the early days of Hitler, when German students were organized to handle foreign students. We were to be guided down the path of admiration for the Nazi movement. The discipline among the German student leaders of the so-called Foreign Students Association was remarkable."

George Mosse, the renowned professor of modern European history who had in fact escaped Hitler's Germany and spent his career studying Nazism and nationalistic mass movements, had a more subtle critique of the Dow protest and its handling. Like many liberal professors, he was against the Vietnam war but considered the Dow obstruction "a terrible mistake." The confrontation inside Commerce marked what he later called an unfortunate "sharp turn away from the intellectualism" that previously had defined the New Left in Madison. Until then, even when he disagreed with his more radical students, he had found them stimulating and serious. But the leaders of the Dow protest, Mosse said, "however erudite they may have appeared, threw out a spark" that moved things in the wrong direction—"from thinking to mindless activity." Any antiwar demonstration that provoked violence was self-defeating, he thought, because it only led protesters into a battle they could not possibly win. Where the visiting Dr. Thompson was struck by the discipline of the protest leaders, and found their manipulative skills analogous to Hitler Youth leaders, Mosse, while disapproving of their tactics, saw them as extemporaneous and disorganized and thus less threatening.

It was with that frame of mind that he rose to speak during the faculty debate. What worried him most was not whether the university was being too lenient, but whether it was exaggerating the danger of a few nihilistic students and worsening the situation by panicking and becoming inflexible. "I have seen more and more students who were never political picketing today," Mosse told his colleagues. It was the sight of violence that propelled them to the picket line, he said, and he feared that a hard-line approach would lead only to more confrontations and "an escalation of violence." He had seen the same cycle at the Free University of Berlin and other campuses around the world. By adhering unwaveringly to rules even at the expense of common sense, Mosse said, the university was becoming "as absolutistic as the students." Would it make sense to invite Dow back the next day if it led to bloodshed? Did it make any sense in the first place, he asked, beyond a determination to follow every rule, to invite Dow to recruit on campus during national Peace Week?

It was typical of Mosse that his words were cheered in the hallway by students he thought were so misguided. But he was surprised by another reaction—hostility from some colleagues inside the theater. He thought he was trying to calm the situation, but as soon as he sat down he felt "a wave of hatred" coming at him. He had greatly underestimated how threatened many professors felt by the student unrest.

From the UW journalism school, Scott Cutlip, a public relations expert, rose in defense of the administration, saying that the state, the faculty, and the students were all "God damn lucky to have Bill Sewell as chancellor"—someone who would stand firm at a time when the university was being paralyzed "by two hundred nihilists."

A professor of engineering, Edward F. Obert, charged that students and sympathetic professors had exaggerated the confrontation and made the injuries to protesters sound worse than they were. The incident was not a case of police brutality, he said, but of "student brutality."

The law school's Ted Finman, who was part of a group taking statements from students who had witnessed the police action inside Commerce, strongly disagreed. "We know enough to say there was police brutality and we ought to have enough guts to say it," he told his colleagues.

William H. Hay, professor of philosophy, said that he had watched the Dow demonstration from the northwest balcony of Bascom Hall and had concluded at the time that the police had made a tactical mistake—that they should have "moved the spectators back before attempting to clear Commerce." The violence was "totally unnecessary," he said, and resulted in large part because people were trapped.

The debate dragged on hour after hour with a circuitous series of motions, amendments, and amendments to amendments. Sewell, feeling buffeted from all sides, eventually rose to defend himself again. He loaded his response with a street-brawling word—"guts"—that was not normally part of the academy lexicon but had been used more than once that night. "This faculty has already put me in a precarious position in its past actions and again here tonight," he said. "You haven't had the guts enough to admit that my reaction was an exact interpretation of what you intended."

In the end Sewell prevailed, though his support was tenuous. By the close vote of 562 to 495, the faculty defeated the resolution that condemned the use of "indiscriminate violence" while saying that the chancellor had made his decisions in "good faith." After that the prosaic Cameron resolution upholding the administration's actions was approved, 681 to 378. And finally, on a voice vote, they decided to cancel the last batch of Dow interviews scheduled for the next day.

After listening for six hours over loudspeakers, their emotions rising and falling, the students outside the theater were left deflated. They felt that their side had lost and that the faculty was interested only in protecting its academic bubble, unwilling to address the moral issues of Dow and the war or the physical facts of the police action. For Paul Soglin, it was another dose of disillusionment. He had always looked up to his teachers—his father was a teacher, the people he admired most were teachers—but now he felt "an overwhelming realization that we could not count on them." Jim Rowen had come to the Union that night believing that the faculty would condemn the police. As professors filed out of the theater, he stood in a crowd lining the South Park Street exit and joined in the subdued, mournful chants of "Shame . . . shame . . . shame."

CHAPTER 27

A LIFE'S WORTH

IN MILWAUKEE the next morning, Friday the twentieth of October, Diane Sikorski was in her bedroom at 4369 North Forty-second Place, the room her father had painted blue. The doorbell rang and she looked out the window and her heart sank at the sight of an earnest soldier standing on the front stoop. The families of men serving in Vietnam knew what it meant when an unexpected uniform appeared at the front door. "They don't come to visit," Diane thought. "They come to tell you what you hope you'll never hear." She left her room, opened the door, and stared into the young man's face, a soldierly mask. Her first reaction was to feel sorry for him. He asked to speak with her father. She turned away and entered the kitchen, suddenly light-headed and exhausted, a numb feeling moving up her arms and legs. Her father and stepmother were drinking coffee. She told her dad about the visitor in uniform, and a look washed over his face that she would never forget. They returned to the living room as a group, Diane and her father and stepmother, and waited for the soldier to speak.

"Are you Edmund Sikorski?" he asked. Then he took out a telegram and began to read. *We regret to inform* . . . Diane watched his lips, but she could not grasp the words, her head was spinning too much. She heard "killed in action" and wanted to scream, but nothing came out. She started to shake and turned to her dad and saw him reaching out for his wife.

The soldier kept reading. Diane heard almost none of it. But she did hear the punctuating grief of her father. *Oh, God! No, not Danny. He was so young. Why couldn't God take me instead?* His wife held him while he wept. Diane wanted to hold him too but couldn't move and stood shaking and feeling cold, as if someone had stripped her of her clothing and left her alone.

Time became a blur. She could not remember the soldier leaving, but he was gone. She went back to her room and collapsed on the bed. Her arms and legs were heavy and aching. Her mother had died suddenly only a few years earlier, and now her big brother, Danny, was gone. He couldn't be dead, she thought. Then she remembered the horrible dream, Danny calling out to her with his stomach missing, and the letter that would arrive in Lai Khe too late.

Her father appeared, his face ashen, eyes red, voice breaking, and held out his arms. Diane asked, "Why does death always happen to our family?"

Edmund Sikorski did not have an answer.

Men in uniforms, faces set in soldierly masks, were trudging up the front steps of homes across the United States that day, delivering the grim news of Black Lions who had been killed in action in the jungle near the Ong Thanh stream. When two immaculate messengers of death reached the door at 11 Conselyea Street in Brooklyn to inform the parents of Paddy Tizzio, Terry Allen's radiotelephone operator, a neighbor saw them before anyone answered the door and rushed out to stop them. The neighbor knew that Paddy's mother was home alone and could not bear the news, so he persuaded them instead to go tell the father, Dominic Tizzio, a supervisor at the Thypin Steel plant in Long Island City. Paddy's sister, Marian, got a call at the plating company where she worked and was told to hurry home. When she arrived, she saw her aunts and uncles and realized someone had died, but presumed it was her father until she heard her mother screaming. Then she knew: Paddy was her mother's light, and when he went out, so did she. She would never celebrate again—no holidays, no religious festivals, nothing for the rest of her life.

At eleven in the morning, mountain standard time, two soldiers arrived at a ranch house outside Helena, Montana, where Eleanor Schroder had been living since her husband, Jack, left for Vietnam on the USNS *Pope* in July. She was the only adult home that day, taking care of her baby son, seven-month-old Larry, and babysitting the three young children of the friends with whom she was staying. She heard the knock on the door and opened it, "and there they were"—the bereavement officers. "You're lying!" she kept insisting when the soldiers told her that Jack Schroder had been killed in action. They handed her a telegram so that she could read it herself. She went into the bedroom and picked up her baby son and rocked him as her tears fell on his chubby face.

The night before, on the nineteenth, she had slept fitfully, but it was unfocused distress, and she had not worried specifically about her young husband in Vietnam. She had always expected him to survive and had not taken it as an omen that day when they had parted, four months earlier, and he had told her that he would rather die than come home crippled. In his absence she had imagined their future lives together; he would finish the dental training he had begun in Milwaukee and set up a shop where he would make false teeth, and together they would bring up a family. Now the future was lost in a daze. She was unable to absorb the reality of his death. At noon her friend came home. Eleanor told her the news and showed her the telegram and became so hysterical that the friend called the closest person who could help, a local veterinarian, who came by to calm the young widow with a tranquilizer.

THREE CHARTERED Greyhound buses idled on Langdon Street outside the Memorial Union late that Friday morning, loading passengers who were going to Washington to march against the war in Vietnam. The detachment of fewer than two hundred riders was slightly smaller than organizers from the Madison Mobilization Committee had expected, with a sprinkling of high school students and townspeople. Some activists at the university, Paul Soglin among them, decided to stay home and push the protest against university administrators and the police. Others, including photographer Michael Oberdorfer and friends from *Connections,* had piled into a Volkswagen minibus the night before and left for Washington on their own. To them the Dow protest signified a line that had been crossed. They had been using the phrase "from protest to resistance" all fall, and now it seemed more than rhetoric. They were no longer interested in marching peacefully or undertaking purely symbolic acts. The confrontation at Commerce only intensified their feelings that they had to do whatever they could, physically, to interfere with the war machine, if not stop the war.

Among the high school students making the bus trip was Alison Steiner, a senior from Madison West, who that fall had become active in a group called Students for Social Justice. They had their own newsletter and tried to distribute *Connections* inside the public schools, though that effort was banned when the alternative paper featured a cover of a nude woman. Steiner's father was an economics professor at Wisconsin; her mother had returned to college to study computer science (and had felt the sting of tear gas on campus that Wednesday). Alison was a budding activist, informed and naïve at the same time. She liked to hang out on campus, where she occasionally audited Harvey Goldberg's lectures on revolutionary France and volunteered at the Wisconsin Draft Resistance Union. Yet until that morning when she boarded the bus for Washington, she had never traveled out of town without her parents, and though she hoped that people would mistake her for a college student, before she left she had to take her mid-semester tests at West High and get a written excuse from her mother, and in her pocket she carried a slip of paper that her parents told her to pull out in case she got arrested or faced some other emergency—the private home telephone number of Senator Gaylord Nelson, a friend of a family friend.

There was deep interest among certain federal authorities as to what these protesters from the heartland were doing. Among the others finding seats in the buses outside the Union were two undercover agents sent by the Army Intelligence Command. Dave Wheadon, a twenty-three-year-old Syracuse dropout who worked as a lab technician at Oscar Mayer on Madison's east side and was recruited to travel to the Washington rally by a friend in his apartment complex, later recalled that two men in their late twenties came aboard wearing trenchcoats and carrying clipboards. They said they were insurance representatives involved in the leasing of the buses and needed the names, addresses, and telephone numbers of passengers for insurance records. In reality the two men were undercover agents, and the names on their clipboard lists went directly into the files of dissidents to be watched by the FBI. Alison Steiner's file began then; an agent accurately recorded that she sometimes wore glasses but wrongly stated that she had blue eyes. The federal effort that fall to monitor dissent—and stifle it—was massive and multilayered. Intelligence agents, some using phony draft cards, not only followed the protesters but also filmed them, photographed them, monitored them on amateur radios, compiled names for future investigations, penetrated most of the groups organizing the demonstrations, attempted to disrupt their activities, and even interrogated bus company owners, pressuring some to drop their charter contracts.

If the action on campus seemed more relevant to some student activists and kept them back in town, there were a few protesters who would not have gone to Washington if not for the Dow protest. One was Judy Genack. The senior European history major had no intention of participating in the national rally until she was stirred to act by what she had witnessed on the Commerce plaza a few days earlier. After that she felt "very drawn toward wanting to connect" with the American anti-war movement, which she related to her experiences in Jerusalem that summer during the Six-Day War. Since she had waited until the last minute before deciding to go to Washington, she traveled by plane rather than bus. Before leaving Friday morning, she made arrangements to stay with a friend of a friend, a young reporter in the Washington bureau of the *New York Daily News* named Steve Matthews, who was covering the antiwar events. Joining a march on the Pentagon was an "impulsive" act and one that did not please her parents, but Genack felt an overpowering need to stand up and be heard.

At the White House President Johnson pressed his aides for updates on the imminent demonstrations while he went through his day with a business-as-usual air. Not long after the buses pulled out of Madison for the long haul east, Johnson was posing for photographers on the South Lawn of the White House with Souvanna Phouma, the royal prime minister of Laos. It was a bright day, and LBJ asked for his sunglasses. After the picture taking the two men conversed through an interpreter.

The Laotian prime minister, as much as Johnson, was preoccupied with the Vietnam war. The North Vietnamese were filtering through Laos along the Ho Chi Minh Trail and using it to stage operations into South Vietnam. At the same time the Laotian military was battling the local communist insurgents, the Pathet Lao. They were losing ten to twenty men a day in that war, Souvanna Phouma told Johnson, and even if they won militarily, they might lose economically without additional American aid. Since "the neutrality of Laos" had to be maintained, he wondered if some "circuitous route" could be found to "relieve these financial pressures." Johnson said the United States had budget problems of its own. His government, he claimed, was now spending $75 billion on defense out of a total $130 billion budget. And his foreign aid program had been cut by one-third. When Souvanna Phouma persisted, asking whether he could get assistance for refugee care and defense needs, the president advised him to talk with Secretary McNamara.

According to a top secret Memorandum of Conversation vetted by

Johnson's national security aid, Walt Rostow, Souvanna Phouma then told Johnson that he had seen "no improvement in the North Vietnamese attitude on the war" since late September when the president had broached the possibility of a bombing pause. Johnson agreed, adding that "in recent days North Vietnam's position was even harsher."

What would the United States do? Would it harden its own stand? Souvanna Phouma asked. Johnson replied that his administration would "keep doing what it has been doing."

Souvanna Phouma hoped for more. He stressed how vitally interested his country was in this question because "most of the North Vietnamese equipment that infiltrated to the South went through Laos." If the United States hardened its stand and heavily bombed all passes from North Vietnam into Laos, "the Lao would be happy," he said. He was afraid that "since North Vietnam has failed to achieve victory" in South Vietnam, "it might very well turn against Laos" and invade his country during the next dry season.

When Johnson asked whether he thought Hanoi's intentions had changed at all since a year earlier, when the two leaders last had met, Souvanna Phouma said that after their earlier visit, when he had returned to the Laotian capital of Vientiane, he had asked a North Vietnamese diplomat what Hanoi would do if the Americans stopped bombing. The diplomat had said that Hanoi "would not accept anything short of a final and unconditional cessation of bombing." It was, the two agreed, the same answer they had been hearing for years.

Johnson was brooding again about his dilemma. How could the war be brought to an end? he asked.

Put pressure on the Soviet Union to exert its influence with Hanoi, Souvanna Phouma suggested.

The Soviets had already tried, Johnson said, but the Chinese were opposed.

He asked if they "were any nearer to peace today than a year ago."

Perhaps, Souvanna Phouma said, but it "was a very difficult question to answer."

IN MADISON that noon hour the student protesters who stayed behind staged a rally on Bascom Hill. It was led by the just-formed Committee on Student Rights, chaired by Paul Soglin and now organized into subcommittees in charge of picketing, safety, petitioning, dorms, faculty, transportation, and a subcommittee to coordinate the subcommittees. This was a flow chart for ambitious plans, but in reality there was not that much to do. The class boycott, into its second day, was already petering out, with departmental deans reporting only negligibly higher absence rates, and those only in the social sciences. Teaching assistant Michael Krasny, the freshman composition instructor whose class inside Commerce had been disrupted Wednesday afternoon, had now turned his sessions into teach-ins about the war and student issues, typical of many of his colleagues sympathetic to the cause. The Bascom Hill rally drew about a thousand people, still considered a healthy crowd, and far greater than most campus rallies before Dow, but only half the size of the day before. The adrenaline rush was going, if not gone.

What should they do next? Soglin and his comrades debated strategy for three hours in the open air near the statue of Abe Lincoln and arrived at a tentative plan. They would stage a march the next day, not unlike the march in Washington, but this one up State Street to the state Capitol. What should the march be about? On that question tension within the committee was apparent. Some student leaders, including Soglin, hoped that it would be about everything: the war, the police action, the establishment, recruiting on campus, the draft, the changing order. But they were now leading a group that included many students who had never protested before, who were not necessarily familiar with foreign policy issues and knew only that they were upset by what had happened two days earlier at Commerce. The group also included many distraught faculty members, who were most upset by the intrusion of police and the bloodshed on campus. Those two factions dominated now, and the majority decision was to limit the march to the events surrounding Dow—the charge of police brutality and the disposition of the cases against sit-in leaders.

Within an hour notices were taped and stapled to trees, telephone poles, and bulletin boards around campus urging people to "March for the Rights of Students & Their Protection." The march would not be a parade, the notices said. "It is not a joyous procession. It is a march of sorrow for the past, and for the future. It is our fear that this might be a funeral march for freedom and human rights on this campus. We march hoping that it is not. . . . We call upon all members of the University community and of the Madison community who are opposed to the action of the police on 18 October to join us. This is your battle, next time, it might be your head."

Inside Bascom Hall letters were beginning to arrive at Chancellor Sewell's office, letters by the hundreds, six bags full. Letters of hate and letters of support, so many letters that one of the chancellor's closest friends, fellow sociologist Bert Fisher, took it upon himself to form a volunteer squad to read and organize them for the appropriate response. There was the telegram from a professor of oncology who complained that he was "ashamed to be a member of the faculty" because of what he called the inappropriate use of tear gas and nightsticks on campus. And there was the letter from a professor of geography who wanted to offer a "positive suggestion." A core of professors with "liberal credentials," he wrote, wanted to offer themselves as replacements for city police when protesters threatened recruitment interviews. These liberal professors would form a cordon to protect access, offering "our bodies and our sensibilities, for we accept the hazards of both violence and vituperation." Only the most hard-core of student activists, he predicted, would attempt violence against them.

Then there was the note from a graduate student in English who said she had been "continually appalled by the permissiveness with which the university has handled unruly demonstrators." And a letter from a third-year law student named F. James Sensenbrenner Jr. saying that he intended to be interviewed by the Central Intelligence Agency when it came to campus in November and expected that those interviews would not be disrupted as the Dow interviews had been. Sensenbrenner, who would be elected to the Wisconsin assembly as a Republican a year later and go on to represent some Milwaukee suburbs in the U.S. House of Representatives, told Sewell that he "would appreciate being informed of the measures being taken to protect the personal safety" of the CIA interviewees and that he planned "to investigate the legal means available to insure adequate protection of persons like myself."

One of the first letters to arrive was a handwritten note on the stationery of Harry Charles Thoma of 4182 Nakoma Road in Madison. "Dear Chancellor," it read. "As an alumnus, a taxpayer, a retired Army officer and father of a son killed in action in Viet Nam I back your stand 100%. Keep it up. Let's hope you get more support in the months ahead. Dissent is a right, but lawlessness and violence cannot and must not be tolerated."

Here, in one note, was an unlikely thread connecting the disparate worlds of war and peace. Harry Thoma's son, Major Charles J. Thoma, had been not only a soldier in Vietnam, but an officer in the Second Battalion, Twenty-eighth Infantry, First Infantry Division. He had been a Black Lion, serving as the battalion operations officer, the same S-3 job later held by Terry Allen Jr. and Big Jim Shelton. On January 12, 1967— ancient history, long, long ago in the war, more than a month before Allen arrived in Vietnam, six months before the C Packet soldiers on the USNS *Pope* got there—Thoma was with the Black Lions on a search- and-destroy mission in the jungle northwest of Saigon, part of the mas- sive Operation Cedar Falls. That day they had found a Viet Cong munitions cache, several hundred tons of rice, and miscellaneous enemy documents. At two twenty in the afternoon, Thoma was shot in the head by a sniper. He died hours later in surgery, at age thirty. He was, as it happened, the first Black Lions officer to die in battle in Vietnam in 1967, and Terry Allen Jr. was the last.

The turmoil at the campus end of State Street consumed the Wis- consin legislature that day. Since Republicans controlled the governor's office, the Assembly, and the Senate, the argument was largely between mainstream conservatives and hard-line right-wingers. In some ways it was a mirror image of the fissure between liberals and leftist radicals on the antiwar side, though with less apparent bad blood. Senator Roseleip was on the loose, pushing for an academic coup d'etat in which state lawmakers would seize operational control of the university, or at least, as a fallback position, make sure that two leftist student organizations, SDS and the W. E. B. DuBois Society, were banned from campus. These groups, Roseleip said, were nothing more than "tools of the Commu- nists." It was left to Jerris Leonard, the Senate majority leader, a moder- ate conservative from the suburbs of Milwaukee, to keep Roseleip under control.

Leonard had ambitions beyond the state legislature. Preparing to challenge Gaylord Nelson for a Senate seat the following year, he had been recruited by the state of Wisconsin's Wall Street bond lawyer, John Mitchell, to chair the state campaign of Mitchell's law partner and polit- ical friend, Richard M. Nixon, the former vice president, who wanted to run in the 1968 presidential primary. Before he could move on to those political pursuits, Leonard had to deal with the problems at the univer- sity. At the time of the Dow protest he was feuding with President Har- rington over construction budgets and tax breaks for private schools, a political fight colored by personal animosity. Harrington was not a par- ticularly beloved figure among state Republicans. They considered him an imperious academic who barely deigned to deal with elected pols, and they loved to point out that he rode in a chauffeured black Cadillac while Governor Knowles used a Rambler built by American Motors in Kenosha. Leonard's distaste for Harrington only increased when word got back to him that the UW president, at a party in Madison, reportedly had declared, "We've got to destroy this guy Leonard."

But there were other factors shaping Leonard's perspective now. Much like Knowles, whose agenda he advanced in the legislature, he wanted to get tough with protesters without disabling the university, which was vital to the economic health of the state, particularly rural areas that relied heavily on the ag school and tended to be represented by Republicans. Furthermore he had come to believe that most student demonstrators were "venting their testosterone" and were not serious threats to the established order. And finally, he had learned a lesson already concerning reckless rhetoric. After an earlier episode on campus, he had criticized the *Daily Cardinal* for employing an editor who happened to room with the son of a Communist Party figure. He had "taken a ration of shit" for that attack and come to regret it as an unfortunate case of guilt by association. All of those things went into Jerris Leonard's reasoning as he took on Senator Roseleip at the Capitol that October Friday.

"You don't outlaw organizations no matter how much you disagree with them," Leonard told Roseleip during the Senate debate. "Everybody has a right to his point of view, even the screwballs in the DuBois Society. Unless you give a method of expression to every point of view in a democracy, you will have riots on the street corners."

"Don't you think this is a conspiracy?" Roseleip thundered back.

"Nobody makes a conspiracy with words," Leonard responded.

In an effort to "cut off hysteria from the right," Leonard and the governor's political team came up with the idea of launching a bipartisan Senate investigation of the Dow incident. The scope of the investigation would be limited to the protest and ways that violent confrontations might be averted in the future. They would stack the committee with moderates and have Jack Olson, the lieutenant governor, serve as chairman. Olson did not want the job but had no choice; Leonard and Knowles considered him mild to the point of boring, just what they wanted. The wording of the resolution was anything but judicious. Blame was already fully assigned as the committee was instructed to gather facts on "the riotous and unlawful activities" of students during the Dow demonstration.

The prospect of an investigation excited Roseleip and his cohorts. "This thing has been swept under the rug too long," said Gerald Lorge of Bear Creek, in support of the legislative inquest. "When you pick up the paper and see the American flag torn down, when people are fighting and dying and being maimed in Vietnam, I think this"—the Dow demonstration—"is the most disgraceful thing I've ever heard of."

For the second straight day Madisonians were picking up the paper and seeing the flag torn down. The *Wisconsin State Journal* devoted nearly half of its Page of Opinion to a Pictorial Editorial headlined "All This Must Go."

What must go? Three things. The first was "Outside 'Help' from San Francisco," rendered in this case by a small photograph of Miss Sifting and Winnowing, under the mistaken assumption that the whiteface mime was a member of the San Francisco Mime Troupe rather than Wisconsin's own Vicki Gabriner. The second thing that had to go was Robert Cohen, who was pictured speaking into a battery-powered bullhorn next to the cutline, "A Teaching Assistant Gives Foghorn Leadership." And the third thing that had to go was the flag cutter, caught in the act atop Bascom Hall again in Norm Lenburg's photograph, this time displayed in four columns.

District Attorney Jim Boll was sitting in his office that afternoon when the phone rang; he picked it up and a male voice said, "I fought in World War II and I was severely wounded and I love the flag. Will you do what you can to apprehend the person who tore down the American flag and desecrated it?" The man had seen the picture, twice, in the paper, and was incensed that the culprit had not been caught. The picture had infuriated Boll too, and now he felt compelled to act. He could laugh it off when a raging young woman protester had shrieked at him, "Boll, you suck cock!" And it was disturbing, but not enough to rouse his prosecutorial fervor, when someone—obviously not an admirer— had slipped into his office the night before and left a white chicken in his chair with a swastika painted on it, and next to the chicken a swastika-decorated egg. Boll didn't consider himself a fascist; he thought of himself as someone who was enforcing the law. He gave the chicken to a janitor, who ate it.

Boll was an officer in the National Guard and his father had fought in the trenches in World War I, and every year at eleven on the morning of the eleventh day of the eleventh month, Veterans Day, no matter what he was doing, he would stand up and turn to the east and pray to honor

the war dead. Once, a few years before the Dow protest, he had performed this annual ritual in the courtroom during the trial of antiwar
demonstrators who had been arrested for blocking a highway near
Truax Field, the local air base. His nation's symbols were deeply felt by
Jim Boll. People could insult him but not the flag.

In his pursuit of the flag cutter, Boll teamed with Vernon (Jack)
Leslie, the Dane County undersheriff, a former marine who had fought
in the Pacific in World War II and who carried a palpable hatred for
the long-hairs who now challenged authority and opposed the war in
Vietnam. They were an unlikely duo, the prosecutor and the sheriff: Boll
bespectacled and mild-mannered, Leslie a hard-drinking gamecock of a
lawman who strutted through town with a menacing air. Whenever
protesters landed in the county lockup, it was Leslie who gleefully ordered their long hair shorn, and in his own private manipulation he recruited a jailed rapist to be the barber. Boll, in describing Leslie, often
told the story of the time they were preparing for another antiwar
demonstration. Leslie had heard students chanting "One, two, three,
four, we don't want your fucking war!" and decided that he could not
tolerate the use of the word "fuck" in that context, so he instructed his
troops to arrest anyone who said it.

"Jack, you can't go arresting people for that," Boll cautioned him.

To which Leslie barked, "Why the fuck can't we?"

Leslie and his men had been called in late, as a backup force, and had
missed the Dow confrontation, and although Boll was among those who
privately felt that the undersheriff's absence was probably for the best,
it had left Leslie unfulfilled. He was eager to bring the protesters into
line. If he could not crack unruly heads inside Commerce, at least he
could haul in the kid who had cut down the American flag. With the
Lenburg photo circulating for a second straight day, Boll and Leslie had
received enough tips to have the name of a prime suspect, a student
named Stielstra. The problem was which Stielstra? Phil or Jonathan?
The search was on.

Detective Tom McCarthy returned to police headquarters for a few
minutes that afternoon of the twentieth. Bandages protected his nose after surgery at Madison General Hospital, the first of many operations on
his sinus passages, which had been permanently damaged. His injury
had been reported in the papers, eliciting a stack of letters, get-well
cards, and telephone messages. Strangers offered him a free trip to Las
Vegas, and a group of lawyers wanted to pay his membership in a down-

town athletic club. Jack Olson, the lieutenant governor, wrote to say that he felt "more secure knowing our peace officers are equal to any occasion."

Nine professors from the UW chemistry department signed a letter to McCarthy saying they "regret terribly your injuries and the deplorable manner in which you and other members of the force were treated by certain students." Local attorney John Fox, an old friend and golfing buddy, sent a jocular note with a hard message. "I am doubly surprised to see that somebody got close enough with a brick to use it on you. I imagine your old age must be causing a slowness in your reflexes," Fox wrote. "Seriously, Tom, I do want to stress my sincere appreciation for your performance as well as the other police officers in this fantastic flaunting of the law by the students. You and I have talked about this in the past and I am sure we both realized that sooner or later this day would come when absolute force would have to be applied in order to impress these people that law and order still must prevail in this city."

The captain of detectives called McCarthy into his office and asked, "Tom, what the hell were you doing *there?*"—meaning how did he end up at the Dow protest. McCarthy explained that he had tried to stay away but was recruited by Inspector Harrington to accompany him to Bascom Hill after the trouble started. "Well," said the captain, smiling, "I'm glad the detective bureau was represented."

This response reflected the swirl of contradictory feelings at the police department in Dow's aftermath. Was it an unmitigated disaster in which the cops were undermanned and overwhelmed, or was it a triumph of absolute force? The prevailing wisdom among the police was a bit of both. Chief Emery, while privately uncertain of the chain of events that sparked the violence, went public that Friday in defense of his officers. He told reporters that his men were "actually fighting for their lives" inside Commerce and that they were "overpowered" by an organized resistance the likes of which they had never seen before on the Wisconsin campus. "We were met by brute force that equaled, and at times exceeded, what we could use," Emery said. "Our use of force certainly wasn't planned or wanted. But our men had to protect themselves and restore order, and I'm proud of the way they did it." Emery's men, especially the thirty or so who had been in the wedge that assembled under the Carillon Tower and marched into Commerce, had not necessarily expected the violence, but many of them were proud of their part. They coined a nickname—the Dirty 30—that boastfully acknowledged their rough methods. The epithet stuck, and for years thereafter, some cops wore Dirty 30 patches on their jacket sleeves to denote that they had fought on the battlefield at Dow.

AS THE BUSES from Madison made the turn around Chicago, Dave Wheadon noticed out the window that they had joined a caravan of chartered coaches carrying citizens from the Midwest to the national rally. It was an exhilarating feeling, he thought, to be part of something larger. The atmosphere inside was all buzz, chatter, and debate. Kent Smith, a sophomore history major from the small town of Cornell near Eau Claire, was still forming his feelings about Vietnam. He had decided to make the trip after reading a leaflet handed out at Sellery Hall; traveling alone, he found himself surrounded by people who made him feel like "the most naïve person" there. To Smith the war seemed "fruitless, wrong and unwinnable," but now he was hearing more sophisticated and cynical explanations for why it was being fought, focusing on American economic imperialism. He listened in amazement as a passenger in the seat in front of him delivered a long, loud lecture about how the United States was in Vietnam not for the Vietnamese but for the profits of Coca-Cola and other American corporations.

By the time the bus caravan reached the Indiana Toll Road, the first of the weekend's protests was under way in Washington, with Yale's chaplain, the Reverend William Sloane Coffin, accompanied by Benjamin Spock, Norman Mailer, and a flock of antiwar notables, gathering on the steps of the Department of Justice. Judy Genack, whose plane had brought her to Washington in time for lunch, was in the audience alongside her new friend, the reporter Steve Matthews. She had never seen anything like this. Dr. Spock, the renowned pediatrician, was someone she had "never imagined could be an activist." And there stood Mailer and the poet Robert Lowell. These were serious people, she thought, real thinkers, different from the hippies and freaks she encountered on the Wisconsin campus. The potent mix of intellect, passion, fame, and mass action thrilled her. She immediately understood what Matthews had told her at lunch: how intoxicating it was to be at that place and time, covering history in the making.

Matthews took notes and Genack listened in awe as Coffin delivered the major speech before going inside to hand over a bundle of draft cards, most collected at rallies earlier in the week, plus some given up now by draft-age men in the crowd. "We cannot shield them. We can only expose ourselves as they have done," Coffin said of the young draft resisters. "We hereby counsel these young men to continue in their refusal to serve in the armed forces as long as the war in Vietnam continues, and we pledge ourselves to aid and abet them in all the ways we can. This means that if they are now arrested for failing to comply with a law that violates their consciences, we too must be arrested, for in the sight of the law we are now as guilty as they." When Coffin and his delegation stepped inside with a bag containing 994 draft cards, they were met not by Attorney General Clark, as he had expected, but by an assistant, who simply refused to accept the draft cards. Coffin dropped the bag on the floor and walked away, complaining that the assistant was "derelict in his duty" for refusing to accept evidence. Mailer, the social historian on the scene, noted "a contained anger in Coffin, much like lawyer's anger, as if some subtle game had been played in which a combination had been based on a gambit, but the government had refused the gambit, so now the combination was halted."

In fact the little drama unfolded precisely the way Clark had laid it out to President Johnson and the Cabinet two days earlier. Still, LBJ was enraged by the act of resistance. He read about the draft-card dumping episode on a wire service ticker stationed near his desk at the White House and was so distraught that he called over an aide, Joe Califano, to read it with him. As Califano later recounted the scene, Johnson "began jabbing at [the UPI report] with his finger" while ordering Califano to let Justice know that the president expected the FBI to investigate.

Early that evening Johnson gave two off-the-record interviews to friendly reporters, first Ernest B. Furgurson of the *Baltimore Sun,* who was writing a laudatory biography of General Westmoreland, then the columnist Joseph Alsop, who supported the war and detested the protesters and was ushered in when Johnson wanted to leak raw intelligence reports detailing the ribald sexuality or political recklessness of antiwar partisans. After Alsop left, Califano accompanied his boss to the White House residence, where two Texas congressmen and their wives were to be dinner guests. As they were sitting in the living quarters before dinner, Califano later wrote, "the president called General Hershey of the Selective Service and delivered a monologue about the need to punish draft protesters." At times LBJ seemed "infuriated," according to

his aide, "but at other times he seemed genuinely struggling to understand what could drive a young American to burn his draft card." His
dismay at the way the Justice Department handled the bagful of cards
seemed to match Reverend Coffin's. He complained to General Hershey
that he wanted to know "who the dumb sonofabitch was who would let
somebody leave a bunch of draft cards in front of the Justice Department and then let them just walk away."

If his attorney general would not act decisively enough against draft-
card burners and protesters disrupting the draft process, LBJ said, he
hoped that Hershey would.

. The old general would indeed act, six days later, by sending a letter
to local draft boards urging them to draft any young men who violated
draft laws or obstructed military recruiters. "I don't want any revenge. I
actually have a lot of confidence in the kids of this country," Hershey
would say, explaining the crackdown. "All I hope to do is to discourage
some of the excesses we have had in the past." Among the sharpest critics of this proposed policy would be Chancellor Sewell at the University
of Wisconsin. It had been twenty-five years since Sewell worked side by
side with Hershey in Washington, analyzing statistics for the wartime
draft, and he still had a soft spot in his heart for his former boss. But now
he would regard Hershey's induct-the-Vietnam-protesters threat as a
reactionary flouting of the First Amendment. It seemed to Sewell in that
autumn of 1967 that defending freedom of speech from attacks by the
left and right was nearly his full-time endeavor. His telegram to Hershey
would go unanswered but be made public, prompting conservatives on
the UW Board of Regents to call for his head, though eventually Sewell's
position would prevail, on the draft issue at least, with the Johnson administration backing away from the plan.

After finishing his long telephone conversation with Hershey that
night of the twentieth, Johnson retired for dinner with Lady Bird and
the Texas congressional couples, Jack Brooks and George Mahon and
their wives. His mind was still locked on the protests. He had considered
issuing a tough public statement, according to Califano, and had gone so
far as to dictate the first sentence but decided it would only bring more
heat his way. At dinner he mentioned the March on the Pentagon
planned for the next day and, as Califano recalled, "worried that 'Communist elements' would take advantage of the situation to 'make sure
that there will be trouble in the Negro ghetto.'" President Johnson
would not be run out of town—he had made that clear from the start—

but now he wondered aloud whether he should ring the White House perimeter with army troops.

IT WAS TWELVE HOURS LATER in Lai Khe, South Vietnam, and the next morning had already broken in sunlight. The men of the Second battalion, Twenty-eighth Infantry—all the Black Lions, including scores of new troops but minus the wounded still in hospitals at Long Binh— gathered outside battalion headquarters for a memorial service to honor the soldiers who died October 17. They lined up in formation: Alpha, Bravo, Charlie, Delta, Recon, Headquarters and Headquarters Company, with Louis Menetrey in command. The First Division brass were there, including Major General Hay and Brigadier General Coleman. There were some words about the brave fight and the great victory and the ultimate sacrifice, but the men were not listening. They stared straight ahead or bowed their heads, lost in thought.

In front of them stood a solitary pair of empty jungle boots, and behind the boots an M-16, bayoneted into the ground. Atop the rifle rested a dusty helmet. It could have been Danny Sikorski's, or Jack Schroder's, or Melesso Garcia's, or Pasquale Tizzio's: it covered all of the dead. In the shade of rubber trees a chaplain read a prayer, a squad of riflemen fired a twenty-one-gun salute, and a mournful bugler played taps. When it was over, Top Valdez, Doc Hinger, David Stroup, and a few others were called forward and pinned with Silver Stars for heroism during the battle, and then more soldiers were called and given Bronze Stars.

Hinger was mortified, not by the honor, but by the timing of the presentation. It was a "miserable, miserable thing," he thought, for those who lived to be given medals at a memorial ceremony such as this. *Some of them died. Some of them were not allowed to.*

Captain Cash was in Lai Khe that day, conducting more interviews for his investigation of the battle. He carried a bulky cassette tape recorder and a notepad and interviewed soldiers individually, scratching names from his list one by one. Giannico. Hinger. Jensen. Phillips. Stephens. Stroup. Troyer. Woodard. Each man's description of the battle was different, conveying only the microcosm of what he saw, but there were places where the stories connected. One thread that wove through the interviews was an overwhelming sense of chaos early in the battle. Was this the usual fog of war or something more? The soldiers, whether in Alpha or Delta, talked about how hard it had been to know where the other friendly forces were. Should they return fire or cease fire? Were they shooting at the enemy or their own side? If the surprise attack gave the Viet Cong fire superiority at the start, the confusion about battlefield positioning helped them maintain it. Some soldiers said they anticipated trouble that morning, but none expected to be defeated. They marched into the jungle with the sensibility that the Black Lions intimidated the Viet Cong and could not lose. It was not until the battle was under way that they realized otherwise.

Defeats can be caused by troop fatigue, poor morale, inferior weaponry, poor training, a lack of preparation, but in this case Cash's interviews indicated that none of those factors was decisive. The information he gathered pointed in other directions, toward mistakes in tactics and communications that allowed the battalion to be surprised, surrounded, and badly outmanned. Terry Allen, as the battalion commander, had to absorb much of the blame. He took even more than he might have deserved because he was dead and could not defend himself or explain away points of contention the way his superior officers were able to do.

As the day progressed, Cash jotted down a preliminary list of lessons learned and other themes he picked up among the "scuttlebutt and complaints" from Delta soldiers:

1) We knew they were there and their general location. Air and artillery should have been used a lot more before we went in, to disrupt their organization, etc. . . . The artillery that preceded us on 17 October amounted to nothing.
2) The companies were nowhere near their normal combat strengths, or what they are expected to be.
3) The smoke located our center of mass to any VC. Smoke can be seen hundreds of meters away. It also obscured our vision. Most of the smoke was coming from the battalion CP [command post]. There was definitely too much smoke used.
4) Personally, I don't believe the battalion commander belongs with the men on the ground.
5) Bn CO [Allen] goofed. He should have let us pull back after we'd retrieved A Co's wounded for them. Instead, we waited around for 40 minutes and that gave Charlie time to horseshoe us and zap us.
6) No mortars were fired at all. I heard the mort. Plat. sgt say "we were aching to go. I've still got it plotted on my board what we

could have done. It's a damned shame." Mortars had been used very effectively by Lt. Welch the day before. On that day they fired mortars constantly on both sides going out there.

At division headquarters Brigadier General Coleman, who had watched the disaster unfold on the seventeenth, outlined his own summary of lessons learned. His intent was not to assess blame but rather to assure that such a disaster would not happen again, yet his long list unavoidably served as a catalog of battlefield mistakes. Among his lessons were: never withdraw leaving wounded; stress to all leaders the proper tactics of conducting a withdrawal; establish a positive succession of command through fire team level; provide backup RTOs and security forces for command groups; designate key individuals to carry red smoke to mark positions of enemy contact; strive for accurate and timely reporting at all levels; improve accuracy and content of journals and logs and perhaps use tape recorders on command [radio] nets; provide workable chainsaws, axes, and machetes in NDP ready for chopper delivery; and at division headquarters record the location of all jungle litters and plastic bags for the dead so they can be delivered to the field as necessary.

There was no mention in Coleman's list of the lesson that ranking officers in helicopters should think twice before check-firing artillery against the advice of commanders on the ground.

At the Twenty-fourth Evacuation Hospital Jim George was still reliving the battle in his sleep. He could hear the gunfire and smell the cordite and hear guys yelling "I'm hit!" over and over again.

Three months earlier, in one of the letters he had written home to Jackie from aboard the USNS *Pope,* he had told her that he would try to be a good soldier, gentleman, lover, and Christian, but now he was struggling with all but the last of those. He thought he had been fighting in a just war, that he had done the best he could and was following orders, but the nightmares persisted. In some ways he felt that he had let his soldiers down, because although he had told them that they "needed to kill as many Viet Cong as they could," he thought his major mission was to get them home safely, and it was hard for him to comprehend the number of casualties. The wounded Alpha captain was overcome by what he called "a powerful love for God and for the soldiers" but had a harder time feeling love for his wife and kids. He knew that he loved them, but the trauma of the devastating event had temporarily diminished his capacity to feel strongly about many things. "Each day's light brings with it more hope, trust & humanity," he wrote to Jackie. "I feel better today. Still haven't had a good night's sleep but that scar will take longer to heal. I finally went to sleep at about 3 this morning. I prayed myself to sleep."

Late that afternoon Major General Hay traveled down to the evacuation hospitals to visit the wounded and hand out more medals. An aide came through the recovery ward ahead of time and briefed Joe Costello, who was to receive a Silver Star. *When they ask your age, make it older than eighteen,* he instructed the young Alpha grenadier from Long Island who had turned around during the retreat in the jungle and helped save soldiers left behind. "Don't give us any grief on that," the aide said.

Costello was unaware until then of a controversy involving the number of eighteen-year-olds getting wounded and killed in Vietnam. When Hay came in with a press entourage, Costello said he was nineteen. "I understand you did a great job out there," Hay said to him. "I want to present you with this Silver Star. You earned it." Before leaving, Hay added, "If there's anything I can do for you, soldier, now or in the future, I want to know about it."

There had been a time, Costello remembered, when he had a chance to get out of the field by volunteering for a clerk's job but didn't because he was not sure that he could type fast enough. That was not going to happen again, he said to himself now.

"Sir, there is," he found himself saying to General Hay. "You can give me some other sort of job. I don't mind working hard, but I saw a lot of my friends go down the other day and I'd like not to see that again."

Hay glanced at an aide, who was taking notes. "Okay," the general said, and moved on to the next bed.

SOMEWHERE IN OHIO the excited conversations lapsed into silence, and by two in the morning, as the peace buses negotiated the darkened mountain curves of the Pennsylvania Turnpike, most of the passengers were asleep. Dave Wheadon, seated near the driver, glanced at the speedometer and blanched at how fast they were going. The buses reached Washington at Saturday dawn and stopped near the Washington Monument. They were all on their own now until the marching was over, with instructions to regroup that night in the parking lot of a Marriott hotel in Arlington, where they would find the buses for the long ride back to Madison.

Steiner and her friends roamed the Mall in the morning sunlight. Wheadon helped people unload protest signs and banners from trucks, then rested under a tree, where his picture was taken by a London newspaper and he was interviewed by a local radio station. He was wearing his finest black linen coat, believing that he should contribute a mature presence to the vibrant scene. Kent Smith crossed the river to Virginia and strolled through Arlington National Cemetery until he found the eternal flame at the gravesite of John F. Kennedy. Jonathan Lipp, a senior at Madison Memorial and, like Steiner, a member of Students for Social Justice, was picked up by prearrangement and driven to someone's house in a vehicle that disoriented him. He expected it to be "a hippie van," but instead they rode in "this very Republican-looking" Ford Galaxy rental car, which struck him as odd because he looked at the world as "the establishment versus everyone else" and the car was "such an establishment thing." After breakfast at Matthews's house, Judy Genack went to Union Station, where she met three friends who had taken the train from Chicago, then walked toward the Mall, past the museums toward the Washington Monument and the Reflecting Pool, disappearing into "the sea of humanity."

The scene was friendly and serious, Genack thought, teeming with people who were there because they cared about their country. In that moment she felt more connected to America than she ever had before. Mike Oberdorfer was feeling something different. He had arrived on the Mall that morning from his mother's house in Bethesda after attending a Friday night gathering of alternative newspaper journalists from New York, Chicago, San Francisco, Berkeley, Boston, Madison, and other seedbeds of the counterculture who had been drawn to Washington for the march. It was a sweet, sun-splashed Indian summer day, but Oberdorfer was not interested in good sensations or mere expressions of solidarity. He thought this was going to be another event like Dow, with massive resistance against the authorities. Those who wanted to stop the war, he believed, now had to be single-minded in that effort and play with a new set of rules.

Two days earlier, in reporting to President Johnson and the Cabinet, Attorney General Clark had estimated from FBI reports that fewer than thirty thousand protesters would attend the rally, but now perhaps four times that number were assembling below the Lincoln Memorial. Here was the typical wide array of American dissent: all ages (though mostly students), moderates and radicals, flower children and hippies and businessmen and mothers and ministers, Marxist-Leninists, socialists, Trotskyites, liberals, Quakers, believers in nonviolence and adherents of physical resistance. To many the war had taken a great nation in the wrong direction; to others it was their own government that had become the enemy. Che Guevara's romanticized visage as the beret-wearing revolutionary martyr could be seen bobbing up and down on posters scattered amid the masses, near signs that read "LBJ the Butcher" and "Beat Army." It was President Johnson, Dr. Spock told the crowd, "who has stubbornly led us deeper and deeper into a bloody quagmire in which uncounted hundreds of thousands of Vietnamese men, women, and children have died—and thirteen thousand young Americans."

A mile away at the White House, LBJ and his men continued their "business as usual" performance, more show than reality. George Christian, the press secretary, later acknowledged that the place was enveloped by "the feeling of siege." For the second day in a row, Johnson hosted Laos's Souvanna Phouma for lunch. As the meal ended, the president called his secretary, Juanita Roberts, "and asked if there was any news he should know about—concerning the Anti-War demonstrations taking place in the District," as the scene was recorded in the White House Daily Diary. "Juanita told him no news other than what had already been given him." At about that time at the rally David Dellinger, the old radical, was predicting that the event marked the "beginning of a new stage in the American peace movement in which the cutting edge becomes active resistance."

At the University of Wisconsin the cutting edge of resistance had been met by the thump of police clubs earlier that week. Now, at the same time that the rally in Washington was unfolding, about two thousand antiwar protesters who had stayed in Madison were turning away from the tactic of physical resistance, instead filing out of the Library Mall to participate in a "funeral procession" up State Street. The decision to hold a peaceful march to the Capitol had been announced the day before, but it nonetheless provoked a two-hour debate beforehand on this Saturday morning. The student activists leading the rally, including Paul Soglin and Ira Shor, a senior from the Bronx, had urged the group to partake in another act of resistance and march up the hill and occupy Bascom Hall. The fact that it was a weekend and the doors might be locked was an obstacle that could be overcome easily, since several teaching assistants had keys to the building. Some sympathetic faculty members strongly opposed that idea and thought even the march up State

Street would be too dangerous. They recommended holding another afternoon of discussions about the war.

That idea was dismissed by the crowd without a vote, rejected with shouts from the crowd of "No guts!" and "Out of order!" A vote was held on the other two alternatives, and rather than count hands or use a voice vote, Soglin and Shor, standing atop the balustrade of the State Historical Society, asked the participants to divide, one side for the sit-in, another side for the march. The vote was "incredibly close," Soglin said later. "Ira and I kind of huddled on the thing for a minute or two, seeing if we both had the same impression, and we were both pretty sure that the crowd that wanted to go up State Street was a little larger than those that sat in." Jane Brotman, among the tenderfoot protesters, voted with the moderate majority.

They wore black armbands and marched single file or in pairs up the sidewalks on both sides of the street, forming a long ribbon of orderly protest that trailed back six blocks. Along the way they passed football fans in town for the Iowa game who were spilling out of bars and restaurants and walking in the other direction, toward Camp Randall Stadium. "Go back to New York!" some shouted. The provincial sensibility that the turmoil on campus was caused by out-of-state students seemed stronger than ever in the aftermath of Dow. When the marchers reached the State Street entrance to the Capitol, they sat down in rows on the cement path. Soglin and Shor walked up the steps and taped a set of demands to the statehouse door: No police or military recruiters on campus. Amnesty for the protest leaders. "We are speaking today to the slogan of police brutality," Soglin told the crowd. "But this is merely a symbol of a society that has tried to ignore the fact that there are serious wounds in all parts of its body." The movement, he added, needed to increase its numbers to "be sure that our legitimate grievances and demands be heard." The protest ended as quietly as it began.

In Washington the speeches at the Lincoln Memorial were ending and part of the huge throng now rumbled south across the Arlington Memorial Bridge to "confront the warmakers" and encircle the evil Pentagon. Leading the way was a brigade of a few hundred radicals who were sympathetic to the other side in the Vietnam war, marching under the red, blue, and gold banner of the National Liberation Front, a posture that infuriated antiwar moderates from mainstream peace organizations. Bands of resistance-oriented activists were scattered about, some in organized units, some congealing extemporaneously, all determined to breach the security ring of bayonet-carrying soldiers and get arrested, but most of the protesters were less confrontational. It took more than three hours for fifty thousand demonstrators to cross the bridge. Mike Oberdorfer was about a third of the way back. Once he reached the other side and saw a few thousand soldiers with bayonets on their rifles, he realized that this was not going to be another Dow. There was no way demonstrators could reach the Pentagon with the army in the way.

Many of those in the rear of the line had no idea what was going on up front. Judy Genack was back there, overcome by the experience. It reminded her of the day that summer in Jerusalem, after the Six-Day War ended, when she had awakened at four in the morning and gone with a cousin to participate in the massive Shavuot holiday pilgrimage to the Western Wall of the Temple Mount, which had been liberated by Israeli parachutists. She had felt so calm that day, one individual among a quarter-million, weaving through the Old City on the way to the wall to pray. And she felt that way again now, marching with other Americans across the bridge toward the Pentagon. As distinct as the two events were, they had the same "unifying" effect on her. Judy Genack did not feel insignificant, her voice too soft for the world. She felt strong, her voice amplified by the realization that she was "thinking and feeling what thousands of other people were thinking and feeling."

The government, in issuing permits for the demonstration, had corralled the protesters into two assembly areas on the Virginia side of the Potomac: a large grassy triangle below the Pentagon and the massive structure's north parking lot. Protesters who broke free of the perimeter and tried to storm the Pentagon were arrested. Hour by hour that afternoon there were thrusts and skirmishes. Two thousand storming from one end, three thousand from another, all repulsed. The sweet autumn air soured with the sting of tear gas. There were taunts, songs, curses, whispers, eggs and bottles tossed, students thrown to the ground and roughed up by wedges of U.S. marshals, scores of protesters suffering minor to moderate injuries, ten soldiers and thirteen marshals among the injured as well; 681 people were arrested before it was over, Norman Mailer among the first, charged with the technical violation of crossing a police line and hauled to a corrections center in Occoquan fifteen miles away, where he spent the night in a jail cell with the linguist Noam Chomsky.

Secretary McNamara watched much of it from his office window, feeling what he later described as an odd mix of terror and exasperation. He was frightened by the mob yet could not help critiquing the tactics of the peace crowd. They did it all wrong, he thought. Had he been in charge, he would have imposed some discipline, and with Gandhi-like peaceful civil disobedience "shut down the whole goddamn place."

In the swarm below, Abbie Hoffman, the hippie pied piper, tripping on LSD and wearing an Uncle Sam hat, was feeling what he would later call "a sense of integration" for pissing on the Pentagon—"combining biological necessity with emotional feeling." His flower brigade was try-ing to ring the building in an effort to levitate it and rid it of evil spirits:

> Ring around the Pentagon, a pocket full of pot
> Four and twenty generals, all begin to rot.
> All the evil spirits start to tumble out
> Now the war is over, we all begin to shout.

Alison Steiner, a face in the crowd, watched young men and women dance up to soldiers and stick flowers in their gun barrels. She knew that some in the antiwar movement believed that "those who didn't resist were doing something wicked," but she did not feel that way herself. There was a banner that said "Bring All the GI's Home" and that is how she felt; the war should end to save everyone, including them. Jonathan Lipp started out the day thinking of the soldiers as the enemy. The Madison Memorial senior stood in the crowd taunting them, calling them "monsters and baby killers and all that stuff." But as he looked into their eyes, he realized that they were his peers, only a year or two older. Some of them were afraid, even crying. He watched a sergeant pull a shaky young soldier out of line and replace him with a new face. He had never thought of soldiers as people before, but it all changed in that mo-ment. They were victims too, he suddenly realized. They all were vic-tims. Lipp walked away not sure whom he was angry at anymore.

He was not arrested, nor was Oberdorfer or anyone else from Madi-son. Kent Smith, carrying a small Instamatic camera, took pictures of the soldiers and Pentagon officials atop the building. On the way back to the departure area Alison Steiner "bopped into the Marriott" to wash her face and saw a group of black protesters having a hard time getting into the establishment, a scene that would stick in her memory. There were hundreds of buses in the parking lot, and trying to find the right one in the darkness was "sort of a scary feeling; you didn't know where you were," Kent Smith thought. Sojourners from the Madison group who found the buses early built a campfire and sang protest songs and passed around different buttons and posters they had collected during the day. The coaches were quiet on the way home. Steiner quickly fell into a deep sleep and dreamed a satisfying dream of fireworks, kaleidoscopic explosions not of warfare but of wonder and joy, like the ones she saw in her Madison childhood on the Fourth of July at the Vilas Park Zoo.

IT WAS WELL INTO Sunday the twenty-second in Vietnam by then. After lunch with his top aides and a conference with South Vietnamese generals in Saigon, General Westmoreland left for Long Binh to visit the evacuation hospitals. His wife, Kitsy, had been a frequent visitor to the Twenty-fourth and Ninety-third in 1967, but this was his first appearance. Charlton Heston, Robert Mitchum, Chuck Connors, Henry Fonda, James Garner, Ephrem Zimbalist Jr., Lana Turner, Ann Landers, Billy Graham, the cast of *Peyton Place,* the actresses Ina Balin and Ann B. Davis, the singers Tina Latin, Joy Eilers, Mary Grover, Susie Chandler, the Rolling Souls, and Dr. James Cain, personal physician to President Johnson—all had visited the hospitals that year before Westmoreland. He came to see the wounded Black Lions.

At four that afternoon his chopper landed on the helipad. It was supposed to be a surprise visit, but the staff knew he was coming. The greeting party included Colonel Jackson Walker, commander of the Ninety-third; P. Evangeline Jamison, the chief nurse, who in her pocket still carried the large pair of scissors she had used to cut open the uniforms of the wounded soldiers; chaplain Bill Wells, who wore a baseball cap with a cross on the brim; and several surgeons. On the way down the covered walkway toward the hospital wards, Westmoreland ducked his head into the first room and asked, "What's in here?" The clerks and orderlies inside were surprised to see the MACV commander and a cordon of staff officers staring at them. Gerard Cygan, a nurse anesthetist, remembered one detail above all others—the fine silk blue lining inside Westmoreland's green baseball cap. Elizabeth Finn, who had joined the U.S. Army Nurses Corps after serving in the religious community at the

Sisters of Charity of Nazareth in Louisville for eighteen years, was struck once again by how "when the generals came around their uniforms were all starched and ironed and had a pleat—they didn't look like they had been in the same country."

The protocol for the visit called for doctors from each wing to stand outside the quonset huts of their wards and greet Westmoreland as he arrived. Chaplain Wells stayed near the general's side, following him down one wing and back the other side. "In one ward we got up to the nurses' station in the center, and before anyone could steer the general to the left, he went to the wing on the right, which was the urology wing," Wells recalled. They approached the first bed, where "a skinny young private was resting on his back."

"What happened to you, son?" Westmoreland asked.

The soldier, mortified, stammered out his answer. "I . . . I . . . was circumcised, sir." Circumcisions were occasionally necessary for men with venereal diseases.

"Well, you don't get a Purple Heart for that!" Westmoreland said gruffly and turned on his heel and marched away.

He was there only to give out Purple Hearts. "Medical wards! I don't want to see medical wards," Westmoreland announced. "I don't want to see those fakers."

The remark stunned Phil Eastman, an army doctor drafted out of his second year of residency at Montefiore Hospital in New York. Eastman now worked in the Ninety-third's medical ward and his patients were anything but fakers, he thought. He made a mental note of the soldiers he had treated that day. There was the case of Japanese B encephalitis, a severe infection with high fever that could cause permanent brain damage, leaving a patient with an IQ of eighty. There was the army truck driver with meliodosis, a severe pneumonia contracted when the soldier had been part of a convoy that rolled across a dry river bed after a bridge had been blown up, raising a dust storm that caused his infection. And there was the patient with cerebral malaria, a virulent form of falciparum malaria, which unlike the more common vivax malaria was prevalent in North Vietnam and resistant to the pills passed out by the U.S. military. This cerebral malaria, Eastman thought, could have been passed along by mosquitoes in areas with close combat between American and North Vietnamese soldiers. These were serious conditions that were in no way the soldiers' fault, Eastman thought. Westmoreland's offhand comment upset him greatly. It also infuriated the medical ward nurses. "He said they were goldbricking," said Elizabeth Finn. "Some of these men were sick as dogs."

In the recovery ward at last, Westmoreland moved down the row of men, pinning Purple Hearts.

"I just want to congratulate you," he said to Bud Barrow, the Delta first sergeant.

"Well, I'm not sure whether you oughta congratulate me or the enemy," Barrow responded. "They're the ones who won that one." His mind raced back to the seventeenth, the denseness of the jungle floor, the Viet Cong shooting from the trees, the terror of being out there, the grief of losing so many of his boys.

Westmoreland pinned a Purple Heart on Barrow's pajamas and said, "Tell me, sergeant. What happened out there?"

"Well sir, we walked into one of the damnedest ambushes you ever seen," Barrow said.

"Oh, no, no, no," Westmoreland replied briskly. "That was no ambush."

"Call it what you want to," Barrow said. The combination of his wounds, the medication, and all he had been through allowed him to speak more bluntly to a general than he would have normally. "I don't know what happened to the rest of the people, but, by God, I was ambushed."

Next came Clark Welch, the Delta commander. Shoes clicked, papers ruffled. Westmoreland pinned a medal and said a few words. They propped up Welch with pillows and snapped pictures of the brave lieutenant and the crisp general. Westmoreland moved on, but his staff aide, a marine major, lingered and asked Welch a question about the battle.

Welch was barely conscious, his thoughts uncensored. He had survived, but the idealism that buoyed him during the early days of forming Delta Company died that day in the Long Nguyen Secret Zone.

Things were totally fucked up, he told the major, as he lay wounded in the hospital bed, his arms and chest wrapped in bandages.

You could try to do everything right, but things were as fucked up as they could be.

Everything was fucked up, from the battalion commander up through the President of the United States. As fucked up as anything he had ever seen. Colonel Allen, even if he was the son of a famous general, was fucked up. The operations officer was fucked up. The entire operation was fucked up. They shouldn't have gone out there like that. They should have had more air support beforehand. They shouldn't have check-fired the artillery. They should have let him fire his mortars.

Just a fuckup from beginning to end, a fuckup that killed Terry Allen and left Danny Sikorski and Jack Schroder and a lot of other young men dead.

A fuckup is what Clark Welch said to the major. He had never felt quite that way before, but it came spilling out of him on that Sunday in Long Binh, feelings that would linger for decades.

On the way out of the hospital Westmoreland passed through the admitting lobby. Peter Miller, another Delta rifleman, the kid drafted out of the Procter & Gamble soap factory in Quincy, Massachusetts, was there. He had just been flown down from Lai Khe, where he had collapsed with a high temperature four days after the battle. He had taken five steps and just fallen flat on his face. He thought it was an infection from an arm wound, but in fact it was malaria. He was so weak that he could barely stand when Westmoreland and his entourage strode by. Salutes were snapped. Miller did not know that Westmoreland might have regarded him as a faker.

After Westmoreland left, Clark Welch wrote home to Lacy for the first time since the battle. Until then he had been too weak to write. He tried to keep his darkest thoughts from her. "My Lacy," he began. "I've been getting your letters right along, and they've really kept me going."

> As you can see, I don't have my own writing
> material: in fact I don't have my own any-
> thing—except your letters. I love you, Lacy.
> I've been on a pretty full schedule since I
> came to the hospital, but now I think I've
> got a pretty good idea what I have to have
> done and what I have to do myself. The two
> machine gun bullets in my left arm took out
> a lot of muscle—that's what concerns the
> doctors. The shrapnel in my back and hands
> & face is no trouble at all. All they did was
> just get it out. There won't even be any scars
> on my hands or face and just a few stitches

in my back. I've been in the O.R. three times
and now they say once more tomorrow
morning, then I'll go to another hospital for
whatever's required. Most of the men with
wounds like mine have been sent to Japan.

After saying that he still hoped he could meet Lacy in Hawaii for R
and R in January, Welch turned to the battle. He had been reading about
it for two days in *Stars and Stripes,* he said, but barely recognized what he
was reading. "So many of our leaders were lost in the action . . . that the
story that does get out has really been distorted." So distorted that the stories did not mention Delta Company at all. "You wouldn't believe the
number of generals, to include Westmoreland, that have been here to see
us. It was a hell of a battle, Lacy, the worst thing that I ever want to see."

In the hospital there was talk of medals earned during the battle.
Welch had heard he was being put in for a Distinguished Service Cross.
"I've thought a lot about medals and I've written to you about them," he
wrote.

It was all over on the 17th. Each man knows
what he did, that's what counts. And I
know what my company did. They did
good. I wish it didn't have to be my men
here in the hospital and going home for
good but we handled it better than anyone
else could have—there were just too many.
I thought I had a pretty good idea of what
"battle" is, but there's nothing like what my
men went through. No man should have to
go through what we were in. If it had to be
done, though, my men did it better than
anyone else could have. There were men
that ran, and men that shot themselves but I
just feel sorry for them. They were just
normal men that reacted normally. All the
others were exceptional, far above what we
have any right to expect from a man.
They're just good men, Lacy, and now most
of them are out. . . . All these men should

> have big signs on them so they could have
> anything they want the rest of their lives.

Welch's fellow company commander, Jim George, in a moment of brutal honesty, realized that during those first few days in the hospital his heart was so focused on God and his soldiers that he barely had room for his wife and sons. Welch told Lacy that he could not have made it through without her.

> I love you Lacy. It looks silly to just see it
> written out there. I remember the second
> time I was hit and couldn't get up or talk or
> do anything anymore. For a second I just
> wanted to be home with my Lacy to take
> care of me. Just to be home, that's what was
> inside me all the time. I love you, Lacy. Tell
> our boys their Dad did the best he could and
> that was all I could do—there were just too
> many of them and too much fire.

IN HANOI THAT VERY AFTERNOON readers of the leading military and political newspapers were learning of both the death of Terry Allen and the Dow protest at the University of Wisconsin. As portrayed by the journals of the North, these events were two signs among many that things were turning their way that October.

The bottom of the front page of the *People's Central Organ of the Vietnam Labor Party* carried a major article about the demonstrations in America under the headline "Supporting Solidarity Day with the Vietnamese People. Tens of Thousands of American Youth Continue to Demonstrate against the Draft and Opposing the War of Aggression in Vietnam. Students of Many American Universities Refuse to Go to Class." It began: "According to all the western news agencies, the closer one got to 21 October, the day the American people organized before the presidential palace [White House] and American Defense Department [Pentagon] a giant demonstration demanding America to terminate the war of aggression in Vietnam, the momentum of indignation of the American people against the American war became more seething and more fierce."

The article recounted the demonstrations against the draft at the Oakland induction center at the start of the week, where students were said to be "defying the savage terrorism of the gang holding power." On the nineteenth of October, the report continued, "more than five thousand students at the University of Wisconsin [Uy-xcon-xin] boycotted in opposition to the board of regents expelling thirteen students after a demonstration on the eighteenth of October of about two thousand students of this school opposing the enemy representative of Dow Chemical Company [cong ty hoa chat Dao] coming to the school to recruit students to come in and work at this company, being a place specializing in producing napalm [na-pan] bombs for the American aggressive gang to use in Vietnam."

The article went on to say that in Washington "the national student committee issued a proclamation supporting the struggle of the University of Wisconsin students. Panic-stricken before the seething struggle of the American people in the previous days, the Johnson group hurriedly had two airplanes bring a unit of the 82nd Airborne division from their base at Fort Bragg in North Carolina state to Washington in order to defend the ministry of defense headquarters."

The official newspaper of the People's Army of Vietnam, *People's Army,* meanwhile, was publishing the first reports in Hanoi of the ambush that Triet's First Regiment had staged on the seventeenth. The article located the battle at Thu Dau Mot, a provincial place name used by the North Vietnamese and Viet Cong to describe an area near the Long Nguyen Secret Zone:

> On the seventeenth of October, the liberation army stopped and fiercely attacked one American battalion of the First Infantry Division about sixty-six kilometers north of Saigon. Providing information about this battle, the UPI wrote that at least fifty-eight people were killed and sixty-one people were seriously wounded in the terrible battle which broke out at 9:50 in the morning of 17 October and continued until almost nightfall. Among those dead were one battalion commander . . . and an important staff officer. This battalion leader crook is the Lieutenant Colonel crook Terry Allen [to-ri an-len], the son of the American crook general crook Allen who formerly commanded the American First Infantry Division in Europe in the second great war. The important general staff officer crook was the crook Major Holleder [Ho-li-do], the

staff officer of the brigade which follows this battalion. The sergeant crook Valdez [van-de-da], still living after the battle spoken
of above, said this: "The enemy arranged themselves to await us
like a cat preparing to pounce out and grab a mouse."

As these reports from Vietnam and America were being hailed
throughout North Vietnam that Sunday, the Politburo was meeting in
Hanoi. This was the midpoint of a critical five-day session, the culmination of ten months of strategic planning that had begun in the first days
of 1967 when General Nguyen Chi Thanh had returned to Hanoi from
the southern jungles and broached the idea of mounting a massive surprise attack on every province of South Vietnam during a holiday. Several military leaders, most notably Vo Nguyen Giap, the national hero,
were skeptical of the idea, fearing that it was premature and would
prove too costly in manpower. But month by month since then the design had taken shape. In April the Politburo and the Central Military
Party Committee dispatched cadres to the battlefields of the South to analyze the military situation and prepare the forces for an offensive. In
June the Politburo approved a resolution underlining its strategic resolve to "achieve decisive victory within a relatively short period of
time"—meaning sometime in 1968. In July the General Staff briefed the
Politburo on plans to use urban warfare to launch a general offensive
uprising in the southern cities and towns. The effort only intensified in
the months after the death of Nguyen Chi Thanh that July. They reorganized the military and political structure in Saigon and its surrounding provinces and improved the combat readiness of troops in the South,
who had increased in number from 204,000 to 278,000 since the beginning of the year and from 126 combat battalions to 190.

Now the Politburo was laying final plans. The military committee
presented the potential problems first. Even if they successfully assaulted
every city and town in the South, they would not have the strength to
hold them. And their overall capacity to launch annihilating attacks was
"still weak." Still, it was believed that "the strategic opportunity had presented itself" and had to be seized. The United States was "still obsti-
nate" but facing more isolation in the world and opposition at home.
And Westmoreland and his generals seemed oddly distracted, obsessed
with the idea that the North was planning another Dien Bien Phu–style
siege somewhere. What the Vietnamese lacked in weaponry, they would
make up for in surprise. The Politburo decided to launch the surprise

offensive even sooner than originally planned. They would strike during Tet Mau Than, the national holiday, at the end of January 1968.

WHEN SUNDAY, OCTOBER 22, arrived in Washington, President Johnson received an early morning briefing on the demonstrations from Joe Califano, then ate breakfast in the White House residence with Lady Bird. At 9:23, after placing a call to Dale Malechek, the foreman of his ranch in the Hill Country of Texas, he went with the first lady and their daughter Lynda to the East Wing exit, where they slipped into the presidential limousine and were driven out past the security ring of soldiers and on toward National City Christian Church. His city was swarming with people who hated him. Even as the president was making his way up the steps of the church, someone in the back of a city bus moving down the street shouted out "Stop the war!" But inside Lyndon Johnson found a sanctuary. The minister, Dr. George R. Davis, was on his side. "There are greater torches by far than the torch of peace," Davis said, referring literally to a peace torch that had been carried to the rally from San Francisco. "The torch of human freedom, and of human dignity."

On the ride back from church, Johnson asked his family if they would like to swing over to the Pentagon to see what was going on. From his morning updates, LBJ knew that most of the protesters had left, but there were still bands of demonstrators roaming the Mall. Several hundred remained encamped near the Pentagon, where they intended to stay. Lady Bird and Lynda agreed, and the little side trip, seen through the eyes of a Secret Service agent, was recorded in the *White House Daily Diary.* "At the Lincoln Memorial, it looked like there were about 150 people sitting on the steps—just scattered around the area. We drove around the memorial one and one-half times—looked at the Mall area and the Reflecting Pool area. Mrs. Johnson particularly noticed the litter and refuse left by those gathered at the memorial yesterday. The president was highly interested in what a hippie looked like, their dress, age groups, and items they carried . . . some were carrying flags, bed rolls, blankets, flight bags, flowers. . . . We then drove across the Memorial Bridge and turned down Shirley Highway—the road was blocked, but we told the Park Policeman we were Secret Service and they let us through. We went around the blockade and up the highway, looking to the right and left—right up to the line of soldiers guarding the highway. We drove slowly, and looked carefully at the Mall entrance of the Pentagon. We circled around, crossed the median strip, and then drove back to the White House."

The peace buses pulled up outside the Memorial Union in Madison at that same hour, after the long overnight drive from Washington. Alison Steiner's mother was waiting to pick her up. The high school senior was exhausted but felt that she had accomplished something. She had said what she had wanted to say. Judy Genack had also returned to Madison, transformed politically and personally by the events of that tumultuous week. What she had seen outside the Commerce Building had compelled her to go to Washington, which had led her to stay at the house of the young journalist, Steve Matthews, who was to become her husband a year later.

There was another rally on campus that Sunday afternoon, a silent vigil on Bascom Hill attended by three hundred students. Later, on the Library Mall, they held another vote and decided to call off the class boycott, which was fizzling in any case. Paul Soglin had resigned as chairman of the Committee on Student Rights. He was upset by the emphasis on police brutality rather than on the war itself, felt caught between moderates and radicals, and thought it was important for students to connect with the outside community, positions that would become only more his own as time went on. It was at that moment that Soglin intensified his political plans and started building the base that would see him elected alderman the following spring and mayor within six years.

The events of that one week in October had changed things, indisputably, but the political implications of that change appeared contradictory. In that sense Wisconsin paralleled the nation. The number of people who now counted themselves in the antiwar movement was increasing, yet also growing was public disdain for confrontational demonstrations.

The conservative backlash involved more than a few veterans organizations and right-wingers in the state legislature. In the aftermath of the bloodshed at Commerce, the Dow Chemical Company announced that a record number of students—at least one hundred and fifty—signed up for later interviews. The university chapter of Young Americans for Freedom also grew to record numbers under the leadership of its Madison-based national chairman, David Keene. Typical of the new recruits was Richard Swearingen, a sophomore who had stood in the crowd outside Commerce and watched Miss Sifting and Winnowing prance in front of him. Swearingen thought the police had gone too far but was more turned off by what he took to be the heedless belligerence of the protesters. He became vice chairman of the local YAF that fall, until his politics shifted back toward the middle again after the assassinations of Martin Luther King Jr. and Robert F. Kennedy in the spring of 1968. Another sign of the conservative reaction was the arrival on campus of the *Badger Herald,* which served as a right-leaning alternative to the leftish *Cardinal* and eventually overtook the *Cardinal* in circulation. The *Herald* was founded by an ally of Keene's in YAF, Patrick Korten (later spokesman for the U.S. Department of Justice during the Reagan era) with behind-the-scenes backing from editors at *Reader's Digest.*

On the national level a Harris survey in the aftermath of that tumultuous week showed the crosscurrents of dissent and reaction. According to the survey 59 percent of the public estimated that "sentiment against the war is rising" and an equal percentage said that "people have the right to feel that way." But those who believed that opponents of the war had the right to demonstrate declined that fall from 61 percent to 54 percent. More than three-fourths of those polled said they felt recent anti-Vietnam demonstrations encouraged the enemy "to fight all the harder." More than two-thirds thought the demonstrations were "acts of disloyalty against the boys in Vietnam." And seven in ten believed the recent demonstrations only hurt the cause of opposing the war.

"THIS WAS A SAD and brooding city Sunday night because everybody seemed to have lost in the anti-war siege of the Pentagon this weekend," James Reston wrote afterward in the *New York Times,* voicing the moderate liberal sentiment. "The majority of the demonstrators who marched peaceably and solemnly to the banks of the Potomac were unhappy because the event was taken over by the militant minority. The leading officials of the government were troubled by the spectacle of so tumultuous a protest against their policy in Vietnam and by the repercussions of this demonstration on their relations abroad."

The weekend of dissent, like much of what he dealt with that October, had indeed left President Johnson only more pessimistic. On the afternoon of Monday, October 23, when the last protesters had left town, he met with his war council for two hours, lamenting his elusive search for answers to his Vietnam dilemma.

"It doesn't seem we can win the war militarily," Johnson told McNa-

mara and Rusk. Then he complained that when he asked the Joint
Chiefs for suggestions on how to shorten the war, all they talked about
were things to do outside South Vietnam.

"We can't win diplomatically either," he said. The Kissinger negotiations had reached a dead end. All that could be done now, he suggested,
was to leak news of their effort so the public would know they had
"tried and failed after going the very last mile."

He could feel it all slipping away. "We've almost lost the war in the
last two months in the court of public opinion," Johnson said. "These
demonstrators are trying to show that we need somebody else to take
over this country."

IN MADISON that Monday afternoon Alison Steiner was called out of
philosophy class at West High and told to report to the assistant principal. He asked why she had been absent Friday. She said she had gone to
Washington to protest the war in Vietnam. The school did not permit
that, he said. Didn't she have nine-weeks exams on Friday? Yes, she
said, but she had taken them early. This did not qualify as an excused absence, he said. The grades would be counted as F's. Eventually the administration would have to back down when Steiner's mother came to
the school to object. On the Wisconsin campus Jane Brotman returned
to her French literature class, assuming naïvely that she could tell her
professor why she had missed the six-weeks exam and that "he would
understand" and let her take it later. Instead, without a trace of anger,
the professor told her that he was sorry but that he had a policy and she
had chosen not to follow it and therefore he would not allow a makeup
test. He was giving her an F for the exam. Brotman, ever the worrier,
was traumatized by the mark of failure but did not regret her choice and
eventually got a B in the course.

The UW faculty reconvened at the Memorial Union Theater that
day for a second long session and this time voted to establish an ad hoc
committee of professors and students that would investigate the Dow
protest and present recommendations for how future confrontations
should be handled. President Harrington opened the meeting. He said
that he had "complete confidence" that Sewell and the faculty would
"find a way to solve our present crisis." His message for students, Harrington said, was "Don't despair for the future of the university or of its
faculty; do not resort to violence or disruption; keep the lines of commu-

nication open to the faculty. I am thinking also of the people of this state, our state, the legislature, which gave this faculty its statutory power, the regents who have extended the area of faculty responsibility. This faculty does not want violence and it will find a way to avoid it. That is our immediate business."

After the debate and the creation of the ad hoc committee, Chancellor Sewell closed the meeting. It was, for the earnest methodologist, an emotional moment. "These recent days have been very trying for every member of the academic community—faculty, students, and administration alike," he said. "No one knows this better than I."

Sewell said that he wanted to reiterate what he had said weeks before the Dow eruption, when he had first addressed the faculty on October 2. "Our students are greatly concerned with what they perceive to be injustice, and some are very active in mounting protests and demonstrations both on campus and in the larger community. . . . Great universities have always been bases of energetic contention and dispute. At no time have students taken matters more seriously than now. The faculty have vigorously supported the constitutional rights of students, which includes the right to dissent and to protest. I trust that we will never deny these rights. I said these things three weeks ago and I wish to affirm these principles today. As I said then and repeat today, there is much for young men and women to be upset about on the national and international scene."

But dissent, he said, had to be based on freedom of speech for all, not obstruction and repression of opposing viewpoints. "I feel it is the obligation of every student, faculty member, and administrative official of this university, as well as every citizen of Wisconsin, to support the expression of any and all opinions and engagements in any and all [legal] activities. If we do not protect the rights of any individual or group on this campus, we jeopardize the rights of all. It is only through such actions that we can provide an example to the state and to the nation that we are committed to maintain a constitutional and civilized society. Thank you."

Sewell left to a thunderous standing ovation.

At the research lab at Oscar Mayer, where Dave Wheadon began another week of work, he was introduced to a new colleague and lockermate, Dennis McQuade, an army veteran who had just returned from Vietnam. When McQuade opened the locker, he noticed a poster of the October 21 March on the Pentagon. What was that doing there? he asked. Wheadon said he had taken the bus to Washington to march against the war, and with that they began a daily conversation about the meaning of war and peace. McQuade would go on to become coordinator of the Madison chapter of Vietnam Veterans against the War.

In a nationally syndicated sports column distributed that day, Red Blaik, the retired army football coach, criticized the March on the Pentagon. "What these demonstrators failed to comprehend is that the career soldier does not commit this country to war—war is the judgment of our civilian leaders elected and appointed. The Pentagon implements this judgment and the career soldier is the one whose duty it is to answer the call of his country—and not to question why. . . . Military men abhor war as they know it in the raw and to them the action of the belligerent demonstrator is incomprehensible." Blaik made this argument in a column paying homage to a former player who had just been killed in Vietnam, the end turned quarterback who led his team to victory over Navy in 1955. No player he ever coached, Blaik said, served as a better example of his favorite axiom: Good fellows are a dime a dozen, but an aggressive leader is priceless. "The priceless leader is now the late Major Don Holleder."

In Milwaukee two soldiers returned to the Sikorski house that Monday, carrying another telegram. It was about Danny's return and burial.

The Army will return your loved one to a port in the United States by first available military aircraft. At the port, remains will be placed in a metal casket and delivered (accompanied by a military escort) by most expeditious means to any funeral director designated by the next of kin or to any national cemetery in which there is available grave space. . . . Forms on which to claim authorized interment allowance will accompany remains. This allowance may not exceed $75 if consignment is made directly to the superintendent of a national cemetery. When consignment is made to a funeral director prior to interment in a national cemetery, the maximum allowance is $150; if burial takes place in a civilian cemetery, the maximum allowance is $300 . . .

"Three hundred dollars," Edmund Sikorski muttered when the soldiers left, the figure from the telegram sticking in his head. "They say my son is worth three hundred dollars."

CHAPTER 28

UNTIL THE ANGELS CAME

A T EIGHT ON THE Tuesday evening of October 24, it seemed that all of El Paso filed into the Harding-Orr & McDaniel funeral home to pay last respects to a favorite son. The chapel pews filled to overflowing for the rosary, and the crowd spilled into the hall. It was a closed casket; the U.S. Army had declared the disfigured body unviewable. Five-year-old Consuelo participated in the ritual, fingering her beads and murmuring in unison with the multitude of strangers: ten Hail Marys, one Our Father. Her sisters were too young to understand. It had been a week since word arrived in front-page banner headlines. Even in El Paso, with sprawling Fort Bliss and its community of military retirees, the war in Vietnam felt distant, unreal, a world apart. But the death of Terry Allen struck hard. The Allens were considered El Paso royalty. The old general and Mary Fran and their officer son had constituted the perfect military home.

Or so it had once appeared. Now the cataclysm of Terry's death had accelerated General Allen's mental disintegration. Family friends Bill and Bebe Coonly had reported to the house on Cumberland Circle as soon as they heard that Terry was missing and had stayed with the Allens the entire week until the body arrived from Vietnam. Hour by hour they had watched the general's condition worsen and his hold on reality slip. "Terry is a good soldier," he would say, using the present tense. "Terry is a good soldier. Terry would never get ambushed." General Allen's mind was stuck again on the Second World War and the little infantry booklets he had written long ago. Friends who came to console him were startled as he reached into his back pocket, took out a booklet, and proceeded to offer instructions on the advantages of night fighting. When he looked at his granddaughter Consuelo, who was the mirror image of her father—the eagle eyes, the sharp nose, the gentle curl of the lips—he thought he was seeing his own boy. He called her Sonny, invited her into his den, showed her old battle maps on the wall, and talked to her about his booklets.

It was left to the general's wife, whose life had been devoted to her family, the military, and the social protocols of El Paso, to hold things together, and Mary Fran Allen showed the steel and poise the task required. Not that she could reconcile herself to her son's death, she told friends. Terry was "such a wonderful young man. He never caused us a moment's worry in his entire life. He was everything that his father and I could ask for," Mrs. Allen wrote in a letter to one of Terry's friends. She was devastated but felt compelled to remain strong, if only for the sake of her three granddaughters. She was dealing not only with an addled husband and a son killed in combat but also with the humiliating situation created by her daughter-in-law, Jean Ponder Allen, who had been living and sleeping with another man at the house on Timberwolf Drive while Terry was in Vietnam. Mary Fran lamented in a letter that Jean's "sadistic behavior" was "a nightmare" for her. "I don't believe there was ever a worse scandal in El Paso. People were so angry at her and the man involved that had he not left town upon hearing of Terry's death I do believe that he would have been tarred and feathered."

The man was gone, but Jean remained. She and Terry had been on the path of divorce, but were still legally man and wife when he died. She came to the rosary and sat there with her three fatherless girls, feeling the scorn of society.

The next morning a letter from Washington was dispatched to Timberwolf Drive. "Dear Mrs. Allen," it began:

> The loss of your husband, Lieutenant Colonel Terry D. Allen Jr., in Vietnam has grieved me deeply. Please accept my personal sympathy.
>
> Our nation is grateful for your husband's selfless and honorable dedication to duty and his country during this conflict to preserve freedom. He shares a revered heritage with other brave men who have fought to achieve ultimate freedom and the blessing of

a free society. I pray that you will be comforted by the deep and lasting sympathy which we have for you and your family.

Sincerely,

Lyndon B. Johnson

Deep and lasting sympathy rarely came Jean Allen's way. One of the few voices of comfort was that of Kiko Schuster, the psychiatrist she had seen that summer during Terry's emergency leave. Schuster, an old friend of Terry's and an honorary pallbearer, thought he understood her mental state after several counseling sessions. "Jean, I think I might be the only person who knows how you feel," he said to her in a phone call after Terry's death. The comment made her weep because she knew he was right. What she had done, she understood, was "horrible for the Allens, horrible for my father, it was tough for a lot of people." She felt that she had no friends. Most of her childhood girlfriends had left town. She was the ridiculed outsider, and from that perspective, beyond the bounds of her prescribed social position, she saw things that she would not otherwise notice, pushing her even further outside. Inattentive to the effects of her own public behavior, she became observant of the private contradictions in the lives of others. She saw clearly now into the double world of El Paso businessmen "who were living this sort of façade and had girlfriends on the side—and who said things about the war that had a lot less to do with what they really thought about it than what they thought they ought to say about it."

Her alienation was nearly complete. She distrusted the United States government, waging a war that she did not believe in. She hated the military, fighting that war. She renounced her faith in the Catholic Church, which to her now seemed part of the establishment and hypocritical. She had been unfaithful to her husband, the fallen soldier. She had shocked El Paso society. One matron approached a Ponder relative and asked how "the family whore" was doing. An old military man who lived next door to Jean on Timberwolf Drive became so enraged that he perfected his golf swing by whacking Titleists against the side of her house. She was the scarlet-lettered woman of El Paso.

The funeral was Wednesday morning, the twenty-fifth, at Fort Bliss. Mass at Saint Michael's Chapel was followed by the burial at Fort Bliss National Cemetery. The black hearse stopped near a fresh hole in the earth dug in section A, row O, not far from the roadway. Allen received full military honors, with taps and a twenty-one-gun salute. The American flag that had draped the coffin was folded with slow-motion precision and handed gently to Terry's mother. The sorrowful scene was bathed in warm desert sunlight. Jean felt more like observer than participant. At the gravesite she looked at her three daughters, who seemed "still and very sad and strikingly solemn for such young children." General and Mrs. Allen showed a "bravery and dignity" that she found heart-wrenching. Jean witnessed everything yet felt cut off from it and the people she loved, including her daughters. She felt she had "no right to even share their grief," enveloped as she was in "a cocoon of shame that seemed quite dark and without any possibility of relief." Yet at the same time she found herself feeling "very angry at the senselessness of Terry's death." From her perspective it was an outrage that no one made mention of the needlessness of the tragedy. It was a hero's burial, and the eulogies were in the vein of LBJ's letter, about a brave man fighting for a free society.

The campaign had begun already for posthumous awards. Harold Durham, the gutsy artillery liaison officer nicknamed Pinky who died calling in howitzer fire near his own position and warning Sergeant Barrow of an enemy charge, was to receive a Medal of Honor; most of the slain Black Lions were getting at least Bronze Stars; and Allen was nominated for a Distinguished Service Cross, the nation's second-highest military award. After the fact, in private, Allen's boss in the First Infantry Division, General Hay, was dismissive of the battalion commander's performance. Hay told a military historian that Allen precipitated "the debacle" by "allowing his lead company to pursue the VC down the trail" instead of forming a perimeter and cloverleafing at the first sign of the enemy. It was a command decision for which he could not forgive Allen, Hay said, especially since everyone knew that a main force enemy unit was in the area.

Allen had made critical mistakes, but Hay's analysis was superficial. He failed to take into account the cloverleafs the Black Lions had indeed conducted that morning, and the perfect silence of Triet's force as it set the trap (not even the extraordinarily observant and cautious Clark Welch saw a sign of trouble until the trap was sprung), and the overwhelming numbers, and the long stretch without artillery fire as they waited for air support, and the pressure that was coming down all the way from Westmoreland to pursue enemy units relentlessly. But Hay placed most of the blame squarely on Allen. "If he would have survived,

I would have relieved him of his command," he told a U.S. Army historian.

Despite this blistering appraisal, Hay nominated Allen for the DSC. He did so, he explained later, "because of the story of Terry's bravery and because he was General Allen's son."

Hay's criticism of Allen, with his decision to nominate him for the Distinguished Service Cross anyway, takes on a deeper and more troubling significance in the context of his own involvement, or lack of involvement, in the battle, and the way that was described and honored later. Hay was in Saigon until the fight was just about over. The senior officers who were involved that day included Brigadier General Coleman, who hovered overhead and made the critical contact with Private Costello; and Colonel Newman, the brigade commander who arrived at the base camp and took over for the fallen Allen; and Major Holleder, who ignored Newman's wishes and rushed fearlessly toward the battlefield and his death; and Lieutenant Colonel Paul Malone, the aviation commander, who was wounded in the right foot as he brought his helicopter down through the trees during the rescue; and Terry Allen, who responded calmly to the ambush and kept trying to hold his unit together after he was wounded. For whatever mistakes any of these officers made before and during the battle, they put their lives on the line and responded bravely. Hay, by all accounts, had little to do with it.

Yet according to records at the Military History Institute in Carlisle, Pennsylvania, Major General John H. Hay, in General Orders Number 174, issued on February 24, 1968, was awarded the Silver Star. The orders read:

> Major General Hay distinguished himself by gallantry in action against a hostile force on 17 October 1967 while serving as Commanding General, 1st Infantry Division, in the Republic of Vietnam. On this date, during Operation Shenandoah II, General Hay received word that two companies from one of his infantry battalions were heavily engaged with an estimated battalion of Viet Cong. He alerted the crew of his command and control helicopter and flew to the scene of the battle. Arriving over the area, General Hay immediately took charge of the situation. Despite heavy ground fire aimed directly at his aircraft, he had his pilot fly at a perilously low level while he adjusted artillery fire onto the insurgents and pinpointed targets for tactical air strikes. He

also directed organization and redeployment of the troops on the ground, who were badly disorganized due to numerous casualties. His cool and calm approach to the situation instilled confidence in the infantrymen, and they regained the initiative over the insurgents. . . . His courage under fire, aggressive leadership and professional competence were responsible for the complete rout of the numerically superior Viet Cong force.

Even more than the inaccurate depictions of the battle concocted earlier by General Westmoreland and his MACV publicists, the Silver Star orders for General Hay described events that were unrecognizable to the Black Lions soldiers whose lives were forever shaped by that single bloody day. The documents supporting his Silver Star award are missing. The commanding general's name does not even appear in accounts of the battle provided by high-ranking officers who would have been in closest contact with him. This was not Handsome John Hay's finest hour. In retrospect his comments disparaging Terry Allen seemed graceless and hypocritical.

Allen was gone but the war was not, and even in places like El Paso, where military service and patriotism were considered synonymous, the burden of war was getting heavier. "Feeling the War," read the headline over an editorial in the *El Paso Times* days after Allen's death. "Every war in modern history has taken its toll of El Paso young men," the editorial began, citing the two world wars and Korea:

Now the war in Vietnam is no different. We have seen stories and pictures in the local newspapers of our young men who have fallen in that far-off land. News came [recently] of the death in action of a member of one of our more prominent families—Lt. Col. Terry Allen Jr., son of a famous general in World War II, a man who has lived among us for a long time and who married an El Paso girl. Every war is brought home to us in one form or another. Our sons lose their lives. Others are wounded. We make sacrifices. Still wars go on and on.

Casualty lists do one of two things: Either they make a nation angry or they make a nation weary. We wonder what casualty lists in the war in Vietnam will do to the American people. Those lists are growing longer and longer. We in El Paso know that only too well.

Friends and family gathered at General and Mrs. Allen's house after the burial. Jean came and was relieved that a few people were friendly to her: Kiko Schuster and Terry's friend Maury Kemp and the Calhouns, a farm family. Bebe Coonly was amazed to see that Jean could plow into this crowd with a smile on her face. In midafternoon Jean left for an appointment, leaving the three girls to stay with their grandmother. She drove to Channel 13, where she worked, and met with a production team from *ABC News* in New York, who were in town to report on the transfer of 437 acres of borderland known as El Chamizal from the U.S. back to Mexico. Vice President Humphrey was coming to El Paso the next day, and President Johnson the day after that.

It was the biggest political story in El Paso in years, and Jean Allen, who knew the local players because of her weekly television show, had agreed to help set things up for the network team. As the meeting started, she apologized if she seemed a bit distracted. "I buried my husband today," she explained.

The production crew was baffled, to say the least.

THE WAVE OF DISSENT that had rolled from the West Coast across America the previous week was now ripping back, like a tide, from the East. Dow and napalm were the focus again of antiwar protests on several college campuses. In Cambridge, Massachusetts, at about the time of Terry Allen's funeral, four hundred students from Harvard and Radcliffe began an eight-hour siege in a conference room, where they held Dr. Frederick Leavitt, director of Dow's eastern research labs, captive. There was no violence, no police charge, but Harvard administrators said the protest leaders would face a year's suspension. At the University of Illinois in Champaign, the Dow recruiter never got to his appointments that day. He was blocked from entering the interview room by demonstrators, who were isolated and waited out by academic officials determined to avoid a replay of the Wisconsin disaster. In Minneapolis, at the University of Minnesota, twenty students began a peaceful sit-in at the campus placement office and announced that they would fast for forty-eight hours to "express compassion for the innocent victims" of napalm.

In Madison the action had moved to the courts, where plaintiff Paul Soglin, lawyer Percy Julian, and the Dow protest leaders were celebrating a minor victory. Federal judge James E. Doyle had temporarily restrained university officials from disciplining students involved in the Commerce clash until he could decide on the constitutionality of the school's regulations on obstructive demonstrations. His decision did not affect the criminal cases being prepared against several students involved in the protest. Michael Oberdorfer, the *Connections* photographer, heard that the police were looking for him soon after he got back in town from the march in Washington. He asked his stepbrother to examine his apartment at 548 West Main Street to see if there was anything incriminating up there. The authorities had Oberdorfer's name and address because he had told them explicitly how to spell his name and where he lived, all in the heat of the protest, in an attempt to show that he had more conviction about his actions than officers who refused to wear their badges had about theirs. Now the police were on their way to charge him with disorderly conduct for pushing an officer.

Curly Hendershot was back in Midland by then, telling Dow colleagues about his harrowing hours inside the Commerce Building. There had been more than a hundred campus protests against Dow in the year since the first were held in October 1966 at Wayne State in Detroit and the University of California at Berkeley, but the sit-in at Wisconsin caused by far the most reverberations; it marked a point where the tactics of protest changed. A line graph charting the number of stories written about Dow during 1966 and 1967 showed two jagged peaks—the first Wisconsin protest on February 22, 1967, and the second Wisconsin incident on October 18. Dow I, as the February protest became known, pushed the number of stories around the country over the thousand mark for the first time. Dow II marked an explosion of coverage, with nearly two thousand newspaper articles and editorials.

To Dow executives the publicity was considered an oddly mixed blessing. They were reassured by the fact that virtually all of the hundreds of editorials were positive about Dow, or negative about the protests, and in any case provided Dow what public relations director Ned Brandt called "fantastic visibility." A public opinion survey that fall, conducted by Dow's in-house marketing pollster, showed that 88 percent of the respondents had heard of the Dow Chemical Company, making it nearly as recognized as U.S. Steel. On the other hand, Dow's increased visibility was tied almost entirely to napalm. Almost half the respondents now identified Dow as a supplier of napalm, a remarkable increase from 1966, when only one person in a hundred could make the connection. And one in five now thought Dow was interested only in war profits.

In the aftermath of the Wisconsin mess, Dow intensified its public relations effort, launching what Brandt called "Phase 2." The first phase, aimed largely at trying to minimize the damage, included Brandt's March 1967 visit to the Pentagon, at which he tried to persuade the Department of Defense to take responsibility for the napalm controversy. The second phase would be more aggressive.

Brandt and his team of publicists started publishing an internal newsletter called "Napalm News" that presented top corporate officials with detailed reports on the latest protests and other events related to napalm. Public relations men were assigned to accompany recruiters to campuses where demonstrations appeared likely, bringing along new press kits that included a revised policy statement on napalm, an annual report, a list of Dow officials and their telephone numbers, a pamphlet on Dow's nine hundred products, and statements by the military about the necessity of napalm. Where before Dow officials sought to avoid napalm debates, they now looked for opportunities to tell their story. Herbert Dow Doan, the president, was pushed forward to serve as the company spokesman, and by necessity overcame his earlier reluctance to take a visible role in the napalm discussion. Doan's byline was placed on an essay Brandt wrote explaining Dow's position on napalm, a piece later published in the *Wall Street Journal.* His essay would be part of a double-barreled media attack, the other half being the release of the letter McNamara had signed back in March.

Dow also undertook an internal program to explain its napalm position to the company's thirty-five thousand employees, of whom only a minuscule few dozen worked on the production of napalm. Discussion groups were formed in Midland to encourage new ways of thinking about the controversy, provoking a constant round of memos circulating through the corporate offices. "Short of ending the war, I don't think it is possible to force a climax of this issue," wrote William B. Seward, one of the public relations men sent out to the campus battlefields. "In considering napalm, I think we should look at it very realistically":

Not during this war, but afterwards, napalm may join the weapons banned by international convention. Today, either by formal or

informal agreement, gasses, poisons, dum-dum bullets, atomic
weapons, and radioactivity . . . are banned. If you remember the
international furor over some relatively mild gas used earlier in
Vietnam, it's plain these agreements carry some weight. The position that napalm is saving American lives doesn't count for too
much in the international forum. So I think we should recognize
the distinct possibility this could be the last war for napalm, just as
World War I was the last war for mustard gas, and that it may be
condemned somewhat retroactively like the World War II air
raid and incineration of Dresden.

To the idea proposed by others that Dow start running full-page ads
in newspapers, Seward said this might invite "the worst situation—a response of full-page ads of napalmed children. I suppose we could respond with dying soldiers, but in the end our objectives wouldn't be
served. At the outset, the protesters would decry full-page ads as the
brute economic strength of the military-industrial complex, but I have
no doubt they would find ample funds to match us inch for inch." Dow
should try to find areas of agreement with the protesters, Seward argued. "Let's draw attention to the theme, 'Are you dedicated to change
for the better? We are!' Let's not get trapped into fighting these issues:
the Vietnam War, Napalm as a Weapon, Defending the Status Quo,
The Military Industrial Complex. For one thing, it would be phony; I
doubt you could muster a majority from the board of directors in support of any of those causes."

One of the questions debated internally within Dow was whether
they should conduct their placement interviews off campus as a way of
avoiding confrontations of the sort that erupted at Wisconsin. They decided to keep going to every campus to which they were invited and to
play up that decision as a way of defining Dow. "We have resisted going
off campus because we want Dow to be seen as a company with spirit
and courage, not like a company that tucks its tail and runs," said Ray
Rolf, the manager of recruiting. "We want to show people that we have
a winning atmosphere here. . . . The only type of person we might be
losing is one who is weak and easily intimidated, and who retreats from
conflict. A person without belief in right or wrong is the only type of person who might be missed because of the demonstrations. . . . We would
miss far more good people if we didn't support the placement office."

From a historical perspective, the most interesting aspect of the controversy swirling around the Dow Chemical Company in October 1967 was that everyone might have been focusing on another chemical product. The controversy was all about napalm then. Napalm, the photographable monstrosity that clung unmercifully to human flesh as it burned at two thousand degrees, had become the brutal symbol of an unpopular war. But here was an instance where the passions of the moment faded with time and something else entirely—virtually ignored during the napalm protests—emerged as the more serious issue. In the long run the chemical product that did the most lasting damage was not napalm but the herbicide Agent Orange (and its cousin, Agent White), manufactured by Dow and six other chemical companies. The defoliants were sprayed in massive doses on much of Vietnam, including the jungles near the Black Lions in Lai Khe, to cut back the protective growth, flush out the Viet Cong, and destroy enemy rice crops. Use of the defoliants began in July 1965, but their heaviest use came in 1967, the year most of the men in this story were in Vietnam. According to later figures compiled by the Veterans Administration, about 4.88 million gallons of Agents Orange and White were dumped on Vietnam in that single year. The effects of the dioxin-laced chemicals were indiscriminate and plagued not only the citizens of Vietnam and their land but the troops on both sides of the war for decades thereafter. Seward, the Dow publicist, was right when he predicted that a company product might be banned from wartime use sometime in the future—but it was Agent Orange, not napalm.

Within three years of the Dow protest in Madison, the federal government halted the use of Agent Orange in Vietnam, concerned that it might cause health problems ranging from cancer to birth defects. Seventeen years later, in 1984, Dow and the other chemical companies agreed to a court settlement establishing a $184-million compensation fund for thousands of Vietnam veterans who suffered from what they believed were Agent Orange–related ailments. The long-term effects of the chemicals became evident decade after decade. In January 2003, thirty-six years after the tumult of 1967, researchers announced that they had found a link between the herbicides used in Vietnam and chronic lymphocytic leukemia. Good intentions and missed connections: there was no way they could have known it then, but if the Dow demonstrators had made Agent Orange their target, their struggle might have linked them more closely in common cause with thousands of returning

Vietnam veterans, and furthered the notion that their protests were meant to save the lives of American soldiers.

WHEN THURSDAY the twenty-sixth of October arrived in Vietnam, Clark Welch felt well enough to take a few hours' leave from the Ninety-third Evacuation Hospital. He described the trip later that night in a letter home to Lacy. Again he presented his most optimistic side, shielding his wife from the life-is-all-fucked-up anger that had overtaken him after the battle:

> I sort of had a pass today and went back to Lai Khe to make sure I left no loose ends in my company. The brigade commander sent his H-13 down this morning at 0600 and I went back to Lai Khe. It was a good day. I know now I left everything in good shape and no regrets. I didn't want to leave this way, of course, but I did it the best way I could. D Company has a new CO and a new first sgt and is back up to strength already. The old timers (before 17 oct) have the run of Lai Khe and we were sure glad to see each other! . . . What we had is still going strong in the 'new' company, too. They'll have just as good a company in a few weeks as we had. Not really, I guess—there will never be anything like the Delta Company that we started, organized, trained and brought into battle. Our 'life cycle' got awfully compressed, but we did more than anyone expected—except what I expected—they did exactly what I knew they would.

The trip to Lai Khe was a welcome relief for Welch, who was bored at the hospital. When he commanded Delta, he told Lacy, work that remained unfinished from the day before awaited him when he started up again at five thirty in the morning, and he would "stay hopping right until about midnight." Now, he complained, all he had to do was get up and make his bed. "Then I'm done. Feels funny." It was also feeling lonelier by the hour. Most of the Black Lions had been released, sent back to the States or transferred to larger hospitals for further treatment. A group of wounded Delta men had left for Japan the day before, leaving the ward to Welch, Sergeant Barrow, and Greg Landon.

Then, while Welch visited Lai Khe, Landon mailed his Purple Heart home, packed his bags, and left as well, going by bus to Bien Hoa, where he was flown to Vung Tau for recuperation at the Thirty-sixth Evacuation Hospital. On the ride to the airport Landon, who had been stuck in the remote countryside around Lai Khe for three months, got his first glimpse of a heavily populated stretch of Vietnam. He recorded the scene like an anthropologist. Noting that he saw more churches than temples, he concluded that the area was "more Catholic than Buddhist." The paved roads, he said, were torn up from large American vehicles, "making the bus ride hell" on his back. He was surprised to see a row of seven car wash establishments along the side of a stream. "Each would pick an American word such as 'Good Chance' car wash or 'Happy' car wash." Nearby was a "Washing Ton Laundry."

Vung Tau closed a circle for Landon, the kid his buddies called Professor. Here was the first Vietnamese ground he had touched three months earlier. The place seemed more welcoming to him now. "Somehow, I plan to have a long recovery," he wrote to his parents in Vestal, New York. His records said he could stay from twenty to sixty days. He was assigned to a ward that held sixty beds in two rows, every face a stranger. "Place looks like a garage, as do most of the hospital developments over here," Landon wrote of the quonset hut architecture. "No trees. I will get down to the beach tomorrow. But there'll be no swimming, just sunning. I imagine it will be January before I get going on the operations again."

The war went on without him. On the day he left for Vung Tau, October 26, 1967, in Vietnam, according to the MACV Office of Information, there were eighteen operations of battalion size or larger. Enemy forces launched a rocket attack on American troops north of Pleiku City, wounding nine men. Most of the action was in the air, where American forces seemed to be answering President Johnson's call to "pour the steel on." Air Force, Marine Corps, and navy pilots flew 142 missions over North Vietnam, pounding the power plant, airfields, rail yards, and storage areas near Hanoi. During the air raids over Hanoi, one Navy F-8 Crusader and two A-4 Skyhawks were shot down. One of the fallen Skyhawks was piloted by a thirty-one-year-old Navy lieutenant commander, who parachuted into White Bamboo Lake after his jet was hit by a surface-to-air missile. Mai Van On, in a nearby bomb shelter with sixty other Hanoi residents, saw the plane plunge into the lake, its tail sheared off by the missile. Instinctively, and against the wishes of those around him, On ran to the lakeshore, grabbed a bamboo pole, and swam out more than a hundred meters to save the American, who had been caught up in his parachute and was struggling below the water's surface. It was John McCain.

To On he was just another human being about to drown, but Hanoi's propagandists knew they had someone special as soon as John S. Mc-Cain III was pulled from the water and processed as a prisoner of war. They immediately began broadcasting radio reports trumpeting the capture of the "crook" son of an American military big shot "crook." McCain's father, John S. McCain Jr., was a Navy admiral, then commander in chief of Europe and soon to take over the Pacific Command.

THE ODD COUPLE of Madison law enforcement, Prosecutor Jim Boll and Deputy Sheriff Jack Leslie, were closing in on the flag cutter that day. They already had made the drive north to Stevens Point to interview William Stielstra, dean of students at UW–Stevens Point and father of the twins Jonathan and Phil Stielstra, to see if he would help the authorities determine which of his sons had snapped the flag lanyard atop Bascom Hall. They had brought with them an FBI enlargement of Norm Lenburg's caught-in-the-act photograph, but it was of no help. In pictures, the father had insisted, he could not tell the twins apart. Leslie grumbled on the way back that the old man must have been lying, but Boll was not so sure. Then Boll and Leslie visited 1215 Drake Street and knocked on the door, where they were confronted by a tall blond-haired young man who identified himself as Philip Stielstra. The flag cutter? They still were uncertain. But Boll noticed that this fellow who answered the door had the makings of a beard, about a quarter-inch of facial hair. The suspect in the picture did not have facial hair. Boll called an expert dermatologist and asked him how quickly someone could grow that amount of facial hair; the dermatologist consulted his European journals and called back with an answer: several weeks. Through process of elimination they had their man at last.

Jonathan Stielstra's arrest jolted his parents, mild and fair-minded Calvinists who had taught their sons to do good in the world. They thought of him as a gentle boy, an Eagle Scout who had earned a God and Country award and had been selected as a model scout at the Boy Scout Jamboree in Valley Forge, and who had been elected president of his sophomore class at Calvin College, following the path of his father, the senior class president there a generation earlier. They knew him, above all, as the product of a family that stressed "being of service to our fellow man." Could this be the same person who struck at the symbol of America and provoked a vengeful manhunt?

On that Thursday the twenty-sixth, eight days after the Dow demonstration, as Boll and Leslie prepared his arrest, Jonathan Stielstra began typing the first of two long letters to his parents in an effort to explain himself. One was political and dealt with his thoughts about Vietnam and his own behavior. He had not only cut down the flag, he had also decided, during that same Stop the Draft week, to resist the draft by sending his draft card back to his draft board. "Now is a time when it is of utmost importance not to think that it's hunky-dory in America," he wrote. "Because right now, 24 hours a day, the people of South Vietnam are being killed. . . . The stakes are very high for anyone who wants to change this society. A very easy way out is available to me as a college student. (Moral abdication is the route of least resistance, especially for those who feel least oppressed.) I could hide behind a 2-S and never worry about a thing—not worry about others, especially those who can't afford to go to college, who are being made to murder Vietnamese and risk their own lives in my place. But my stakes are meager compared to a Vietnamese peasant's. Really meager."

In the other letter, which he titled "A Little Manifesto," Stielstra drew heavily from the philosophy classes he was taking and from the counterculture lingo of the sixties. It was an abstract articulation of what he called his "philosophy of life." What it boiled down to, in its own way, was an attempt by a young man to cut the apron strings and perhaps to prepare his parents for difficulties to come. "It is incumbent on he who would criticize me to attempt to understand the kind of life I aspire for, and it is incumbent on me to live faithfully in accord with those aspirations," he wrote.

> More concretely, I will structure my own life creatively vis-à-vis the tyrannies of a less-than-democratic location of state power and university power, over-structured curriculums and formalized class learning, programmed social existences which falsify and dehumanize life, and vis-à-vis authority figures and parents when they come into danger of exercising unwarranted hegemony over my life by threatening to mold me in a particular prescribed fashion. Parent hegemony is a natural and beneficent relationship to the helpless child in the process of growing up, but becomes unnatural and malicious when it interferes with the child's acquiring

his own capacities for awareness (intellectual and artistic) and for forming positive, intimate feelings and relationships. This is no allegation or sermon; it's just an explanation of where I want to stand as a human being. I write this because I love you in a manner which you may not suspect.

Jon

Where Stielstra stood as a human being then was on the verge of copping a guilty plea with a sentence of thirty days in jail. They had him cold, Boll and Leslie did. Percy Julian would represent him, as he did most student protesters, but there was no argument the lawyer could conjure up that would erase Norm Lenburg's photograph.

For the family of Danny Sikorski, eighty miles away in Milwaukee, Thursday the twenty-sixth was a day they wanted to forestall. That morning Diane Sikorski and her father and stepmother rode in silence to the Max A. Sass & Son Funeral Home at 1515 West Oklahoma Avenue in south Milwaukee. On the way they got in an accident. Another driver plowed into their rear fender. In a daze Edmund Sikorski got out and told the woman driving the other car that it was okay, no need to exchange insurance cards, he would handle it later, but now he was on his way to his son's funeral. When they arrived at Sass's, Diane glanced at the closed casket and started crying. The night before, at the visitation for Danny, she had tried to cry but no tears came. Now they cascaded out of her. "I wanted him alive. I wanted to rip the cover off to see if he was really in there. This was my last chance. I felt so helpless and angry," she recalled later. After Father Czaja said a prayer, Diane approached the casket. In her next conscious moment she was looking up from the floor at her father and the funeral director, who were trying to lift her into a chair. She had fainted while blessing her brother.

The funeral mass was held at Saint John Kanty's Church. The family had sat in the same row three years earlier for the service for Danny and Diane's mother. Time now circled back for Diane and the two moments merged. Father Czaja, in his homily, talked about Danny as a child and a young man and revealed that Danny had visited him on his leave before going to Vietnam and asked for the priest's blessing because he knew he wasn't coming home. Prayer cards were distributed. The photograph showed Danny in army dress, looking a little pudgy. *Merciful Jesus, grant him eternal rest (7 years and 7 quarantines). Sweet Heart of*

Mary, be my salvation (300 days' indulgence). My Jesus, mercy! (300 days' indulgence).

Then the burial at Saint Adalbert's Cemetery, in the veterans section, not far from where Diane had stood five years earlier, on Memorial Day 1962, and delivered the only public speech of her life. She was selected because she had written "Freedom As America Knows It," the winning entry in an eighth-grade essay contest. "Even before 1776 the world looked upon America as a refuge for the persecuted, a land of social equality—a land of opportunity," she had written. "It took a cost of hardship and heartache, labor and loneliness to purchase these freedoms. Liberty is a thing of the spirit—it is freedom to worship, to think, to hold opinions and to speak without fear. Freedom to challenge wrong and oppression with surety of justice. Liberty is far more valuable than money or riches, more valuable even than our country and friends."

Now she was looking at the Stars and Stripes draped over her brother's casket. The same symbol that had enraged Jonathan Stielstra comforted Diane Sikorski. She wished that the American flag could be buried with her brother to keep him warm in his grave.

In Madison a few hours later, at seven that night in Capitol building room 421 south, the Senate Select Committee continued its hearings into "the Riotous and Unlawful Activities the Week of October 16, 1967 Occurring on the Madison Campus of the University of Wisconsin." This was a prime-time show: Chancellor Sewell was at the witness table. At his side was Richard Cates, one of Madison's toughest lawyers, who represented the university in the three-ringed legal case that surrounded Dow: the legislative hearings, the Soglin-led court challenge to university rules, and the university discipline hearings against thirteen suspended student leaders. Five years later Cates would be in Washington, working for the House Judiciary Committee as it investigated the Watergate-related crimes of the next president of the United States. Now he advised Bill Sewell as the state senators and their counsel took the chancellor through the sequence of events of October 18 minute by minute, pressing him on why the protesters were allowed to enter the Commerce Building at all, why the Madison police were called, and how Sewell had expected the confrontation to be resolved.

An hour into the questioning, Senator Walter Chilsen noted that Sewell's field was sociology. "I wonder if you would like to comment on the sociological impact of the demonstrations of a week ago," Chilsen said. "Have you changed your attitude about the sociological meaning of that demonstration and of other demonstrations around the country? I suppose we can tolerate a short dissertation."

Chilsen assumed that Sewell's specialty was collective behavior, but Sewell corrected him. "Oh, no. My major interests in sociology are in research methodology, in which I think I have made some significant contributions in the field of personality and social structure . . . but I am not a specialist in collective behavior," Sewell said. And he had not had time in the seven days since the Dow demonstration, he added, to reflect on the sociological meaning of the events. But he then offered what, in a sense, amounted to a classic liberal variation of Diane Sikorski's eighth-grade essay on American freedom. "If you ask me, what do I think is the effectiveness of protest sociologically, then I believe that in general the effective protest makes people who would otherwise be unaware of the feelings of those who protest aware of the nature of their cause." He went on:

And it seems to me, sir, that in a democratic constitutional society this is a very necessary, indeed an inevitable means for people to make known their feelings, their attitudes on questions that are near and dear to them and . . . may not be as important to other people. And it is for that reason that we have tolerated in our society those who speak out against what they see to be wrong with society. . . . And it is true that the legislative process, whether at the state or at the federal level, is slow to recognize the demands of people.

You can speed this process up doubtless by making yourself heard, by bearing witness to your cause. This I see as a great sociological, a great moral value of protest. It seems to me on the other hand that when you come to the point where you . . . you are not arousing enough attention to your cause by lawful, orderly protest, that you must resort to disorder, you must resort to disruption, to the invasion of the rights of others, then you may get yourself on television. You may get yourself headlines in the newspapers. But my guess is that you lose supporters and respect for your cause. This I think is carried to the extreme when you are willing to resist lawful authority even after it is called to your attention. . . .

And again, since you offered me the opportunity, sir, to digress and to lecture a bit, I want you to know, and I think it is only fair that you should know, that I have personally from the beginning opposed the policies of our government in Vietnam. I have signed petitions to that effect. I have written letters to our representatives. I have written letters to the president. And not more than four days before this event took place, I had again signed a petition opposing our policy in Vietnam. I do that as a free citizen in a free country. It is a recourse that is available to me as a free citizen in a free country. It is a right that I have as a citizen regardless of what my position may be in the university. It is a right that I guard more than any other right, the right of freedom of speech, freedom to dissent.

Later in the hearing it became clear that some state legislators were furious with Sewell for his reluctance to rid the university of radical teachers who were on the state payroll, either as faculty members or untenured teaching assistants, and were inciting radical behavior. Senator Robert W. Warren of Green Bay, who later would become a federal judge, pressed the issue most closely with Sewell.

> **Warren:** Chancellor, I think that all of the witnesses that have preceded you would probably agree with the statement that there is a hard core of extremely radical, revolutionary militants on our University of Wisconsin campus. Would you agree with that statement?
> **Sewell:** I hate to agree with other people's statements, sir.
> **Warren:** All right. Let's go ahead this way then. What I am interested in getting at is that most people prior to you indicated that they would acknowledge the existence of a very militant minority on the University of Wisconsin campus. They talk about rights and all of us on this committee are perfectly willing to recognize the existence and the vital necessity of protecting those rights, but we on this committee and in this legislature and in this Capitol also have the responsibility of determining how we are going to allocate the financial resources of the state of Wisconsin. In the past I think that the legislature has been highly generous with the university . . . and the problem that arises is we keep finding this hard core of people who I personally feel are not entitled to the protection—well, let me state it differently, who are not entitled to my financial support in the long run—and we seem to

be utterly unable to reach this cancerous sore and we keep finding them coming in greater and greater numbers in certain areas of the university. Is the only way in which we are going to be able to return to what at least I consider some quality to some of this university faculty by the fiscal appropriation route, is that all we can do? For instance, do we have to say that the college of philosophy is going to lose X amount of dollars? What can we do in your opinion to take care of—I am not talking about freedom of speech now. I am talking about violent revolutionaries—

Sewell: You are speaking of faculty of the university?

Warren: Yes. I have watched faculty members jump up and down when the youths talk about imperialism.

Sewell: I am afraid, sir, you have lost me completely.

(Laughter from the audience.)

Sewell: No . . . I am trying to be honest with you. But you have made what sounds like a speech rather than a question. But let me say as follows: that you surely will never have a great university— and you have had one for a hundred years in this university—if you are going to say that the political views of professors are somehow going to be screened. Is that your question?

Warren: I agree with that statement.

Sewell: Okay. Then what are you saying? That a professor can't condemn imperialism?

Warren: No, I am saying—

Sewell: Or condemn our policy in Vietnam?

Warren: No, no, not at all.

Sewell: Okay, then what are you saying about imperialism?

Warren: What I am trying to say, it seems to me if in fact you as an employer can no longer fire a faculty member apparently—

Sewell: Oh yes, I can.

Warren: Not without a hearing.

Sewell: Well, obviously not. This is the United States of America, sir, where people have . . . where there is due process.

Full of vigor, emerging from the despair that had engulfed him in the hours after Dow, Sewell might have won the rhetorical debate with the legislators, but his arguments, presented with what his interlocutors considered an air of arrogance, situated him, more than ever, in the middle of an impossible situation. Student antiwar leaders felt betrayed by him and blamed him for sending in the cops. Now more legislators disliked him too. The Senate investigation would go on for two more weeks, attracting headlines but leading to no major findings.

THE HOMECOMING PARADE was held the next day, Friday the twenty-seventh. "If you want to be a Badger, just come along with me, by the bright shining light . . ." The old-style University of Wisconsin scene of bratwurst and red sweaters and cheerleading and the stench of stale beer in the Var Bar and panty raids and fraternity bonhomie was on display again, competing for attention with the emerging sixties counterculture. A northern chill blew into Madison as crowds lined the sidewalks to watch the fraternity and sorority floats glide around the Capitol square and down Langdon Street. There was Popeye and his can of spinach, the work of the Tri Delts and Alpha Epsilon Pi. Here came Delta Gamma and Phi Gamma Delta's float showing Bucky Badger dunking a Northwestern Wildcat in a shower. Dennis the Menace, Pogo, Snoopy, Snuffy Smith—one after another the cartoon characters rolled into view and drew laughs and claps and cheers and rolled on down the street.

What a classic fall football weekend this promised to be. The Chi Phis were preparing for a special guest, one of their old fraternity brothers, Charles S. Robb, who had marched proudly around campus and up Langdon Street in his drill uniform as the ROTC brigade commander during his senior year at Wisconsin in 1961, an era just before the rise of the Anti-Military Ball. Robb was now a U.S. Marine Corps major stationed at the White House in Washington and engaged to marry Lynda Bird Johnson, the president's daughter. He already had papers to leave for Vietnam early in 1968, not long after their December wedding, but that seemed distant. He and his famous fiancée were mostly oblivious to the political and cultural changes swirling around them, preoccupied, as Robb later said, by the "whirlwind of prenuptial activities." Those included, for this one weekend, a football game at Camp Randall Stadium, where they would be greeted by Chancellor Sewell; a dinner with old fraternity brothers in New Glarus; and then a reception the next day at his parents' house in Milwaukee. Robb's father, a regional representative for American Airlines, had switched his party affiliation to LBJ's Democrats by then, but he could not yet say the same for his military son.

There were no antiwar demonstrations in Madison to counter the Homecoming hoopla. Paul Soglin was preoccupied with a valuable bit of information that his ex-girlfriend, Cathy Dietrich, had passed along to him when she knocked on his Bassett Street apartment the night before. She had worked late as a waitress in a private room at the Madison Club, and while serving a table of state senators, she overheard them discussing ways to embarrass the protest lawyer, Percy Julian, and to go after Soglin and other out-of-state students. They were going to go after Julian for using the state telephones inside the Capitol to make free long-distance calls. The word went out quietly; people were exhausted, regrouping, or, in a few cases, hiding.

They had been scrapping away at the war for years, this messy, bedraggled student band, with no money or power, only the will to dissent. The selfless and the self-involved, the peaceful and the reckless, the righteous and the contentious, their differences were covered over by their overwhelming opposition to U.S. military involvement in Vietnam. It was simplistic to say that events were turning because of them or in spite of them; the culture was accepting, rejecting, co-opting, adapting, disapproving, and absorbing them at the same time, and the results were complex and contradictory. If citizens outside the cauldron of the university were offended by the excesses of young radicals, more of them were growing anxious about Vietnam and what it was doing to America, and in that sense the chaotic Wisconsin protesters were in the vanguard of a movement that would be embraced by millions of people from all walks of life.

The most dramatic antiwar action that Friday took place at a Selective Service office in Baltimore. A minister for the United Church of Christ stood watch at the door as the Catholic priest Philip Berrigan and two other men opened plastic vials and poured their own blood into open file drawers containing draft records. The act, Berrigan said, was done in protest of "the pitiful waste of American and Vietnamese blood" on the other side of the world. "We shed our blood willingly and gratefully in what we hope is a sacrificial and constructive act. We charge that America would rather protect its empire of overseas profits than welcome its black people, rebuild its slums and cleanse its air and water." The men were arrested by the FBI, and Berrigan refused to post bond, preferring to spend the weekend in jail.

In Madison the one reminder of the tumult in the world outside came from an unlikely source. After the parade the Homecoming floats were parked on the front yards of fraternity houses on Langdon Street. There, not far from the Chi Phi house, was the float constructed by Pi Beta Phi and the Evans Scholars, with a theme that lightheartedly connected the turmoil of the Vietnam war with the merriment of a football weekend. It was a likeness of President Johnson, Chuck Robb's future father-in-law, with his long countenance, huge ears, and pronounced jowls, his right hand cocked and holding a football, his face rising above a stadium scoreboard, wearing not a helmet but a huge ten-gallon hat with a bright red W on it. The theme of the float was "Victory at Hand."

College kids with the optimism of General Westmoreland. The Badgers would lose the next day to Northwestern, another notch in a winless season. As for the war, as 1967 neared an end, the American embassy in Saigon would beckon guests to a New Year's party with the encouraging words: "Come see the light at the end of the tunnel."

IT WAS COINCIDENCE, but nevertheless odd, that within a twenty-four hour period starting on that Friday, October 27, 1967, so many political players of war and peace were converging on the cities of Madison, El Paso, and Milwaukee.

The president's daughter and her fiancé were in Madison. Vice President Humphrey was delivering the keynote address at a two-day conference with Mexican officials in El Paso, where Terry Allen's funeral, forty-eight hours old, was now overwhelmed by other stories. Humphrey visited wounded Vietnam soldiers at the army hospital and handed out medals and worked the rope lines outside, greeting a throng of military wives, many of whom handed him notes that he promised to deliver to their husbands when he reached Vietnam, his next stop. President Johnson, who was also on his way to El Paso for the signing of the El Chamizal treaty transferring some borderland back to Mexico, had given Humphrey his own special message to carry to Vietnam. It was an urgent note warning President Thieu, whose inauguration Humphrey would attend, to "get moving" on economic and social reforms.

While Humphrey was in El Paso, Senator Robert F. Kennedy of New York, the war critic Johnson feared most, arrived in Milwaukee that Friday to speak at a dinner for Wisconsin Senator Gaylord Nelson. The heat was turning up: Senator Eugene McCarthy of Minnesota had been quoted in the morning papers saying that perhaps someone should challenge LBJ in the Democratic primaries. Nowhere did Johnson seem more vulnerable than in Wisconsin, one of the key primary states. And now, hours after Kennedy, here came Richard Nixon, the former vice president, sliding into Milwaukee himself for his first Wisconsin visit in preparation for his 1968 run for president. The time seemed right, Nixon said, for a "peace candidate." He was speaking of himself, though he added that his notion of a peace candidate might not be the same as anyone else's.

Clark Welch and Sergeant Barrow were by then being evacuated from Vietnam to another recuperation hospital in Japan. Greg Landon, in Vung Tau, was writing a letter home about the beach he had visited that day and how he had looked out at the coastline of the South China Sea, so blue and peaceful, where the C Packet troops had come ashore almost exactly three months earlier. And across the world, in the middle of America, Jack Schroder was being buried. Machine Gun Red or Airborne Schroder, one of Welch's kids in Delta Company, dead at twenty years of age.

It was ten days after the battle of Ong Thanh. The funeral was held in tiny Clay Center, Nebraska, eighty miles southwest of Lincoln. Clay Center, population 860, was known for its Old Trusty poultry incubators and its Spring Wing Ding celebrating the waterfowl migration of millions of snow, blue, and whitefront geese. This was Jack's home turf, the people he had left behind to study as a dental technician in Milwaukee. It seemed that every person in Clay Center knew Jack's mother, Helen. They all knew Jack's grandparents, Florence and Samuel Moger. And they all knew Jack and knew that he had been killed in Vietnam and that he had a young wife and son living in Montana. News of his death spread quickly through town by word of mouth, then was recounted in turn-of-the-century formalized prose in the local weekly newspaper: "And thus there comes into the Clay county scene a third generation that has been touched by and felt the anxiety of war and its dread sorrow, and another young life is a sacrifice the families affected must shoulder. The sympathy of the public is often more verbal than sincere, but in their hour of tragedy and sorrow the Moger family in Clay Center has the sincerest sympathy of a large circle of Clay county people and friends of the family. Death, whose countenance may be friendly or not, in this instance did not come friendly and soothing, but as a terrible shock."

On the flight from Helena, Eleanor Schroder thought about what Jackie Kennedy had endured. *You just do it,* she said to herself. *You walk through it like a maze. You can't do anything about it. You just have to accept it and go.* Her family came out from Wisconsin, but she could barely remember talking to them. She wanted to see the body, but the men would not let her. Another closed casket; only Grandfather Moger and the mortician saw Jack's remains. Eleanor couldn't believe all the people dropping by with food and flowers. "Have a fast trip back to the states," Jack's mother had written in a letter he read in Fort Lewis in early July, the day he started keeping a journal. It was too fast, this trip back.

It rained the morning of his burial. Military rites were conducted by American Legion Post 87, whose veterans later renamed their baseball diamond Mills-Schroder Field in honor of Jack. Larry Schroder would grow up in Clay Center and play ball on that field as a teenager and would hear the checkout lady at the grocery remark on how much he looked like the dad he never knew. And eventually he would be given a box containing the .38 Smith & Wesson that Jack had pestered Eleanor to send him in letters he wrote from the jungles of the Long Nguyen Secret Zone. The box had made its way to the Black Lions in Lai Khe a few days after Jack was killed; it came back stamped undeliverable. It would remain forever unopened, a reminder of the unfulfilled promise of a soldier's short life. As the coffin descended into the wet Nebraska clay, Eleanor clutched tightly her baby son; her savior, she called him. And the world, as the poet said, would bend into the cruel angles.

EPILOGUE

WHEN CATHAY PACIFIC flight 765 from Hong Kong touched down at Ho Chi Minh City on the morning of January 27, 2002, here I was, finally, decades late, the fucking new guy. This was my first visit to a country that I only had imagined, for better and worse. With my wife at my side, I looked out the window from seat 45C as the airplane rolled toward the terminal. Everything seems exotic the first time: guard towers, machine guns, uniforms of deep olive green and dark red; motorbikes racing our jet on a parallel dirt road, three-packs of teenaged boys clinging to each seat; a hive of gray hangars, giant, culvertlike cement half-moons that once provided cover for U.S. helicopters; patient queues of travelers at the checkpoints inside; more soldiers, stone-cold serious, born after the war was over; a clattering, expectant sea of people waiting outside, fingers gripping the chain-link fence, heads straining for the first glimpse of arriving relatives bringing appliances and cardboard boxes full of other material wonders from the world beyond. Then into the sunlight and a surprising jolt of exhilaration in the steamy Saigon heat.

Connections are what fascinate me, the connections of history and of individual lives, the accidents, incidents, and intentions that rip people apart and sew them back together. These interest me more than ideological formulations that pretend to be certain of the meaning of it all. I came to Vietnam looking for more connections. And I brought some connections with me.

I grew up in Madison, where half the events recorded in this book would take place. During the days in October 1967, when the Black Lions were fighting and dying in the jungle of the Long Nguyen Secret Zone and antiwar protesters were staging a sit-in at the Commerce Building, I was a naïve freshman at the University of Wisconsin. I observed the Dow demonstration from the edge of the crowd, and felt the sting of tear gas, and saw a few things that I mostly forgot. Three years later I received a low number in the draft lottery in 1970 and rode the bus to Milwaukee for an induction physical but was declared 4-F because of chronic asthma that I'd had since childhood. Campus demonstrations were still going on, and I began covering them in newspaper and radio reports. None of this was enough to warrant making myself a character in a book of history. I had no intention of including myself in any case, beyond the extent to which all authors of nonfiction or fiction are hidden characters in anything they write. But I was *of* Madison. I was steeped in its progressive tradition, honoring the right to dissent, and I carried that with me wherever I went, and in that sense I was making a connection as soon as I landed in Ho Chi Minh City, bringing the Wisconsin side of the story to the Vietnam side.

In the lobby of the Hotel Continental a few hours later, there stood Clark Welch, the great soldier of Delta Company, at age sixty-two his stomach filled out and his crewcut turned gray, but still with that characteristic forward lean and disarmingly sheepish smile. He was back in Vietnam for the first time in three decades, and he looked exactly like what he was: American veteran and tourist, wearing a short-sleeved striped shirt and fanny pack, his keen blue eyes occasionally darting around the room, always scouting the territory. And next to him was Consuelo Allen, oldest daughter of Lieutenant Colonel Terry Allen Jr., the battalion commander who was killed thirty-five years earlier on that bloody autumn day. People had always commented that Consuelo was the spitting image of her father, and the resemblance was now stronger than ever.

For more than thirty years after the battle, Clark Welch burned with hostile feelings about Commander Allen and the flawed leadership decisions that sent the 2/28 Black Lions into the jungle that morning. He had thought about the battle every day since, and as he rose through the ranks to captain, major, and colonel, he committed himself to the promise that no one who trained under him would get caught in a similar situation. Welch knew that Allen had three daughters but was wary of meeting them. He was concerned for himself and them: afraid that they would not like him and that seeing them would only bring him pain. But in the final few years of the twentieth century, after he had retired, he was tracked down by his old comrade, Big Jim Shelton, who had been Terry Allen's closest friend in Vietnam. Shelton told him about the Allen girls and how bright and curious they were, and it started Welch on the path of wondering.

"I'm going to ask you something: where are Terry Allen's daughters and what do they think of me?" Welch asked me at the end of our first long interview, conducted in the lobby of a Denver hotel on a summer's day in 2000.

I told him the daughters were in Texas—El Paso and Austin—and that they did not know enough about Welch to think much about him at all, except that he was a soldier with their father and that he had lived and their father had died.

"I dream about them," Welch confided. "I want them to be wonderful people."

Now here they were, together, Clark Welch and Consuelo Allen, connected for this mission in Vietnam. Consuelo came with questions. Where did her father die? What did it look like? What must it have felt like? How has it changed? Welch had fewer questions; he thought he knew the answers. He anticipated that the experience would be difficult, that his mind would ricochet endlessly from present to past to present to past.

Once, long ago, on an early summer evening in 1967 after he had flown over his little section of Vietnam in a helicopter, Lieutenant Welch wrote to his wife: "This place can be beautiful! The winding rivers, the little hamlets, the neat rice paddies, and little gardens are very tranquil looking. And the rivers are either bright blue or brown, the fields and forests are deep green, and the shallow water on the rice looks silver from up there. Riding in the chopper with the doors off—there's a nice cool breeze, too. Maybe we could come back here some day when it's as peaceful and beautiful on the ground as it looks from the sky."

Nothing is that peaceful, ever, and certainly not the Democratic Republic of Vietnam, but now the war was long over and Clark Welch was back. He was eager to see the beauty of the country again; and to reflect on what had happened in 1967 and how things might have gone differently, in the battle and the war; and to be there when and if I found soldiers who had fought that day for the other side, the VC First Regiment. And he and Consuelo would come with me to walk the battlefield in the Long Nguyen Secret Zone south of the Ong Thanh stream. Big Rock was ready: he had his old army pictograph map with the coordinates of the battle and a little global positioning system (GPS) location finder that dangled from his neck like a good luck pendant.

IN THE SUMMER OF 2001, my wife and I had returned to Madison for three months of research on the Wisconsin side of the book. On my first day back I walked into the offices of the *Capital Times,* my home away from home. My father, Elliott Maraniss, had been an editor of the *Cap Times,* and I had begun my journalism career there covering high school football games and writing movie reviews.

Ron McCrea, the city editor, saw me approaching and said, "Hey, Dave, isn't that an amazing coincidence about your book?"

"What coincidence?" I asked. I had no idea what he was talking about.

One of McCrea's best friends was Dave Wagner, a veteran journalist who had worked at the *Capital Times* in the early 1970s before moving on to editing jobs in Waukesha and Phoenix. Before that Wagner had been part of the antiwar movement at the University of Wisconsin and a founding journalist at the alternative newspaper *Connections.* More writer and intellectual than activist, he was not one of the people inside Commerce when the Dow confrontation began on October 18, 1967, but got there in time for the scrum on the Commerce plaza and the tear gas—and was assigned by editor Bob Gabriner to help put out the *Connections* special issue called "The Great Dow War."

Wagner and his wife, Grace, who had witnessed the Dow protest, have two adult children. Their son Ben was born a year after Dow. He came back to the University of Wisconsin in the late 1980s to get a degree in philosophy, then returned to the Phoenix area in 1991. Ben found a job at the AT&T call center in Phoenix, where he sat next to a vibrant young woman named Theresa Arias. They had a constant patter going, and Ben thought Theresa was "a terrible smart-ass," contradicting him all the time. In other words, he was taken by her. They started dating and never stopped and were married on October 19, 1996. Two days before the wedding, as he did every year on October 17, Theresa's father, Michael Arias, visited a cemetery in Phoenix to pay respects and place a can of beer at the gravestone of his old Vietnam buddy, Ralph Carrasco. This was the same Michael Arias who had served as a radiotelephone operator in Alpha Company of the 2/28 Black Lions and who had taken the compass and helped lead Jim George and his wounded band out of the jungle. Ralph Carrasco was one of the dead soldiers they had to leave behind.

After visiting the grave, Arias went to dinner at a Chinese restaurant in Scottsdale with Ben's father, Dave Wagner. The two men were meeting for the first time. Ben Wagner had told his father about the military decorations on a wall at the Arias home—an M-16 and various pictures and awards. Theresa Arias knew a bit about the Wagner family history—white, liberal, antiwar agnostics from the north. They were worried how the meeting would go. It went fine; the war did not come up.

In the crowd at the wedding were some of Michael Arias's military buddies, including Randy Brown and Ernie Buentiempo, and Wagner's old newspaper friend Ron McCrea, who was Ben Wagner's godfather.

Years later, at a family gathering, Arias and Wagner got to talking about Vietnam and found that they agreed more than they disagreed. Theresa mentioned that a writer for the *Washington Post* had recently interviewed her father about an awful ambush his battalion had marched into on October 17, 1967. Wagner said that he knew one reporter at the *Post,* David Maraniss. That's him, Michael Arias said.

Wagner passed the word back to McCrea, who told me when I reached Madison. The odds were infinitesimal—but there it was, a marriage connecting the worlds of war and peace in 1967, the Black Lions soldiers of Vietnam and the student demonstrators of Wisconsin. There were no great lessons to be drawn from this improbable marriage except a reminder of how people and groups are ripped apart and sewn back together. This has less to do with the overwrought notion of healing than with the unpredictability of life and the relentless power of the human spirit. Theresa and Ben Wagner were expecting twins late in the summer of 2003. In my mind's eye I've added the picture of their young family to the last page of my mental catalog of Vietnam images, which begins with that napalmed little girl screaming as she runs naked down the street.

Many of the protesters who had been arrested in the Dow demonstration were, as one might expect, gone from Madison when I came back thirty-four years after the event. Evan Stark, the movement orator, left Madison days after the protest, officially withdrew from school in November, and never returned. He ended up later teaching at Rutgers-Newark in New Jersey, doing important work on spousal abuse. In terms of university discipline, seven other students were expelled or withdrew before they could be kicked out, and six who had been identified as protest leaders were placed on probation. In the courts Mike Oberdorfer, Robert Cohen, and four other students were found guilty of disorderly conduct and sentenced to short jail terms, most for thirty days. Cohen, the best known of the defendants, struck a side deal with the judge: he could plead guilty and avoid jail if he promised to leave Madison and never come back. District Attorney Jim Boll heard about the informal plea bargain on the radio and was shocked. When he confronted the judge, William Sachtjen, he was told that it was true. "I was sitting in my office and Bob Cohen walked by," the judge told Boll. "And I told him to come on in and we had a little discussion and I made this deal with him and I didn't think you would care." Cohen drifted east.

Jonathan Stielstra, who had cut down the flag atop Bascom Hall, spent twenty-three days in the Dane County jail during the early winter of 1967, then continued a Zelig-like existence that took him to virtually every memorable event of the counterculture and New Left in the sixties. Stielstra was, consecutively, at Columbia and in Paris, briefly, during the student rebellions of spring 1968; in Hanoi with a delegation of SDS leaders in May; on the streets at the Democratic Party convention in Chicago that summer, and later at both Woodstock and Altamont, the alpha and omega of sex, drugs, hippies, and rock and roll. "Hitched out here with 3 Madison friends," he wrote to his parents after Woodstock. "It had to be the most incredible event: combination rock concert, be-in, Boy Scout jamboree, massive traffic jam, downpour during a Big Ten football game . . . all on a very-unbelievable-for-all scale." He had another run-in with the law in 1971 when he refused induction into the U.S. Army but received three years probation after promising to undertake alternative civilian service. In 1974 he returned to Madison and started a natural foods grocery.

What once had seemed certain to Stielstra by the late 1970s appeared more complicated. If he had to do it over again, he believed, he would not have cut down the flag. It was a spontaneous act, he said, so he did not entirely regret it, but neither did he feel that it had any beneficial effect. As for refusing induction, he now felt that every person should fulfill some obligation to the country, though not necessarily military. His attitude toward the University of Wisconsin also changed. More than a decade after the Dow demonstration, he re-enrolled in school to obtain a degree in accounting. Most of his courses were in the very building where it all started, Commerce. From there he became a family man and accountant, living on a cul-de-sac in a quiet middle-class neighborhood on Madison's west side, not far from the former district attorney who had prosecuted him.

Paul Soglin emerged from the Dow protest determined to broaden both the antiwar movement and his own political ambition, working— as young people were implored to do in the sixties—within the system. At the invitation of church groups, he spoke at forums on the east and west side about the meaning of the Dow protest and the Vietnam war.

By year's end he was plotting his race for Madison alderman in the city's student-dominated eighth ward. He won that election in April 1968 and within five years was mayor, a job he held from 1973 to 1979 and again from 1989 to 1997, and which he sought again, a third go at it, in spring 2003. (By then he was regarded as the "conservative" candidate—and he lost.) As years and decades went by, and as Madison prospered, making virtually every list of America's most livable cities, Soglin came to be seen not as a threatening radical but as a cultural and political totem of a progressive town. When he grew tired of politics, he retired and went into the financial consulting business and moved with his second wife and their daughters into a modernist house on Madison's west side. He also began teaching public policy at the university. His classroom was in the old Commerce Building (now called Ingraham Hall), on the first floor, around the corner from where his back and legs had been bashed by billy clubs that long-ago October day. That same building also now housed the offices of Wisconsin's center for Southeast Asian studies.

Soglin's first chief of staff in the mayor's office was Jim Rowen, who had been in the Commerce Building during the Dow protest and watched Soglin curl into the fetal position as he was being beaten. They barely knew each other beyond that. The intervening five years had been mercurial for Rowen. As an investigative journalist, he had written an influential series on Wisconsin's connections to the Pentagon through the Army Math Research Center on campus. In the darkest hour one morning in August 1970, a massive explosion shattered Sterling Hall, the building housing the army math center, killing a young physicist who had been working on experiments in another part of the building. Four young men were charged with the crime, and three—Karl and Dwight Armstrong and David Fine—were apprehended; the fourth, Leo Burt, never resurfaced. Rowen had nothing to do with the bombing. His writings were expository, not incendiary, but he was haunted by that event.

The destruction of the Army Math Research Center was a pivotal moment in the national antiwar movement, and its effect was most profound in Madison. The intense antiwar movement that turned white hot in October 1967 with the Dow demonstration kept going for years, into the early seventies, through the protests against the invasion of Cambodia, but there was a sense that things changed when Sterling Hall tumbled down and took an innocent life with it. By 1972 Rowen was involved in a different world, traveling the country with his wife, Susan, on behalf of the presidential campaign of his father-in-law, the antiwar candidate Senator George McGovern. It was within a year of McGovern's loss that Rowen returned to Madison and began a long, successful career moving between the worlds of municipal government and journalism in Madison and Milwaukee, his sensibilities shaped by feelings of outsiderness that came over him when the police marched into the Commerce Building.

Jane Brotman and Betty Menacher, who as naïve freshmen watched the events of Dow unfold—Brotman from the plaza outside, Menacher from the hallway next to her classroom—were each permanently touched by October 18, 1967. Three and a half decades later, the two women would attribute the course of their lives to changes that began that day. Menacher became a VISTA volunteer after graduating and eventually developed a career in educational policy in Milwaukee. Brotman grew more and more involved in the antiwar movement, started to develop a more internationalist perspective, and studied to become a psychologist. She left Madison in 1972, then moved back two decades later when her husband, a cardiologist, took a post at the University of Wisconsin. The job offer came on October 18, 1992. "There is something about that day for me," Brotman would say.

Bill Kaplan, the junior from Wilmette who escaped into the Commerce bathroom when the police stormed the building, became temporarily radicalized by the events of that day, beginning a process of political maturation in which he first swung left into the SDS, and then gradually eased back toward the center-left, settling in the Washington area as a liberal Democrat. He looked back with self-reproach at some of his actions during the sixties and early seventies. What especially troubled him was the fraying of his relationship with his older brother. Jack T. Kaplan graduated from Wofford College in 1969, was commissioned through ROTC as a second lieutenant, then went through Special Forces School and headed to Vietnam in 1970. During that time, the brothers barely spoke. More than two decades later, in the 1990s, after their mother's death, they began a reconciliation. "I wrote my brother a long letter saying, 'I'm ashamed that while you were in Vietnam, I never wrote you, and I feel bad about it,' " Bill Kaplan told me, his eyes filling with tears, at the end of a long interview. "Jack then said to me that he didn't feel bad about it because he remembered when I went to the airport with him when he left for Vietnam, and he never forgot that. I hadn't realized that meant anything to him. I really spilled my guts and said, 'I feel like an asshole, here you were, you could have been killed, and I'm not even writing you a letter because we were on different sides on the war.' And that was wrong and I regret it enormously."

On October 27, 2001, in the aftermath of the terrorist attack on the World Trade Center in New York, Kaplan wrote a guest column for the *Wisconsin State Journal* in Madison saying that he supported the U.S. military action in Afghanistan, where Jack Kaplan was again on the firing line with the Special Forces. "AntiVietnam War leader backs this effort," read the headline. Kaplan drove his brother to the airport again, just as he had thirty-one years earlier, but "this time," he wrote, "he not only has my love, but also my political support." On Vietnam, however, Kaplan's views had not changed. "I'm still against that goddamned war." He was also opposed to the invasion of Iraq.

William Sewell's chancellorship was short and unsweet. He resigned within a year of the Dow demonstration and took a year's leave to study at the Russell Sage Foundation in New York, then returned to Wisconsin and continued his highly regarded career in sociology. The strains of the administrative job, with the constant pressure of dealing with radical students and a conservative legislature, did nothing to help his angina problems, yet he went on to live an extremely long and productive life. When I first interviewed him, he was ninety years old and still reporting to his office every day in the Social Science Building, monitoring the major project of his career, a longitudinal study of people who graduated from high school in Wisconsin in 1959, tracing their education levels, goals, and accomplishments. During the seventies and eighties he was interviewed for oral histories of the university. He had acute observations on the antiwar leaders he dealt with during his year as chancellor and seemed especially fascinated by Paul Soglin. Soglin, he said, was "one of the second- or third-rate people in the movement," nowhere near as influential as Evan Stark or Robert Cohen, yet the one who rose politically. "He's clever," Sewell told an oral historian, "and he was by far the most consummate politician of all of them. . . . I don't think Paul ever did anything in his life that he didn't test the water pretty thoroughly first. But he's managed, you know. I think he's managed to do very well at it."

Sewell managed too, even though, three decades after the fact, he still worried that he would be remembered only for a single violent day in a long-ago October. One spring morning in 2001 Sewell suffered a stroke while climbing up the steep hill from a parking lot near Lake Mendota to the side entrance of the Social Science Building. He drifted in and out of consciousness for several weeks before dying on June 24, 2001. Old friends and colleagues trooped to his bedside in his final days, and one afternoon he and some colleagues got to talking about the troubles of the sixties. Sewell said that he had no regrets and no hard feelings, though he still could do without Evan Stark.

Charles S. Robb, the University of Wisconsin graduate and Marine Corps captain who had married President Johnson's daughter Lynda, sat in the family box in the gallery one night in January 1968 and listened to his father-in-law deliver the State of the Union address. Robb wore his "regular Marine greens" for the occasion, as President Johnson had asked him to do. He and Lynda "waited and waited" that night to hear words of resignation that President Johnson had confided to them he would utter, but the words were never spoken. Then came the Tet Offensive, and the candidacy of Eugene McCarthy, and McCarthy's winning of 42.2 percent of the vote in New Hampshire, and the emergence of Robert F. Kennedy. On the evening of March 31, 1968, Robb was in Okinawa, on his way to Vietnam, when President Johnson gave a nationally televised speech. Lynda Robb had said goodbye to her husband from Camp Pendleton the day before and had returned to the White House distraught and in tears, challenging her father to explain the war. The family was in emotional meltdown. The president himself seemed more upset than at any time since his mother's death. Now, here came the words: "I shall not seek, and I will not accept, the nomination of my party for another term as your president . . ."

The Democratic primary in Wisconsin was held two days later, on April 2. It was common wisdom by then that Johnson could not win that primary. As the notes of the president's war council later revealed, and as Chuck Robb and other family members later noted, LBJ was leaning against seeking reelection long before then, but nonetheless the prospect of defeat in Wisconsin might have been the final trigger to his decision.

During his years at the University of Wisconsin, political science graduate student Richard Cheney wanted nothing to do with Vietnam. He supported the war but did not want to serve in it, and was barely interested in it one way or another. He and his wife, Lynne Cheney, were on campus during the Dow demonstration in October 1967, but only vaguely remembered the protest, nothing more than Lynne's recollection of a mime troupe prancing in white face. They just wanted to do their work and move on. Life works in odd ways: Cheney, like some other politicians who moved through the Vietnam era barely touched by it, would spend the rest of his career with Vietnam often on his mind. It was easier for him to ignore it while it was going on than after it was over.

Cheney left for Washington after his Madison interlude, first working as an aide to Wisconsin congressman William Steiger. In 1969, Steiger was a leading member of a group of young House Republicans who, at the request of President Nixon, conducted an investigation to determine whether universities that had been disrupted by radical protests should lose federal funding. Cheney did the advance work for the group's trip to the University of Wisconsin, where the delegation met with faculty members and attended an SDS-sponsored event. The congressmen decided that Nixon should not cut university funding.

Six years later, when Saigon fell on April 30, 1975, Cheney was in the White House, working as a top aide to President Ford's chief of staff, Donald Rumsfeld. He watched Ford announce on television that everyone had been evacuated from the U.S. embassy, but then word came to their office that the announcement was premature. Sixteen years later, Cheney was sitting in the Pentagon office that Robert McNamara once occupied, dealing with questions of war and peace. He had never served in the military, had no qualms about avoiding service in Vietnam, and here he was, a defense secretary dealing with top generals, Colin Powell and Norman Schwarzkopf, whose entire perspectives were shaped by their experiences as young commanders in Vietnam. At dawn one day as the Gulf War was about to begin, Cheney visited the Vietnam Memorial. He was alone, except for his security detachment. "I wanted to be reminded what the cost was if you blew it," he told me later. "And there was no better, no more stark symbol of the cost if you didn't get it right than those fifty-eight thousand names on the wall." Cheney was talking to me twelve years later in his office in the West Wing of the White House. He was vice president now, a leading hawk of the Bush administration. Reminders of Vietnam echoed all around him as he led the push toward war with Iraq.

Coming the other way, from Washington to Wisconsin, and making another unlikely connection between the worlds of soldiers and protesters, was John A. Cash, the army officer and military historian who had been sent to Lai Khe to interview survivors after the Black Lions ambush. Cash, a career army man, arrived in Madison during the summer of 1969 for graduate work in Latin American studies. Professor Thomas Skidmore oversaw his work, which was to prepare him to be a military attaché in Brazil. Cash took language labs in Portuguese and courses on Brazilian history and culture. On the first day of his first course, he arrived early and noticed that when other students came in, they pushed their desks to the other side of the room, isolating him. Someone told him they didn't want to sit near a paid killer. "He was a bit shaken by this," Skidmore told me later. "But by the end of the year he was quite comfortable talking to the students and almost wished he could switch over and be in the academic world." His friends back at the Office of the Chief of Military History in Washington remember him calling back and saying, only half joking, "Man, this is rougher than Vietnam!" His first marriage was crumbling then, in part because his wife intensely opposed the Vietnam war, voicing the same arguments that Cash was hearing in Madison.

One legacy of Cash's time at the University of Wisconsin was a daughter born to a woman with whom he had a relationship there. Martha White, bright and lithe, grew up in Madison with the sensibilities of an artist and a touch of the local counterculture. By the time I interviewed her, in the spring of 2002, John A. Cash had been dead for three years, buried in section 67, grave 3909 at Arlington Cemetery. Martha revered her father but wanted nothing to do with war or the military.

ONE OF THE blessings of the Internet is the way that it has linked soldiers who long ago shared the most unforgettable experience of their lives, none more than veterans of Vietnam. Most of the soldiers who survived the battle of October 17, 1967, returned to the United States and went their own ways. Because of the way the nation received them, with neglect if not hostility, many of them decided to bury their pasts, never talk about Vietnam, and not seek out their old buddies. This resolution changed noticeably in the early 1990s, as the Internet age began, and underwent a dramatic shift as the Internet exploded at the same time that Vietnam vets reached their mid fifties and early sixties, when they were once again feeling their own mortality. The result has been an endless stream of e-mail conversations, a profusion of websites created by and devoted to veterans of scores of military units, with guest books and photographs, and more frequent reunions with greater attendance. The Black Lions, like every group, rely on networkers to connect them together, and they are lucky to have two men devoted to that cause.

The first is Tom Hinger, the medic who marched into battle with Alpha Company and worked heroically to save lives that day but felt nonetheless that he had failed his fellow soldiers because so many men died. In the weeks after the battle, Hinger and his fiancée, Jane, exchanged calendar letters and crossed out the days until his return. He made it back; they married and moved to Florida, where she became a teacher and he worked for the utility company and became an expert guide for bass fishermen, and he tried to live a normal life, although sometimes, especially around October 17, the memories of Vietnam and the battle would overwhelm him, and he would sleep on the floor and guard the yard as though it were a dangerous perimeter. Then, more than twenty years after the battle, he started reconnecting with a few of his fellow Black Lions, brought together because a television production company was doing a story on famous athletes killed in battle, including Donald Holleder, the All-America football player from Army. Doc Hinger had cradled Holleder in his arms as he died.

Through a series of searches and coincidences, a group formed around Hinger and the Holleder story. It included Jim Shelton, who had risen through the ranks to become a brigadier general before he retired. Shelton, who, along with being Terry Allen's best friend in Vietnam, had played college football against Holleder, had an irrepressible personality that made it easy for him to engage with enlisted men like Hinger and the guys, which he found preferable to sipping cocktails with other generals. Then there was Joe Costello, the Alpha grenadier who had marched into the jungle next to Hinger and who had bravely returned to the battlefront to help some stranded men. Costello had earned a Silver Star by his actions, along with something far more valuable—a rare and hard-earned peace of mind that allowed him to continue his life without feelings of regret or fear. He came back from Vietnam with an attitude that the rest of life was "all gravy." He returned to school, studied criminal justice, and became a progressive-thinking warden in the New York prison system. Tom Grady, who had served as the executive officer of Alpha Company, also joined the group, as did Steve Goodman, the Black Lions provisioner, and Carl Woodard, the Alpha squad leader; all three shared Costello's feeling that they were among the lucky ones. Grady had made it to colonel in the army reserve, while also doing well in the corporate world; Goody had entered the trucking business when he escaped the army; and Woody developed his talents in military security and intelligence.

These six men, four enlisted guys and two officers, formed the core of a larger gang that began meeting one football weekend every autumn at West Point for what Hinger dubbed the November Nightmare. Only Shelton had known Holleder, who was the original reason they got together, and none of them had attended West Point, but that barely mattered. After year-round reminders and e-mail updates from Hinger, a prodigious search engine all to himself, they descended on the United States Military Academy and environs for three days—paying homage to Holly, walking through the West Point graveyard, relaxing in a makeshift command post in a modest roadside motel, drinking and laughing and wolfing down hoagies and snoring and lying. Grady would tell the same joke every year and get louder laughs each time, and Goody would entertain the crowd with his uncanny ability to get better tickets for the Army game, and Doc would take his sarcastic jibes at the officers. And at some point, inevitably, they would rehash the events of October 17, 1967. Their "fearless leader," Big Jim Shelton, was obsessed by the battle; he began writing his own account of it. He was driven in part by the unanswerable question of whether things might have unfolded differently had he been at Allen's side that week, as his operations officer, instead of back in Lai Khe with the division brass. "It is etched into our souls," Shelton said to me once. "Every night we refight the battle."

As I began researching this book, these old soldiers took me in. Though I never served in the military and never experienced a battle, they allowed me to see the best of soldiering, a bond of love and respect that for all the hyperbole flying around was incomparably meaningful.

One recent year the November Nightmare had its first women guests. They were two of the Allen sisters, Consuelo and Bebe. They had known General Shelton for years, but this was the first time they would meet soldiers who were actually in the battle when their father was killed. In the motel room command post late on the first night, after hours of merriment, Joe Costello turned to Bebe and said, "I just wanted you to know something about your father. I might have been one of the last people to see your father alive." As Costello talked, in his clear, soothing way, Bebe's eyes filled with tears. She was confronting a subject that she had avoided for decades. Now here it was, the reality. "When I came by him during the battle he was calm and in complete control," Costello said, and then he talked more about the battle and Terry Allen. Consuelo, sitting nearby and overhearing the conversation, said, "I have to keep myself together, I can't have both of us crying." But she felt the same pull on her deepest emotions, and all weekend she kept asking more questions about the battle and the death of her father.

The second Black Lions networker was Fred Kirkpatrick, the Delta Company point man who by chance had escaped the battle because the army let him go to Japan on R and R that week, his second vacation of his tour. After his year in Vietnam, Kirkpatrick returned to Stow, Ohio, haunted by the fact that he was not there on October 17. He did not know how to channel his feelings until a few decades later, when he received a letter from the mother of Jackie Bolen, who was looking for information about how her son had died. This set Kirkpatrick on a path that became his life's mission, giving meaning to his sense of loss. With the advent of the Internet his effort became easier and more rewarding, as he tracked down survivors and families of the dead soldiers. He began organizing Black Lions reunions in Las Vegas, gatherings that centered on a memorial service on October 17, helping soldiers connect for the first time in decades.

It was at a Las Vegas reunion in October 2000 that Clark Welch saw his old first sergeant, Bud Barrow, for the first time since they had been in the hospital together in 1967. I was sitting with Welch at a table in the Black Lions hospitality suite when Barrow walked in, and I'll never forget the look that washed over his face. "There he is! You sonofabitch!" That said it all, and he rose and engulfed Barrow in a tearful embrace.

By the time of the 2002 reunion, Kirkpatrick had found most of the surviving enlisted men from the original C Packet, and many of them came to Las Vegas. Greg Landon, called the Professor, was there with his wife. He had returned to Amherst after his Vietnam tour and was now a military contract specialist. Mike Troyer, Bill McGath, Mike Taylor, Doug Cron, Terry Warner, and Tom Colburn sat around a table, all together for the first time since 1967. Nearby were Ernie Buentiempo, Santiago Griego, and Faustin Sena. Each man was dealing with past and present in his own way. I felt a special affinity with Sena, a poetic Mexican-American who happened to be a huge Green Bay Packers fan, an unlikely cheesehead. One day when we were talking, I asked why he came to these reunions. I had met him a year earlier at another Black Lions reunion at Fort Jackson, South Carolina, which he and Griego reached by driving twenty-seven hours nonstop from New Mexico. "I have a headache every day of my life," Sena explained. "Except when I am here, with these guys, my headache goes away."

More than a year before the 2002 reunion, as I was working the telephone trying to track down survivors of the battle, I reached Tom Colburn at a number in Michigan. His voice was soft and shaking, and when I told him that I was trying to interview men who had fought with the Black Lions on October 17, 1967, his voice quavered more. He said he was still getting treatment for that day and was not ready to talk about it. Now, here he was, in Las Vegas, sitting at a table with his Ohio squadmates—Baby-san at age fifty-three.

It will be hard for me to think about war ever again without considering Tom Colburn. He was barely eighteen, in the jungle, all hell breaking loose, bullets raining down from the trees, a buddy wounded, within sight, in the sunlight only yards away, calling his name, pleading for help, and there was Colburn, behind a tree, shaking with fear that if he moved to help, he would get killed. Those few awful minutes cruelly defined his sense of self for all the years to come. When he came back to Michigan, he pushed everybody away, refused to go outside, and when he had to attend family events, he sat in a corner by himself. He was always looking for the closest exit, preferring doorways, where he could escape. Thunder made him jump. He had a hard time being near people. For a time he mowed lawns for the Pontiac parks department. More recently he worked for a moving company, but that ended sadly. The younger men on his crew discovered that loud noises spooked him. They were insensitive slugs with no knowledge of his history, and they thought it was fun to slam things around and watch him shudder. Finally, when they lit a pack of firecrackers, Colburn walked off the job and kept walking, right up the hill, ghostly white, sweating profusely, until he reached Shenanigans bar on Kennett Road.

By the time of the reunion Colburn was on 50-percent disability. "I still shake a lot," he said. "Sometimes I'm holding a glass of water and it slips out of my hand." His hand trembled as he spoke.

On the day before Thanksgiving 1967, an envelope arrived at the Sikorski family home in Milwaukee. It was stamped "Verified Deceased, Return to Sender." It was the letter that Danny Sikorski's sister, Diane, had written him on October 17 after waking from a dream in which she heard his voice and saw an image of him with a hole where his stomach should have been. In the years after Danny's death, Diane heard about someone who got pregnant to try to keep her boyfriend out of the draft. Another person gained weight to keep out of the draft. She worked with a woman she admired greatly whose son fled to Canada to avoid the draft. His mother wanted him to come home; he was safe but not free.

In 1972 Diane married Ron Kramer, a man she met at the manufacturing plant where they both worked. She was relieved that he was 4-F.

For thirty-four years, until the time I went to interview her in a Milwaukee suburb in the summer of 2001, Diane felt "hatred, denial, despair,
depression" whenever she thought about Vietnam and her brother's
death. Then, in the aftermath of our conversations, she said she "was finally able to let go." She ordered a bronze nameplate for Daniel Sikorski
to be placed at Saint Adalbert's Cemetery and a personalized brick with
his name on it for the Vietnam Veterans Memorial at Veterans Park. In
the summer of 2002 she felt ready, finally, to visit the Vietnam Memorial
in Washington for the first time. She stopped at block 28 E of the sloping wall and left a memory box on the ground. Starting with Terry
Allen in Row 25, fifteen rows in that single granite block are taken up by
soldiers killed in the battle of Ong Thanh. Diane found her brother's
name in Row 31.

On January 22, 2002, on my way to Vietnam, I stopped in San Francisco and met with Jean Ponder Allen Soto. I had interviewed her at
length already, and this was more a conversation. The Soto in her name
came from her second husband, whom she had married within a year of
Terry Allen's death. They both had worked as VISTA volunteers in the
colonias of El Paso. Soto was a stepfather to the three Allen sisters, who
had a difficult time with him, and eventually he and Jean divorced. Now
she was living in Richmond, California, and finishing her doctoral studies at the Graduate Theological Union at Berkeley on sexuality and the
Catholic Church. She and her three daughters all had obtained undergraduate degrees from schools in Boston. Of all the characters in my
book, Jean was in many ways the most complicated for me. She had invested trust in me by telling me her story, with all of its unflattering details. I wanted to present her actions accurately, all the while realizing
that many people would dislike her because of what she had done. But
of course she understood that better than I; she had dealt with it for
three and a half decades.

It was not until many years after Terry Allen's death that she was able
to mourn him, she told me. The process began when his mother died
and Jean went through her effects and found letters expressing grief at
Terry's death. "I surprised myself because I wept so at these," she said.
She began thinking about Terry and their relationship and the struggle
of soldiers in Vietnam in a new way. Before, she had thought that "anybody who was in the war was a bad guy," but now she realized how

wrong that was, and she came to think of them as sympathetic figures in a national tragedy. This took her through another painful process, unearthing emotions that she had buried. One day, watching a documentary on the Civil War, she saw old veterans of North and South embrace, and she found the reconciliation a wondrous mystery and hoped that something similar could happen as the sides of war and peace from the Vietnam era reached old age. "We set these structures that we are so deadly serious about," she said. "And they become issues of life and death and matters of betrayals and hatreds, and yet somehow, sometimes, that is what in the end creates the possibility of the two sides joyously embracing."

Here we sat, across from each other at a long conference table in a quiet room inside the offices of the foreign ministry in Ho Chi Minh City: Clark Welch and I on one side, Vo Minh Triet and two interpreters on the other. It was eight thirty on the morning of January 30, 2002. Two days earlier I had given the Vietnamese press office Triet's name, which I had seen on U.S. military documents: intelligence reports from the late 1960s and more recent reports regarding MIA searches in Vietnam. Now Clark and I were looking at Triet in the flesh, the officer who had commanded the First Regiment in 1967. I was afraid that he might not remember anything about the battle, and I wanted to learn as much as I could from him about his life and times anyway, so I asked him questions for the first few hours that had nothing to do with October 17, 1967. Clark thought this was a waste of time, though he was polite enough to tolerate it.

Then finally, after a lunch break, we pulled out our maps of the area north of Lai Khe in the Long Nguyen Secret Zone, and I started to say a few things about the Black Lions and what they were doing on search-and-destroy missions that October leading up to the battle. Triet rose from his chair, examined the maps for a few minutes, which seemed like forever, and at last put his finger right on the coordinates of the battlefield and said something in Vietnamese, which was translated by my interpreter, Kyle Horst. The words gave me chills.

"Of course I remember," Triet said. "We weren't supposed to be there. Let me tell you how it happened."

For the next two hours he talked about the battle and the days before and after, providing details that I later used to fill out the narrative. The more he talked, the more it seemed that Welch's comprehension of Vietnamese, which he had studied briefly before being sent to Vietnam in 1967, came back to him. The two old soldiers were talking the same language, communicating, even when they did not understand everything the other was saying. At the end of the interview I asked whether Colonel Triet would be willing to ride with us the next day to the battlefield. He said why not, he had nothing better to do. He was seventy-two years old and retired; he spent his days now as a functionary in Ho Chi Minh City's Ward 14, promoting population control.

At eight the next morning our entourage piled into a van for the bumpy ride north up Thunder Road. Triet was there, and Clark Welch, and Consuelo Allen, and her friend Rob Keefe, and Kyle Horst, my guide and interpreter. Also my wife and I, and a driver and our Vietnamese minder, Madam Ha. Before the van pulled away from the Hotel Continental, Triet turned to Clark Welch, soldier to soldier, and said of that long ago battle on the ground we were revisiting, "No one won that day."

It was a statement with several levels of meaning, but above all, it was a grace note, a way of connecting men who had once tried to kill each other. Triet later made the same comment to Consuelo Allen.

Kyle was fluent in Vietnamese and seemed to know everyone in the country, having lived there off and on since the early 1980s, when he worked on refugee issues for the United Nations. He had been to the battle area several months earlier on a scouting mission. Clark Welch had tried to get there a few days earlier, before I'd arrived in Ho Chi Minh City, and had gotten close but couldn't quite find it. He did encounter a friendly family that farmed a small plot of land a few miles away. From them, using his basic Vietnamese, he learned that they had supported America and South Vietnam and had fled to the village of Chon Thanh during the war and that after, the father had been sent to a prison reeducation camp for many years.

This time, executing a few turns at intersections that were not apparent on every map, we made it to an unmarked road closer to the battlefield. We drove down that road until it became impassable, then got out and walked. Our destination was the bamboo and tin house of Nguyen Van Lam, another local farmer. Lam had supported the Viet Cong during the war. He had served as a company commander in Rear Service Group 83 and fought in the October 17 battle. When we arrived at Lam's, he was out. A son said he was attending a wedding, but Lam showed up shortly thereafter, the word having spread quickly about the appearance of the bearded American (Kyle) and some other strangers with big noses.

Nguyen Van Lam had ten sons, the youngest ten years old. At the entrance to his house they kept squirrels in a cage. In a muddy little enclosed pond in the side yard, they raised eels. There were several framed portraits and certificates on the walls of his living area, some honoring Lam for his war service, others honoring his wife's brother, who was considered a martyr, killed "opposing the Americans to save the country."

When Lam arrived from the wedding, Triet immediately recognized him, even though they had only been together for a few days thirty-five years earlier. "Oh my God," Lam said. "You are still alive?"

They hugged and sat down in the shaded opening to the house, clasping hands much of the time as they talked. When Triet heard that Lam had ten children, he chastised him. "You give birth like chickens," he said, and asked whether Lam and his wife had ever heard of population control.

Are you sick at all? Triet asked.

No, Lam said. He had some hearing loss from air strikes and a cluster bomb pellet in his lung, but other than that he was fine.

Do you have AIDS? Triet asked.

Lam laughed. Triet was still ribbing him for his prodigious family.

Soon we were off, walking tentatively across a creaking bamboo monkey bridge over the Ong Thanh stream, following a narrow path through the manioc fields, passing a herd of water buffalo, and moving south toward the battlefield. Our first stop was where the Black Lions had set up their night defensive position on October 16. There were still a few holes in the field, remnants of American bunkers. The open land we walked through next had been dense jungle in 1967. Clark Welch, checking his GPS location finder, said we were right on target, but he kept repeating, "It looks so different. Everything has changed."

Lam said that in the days after the battle, the area was heavily bombed and then defoliated so that there were no trees left. Years later everyone in the area started getting headaches, he said. Not long ago a few local people in their forties and fifties had terrible headaches for three days and then died. The villagers thought it was because of Agent Orange.

As we moved closer to the battlefield, Triet and Welch seemed like they were in their own world again, the two proficient soldiers reliving the battle. They would walk off together and point and say a few things, describing the line of march of the American companies and the positioning of Triet's three battalions. We stopped a few more times, once for Lam to describe a spot where a huge tree once stood. Was it the tree near where Donald Holleder was killed? Perhaps. We were near the area that the Americans called the draw, an intermittent stream. At our next stop Lam pointed to a depression in the ground and said this was where he and his men, on the morning after the battle, had found the torso of an American soldier that had been ripped apart by wild pigs. I wondered whether it could have been Hargrove or Fitzgerald, the two MIAs. *What color was it?* I asked. Hargrove and Fitzgerald were black. *White,* said Lam. So I presumed the torso was found by the American recovery party later that day.

A hundred meters further, Clark checked his GPS and his maps and said we were nearing the ground of the battle. We had to move to our right, or east, a few hundred meters, he said, so we turned and walked that direction. In 1967 this had been dense jungle; now it was a government rubber plantation, a grove of medium-height trees planted in neat rows. It was refreshingly cool, away from the ninety-degree heat, and sunlight dappled gently through the grove. It felt as though we were walking into a cathedral. The ground was covered with dry brown leaves that crunched softly as we walked. And then Clark pointed to a spot that matched the coordinates of where Terry Allen and the battalion command were killed.

An anthill happened to be right there, just as there had been during the battle. A different anthill, obviously, but it served as a symbolic memorial nonetheless. I asked our Vietnamese companions to keep quiet so we could pay our respects. Clark Welch bit his lip and winced, memories of that day cascading through his mind. Tears streamed down Consuelo Allen's face as she studied the lonely spot where her father had died. The moment that he was killed and this moment, as she stood on the same ground, separated by thirty-five years, now seemed as one. Her mother had written a poem that she wanted me to read if and when we reached this spot. She called it "A Prayer for the Journey to the Battlefield."

> Through this pilgrimage
> may you illumine
> the battle's grace
> the noble face
> of those who fought
> May your footsteps

> where blood was found
> turn that ground
> to wide forgiveness
> And heal and free
> those left behind
> deep peace find
> that passes understanding
> Blessed are the peacemakers

The next day while I was conducting interviews in Ho Chi Minh City, Clark, Consuelo, my wife, and the rest of our group walked through the city. As they passed a crowd of young boys selling postcards, someone, unseen, slipped open Clark's fanny pack and stole his wallet. It was the only unkind act we encountered during our days there. On the following day Consuelo returned to the United States, my wife and I took a weekend flight to Hanoi, and Clark stayed in Saigon, awaiting our return. I had no qualms about leaving him alone. He had a way about him that made him an endearing figure in our little quarter of old Saigon near the Hotel Continental. Ha and Phuong, two charming and street-smart girls, adept in colloquial English—which they had learned by interacting with tourists, selling them postcards and books—took great care of Clark, guiding him on his ventures around the city. Little Ha, a four-foot-six teenager who looked hip in her black Nike stocking cap, had warned Clark to watch his wallet and had scolded him when she had learned that it was gone. They showed him where to eat, what to drink, and how to work the system. They poked his belly and pulled the hair on his big arms. The cyclo drivers loved him too. "Clark our friend, Clark our friend!" they would say, looking for him, holding his business card and lifting an arm high above their heads to depict the tall American.

All of this at times overwhelmed Clark. He delighted in his friendship with Ha and Phuong and the cyclo drivers and felt "an extraordinary attachment" to the soldiers from the other side. "We once fought against each other; now we are becoming old soldiers together—on both sides," Clark wrote later, looking back on his experience. "We together admire the toughness and bravery of our magnificent soldiers—on both sides. We together grieve for the terrible losses—on both sides."

The day after we returned from Hanoi, Clark and I drove north again up Thunder Road. Our first stop was Lai Khe. The American soldiers were long gone, but the village remained. Some women there told us that until a decade ago, some of the barracks had housed hundreds of Amerasian children, the progeny of First Division soldiers. They were all gone now. Most of them were in the United States. We saw the remnants of the old Big Red One ice cream factory and met two women who had worked at a bar in the village in 1967. Ho Thi Bang said that she was twenty-eight then, too old to be a bar girl, so she washed dishes. From there we drove up the highway and around the unmarked dirt roads again to Nguyen Van Lam's house. There was too much else going on during our first meeting, as we toured the battlefield, for me to interview him, so now we sat down and talked. When we were done, he introduced us to his family—all of the boys, his wife, a daughter-in-law, and a grandchild. His seventh son was maimed, one hand cut off at the wrist. He had been weeding around the family rubber trees in their garden across the road, they said, and an old grenade from an American M-79 came out of the ground and exploded, shattering his right hand.

There was still a lot of ammo around, Lam said. He pointed to a pile near the squirrel cage. "My, my, my," Clark said, looking at a collection of bullets and pieces of shrapnel hidden under a banana tree. Lam reached down and picked up some shrapnel and said, "You left these behind." Nearby was a live U.S. mortar round.

When we finished our visit, Kyle Horst told me about something he had heard the last time he was in the area, something about a memorial not too far away. One of Lam's sons said he knew where it was, so he came along with us. We got lost, stopped for directions, and backtracked twice, but finally found someone who could take us there. Our van stopped in the middle of nowhere, it seemed. There was a forest to our right, and we walked several hundred yards through the brush and the trees until we reached a small clearing, and there stood a large marker. It loomed several feet above us, shiny marble, with intricate maps and a battle flag and writings etched on both sides. Someone had put a lot of effort into creating the marker, but no one had bothered to maintain it. For all practical purposes, it was a lost memorial, with no guides, no signs telling people how to get to it, nothing. "You wouldn't just stumble on it," said Clark. The Vietnamese locals told us we were the first foreigners ever to visit this spot.

One part of the marker read, in Vietnamese: "From 4 P.M. 26 April 75 to 11:30 30 April 75, this HCMC [Ho Chi Minh Campaign] headquarters commanded a decisive battle to capture and liberate all of Saigon and the provinces of the Mekong Delta, concluding the historic Ho Chi Minh campaign, completing victory in the American imperialist war of aggression and completing the democratic national revolution in the entire nation."

Who could have guessed that here, only a few kilometers from where the Black Lions fought and died on October 17, 1967, the command of the North Vietnamese Army, eight years later, would organize the final battle of the long war.

ON FEBRUARY 7, our last full day in Vietnam, we rode a Russian-built hydrofoil down the Saigon River to Vung Tau, the resort town on the South China Sea. A cabbie drove us across the peninsula to what was known as Back Beach. It was lined with restaurants and resort hotels, and if you didn't look at the Vietnamese lettering, you could have thought you were at Port Aransas or Mustang Island along the Texas coast. We stopped in a parking lot, and Clark Welch walked with me toward the beach and pointed to the spot where he and Bud Barrow stood with their makeshift Delta Company flag, waiting for their new soldiers. Then we took a cyclo ride over to Nui Nho, the little mountain, and climbed to the top. The steep, winding path was lined with benches, each one donated by a Catholic parish in the States. There were hundreds more on the mountaintop, more than ever could be used. They were meant for the mind more than the body, reminders, connections, from past to present, there to here. Etched into each bench was the name of an American city, from Atlanta to West Chester, all the places where Vietnamese refugees had resettled when they fled their country after the war. Rising above the benches was a giant statue of Christ, his head encircled by a halo, his arms outstretched, facing the sea. This odd little mountain of Catholic belief at the entryway to a communist land.

It was such a soothing afternoon, with a refreshing breeze. A Vietnamese boy in a hang glider soared and looped silently, like an angel, above our heads. I sat on a bench at the edge of the mountain, the statue rising behind me, and looked down past two old French cannons to the arc of white sand and blue-green sea far below, and thought about the USNS *Pope,* and how once, long ago, it came to a stop right at that spot, and the young soldiers of C Packet—George, Grady, Landon, Troyer, Sena, Farrell, Griego, Colburn, Cron, Nagy, Garcia, Reece, McMeel, Warner, Tallent, Miller, Taylor, McGath, and Schroder—clambered down the Jacob's ladders, rolled in on the landing craft, made their way ashore, and marched into sunlight.

NOTES

T HE NARRATIVE of this book is based on primary sources: hundreds of letters and journal entries, thousands of archival documents, and interviews with 180 people. Many subjects were interviewed several times; they are usually listed by date of the first interview. The vast majority of documents were found at ten exceptional archives:

National Archives at College Park, Md. (NARA)

U.S. Army Center of Military History, Fort McNair, Washington, D.C. (CMH)

U.S. Military History Institute, Carlisle Barracks, Carlisle, Pa. (MHI)

University of Wisconsin–Madison Archives Oral History Project, Steenbock Memorial Library, Madison (UW)

State Historical Society of Wisconsin, Madison (SHSW)

LBJ Presidential Library, Austin, Tex. (LBJ)

First Division Museum at Cantigny, Wheaton, Ill. (FDM)

National Personnel Records Center, St. Louis, Mo. (NPRC)

University of Texas at El Paso Library Special Collections Department (UTEP)

Post Street Archives, Midland, Mich. (PSA)

CHAPTER 1: SAILING TO VUNG TAU

PAGE

3   *No one at the military base:* Ints. Jim George, May 27, 2001; Tom Grady, March 5, 2000.

4   *When they could, the bored:* Ints. Greg Landon, June 19, 2002; Mike Troyer, August 21, 2002; Peter Miller, August 27, 2002.

4   *"Morale of the men":* Greg Landon letters to parents, June 8–30, 1967.

5   *Schroder was a quiet:* Int. with Eleanor Schroder Clark, January 3, 2001.

6   *"Was woke up this morning":* Journal of Pvt. Jack Schroder, July 5, 1967.

6   *That evening a posse of privates:* Michael Taylor letter to parents, July 5, 1967.

6   *at their own private going-away:* Int. Tom Grady, March 5, 2000.

7   *It was the USNS* General John Pope: *Dictionary of American Fighting Ships,* Department of the Navy, Washington, D.C.

7   *When sunlight hit:* Ints. Tom Grady, March 27, 2002; Faustin Sena, October 18, 2002.

7   *Not long after they shoved off:* Schroder journal; ints. Faustin Sena, October 18, 2002; Michael Taylor, October 19, 2002; Santiago Griego, October 19, 2002; Bill McGath, October 19, 2002.

8   *The only good part of the voyage:* Int. Tom Grady, March 5, 2000.

9   *Private Landon, who also kept a diary:* Greg Landon shipboard journal, July 5–28, 1967.

9   *News from the outside world: Pope Pourri,* editions of July 15–20, 1967. The front page of the shipboard newspaper on the 15th featured an illustration of a bikini-clad woman wearing a USNS *Pope* float around her middle. Each day's edition included a position report. On the 15th they were at 30 06 N latitude and 175 06 W longitude. The *Pope* had steamed 3,007 miles and had 3,063 to go. Also ints. Santiago Griego, October 18, 2002; Mike Taylor, October 19, 2002; Greg Landon, June 19, 2002.

10   *That last sigh of relief:* Int. Jim George, May 27, 2001. Also George letters to wife Jackie, July 7–28, 1967.

11   *Thoughts of killing also raced:* Ints. Mike Troyer, August 21, 2002; Peter Miller, August 27, 2002; Bill McGath, October 19, 2002; also letters of Mike Taylor from USNS *Pope* to parents, July 8–27, 1967.

12   *Whether it was mass dyslexia:* Jack Schroder journal, July 5–28, 1967. Also ints. Faustin Sena, May 27, 2001; Santiago Griego, October 18, 2002.

12   *They reached Okinawa at nine:* Jack Schroder journal, July 22, 1967; Greg Landon journal, July 22, 1967; int. Mike Troyer, August 21, 2002.

12   *The troops who scrambled off:* Ints. Tom Grady, March 27, 2002; Jim George, May 27, 2001; Jack Schroder journal, July 5–28, 1967.

13   *The morning sunrise was soothing:* Mike Troyer letter to parents, July 24, 1967. Ints. Jim George, May 27, 2001; Peter Miller, August 27, 2002.

15   *Soldiers line the deck:* NARA military film archive, October 7 landing by 1st Infantry cameraman Bigley. Carland, *Stemming the Tide,* 66.

15   *The four-star general and the ao dai wisps:* Int. Doug Tallent, October 19, 2002.

15   *modern-day Don Quixote and Sancho Panza:* Ints. Clark Welch, January 28–February 8, 2002; Clarence Barrow, October 16, 2000.

16   *It was raining when they arrived:* Ints. Greg Landon, June 19, 2002; Mike Troyer, August 20, 2002; Jim George, May 27, 2001; Tom Grady, March 27, 2002.

CHAPTER 2: TRIET'S MARCH SOUTH

18   *He was a southerner, the sixth son:* Descriptions of Triet's early life, experiences march-
     ing south down the Truong Son range in 1961, and service with the 1st Regiment based
     on author interviews with Vo Minh Triet in Ho Chi Minh City, Vietnam, January 30,
     31, February 7, 2002, Kyle Horst translator.
18   *Nguyen Dinh Chieu, the great blind poet:* "Funeral Oration for the Partisans of Can
     Giuoc, Nguyen Dinh Chieu," *Vietnamese Literature,* Hanoi, 1980.
19   *It was to be a temporary separation: Documents Related to the Implementation of the
     Geneva Agreements Concerning Vietnam,* 181–83; United States Senate, Committee on
     Foreign Relations, *Background Information Relating to Southeast Asia and Vietnam,*
     1967.
19   *In the official military history: Su Doan 9,* People's Army Publishing House, Hanoi,
     translated by Foreign Broadcast Information Service, 8.
22   *knew much about these arriving Americans:* James G. Zumwalt ints. with 9th Division
     Col. Ta Minh Kham, 1995, and Nguyen Song, political commissar for 2nd regiment,
     9th Division. Zumwalt, a Marine Corps Vietnam veteran and son of the late Admiral
     Elmo Zumwalt Sr., spent several years interviewing former Viet Cong and North
     Vietnamese Army veterans. His interest began after the death of his brother, Elmo
     Zumwalt Jr., another Vietnam veteran who served in heavily defoliated areas and
     whose cancer was believed to have been caused by exposure to the herbicide Agent Or-
     ange. James Zumwalt and his father helped pressure the U.S. government to recognize
     health problems related to Agent Orange. During his many trips to Vietnam, James
     Zumwalt became curious about the daily lives of people fighting on the other side. His
     fascinating but as yet unpublished manuscript, *Bare Feet, Iron Will,* is based on the al-
     most 200 interviews he conducted from 1994 to 2000.

CHAPTER 3: LAI KHE, SOUTH VIETNAM

25   *Before a massive repair job:* "Thunder Road," *Danger Forward,* the magazine of the Big
     Red One, Vietnam, September 1967.
25   *There was no one comparable:* Descriptions of Clark Welch based on letters from Welch
     to his wife Lacy, June–October 1967; documents of the 1st Infantry Division in Viet-
     nam, NARA; and author interviews with Welch, January 28–February 8, 2002.
32   *He would go nowhere without the new first sergeant:* Ints. Clark Welch, January 28–
     February 8, 2002; Clarence Barrow, October 16, 2000, October 18, 2002.
34   *"We are called the Black Lions":* Jack Schroder letter to wife Eleanor, August 3, 1967.
35   *Mike Troyer wrote home:* Mike Troyer letter to parents, July 30, 1967.
35   *A more subdued account:* Greg Landon letter to parents, July 31, 1967.
35   *Sometimes the truth stretching:* Clark Welch letter to wife Lacy, August 9, 1967. In this
     letter, along with the story of the Walter Mittyish soldier, Welch related the psycho-
     logical aspects of being a company commander. "I've got all the personnel problems of
     175 men!" he wrote. "So far this has involved sending 2 back to the States and coun-
     seling 7 others. . . . I was a little bit concerned about all the counseling I've had to do
     until I heard what the other new Delta company here has had. They've got 5 AWOL
     and many, many other assorted things going on."
37   *"We had a beer party last night":* Jack Schroder letter to wife Eleanor, August 10, 1967.
38   *Mere days in country:* Letters from Greg Landon, Mike Troyer, Clark Welch, August
     1–12, 1967.

39 *There were always fucking new guys:* Ints. Tom Hinger, March 12, 2000; Joe Costello, November 3, 2000; Michael Arias, March 1, 2001; Steve Goodman, November 20, 2000.

42 *Danny Sikorski was another gunner:* Ints. Diane Sikorski Kramer, July 28, 2001; Edmund Sikorski, August 5, 2000; scrapbooks of Danny Sikorski and Diane Sikorski.

44 *When Clark Welch took command of Delta:* Ints. Tom Grady, March 27, 2002; Jim George, May 27, 2001; Clark Welch letter to wife Lacy, August 5, 1967.

CHAPTER 4: EL PASO, TEXAS

47 *El Paso, on the verge of a boom: Fort Bliss–Past and Present,* Fort Bliss Visitors Bureau, January 1968. Ints. Consuelo Allen, February 2, 2001; Albert Schwartz, February 2, 2001, Jonathan and Pat Rogers, February 4, 2001.

48 *In from the above-ninety heat:* Ints. Bill and Genevieve (Bebe) Coonly, February 2, 2001.

49 *"My dear Sonny":* Maj. Gen. Terry de la Mesa Allen Sr. letter to son, Terry Allen Jr., December 8, 1942, UTEP. The father signed off that letter, "A very merry Xmas, Old Top Pops."

50 *The soldier's life went back:* "Allen and His Men," *Time,* August 9, 1943, 32–36.

51 *Ernie Pyle occasionally slept in his tent:* Ernie Pyle, *Here is Your War, America's Favorite Correspondent Tells the Story of Our Soldiers' First Big Campaign,* 187–88.

51 *General Omar Bradley yanked Allen from command:* Terry Allen Sr. letters, 1943, UTEP; Michael D. Pearlman, *To Make America Safe for Democracy,* 249; "Allen and Huebner: Contrast in Command," Col. Bryce F. Denno, Army, 1984.

51 *Terry Allen Sr. was a skilled polo player:* Ints. Consuelo Allen, February 2, 2001; Albert Schwartz, February 4, 2001; *El Paso Times Sunday Magazine,* February 21, 1965; "Cavalryman versus Cowboy," *True West,* September–October 1965. The *True West* article repeated an incident from the race first reported in the *Brooklyn Daily Eagle* of December 21, 1922: "The Major had stopped in a restaurant for breakfast and had ordered bacon and eggs. While waiting for the cook to fill the order, the old gentleman proprietor of the restaurant stopped at the Major's table and remarked that the race between a soldier and a cowboy was surely on the lips of half the country. ''Course,' he drawled, 'Major Allen don't have a chance to beat Key Dunne. That cowboy will wear out the Army officer; he's too strong for him. That Army horse hasn't a chance to stick it out with a mustang in a 300-mile race.'

"'Oh, I don't know,' Major Allen replied. 'I can't say as to the outcome of the race yet, but I'm Major Allen and I'm out in front at the present time and still in good condition. Up to the present, the joke is on you, so hurry on with the ham and eggs.'

"'The joke is not only on me,' replied the restaurant owner, with a chuckle, 'but the ham and eggs as well.'"

52 *From the war zone in Europe in 1945:* Terry Allen Sr. letter to Charles Meurisse and Co., Chicago, April 4, 1945, UTEP.

52 *"I have avoided seeking political influence":* Terry Allen Sr. letter to Capt. Reese Cleveland, September 17, 1944, UTEP; letter to Alfred P. Wechsler, October 4, 1944, UTEP.

53 *As a cadet in Company H-1: Howitzer* yearbook, 1952; Assembly, December 1975; Red Blaik letter to Mrs. Terry Allen, January 21, 1949, Allen family papers.

54 *Terry Sr. was watching his son's progress:* John C. Schuller letter to Terry Allen Sr., December 20, 1955, UTEP.

54 *and then was sent west to Colorado Springs:* Ints. Bebe and Bill Coonly, February 2, 2001.

55 *General Allen and Mary Fran lived:* Ints. Conseulo Allen, February 2, 2001; Bebe and Bill Coonly, February 2, 2001; Jean Ponder Allen Soto, February 3, 2001; *El Paso Times,* February 2, 1965.

56 *Always on the lookout to help his son:* Terry Allen Sr. letter to Major Gen. R. W. Porter, September 1965, Allen family papers; *El Paso Times,* October 1, 3, 8, 1961.

57 *After a honeymoon on the Riviera:* Int. Jean Ponder Allen Soto, February 3, 2001; Jean Allen letter to Mary Frances Allen, September 12, 1962, Allen family papers.

57 *"Your considered counsel has always been":* Terry Allen Jr. letter to father, September 3, 1963, Allen family papers.

58 *Out of whimsy and desperation:* Int. Jean Ponder Allen Soto, February 3, 2001.

59 *Holding on dearly to reminders:* Ints. Consuelo Allen, February 2, 2001; Jean Ponder Allen Soto, February 3, 2001; Albert Schwartz, February 3, 2001.

59 *"I was thrilled to receive three letters":* Terry Allen Jr. letter to wife Jean, March 25, 1967, Allen family papers.

62 *How different that world:* Int. Jean Ponder Allen Soto, February 3, 2001.

63 *"This is for all the women":* Int. Consuelo Allen, February 2, 2001.

63 *"A very special place": The Officer's Guide,* 1967–68 edition, 104.

63 *She struck up a relationship:* Int. Jean Ponder Allen Soto, February 3, 2001.

64 *He drove over to 5014 Timberwolf:* Ints. Bebe and Bill Coonly, February 2, 2001; Consuelo Allen, February 2, 2001; Jean Ponder Allen Soto, February 3, 2001.

65 *Tad Smith was not a divorce lawyer:* Int. Tad Smith, December 12, 2001.

66 *"You can't leave!":* Ints. Consuelo Allen, February 2, 2001; Jean Ponder Allen Soto, February 3, 2001.

CHAPTER 5: SONG OF NAPALM

69 *On the Sunday morning of March 12, 1967:* Int. E. N. Brandt, April 12, 2001; internal Dow document from W. H. Coffey to Dr. A. P. Beutel, "Napalm Meeting with Department of Defense Officials," March 9, 1967, PSA.

69 *Dow Chemical was not one of the big boys:* Department of Defense contractors list, 1967; ints. E. N. Brandt, April 12, 2001; Herbert Doan, April 12, 2001; Dave Coslett, April 26, 2001; Bill Seward, April 27, 2001; Ray Rolf, May 1, 2001; name file, Dow Chemical Co., LBJ. "Dear Jimmy, I have on the handsome tie you sent me," Johnson aide Walter W. Jenkins wrote to Dow's Jimmy Phillips. "I want you to know how proud I am of it. Many thanks, my friend, for thinking of me."

70 *Napalm was cheap and easy to make:* E. N. Brandt, *Growth Company* (Michigan State University Presss, 1967), 351–70; ints. Herbert Doan, April 12, 2001; E. N. Brandt, April 12, 2001.

70 *Dow in turn became the most visible target:* Dow internal document, 1967 list of campus protests, PSA; Brandt, *Public Relations Journal,* July 1968.

71 *"the 'Merchants of Death' label":* J. J. Boddie internal memorandum, December 12, 1966, PSA.

71 *Before then, as Brandt once explained:* Brandt, *Public Relations Journal,* July 1968. Also *NYT,* March 11, 1967, 17.

72 *The* Ramparts *piece:* Pepper, "The Children of Vietnam," *Ramparts,* January 1967. The preface was written by Dr. Benjamin Spock.

73 *Pepper's base number of 415,000 civilian deaths:* Langguth, *Our Vietnam,* 622. "Civilian casualties were impossible to estimate," Langguth wrote, describing the situation at the

time of the Paris Peace Talks in 1973. "They may have run to a million men, women and children." Also Summers, *Vietnam War Almanac,* 112: "Further estimates are that some 300,000 South Vietnamese civilians died in the war. Additionally, North Vietnamese civilian deaths from American bombing totaled some 65,000. These statistics on civilian casualties are a matter of considerable controversy and the true numbers will probably never be known." *Impact of the Vietnam War,* United States Senate, Committee on Foreign Relations, 1971. In the introduction, the report states that "the survey spells out the casualty figures ... over a million civilian casualties in South Vietnam"; *CBS Evening News* interview, May 12, 1967, with physician members of Committee of Responsibility.

74 *veteran War correspondent Martha Gellhorn: Ladies' Home Journal,* January 1967, republished in *Reporting Vietnam,* Part One, 1998.

75 *When Ned Brandt and two associates:* Int. E. N. Brandt, April 12, 13, 2001.

76 *"Dear Mr. Doan":* Letter written for Robert S. McNamara by Dow public relations department, published in newspapers in December 1967, PSA.

CHAPTER 6: MADISON, WISCONSIN

77 *The 1967 fall term: Daily Cardinal,* October 4, 1967; *Wisconsin State Journal,* October 5, 1967; Letters of Betty Menacher, September–October 1967; *Capital Times,* October 1–15, 1967.

80 *There were 5,385 freshmen: Characteristics of 1967 Freshman Class,* UW Registrar records; *Wisconsin Alumnus* magazine, vol. 69, December 1967.

82 *"Our image, Arlie":* Harrington letter to Mucks, March 6, 1967, UW, box 57.

82 *Otto Festge, Madison's liberal mayor:* Int. Otto Festge, July 6, 2001.

82 *On the night of May 15, 1935: Scotton Report on the Anti-Dow Protests,* December 1967: Journalist James W. Scotton was commissioned by the University of Wisconsin News and Publication Service to answer questions raised by the Dow demonstration. His report, a model of evenhandedness, placed the 1967 protest in the context of dissent on campus, going back to the 1930s.

83 *Jane Brotman, after graduating:* Ints. Jane Brotman, January 24, 2001, April 9, 2002.

83 *her father, a lumber salesman:* Ints. Betty Menacher, April 27, 2001, April 8, 2002.

83 *"We ended up lost in Chinatown":* Menacher letter to Mary Mahaney, June 23, 1967.

84 *"Lately everyone has been stealing food":* Menacher letters to Mary Mahaney, August 16–20, 1967.

86 *Betty was Catholic but:* Ints. Betty Menacher, April 27, 2001, April 8, 2002.

86 *"Do you ever have panty raids?":* Menacher letter to Mary Mahaney, October 7, 1967.

87 *Jane Beth Brotman followed a well-worn path:* Ints. Jane Brotman, January 24, 2001, April 9, 2002.

CHAPTER 7: SOGLIN'S THRILL

91 *The lead editorial: Daily Cardinal,* September 28, 1967. Soglin's career as a columnist lasted less than a year.

92 *Their latest intellectual forum was* Connections: The first sixties-style underground paper in Madison, *Connections* had begun publication the previous spring. Copies are archived at the Wisconsin State Historical Society, which has a vast collection of alternative newspapers, shepherded by the leading expert on that genre, James Danky.

93 *Boston, Tampa, Buffalo, Cincinnati:* Warren Christopher papers, Urban Riots, August 11, 1967, LBJ.

93 *Many students who had headed south:* The graduate schools at Wisconsin were bubbling with students who had been active in the civil rights movement. Bob Gabriner, the editor of *Connections* and a graduate student in history, had spent several summers organizing voting drives in rural western Tennessee. He made a return trip through the South in the summer of 1967 with his wife, Vicki Gabriner, recording oral histories of rural and otherwise unknown and unrecognized black civil rights participants. By the end of that summer, Gabriner said, he felt that the Black Power movement was pushing him away, so he turned more of his attention to the war.

93 *All summer long, a rumor had spread:* Int. Robert Swacker, May 2, 2002; *Crisis,* newsletter of the Committee to End the War in Vietnam, vol. IV, no. 1, September 11, 2002.

94 *The military was not an institution:* Ints. Paul Soglin, June 22, 2001, August 3, 2001, April 10, 2001.

95 *aboard the SS* Patricia: List or Manifest of Alien Passengers for the United States Immigration Officer at Port of Arrival. Required by the regulations of the Secretary of Commerce and Labor of the United States under Act of Congress approved February 20, 1907. S.S. Patricia sailing from Hamburg November 8th 1912. Also, S.S. Patricia sailing from Hamburg June 2, arriving Port of New York June 16, 1905, Soglin papers.

95 *Paul's father, Albert Soglin:* Descriptions of Soglin's early life from ints. Paul Soglin, June 22, 2001, August 3, 2001, April 10, 2002. Also *Paul Soglin, Former UW Student,* UW Oral History Project, interview by Laura Smail, December 21, 1977. In the late 1970s Smail conducted first-rate interviews with key figures of the antiwar years on campus, including most UW administrators and some student leaders; unpublished Soglin memoir, Soglin papers.

97 *An editorial in the* Cardinal: *Daily Cardinal,* October 19, 1963.

98 *He gradually switched his concentration:* Int. Paul Soglin, August 3, 2001; Mosse, *Confronting History,* 150–70; *History Digest,* January 1970; Williams, *America in Vietnam,* 1985; William Appleman Williams, *Roots of the Modern American Empire: A Study of the Growth and Shaping of Social Consciousness in a Marketplace Society;* William Appleman Williams letter to George Mosse, January 13, 1969, UW. Williams had left Madison for Oregon State. He had finished the manuscript of *Roots of the Modern American Empire,* as he told his former colleague Mosse: "I managed to finish the big book on the agricultural businessmen just as school started, and Random House is now inching it through the production process. It is big, some 800 typescript with footnotes, so it won't be out till summer or early fall. I cast it very largely in terms of the development and shaping of social consciousness in a marketplace society, trying to show how the metropolis and the country came to a consensus on imperial marketplace expansion as a way of resolving economic and political difficulties. I think you will enjoy it a good bit." For Mosse lecture on cemeteries, Mosse papers, UW.

102 *"One cannot understand one's own history":* Mosse, *Confronting History,* 171–86.

102 *The "one rule," Soglin recalled:* Soglin interview, UW Oral History Project; also Soglin ints. with author, August 3, 2001, April 10, 2002.

103 *It was the draft that provoked:* Ints. Jim Rowen, April 8, 2002; Paul Soglin, April 10, 2002; Robert Swacker, May 2, 2002; William Kaplan, March 28, 2001; Bob Gabriner, May 31, 2002; Evan Stark, July 16, 2002; Morris Edelson, May 10, 2002. Also transcript of Soglin interview, *The War at Home* papers, SHSW.

105 *"Please excuse the way":* Soglin letter to Harrington and response, Harrington file, UW.

106 *When the Dow Chemical Company visited: Capital Times,* February 18–24, 1967; *WSJ,* February 17–25, 1967; *Daily Cardinal,* February 20–25, 1967; transcript of interview with Henry Haslach, *The War at Home* papers, SHSW; Ints. Paul Soglin, August 3, 2001; Art Hove, June 20, 2001; Joe Kauffman, June 19, 2001; Jack Cipperly, June 19, 2001; Ralph Hanson family papers; Robben Fleming papers, UW.

110 *"After the thing had kind of broke down": Paul Soglin, Former UW Student,* UW Oral History Project interview, December 21, 1977.

110 *Richard B. Cheney counted himself in that group:* Int. Vice President Richard B. Cheney at his office in the White House, June 19, 2002.

110 *His wife, Lynne, was teaching:* Int. Lynne Cheney, May 13, 2002, with follow-up e-mail correspondence.

112 *If Cheney had no "moral":* Int. Vice President Cheney, June 19, 2002. In explaining his draft status, Cheney said: "I graduated from high school in 1959. I was eighteen and that's when I registered for the draft. I was, in the early sixties, at various times either a student, which was 2-S, or 1-A, because I had a spotty academic career. I got kicked out of Yale twice. During those periods when I wasn't in school, I was working full-time building power line transmission lines and would be reclassified 1-A during those periods. But this was the early sixties before the war had heated up. Got married in '64, and in '66 I went to Madison. And our first daughter was born in July of '66. That shifted me to 3-A and I turned 26 in January 1967. So I was on the front edge. I never served. When I was 1-A back in the early sixties, they were taking older guys first. So I never served."

113 *During the run-up to the election:* Ints. Paul Soglin, April 10, 2002; Cathy Dietrich, May 5, 2002.

117 *When the new school year began: Daily Cardinal,* September 18–29, 1967; ints. Paul Soglin, August 3, 2001; Robert Swacker, May 2, 2002.

CHAPTER 8: SEWELL'S PREDICAMENT

119 *Student problem? Sewell's mind:* Ints. William Sewell, August 10, 2000, September 15, 2000. Sewell, who died a year later, was physically active and retained his acute intelligence past his 90th birthday. He still reported to work at the Social Science Building virtually every day, to a book-crammed office with windows looking out on Lake Mendota.

121 *It was with this sensibility:* Ints. Hal Winsborough, July 10, 2001; William Sewell, August 10, 2000.

121 *Vietnam teach-in on campus:* Ints. William Sewell, April 10, 2001; Evan Stark, July 16, 2002; Robert Swacker, May 2, 2002; *Daily Cardinal,* April 1–3, 1965; *The War at Home Papers,* SHSW.

122 *Hershey was a relic:* Int. William Sewell, September 15, 2000; Baskir, *Chance and Circumstance,* 17.

124 *Days after Japan surrendered:* Int. William Sewell, September 15, 2000; *The United States Strategic Bombing Survey, The Effects of Strategic Bombing on Japanese Morale,* Morale Division, 1947.

125 *Sewell soon turned from one twentieth-century trauma:* Sewell, "Infant Training and the Personality of the Child," *American Journal of Sociology,* vol. LVIII, no. 2, September 1952.

126 *Since its founding in 1917: Capital Times,* Special Monday section, July 5, 1971. The newspaper that day, in recognition of the U.S. Supreme Court decision allowing the

New York Times and *Washington Post* to publish the Pentagon Papers, ran a full-page collage of twenty-seven antiwar editorials it had published since 1965, only a small portion of the total number.

127 *A defining point on the timeline: Vietnam Hearings, Voices from the Grass Roots:* A transcript of testimony given at the hearing on the war in Vietnam conducted by the Hon. Robert W. Kastenmeier, Member of Congress, 2nd District, Wisconsin; also transcript of Babe Rohr interview, *The War at Home* papers, SHSW.

132 *Bill Sewell lived on the west side:* Int. William Sewell, August 10, 2000; Personal Data and Professional Experience of William Hamilton Sewell, Fall 2000; "Students and the University," William H. Sewell, *American Sociologist,* May, 1971.

133 *Sharp humor was Sewell's favorite:* Ints. Margaret Bright, July 19, 2001; Hal Winsborough, July 10, 2001; Robert Hauser, July 28, 2001; testimonials by family at Sewell funeral in Madison, June 28, 2001.

134 *Joseph Kauffman, the forty-six-year-old:* Int. Joseph F. Kauffman, June 19, 2001.

137 *At the first special faculty meeting:* Int. William Sewell, August 10, 2000; faculty minutes, February 23, 1967, UW.

CHAPTER 9: "WHAT A FUNNY WAR!"

141 *Clark Welch was in a spirited mood:* Welch letter to wife Lacy, August 6, 1967.

141 *Life is all in the perspective:* Greg Landon letter to parents, August 6, 1967.

142 *At the* New York Times *bureau:* R. W. Apple, NYT, August 6, 1967, 1.

143 *From the day he started training Delta:* Clark Welch letters to wife Lacy, August 15–September 25, 1967. Welch wrote his wife almost every day, sharing his war with her.

144 *Late on the afternoon:* In addition to Welch letters, int. Clarence Barrow, October 15, 2000.

145 *And these soldiers of whom Welch was so proud:* Mike Taylor letter to parents; Greg Landon letter to parents; Jackie E. Bolen letter to grandmother; Mike Troyer letter to parents, September 20, 1967.

147 *One night, as he was writing Lacy:* Welch letter to wife Lacy, September 4, 1967.

149 *Welch was haunted:* Ints. Clark Welch, January 28–February 8, 2002.

151 *The assignment was to patrol:* Ints. Jim Shelton, March 13, 2000, April 29, 2000; Michael Arias, June 2, 2001; Letter of Appreciation, September 18, 1967, from Col. Seibert to Lt. Col. Allen: "Your constant movement and the ability of your units to cover so large an area was largely responsible in keeping Viet Cong activities to a minimum. This contributed immeasurably toward the success of the recent election in Duc Tu and Cong Thanh districts"; James A. Snow letter to Terry Allen Sr., October 23, 1967, Allen family papers.

154 *when the phrase was coined:* Maclear, *The Ten Thousand Day War,* 157. Maclear quoted DePuy as saying, "It was an unfortunate choice of words."

154 *DePuy often used Thunder Road:* Browne, *The New Face of War,* 60–61, excerpts from transcript of press conference given October 6, 1964, in Saigon by Brig. Gen. William E. DePuy, operations officer of the U.S. MACV. Browne, writing in 1964, concluded his "Ambush" chapter with a perceptive look backward and forward: "The history of the Indochina War shows the French never found an adequate solution to the ambush problem. Even after the Viet Minh shifted gears from guerrilla warfare to full-scale mobile warfare, their basic operating pattern remained the ambush, on a huge scale. One after another, French regimental combat teams were hacked to pieces simply moving from one place to another, and this kind of thing continued right up to the end

of the war. The ambush appears to me to be a key element in the new face of war. I think the Free World faces the choice of living with this fact, or dying with it."

155 *the First Division had been searching:* Sigler, *Vietnam Battle Chronology;* DePuy interview notes, October 7, 1977, at his Virginia home; George L. MacGarrigle, CMH; MacGarrigle, *Taking the Offensive;* also First Infantry Division Unit Histories, March, 1968; United States Military Assistance Command, Vietnam, Command History 1967, vol. 1, prepared by the Military History Branch, Office of the Secretary, Joint Staff, MACV, MHI.

156 *The other side was fully aware:* Ints. 1st Regiment commander Vo Minh Triet, January 30, 31, February 7, 2001; Col. Ta Minh Kham interview with James Zumwalt, 1995.

157 *the military rhetoric from Hanoi:* Article by Brig. Gen. Vuong Thua Vu, Hanoi Domestic Service, November 1967, translated by Central Intelligence Agency. CIA Files, RG 263, NA.

157 *liberation forces were holding: Su Doan 9, Hanoi;* also int. Robert DeStatte, January 15, 2002.

159 *In the special intelligence estimates: Special Intelligence Estimate for 1st Division to Discuss Destruction of the 271st Regiment and Its Logistical Support Base,* October 1967, MHI.

160 *The young soldiers of Delta Company:* Greg Landon letter to parents; September 27, 1967; Mike Troyer letter to parents, October 1, 1967; Jack Schroder letters to wife Eleanor, September 18, 24, 1967.

161 *"the 1st Infantry Division has got quite":* Clark Welch letter to wife Lacy, September 29, 1967.

161 *On the night of October 4:* Account of Delta Company activity in first days of Shenandoah II based on letters home from Clark Welch, Mike Troyer, Jack Schroder, Mike Taylor, Greg Landon, Michael Arias, and Ray Albin. Also ints. George Burrows, March 15, 2001; Ray Albin, January 23, 2001; David Laub, March 5, 2001; Michael Arias, March 11, 2001; Douglas Ikerd, May 26, 2001; Santiago Griego, May 28, 2001; Mike Troyer, August 21, 2001.

CHAPTER 10: GUERRILLA THEATER

166 *First stop, Minneapolis:* Contact list, Commedia Dell'Arte Tour, Fall/Winter 1967, San Francisco Mime Troupe Papers, archived at the Wisconsin State Historical Society. The tour schedules were mimeographed and distributed to members of the troupe.

166 *Davis, who founded the troupe:* Int. Ronald G. Davis, May 8, 2002; Davis, *The San Francisco Mime Troupe, the First Ten Years.*

167 *"The greatest error":* Draft of Davis "platform" for the S.F. Mime Troupe, April 1967, SHSW.

168 *The main play for the Midwest: L'Amant Militaire,* S.F. Mime Troupe papers, SHSW. "Adaptation may be a misleading term for the relation of our commedia shows to their originals," Davis wrote in the publicity papers for the tour. "We do not usually set ourselves the task of translating an author's intentions; rather, we exploit his work to suit our own; using what we can and discarding the rest, writing in new scenes and characters, to say nothing of new emphases."

169 *Before leaving for the Midwest:* Ints. Ronald G. Davis, May 8, 2002; Morris Edelson, May 10, 2002.

171 *In his first appearance before the faculty:* Faculty minutes, October 2, 1967, UW.

172 *The dean of student affairs began:* Ints. Joseph F. Kauffman, June 19, 2001; Jack Cip-

perly, June 19, 2001; Art Hove, June 20, 2001; Joel Skornicka, August 13, 2001; Hanson family papers; *Scotton Report.*

172   *One student who seemed approachable:* Int. Robert Swacker, May 2, 2002; Scotton report, UW; "Meetings with Anti-Dow Coordinating Committee," Memorandum from Peter Bunn to Kauffman, November 1, 1967, appended to *Scotton Report.*

174   *Who would issue the warning?:* Ints. William Sewell, August 10, 2000; Joseph Kauffman, June 19, 2001; *Daily Cardinal,* October 11, 1967.

174   *When Paul Soglin read it:* Ints. Paul Soglin, August 3, 2002; Percy Julian, August 24, 2001; Robert Swacker, May 2, 2002.

175   *The report was a remarkable document: Officer's Report.* Madison Police Department, Special Assignment, October 13, 1967, "Attention: Chief of Police, re Dow Plans."

179   *Wilbur Emery, the recipient:* Ints. Tom McCarthy, August 8, 2000; Al Roehling, August 17, 2001; Otto Festge, July 6, 2001; Jim Boll, August 9, 2001.

180   *He had come onto the force:* Int. Tom McCarthy, August 8, 2000.

181   *Hanson took over:* Hanson papers, unprocessed. In the summer of 2001, a few years after Hanson's death, his widow, Lucille Hanson, told the author that she had "some of his papers" in her garage. The papers were stored in six boxes. They included documents, letters, a scrapbook, newspaper clippings, and a partial autobiographical manuscript.

184   *six-point plan on police guidelines: Dow Placement Interviews and Police Operations,* University of Wisconsin, Madison Campus, October 17–20, 1967, Ralph E. Hanson, Director, Department of Protection and Security, October 12, 1967, appended to *Scotton Report.*

CHAPTER 11: JOHNSON'S DILEMMA

185   *American and allied forces were in the field:* Office of Information, United States Military Assistance Command, Vietnam, release number 289-67, October 15–16, 1967. MHI.

186   *Readers of the* New York Times: Taylor, *NYT Magazine,* October 15, 1967.

186   *From aide William Leonhart:* Leonhart Memos, October 13, 1967, NSF File, LBJ.

186   *Every few months in 1967:* Gallup Poll Index, 1967.

187   *"Avast, belay":* Telegram October 2, 1967, Ellsworth Bunker to wife, LBJ.

187   *Locke responded to the urgent plea:* "For the President from Ambassador Locke, Subject: Measurements of Progress in South Vietnam," Saturday, October 7, 1967, LBJ.

188   *"like an ox bone stuck":* Liberation Radio commentary, October 15, 1967, CIA files, RG 263, box 48, NARA.

189   *He had closed September: Public Papers of the President of the United States,* LBJ, 876–81.

189   *On the evening of October 3:* "Notes of the President's Meeting with Secretary Rusk, Secretary McNamara, Mr. Rostow, CIA Director Helms, and George Christian," Tom Johnson notes, Box 1, LBJ.

193   *The same group, minus Helms:* "Notes of the President's Meeting with Secretary McNamara, Secretary Rusk, Walt Rostow, George Christian, Cabinet Room, October 4, 1967," Tom Johnson Notes, box 1, LBJ.

194   *Douglass Cater, another White House:* Memorandum to the President from Douglass Cater," Wednesday, October 4, 1967, 4:50 P.M., Office Files of Douglass Cater, box 17, LBJ.

194   Life *magazine, once a pillar:* "Life Rumored Ready to Shift War Stand," *NYT,* October 10, 1967.

195   *latest analysis from General Giap:* Int. Huu Mai, Giap's longtime associate, Hanoi, Feb-

ruary 4, 2002; "Pacification Foiled, Gen. Giap Declares," Hedrick Smith, *NYT,* October 10, 1967, 1. Reports followed in the *Washington Post* and other major American newspapers over the following week.

196 *local Viet Cong officials had been lectured:* Military Assistance Command, Vietnam, intelligence report, October 1967, MHI.

196 *Speaker John W. McCormick: NYT,* October 12, 1967.

196 *"a little stronger chemical":* "Notes of the President's Meeting with Secretary McNamara, Secretary Rusk, Walt Rostow, President's Office," October 5, 1967, Tom Johnson Notes, box 1, LBJ.

196 *Dirksen was talking primarily: Washington Post,* October 10–15, 1967, daily coverage of Senate debate on the war.

197 *pushing hard for a United Nations role:* Mansfield letter to President Johnson, October 9, 1967, Mansfield File, LBJ.

197 *memorandum to the White House:* "Memorandum for the President. From: Senator George McGovern. Subject: Vietnam," October 12, 1967, LBJ. While McGovern pushed for a bombing halt, another future Democratic presidential candidate, Sen. Walter Mondale of Minnesota, remained supportive of the White House position, while lamenting how difficult it was to hold his ground. In an October 12 memo to Secretary Rusk, National Security Adviser William P. Bundy wrote that Mondale had called him that morning. "Mondale went on to expound at length on the difficulties of liberal senators like himself who were still standing fast against public and easy endorsement of the UN solution or stopping the bombing in return for talks. He noted that, with Gene McCarthy and others such as Percy taking these easy avenues, it was increasingly putting him and others like him on the spot. He said that he was losing support in Minnesota from peace groups and others who had strongly supported him in the past—which was not critical for him since he does not come up in 1968—but was typical of the problems many others faced."

198 *CIA had been given:* Gibbons, *The U.S. Government and the Vietnam War, Part IV: July 1965–January 1968,* 851–60. Also Wells, *The War Within,* 184.

198 *a report about the international connections: The Peace Movement: Confusion, Coordination, and Communism,* CIA report, October 1967; DeBenedetti, *A CIA Analysis of the Anti-Vietnam War Movement,* October 1967; U.S. Senate, 94th Congress, *Final Report of the Select Committee to Study Governmental Operations with Respect to Intelligence Activities (Church Committee),* 1976, vol. III, 152–54.

201 *it prepared a footnoted: The North Vietnamese Role in the War in South Viet-Nam,* Department of State, Bureau of Public Affairs, October 1967, LBJ.

203 *"Dean, I want to know":* "Notes of the President's Meeting with Secretary Rusk, Secretary McNamara, Walt Rostow, CIA Director Helms and George Christian, October 16, 1967," Tom Johnson Notes, box 1, LBJ.

CHAPTER 12: NO MISSION TOO DIFFICULT

205 *The fourteenth had been a miserable day:* Ints. Clark Welch, January 28–Feb 8, 2002; Jim George, May 27, 2001, Ray Albin, January 29, 2001; Michael Arias, June 2, 2002; Gerald Thompson, May 26, 2001; Carl Woodard, May 27, 2001; Greg Landon, June 19, 2002; Mike Troyer, August 21, 2002; Bill Erwin, May 27, 2001.

207 *Erwin's recon platoon and Kasik's Bravo:* Int. Bill Erwin, May 27, 2001; Report of Jim Kasik on Bravo Company, October 9–17, 1967, Kasik papers, May 1, 1989.

208 *George went along:* Int. Jim George, May 27, 2001.

208 *Joe Costello, the grenadier:* Int. Joe Costello, November 3, 2000.

209 *Kirkpatrick had put in for the vacation:* Int. Fred Kirkpatrick, October 16, 2000. Kirkpatrick documents, unprocessed. Kirkpatrick, of Stow, Ohio, has done more than anyone else to reconnect enlisted men who served with 2/28 Delta in Vietnam in 1967. He has also organized reunions of the Black Lions in Las Vegas every October .

210 *When the sergeant finished:* Ints. Clark Welch, January 28–February 7, 2002; Ray Albin, January 29, 2001; Clarence Barrow, October 15, 2000; John Durham, October 18, 2002; Durham family papers, unprocessed.

211 *Back at Lai Khe, Lieutenant Tom Grady:* Int. Tom Grady, March 27, 2002.

211 *General Westmoreland took leave:* "Schedule of Events for William C. Westmoreland, Sunday, October 15, 1967," Westmoreland Papers, MHI; *Senior Officer Oral History Program,* General William C. Westmoreland, USA, Retired, interviewed by Lieutenant Colonel Martin L. Ganderson, USA, MHI; "Westmoreland in Vietnam, Pulverizing the Boulder," *Army* magazine, February 1976.

212 *Steve Goodman, a Black Lions armorer:* Int. Steve Goodman, November 20, 2000.

212 *Fergusson's son Bob:* Telex exchanges between Gen. Westmoreland and Gen. Furgusson, October 8–30, 1967, Westmoreland papers, MHI.

215 *Gavin's visit was by far:* Telexes from Gen. Wheeler to Gen. Westmoreland, October 6, 17, 1967; telex from Gen. Westmoreland to Lt. Gen. Brown, asst. to the chairman, October 11, 1967, Westmoreland papers, MHI. Biggs, *Gavin,* 135–70; Malcolm Muir, ed., *The Human Tradition in the World War II Era* (Scholarly Resources, Wilmington, Del., 2000), 191.

216 *the "cross-over" point:* Transcript of Westmoreland press briefing in Saigon, June 29, 1967. In attendance were U.S correspondents John Apple, Joseph Fried, Sanders, Coffey, Tuckman, Erlandson, Stewart, Pisor, Randolph, Brannigan, Hughes, Martin, Kalb, Dillin, and Steinman, JUSPAO files, NARA.

217 *Hay was too slow: Senior Officer Oral History Program, Lieutenant General John Hay, USA Retired,* interviewed by Lt. Col. James Thomas, October 4, 1980, MHI; Hay interview with military historian George L. MacGarrigle, April 29, 1980; telex from Gen. Westmoreland to Gen. Johnson, CSA, Washington, October 12, 1967; Record of COMUSMACV FONECON, Westmoreland and Weyand, February 22, 1968, Westmoreland papers, MHI; Int. Jim George, May 27, 2001.

219 *Clark Welch's Delta led the way:* Ints. Clark Welch, January 28–February 7, 2002; Paul D. Scott, August 25, 2002; Clarence Barrow, October 15, 2000; Peter Miller, August 27, 2002; Greg Landon, Terry Warner, October 19, 2002; Doug Cron, October 19, 2002; 2/28 *Daily Journal and Officer's Log,* October 16, 1967, NARA; Clark Welch letter to wife Lacy, October 24, 1967.

225 *He was not a martinet:* Ints. Bill Erwin, May 27, 2001; Jim George, May 27, 2001; Clark Welch, January 28–February 7, 2002; Thomas F. Reese, March 8, 2001.

225 *Gerard Grosso, the S-3 air:* Int. Gerard Grosso, December 13, 2002. Also Grosso letter to Jim Shelton, Spring 2002.

226 *here came the troops:* Ints. Clark Welch, January 28–February 7, 2002; Clarence Barrow, October 18, 2002; Santiago Griego, October 17, 2002; Faustin Sena, October 17, 2002; Jim George, May 27, 2001; Bill Erwin, May 27, 2001; Jim Shelton, April 28, 2000; Report of Jim Kasik on Bravo Company, October 9–17, 1967, May 1, 1999, e-mail correspondence.

231 *In their bunkers the troops were apprehensive:* Michael Arias letter to mother, October 16, 1967; ints. Carl Woodard, May 27, 2001; Peter Miller, August 27, 2002; Joe Costello, November 3, 2000; Ray Albin, January 29, 2001.

CHAPTER 13: MICHIGAN MEN

233 *Curly Hendershot at age fifty-five:* Ints. E. N. Brandt, April 12, 2001; Herbert Dow Doan, April 12, 2001; Sherlynn Hendershot, April 16, 2001; Bill Seward, April 27, 2001; Ray Rolf, May 1, 2001; transcript of oral interview of E. N. Brandt by James J. Bohning in Midland, Michigan, June 17, 1992, PSA.

235 *From the outside Dow appeared:* Ints. Herbert Dow Doan, April 12, 2001; E. N. Brandt, April 12, 2001; transcript of oral interviews of Carl A. Gerstacker, July 21, 1988; E. N. Brandt, June 17, 1992; Herbert Dow Doan, July 29, 1988, by James J. Bohning and Arnold Thackray, PSA. Also Brandt, *Growth Company.*

237 *"the patriotic generation":* Ints. Donalda Doan, April 16, 2001; Herbert Dow Doan, April 12, 2001.

239 *Jonathan Star Stielstra was a transfer student:* Ints. Jonathan Stielstra, August 20–21, 2001; Stielstra papers, unprocessed.

241 *The same undercover agent: Officer's Report,* Madison Police Department, Special Assignment, October 16, 1967; *Daily Cardinal,* October 17, 1967.

CHAPTER 14: FOR WANT OF RICE

243 *This was his home territory:* Ints. Nguyen Van Lam, January 31, February 5, 2002, at his home near the Ong Thanh stream in the Long Nguyen Secret Zone, Kyle Horst interpreter.

244 *A military doctor from Hanoi:* Zumwalt, *Bare Feet, Iron Will;* also int. James Zumwalt, May 20, 2001.

244 *the logistical command flowed: Final Report on Rear Service Operations for the Nam Bo–Extreme South Central Region during the War of Resistance against the Americans,* edited by Nguyen Viet Phuong and Tu Quu, published by General Protectorate for Rear Services, 1986, for internal distribution within armed forces; *The History of Group 559, The Truong Son Troops and the Ho Chi Minh Trail,* edited by S. Col. Phan Huu Dai, 1999, with translations by Robert DeStatte.

246 *In practice things were different:* Ints. Vo Minh Triet, January 30, February 7, 2002; Nguyen Van Lam, January 31, February 5, 2002.

CHAPTER 15: "THE TREES ARE MOVING"

249 *The night before:* Ints. Clark Welch, January 28–February 7, 2002; Clarence Barrow, October 15, 2000; also Clark Welch letters to wife Lacy, October 22–30, 1967.

250 *Men were moving faster:* Ints. Frank McMeel, March 12, 2000; Mike Troyer, August 21, 2002; Ernest Buentiempo, June 9, 2002; Michael Arias, June 2, 2002; Joe Costello, November 3, 2000.

250 *early evening in Washington: White House Daily Diary,* October 16, 1967; "Memorandum for the President, Subject: Notes for Use in Talking with Reporters," from Gordon Ackley, October 13, 1967, LBJ.

251 *At the same approximate time:* CIA reports on Hanoi broadcasts and Moscow Tass International Service, NARA, CIA box 39.

252 *The Black Lions began gathering: Daily Staff Journal, Duty Officer's Log, 2d Bn, 28th Inf, 1st Inf Div.,* 17 October 67, NARA; Department of the Army, Headquarters, 1st Infantry Division, *Combat After Action Interview Report, Battle of Ong Thanh, 2-28 Infantry, 17 October 1967,* CMH files.

252 *The morning opened:* Int. Joe Costello, November 3, 2000; 28th Infantry Regiment, Vietnam Unit History, Koch recollections.

253 *Alpha came out:* Ints. Jim George, May 27, 2001; Michael Arias, June 2, 2002; Ernest Buentiempo, June 9, 2002; correspondence with Thomas V. Mullen, April 10, 2002; 2LT Peter J. Edwards interview with SP4 Williams, 17th Military History Detachment, October 24, 1967, CMH; Sgt. Donald W. Pipkin interview with Capt. Cash, Military Historian, October 24, 1967, CMH.

254 *Private Costello was positioned:* Int. Joe Costello, November 3, 2000; *Pvt. Joseph P. Costello Interview with Major William E. Daniel, 17th Military History Detachment,* October 20, 1967, CMH.

254 *a walking skeleton:* Int. Thomas Hinger, March 12, 2000; *SP4 Thomas M. Hinger interview with Capt. Cash,* October 21, 1967, CMH.

254 *Welch's Delta started moving: Daily Staff Journal, Duty Officer's Log, 2d Bn., 28th Inf., 1st Infantry Division, 17 October 67,* NARA; ints. Clark Welch, January 28–February 8, 2002; Peter Miller, August 27, 2002; Paul D. Scott, August 25, 2002; Clarence Barrow, October 16, 2000; *2LT David H. Stroup interview with Capt. Cash, October 21, 1967,* CMH.

255 *Delta's second was led:* Ints. Dwayne Byrd, October 16, 2000; Mike Troyer, August 21, 2002; Doug Cron, October 19, 2002; Faustin Sena, October 18, 2002; Fred Kirkpatrick, October 16, 2000, October 18, 2002.

256 *"I got off the M-60":* Jack Schroder letter to wife Eleanor, October 10, 1967.

256 *His little sister, Diane:* Int. Diane Sikorski Kramer, July 28, 2001.

256 *On the right file Greg Landon:* Int. Greg Landon, June 19, 2002; Landon letters to parents, October 10–15, 1967.

257 What are we doing this for?: Ints. Clark Welch, January 28–February 8, 2002.

257 *With every step southward:* Ints. Jim George, May 27, 2002; Michael Arias, June 2, 2002; Ernest Buentiempo, June 9, 2002; Tom Hinger, March 12, 2000; *Combat After Action Report, Battle of Ong Thanh, 2-28 Infantry, October 17, 1967,* CMH.

257 *another F-100 overhead:* Notes and papers of John Cash investigation of Battle of Ong Thanh, CMH; *Contemporary Historical Evaluation of Combat Operations Report, Ambush at XT 686575,* Department of the Air Force, December 29, 1967, CMH.

259 *From his position with Delta:* Ints. Clark Welch, January 28–February 8, 2002; Peter Miller, August 27, 2002; Michael Arias, March 11, 2001; Tom Hinger, March 12, 2000; *Combat After Action Report, Battle of Ong Thanh, 2-28 Infantry, 17 October 1967,* CMH; *Daily Journal, 2-28, 1st Infantry Division,* October 17, 1967, NARA.

CHAPTER 16: AMBUSH

260 *The fresh tracks along the trail:* Ints. Vo Minh Triet, January 30–31, 2002; Nguyen Van Lam, February 5, 2002.

261 *Private first class Breeden:* Ints. Ernest Buentiempo, June 9, 2002; Michael Arias, March 11, 2001; *Combat After Action Report,* October 17, 1967, CMH; *José B. Valdez Interview with Major Daniel, 17th Military History Detachment,* October 18, 1967, CMH.

261 *The opening fusillade echoed back:* The narrative of the battle, drawn from primary documents and interviews, is the author's attempt to convey the chaos of the firefight while giving it some measure of coherence. It was accomplished by piecing together the accounts provided by dozens of participants in interviews conducted by Capt. Cash and military historians in the days after the battle, supplemented first by contemporaneous letters and tape recordings, next by the official military logs, journals, investiga-

tions, and after action reports, and finally by author interviews with dozens of participants decades later.

Transcripts of interviews conducted by military historians in October 1967 included those of the following battle participants: Clarence Barrow, Jimmy Cheatwood, William Coleman, Joe Costello, Peter Edwards, Jim George, Paul Giannico, Tom Hinger, Robert Jensen, Willie Johnson, James Jones, Carl Kiser, Larry Lowe, Paul Malone, George Newman, Raymond Phillips, Donald Pipkin, Paul D. Scott, John Sloan, George Smith, Roy Stephens, David Stroup, Thomas Suttle, Mike Troyer, José Valdez, Thomas Wagner, James White, Clark Welch, and Carl Woodard, CMH.

In addition, battle participants interviewed by the author included: Tom Hinger, Clark Welch, Jim George, Joe Costello, Tom Grady, Frank McMeel, Michael Gormley, Dwayne Byrd, Clarence Barrow, Ray Albin, James Shelton, Gary Malone, Jim Gilliam, David Laub, Michael Arias, Faustin Sena, Santiago Griego, Bill Erwin, Carl Woodard, John Fowler, Ernest Buentiempo, Greg Landon, Dave Berry, Mike Troyer, Paul D. Scott, Peter Miller, Thomas V. Mullen (written communications), Mike Taylor, Doug Cron, Doug Tallent, Terry Warner, Bill McGath, Thomas Colburn, Mark Smith, Gerard Grosso, Vo Minh Triet, and Nguyen Van Lam. These accounts were bolstered by contemporaneous letters and tapes from Clark Welch, Greg Landon, Jim George, Mike Taylor, Michael Arias, Ray Albin, and Mike Troyer.

Also helpful were MacGarrigle, *Taking the Offensive,* 349–61; Shelton, *The Beast Was Out There;* and various uncatalogued papers provided by Jim Shelton and Fred Kirkpatrick.

CHAPTER 17: HOLLEDER'S RUN

285 *one of a small band of Black Lions:* Ints. Joe Costello, November 3, 2000; Clarence Barrow, October 18, 2002; Bill McGath, October 19, 2002; Randy Brown, October 19, 2002; Doug Cron, October 19, 2002.

286 *Costello got on the radio:* Int. Joe Costello, November 3, 2000; *Joe Costello Interview with Major Daniel, 17th Military History Detachment,* October 20, 1967; *William Coleman interview with Capt. Cash,* October 21, 1967; "Memorandum for Commanding General," from William S. Coleman, October 21, 1967, CMH.

287 *For the Black Lions who had remained:* Ints. Ray Albin, January 29, 2001; Terry Warner, October 19, 2002; Doug Tallent, October 19, 2002.

288 *The key point for Albin's platoon:* Ints. Ray Albin, January 29, 2001; Terry Warner, October 19, 2002; Clark Welch, January 28–February 8, 2002; *John F. Sloan Interview with Military Historian Capt. Cash,* October 22, 1967, CMH.

288 *The relationship between the brigade:* Int. Gerard Grosso, December 13, 2002; *John F. Sloan Interview,* CMH; transcript of statement of 1st Lt. Lester T. Scott in Cash papers, October 1967, CMH.

290 *situation grew bleaker:* 28th Infantry Regiment, Vietnam Unit histories, recollections of Koch and Watson, www.28thinfantry.org; Int. Ray Albin, January 31, 2002.

290 *Lieutenant Erwin's scout platoon:* Int. Bill Erwin, May 27, 2001; *2d Lt. William D. Erwin interview with Major Daniel, 17th Military History Detachment,* November 19, 1967.

291 *When Holleder arrived in Vietnam:* Portrait of Maj. Donald Holleder drawn from interviews with James Shelton, March 14, 2000; Bill Crites, January 23, 2001; Pete Vann, January 25, 2001; Edwin J. Messinger, February 20, 2001; papers of Col. Earl (Red) Blaik, papers of Donald Holleder, U.S. Army Military Academy; also Blaik, *The Red*

Blaik Story, 336–57; Donald Walter Holleder obituary, *Assembly,* Fall 1969, by classmate Maj. Perry M. Smith; *Sports Illustrated,* December 5, 1955.

294 *Doc Hinger was far behind:* Int. Tom Hinger, March 12, 2000; *Narrative Account, Death of Major Donald W. Holleder,* October 25, 1967, CMH.

295 *actions of Vo Minh Triet's regiment:* The 9th Division history, translated by Foreign Broadcast Information Service, October 1995; Vuong Thu Vu, "The Victories in Binh Long and the First Fresh Lessons," November 29, 1967, Hanoi Domestic Service, CIA Files, NARA; ints. Nguyen Van Lam, February 5, 2002; Vo Minh Triet, January 30–31, 2002.

297 *Grady was in Lai Khe:* Int. Tom Grady, March 27, 2002; Grady letter to Capt. George, October 24, 1967.

298 *Back toward the jungle:* Ints. Tom Grady, March 27, 2002; Bill Erwin, May 27, 2001; Mark Smith, October 19, 2002; Ray Albin, January 29, 2001; Tom Hinger, March 12, 2000;, Steve Goodman, November 20, 2000; George Burrows, March 15, 2001; Thomas F. Reese, Clarence Barrow, October 18, 2002, March 8, 2001; Jim Kasik, report to Jim Shelton, May 1, 1989.

302 *It was easier to find the fallen:* Coleman, "Memorandum"; MacGarrigle oral history interview with Col. Paul B. Malone III, CMH; *Major Larry E. Lowe Interview with Major William E. Daniel, 17th Military History Detachment,* October 28, 1967, CMH; Int. Joe Costello, November 2, 2000; correspondence of Thomas V. Mullen, Shelton papers; *Col. George E. Newman Interview with Military Historian Capt. Cash,* October 22, 1967; George E. Newman letter to Mike Dinkins, January 11, 1989.

305 *At Lai Khe late that night:* Ints. Jim Shelton, March 14, 2000; November 4, 2001.

307 *The camp was full of dazed men:* Ints. Michael Arias, March 11, 2001; Tom Grady, March 27, 2002; Ray Albin, January 31, 2001; George Burrows, March 15, 2001; Tom Hinger, March 12, 2000.

CHAPTER 18: "THE NEWS IS ALL BAD"

310 *Johnson had just left a meeting: White House Daily Diary,* October 17, 1967. ("The President walked w/ Prime Minister Lee—through the center door to his office—en route to the West Lobby to say goodbye and to escort the Prime Minister to his car.")

310 *As historian Henry Graff:* "How Johnson Makes Foreign Policy," *NYT Magazine,* July 4, 1965; also Graff, *The Tuesday Cabinet,* 5, 17.

310 *Johnson mentioned that he was impressed:* "Notes of the President's meeting with Secretary McNamara, Secretary Rusk, General Wheeler, CIA Director Helms, Walt Rostow, George Christian, in the Mansion," October 17, 1967. Meeting began 1:40. Tom Johnson Notes, box 1, LBJ.

311 *his entire five-minute report:* "Front Line Report," 6:55 A.M., WTOP Radio, October 17, 1967, republished in *The Pentagon Papers,* vol. 4, 209–10.

311 *"NVN is paying heavily":* JCSM-555-67, October 17, 1967, "Memorandum for the Secretary of Defense. Subject: Increased Pressures on North Vietnam," *Pentagon Pagers,* vol. 4, 210–11.

312 *The second October 17 memo:* "Memorandum for the President, October 17, 1967. Subject: Vietnam—October 1967." McG. B., LBJ; transcript of news conference #1013-A, "At the White House with George Christian," 11:05 A.M. EDT, October 17, 1967, LBJ.

313 *from presidential aide Joseph Califano:* "For the President, From Joe Califano. The White House, Washington, 12:40 P.M., Tuesday, October 17, 1967," LBJ. The president

signed off on his one-sentence response at 1:40; a handwritten notation on the memo says, "Relayed by phone to JC in Cater's office."

314 *The second note came:* "Memorandum for the President, Tuesday, October 17, 1967, 1:00 P.M., White House Situation Room," LBJ. The 6:30 A.M. Vietnam memo from the White House Situation Room provided a brief report on the October 16 firefight involving Clark Welch and his company but not on the October 17 ambush, though it already had taken place.

314 *Johnson sat down:* "Notes of the President's Meeting," October 17, 1967, Tom Johnson Notes, box 1, LBJ.

315 *That afternoon in El Paso:* Ints. Jean Ponder Allen Soto, February 3, 2001; Bill and Bebe Coonly, February 2, 2001; Jonathan and Pat Rodgers, February 4, 2001; Albert Schwartz, February 3, 2001.

CHAPTER 19: THE SPECTACLE

316 *They settled for a prefabricated:* Int. Jim Rowen, April 8, 2002; various correspondence with Jim Rowen and Susan McGovern.

319 *From the front bedroom:* Ints. Paul Soglin, April 10, 2002, June 22, 2001.

320 *William Sewell, the chancellor, had arrived:* Ints. William Sewell, August 10, 2000, April 22, 2001; William H. Sewell oral history interviews conducted by Laura Smail, 1977, 1983, 1985, University of Wisconsin archives.

320 *Hanson had been up since four:* Unprocessed Hanson papers; int. Lucille Hanson, June 11, 2001; Robben Fleming letter, June 28, 1967. The final paragraphs of the letter read: "You may note that I have given you a new tie. Thus, you are forever identified with the University of Wisconsin, even though you are soon to leave us for Michigan. I don't know whether or not you have a pastime, but I do know that you keep your cool on the barricades. This has been inspirational to many of us and I know your presence will be sorely missed here on the Madison campus."

322 *The demonstration began at nine thirty: Capital Times,* October 17, 1967, *Scotton Report.*

323 *This caught the attention of:* Testimony of Ralph Hanson at SSC, November 2, 1967, Legislative Reference Bureau; Stark, "In Exile," *History and the New Left,* ed. Paul Buhle, 166–77; Evan Stark interview transcript, *The War at Home,* SHSW; int. Evan Stark, July 16, 2002; Joseph F. Kauffman letter to Chancellor R. W. Fleming, March 10, 1967, Fleming papers, UW.

324 *the demonstrators gathered for an hour:* Video and tape recording of October 16 demonstration, original film by Blake Kellogg, WKOW-TV, SHSW; "Why We Sit In," appendix D, Scotton report; "Memo to: Dean Joseph F. Kauffman, from Jack W. Cipperly, Subject: Description of the events of October 17 and 18, 1967," unprocessed Cipperly papers.

327 *a spectacle of another form:* "Memorandum to Dean Kauffman, from Peter Bunn, Re: Meetings with Anti-Dow Coordinating Committee, October 9–17, 1967," appendix F, Scotton report; "The Great Dow War," *Connections,* November 1, 1967.

328 *Into this unsettled place:* Ints. Ronald G. Davis, May 8, 2002; Morris Edelson, May 10, 2002; Michael Oberdorfer, January 3, 2003; Jim Rowen, April 8, 2002; Coyote, *Sleeping Where I Fall;* Davis, *The San Francisco Mime Troupe.*

CHAPTER 20: "THAT'S ALL THERE IS?"

330 *The morning after the battle:* Int. Vo Minh Triet, January 30–31, 2002.

330 *Soldiers from Rear Service Group 83:* Int. Nguyen Van Lam, February 5, 2002; also discussions by Triet and Lam during tour of battlefield with author, Clark Welch, and translator Kyle Horst, January 31, 2002.

331 *When men from Bravo and Charlie companies:* Int. Thomas F. Reese, March 8, 2001; Sloan interview; Kasik report; 28th Regiment Vietnam Unit History, Koch recollections.

333 *when Lieutenant Grady held muster:* Ints. Tom Grady, March 27, 2002; Tom Hinger, March 12, 2000.

334 *The only job to be done:* Ints. Gerald Thompson, May 26, 2001; Mike Troyer, August 21, 2002; Tom Colburn, October 19, 2002; Larry McDevitt, March 16, 2001; Tom Grady, March 27, 2002; Jim Shelton, March 13, 2000.

336 *This is not Vietnam:* Ints. Joe Costello, November 3, 2000; Jim George, May 27, 2001; letters from Jim George to wife Jackie, October 18–31, 1967.

336 *The Ninety-third had more of the atmosphere: Daily Staff Journal or Duty Officer's Log, 93rd Evac Hosp, 1 July 67 to 21 October 67,* NARA; *Report of Army Medical Service Activities,* 93rd Evacuation Hospital, Calendar Year 1967.

337 *Clark Welch was taken:* Ibid.; Ints. Clark Welch, January 28–February 8, 2002; Clarence Barrow, October 16, 2000; Greg Landon, June 19, 2002; Dwayne Byrd, October 18, 2000; Santiago Griego, October 17, 2002; John Fowler, January18, 2001; Faustin Sena, October 18, 2002.

339 *It had been a typical morning:* "Schedule of Events for General W. C. Westmoreland, Sunday October 15 to Monday, October 23," Westmoreland papers, MHI; "General Westmoreland's History Notes, 16 October–12 November 1967," MHI.

340 *Lieutenant Grady was just leaving:* Ints. Tom Grady, March 27, 2002; Louis Menetrey, April 28, 2000; Gerard Grosso, December 13, 2002.

341 *how to explain this:* "General Westmoreland's History Notes, 16 October–12 November 1967," MHI; notes of John Hay interview with oral historian George MacGarrigle, CMH; ints. Bert Quint, August 16, 2001; Kurt Volkert, August 16, 2001; "Radio-TV Defense Dialog," broadcasts of October 19, 1967, transcript of *CBS Evening News* broadcast, 6:30 P.M., "Big Red One Catastrophic Battle," Lichty archives. At his old Victorian house in Evanston, Illinois, Northwestern University professor Lawrence Lichty has developed an unmatched private archive of documents concerned with the media and war, especially television and Vietnam. His interest began in the 1960s when he taught at Wisconsin.

343 *"I want every man right now":* Int. Tom Grady, March 27, 2002; letters from Michael Arias, Ray Albin, Mike Taylor, Mike Troyer, Jim George, Greg Landon, October 18, 1967, from Lai Khe and evacuation hospitals.

345 *"Elements of the U.S. Army's 1st Brigade":* News release, Office of Information, United States Assistance Command Vietnam, 18 October 1967, MACV Communiqué.

346 *the young anchor Peter Jennings:* Radio-TV Defense Dialog, broadcasts of October 18, 1967, 6:30 P.M. "Peter Jennings and the News, ABC-TV, Comments on the Ambush Near Saigon," Lichty archive.

CHAPTER 21: DOWN WITH DOW

348 *a battalion of students:* Ints. Paul Soglin, April 10, 2002; Jim Rowen, April 8, 2002; Jonathan Stielstra, August 20–21, 2001; Michael Oberdorfer, January 3, 2003; Stuart Brandes, August 6, 2001; William Kaplan, March 28, 2001; account of Stuart Brandes, written 3–5 P.M., October 18, 1967. Brandes, the history doctoral student, wanted to record his observations for history, which he did immediately after the demonstration. His account began: "I am now sitting in my carrel in the State Historical Society of Wisconsin. I have just witnessed the first riot of my young life. As an historian I know how inaccurate accounts of riots are, and I would like to set down my observations while they are clear in my mind."

349 *That would be the San Francisco:* Ints. Ronald G. Davis, May 8, 2002; Vicki Gabriner, December 27, 2001; Coyote, *Sleeping Where I Fall.*

350 *ragged but diversely attired line:* Ints. Paul Soglin, June 22, 2001; April 10, 2002; Jim Rowen, April 8, 2002; Jonathan Stielstra, August 21, 2001.

351 *From his office window:* Sewell testimony before Senate Select Committee, October 25, 1967, Legislative Reference Bureau; int. with William Sewell, August 10, 2000.

352 *Harrington, the university president, left Madison:* Harrington testimony before SSC, October 24, 1967, LRB; *Scotton Report.*

352 *Ralph Hanson assembled his troops:* Testimony of Ralph Hanson before SSC, November 2, 1967, LRB; *Scotton Report.*

353 *Schiro and his men observed quietly:* George Schiro testimony before SSC, November 3, 1967, LRB; *Scotton Report.*

354 *Center descended from his office:* Charles C. Center, "Statement prepared as an eyewitness account of the episode of violence on the Madison campus," October 18, 1967, UW; Hanson testimony at SSC, November 2, 1967, LRB.

355 *Hanson targeted three student leaders:* Ibid.; *Scotton Report.*

356 *Emery took the call:* Testimony of William Emery at SSC, LRB; int. James Boll, August 9, 2001.

356 *Consuelo Allen and her younger sisters:* Ints. Jean Ponder Allen Soto, February 3, 2001; Bill and Bebe Coonly, February 3, 2001; Consuelo Allen, February 2–4, 2001; Albert Schwartz, February 3, 2001.

357 *curious bystanders like Jane Brotman:* Ints. Jane Brotman, January 23, 2001, April 8, 2002.

358 *a platoon of sociology professors:* Int. Hal Winsborough, July 10, 2001.

358 *Jack Cipperly was standing:* Cipperly memo to Dean Kauffman, "Description of Events of October 17 and 18, 1967"; int. with Jack Cipperly, June 19, 2001.

359 *The lot was full:* Testimony of Sgt. Kenneth Buss at SSC, November 3, 1967, LRB; ints. Percy Julian, August 24, 2001; Al Roehling, August 17, 2001.

360 *tensions evident within that foursome:* Ints. William Sewell, August 20, 2000; Joseph F. Kauffman, June 19, 2001; Sewell testimony at SSC, October 25, 1967, LRB.

360 *Hanson shared Sewell's caution:* Hanson testimony at SSC, November 2, 1967, LRB; Marshall Shapiro, August 16, 2001; Shapiro testimony at SSC, October 23, 1967, LRB.

361 *Stark and three escorts:* "The Great Dow War," *Connections,* November 1–14, 1967; *Scotton Report,* UW; transcripts of Sewell, Hanson, Kauffman, and Emery testimony at SSC, October 23–November 9, 1967; ints. Evan Stark, July 16, 2002; Percy Julian, August 24, 2001; William Sewell oral history interviews by Laura Smail, 1977, 1983, 1985.

CHAPTER 22: MOMENTS OF DECISION

363 *Miss Sifting and Winnowing pranced:* Int. Vicki Gabriner, December 27, 2001; communications with Richard Swearingen, January 15, 2003.

363 *William Bablitch, a third-year law:* Testimony of William Bablitch at SSC, October 23–November 7, 1967, LRB.

364 *Betty Menacher, the freshman:* Ints. Betty Menacher, April 27, 2001, April 8, 2002; Jerrilyn Goodman, August 8, 2001; Michael Krasny, May 2, 2001; John Pickart, April 8, 2001; Everett Goodwin, May 17, 2001; John Pickart letter to Pam Crane, October 19, 1967.

366 *To make the detention process:* Transcripts of testimony of William Emery, Ralph Hanson, and Marshall Shapiro at SSC, October 23–November 9, 1967, LRB; *Scotton Report*; private uncatalogued papers of Ralph Hanson.

367 *Stuart Brandes, looming:* Ints. Stuart Brandes, August 6, 2001; William Kaplan, March 28, 2001; Jim Rowen, April 8, 2002; Robert Swacker, May 2, 2002; Jonathan Stielstra, August 21, 2001, Michael Oberdorfer, January 3, 2003; account of Stuart Brandes, written 3–5 P.M. October 18.

368 *Hanson found his way out:* The narrative account of the confrontation inside Commerce is based on primary documents and interviews. Ints. Paul Soglin, Jim Rowen, Stuart Brandes, Blake Kellogg, Marshall Shapiro, Michael Oberdorfer, Dennis Connor, Bob Swacker, William Kaplan, Al Roehling, Bob Hartwig, Jack Cipperly, Joel Skornicka, James Ozark, Jonathan Stielstra, Vicki Gabriner, Tom Beckman, William Sewell, Joseph Kauffman, John Pickart, Evan Stark, Everett Goodwin, Eric Nathan, Betty Menacher, Michael Krasny; testimony of Hanson, Schiro, Buss, Bablitch, Lederer, Wade, Shapiro at SSC, October 23–November 7, 1967, LRB; Smail oral history interviews with Paul Soglin and William Sewell; *Scotton Report;* account of Stuart Brandes, written 3–5 P.M. October 18; John Pickart letter to Pam Crane, October 19, 1967; unprocessed papers of Ralph Hanson. Also "The Great Dow War," *Connections,* November 1–14, 1967, and accounts in the *Capital Times,* October 18, 1967, and *Daily Cardinal* and *WSJ,* October 19, 1967.

CHAPTER 23: STARS AND STRIPES

380 *Downtown at police headquarters:* Ints. Tom McCarthy, August 8, 2000; Perry Pierre, April 2, 2001.

382 Where did this driver come from?: Ints. Paul Soglin, April 10, 2002, June 22, 2001; Robert Samp, August 14, 2001; Michael Oberdorfer, January 2, 2003; "Memo to Chancellor William H. Sewell from Robert C. Hickey, Department of Surgery," October 25, 1967, UW.

383 *They were just "livid, outraged":* Ints. Jim Rowen, April 8, 2002; Al Roehling, August 17, 2001; Michael Oberdorfer, January 2, 2003.

384 *Jonathan Stielstra was nearby:* Ints. Jonathan Stielstra August 20–21, 2001.

385 *Jim Boll, the district attorney:* Int. James Boll, August 9, 2001.

385 *Radio newsman Marshall Shapiro:* Testimony of Marshall Shapiro at SSC, October 23–November 7, 1967, LRB; int. Marshall Shapiro, August 16, 2001.

386 *Dave Wagner, a senior:* Ints. Dave Wagner and Grace Wagner, June 2, 2002.

387 *a* Connections *production:* Ints. Mike Oberdorfer, January 3, 2003; Bob Gabriner, May 31, 2002; David Westley, January 3, 2002.

388 *Detective McCarthy was standing:* Ints. Tom McCarthy, August 10, 2000; Jack Cipperly, June 19, 2001; Bob Hartwig, August 16, 2001; testimony of Ralph Hanson, George Schiro, Bob Hartwig at SSC, October 23–November 7, 1967, LRB; *Scotton Report.*

389 *Tear gas had never been released:* Ints. Jack Cipperly, June 19, 2001; Jane Brotman, April 9, 2002; Betty Menacher, April 8, 2002; Eric Nathan, January 30, 2001; Tom Beckmann, August 17, 2001; testimony of William Emery, Ralph Hanson, Warren Wade at SSC, October 23–November 7, 1967, LRB; Stark, "In Exile," *History and the New Left.*

391 *Jonathan Stielstra had returned:* Account of Stielstra's flag cutting drawn from ints. Jonathan Stielstra, August 20–21, 2001; Norm Lenburg, August 20, 2001; Jim Rowen, April 8, 2002; Bob Rennebohm, September 4, 2001.

393 *"just sort of in a daze":* Int. Jim Rowen, April 8, 2002; communications from Eleanor McGovern, November 2002.

394 *By the time Paul Soglin:* Ints. Paul Soglin, June 22, 2001, April 10, 2002; Percy Julian, August 24, 2001.

396 *News of the calamitous events:* Accounts in *WSJ* and *Capital Times,* October 19, 1967.

397 *There was a mass meeting:* Ints. Jim Rowen, Jane Brotman, Paul Soglin, Betty Menacher, Morris Edelson, Ronald Davis, Bill Kaplan, Mike Oberdorfer, Jonathan Stielstra, Jack Cipperly; John Pickart letter to Pam Crane, October 19, 1967; *TAA Review—The Sequence of Events,* November 1967, SHSW.

399 *Kauffman's wife and teenaged son:* Ints. Joseph Kauffman, June 19, 2001; William Sewell, August 10, 2000; unprocessed papers of Ralph Hanson.

CHAPTER 24: "BOMBING WASHINGTON"

400 *At a midday Cabinet meeting: White House Daily Diary,* October 18, 1967, LBJ. Johnson attended the Cabinet meeting after a noontime visit to the Church of the Epiphany on G Street NW to mark the National Day of Prayer; "Minutes of Cabinet Meeting of October 18, 1967, The White House," LBJ; *State Journal* editorial page, October 19, 1967.

402 *President Johnson reconvened:* "Notes of the President's Wednesday Night Meeting in the Cabinet Room," Tom Johnson Notes, box 1, LBJ.

407 *The Politburo in Hanoi:* Ho Khang, *The Tet Mau Than 1968 Event in South Vietnam.*

CHAPTER 25: BODY COUNT

408 *On the morning of October 19:* Int. Jim Shelton, November 6, 2002.

408 *At Alpha Company's camp:* Int. Tom Grady, March 27, 2002.

409 *On the other side of Lai Khe:* Ints. Gerry Grosso, December 13, 2002; Ray Albin, January 29, 2001, David Laub, March 5, 2001.

409 *"unbelievable" mismanagement: Hearings before the Special Subcommittee on the M-16 Rifle Program of the Committee on Armed Services,* House of Representatives, May 15–August 22, 1967, report released October 18, 1967.

410 *Of most interest to Goodman:* Int. Steve Goodman, November 20, 2000.

411 *They had a dual meaning:* S.L.A. Marshall, *Men Against Fire,* 54–57; Russell W. Glenn, *Reading Athena's Dance Card,* 49.

411 *John A. Cash, an army historian:* Ints. Vince Demma, March 28, 2001; John Albright, March 29, 2001; George MacGarrigle, March 30, 2001; Alan Sandstrom, April 2, 2001; Martha White, April 9, 2002; Cash notes and documents, CMH.

415 *To protect both their own careers:* William M. Hammond, *Public Affairs: The Military*

and the Media, 1962–1968; Release of Casualty Information; Adm. Sharp telex to Gen. Westmoreland, October 15, 1967, Westmoreland papers, MHI.

416 *The battle was only a few days gone:* Ints. Ernest Buentiempo, June 9, 2002; Gerard Grosso, December 13, 2002; Phil Duncan, March 5, 2001; Carl Woodard, May 27, 2001; Tom Grady, March 27, 2002; Mike Taylor letter to parents, October 19, 1967; reel-to-reel tapes sent home by Mike Troyer, October 19, 1967; letters from Greg Landon in 93rd Evacuation Hospital and from Jim George in 24th Evacuation Hospital, October 19, 1967.

CHAPTER 26: "TRAGEDY BEYOND OUR WORDS"

420 *Bill Sewell awoke:* Int. William Sewell, September 15, 2000; Smail, *Three Interviews.*

420 *Paul Soglin had run through:* Ints. Paul Soglin, June 22, 20001, April 10, 2002.

421 *The circus atmosphere:* Int. Ronald Davis, May 8, 2002; Davis, *The San Francisco Mime Troupe.*

421 *In place of the mime agitators:* Ints. James Hadden, April 3, 2001; accounts in *Capital Times, Daily Cardinal, WSJ,* October 19–20, 1967; *TAA Review.*

423 *The first picketers stationed:* John Pickart letter to Pam Crane, October 19, 1967.

424 *Jane Brotman, although:* Ints. Jane Brotman, January 24, 2002, April 9, 2002; Jane Brotman letter to father, October 19, 1967. The letter struck a chord with Brotman's father, who until then had been dismissive of her reaction to the Dow protest. He was so impressed by what she wrote that he gave a copy of the letter to the local newspaper, the *News Record* in South Orange, which later republished it, without using Brotman's name, as part of an editorial titled "Credo of Today's Youth." The editorial writer, commenting at the end of the letter, wrote: "Can anyone challenge the thinking in this sincere and revealing letter? I'm proud of this young woman and the generation she represents. We're going to be in good hands."

426 *an hour-long conversation:* "Notes of the President's Meeting with Robert Manning of *The Atlantic,"* October 19, 1967, LBJ.

427 *Norman Lenburg's second-to-last day:* Int. Norm Lenburg, August 20, 2001; *WSJ,* October 19, 1967.

428 *At least one reader:* Ints. Jonathan Stielstra, August 21, 2001; Michael Oberdorfer, January 3, 2003; Bob Gabriner, May 31, 2002; *Connections,* October, November, 1967.

430 *Appropriating a favorite word:* "The Spectacle of Violence," *Capital Times,* October 19, 1967.

432 *When the special meeting:* Narrative account of faculty meeting drawn from *Special Meeting of the University of Wisconsin Faculty, 3:30 P.M. Thursday, October 19, 1967, Memorial Union Theater,* UW; Ints. William Sewell, September 15, 2000; Joseph Kauffman, June 19, 2001; Samuel Mermin, August 7, 2001; Paul Soglin, June 22, 2001; Mike Oberdorfer, January 3, 2003, Robert Barnett, March 19, 2002; Jane Brotman, April 9, 2002; Kenneth W. Thompson memo to Chancellor Sewell, *Mermin Report,* 1968 UW; Mosse, *Confronting History.*

435 *In Japan by then:* Ints. Fred Kirkpatrick, October 16, 2000, October 18, 2002; correspondence of Fred Kirkpatrick. *Stars and Stripes,* vol. 23, No. 292, Friday, October 20, 1967.

CHAPTER 27: A LIFE'S WORTH

441   *In Milwaukee the next morning:* Ints. Diane Sikorski, July 28, 2001; Edmund Sikorski, April 8, 2001; Sikorski family scrapbook.

442   *Men in uniforms:* Int. Marian Tizzio, November 6, 2002; Tizzio family scrapbook.

442   *a ranch house outside Helena:* Ints. Eleanor Schroder Clark, January 3, 2001, December 10, 2002; papers of Moger family.

443   *fewer than two hundred riders:* Ints. Paul Soglin, June 22, 2001, April 10, 2002; Mike Oberdorfer, January 3, 2003; Dave Wheadon, December 23, 2002; John Lipp, December 22, 2002; Alison Steiner, December 26, 2002; Judy Genack, December 26, 2002; Kent Smith, December 29, 2002; David Westley, January 3, 2002; accounts in *Capital Times, WSJ,* October 20–21, 1967; Gibbons, *The U.S. Government and the Vietnam War,* 853–60.

445   *South Lawn of the White House:* Department of State, "Memorandum of Conversation, October 20, 1967, 12:30 P.M. Subject: War in Southeast Asia and Prospects for Peace. Participants: The President, Prince Souvanna Phouma, Prime Minister of Laos, A Toumayan, Interpreter," LBJ.

446   *In Madison that noon hour:* Accounts in *Capital Times,* October 19, 1967; ints. Michael Krasny, May 2, 2001; Paul Soglin, June 22, 2001; David Cherry papers, SHSW.

448   *letters were beginning to arrive:* Sewell papers, UW. The letters to Sewell were more evenly divided than letters written to the newspapers or to legislators, which were more often harshly critical of the students. Elaine Sacarny Zack, from the Wisconsin class of 1946, wrote Sewell that in one week, her daughter, who had followed her to Madison, "was welcomed into the freshman honorary society in recognition of high achievement in pursuit of knowledge, and brought to tears, as stunned, she witnessed a melee outside the Commerce Building. I pray there will be no fear, tear gas, or violence on the campus of the University of Wisconsin again."

449   *Since Republicans controlled:* Int. Jerris Leonard, May 21, 2001; accounts in *Capital Times, WSJ,* October 20–22, 1967.

451   *District attorney Jim Boll was sitting:* Int. James Boll, August 9, 2001.

452   *Bandages protected his nose:* Int. Tom McCarthy, August 8, 2000; McCarthy scrapbook of letters and cards.

454   *As the buses from Madison:* Int. Dave Wheadon, December 23, 2002.

454   *the first of the weekend's protests:* Gibbons, *The U.S. Government and the Vietnam War,* 862–63; accounts in *NYT,* October 21, 1967; Wells, *The War Within,* 195; Joseph A. Califano, *The Triumph and Tragedy of Lyndon Johnson,* 198–99; int. Judy Genack, December 26, 2002; *White House Daily Diary,* October 20, 1967, LBJ.

457   *It was twelve hours later:* Ints. Tom Grady, March 27, 2002; Michael Arias, June 2, 2002; Tom Hinger, March 12, 2000; 2/28 News Release No. 4015, Slug: "Black Lions Memorial Service." SP5 Dick Claprood wrote: "Setting aside their rifles for a few moments of prayer, the 1st Inf Div's 2d Bn, 28th Inf, briefly suspended their relentless pursuit of the Viet Cong. But the war was still foremost in each man's mind as the 'Black Lions of Cantigny' were conducting a memorial service for the 57 American soldiers who gave their lives. . . ."

457   *Captain Cash was in Lai Khe:* Oral history interviews conducted by Capt. John A. Cash, October 21, 1967, CMH.

459   *Brigadier General Coleman:* "Office of the Assistant Division Commander, Subject: Summary of Lessons Learned. Reference: 2/28 Contact, 17 October 1967," CMH.

459 *Jim George was still reliving:* Ints. Jim George, May 27, 2001; Joe Costello, November 2, 2000; letter from Jim George to wife Jackie, October 21, 1967.

460 *The buses reached Washington:* Ints. Dave Wheadon, December 23, 2002; Alison Steiner, December 26, 2002; John Lipp, December 22, 2002; Kent Smith, December 29, 2002; David Westley, Judy Genack, December 26, 2002; Michael Oberdorfer, January 3, 2003; Wells, *The War Within,* 194–96; Norman Mailer, *The Armies of the Night; White House Daily Diary,* October 21, 1967, LBJ.

462 *"funeral procession" up State Street:* Ints. Paul Soglin, June 22, 2001; Jane Brotman, April 9, 2002; accounts in *Capital Times,* October 21, *WSJ,* October 22, 1967.

463 *Leading the way was a brigade:* Wells, *The War Within,* 196; accounts in *Washington Post, WSJ,* October 22, 1967; *White House Daily Diary,* October 21, 1967, LBJ; Ints. Michael Oberdorfer, January 3, 2003; Judy Genack, December 26, 2002; Alison Steiner, December 26, 2002; Kent Smith, December 29, 2002.

466 *After lunch with his top aides:* "Schedule of Events for General W.C. Westmoreland, October 22, 1967," MHI; "General Westmoreland's History Notes, 16 October–12 November 1967." The brief journal account that day read: "On Sunday I had lunch with General Palmer and visited General Weyand's headquarters where we discussed future plans and I gave him appropriate guidance. I then visited the 93rd and 24th Evacuation Hospitals, primarily to see the casualties from the 2/28th Infantry resulting from their recent sharp engagement along the Binh Long–Binh Duong border. Upon return to my headquarters I met with the visiting AFL-CIO executives who are in strong support of our war efforts." *Report of Army Medical Service Activities,* 93rd Evacuation Hospital, Calendar Year 1967, NARA; ints. Elizabeth Finn, March 13, 2002; Donald Parlee, March 13, 2001; P. Evangeline Jamison, March 8, 2004; Edward Amorosi, March 7, 2001; Phil Eastman, March 7, 2001; Gerald Cygan, March 6, 2001; Bill Wells, March 5, 2001; Jackson Walker, April 2, 2001; Clark Welch, January 28–February 8, 2002; Clarence Barrow, October 16, 2000; Peter Miller, August 27, 2002; Clark Welch letter to wife Lacy, October 22, 1967.

471 *In Hanoi that very afternoon: People's Central Organ of the Vietnam Labor Party,* October 22, 1967, *People's Army,* October 22–23, 1967, Hanoi, translated by Anthony Broadman and Kyle Horst.

473 *the Politburo was meeting:* Khang, *The Tet Mau Than 1968 Event,* 31, 33.

474 *When Sunday, October 22, arrived: White House Daily Diary,* October 22, 1967, LBJ.

475 *The peace buses pulled up:* Ints. Alison Steiner, December 26, 2002; Paul Soglin, April 10, 2002.

475 *The events of that one week:* Dow Chemical internal memos, October–November 1967, PSA; ints. David Keene, May 15, 2002; Richard Swearingen, January 15, 2003; Gibbons, *The U.S. Government and the Vietnam War,* 867–68.

476 *"This was a sad and brooding city": NYT,* October 23, 1967.

477 *"It doesn't seem we can win":* "Notes of the President's meeting with Secretary Rusk, Secretary McNamara, Walt Rostow, Richard Helms, George Christian, General Wheeler, in the Mansion," October 23, 1967. Tom Johnson Notes, box 1, LBJ.

477 *In Madison that Monday:* Int. Alison Steiner, December 26, 2002.

477 *The UW faculty reconvened: Minutes of Second Special Session of University of Wisconsin faculty, 4:30 P.M., October 23, 1967, Memorial Union Theater,* UW.

478 *At the research lab:* Ints. Dave Wheadon, Dennis McQuade, December 23, 2002.

479 *Red Blaik, the retired:* Col. Red Blaik Syndicated Football Series, Holleder file, USMA archives.

479 *In Milwaukee two soldiers:* Ints. Edmund Sikorski, Diane Sikorski, July 28, 2001; Sikorski family scrapbook.

CHAPTER 28: UNTIL THE ANGELS CAME

480 *The chapel pews filled to overflowing:* Narrative of Terry Allen's funeral drawn from ints. Jean Ponder Allen Soto, February 3, 2001; Conseulo Allen, February 2–4, 2001; Albert Schwartz, February 3, 2001; Jonathan and Pat Rodgers, February 4, 2001; *El Paso Times,* October 20–24, 1967; Terry Allen file, LBJ; letter from Mary Fran Allen to Jim Shelton, November 4, 1967.

483 *General Hay, was dismissive:* Hay oral history interview with George MacGarrigle, April 29, 1980, CMH; "Citation, By Direction of the President, The Silver Star (Second Oak Leaf Cluster) Presented to Major General John H. Hay Jr., United States Army, For Gallantry in Action, General Orders Number 174, 24 February 1968," MHI.

486 *Dow and napalm were the focus:* Dow Chemical Co. internal memos, October–November, 1967, PSA; accounts in *Washington Post, WSJ,* October 26, 1967.

486 *the action had moved:* Ints. Percy Julian, August 24, 2001; Paul Soglin, April 10, 2002; Mike Oberdorfer, January 3, 2003.

487 *Curly Hendershot was back:* Ints. E. N. Brandt, April 12, 2001; Herbert Dow Doan, April 12, 2001; Dave Coslett, April 26, 2001; Bill Seward, April 27, 2001; unprocessed papers of Bill Seward; Dow Chemical Co. internal documents, Agent Orange files, PSA.

491 *Clark Welch felt well enough:* Welch letter to wife Lacy, October 26, 1967; ints. Clark Welch, January 28–February 8, 2002.

491 *Landon mailed his Purple Heart:* Greg Landon letters to parents, October 26–27, 1967; int. Greg Landon, June 19, 2002.

492 *One of the fallen Skyhawks:* Hanoi Radio broadcast, translated by CIA, October 26, 1967, NARA; "McCain's Vietnam Rescuer Talks," Associated Press, February 24, 2000.

493 *The odd couple of Madison:* Ints. James Boll, August 9, 2001; Jonathan Stielstra, August 20–21, 2001; scrapbook of Jonathan Stielstra.

495 *family of Danny Sikorski:* Ints. Edmund Sikorski, Diane Sikorski, July 28, 2001; Sikorski family scrapbook.

496 *a prime-time show:* William Sewell testimony at SSC, October 25, 1967; ints. William Sewell, August 10, 2000; Richard Cates, June 26, 2001.

500 *The Homecoming parade:* Accounts in *Capital Times,* October 27, 1967, *WSJ,* October 28, 1967; ints. Charles S. Robb, January 27, 2003; Paul Soglin, June 22, 2001.

502 *As for the war:* David Halberstam, *The Best and the Brightest,* 737.

502 *so many political players:* Accounts in *El Paso Times, Milwaukee Journal, WSJ,* October 28, 1967.

503 *The funeral was held:* Ints. Eleanor Schroder Clark, January 3, 2001; Larry Schroder, October 18, 2002; Schroder family scrapbook; Weigl, "Elegy," *Archaeology of the Circle,* 94.

Selected Bibliography

Adams, Sam. *War of Numbers*. Steerforth Press, South Royalton, Vt., 1994.

Basker, Lawrence M., and William A. Strauss. *Chance and Circumstance*. Random House, New York, 1978.

Biggs, Bradley. *Gavin: A Biography of General James A. Gavin*. Archon Books, New York, 1980.

Browne, Malcolm W. *The New Face of War*. Bobbs-Merrill, New York, 1965.

Buhle, Paul, ed. *History and the New Left: Madison, Wisconsin, 1950–1970*. Temple University Press, Philadelphia, 1990.

Bunzel, John H. *Political Passages: Journeys of Change through Two Decades, 1968–1988*. Free Press, New York, 1988.

Califano, Joseph A., Jr. *The Triumph and Tragedy of Lyndon Johnson*. Simon & Schuster, New York, 1991.

Carland, John M. *Stemming the Tide, May 1965 to October 1966, Combat Operations, the United States Military in Vietnam*. U.S. Army Center of Military History, Washington, D.C., 2000.

Chomsky, Noam. *Understanding Power*. New Press, New York, 2002.

Clausen, Aage R. *How Congressmen Decide: A Policy Focus*. St. Martin's Press, New York, 1973.

Clymer, Kenton J., ed. *The Vietnam War: Its History, Literature and Music*. Texas Western Press, El Paso, 1998.

Coyote, Peter. *Sleeping Where I Fall*. Counterpoint, Washington, D.C., 1998.

Dai, Colonel Phan Huu, ed. *The History of Group 559, The Truong Son Troops and the Ho Chi Minh Trail*. People's Army Publishing House, Hanoi, 1999.

Davis, R. G. *The San Francisco Mime Troupe: The First Ten Years*. Ramparts Press, Palo Alto, 1975.

DeBenedetti, Charles, and Charles Chatfield. *An American Ordeal: The Antiwar Movement of the Vietnam Era*. Syracuse University Press, Syracuse, 1990.

Debord, Guy. *The Society of the Spectacle*. Buchet-Chastel, Paris, 1967.

Dixon, Norman. *On the Psychology of Military Incompetence*. Pimlico, London, 1994.

Duiker, William J. *Ho Chi Minh*. Hyperion, New York, 2000.

Dunnigan, James F., and Albert A. Nofi. *Dirty Little Secrets of the Vietnam War*. St. Martin's Press, New York, 1999.

Fall, Bernard B. *Hell in a Very Small Place*. J. B. Lippincott, Philadelphia, 1966.

FitzGerald, Frances. *Fire in the Lake*. Atlantic Monthly Press, Boston, 1972.

Giap, Vo Nguyen. *The Unforgettable Days*. GIOI Publishers, Hanoi, 1994.

Gibbons, William Conrad. *The U.S. Government and the Vietnam War, Part IV: July 1965–January 1968*. Princeton University Press, Princeton, 1995.

Glenn, Russell W. *Reading Athena's Dance Card: Men against Fire in Vietnam.* Naval Institute Press, Annapolis, 2000.

Graff, Henry F. *The Tuesday Cabinet.* Prentice-Hall, Englewood Cliffs, N.J., 1969.

Graubard, Stephen R., and Geno A. Ballotti, eds. *The Embattled University.* George Braziller, New York, 1970.

Gray, John. *Two Faces of Liberalism.* New Press, New York, 2000.

Greene, Graham. *The Quiet American.* William Heinemann, London, 1955.

Halberstam, David. *The Best and the Brightest.* Random House, New York, 1972.

Hammond, William M. *Reporting Vietnam.* University Press of Kansas, Lawrence, 1998.

Harris, David. *Our War.* Times Books, New York, 1996.

Hoopes, Townsend. *The Limits of Intervention.* David McKay, New York, 1969.

Hynes, Samuel. *The Soldiers' Tale: Bearing Witness to Modern War.* Viking Penguin, New York, 1997.

Jones, Bruce E. *War Without Windows.* Vanguard Press, New York, 1987.

Just, Ward. *To What End.* Houghton Mifflin, Boston, 1968.

Kaiser, Charles. *1968 in America.* Grove/Atlantic, New York, 1988.

Kaiser, David. *American Tragedy.* Harvard University Press, Cambridge, 2000.

Karnow, Stanley. *Vietnam: A History.* Viking, New York, 1983.

Kearns, Doris. *Lyndon Johnson and the American Dream.* Harper & Row, New York, 1976.

Khang, Ho. *The Tet Mau Than 1968 Event in South Vietnam.* GIOI Publishers, Hanoi, 2001.

Khoi, Hoang. *The Ho Chi Minh Trail.* GIOI Publishers, Hanoi, 2001.

Langguth, A. J. *Our Vietnam.* Simon & Schuster, New York, 2000.

Leebaert, Derek. *The Fifty-Year Wound.* Little, Brown, Boston, 2002.

Macdonald, Peter. *Giap.* W. W. Norton, New York, 1993.

MacGarrigle, George L. *Taking the Offensive, October 1966 to October 1967, Combat Operations, the United States Military in Vietnam.* U.S. Army Center of Military History, Washington, D.C., 1998.

Maclear, Michael. *The Ten Thousand Day War, Vietnam 1945–1975.* St. Martin's Press, New York, 1981.

Mahler, Michael D. *Ringed in Steel, Armored Cavalry, Vietnam, 1967–68.* Presidio Press, Novato, Calif., 1986.

Mailer, Norman. *The Armies of the Night.* New American Library, New York, 1968.

Mangold, Tom, and John Penycate. *The Tunnels of Cu Chi.* Random House, New York, 1985.

Mann, Robert. *A Grand Delusion.* Basic Books, New York, 2001.

Marshall, S.L.A. *Men Against Fire.* McLeod Ltd., Toronto, 1951.

Marwick, Arthur. *The Sixties.* Oxford University Press. Oxford, 1998.

McMaster, H. R. *Dereliction of Duty: Lyndon Johnson, Robert McNamara, the Joint Chiefs of Staff, and the Lies That Led to Vietnam.* HarperCollins, New York, 1997.

Meconis, Charles A. *With Clumsy Grace: The American Catholic Left 1961–1975.* Seabury Press, New York, 1979.

Mosse, George L. *Confronting History, A Memoir.* University of Wisconsin Press, Madison, 2000.

Mosse, George L. *The Nationalization of the Masses.* Cornell University Press, Ithaca, 1975.

Ninh, Bao. *The Sorrow of War.* Martin Secker & Warburg, London, 1993.

Pentagon Papers, ed. Senator Mike Gravel, Vols. 1–4. Beacon Press, Boston, 1971.

Phuong, Nguyen Viet, ed. *Final Report on Rear Service Operations for the Nam Bo–Extreme South Central Region Theater during the War of Resistance against the Americans.* General Directorate for Rear Services, Hanoi, 1986.

Pike, Douglas. *Viet Cong.* M.I.T. Press, Cambridge, 1966.

Pribbenow, Merle L., trans. *Victory in Vietnam: The Official History of the People's Army of Vietnam, 1954–1975.* The Military History Institute of Vietnam, Hanoi, 1998.

Pyle, Ernie. *Here Is Your War.* Henry Holt, New York, 1943.

Rowe, John Carlos, and Rick Berg, eds. *The Vietnam War and American Culture.* Columbia University Press, New York, 1991.

Sheehan, Neil. *A Bright Shining Lie: John Paul Vann and America in Vietnam.* Random House, New York, 1988.

Shelton, James. *The Beast Was Out There.* Cantigny Military History Series, Wheaton, Ill., 2002.

Sieg, Kent, ed. *Foreign Relations of the United States, 1964–68. Volume V: Vietnam 1967.* United States Government Printing Office, Washington, D.C., 2002.

Silber, Glenn, and Barry Brown. *The War at Home,* a film. First Run Features, New York, 1979.

Snepp, Frank. *Decent Interval.* Random House, New York, 1977.

Summers, Harry G., Jr. *The Vietnam War Almanac.* Presidio Press, Novato, Calif., 1995.

Turner, Fred. *Echoes of Combat: Trauma, Memory and the Vietnam War.* Anchor Books, New York, 1996.

Weigl, Bruce. *Archeology of the Circle.* Grove Press, New York, 1999.

Wells, Tom. *The War Within: America's Battle over Vietnam.* University of California Press, Berkeley, 1994.

Williams, William Appleman, ed. *America in Vietnam: A Documentary History.* Norton, New York, 1989.

Wilson, George C. *Mud Soldiers: Life Inside the New American Army.* Scribner, New York, 1989.

ACKNOWLEDGMENTS

Cᴏᴜɴᴛʟᴇss ᴛɪᴍᴇs while I was writing this book, I read the eighteen lines of "Elegy." The poetry of Bruce Weigl inspired me, and I apologize for inverting his phrase in the title.

For three months in the summer of 2001, my wife and I moved back to Madison, our hometown, so that I could report the Wisconsin side of the story. Many generous friends helped us while we were there, foremost Kim Vergeront and Andrew Cohn, who proved to be a master in finding documents; Judy and Ben Sidran, who brought music to our summer; Doug and Bette Moe, the great provisioners, who helped us find our rental home and our way; and also Dave Zweifel, Ron McCrea, John Nichols, and the staff of *The Capital Times;* and Dan Siebens, Dave Foster, Suey Wong, Steve Marvin, Sam Schwartz, Bob Freed, Sue Brausen, Linda Berman, Chris Hall, and Jim and Julie Hopson.

I come from a family of librarians and editors and have immense respect for all librarians and archivists. They were, as always, invaluable as I researched this book. The University of Wisconsin and the State Historical Society of Wisconsin contain world-class archives on the sixties. Helping me at Wisconsin with various collections were James Danky, Harold Miller, Steve Masar, and Bernard Schermetzler. Also generous with their time and knowledge were Blake Kellogg, Lawrence Lichty, Jack Cipperly, Liz Beyler, Alfred W. McCoy, Sam Mermin, Jeff Smoller, Stuart Levitan, Bob Newton, Mike Fellner, and Glenn Silber.

At archives around the country, pointing me in the right direction and offering helpful research advice were Dr. Timothy Nenninger and archivists Susan A. Francis-Haughton and Rich Boylan at the National Archives at College Park; Lieutenant Colonel Edwin M. Perry, David Keough, Richard J. Sommers, James T. Baughman, and Nancy Baylor, at the U.S. Army's Military History Institute; John M. Carland at the Center of Military History; Dr. John F. Votaw and archivist Andrew Woods at the First Division Museum; Alan Aimone at the United States

Military Academy special collections; Nancy Barr at the Military Sealift Command; David L. Petree of the National Personnel Records Center; and Mike Parrish and Linda Seelke at the LBJ Library. At various points in researching this book, four industrious young men helped me track down documents: Dan Alexander, James Alexander, Michael Penn, and Anthony Broadman.

Researching the Vietnam side of this book was made immeasurably easier, and more pleasurable, by the selfless assistance of Fred Kirkpatrick and Tom Hinger, whom I've described as one-person search engines, and by the ebullient goodwill of Jim Shelton, my fellow author, and the other Black Lions from the November Nightmare—Tom Grady, Joe Costello, Steve Goodman, and Carl Woodard. Thanks also to Diane Sikorski Kramer, Jim George, Michael Arias, Greg Landon, Rick Calef, Ray Albin, Eleanor Schroder Clark, Mike Taylor, Mike Dinkins, and Mike Troyer for sharing their letters, photographs, and tapes.

This book would not have been possible without the unending generosity of my employers at the *Washington Post,* including chairman Don Graham, who took time from his swamped schedule to read the manuscript and provide sound advice, publisher Bo Jones, executive editor Len Downie, and managing editor Steve Coll. Researchers Madonna Lebling, Bobbye Pratt, and Margot Williams, and transcriptionist Carol Van Horn are treasures of the *Post.* Sarah Cohen saved me from a computer disaster. Thanks also to friends Maralee Schwartz, Valerie Strauss, Ellen Nakashima, Anne Hull, Bill Hamilton, Bob Kaiser, Bea Harwood, John Feinstein, Bob Woodward, Michael Weisskopf, David Von Drehle, Henry Bryan, and Chip Brown. Rick Atkinson, my fellow scribbler, opened the doors to the military world for me and lit the path from beginning to end. The philosophy of Pat Toomay was always thought-provoking. When I think of the Vietnam experience, I think first of two good men, my dear old friends Michael Norman and Tilt Meyer, and of Beth Norman. Jim Warren, Blaine Harden, and Whitney Gould were careful readers, again. I consider myself lucky to have Rafe Sagalyn as my agent, and Simon and Schuster as my publisher. Alice Mayhew, my editor, has meant more to me every year, and I cherish our professional relationship and personal friendship. Dealing with her trusty right hand, Roger Labrie, is a pleasure. Thanks also to the copy editors, Peg Haller and Loretta Denner, and to Simon and Schuster's Carolyn Reidy, David Rosenthal, Victoria Meyer, Aileen Boyle, Rebecca J. Davis, and Anja Schmidt.

Nothing gives me more satisfaction than sending chapters to Milwaukee for my parents, Elliott and Mary Maraniss, to pencil their way through. They are great editors, and offer extemporaneous comic relief when they start arguing points of grammar between themselves and forget that I'm on the other end of the line. Since I was a young boy, I've been awed by the intellect of my older brother and sister, Jim Maraniss and Jean Alexander. I write with a photograph of my sister Wendy nearby.

The journey to Vietnam was a highlight of my career, made especially rewarding by the people who came with me in what we called the Saigon Seven: Clark Welch, the great soldier, Consuelo Allen, the soulful daughter, Rob Keefe, the bright comic, Connie Doebele, the goodnatured book chronicler, and Kyle Horst, the multilingual Eagle Scout. It is an understatement to say that Kyle is the best guide and interpreter around. Madam Ha, our handler from the foreign ministry, could move the earth, and often did; unlike many press officers, she was more interested in getting us what we wanted than in keeping things from us. The other member of the Saigon Seven was my wife, Linda, who embraced this book with her boundless warmth and exuberance and was with me all the way, taking photographs, offering insights, reading every word, making invariably good suggestions. With Linda at my side, and with the love of Andrew, Sarah, and her Tom, no one could ask for more sunlight.

INDEX

Kraft, Joe, 310
Krasny, Michael, 365–66, 377, 378, 447
Krische, John D., 286
Ky, Nguyen Cao, 151

LaFollette, Bronson, 175
LaFollette, Robert M., Jr., 123
Lai Khe: as First Infantry base, 16–17, 24–46;
  French rubber plantation near, 24; ice cream
  plant at, 212, 527; location of, 24; Viet Cong
  mortar attacks on, 27, 30, 35; villagers supporting Viet Cong, 24, 156; after the war, 526–27
Laird, Melvin, 111–12
Lam, Nguyen Van, 243–44, 246, 248, 296, 330–
  331, 347, 523–25, 527
Lancaster, Jerry, 261, 284
Landon, Gregory, 5; arrives in Vietnam, 15, 16; at
  Black Lions reunion, 519; en route to Viet-
  nam, 9, 10, 12, 13; evacuation from battlefield,
  307; at Fort Lewis, 4–5; at Lai Khe, 35, 36–37,
  38; letters home after battle, 345–46, 418–19;
  at Ninety-third Evacuation Hospital, 337–38;
  in operation of October 17, 256–57, 273, 274,
  282–83; in operations of early October, 160; at
  Thirty-sixth Evacuation Hospital, 491–92,
  503; during training, 141–42, 145
Langguth, A. J., 73
Lao Dong Party, 196, 201, 202
Laos, 244, 445–46
Laub, David, 279, 281, 283, 409
Lawrence, David, 402
Leavitt, Frederick, 486
Lederer, John, 369, 372–73
Le Duan, 202
leeches, 20
Lee Kuan Yew, 310
Lenburg, Norman, 391, 427–28, 451, 493, 495
Leonard, Jerris, 449–50
Leonhart, William, 186
Leslie, Vernon (Jack), 452, 493, 494, 495
Lester, Dewey, 256
Lichty, Lawrence, 547n
Life magazine, 194–95
Lincoln, Gary, 284, 334
Lipp, Jonathan, 461, 465
Lipski, Donald, 372
Locke, Eugene M., 187–88
Lonefight, Reynolds, 273, 283, 338
Long Nguyen Secret Zone: CS attack in, 162–63;
  First Infantry Division operating in, 155, 162,
  197, 205, 207; First Viet Cong Regiment in,
  159, 163, 207, 246–48; location of, 24; Rear
  Service Group 83 in, 243, 245
Lorge, Gerald, 451
Lovato, Joe, Jr., 221, 224, 272, 277, 282, 284
Lowe, Larry E., 302, 304
Lowell, Robert, 454
Lowenstein, Allard, 79, 115
Luberda, Andrew, 256, 259, 267, 277, 280, 281–
  282, 284

Lucas, Jim G., 11
Luce, Henry, 195

Madison (Wisconsin): Capital Times newspaper,
  126–27, 429–32, 508, 536n; contingent to
  Washington rally of October 1967, 443–45,
  454–55, 460–62, 466, 475; demonstration on
  October 21, 447, 462–63; as east side–west side
  town, 126, 137; four factors in, 80; map of, 77;
  police culture in, 179–80; San Francisco Mime
  Troupe in, 169–70; Soglin becomes mayor of,
  376, 475, 510. See also Wisconsin, University of
Mahon, George, 456
Mailer, Norman, 401, 454, 455, 464
mail service, 212
Malone, Paul B., 302, 304, 484
Manning, Robert, 426–27
Mansfield, Mike, 197
Maraniss, Elliott, 508
Marcovich, Herbert, 189, 403
Marshall, S. L. A., 411, 417
Mate, Kenny, 181
Matthews, Steve, 445, 454, 461, 475
McCafferty, Arthur, 314
McCain, John S., Jr., 492
McCain, John S., III, 492–93
McCarthy, Eugene, 502, 514, 540n
McCarthy, Joseph R., 126, 430
McCarthy, Tom, 180–81, 380–81, 388–89, 396,
  452–53
McCormack, John W., 196
McCrea, Ron, 99, 508, 509
McDevitt, Larry, 335
McFadden, James, 175
McGath, Bill, 5; at Black Lions reunion, 519; en
  route to Vietnam, 7, 8, 11; in operation of
  October 17, 287
McGovern, George, 197, 316, 512
McGovern, Susan: campaigning for her father,
  511–12; in Dow Chemical protest of October
  1967, 319, 324, 329, 348, 350, 351, 367, 374, 376,
  383, 393; and the draft, 318; father George
  McGovern, 197, 316; marriage to Jim Rowen,
  316–17
McMeel, Frank, 5; in evacuation hospital, 338;
  letter home after battle, 345; in operation of
  October 14, 206; in operation of October 17,
  271–72, 279, 281, 283
McMillin, Miles, 126, 430–32, 434
McNally, Jim, 380–81
McNamara, Robert S.: and budget problems,
  250–51; Dow requesting letter from, 75; on
  halting bombing, 203–4, 405; Johnson expresses his pessimism about the war, 476–77;
  as losing confidence in the war, 193; at meeting with Johnson on October 3, 189; at Tuesday lunch, October 17, 310, 311; at war council
  of October 18, 402, 405; on Washington
  antiwar rally, 190–91, 465
McParland, Leland, 396

ABOUT THE AUTHOR

David Maraniss is an associate editor at *The Washington Post* and the author of two critically acclaimed and bestselling books, *When Pride Still Mattered: A Life of Vince Lombardi* and *First in His Class: A Biography of Bill Clinton*. He has won virtually every major award in journalism, including the 1993 Pulitzer Prize for National Reporting. He lives in Washington, D.C.